HANDBOOK OF PERCEPTION
Volume VII

Language and Speech

This is Volume VII of

HANDBOOK OF PERCEPTION

EDITORS: *Edward C. Carterette and Morton P. Friedman*

Contents of the other books in this series appear at the end of this volume.

HANDBOOK OF PERCEPTION

VOLUME VII

Language and Speech

EDITED BY

Edward C. Carterette and Morton P. Friedman

Department of Psychology
University of California, Los Angeles
Los Angeles, California

ACADEMIC PRESS   New York San Francisco London   1976

A Subsidiary of Harcourt Brace Jovanovich, Publishers

ACADEMIC PRESS, INC.
111 Fifth Avenue, New York, New York 10003

United Kingdom Edition published by
ACADEMIC PRESS, INC. (LONDON) LTD.
24/28 Oval Road, London NW1

Library of Congress Cataloging in Publication Data

Main entry under title:

Language and speech.

   (Handbook of perception ; v. 7)
   Includes bibliographies.
   1.   Language and languages—Addresses, essays, lectures.   2.   Languages—Psychology—Addresses, essays,
lectures.   3.   Speech—Addresses, essays, lectures.
I.   Carterette, Edward C.   II.   Friedman, Morton P.
III.   Title.   [DNLM: 1.   Language.   2.   Speech.
3.   Perception.   4.   Language disorders.   5.   Speech
disorders.   WL700 H234 v. 7]
P106.L316   410'.1   76-6946
ISBN 0—12—161907—9 (v. 7)

PRINTED IN THE UNITED STATES OF AMERICA

CONTENTS

PART I.   FUNDAMENTAL ASPECTS
OF LANGUAGE AND SPEECH

Chapter 1.   The Formal Nature of Language and
Linguistic Theories

Victoria A. Fromkin

Chapter 2.   Research Methods in Psycholinguistics

Gary M. Olson and Herbert H. Clark

Chapter 3.   The Production of Speech and Language

Peter MacNeilage and Peter Ladefoged

Chapter 4.   Neurobiology of Language

Harry A. Whitaker

Chapter 5.   The Development of Speech

Jacqueline Sachs

PART II.   CODING, PERCEPTION, AND HEARING

Chapter 6.   The Perception of Speech

C. J. Darwin

Chapter 7.   Phonetic Coding and Serial Order

Wayne A. Wickelgren

Chapter 8.   Semantics: Categorization and Meaning

James Deese

Chapter 9.   Sentence Comprehension: A Case Study in the Relation of Knowledge and Perception

J. M. Carroll and T. G. Bever

Chapter 10.   Language and Nonverbal Communication

John Laver

Chapter 11.   Language Teaching and Language Learning

Evelyn Hatch

PART III.   DISORDERS OF LANGUAGE AND SPEECH

Chapter 12.   Language Disorders (Aphasia)

H. Goodglass and N. Geschwind

Chapter 13.   Disorders of Speech Production
Mechanisms

Harry A. Whitaker

PART IV. TRENDS IN PSYCHOLOGICAL TESTS OF LINGUISTIC THEORY

Chapter 14. Disintegrating Theoretical Distinctions
and Some Future Directions
in Psycholinguistics

P. L. French

LIST OF CONTRIBUTORS

Numbers in parentheses indicate the pages on which the authors' contributions begin.

T. G. BEVER (299), Psycholinguistics Program, Columbia University in the City of New York, New York, New York

J. M. CARROLL (299), Psycholinguistics Program, Columbia University in the City of New York, New York, New York

HERBERT H. CLARK (25), Department of Psychology, Stanford University, Stanford, California

C. J. DARWIN (175), Department of Psychology University of Sussex, Brighton, Sussex, England

JAMES DEESE (265), Department of Psychology University of Virginia, Charlottesville, Virginia

P. L. FRENCH (445), Department of Psychology, University of California, Los Angeles, Los Angeles, California

VICTORIA A. FROMKIN (3), Department of Linguistics, University of California, Los Angeles, Los Angeles, California

N. GESCHWIND (389), Harvard University School of Medicine and Veterans Administration Hospital, Boston, Massachusetts

H. GOODGLASS (389), Veterans Administration Hospital, Boston, Massachusetts

EVELYN HATCH (363), Department of English, University of California, Los Angeles, Los Angeles, California

PETER LADEFOGED (75), Linguistics Department, University of California Los Angeles, Los Angeles, California

JOHN LAVER (345), Department of Linguistics, University of Edinburgh, Edinburgh, Scotland

PETER MACNEILAGE (75), Departments of Linguistics and Psychology, University of Texas at Austin, Austin, Texas

GARY M. OLSON (25), Department of Psychology and Human Performance Center, University of Michigan, Ann Arbor, Michigan

JACQUELINE SACHS (145), Departments of Speech and Linguistics, University of Connecticut, Storrs, Connecticut

HARRY A. WHITAKER (121,429), Departments of Psychology and Neurology, University of Rochester, Rochester, New York

WAYNE A. WICKELGREN (227), Department of Psychology, University of Oregon, Eugene, Oregon

FOREWORD

The problem of perception is one of understanding the way in which the organism transforms, organizes, and structures information arising from the world in sense data or memory. With this definition of perception in mind, the aims of this treatise are to bring together essential aspects of the very large, diverse, and widely scattered literature on human perception and to give a précis of the state of knowledge in every area of perception. It is aimed at the psychologist in particular and at the natural scientist in general. A given topic is covered in a comprehensive survey in which fundamental facts and concepts are presented and important leads to journals and monographs of the specialized literature are provided. Perception is considered in its broadest sense. Therefore, the work will treat a wide range of experimental and theoretical work.

This ten-volume treatise is divided into two sections. Section One deals with the fundamentals of perceptual systems. It is comprised of six volumes covering (1) historical and philosophical roots of perception, (2) psychophysical judgment and measurement, (3) the biology of perceptual systems, (4) hearing, (5) seeing, and (6) feeling, tasting, smelling, and hurting.

Section Two, comprising four volumes, will cover the perceiving organism, taking up the wider view and generally ignoring specialty boundaries. The major areas include (7) language and speech, (8) perception of space and objects, (9) perception of form and pattern, and (10) aspects of cognitive performance, information processing, perceptual codes, perceptual aspects of thinking and problem solving, esthetics, and the ecology of the perceiver. Coverage will be given to theoretical issues and models of perceptual processes and also to central topics in perceptual judgment and decision.

The "Handbook of Perception" should serve as a basic source and reference work for all in the arts or sciences, indeed for all who are interested in human perception.

EDWARD C. CARTERETTE
MORTON P. FRIEDMAN

PREFACE

Language is exceedingly complicated.
GEORGE ARMITAGE MILLER—1965

Language and speech is a vast, fertile, fascinating, and bewildering domain. Its methods are the methods of most of the scientific and some of the humanistic disciplines. Important phonetic and cognitive data are contained in descriptive field reports, such as the developmental diaries of a single child. Another class of information comes from mathematical and computer methods—such as linear predictive coding, Fourier analysis, or digital filtering—which are used in the analysis and synthesis of speech and models of the vocal tract. In between are the data and methods of phonetics, formal linguistics, experimental psycholinguistics, speech perception, and psychoneurology, to name an obvious several.

The topics we have chosen to cover in this volume are those which are most essential to the central concern of *The Handbook,* that is, to perception. Therefore large, important, and active areas have been omitted. Anthropological and sociological linguistics, philosophy and logic of languages, animal communication, schizophrenic speech, speech interaction in psychotherapy, verbal learning, and verbal behavior, are examples. In each of these cases there exists a large and substantial literature. There are also some newer and rapidly developing areas of research that this volume does not cover, although some are alluded to, such as generative semantics, speech understanding systems, or computer models for understanding natural language.

We turn now to the present volume. Part I on *Fundamental Aspects of Language and Speech* begins with Fromkin's account of the formal nature of language and linguistic theories. She succinctly characterizes the view of linguists working within Chomsky's general deductive theory whose concern is "constructing a theory of language that will account for and *explain* the observable end result of the speech production and perception process."

Olson and Clark (Chapter 2) tell us that the methods of psycholinguistic research are generally ordinary, except in speech perception, where advanced electronic and computer methods have revolutionized research. "But what psycholinguistics lacks in methodological techniques it makes up for in difficult methodological issues." Olson and Clark's treatment of research methods in language acquisition, comprehension, and memory therefore surveys both the methods and the conceptual foundations that condition them.

A considerable amount is now known about the prediction of speech, including the physiological mechanisms of individual speech sounds. MacNeilage and Ladefoged review this somewhat technical knowledge. Their account of productive mechanisms, particularly articulatory dynamics, leads them to emphasize the importance of performance variables in formulating linguistic theory.

"A goal of the study of the neurobiology of language," says Whitaker (Chapter 4), "is a general biological theory of language." Such a theory has not yet been proposed, but in his view some of its components are reasonably well established. In dealing with these components Whitaker considers both innate and acquired components. He also discusses neurolinguistic models in the light of data obtained by the classical lesion method, and by the electroencephalographic method used with normal subjects.

"Children undoubtedly are suited for acquiring linguistic systems, partly in terms of inborn characteristics (such as certain aspects of speech perception), partly in terms of their cognitive abilities, and partly in terms of the sorts of strategies they use to process the input they receive." These are aspects of the review by Sachs (Chapter 5) of the problems of how and why a child comes to be a speaker of a language.

Coding, Perception, and Hearing of language (Part II) begins with Darwin's contemporary and informed Chapter 6 on "The Perception of Speech. The unity of his treatment derives in considerable part from the notion of reconstruction. The listener follows the meaning of the speaker, which is somehow extracted from speech segments that are not directly accessible. The listener reconstructs properties of the stimulus from that which he knows about higher level categories. Darwin pursues the implications of this reconstruction for perception by following the changes that "take place in semantic elements as they are described linguistically at different levels. In Chapter 7, "Phonetic Coding and Serial Ordering," Wickelgren deals with the theoretical units of coding that are useful in accounting for the phenomena of speech perception and articulation. His concern is with coding and serial order in the phonetic domain, which includes everything between the syntactic–semantic domain of the speaker and that of the hearer. We note that the views of Wickelgren and of MacNeilage and

Ladefoged (Chapter 3) about the motor control of serial ordering of speech are quite different.

Deese has previously argued that the cognitive categories that underlie semantic relations ultimately derive from modes of perceiving. In Chapter 8, *Semantics: Categorization and Meaning* he has retained this principle for discussing the semantic structure of the lexicon, and the nature and role of larger linguistic units in understanding. Deese comes full circle in Section IV by asking of the relation between perception and semantic structures, "How can the one be converted into the other?"

Carroll and Bever undertake in Chapter 9 to show how the study of sentence perception can serve as a model for the study of relationship between knowledge and behavior. They hold that linguistic structures are behaviorally pertinent only as a result of perceptual operations. Research has disabled two earlier phases—that grammatical transformations are psychological processes and that linguistically defined structures have psychological reality.

It is well argued by Laver in Chapter 10 that "language and nonverbal communication have an important degree of mutual relevance, if one views the communicative resources exploited in face-to-face interaction as a unified, total system rather than in the more traditional atomistic way." Laver is very brief but he covers a surprising amount of material clearly and objectively.

Hatch (Chapter 11) chronicles the vicissitudes of the fact that language teaching techniques reflect what linguists, psychologists, and philosophers tell teachers about language and language learning. She reviews the research of the structural and transformational periods and tells what of value was wrested by language teachers from it and at what cost. Hatch concludes that teachers have to commit themselves to research "and begin looking for the answers ourselves."

Part III, entitled *Disorders of Language and Speech,* begins with a fascinating, comprehensive account of Aphasia by Goodglass and Geschwind [Chapter 12, *Language Disorders (Aphasia)*]. The authors being psychologist and neurologist, respectively, are uniquely suited to give a clear and authoritative account of the major knowledge about brain and language as inferred from aphasias.

In Chapter 13, Whitaker reviews *Disorders of Speech Production Mechanisms.* In his treatment Whitaker notes that expressive motor aphasia syndromes tend to be identified as some variety of speech disorder rather than aphasia and other than dysarthria. Accordingly he sets out to make a theoretical case for distinguishing the phonological, linguistic, asphasic aspects of these syndromes from the purely productive dysarthria components.

Part IV, *Trends in Psychological Tests of Linguistic Theory* contains a single chapter by French, which deals with *Disintegrating Theoretical Distinctions* and *Some Future Directions in Psycholinguistics*. She takes up the evidence for the dissolution of the distinctions of competence/performance and of syntax/semantics. Her aim is to detail the development in linguistics and psycholinguistics after the Chomskyan revolution. We were led, she believes, to "an even more radical shift," to include meaning and cognition in the study of human language.

Some topics of considerable interest in the perception of language and speech happily will be included among the last three volumes of *The Handbook* (8, 9, and 10). For example, there will be chapters on the perception of letters and words in visual displays, the relationship between verbal and perceptual codes, representation of objects, auditory patterns, the psychology of reading, and disorders of perceptual processing. There are two chapters relevant to speech and language in Volume 4 (*Hearing*)— "Pathologies of Hearing" by D. D. Dirks, and "Perception of Music" by J.-C. Risset.

We thank Mrs. Cheryl Grossman and Miss Esther Zack for their help in organizing the table of contents, readying the volume for the printer, and proofreading. Editors of Academic Press both in New York and San Francisco have been enormously helpful in smoothing our way.

Financial support has come from The National Institute of Mental Health (Grant MH-07809), The Ford Motor Company, and The Regents of The University of California.

Part I

**Fundamental Aspects
of Language and Speech**

Chapter 1

THE FORMAL NATURE OF LANGUAGE AND LINGUISTIC THEORIES

VICTORIA A. FROMKIN

I. INTRODUCTION

Wherever and whenever man has lived, one finds speculations, observations, and arguments about the nature of human language. In different periods, however, one finds different emphases and different goals. The history of linguistics, like the history of all sciences, reveals a series of scientific revolutions in the Kuhnian sense (Kuhn, 1962). A major revolution, which posed new questions, was ushered in with the publication of Chomsky's *Syntactic Structures* in 1957. Linguistics was no longer conceived of as merely a "classificatory science" (Hockett, 1948). Explanation rather than mere description was sought. The aim of constructing a theory of linguistic universals—which would define the class of all possible human languages, thus revealing the nature of language—replaced the view that "languages could differ in innumerable ways [Joos, 1958]." The inductive methods of the earlier paradigm (Bloomfield, 1933) were replaced by a deductive theory.* Chomsky's view (1972) that "the major contribution to the

---

* Cf. Einstein (1934, p. 69): "The predominantly inductive methods appropriate to the youth of science are giving place to tentative deduction."

study of language will lie in the understanding it can provide as to the character of mental processes and the structures they form and manipulate" was a sharp break with the earlier view that linguists "must study the way people talk without bothering about the mental processes that we may conceive to underlie or accompany these habits [Bloomfield, 1922]." Thus, linguists working within this new paradigm have been concerned with constructing a theory of language that will account for and *explain* the observable end result of the speech production and perception process.

The goals of modern linguistics, then, are vastly different from those that immediately preceded. The basic aim is to construct a theory that can account for the "creative aspect" of language use (Chomsky, 1965, 1966), i.e., the fact that a speaker of a language can produce and comprehend novel sentences. Furthermore, the theory aims at revealing other aspects of a speaker's linguistic competence—his tacit knowledge of structural ambiguities, related sentence types, grammatical versus nongrammatical sentences, possible versus impossible (or improbable) "words," etc. This theory would represent a set of general constraints on all human languages and define the notion "possible human language."

The grammar of a particular language, constrained by the general theory, represents a model or theory of a speaker's linguistic competence. Each particular grammar constructed by the linguist is aimed at representing a psychologically real grammar.* In other words, it is not enough for the linguist's grammar to be formally elegant and account for the data; rather, it "aims at finding a true theory or description [of linguistic knowledge] which shall also be an explanation of the observable facts [Popper, 1963, p. 103]."

Another demand placed on both the general theory and each particular grammar is that they be formally stated, i.e., explicit, and therefore testable. The general theory must be rich enough to account for the facts of any human language and constrained so that it will include only human languages in its domain.

In the discussion that follows, some of the formal aspects of linguistic theory will be presented. Due to length limitations, the discussion will deal almost exclusively with the syntactic aspects of natural language.

II. FINITE GRAMMARS AND INFINITE LANGUAGES

A language can be defined formally as an infinite set of well-formed sentences. The set is infinite since, for every sentence of n length, in any

---

* This is not unlike the position maintained by Sapir in 1933.

language, there is a sentence of $n + 1$ length. This can be exemplified by the jingle about what went on in the famous or infamous "house that Jack built." That is, one can say

(1) *This is the house that Jack built.*

or

(2) *This is the malt that lay in the house that Jack built.*

or

(3) *This is the farmer sowing his corn, that kept the cock that crowed in the morn, that waked the priest all shaven and shorn, that married the man all tattered and torn, that kissed the maiden all forlorn, that milked the cow with the crumpled horn, that tossed the dog, that worried the cat, that killed the rat that ate the malt that lay in the house that Jack built.*

Speakers of a language are capable of producing and understanding any member of this infinite set; they have the ability to produce and understand sentences never produced or heard before.

Given the finite capacity of the brain, we cannot store an infinite set of sentences. What is stored is a finite *grammar,* a device for generating these sentences, i.e., for enumerating the set in an explicit way. Such a grammar must contain some *recursive* device, which can be applied and reapplied to generate the infinite set required.

The grammar of a language, then, can be conceived of as a finite set of primitive elements or units and a finite set of rules for combining these units to form all, and only, the sentences of the language. The sentences produced by this device must have associated with them a particular phonological or phonetic representation and a semantic representation. That is, the grammar must be a device that relates certain sounds with certain meanings.

Every speaker of a language knows the grammar of that language. (This knowledge, is, of course, tacit knowledge.) He knows the basic elements—the vocabulary—and the rules to combine these elements to form "grammatical" (well-formed) sentences. He knows how to pronounce these sentences and what they mean and how to combine sentences and change them into other sentences.

In the standard version of transformational theory (Chomsky, 1965), the grammar consists of a number of parts or components: a *phonological component,* a *semantic component,* and a *syntactic component* (which includes the vocabulary or *lexicon*).

A. The Phonological Component

Assuming that a grammar is a mechanism for pairing certain sound sequences with certain meanings, one part of the grammar must make explicit what speakers know about the sounds and sound patterns of the language. This is the function of the *phonological component*.

Part of a speaker's knowledge about his language is knowledge of the sounds and sound sequences that can occur. Thus, for example, the grammar of English should account for the fact that the "p" sound occurs in the language, while the grammar of Yoruba must show that the "p" sound does not occur. Such facts will be partially revealed by the way in which words are represented in the lexicon. In English, *pit* and *spit* will be listed, since they are both part of the English vocabulary, and both words will include a phonological segment (symbolized here as /p/, to differentiate it from the letter "p"). Phonetically, however, the /p/ in the two words are different sounds; the /p/ that occurs in *pit* (and in all words in which it is the initial consonant) is phonetically an aspirated sound, [pʰ], while the /p/ that occurs after /s/ in all words is an unaspirated sound, [p]. (The symbols within square brackets represent the phonetic pronunciation of the segment.) It is not the aim of this chapter to discuss the details of phonetics but rather to illustrate the nature of phonological rules. When a /p/ is aspirated and when it is unaspirated is predictable in English; aspiration is a redundant feature. This is true for all words in which a /p/ occurs. In fact, the predictability of aspiration also pertains to /k/ and /t/, i.e., to the class of voiceless stop consonants that can be defined by the phonetic features

$$
\begin{bmatrix}
+ \text{ consonantal} \\
- \text{ voiced} \\
+ \text{ stop}
\end{bmatrix}
$$

To reveal the generalization concerning these variant forms, the phonological component will contain a formal rule, as follows:

(4) a.
$$
\begin{bmatrix}
+ \text{ consonantal} \\
- \text{ voiced} \\
+ \text{ stop}
\end{bmatrix} \rightarrow [+ \text{ aspirated}]/\# \underline{\qquad}
$$

which is to be read: A voiceless stop consonant becomes (→) aspirated in the environment (/) after a word boundary (#).

Notice that by using features to define the class of sounds, the rule will apply to /p/, /t/, and /k/; one need not state each individual sound. Were we to list each sound segment, the generalization would be obscured; that is, the rule would not show why it is just these three segments that are aspirated in this context. By using features, the similarity of the three sounds is revealed. Such features therefore become part of the formal apparatus of linguistic theory.

Phonological rules of this kind are "pronunciation rules." They relate the abstract lexical representation of vocabulary items to their phonetic representation. /p/ is an abstract phonological segment, usually called a *phoneme;* unaspirated [p] and aspirated [pʰ] are phonetic segments derived by application of the general rule. We do not pronounce phonemes; rather, we pronounce phonetic segments.

Words of course are not the most elementary units of meaning in a language as can be seen from the following:

A	B
sign	signature
malign	malignant
design	designate
paradigm	paradigmatic

All the words in the B column contain the corresponding words in the A column. *Sign* is composed of one basic element of meaning, which is called a *morpheme; signature* is composed of this morpheme plus the suffixal morpheme *-ature.* It is clear from the above examples that a morpheme may have alternative pronunciations. All the words in the A column are pronounced without a [g], while the same morphemes in the B column are pronounced with a [g]. When one pronounces a [g] and when one does not is predictable, in the same way that aspiration is predictable, as is shown by rule (4b):

(4) b. $\qquad$ $g \rightarrow \emptyset /$ _____ [+nasal] #

(i.e., /g/ becomes zero when it occurs in the environment before a nasal segment followed by a word boundary).

If the phonological representation of the morphemes *sign, malign,* etc. and the words *sign + ature, malign + ant,* etc. include a /g/, this phonemic segment will be deleted only when no suffix is attached. This is a general fact about English, and it is thus to be revealed as a general rule, rather than as an idiosyncratic aspect of any of the above pairs. The rule will also apply to *phlegm/phlegmatic, resign/resignation, repugn/repugnant,* etc.

The phonological components of all grammars will contain such rules, although they will differ in detail according to the specific characteristics of the sound system of each language. The rules will operate on strings of morphemes in their lexical phonemic representation organized into hierarchical structures called *surface structures.* The output of the rules will be the phonetic representations of the sentences of the language, which reveal our knowledge of the pronunciation of sentences.

B. The Semantic Component

The *semantic component* of a grammar consists of *semantic rules* that have the function of representing the meanings of the sentences in the language. That is, the meanings of the words *eat* and *like* in sentences (5) and (6) are identical, but the sentences mean different things.

(5)   *I like what I eat.*

(6)   *I eat what I like.*

The rules of the semantic component provide semantic interpretations of sentences. In this model, the meanings of sentences are uniquely determined by structures, which are called the *deep structures* of sentences. The meanings of the individual lexical items or words are represented in these deep structures.

C. The Syntactic Component

The *syntactic component* of a grammar contains rules of "sentence formation." The recursive property of the grammar—that property which permits the generation of an infinite set of sentences—is a property of the *syntactic rules.* All combinations of words do not constitute possible or grammatical sentences of a language. The syntactic rules must generate sentences like (5) and (6) above but not sentences like (7) through (10).

(7)   * *Like I what eat I.**

(8)   * *Like I I what eat.*

(9)   * *Like eat what I I.*

(10)   * *I I eat like what.*

Syntactic rules also account for the fact that sentences (11) through (14), are, in some sense, similar in structure.

(11)   *It will shock Mary.*

(12)   *The news will shock Mary.*

(13)   *George's announcement will shock Mary.*

(14)   *George's entering a monastery will shock Mary.*

* Asterisk '*' before a sentence designates that it is "ungrammatical" or "deviant" in some way.

That is, there is some sense in which *it, the news, George's announcement,* and *George's entering the monastery* are structures of the same sort, i.e., they belong to the same category, which we can call *noun phrase* (NP).

If the grammar truly represents a speaker's knowledge of the language, then the syntactic rules must account for the fact that a sentence like (15a) is ambiguous, i.e., can be interpreted as either (15b) or (15c):

(15) a. *Sylvester likes Guinevere more than Lochinvar.*
    b. *Sylvester likes Guinevere more than Lochinvar likes Guinevere.*
    c. *Sylvester likes Guinevere more than Sylvester likes Lochinvar.*

but that (16), which seems to have the same structure as (15), is not ambiguous.

(16)   *Sylvester likes bagels more than doughnuts.*

Similarly, (17a) can be interpreted as (17b) or (17c), but (18) has only one interpretation:

(17)   a. *Visiting professors can be boring.*
           b. *Professors who visit can be boring.*
           c. *To visit professors can be boring.*

(18)   *Smiling professors can be boring.*

The syntactic rules must also account for the fact that speakers of the language know that (19a) can be changed into (19b):

(19)   a. *Clarence turned down the job.*
           b. *Clarence turned the job down.*

but (20a) cannot similarly be changed into (20b):

(20)   a.   *Clarence turned down the alley.*
           b. * *Clarence turned the alley down.*

Finally, the syntactic rules must account for the fact that other pairs of sentences that appear on the surface to be similar in structure must derive from different underlying structures, as exemplified by (21) and (22):

(21)   *Gerald is difficult to please.*

(22)   *Gerald is eager to please.*

Example (21) can be expressed as (21a) or (21b):

(21)   a. *It is difficult (for someone) to please Gerald.*
           b. *Gerald is difficult (for someone) to please.*

That is, in (21), *Gerald* is the logical object of the verb *please* (but the surface subject of the main clause). Example (22) can be paraphrased as (22a) but not as (22b).

(22)   a.   *Gerald is eager to please (someone).*
            b.   * *It is eager (for someone) to please Gerald.*

In this sentence, *Gerald* is the logical subject of *please* as well as the surface subject of the main clause.

We have listed just some of the aspects of a speaker's syntactic knowledge that must be accounted for in a grammar. The theory must provide the mechanisms by which such linguistic knowledge can be accounted for. Since all languages are characterized by these general properties, the grammars of all languages will contain similar components and similar kinds of rules.

D. The Lexicon

Every grammar must also contain a *lexicon,* which includes a finite number of lexical items. Each lexical entry must include everything a speaker knows about that item. Such knowledge includes how the item is pronounced (i.e., its *phonological* representation), what it means (i.e., its *semantic* properties), and how it can be combined with other items to produce well-formed, grammatical sentences (i.e., its *syntactic features*).

III. PHRASE STRUCTURE RULES

To permit the generation of an infinite set of sentences, all of which are well-formed or grammatical, the syntactic component of any grammar contains a set of rules called *phrase structure rules* (or "rewrite" rules).

Phrase structure (PS) rules are of the form: A → B, where A is a single symbol and B one or more symbols, and the rule is to be interpreted as "Rewrite or replace A by B."

A grammar containing such rules is called a *context-free phrase structure grammar.* This is an algebraic notion most thoroughly studied by Chomsky. The version given here is highly oversimplified, but it will hopefully reveal how certain properties of natural languages may be described formally by the use of such grammars.

In order to reveal generalizations in the rules, a number of *collapsing conventions* are required.

If the grammer contains two rules of the form A → BC and A → B, we collapse these into one rule by the use of parentheses: A → B(C). Given this "collapsed" rule one can expand the A into either BC or B.

If the grammar contains two rules of the form A → B and A → C, the two may be collapsed by using a brace notation:

$$A \rightarrow \begin{Bmatrix} B \\ C \end{Bmatrix}$$

All phrase structure grammars contain an *initial symbol,* which occurs on the left side of the arrow in at least one rule. There are also *terminal symbols,* which occur only on the right side of the arrow.

To generate sentences by means of such a phrase structure grammar one proceeds as follows:

(*i*) Write down the initial symbol.
(*ii*) Apply any rule that has the initial symbol to the left of the arrow.
(*iii*) Repeat for each symbol, until only terminal symbols are in the string.

The following rules represent a phrase structure grammar:

1. $A \rightarrow (B)C$

2. $B \rightarrow \begin{Bmatrix} D(E) \\ F \end{Bmatrix}$

3. $C \rightarrow \begin{Bmatrix} G \\ A \end{Bmatrix}$

To derive a sentence of this language we write down the initial symbol:

$$A$$

We now expand this as stipulated into C or BC.* This can also be done by constructing a tree diagram (*phrase marker*)†:

$$
\begin{array}{ccc}
 & A & \\
 & \diagup\diagdown & \\
B & & C
\end{array}
$$

We now must expand B, since B occurs on the left of the arrow in rule 2.

$$
\begin{array}{ccc}
 & A & \\
 & \diagup\diagdown & \\
B & & C \\
\diagup\diagdown & & \\
D \quad E & &
\end{array}
$$

We cannot expand D or E, since they are terminal symbols (i.e., they do not occur on the left of the arrow in any rule). But C must be expanded:

$$
\begin{array}{ccc}
 & A & \\
 & \diagup\diagdown & \\
B & & C \\
\diagup\diagdown & & | \\
D \quad E & & A
\end{array}
$$

* We shall illustrate by expanding only one of the possibilities for each rule.

† A branching diagram or tree is called a *phrase marker,* since it delineates or "marks" and labels the phrases, i.e., the constituents of which the sentence is constructed. The phrase marker represents the *structural description* of a derived sentence.

A is "nonterminal," so it must be expanded:

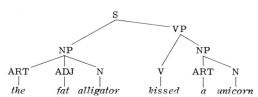

The derived string D E C now consists of only terminal symbols, and is a "sentence" generated by the grammar.

The "generative capacity" of a grammar, for a natural language consisting of terminal lexical elements and a set of phrase structure rules, may be exemplified by the following:

LEXICON:

$$N \rightarrow \textit{boy, girl, alligator, unicorn, etc.} \quad (N = \text{noun})$$
$$V \rightarrow \textit{saw, kissed, strangled, etc.} \quad (V = \text{verb})$$
$$ART \rightarrow \textit{a, the} \quad (ART = \text{article})$$
$$ADJ \rightarrow \textit{little, big, fat, stupid} \quad (ADJ = \text{adjective})$$

PS RULES:

    a. S → NP VP   (Replace S [sentence] by NP [noun phrase] followed by VP [verb phrase])

    b. NP → ART (ADJ) N

    c. VP → V NP

By applying these rules according to the instructions given, we can construct a *derivation,* or *tree diagram,* of the sentence *The fat alligator kissed a unicorn.*

```
                      S
              _____|_____
             NP               |‾‾‾VP
          ___|___             |    ‾‾‾‾‾
         |   |   |            |    NP
        ART ADJ  N            V   ART  N
         |   |   |            |    |   |
        the fat alligator  kissed  a  unicorn
```

This little grammar can generate 3264 sentences, all of them well-formed strings of English; some of them are:

(23)   a. *A fat alligator kissed a unicorn.*
           b. *A fat alligator kissed the unicorn.*
           c. *A fat alligator kissed a fat unicorn.*
           d. *A fat alligator kissed the fat unicorn.*
           e. *A fat boy kissed the unicorn.*
           f. *The stupid boy strangled the little alligator.*
           g. *The big unicorn kissed the stupid alligator.*

Not only does this small grammar derive many sentences but all the sentences are well-formed sentences of English. The kinds of rules that have been written guarantee this. If rule b were written as b':

b'. NP → ART N (ADJ)

it would generate "ungrammatical" strings in English (e.g., *The alligator stupid strangled a unicorn fat.*), although it could generate well-formed strings in French if the lexicon contained French words. It can be seen that a grammar so constructed, because of its formal character, is testable. If it derives ungrammatical sentences it is clearly *not* a model of a speaker's knowledge of his language.

But such a grammar accounts for more than what is or is not a well-formed sentence. It "explains" *why* a sentence is well-formed and accounts for a speaker's knowledge of the fact that, for example, *the boy, the stupid boy, the fat boy, the big alligator,* etc. are phrases of the same kind—noun phrases—and therefore can occur either as the "subject" of a sentence or the "object" of a verb (as part of the verb phrase). It accounts for why *the boy kissed the girl* is well-formed but **boy the kissed girl the* is not, since the rules explicitly state that ART precedes N.

Clearly, by increasing the number of items in the lexicon, the grammar could generate an astronomical number of sentences, but it still would not generate

(24)   *The big, fat, stupid alligator kissed the girl.*

This is a trivial problem and easily can be remedied by changing rule b to b":

b". NP → ART $(ADJ)_0^n$ N

where the subscript means "no occurrences" and the superscript means "any number of occurrences" (i.e., zero or any number of ADJ). Using this rule, one could (with proper additions to the lexicon) derive a sentence such as:

(25) *The big, blond, cross-eyed, pigeon-toed, loud-mouthed, fascistic bitch swatted the skinny, gnarled, yellowing, ageless dwarf.*

A grammar of this kind also makes explicit the long-accepted notion that sentences have a hierarchical structure.

The tree diagram or phrase marker on page 12 clearly shows that a sentence is composed of a noun phrase and a verb phrase, and the categories that constitute each. It reveals that *the fat alligator* is an NP and is a phrase of the same type as *a unicorn,* which is also an NP. Each "node" or "branching point" in the tree represents what has traditionally been called a "constituent" of the sentence.

By the addition of rule b″, which permits us to generate a sentence with any number of adjectives, we have provided the grammar with the power to generate an infinite set of sentences. Obviously, when we actually use our knowledge of the language in speaking or in the perception of utterances, we never use this ability to produce a sentence with an unlimited number of adjectives. On the other hand, it is clear that *in principle* we have the ability (if not the stamina or immortality) to go on adding adjectives forever.

To generate sentences like:

(26)   *The boy kissed the unicorn and the girl kissed the alligator.*

we can add rule a′ to the grammar:

$$\text{a'. } S \rightarrow S \text{ (and S)}_0^n$$

Using the other rules as given, we can now derive an infinite set of phrase markers, including the following:

(*i*)

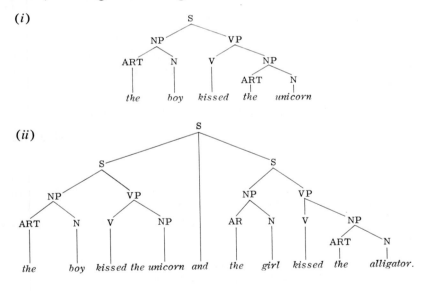

(*ii*)

(*iii*)

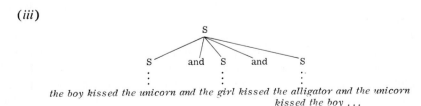

the boy kissed the unicorn and the girl kissed the alligator and the unicorn
kissed the boy . . .

By permitting a symbol to appear both on the left and on the right of the arrow, the grammar includes the recursive property needed to generate an infinite set of sentences.*

A. The Capacity of Phrase Structure Grammars

Phrase structure grammars (PSGs) are therefore powerful devices for generating the sentences of a language and associating a structure with each sentence. They can generate an infinite set of sentences by means of such recursive rules as S → S (and S). They can provide adequate representations of hierarchical relations, as shown by the two tree diagrams below for sentence (27):

(27)   *John and Mary or Bill will come.*

a.

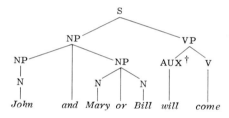

b.

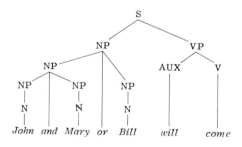

---

* The rules and phrase markers are provided merely to exemplify the notions presented. No claims are made as to whether these are the actual rules or phrase markers in the grammar of English.

† The simple grammar given above does not include many category symbols which are needed in a full grammar, e.g., AUX [auxiliary], PRO [pronoun], PN [proper noun], etc.

Diagram a represents the sentence that means *John and Mary will come or John and Bill will come,* and diagram b represents the sentence that means *John and Mary will come or Bill will come.*

By providing labels (the symbols in the rules which represent the nodes of the branches in the tree diagrams), similar strings of PSGs reveal the similar syntactic categories, as shown by diagrams (28a–c):

(28) a.

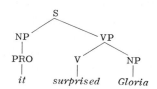

b.

c.

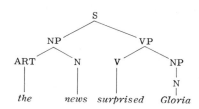

These three phrase structures can be derived by a phrase structure rule:

$$NP \rightarrow \begin{cases} PN \\ ART \\ NP \text{ (that S)} \end{cases}$$

which shows that *it, the news,* and *the fact that Seymour was a dropout* have something in common, they are all NPs.

B. Transformational Rules

It is clear that any grammar of a language must include phrase structure rules. But there are other aspects of our linguistic knowledge that they cannot adequately account for.

I will illustrate the problems of phrase structure grammars by just one simple example. Consider sentences like the following:

(29)   a. *Minerva looked up the number.*
                 b. *Minerva looked the number up.*

(30)   a. *Thor threw down the hammer with a bang.*
                 b. *Thor threw the hammer down with a bang.*

(31)   a. *Zeus took out the garbage.*
                 b. *Zeus took the garbage out.*

If the grammar contained only phrase structure rules, we would have to derive the "a" sentences and the "b" sentences by different rules. The rule for the "a" sentences would be something like

c′. VP → V (PART) NP (where PART = particle)

and the rule for the "b" sentences

c″. VP → V NP (PART)

Notice however that, in (32), sentence b is grammatical but sentence a is not:

(32)   a. * *Zeus took out it.*
                 b.   *Zeus took it out.*

The rules would have to be much more complicated than those given above if such ungrammatical occurrences were to be avoided.

That is, if NP is expanded into PRO, the particle *must* occur after the noun phrase, but if NP is expanded into ART and N, then the particle can occur either before or after the NP. Since this expansion must occur prior to deciding which rule to apply, the two rules above will not work. Furthermore, including these two rules in the grammar would fail to show the relationship between the "a" sentences and the "b" sentences.

To account for such phenomena, grammars contain, in addition to phrase structure rules, *transformational rules* (T-rules). These rules differ from phrase stucture rules in that they do not rewrite strings of symbols, but rather, apply to entire structures or trees. Each T-rule contains two parts: a *structural description* (SD), which states the conditions under which the rule applies, and a *structural change* (SC), which states what change is to occur.

Suppose the grammar contained the PS rule c′ given above to derive the "a" structures. A T-rule of particle movement might then be stated as:

(33) SD: *X* V PART NP *Y* (where *X* and *Y* are variables and may be null)

   SC: *X* V NP PART *Y* (which states that the structure specified by the SD is to be changed into the structure specified by the SC).

This rule can apply to an infinite set of phrase markers—all of which are generated by the PS rules—as long as they include the structure "V PART NP." This is illustrated by the diagrams below.

(34) a.

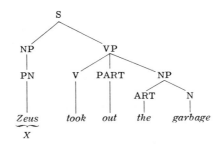

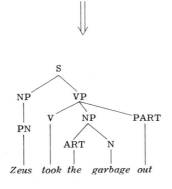

(34) b.

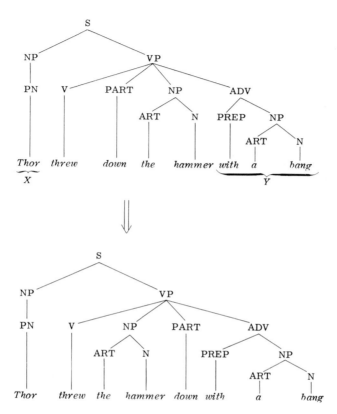

This is a rather trivial example of the power of T-rules. Transformational rules can account for a great deal of a speaker's syntactic knowledge not revealed by phrase structure rules.

Phrase structure rules derive what may be called the *deep structures* of sentences (or underlying structures), and transformational rules map these deep structures onto *surface structures*. T-rules can derive a single surface structure from two or more underlying deep structures, thus accounting for the ambiguity of sentences like:

(35)   a. *George wanted the presidency more than Martha.*

A T-rule can be formally stated that specifies which items can be deleted. Thus sentence (35a) can be derived from (35b):

(35) b. *George **wanted the presidency** more than Martha **wanted the presidency.***

where the identical structure of the second clause *wanted the presidency* is deleted.

Sentence (35a) can also be derived from

(35) c. **George wanted** *the presidency more than* **George wanted**
         Martha.

where again the identical structure *George wanted* is deleted.

We stated above that the rules of the semantic component operate on the deep structures of sentences, that is, they apply before transformational rules derive the surface structures. The reason for this is provided by examples (35a–c). Since there are two different deep structures, there are two different meanings that can be assigned to one surface structure.

T-rules can also derive two different surface structures from one deep structure, as is shown by the particle movement above.

T-rules can substitute one lexical item for another:

(36)   *Jane has* **some** *money* $\Rightarrow$ *Jane doesn't have* **any** *money.*

where *some* becomes *any* under negation.

In (37), the T-rule that maps a onto b moves the NP *John* to subject position and also deletes the underlying NP *it*:

(37)   a. *It is easy to please John* $\Rightarrow$
                               b. *John is easy to please.*

We can see now why we know that *John* is the object of *please* in (37b), but since (37b), *John is eager to please,* cannot derive from (38):

(38)   * *It is eager to please John.*

the different interpretations of the similar surface structures are revealed.

But grammars cannot consist entirely of transformational rules, since these require input structures on which to operate, and it is just these input structures—the deep structures—which are the output of the phrase structure rules and the lexicon.

This view of a grammar—as a formal device for generating sentences with structural descriptions and with phonetic and semantic representations—accounts for much of what can be considered a speaker's linguistic competence. Furthermore, it does this in an explicit and testable fashion.

Since this model of a grammar was first put forth (Chomsky, 1957), the theory has been expanded and revised (Chomsky, 1965). Transformational theory has generated a great deal of research and provided exciting new insights into the nature of language and grammars. But, as is to be expected in a developing science, new problems have arisen in the course of applying the theory, which have promoted new debates within the paradigm.

The "standard model" of transformational grammar assumed that transformations do not change meaning, i.e., transformational rules are meaning-preserving operations (Katz & Postal, 1964), that the semantic and syntactic components of a grammar are independent, and that the "meaning" of sentences was completely determined by the deep structures of sentences.

Sentences characterized as having *logical predicates* (including quantifiers like *all, every, many, some,* etc. and the negative element *not*) presented problems for the "standard model," as is shown by the following:

(39)   *Many arrows didn't hit the target.*

(40)   *The target wasn't hit by many arrows.*

In the "standard model," sentence (40) is related to sentence (39) by a *passive transformation,* and, therefore, the two sentences should mean the same thing. This is not the case, since (41) is an acceptable sentence but (42) is not:

(41)   *Many arrows didn't hit the target, but many did.*

(42)   * *The target wasn't hit by many arrows, but many arrows did hit the target.*

Similarly, the passive sentence (44) is not synonymous with (43):

(43)   *Everyone loves someone.*

(44)   *Someone is loved by everyone.*

Sentences such as these showed that changes in the standard theory were required. Two different approaches were developed to account for these facts, one known as the extended standard theory (EST) (Chomsky, 1970) or interpretive semantics (Jackendoff, 1972) and the other as generative semantics (GS) (Lakoff, 1969; Postal, 1970, 1971; Ross, 1969).

In the EST, the assumption that transformations are meaning-preserving is discarded to a certain extent, and an additional set of *"surface interpretation rules"* are added to the grammar. These new rules operate on derived surface structures. The "meaning" of a sentence, according to EST, depends on both the deep syntactic structure and the derived structure. The distinctness between the syntactic and semantic levels is maintained.

The generative semanticists, on the other hand, maintain the meaning-preserving nature of transformations but discard the separation between syntax and semantics. They suggest that the sets of formal objects that represent semantic and syntactic structures (or trees) are identical. In other words, in the GS grammar, the semantic representation of a tree is the deep structure of that tree. If two sentences (surface structures) have different meanings, then they must be derived from different deep structure trees. The generative semanticists also maintain that, if two sentences are synonymous, they have the same deep structures. According to this theory, then, sentences (39) and (40) and sentences (43) and (44) would not be transformationally related but would be derived from different deep structures. In addition, sentences (45), (46), and (47) would have identical deep structures (Postal, 1970):

(45)   *John strikes me as being similar to Harry.*

(46)   *It strikes me that John and Harry are similar.*

(47)   *John reminds me of Harry.*

The deep structure from which these three sentences are derived would of necessity be much more abstract than the deep structures generated in the EST.

Neither of the two new models has been formalized to the extent of the "standard theory." Each raises problems that are answered by one and not the other, or by neither.

The limits of this chapter preclude the possibility of dealing with some of the phenomena of natural language that have given rise to the current debate.

It should also be noted that none of these theories attempt to model how a speaker–listener produces or comprehends utterances, i.e., how he utilizes his grammar (linguistic competence or knowledge) in real-time linguistic behavior.

We should not be surprised that there is at present no totally acceptable or complete theory of language. Natural language may well be the most complex phenomenon to be studied scientifically.

No theory represents the final "truth." What is important is that the developments of the last several years have set new demands on linguistic theory and have managed to account for a number of aspects of human language. Much has been discovered and explained, despite the questions that still await answers.

References

Bloomfield, L. Review of *Language* by E. Sapir. *The Classical Weekly,* 1922, **15.**
Bloomfield, L. *Language.* New York: Holt, 1933.
Chomsky, N. *Syntactic structures.* The Hague: Mouton, 1957.

Chomsky, N. *Aspects of the theory of syntax.* Cambridge, Massachusetts: M.I.T. Press, 1965.

Chomsky, N. *Cartesian linguistics.* New York: Harper, 1966.

Chomsky, N. Deep structure, surface structure and semantic interpretation. In R. Jakobson & S. Kawamoto (Eds.), *Studies in general and oriental linguistics presented to Shiro Hattori.* Tokyo: TEC Co, 1970. Pp. 52–91.

Chomsky, N. *Language and mind.* (Enlarged ed.) New York: Harcourt, 1972.

Einstein, A. *Essays in science.* New York: Philosophical library, 1934.

Hockett, C. A note on 'structure'. *International Journal of American Linguistics,* 1948, **14,** 269–271.

Jackendoff, R. *Semantic interpretation in generative grammar.* Cambridge, Massachusetts: M.I.T. Press, 1972.

Joos, M. *Readings in linguistics.* New York: American Council of Learned Societies, 1957.

Katz, J., & Postal, P. M. *An integrated theory of linguistic descriptions.* Cambridge, Massachusetts: M.I.T. Press, 1964.

Kuhn, T. S. *The structure of scientific revolutions.* Chicago: Univ. of Chicago Press, 1962.

Lakoff, G. On generative semantics. In D. D. Steinberg & L. A. Jakobovits (Eds.), *Semantics? An interdisciplinary reader in philosophy, linguistics, anthropology and psychology.* New York: Cambridge Univ. Press, 1969.

Popper, K. R. *Conjectures and refutations: The growth of scientific knowledge.* New York: Basic Books, 1963.

Postal, P. On the surface verb *remind. Linguistic Inquiry,* 1970, **1**(1), 37–120.

Postal, P. *Crossover phenomena.* New York: Holt, 1971.

Ross, J. R. Guess who. In *Papers from the 5th Regional Meeting of the Chicago Linguistic Society,* 1969.

Sapir, E. The psychological reality of phonemes. In D. G. Mandelbaum (Ed.), *Selected writings of Edward Sapir in language, culture and personality.* Berkeley: Univ. of California Press, 1949.

Chapter 2

RESEARCH METHODS IN PSYCHOLINGUISTICS

GARY M. OLSON AND HERBERT H. CLARK

I. INTRODUCTION

Scientists are captives of their methods. Their theories are only as meaningful and as satisfying as their procedures for collecting and analyzing data allow. Methods are the ground rules for scientific inquiry and the definition of its limits. But methods cannot exist *in vacuo,* for methodology is a reflection of theory and is determined as much by hypothesis as by expediency or technology. This is not surprising. Without theories, observations would have no interpretation or structure. As a consequence, a survey of the methods of a field is in part a survey of its conceptual foundations.

Research methods in psycholinguistics are, as a class, rather ordinary. Except in the area of speech perception, which will not be treated in this chapter, few research techniques stand out for their technical complexity or originality. But what psycholinguistics lacks in methodological techniques it makes up for in difficult methodological issues. This is largely due to the kinds of theories assessed in psycholinguistic experiments. Psycholinguistics has borrowed many productive ideas from related fields like linguistics, computer science, and philosophy. Yet theoretical constructs derived from metatheoretical and conceptual principles different from psychology have an unclear status for models of language performance. Further, these fields are constantly changing, and psychological theory which depends on them must be continually revised and rethought. One investigator may design an experiment with an eye on syntactic variables, only to have his design criticized by the next investigator for its lack of control of the semantic variables that have resulted from a more sophisticated linguistics. This is related to the problem of competing theoretical traditions within psychology. Psycholinguists have come from a variety of backgrounds, and their ideas about how to do experiments reflect this fact. An investigator with a background in verbal learning feels it is important to control the frequency of occurrence of words. The next investigator, with a background primarily in linguistics, thinks such control is unnecessary, perhaps even too restrictive, since frequency per se can never play a role in his psycholinguistic theories. And finally there is the more usual problem of designing experiments that are powerful enough to test alternative explanations. All too often there are several plausible models for some set of facts, with no evidence available to decide among them.

There of course have been methodological advances associated with technical breakthroughs. The ability to synthesize speech sounds, dependent on modern electronic capabilities, has revolutionized the study of speech perception. Techniques for the recording of central nervous system activity have allowed significant study of the localization of speech processing in the brain. Computers have made the statistical analysis of enormous quantities of data commonplace, and this, coupled with on-line data collection via minicomputers, has allowed the study of problems whose scope, precision, and detail was impossible only a few years ago. Computers have also led to the development and testing of complex simulation models of language processing. Nevertheless, the bulk of psycholinguistic research has been characterized by the application of old—sometimes very old—techniques. For example, the study of additive factors in mental operations via reaction times is at least as old as Donders in 1869, but the interpretation of facts about language structure in light of such procedures is a new and important issue. Similarly, the recording of children's speech in natural settings can be traced back at least to the eighteenth century, although the analysis of such corpora in terms of transformational grammars and hypotheses about language universals is a contemporary problem.

Our first order of business will be to consider some of the issues that arise from the interaction between linguistics and psychology. From there we will go on to a detailed consideration of some of the major methodologies of various areas of psycholinguistics. Space limitations prevent us from discussing all or even most of the methods in psycholinguistics, so we have chosen a representative sample from the areas of language acquisition, language comprehension, memory for linguistic material, and semantic memory. Other chapters in this volume can fill in many of the gaps in our coverage.

II. RELATIONS BETWEEN PSYCHOLINGUISTICS AND LINGUISTICS

Any specialty has ties with many other fields, and psycholinguistics is no exception. Philosophers and logicians study the syntax, semantics, and pragmatics of natural and artificial languages; mathematicians study the formal characteristics of automata; biologists study the communication systems of animals; neurophysiologists study the functional characteristics of language centers in the brain; and computer scientists attempt to develop programs capable of processing natural language. Each of these is a topic of importance for psycholinguistics and deserves our attention. However, we shall limit our discussion to the discipline that has influenced psycholinguistics the most, namely, linguistics. Its influence has been direct and widespread, but it has also been the source of some of the most serious questions about psycholinguistic theory and methodology.

To many, the relationship between linguistics and psycholinguistics might seem to be especially straightforward. The linguist, it might be said, is concerned with *competence,* while the psycholinguist studies *performance.* This historically important distinction has often been misleading. The conceptual dangers inherent in the simplistic view just mentioned have been succinctly summarized by Fodor and Garrett (1966):

> There are in short two performance/competence distinctions more or less confused in the methodological literature of psycholinguistics. The first, which insists upon the distinction between studying behavior and studying the mechanisms underlying it, seems to us pre-eminently worth honouring . . . .
> The second is, however, less obviously sound; for the contrast between lin-

> guistic information and "psychological mechanisms" is often interpreted not
> as a point of methodology but rather as a theory (or proto-theory) of the
> way speech is produced. It suggests that a performance model ought to con-
> sist of a model of linguistic competence (a grammar) plus some further
> component or components at present unknown; jointly these components are
> somehow to issue in the utterance or understanding of sentences [p. 138].

They go on to say,

> It is one thing to say that a grammar formalizes the speaker's linguistic infor-
> mation. It is quite another thing to argue that a grammar is *therefore* a
> component of whatever system of mechanisms is involved in the production
> of speech [italics in original, p. 139].

Psychologists are ultimately interested in the mechanisms that generate
behavior. However, the goal of linguistic theory is to obtain an axiomatiza-
tion of language, a grammar, that formally accounts for the structural relations among elementary constituents, "a system of rules that in some explicit and well-defined way assigns structural descriptions to sentences
[Chomsky, 1965, p. 8]." According to the contemporary transformationalists, the intuitions of the native speaker about such things as grammaticality or acceptability, paraphrase and ambiguity, and the like are primary
data for the evaluation of grammars. In this sense the grammar represents
the "tacit" knowledge of the speaker. But what this means is controversial
(Fodor, 1968; Morganbesser, 1969; Nagel, 1969) and has been the source
of much error in psycholinguistics. As Lyons (1970) has pointed out, the
mathematical language of abstract automata has misled many into thinking
that rewrite rules are descriptions of actual mechanisms of language production. But grammars are not theories about the mechanisms of production or of comprehension. The criteria used to justify them are largely
formal ones having nothing to do with possible mechanisms, and the formalisms of generative grammars are no more appropriate for production
than for comprehension.

The confusion here is not entirely due to the psychologist. As Greene
(1972), Pylyshyn (1972), and Watt (1970, 1971) have argued, linguists
have been unclear in what they have said about the relation of linguistics
to psychology. Greene (1972), for example, pointed out that Chomsky—the linguist most influential in the recent growth of interest in psycholinguistics—has been equivocal about the relation. In *Language and Mind*
he writes: "At the level of universal grammar, [the linguist] is trying to
establish certain general properties of human intelligence. Linguistics, so
characterized, is simply the sub-field of psychology that deals with these
aspects of mind [Chomsky, 1968, p. 24]." But when faced with specific
applications of linguistics to psycholinguistics, Chomsky has tended to cau-

tion the psychologist on the use of linguistics as psychological theory. Thus, in *Aspects of the Theory of Syntax* he says:

> When we speak of a grammar as generating a sentence with a certain structural description, we mean simply that the grammar assigns this structural description to the sentence. When we say that a sentence has a certain derivation with respect to a particular generative grammar, we say nothing about how the speaker or hearer might proceed, in some practical or efficient way, to construct such a derivation [Chomsky, 1965, p. 9].

If linguistics does not describe the actual mental operations the hearer or speaker goes through in comprehending or producing speech, then what "general properties of human intelligence" does it establish? If this were clear, it would be straightforward to see where linguistics fits within psycholinguistics. Watt (1970, 1971) questioned the whole foundation of linguistics on these grounds. He pointed out that linguistics is based on the criterion of structural or rule economy. But it could just as well be based on some other criterion, for instance a criterion of economy in performance, with psychological data playing a central rather than a peripheral role in the determination of linguistic theory.

Obviously linguistics has played and will continue to play a central role in psycholinguistic methodology, no matter how this issue is resolved. Its main influence, though often overlooked, has been in the theoretical language of psycholinguistics. Every psycholinguistic theory has been stated in terms of technical notions like "word," "noun," "adjective," "phrase," "sentence," "clause," to say nothing of more abstract notions like "transformation," "deep structure," "surface structure," "markedness," or "presupposition." Investigators have often appeared to assume these terms were nontheoretical ones, useful for the neutral description of speech as behavior but implying no more. However, even a term like "word" is a technical concept with important methodological consequences. Does each "word" have a simple meaning attached to it, as previous investigators of verbal learning and linguistic memory have supposed, or should some words be thought of as combinations of simpler notions, i.e., as equivalent to more than one simpler word, as new linguistic analyses would have it? How one answers questions like this will determine what experiments one sets up, what controls one uses, and what analyses one carries out on the resulting data.

Perhaps the most beneficial influence of linguistics has been to raise the level of sophistication about language within psychology. Not too long ago, psychologists interested in language felt they could study it with little or no knowledge about linguistics, since after all it appeared to have little to do with behavior. Nowadays, these same psychologists find it imperative to know as much as they can about linguistics. For one thing, ignorance of linguistic structure often leads to naive experimental designs, studies in which obvious properties of language are confounded with the effects of interest. For another, knowledge of linguistics can lead to more sophisticated psychological theories, even when they are clearly distinguishable from the relevant linguistic theories. This has happened recently in the areas of syntax and phonology, where linguists have concentrated most of their effort, and it is beginning to happen in semantics, where more and more linguists are turning for exciting new discoveries about language. It has become impossible to study psycholinguistics without a thorough knowledge of relevant work in linguistics.

III. LANGUAGE ACQUISITION

As Blumenthal (1970) has observed, "With the rise of modern psychology the acquisition of language by children has been the most frequently investigated subject [p. 79]." Yet perhaps in no area of psychological inquiry into language have technical advances played a smaller role. One of the most important sources of evidence is still the simple observation and recording of child speech in natural settings. Though we now have audio- and videotape recorders to improve the reliability of such observations, the basic technique differs little from that employed in the numerous diary studies of child language that began to appear in the late eighteenth century. But recent developments in linguistic theory have led to new and sophisticated analyses of child speech, replacing the earlier anecdotal and unsystematic observations. Further, the collection of child language samples is now increasingly supplemented with simple experiments designed to test what the child knows about phonology, morphology, syntax, and semantics. The few controlled observations carried out by diarists were usually very informal and would not be called experiments by today's standards. These two classes of procedures—naturalistic observation and planned experiment—define the poles of a continuum, and many investigations combine aspects of both. Nonetheless, we shall organize our discussion on the basis of these two extremes. (See McNeill, 1970, for a more elaborate classification of child language research methods.)

A. Observing and Recording Language Behavior in Natural Settings

Scientific inquiry begins with simple observation and description, and this remains a very productive form of study in developmental psycholinguistics. Dietrich Tiedemann's careful and detailed report of his observations of the development of his son Friedrich, which appeared in 1787 (see Murchison & Langer, 1927, for an English translation), was the model for a number of such descriptions that appeared throughout the nineteenth and twentieth centuries. These reports were typically based on the author's observations of his own children, and their extensive detail about context and semantic significance has proved to be useful to contemporary investigators. These diarists recorded and discussed a wide range of language phenomena, including phonological development, the acquisition of vocabulary, morphological changes, the development of sentential syntax, and the relation of these to general intellectual development. Since the keeping of diaries continues to be of interest to parents with some linguistic or psychological sophistication, it would be useful for any prospective diarist to examine the guidelines proposed by Berko and Brown (1960) for the keeping of such records.

Modern longitudinal studies are no different in kind from these earlier diary studies, although they do reflect procedural refinements that have made them more useful. The typical scenario for such studies is to have the investigator periodically visit the subject—now usually not the investigator's own child—and record a sample of language behavior of several hours' duration. Usually a simple tape recording is made of the child's speech and the speech of adults in the room, while the investigator takes notes on nonlinguistic actions and possible interpretations for deictic, anaphoric, or potentially ambiguous constructions. Videotaping the child's speech and activities can provide essential contextual information important to the study of semantic development (e.g., Bloom, 1970, 1973).

Recording the speech and the accompanying extralinguistic context is not difficult, but what comes next is. Several things can be done with the set of utterances. One can try to formulate grammars for various stages of development, attempting to give a broad view of the child's overall linguistic abilities. Such grammars consist of a set of rules—much like those found in adult grammars—that capture the distributional properties of the corpus. The idea is to play linguist and describe the child's language as if it were an exotic language recently discovered on some remote island. This kind of analysis is best represented by the work of Roger Brown and his associates in their studies of Adam, Eve, and Sarah (Brown, 1973). Brown and Fraser (1963) have discussed in detail how such analyses are done. Braine (1963) and Ervin (1964) have done very similar analyses.

McNeill (1970) pointed out two sources of difficulty associated with such comprehensive analysis. First, what one really wants is a description of underlying competence, the underlying language ability that yields the sample of productions. But the writing of relatively complete grammars based on a distributional analysis of the utterances ends up being a description of the corpus, not of the child's ability. The analysis of early two-word utterances into pivot and open classes (Braine, 1963; Brown & Fraser, 1963; Miller & Ervin, 1964) has recently been criticized on these grounds (e.g., Bloom, 1970, 1971; Bowerman, 1973). The pivot–open distinction is based exclusively on distributional criteria, yet the study of the child's use of two-word utterances in context shows that there is a rich implicit structure to them that is not evident from distributional criteria alone. The second difficulty McNeill raised is that the analysis of the grammar of a particular child at a particular stage of development is invariably confounded with the adult's own linguistic knowledge. Distinctions are made during analysis that reflect the adult's knowledge of where the language will eventually end up. It is clear that at some point the distinctions in the adult's language will be reflected in the child's. But the identification of the exact point at which this happens is a critical issue which requires that distinctions functional in the child's grammar be separated from projections of the adult's grammar.

The extensive corpora of longitudinal researches are also useful for tracing the development of specific linguistic forms. For instance, the child's mastery of negation (Bellugi, in press; Bloom, 1970; Klima & Bellugi, 1966), of questions (Brown, 1968; Klima & Bellugi, 1966), of noun and verb inflections (Brown, 1973; Cazden, 1968), and of simple transformations (Brown & Hanlon, 1970) have been explicated on the basis of longitudinal data. In these cases, the investigators have described the successive approximations children make to adult forms, so here the adult's knowledge of what rules the children are attempting to learn plays a central role. Klima and Bellugi (1966), for example, noted the complex rules for negation in adult language and then followed the child through separate stages in the acquisition of successive parts of the adult rules. This kind of analysis is much less useful for studying linguistic forms that are not so clearly marked.

Either of these kinds of analysis, writing complete grammars for a given developmental stage or tracing the development of a specific adult form through longitudinal data, presents a serious methodological question. How do we know that the rules we use to describe the child's ability are correct? A grammar can be erroneous in two different ways: (a) it can fail to generate sentences that are in fact grammatical and (b) it can generate sentences that are ungrammatical. By methodological convention the utterances of a corpus provide a rough check for (a). But, as Braine (1971) suggests, (b) is a trickier problem, since nothing in the corpus provides direct evidence of what is ungrammatical for the child. Asking the child for judgments of grammaticality is usually not very helpful, for young children have difficulty distinguishing formal correctness from semantic truth value—though see Gleitman, Gleitman, and Shipley (1972) and de Villiers and de Villiers (1972) for some recent evidence on this. Therefore, evidence internal to a corpus itself must be used, and Braine (1971) examined a number of these techniques in detail. One is to use replacement sequences like those in

(1)   *Want more. Some more. Want some more.*

(2)   *Truck fall down. Big truck fall down. This fall down.*

to provide evidence for the kinds of formal manipulations allowable in the child's grammar. The relative frequency of constructions offers another source of indirect evidence for the evaluation of grammars. Braine also suggested that the formal criterion of the overall simplicity of a grammar with respect to a corpus, and judicious use of the investigator's knowledge of adult grammar, provide additional constraints in the absence of direct evidence of ungrammaticality. Ervin (1964) used imitation tests as a means of evaluating grammars based on five children's corpuses. Braine's excellent discussion of these various means for assessing grammatically should be consulted for additional details.

The diary studies have provided evidence for phenomena that would be infeasible to study experimentally. For instance, E. Clark (1973b) has combed these for examples of what she has called "over-extensions," cases where the child uses a word like *doggie* to refer to horses, cows, and cats as well as dogs. Clark used the diary data to draw systematic conclusions about the properties of over-extensions, their time of appearance, and their implications for semantic development. Ingram (1971) made similar use of the diary accounts in his study of the holophrastic speech of very young children.

B. Interactive Observation and Experimentation

The analysis of samples of naturally occurring utterances offers an opportunity for a comprehensive description of linguistic abilities and, as Braine (1971) has observed, provides one of the most natural techniques for the study of language development in very young children. However, such data are primarily relevant to the study of production and provide only indirect evidence, if any, for comprehension. Mother–child interactions often give fortuitous examples of comprehension phenomena, but these lack the kind of careful control that is needed to study a particular ability in detail. Consequently, many investigators have turned to experimental methods. The investigator presents either linguistic or nonlinguistic material to the child and then asks for a critical response, which can serve as an indicator of linguistic ability. Such methods have been used to study the child's understanding of word morphology, the process of imitation, the child's interpretation of various linguistic forms, and even the process of production, which has been so successfully studied via spontaneous speech samples.

Berko's (1958) study of English morphology is a justly famous example of the application of experimental techniques to child language acquisition. The elegance of her method can be illustrated with an example. One class of morphological rules she studied were those for pluralization. The child's knowledge of these rules was tested by showing him a line drawing of a hypothetical animal, and saying, "This is a wug." A second drawing was presented containing two of the animals, and the experimenter said, "Now there is another one. There are two of them. There are two _____." The experimenter paused, and the child was required to fill the pause with the correct response, in this case *wugs* with the morph/–z/ in the terminal position. The use of a nonsense word ensured that a correct response was due to the relevant morphological rule and not to having memorized a particular plural heard before. Other systems of rules were studied in the same way by Berko.

Experimental studies of imitation grew out of the observation in diary studies that children tend to simplify sentences when imitating them. This phenomenon has now been examined in experiments where investigators had full control over the sentences the children were asked to imitate (Fraser, Bellugi, & Brown, 1963; Menyuk, 1963, 1969; Slobin & Welsh, 1973). Slobin and Welsh (1973), for example, found that their imitation task could be used as a gauge of comprehension as well as of production. Complex sentences that were understood by the child were routinely simplified, as in (3), but those that exceeded the child's capacity for comprehension were simply jumbled, as in (4).

(3) *The man who I saw yesterday got wet → I saw the man and he got wet*

(4) *The boy the book hit was crying → Boy the book was crying*

It has been the study of comprehension that has received the greatest impetus from carefully controlled experiments. Typically, the child is read a sentence and is asked to choose which of two pictures the sentence describes, or to act out the sentence with the toys in front of him. For example, Donaldson and Wales (1970) studied the comprehension of relational terms like *more, less, same,* and *different* by asking children to point to an object in an ordered array. Objects differing in height might be presented to the child, and he would be asked, "Point to the biggest one." Shipley, Smith, and Gleitman (1969) had children respond to simple commands that either did or did not contain extra nonsense words. They were interested in the effects on comprehension of incidental material that the child did not know. E. Clark (1971, 1972), in her studies of the meaning of *before, after, in, on,* and other such terms, gave children instructions to carry out an action or series of actions. She could then assess just how the children understood these words by noting what mistakes they made in acting out the instructions. C. Chomsky (1969), in a model study of comprehension, examined a variety of constructions (e.g., *John is easy/eager to please*) and lexical items (e.g., *ask, tell,* and *promise*) by requiring children from 5 to 10 years of age to act out instructions containing these materials. By use of this technique, Chomsky was able to give a sequence for the acquisition of these linguistic entities in far greater detail than would be possible from observations of spontaneous speech of children in that age range. Her techniques have since been elaborated by Cromer (1970, 1972) and Maratsos (1974).

There have been some difficulties with these methods, however. Fraser *et al.* (1963) used a battery of related tests to study imitation, comprehension, and production, and argued from their data that children could imitate sentences they could not comprehend and comprehend sentences they could not produce. Recently, Baird (1972) and Fernald (1972) questioned the logic of that experiment. Both noted that the three tests had quite different probabilities of chance success, so that the criterion scores for imitation, comprehension, and production were not comparable. They argued that one cannot draw any firm conclusions from this or similar studies until some solution to the criterion problem is reached. Fernald (1972), in fact, reran the Fraser *et al.* study, using an appropriate scoring technique, and failed to find the differences reported in the original study. In quite a different respect, McNeill (1970) noted that comprehension studies of the kind described above are limited by the restricted range of what he called the "portrayable correlates of various grammatical contrasts and classes [p. 13]." But, as McNeill pointed out, this methodological stricture can be circumvented by studying spontaneous dialogues in longitudinal data or by using controlled imitation for examining both comprehension and production of syntactic forms (see Slobin & Welsh, 1973). Finally, E. Clark (1973a) and Maratsos (1974) have noted that care must be taken to distinguish between responses based on linguistic knowledge and responses based on nonlinguistic strategies or contextual information. Incorrect conclusions about the nature and extent of the child's linguistic knowledge could result if such factors were ignored.

There is a more serious limitation of experimental studies of acquisition whose magnitude has not been completely assessed. Donaldson (1970, 1972) has discussed the effects that the formal situation of the experiment itself might have on the linguistic behavior displayed by the child. This is a general methodological problem in any psychological experimentation with human subjects, but there is some indication that it might be an especially acute problem with children's linguistic abilities. For instance, there is the dramatic work of Labov (1970) on the unrepresentativeness of verbal behavior elicited from black children by white investigators or even unsympathetic black investigators. A black child who is virtually silent before a white experimenter going through the formal ritual of psycholinguistic tasks becomes highly verbal and displays great linguistic sophistication with a black investigator who understands the dialect and ways of life of the black ghetto. The linguistic as well as social implications of this problem are obvious in the case of studies of black English. But how representative is the output of a white child in the presence of a white investigator? Such problems can be minimized through intelligent and sensitive efforts to build rapport, but it must be remembered that in any artificial, contrived situation we will probably not be viewing the full extent of the child's linguistic abilities. Hopefully, more serious interactive influences are not present, but no one has systematically evaluated such possibilities.

C. Other Techniques for Studying Language Acquisition

We have briefly covered some representative methods in developmental psycholinguistics, and interested readers will have to consult the cited sources for more complete discussion. However, two additional methods must be mentioned here. First, language learning can be studied as a formal problem, either through mathematical studies of possible language learning systems (Feldman, Gips, Horning, & Reder, 1969; Gold, 1967; Wexler & Hamburger, 1972) or through computer modeling of specific learning systems (Anderson, 1975; Reeker, 1970; Siklóssy, 1971, 1972). Little of this work has made any pretense of being directly relevant to questions of first language acquisition in the child. Since relatively little is known about acquisition, an attempt to model development in detail would be forced to make many premature and arbitrary assumptions. But, as more is learned, such models will become increasingly important. Of course, formal results can always serve as general constraints on theories of language development. For instance, the work of Feldman et al. (1969) has shown how important the order of input strings is in determining the learnability of a grammar. Although adults probably manipulate their language input to children in order to conform to some informal optimality criterion, the burden of selecting and organizing probably falls upon the child (see Pfuderer, 1969, who finds that there are some changes in adult inputs as the child develops). Thus, strategies involved in the acquisition of language are probably intimately related to criteria for the child's selection of language inputs for hypothesis testing (see Ervin-Tripp, 1971; Macnamara, 1972).

A second method is the study of language by laboratory analogies with adult subjects. Various symbolic systems have been contrived and taught to adults, demonstrating that artificial materials with rulelike properties similar to natural languages can be learned. Usually these studies represent little more than exercises in the cleverness and ingenuity of adult subjects in deriving relations coded implicitly in nonsense materials (e.g., Foss, 1968; Miller, 1967; Reber, 1967; Smith & Braine, in press; Smith & Gough, 1969; Smith, 1970), although occasionally such work is explicitly proposed as an analogy for some aspect of natural languages (e.g., Palermo & Eberhart, 1968; Palermo & Howe, 1970; Palermo & Parrish, 1971). Slobin (1971a) has presented a number of objections to Palermo's approach, showing how difficult it is to capture faithfully the characteristics of English in a contrived symbol system and how difficult it is to simulate the conditions of child language learning. Miller (1967) listed a number of reasons why the learning of artificial materials in the laboratory is not like a child learning his first language, many of which are obvious but important: (a) the subjects are not infants in their mental abilities and (b) they already know at least one natural language; (c) the artificial language has no semantics nor (d) any use outside the laboratory; (e) the experience with the language lasts only an hour or so; and (f) the symbolic inputs are usually visual instead of auditory. Slobin (1971a) raised similar points. Thus, while these studies are interesting and are relevant to the study of adult inferential behavior, they are limited in how much insight they offer into developmental psycholinguistics.

D. Resources

We have already referred to the useful discussions of methodological issues in Berko and Brown (1960), McNeill (1970), and Braine (1971). Recent collections of papers edited by Slobin (1971b), Huxley and Ingram (1971), Reed (1971), Moore (1973), and Ferguson and Slobin (1973), raise a number of methodological points in the context of specific substantive problems. An excellent summary of research techniques is available in the manual edited by Slobin (1967), which was specially prepared as a guide for cross-cultural studies of language acquisition.

IV. COMPREHENSION

Psychologists have frequently asked whether the structures studied by linguists have any "psychological reality," whether they in any way predict performance in tasks with linguistic stimuli. This is a weak theoretical question for cognitive psychology, since it usually is based on unprincipled extrapolations of results from linguistic analysis to performance conditions whose dominant variables are not specified. Nonetheless, it is a question that has been tackled frequently, and a variety of techniques have been applied to its analysis. Some of the procedures antedate the influence of transformational grammars on psycholinguistics, although linguistic theory since Chomsky (1957) has given psychologists many more specific ideas whose "reality" seems to be of interest.

Prior to transformational grammars, the development of information theory in communications research gave the psychologist a formal way of discussing the role of grammar in language performance. Grammatical structures were seen as the basis for establishing sequential constraints, grammatical factors making words more predictable or less informative in the technical sense of information. Thus, our knowledge of the rules of English allows us to reduce the range of possible completions for

(5)   *The tall _____ kicked the football.*

enormously, although of course to be accurate we would have to admit that both semantic and syntactic constraints are involved. Sequential constraints were studied with procedures developed by Miller and Selfridge (1950) and by Taylor (1953), while information theory (Garner, 1962; Miller, 1951; Miller & Chomsky, 1963) provided formalizations for quantifying these constraints. Mathematical studies of the structure of grammars revealed the inadequacies of Markovian processes as models of language or language users (Chomsky, 1963; Chomsky & Miller, 1963; Miller & Chomsky, 1963), and this has reduced the interest in analysis of linguistic strings based on information theory. Nevertheless, such analysis might be useful in situations where quantitative approximations to various unspecified underlying processes are sufficient (see, e.g., Clark, 1965).

The development of nonmetric scaling and clustering techniques has offered new tools for the study of the "psychological reality" of grammars. For instance, Levelt (1970) and Martin (1970) have applied Johnson's (1967) hierarchical clustering procedures to the psycholinguistic study of syntax. Subjects are asked to rate the relatedness of pairs of terms from a sentence (Levelt, 1970) or to group or cluster the words "into whichever and however many parts seem intuitively natural to you [Martin, 1970,

p. 160]." Data from many subjects are collapsed into confusion matrices for input to the clustering routine. The output of the clustering is a tree that represents the "subjective phrase structure." However, it is difficult to know exactly what these trees represent. Undoubtedly the judgments that form the data of the confusion matrices have much in common with the judgments used by linguists in writing grammars, but the criteria for the former are much less clear. The use of unconstrained judgments probably confounds a variety of theoretically important relationships, such as that between the underlying conceptual structure and the surface structure. While the kinds of distinctions made by linguists may not turn out to be operative in language performance, where there are theoretical reasons for wanting to be clear about several possible levels of structure, these scaling techniques must be evaluated carefully. Other discussions of scaling are available in Danks and Glucksburg (1970) and Degerman and Mather (1972).

Many other techniques have been used to assess the "reality" of various structures proposed by transformational grammarians. We will examine one of these—the so-called "click" experiment—in detail for several reasons. First, it has been widely cited as an important technique for the study of sentence processing. For example, Bever (1970a,b) and Fodor, Bever, and Garrett (1974) have made considerable use of the "click" results in discussions of comprehension strategies. Second, the technique has been plagued by a host of more or less serious methodological problems. And third, it gives us a chance to look closely at a problem whose theoretical implications are intimately related to methodological issues.

A. The "Click" Experiments

Methodologies are founded on assumptions about relations between variables of interest and presumed invariances that can form the basis for control. One such invariance, which has been exploited frequently in psycholinguistic research, is the limited capacity of the human information processor's input channels (Moray, 1969; Broadbent, 1971; Kerr, 1973). The simplest assumption is the strongest one, namely, that only one thing can be done at a time. Thus, if we require a subject to do two things at once, competition for the limited capacity should produce patterns of behavior that are of theoretical interest. The following general paradigm will recur in several forms in this chapter. A sentence or other linguistic string is presented to a subject for comprehension and some second criterion task is presented at the same time. The pattern of behavior on the second task is predicted on the basis of hypotheses about language processing and the relation of this processing to the competition for limited capacity. A schematic of this strategy is shown in Fig. 1. The investigator monitors the criterion task for theoretically interesting patterns of performance, with some kind of additional check to make sure the subjects are not cheating, that they are in fact understanding the materials. It is usually assumed that the real-time processing of language is discontinuous, that it is organized into units of less than sentence size, which themselves are wholes that cannot be further segmented. The processing necessary to carry out the criterion task must therefore be carried out in relation to the processing of these units of analysis.

Let us assume that the units of speech analysis—whatever they may be—affect performance on the secondary task in some systematic way. We can then work backwards from the performance on the secondary task to confirm or disconfirm hypotheses about the units of speech processing. This is the logic behind the "click" studies. Although the technique of superimposing a nonlinguistic click over speech and then measuring some response to the click was first used by Ladefoged and Broadbent (1960), the procedure is most widely known from the work of Bever and his associates (Abrams & Bever, 1969; Bever, 1973; Bever, Lackner, & Kirk, 1969; Bever, Lackner, & Stolz, 1969; Fodor & Bever, 1965; Fodor, Bever, & Garrett, 1974; Garrett, Bever, & Fodor, 1966). The issue raised by Bever was whether the syntactic processing of a sentence can influence the subjective localization or the time of detection of the clicks. First we will look at an example of this paradigm in use, Fodor and Bever's (1965) original study. Then we will examine a series of issues that have been raised by Bever and by other investigators interested in the technique. In line with Bever's research we shall concentrate on the use of the "click" paradigm for studying the influence of language structure on comprehension, although some of the investigations we shall mention were interested in other questions as well.

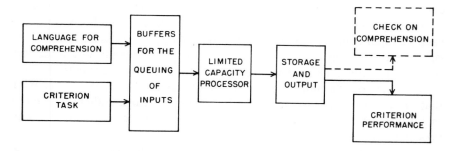

Fig. 1. General scheme for studying language comprehension using the assumption of a limited capacity input channel.

Fodor and Bever (1965) used sentences like

(6)   *That he was happy was evident from the way he smiled.*
         ′ ′ ′ ′ ′ ′ ′ ′ ′

The constituent structure of (6) is shown as

(7)   [[[*that*][[*he*][[*was*][*happy*]]]]
         [[*was*][[*evident*][[*from*][[[*the*][*way*]][[*he*][*smiled*]]]]]]]]

The major syntactic break in this sentence is between *happy* and *was,* and
Fodor and Bever hypothesized that this break defines a major discontinuity
in the processing of the sentence. On the assumption that sentence processing and click perception will be competing for access to limited resources,
clicks that occur near this syntactic boundary should be perceived as
though they had occurred in the boundary, while clicks already at the
boundary should be perceived accurately. In other words, the subjective
location of the clicks should be displaced toward major syntactic
boundaries.

Sentences like (6) were recorded on one track of a stereo tape and
a signal that triggered a nonlinguistic click was located at a prespecified
point in a second track of the tape. For the sentence in (6) the objective
location of the click could be any of the nine tick marks shown below
the sentence. It should be noticed that the clicks are symmetrically located
around the major syntactic boundary, so that any tendency for the clicks
to be mislocated for some other reason should cancel out. The sentences
were played into one ear, the click into the other. Subjects listened to this,
wrote down the sentence, and put a slash where they thought the click
had occurred. The data showed that the majority (66%) of the errors
made for clicks objectively outside the major break were located closer
to the break, while clicks objectively in the break were located more accurately than those outside it. This pattern of results was taken as support
for the view that the syntactic structure of the sentence plays an active
role in the perception and comprehension of speech.

The "click" technique depends on a long chain of assumptions—from
the analysis of linguistic structure, through the assumed cognitive activities
mediating sentence processing, to the precise click displacements found.
It is not surprising, then, that it has been subjected to close scrutiny. Various investigators have looked at the role of linguistic structure, click distributions, response biases, memory, and familiarity in this paradigm. As we
will see, consideration of these variables cannot be divorced from theoretical questions. We shall examine these variables under five headings.

1. *What features of the sentence cause subjective shifts in the perceived
location of the clicks?* Fodor and Bever were interested in the role of con-

stituent structure and did not draw a distinction between superficial and underlying structure. In fact, most of the major syntactic boundaries in Fodor and Bever's material were simultaneously superficial and underlying boundaries. Bever, Lackner, and Kirk (1969) pitted surface against deep structure boundaries and concluded that the latter were the important influence on the subjective location of clicks. However, Chapin, Smith, and Abrahamson (1972) were critical of the Bever *et al.* (1969a) procedure for testing the two possibilities, and designed their experiment so that clicks were objectively located halfway between a superficial boundary and a deep boundary without superficial marking. They found that superficial boundaries were the major determinant of shifts in the perceived location. Chapin *et al.* noted how difficult it is to construct sentences that adequately represent the hypotheses being contrasted in a design like theirs, a point that Fodor, Bever, and Garrett (1974) exploited in a critique of the Chapin *et al.* results. This is especially acute in light of controversies in linguistics about the nature and form of underlying structures. Thus, studies which have found little evidence for syntactic effects (e.g., Reber & Anderson, 1970) have defined the break between NP and VP in simple declarative sentences as a major syntactic break, while studies showing very strong effects (e.g., Holmes & Forster, 1970, 1972a; Seitz & Weber, 1974) have used the break between clauses separated by a conjunction or a major pause. There seems to be little agreement as to what constitutes a major break, and there are grounds for quibbling with what is or is not a break in underlying structure (Fodor *et al.,* 1974). Attempts to compare the relative effectiveness of major and minor breaks within the same sentence have yielded inconclusive results (Bever *et al.,* 1969a; Chapin *et al.,* 1972; Holmes & Forster, 1970, 1972a).

Factors other than syntactic structure can play a role in the perception of clicks, and this raises the theoretical issue of what factors are actually the most salient. Fodor and Bever (1965), Garrett *et al.* (1966), Bever *et al.* (1969a), and Abrams and Bever (1969) included various controls for the effects of surface cues like pauses and stress, effectively eliminating these as confounding variables in these studies. However, Bond (1971) and Lehiste (1972) found consistent effects for stress and minimal effects for syntactic structure when the design included an opportunity to examine both variables.

2. *Do the clicks migrate or fade?* The series of studies by Bever have focused on the assumption that the competition for limited perceptual processing capacity causes the superimposed clicks to be misperceived as falling closer to syntactic junctures than is objectively the case, and in general the data of Bever and his colleagues supports this. But Holmes and Forster (1970, 1972a) have emphasized accuracy of click location rather than

a perceptual drift, finding that clicks at the syntactic boundary are more accurately localized than those not at the boundary. They find no evidence of drift. Seitz and Weber (1974) find drift when subjects must remember the sentence as well as localize the click, but find only differential accuracy effects like Holmes and Forster's when subjects are given a script and asked to mark the location.

3. *How are the clicks distributed?* Much of the difference between migration and fading can be attributed to differences among investigators in where they put the clicks in the first place. We saw in sentence (6) that Fodor and Bever distributed the objective locations of the clicks around the major syntactic boundary, and most other studies have followed suit by locating most of the clicks very close to whatever structure was being studied. However, Chapin *et al.* (1972) located clicks midway between two structures of theoretical interest and observed which way they tended to drift. Studies that have emphasized general preposing strategies or other broad response biases have generally distributed the objective click locations more widely throughout the sentence and sometimes have not even been too concerned about locating them with respect to syntactic boundaries (Ladefoged & Broadbent, 1960; Chapin *et al.*, 1972; Bertelson & Tisseyre, 1970; Reber & Anderson, 1970; Holmes & Forster, 1972a).

4. *What kinds of response biases do subjects have in such tasks?* The issue of the objective click locations becomes critical when subjects' response biases are taken into account. We have already mentioned that many investigators have found a tendency for subjects to prepose clicks, to locate them on the average somewhat earlier in the sentence than their objective location. But other, more serious kinds of response biases have been found. Ladefoged (1967), Reber and Anderson (1970), and Bever (1973) had subjects locate clicks for sentences that objectively had no clicks at all, subjects being told they were in an experiment on subliminal perception or that the clicks were quite faint and hard to hear. The protocols showed that clicks were generally placed in or near major syntactic boundaries. Reber and Anderson (1970) found that analyses of such response biases accounted for the major portion of the error pattern obtained for a second group of subjects, who did have clicks in their sentences. What constitutes a reasonable measure of response bias in these location tasks is unclear. Bever (1973) and Fodor *et al.* (1974) emphasize that response bias data must be collected under conditions where the subject is attending to the structure and meaning of the sentence, and cite unpublished experiments that apparently show "a click displacement effect over and above any response bias [Fodor *et al.*, 1974, p. 332]." But in any event the response biases are large and systematic, and are similar to predicted patterns of response based on perceptual competition arguments,

so their assessment is essential in order to interpret any studies using this technique.

5. *Does the interposition of a delay and sentence recall influence the pattern of results?* Fodor and Bever had subjects recall the sentence and write it down prior to indicating where they thought the click had occurred. This intervening memory activity made it impossible to confirm Fodor and Bever's original hypothesis that the click misperception phenomena reflect the perceptual segmentation of linguistic materials. Procedural variations have been introduced by various investigators to minimize the role of memory. Studies using Fodor and Bever's procedure of sentence recall prior to click localization show the strongest effects of syntactic structure (Fodor & Bever, 1965; Garrett *et al.,* 1966; Abrams & Bever, 1969; Bever *et al.,* 1969a,b; Holmes & Forster, 1972a; Seitz & Weber, 1974), while those using localization without recall, by having subjects mark printed sentences given to them by the experimenter, show moderate, mixed, or negligible effects (Reber & Anderson, 1970; Bond, 1971; Lehiste, 1972) and those using reaction time to the click, rather than localization, have found that the pattern of times does not correspond at all to the pattern of location drifts (Abrams & Bever, 1969; Bond, 1971; see, however, Holmes & Forster, 1970, for an exception, though their clause breaks were also major acoustic breaks.) Fodor *et al.* (1974) emphasize the importance of having subjects attend to the meaning of sentences under conditions where they will not have to recall them, a flaw that vitiates the nonrecall condition of Seitz and Weber's (1974) experiment. A similar flaw appeared in the study by Lehiste (1972), which used a single sentence that was presented over and over again with variations only in stress and in the location of clicks. Undoubtedly syntactic structure effects would be minimized under such conditions, since subjects probably no longer attended to the meaning or form. Fodor *et al.* (1974) and Bever (1973) report unpublished results that apparently show a reliable click misperception effect under conditions of no sentence recall.

B. Summary of the Click Experiments

The multiplicity of methodological and theoretical tangles surrounding the use of the click paradigm precludes any simple evaluation of its usefulness. It is safest to assume, given present evidence, that the basic validity of the technique for assessing syntactic processing has not been unambiguously established. Further, given its apparent insensitivity to minor syntactic effects, there may be little the procedure can show beyond the demonstration that the major clause boundaries of sentences have psychological reality. Fodor *et al.* (1974) promise that unpublished data of theirs will clarify many of these difficulties and confirm the basic validity of the procedure for showing these effects.

C. Other Sentence Perception Tasks

The phoneme monitoring task is another technique that requires the subject to divide his attention between two activities. It is based on the same limited capacity assumptions as the click studies, but is not vulnerable to most of the criticisms leveled at those studies. A subject is required to listen to a sentence, knowing that later he will be asked questions that require comprehension, and is asked to press a button as quickly as possible whenever he hears a word beginning with /b/ or some other phoneme. If comprehension is difficult immediately preceding the word with /b/, the subject should take longer to react because he will be attending more to comprehension than to monitoring. This technique has been used quite successfully by Foss, Hakes, and their associates (Foss, 1969, 1970; Foss & Lynch, 1969; Cairns & Foss, 1971; Hakes & Foss, 1970). For example, Foss (1969) found that latencies for monitoring a /b/ were longer following a difficult lexical item (like *incarcerate*) than an easy one (like *imprison*), while Hakes and Foss (1970) showed that self-embedded sentences with relative pronouns (*The man that the boy knew left*) yielded quicker reaction times than the same sentence without the pronouns (*The man the boy knew left*). The pronouns were presumed to facilitate comprehension by providing explicit indicators in the surface structure of the underlying logical relations. Because these studies require an immediate response which shows prima facie evidence of difficulty in processing, these phoneme monitoring tasks are not subject to criticisms about response bias, memory complications, or distribution artifacts. But the procedure is apparently a difficult one to use, often requiring large numbers of subjects and sentences to uncover reliable differences.

Forster (1970), Forster and Ryder (1971), and Holmes and Forster (1972b) employ another procedure for assessing perceptual processing of sentences, which they call the rapid serial visual presentation (RSVP) technique. Each word of the sentence is presented singly and rapidly, with the subject required to write down the sentence after the presentation. This procedure also seems to show some promise.

D. Mental Chronometry

Sternberg (1969, 1971) has documented the history and the recent renaissance of Donders' procedure for the decomposition of mental processes with reaction time data. These procedures have been applied to psycholinguistic phenomena with much success. We shall focus on simple verification tasks where subjects must make "true"–"false" judgments of a sentence–picture or sentence–sentence display. Let us consider an example in some detail.

A recent series of papers (Clark, 1970, 1975; Clark & Chase, 1972; Chase & Clark, 1972; Trabasso, Rollins, & Shaughnessy, 1971) have outlined a model to account for the mental processes underlying the verification of positive and negative sentences. The power of the model has been demonstrated by showing that with relatively simple assumptions it can be made to account for the bulk of the previous psychological data on the comprehension of negatives. We will only briefly outline the model, its rationale, and its predictions, and recommend that the interested reader consult the original papers for a more complete explication and justification.

The model was designed to account for the time it takes people to decide whether a sentence is true or false of a picture. In a typical experiment (Clark & Chase, 1972), the subject is shown a display containing a sentence and a picture. He is to read the sentence, view the picture, and then press a "true" or "false" button as quickly as possible. He is timed from the moment the display is shown until he presses a button. In the simplified example we shall use, there are just four sentences, each to be compared against a picture of an A above a B: (a) the true positive sentence *A is above B;* (b) the false positive *B is above A;* (c) the true negative *B isn't above A;* and (d) the false negative *A isn't above B.*

According to the model, the process of carrying out this task consists of four stages. At Stage 1, the subject represents the sentence he is to verify and stores this representation in immediate memory. The true negative sentence *B isn't above A,* for example, might be represented as in

(8)   false *(above (B, A))*

The claim is that a negative sentence consists of two parts, a positive proposition *B is above A,* represented here as a function with two arguments *above (B, A),* (the *embedded* function) and another proposition into which the first is embedded, namely, *It is false that S,* represented here as a single-argument function *false (S)* (the *embedding* function). At Stage 2, the subject must represent the picture in some form that he can compare to the representation in (8). Thus, the picture of an A above a B is represented as in

(9)   *above (A, B)*

The crucial comparison process occurs at Stage 3. There, the subject must keep track of a truth index that tells him whether the sentence is ultimately true or false. The value of this truth index is determined by how the representations of (8) and (9) match with each other. The model assumes that the truth index has only two possible values, *true* and *false,* and that the initial value is *true.* Then Stage 3 consists of the two simple rules shown in (10):

(10) RULE 1: *If the embedded functions do not match, change the truth index.*
RULE 2: *If the embedding functions do not match, change the truth index.*

For the true negative sentence represented in (8), the process would go as follows. First, Rule 1 would compare *above* (*B, A*) in (8) against *above* (*A, B*) in (9), find a mismatch, and change the truth index from *true* to *false.* Second, Rule 2 would compare the *false* (*S*) of (8) to the absence of an embedding function in (9), find a mismatch, and change the truth index from *false* to *true.* Similar processes would be carried out for the other types of sentences. At Stage 4, the outcome of Stage 3—the final value of the truth index—would be converted into an overt response, in this case a button press.

The important property of this model is that each of the component processes is assumed to consume a fixed and additive amount of time. Specifically, negatives take longer to represent at Stage 1 than affirmatives, by an increment of time b; Rule 1 takes an increment c whenever it is required; and Rule 2 takes an increment d whenever it is required. All the time not included in these increments is thrown into a base time t_0. Thus, the model predicts that the latencies of *true affirmative, false affirmative, true negative,* and *false negative* sentences are composed of the components shown in Table 1. For example, this model predicts—not surprisingly—that negatives should take longer than affirmatives, and this by an amount equal to $(b + d)$. But the unique prediction of this model is that whereas true should be faster than false when the sentences are positive, true should be slower than false when the sentences are negative. Moreover, the model claims that the time advantage that true has over false for positive sentences—the parameter c—is exactly the same time advantage that false has over true for negative sentences. So the model makes quite specific predictions, which have been confirmed by recent research. The actual latencies of one experiment (Clark & Chase, 1972) are shown in Table 1. These latencies were used to estimate the base time t_0 (the time taken for the simplest sentence) as 1810 msec, parameter c (the time for a mismatch of embedded functions) as 187 msec, and the combined parameter $(b + d)$ (the time for negatives) as 685 msec. As Table 1 shows, the latencies predicted by these formulas and these parameter estimates

TABLE I

LATENCY COMPONENTS, ACTUAL LATENCIES, AND PREDICTED LATENCIES[a]

Type	Components of latency	Actual latencies (msec)	Predicted latencies (msec)
True affirmative	t_0	1810	1810
False affirmative	$t_0 + c$	1997	1997
True negative	$t_0 + c + (b + d)$	2682	2682
False negative	$t_0 \quad + (b + d)$	2495	2495

[a] Data from Clark and Chase (1972), on Explicit Negatives.
NOTE: t_0 = 1810 msec.
c = 187 msec.
$(b + d)$ = 685 msec.

exactly equal the actual latencies of the experiment. In other experiments, the model is not quite so accurate, but it is typically within the range of random error in the latencies.

This technique says nothing about the way in which the encodings of the sentence and the picture are derived; it only specifies their representation. Yet the range of linguistic phenomena that have been treated by the procedure (see Clark, 1975, for a review) attest to its usefulness. We shall see in a later section that it is also a useful technique for analyzing individual lexical items into components.

E. Other Procedures

The procedures we have emphasized, many of them using reaction time, treat the immediate processing of sentences. Where comprehension stops and retention begins is difficult to say, for they are clearly intimately related. However, many procedures that have been used to assess the "psychological reality" of linguistic structures have been more accurately studies of retention, and the interposition of memory processes—even over very brief intervals—can markedly alter the character of the findings. We have already seen evidence of the problem of memory creeping in to contaminate comprehension measures in the click studies, and Fillenbaum (1970) discusses other examples of the same problem.

Although our emphasis has been on immediate and rather direct measures of sentence processing, other techniques can be found. First, there are rating techniques. The subject is given a sentence that violates some particular syntactic or semantic constraint and is asked to rate it for its acceptability (e.g., Clark & Begun, 1968, 1971; Danks, 1969; Danks & Glucksberg, 1970; Downey & Hakes, 1968). Or he might read a sentence and be asked to judge how difficult it was to comprehend (e.g., Schwartz, Sparkman, & Deese, 1970; Wang, 1970a,b). These techniques, though indirect, have been shown to be reliable and have led to some interesting, nonobvious conclusions. Second, there are techniques that attempt to get at the particular interpretation people give to sentences. Johnson-Laird (1969, 1970a) gave subjects sentences like *All children like some toys* and got his subjects to reveal how they interpreted them by having them enumerate situations the sentences described. Taplin (1971) used a similar technique for studying *if–then* conditionals. Third, there are techniques that use the fact that reasoning problems demand prior comprehension of linguistic materials. One such reasoning task (e.g., Clark, 1969) has made use of the so-called three-term series problem (e.g., *If John is better than Dick, and Pete is worse than Dick, then who is best?*). Another has required subjects to decide whether a rule like *All cards with an even number on one side have a vowel on the other* is true or false (see Johnson-Laird & Wason, 1970; Wason, 1968). In a sense these latter techniques are simply extensions of simpler ones already discussed, although the added complexity does raise new issues.

F. Resources

Surveys by Miller and McNeill (1969), Johnson-Laird (1970b), Fillenbaum (1971b, 1973), Slobin (1971b), and Fodor *et al.* (1974) offer a more extensive treatment or an alternative viewpoint for many of the comprehension paradigms we have considered. More dated surveys by Herriot (1970) and Hörmann (1971) provide better coverage of earlier paradigms, especially those closely tied to traditional verbal learning. Clark (1975) and Fodor *et al.* (1974) attempt to bring theoretical order to a wide range of data on comprehension.

V. MEMORY

We shall group studies of memory under two categories. Studies of *retention* are those that investigate the remembering of specific linguistic inputs over short or long periods of time. Studies of *semantic memory* are those that investigate the properties of the relatively permanent store of information or knowledge that is used over and over in various language-related tasks.

A. Studies of Retention

The dominant issue in the study of the retention of linguistic materials has been the question of what is retained. This is not an easy question to investigate, since there are many possibilities and it is difficult to arrange the experimental conditions to differentiate clearly among them. The most frequently discussed candidates for memory representations have been associations among words or among other abstract linguistic entities, surface structure, deep structure, mental images, and semantic or conceptual structures. Not all of these candidates are well-defined, so it is often hard to say whether a given pattern of results supports or fails to support a given model. But even more important from a methodological point of view is the question of what interaction there might be between the memory representations and the strategies and processes of storage, search, and retrieval. In earlier psycholinguistic experiments little attention has been given to the classic issues of the psychology of remembering, with unfortunate results (Johnson-Larid, 1970b; Fillenbaum, 1971b, 1973). But, as more psychologists with an interest in memory have attacked psycholinguistic questions, the sophistication of research has risen (e.g., Anderson & Bower, 1973; Kintsch, 1974).

It is always difficult to know exactly what any given retention test is testing, but the problem seems especially troublesome in psycholinguistics. For instance, serious problems of scoring arise whenever we have subjects free-recall sentences. How should we score synonyms and paraphrases? What are our criteria for determining whether or not two expressions are synonymous? If we score for exact verbatim recall, we must be prepared to limit our generalizations to what must be an unrepresentative kind of language use. To minimize problems of scoring, investigators of retention often use paradigms which give more control over possible responses—for example yes–no or multiple-choice recognition tests. But this leads to other problems. Do our hypotheses about possible memory representations for language blind us in the design of our experiments so that we fail to detect significant clues to memory structures? Let us look at some studies to see the importance of these questions.

Miller (1962) attempted to incorporate the insights of the new linguistics into psychology by formulating a memory model based on Chomsky's (1957) earlier version of a transformational grammar. He proposed that sentences are stored in memory as a kernel string plus a transformational tag, the string representing the logical relationships among sentence constituents and the tag indicating the formal operations needed to map the kernel into an acceptable surface form. Miller assumed the kernel strings could be remembered independently of the transformational tags. Further, the tags were presumed to have a much more labile trace. This might mean that the sentence

(11)   *Hasn't the ball been hit by the boy?*

whose appropriate memory representation is

(12)   *The boy has hit the ball.* (Pas, Neg, Ques)

could lose its Neg tag and be misremembered as

(13)   *Has the ball been hit by the boy?*

Mehler (1963) tested this hypothesis by having subjects recall sentences and then examining the pattern of syntactic errors in recall protocols. Subjects were very good at recalling sentences that had no transformations (or, in later terminology, no optional transformations) and tended to simplify other sentences by deleting certain transformations. This appeared to confirm Miller's model. However, Foa and Schlesinger (1965) examined Mehler's data and found that virtually all of the errors made by subjects were meaning preserving (e.g., active–passive confusions but very rarely active–negative ones). This suggested that instead of a syntactically based representation subjects stored the sentence in semantic terms. The trend of subsequent data has proved Foa and Schlesinger's reinterpretation valid.

Structures may be simple or complex, and an obvious parameter for any hypothesis about comprehension or retention is some measure that relates complexity of the linguistic materials to the relative difficulty of processing. A study by Savin and Perchonock (1965) examined the role of transformational complexity in the retention of simple sentences, and their methodology has often been cited for its ingenuity. Subjects memorized a sentence and a list of eight words, followed by immediate recall of both the sentence and the list. Savin and Perchonock reasoned that sentences with greater complexity, in this case more transformational tags, should take up more space in memory and thus lead to poorer recall of the accompanying word list. In a slight variation of the paradigm summarized in Fig. 1, they assumed that the sentence and the list were competing for storage in a limited capacity device, and that more complicated sentences would displace list words from memory. Thus, subjects correctly recalling a simple active declarative sentence should be able to recall more of the list words than subjects recalling a negative question, since the latter requires two more optional transformational tags than the former (by Miller's, 1962, hypothesis). Their results supported their predictions.

However, there are difficulties with their interpretation. First, as we mentioned before, the validity of the transformational tag model on which they based their predictions has been challenged by many other studies. It is possible, of course, that they could still come up with different formalisms that might capture the same ordinal predictions relating complexity to remembering. The second and more serious difficulty is that subsequent investigations have not been able to replicate Savin and Perchonock's results or have replicated them only at the expense of uncovering serious confoundings in their design that leave the interpretation of their data wide open. Matthews (1968) could not replicate the original results using essentially the same design. Epstein (1969) found that the effect of transformational complexity disappeared when the word lists were recalled before the sentence rather than after, indicating that the effect was due not to conflicting storage demands but to some kind of output interference. Glucksberg and Danks (1969) observed that transformational complexity in Savin and Perchonock's study was almost perfectly correlated with recall delay, a serious confounding that Glucksberg and Danks could not eliminate as a possible explanation. The data of Foss and Cairns (1970) lend further support to the idea that output interference or some kind of interruption of rehearsal, rather than an interaction of syntax and limitations of memory capacity, are involved in this paradigm. Thus, although ingenious, the Savin and Perchonock study was an unsuccessful attempt to demonstrate the predictive validity of a particular complexity measure.

The weighing of syntactic versus semantic factors has been important, and a number of procedures have been designed to examine the issue more directly. For instance, Sachs (1967, 1974) demonstrated that subjects are very good at recognizing changes that alter the meaning of sentences they have studied, but are very poor at recognizing changes that alter structural or lexical characteristics while preserving the meaning. Her subjects listened to recorded prose passages, and at some point the passage was interrupted and a test sentence presented. These test sentences were identical to a sentence presented earlier, were altered to change the form but preserve the meaning, or were altered to change the meaning. If (14) represents a sentence originally in the passage, (15) is a sentence with the meaning changed, while (16) and (17) have altered structure but the same meaning:

(14) *He sent a letter about it to Galileo, the great Italian scientist.*

(15) *Galileo, the great Italian scientist, sent him a letter about it.*

(16) *A letter about it was sent to Galileo, the great Italian scientist.*

(17) *He sent Galileo, the great Italian scientist, a letter about it.*

Subjects were very good at correctly discriminating an original sentence from any of the changed sentences on an immediate test, but when the test sentence was given after subjects had listened to intervening prose they could accurately recognize only changes that altered meaning. Wanner (1968) found the same pattern in a novel procedure where he tested subjects on the instructions for a task they thought was going to follow. Fillenbaum (1966) found similar results in a slightly different study, where subjects most often confused the correct *open* with the incorrect *not closed* in the test sentence in (19) whose original is shown in (18):

(18) *The door was open.*

(19) *The door was* (a) *open* (b) *not open* (c) *closed* (d) *not closed.*

These general demonstrations provide little evidence about the specific form of the memory representations, so let us look at some experiments that have attempted to deal with this. One of the most influential hypotheses about what is remembered postulates that the representation of a sentence in memory is very closely related to its linguistically specified deep structure. One of the most famous tests of this hypothesis was performed by Blumenthal (1967; Blumenthal & Boakes, 1967). He proposed that the scope or range of a lexical item's function in the deep structure should predict the effectiveness of that item as a prompt for recall of the entire sentence. Items with greater scope, that is, items inserted into the phrase-marker closer to the initial S symbol, should be more effective prompts. For instance, the pair of sentences (20a) and (21a) have equivalent surface structures but differ in their deep structures [shown in (20b) and (21b)]:*

(20)　　a. *Gloves were made by tailors.*
　　　　b. $[[tailors]_{NP}[[made]_V[gloves]_{NP}]_{VP}]_S$

(21)　　a. *Gloves were made by hand.*
　　　　b. $[[someone]_{NP}[[made]_V[gloves]_{NP}[by\ hand]_{MANNER}]_{VP}]_S$

Blumenthal reasoned that *tailors* should be a more effective recall cue than *hand,* since *by hand* is only part of the verb phrase whereas *by tailors* is a passified logical subject. As the sentence's logical subject, *tailors* has greater scope or range of function in (20) than does *hand* in (21). Similarly, consider the pair of sentences in (22a) and (23a):

(22)　　a. *John is eager to please.*
　　　　b. $[[John][[be\ eager]_V[[John]_{NP}[[please]_V[someone]_{NP}]_{VP}]_S]_{VP}]_S$

(23)　　a. *John is easy to please.*
　　　　b. $[[[it][[someone]_{NP}[[please]_V[John]_{NP}]_{VP}]_S]_{NP}[be\ easy]_{VP}]_S$

* The following symbols appear in the examples: NP = noun phrase, VP = verb phrase, V = verb, S = sentence, MANNER = adverb of manner.

Eager in (22a) is a nominal modifier [see (22b)], while *easy* in (23a) is a sentence modifier [see (23b)]. Thus, *easy* should be a more effective prompt for the recall of the entire sentence than should *eager*. Blumenthal's data were consistent with these predictions.

Blumenthal's data were also consistent with a different deep structure parameter, offered by Wanner (1968). He reasoned that the number of times a lexical time is repeated in deep structure, not its scope or range, should determine its effectiveness as a prompt. In a new experiment Wanner used sentences like those in (24a) and (25a), pitting his proposal against Blumenthal's:

(24) a. *The governor asked the detective to cease drinking.*
      b. [[*governor*][[*ask*][*detective*][[*detective*][[*cease*][[*detective*]
          [*drink*]]]]]]

(25) a. *The governor asked the detective to prevent drinking.*
      b. [[*governor*][[*ask*][*detective*][[*detective*][[*prevent*][[*someone*]
          [*drink*]]]]]]

Governor appears equally often in the deep structure of these sentences (once), while *detective* appears twice in the deep structure of (25a) and three times in the deep structure of (24a) [shown schematically in (24b) and (25b)]. Nor do *governor* and *detective* differ in their scope in the two sentences. Subjects first free-recalled sentences like these, then were given the equivalents of *governor* or *detective* as recall prompts. Wanner calculated the relative improvement in sentence recall with the prompts compared to the free recalls, and examined this as a function of the number of occurrences of the prompt in the deep structure. The results supported Wanner's hypothesis—the effectiveness of the prompt increased with the number of its occurrences. Since Wanner did not independently vary the scope or range of the deep structure, while keeping the number of its occurrences constant, his experiment does not rule out the possibility that Blumenthal's measure has some predictive validity as well.

Many studies testing features of the deep structure model have used the strategy of presenting sentences with similar or identical surface forms but differing deep structures (Blumenthal, 1967; Blumenthal & Boakes, 1967; Davidson, 1968; Davidson & Dollinger, 1969; Rohrman, 1968, 1970; Rohrman & Polzella, 1968; Suls & Weisberg, 1970; Wanner, 1968). This is a logical and elegant research strategy, but it must be kept in mind that these kinds of changes cannot be made without concomitant alterations in meaning. Thus, data consistent with the deep structure model will of necessity be consistent with any more abstract model that includes deep structure relations as a subset. Since many aspects of meaning do not have corresponding manifestations in deep structure (at least in the standard theory of Chomsky [1965, 1971] most often discussed by psycholinguists), a method is available for testing the empirical adequacy of the deep structure model of memory. Let us look at one relevant study.

Bransford, Barclay, and Franks (1972) demonstrated in a series of experiments that subjects remember the situation a sentence describes, not the linguistic deep structure of the sentence. Consider the set of four sentences that result from the two binary choices of words in (26).

(26) *Three turtles rested (on/beside) a floating log and a fish swam beneath (it/them).*

If *on* is chosen as the preposition, then completing the sentence with either pronoun results in a description of the same situation, whereas when *beside* is the preposition the two pronouns yield descriptions of different situations. If subjects are remembering what is described, rather than deep structures, they should have more trouble distinguishing *it/them* variants of (26) when *on* was the original preposition than when *beside* was (assuming they had studied only one version). For a variety of relationships using this logic, Bransford *et al.* found that subjects' recognition errors did follow a pattern inconsistent with the deep structure model. In fact, a variety of other recognition data follow a very similar pattern (e.g., Anisfeld, 1970; Bransford & Franks, 1971; Bransford & Johnson, 1973; Fillenbaum, 1966, 1971a; Franks & Bransford, 1972; Olson, 1971).

B. Semantic Memory

Many things that we ask subjects to do in our laboratories tap their permanent store of knowledge. This includes commonly used tasks like word associations, free recall, serial learning, paired associate learning, and recognition learning. But various complicating processes, many of them poorly understood, intervene in all of these, making them inefficient ways of studying the nature of semantic memory itself. So in this section we will consider some more direct techniques.

Distance or space is a dominant metaphor in theories of semantic memory, largely because it is easy to translate into simple empirical indicators. Traveling distance should take time, so reaction time becomes an obvious index of semantic relations. Similarly, items in the same neighborhood ought often to appear together in performance, if we assume memory search is primarily associative (Frijda, 1972). Clustering effects or confusion data can be used to assess this.

Let us look first at the use of clustering or confusion data. Miller (1969) had subjects sort words into subjectively defined categories of semantic

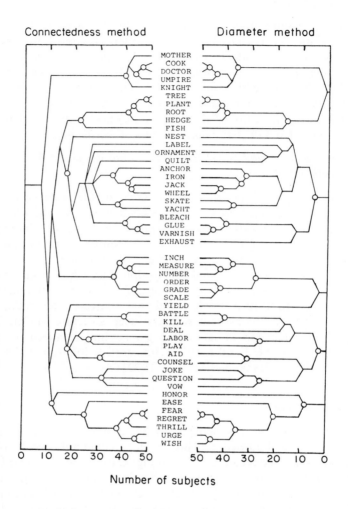

FIG. 2. Tree structures obtained by clustering analysis for data on 48 English nouns. [From Miller (1969), reproduced by permission.]

similarity and pooled the data over subjects to yield a matrix of proximities. These pooled data were then analyzed with Johnson's (1967) hierarchical clustering algorithms to recover their implicit structure. The results of such an analysis for 48 English nouns are shown in Fig. 2.* These tree diagrams

* The two solutions obtained by the connectedness and diameter methods are technical variants of the clustering algorithm. Their precise meaning can be found in Johnson (1967) and Miller (1969). It is apparent from Fig. 2 that they yield very similar solutions for these data.

make explicit the semantic relations implicit in the sorting data, and the figural representation is much more easily interpreted than the original matrix of proximities. Fillenbaum and Rapoport (1971) used similar procedures, and data for English pronouns are shown in Fig. 3. The two-dimensional solution from multidimensional scaling analysis (Shepard, 1962a,b; Kruskal, 1964) has been combined with the clustering analysis by showing the clusters as contours superimposed on the spatial solution. Fillenbaum and Rapoport (1971) also analyzed color names, kinship terms, emotion names, prepositions, conjunctions, and several classes of verbs, while Miller (1972) has looked at verbs of motion and Anglin (1970) has studied the development of semantic memory. However, there are limitations to the use of these techniques (see, e.g., Shepard, 1972). Fillenbaum and Rapoport (1974) repeated some of their studies with the linguist Charles Fillmore as a subject, and, with such an articulate and sophisticated person, were able to pinpoint some serious methodological problems. For instance, Fillmore reported that he was unable to use the same criterion of semantic similarity throughout the task, instead often shifted criteria from pair to pair. This clearly obscures the interpretation of the scaling solution, and, as Fillenbaum and Rapoport suggest, such conditions of shifting criteria are probably the rule rather than the exception. The reader interested in the structural analysis of similarity data is urged to consult their paper for further details.

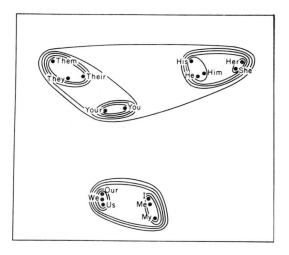

Fig. 3. Two-dimensional Euclidean representation obtained from multidimensional scaling analysis of English pronouns, with hierarchical clustering results shown as contours. [From Fillenbaum & Rapoport (1971), reproduced by permission.]

Frijda (1972) emphasized that the ability to provide information for true–false judgments about statements is an important property of human long-term memory. This ability is central to tasks that use reaction time for studying semantic memory. The time it takes a subject to make a true–false judgment is taken as an index of underlying semantic structures, and the distance metaphor plays an important role. Semantic relations whose constituents are stored far apart in memory should take longer to compare or verify than those whose constituents are close together. Research using this logic is concerned both with the properties of the semantic space over which distances are computed and with the independent validation of the structures revealed by reaction time data.

A study by Collins and Quillian (1969) will serve to illustrate the research issues involved. They studied the ability of subjects to verify simple statements like *A canary can fly* or *A canary is an animal*. On the basis of hypotheses about the storage of lexical information in memory (Quillian, 1968, 1969), the hierarchy shown in Fig. 4 was proposed as a representative structure from semantic memory. This proposal has two important properties. First, the hierarchical structure is a proposal about the overall organization of information in memory. Second, the storage of properties only at the highest relevant superset node is a proposal about economical information storage. To know that a canary has skin requires knowing that a canary is an animal and that animals have skin. Such inferential derivations lead to the predictions about reaction time that Collins and Quillian tested. It is assumed that statements are verified by tracing through the graph from the nodes representing the two concepts until an intersection

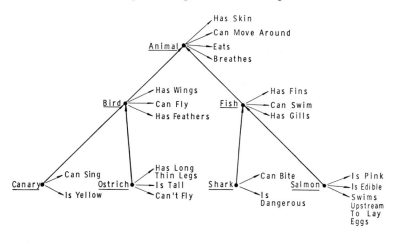

Fig. 4. Hypothetical semantic memory structure. [From Collins & Quillian (1969), reproduced by permission.]

is found. This search emanates in parallel from a node in all directions. Constant increments of time are accrued for each internode link traveled and for each property list examined prior to finding an intersection. Thus, verifying *A canary has skin* should take longer than verifying *A canary is yellow*. The data shown in Fig. 5 appear to confirm Collins and Quillian's hypothesis, since reaction time increases linearly with the number of nodes searched, and a constant time is added for accessing a property at any given level of the hierarchy.

The question of the representativeness of the structures examined by Collins and Quillian has important methodological implications. Structures like the one in Fig. 4 were derived from rationalistic, a priori speculation about the nature of semantic information storage. Are important properties obscured or confounded by constructing the structures in this fashion? The alternative is to use some other empirical measure as a source of predictions or as a check on rationalistic construction. Conrad (1972) confirmed that reaction times can be predicted on the basis of the hierarchical structure proposed by Collins and Quillian, but found no evidence for the economical encoding of properties when she controlled for the relative fre-

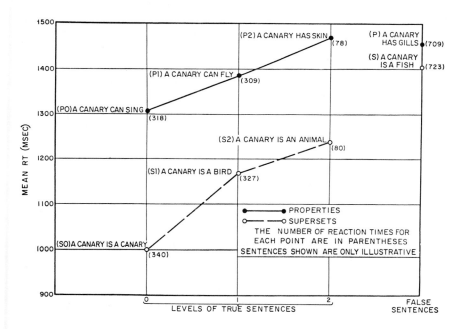

FIG. 5. Average reaction times for different types of sentences that have been verified against information in semantic memory. [From Collins & Quillian (1969), reproduced by permission.]

quency with which a property is associated with a word. The important methodological variation in her experiment was that she had an independent group of subjects provide normative data for use in setting up materials, with proper controls for properties like those just mentioned. Rips, Shoben, and Smith (1973) went one step further. They had independent groups of subjects generate the entire semantic structure by using scaling and clustering procedures like those discussed earlier. These changes in the way in which stimulus materials are selected have introduced a different picture of the structure of semantic memory. On the basis of data like those of Conrad (1972), Rips *et al.* (1973), and others, very few would hold that the semantic structure shown in Fig. 4 is representative of the general organization of memory. The general problem of sampling biases in the selection of stimulus materials will be discussed again at the end of this section.

In the section on comprehension we examined the use of mental chronometry in analyzing explicit negation. Similar techniques can be applied to the analysis of individual lexical items, although the matter is slightly more complicated. Many lexical items are inherently or implicitly negative. H. Clark (1971) has summarized evidence which shows that, for instance, *absent* behaves as though it were *not present,* and *different* as though it were *not same.* However, an even more impressive demonstration of the use of mental chronometry to dig out the characteristics of a lexical item have been provided by Just and Clark (1973) for the pair *remember to–forget to.* These are interesting items, because their implicit negation affects some parts of their meaning but not others.

In particular, we must make a distinction between the presuppositions and the implications of sentences containing these verbs. Consider the following sentences:

(27)   a. *John remembered to let the dog out.*
         b. PRESUPPOSITION: *John intended to let the dog out.*
         c. IMPLICATION: *John let the dog out.*

(28)   a. *John forgot to let the dog out.*
         b. PRESUPPOSITION: *John intended to let the dog out.*
         c. IMPLICATION: *John didn't let the dog out.*

According to Karttunen (1971), (27a) and 28a) can be said to presuppose the propositions in (27b) and 28b) and to imply the propositions in (27c) and (28c). To say that John forgot to do something is to presuppose that John had some intention of doing it and to imply that because of a memory lapse of some sort he failed to do it. The interesting property of this pair of sentences is that, while the implications of *remember* and *forget* are positive and negative, respectively, the presuppositions of both are positive. Thus, if subjects are required to access and verify the implications of *remember* and *forget, remember* should show the pattern of latencies characteristic of positive sentences and *forget* the pattern of negative sentences. However, if subjects are asked to access the presuppositions, both *remember* and *forget* should show patterns characteristic of positive sentences. In other words, *forget* should look like a negative whenever its implications are examined, but a positive whenever its presuppositions are examined.

Just and Clark required subjects to give true–false judgments for a large variety of statements like those in (29):

(29) a. *If John remembered to let the dog out, then the dog is in.*
   b. *If John forgot to let the dog in, then the dog is out.*
   c. *If John remembered to let the dog in, then the dog is supposed to be in.*
   d. *If John forgot to let the dog out, then the dog is supposed to be in.*

Sentences (29a) and (29b) require subjects to access the implications of *remember* and *forget,* whereas sentences (29c) and (29d) require them to access the presuppositions: Although *supposed to* in (29c) and (29d) was perhaps not the best paraphrase of the presuppositions of *remember* and *forget,* it was adequate for the experiment by Just and Clark. Subjects were timed from the moment they began reading the sentence to the moment they pressed a "true" or "false" button.

The mean latencies are shown in Table 2 and bear out the predictions. When the subject was required to access the implication, then *remember* patterned like a positive sentence, with "true" faster than "false," and *forget* patterned like a negative one, with "false" faster than "true." But when the subject was required to access the presuppositions, both *remember* and *forget* patterned like positive sentences, with "true" faster than "false." Further, *remember* was dealt with around 580 msec faster than *forget,* and this is also consistent with *remember* being positive and *forget* negative. The specificity of the negative element in *forget* is evident in the different patterns of latencies for the implication and presupposition of the term, and this is consistent with the linguistic fact that the negative element contains the implication within its scope but not the presupposition.

C. The Language-as-Fixed-Effect Fallacy

Coleman (1964) criticized psychological research using language for failing to perform appropriate analyses that would allow generalization be-

TABLE II

LATENCY COMPONENTS, ACTUAL LATENCIES, AND PREDICTED LATENCIES[a]

Type	Components of latency	Actual latencies (msec)	Predicted latencies (msec)
Implication			
True *remember*	t_0	2814	2829
False *remember*	$t_0 + c$	3252	3226
True *forget*	$t_0 + c + (b + d)$	3670	3807
False *forget*	$t_0 + (b + d)$	3536	3410
Presupposition			
True *remember*	$t_0 + e$	3564	3639
False *remember*	$t_0 + c + e$	4100	4036
True *forget*	$t_0 + (b + d) + e$	4183	4220
False *forget*	$t_0 + c + (b + d) + e$	4664	4617

[a] Data from Just and Clark (1973), on statements containing *remember* and *forget*.

NOTE: t_0 = 2829 msec.

c = 397 msec.

$(b + d)$ = 581 msec.

e = 810 msec.

yond the language sample used. If we are studying differences between nouns and verbs, we typically want to generalize to all nouns and verbs in the language, not just to the sample used in our experiment. Thus, in the argot of analysis of variance (Scheffé, 1959; Winer, 1971), language should be treated as a random effect, not a fixed one. Very few investigators do this. Clark (1973) has recently revived and expanded upon Coleman's criticisms in the context of current studies of word perception and semantic memory. He examined in some detail a series of studies by Rubenstein and his associates (Rubenstein, Garfield, & Millikan, 1970; Rubenstein, Lewis, & Rubenstein, 1971a,b) and demonstrated that the conclusions reached in these papers could not be supported when analyses appropriate for generalization beyond the language sample were performed. This serious methodological problem is not unique to this series of experiments, and Clark pointed out similar difficulties with a number of other well-known studies (e.g., Collins & Quillian, 1969; Conrad, 1972; Meyer, 1970).

How can we be sure our results will generalize beyond our language sample? Clark (1973) discussed in detail several remedies. One of the most obvious is to use proper statistics, although there are technical complications with random-effects designs. Other remedies include choosing an appropriate design, and sampling language by a systematic procedure. Of course it is possible that in certain instances we will want to examine the properties of specific words or sets of words, as in the work of Just and Clark (1973) reviewed earlier (see also Clark, 1969, 1975; Olson & Laxar, 1973, 1974). Whichever kind of research one chooses to do, one must be explicit about it and modify the design and analysis of the experiments appropriately.

D. Comprehensive Theories of Memory Structure

Research on language processing programs in computer science (e.g., Quillian, 1968, 1969; Schank & Colby, 1973; Schank, 1972; Simmons, 1972; Winograd, 1972; Woods, 1970; and reviews by Frijda, 1972; Siklóssy & Simon, 1972; Simmons, 1965, 1970) has stimulated a number of psychologists to develop comprehensive models of human memory that synthesize many ideas about language and memory (e.g., Anderson & Bower, 1973; Collins & Quillian, 1972a,b; Kaplan, 1972; Kintsch, 1972, 1974; Rumelhart, Lindsay, & Norman, 1972; Norman & Rumelhart, 1975). The techniques involved in theoretical work of this kind are beyond the scope of a brief chapter on methodology, since the development of program structures and the coding of these into appropriate formal languages are often involved. Many of these models reach the stage of being operating programs, allowing for a variety of simulations of psycholinguistic phenomena as well as providing derivations for new laboratory tests. It is already clear that these efforts represent an increasingly important aspect of psycholinguistic research on the comprehension and retention of language.

E. Resources

Reviews of research on the retention of language are available in Fillenbaum (1971b, 1973), Johnson-Laird (1970b), Anderson and Bower (1973), and Kintsch (1974). Frijda's (1972) review treats issues of semantic memory. The references cited in the preceding paragraph can serve as useful introductions to general questions of memory in psycholinguistic research, and recent collections of papers by Norman (1970), Carroll and Freedle (1972), Melton and Martin (1972), and Tulving and Donaldson (1972) and the recent text by Murdock (1974) provide useful background material for the general study of memory.

VI. CONCLUSION

The most bothersome methodological issues in psycholinguistics arise at the interface between psychology and linguistics. For instance, playing off syntax and semantics in the design and analysis of experiments is a direct translation of a linguistic distinction into a psychological one. Is such a translation justifiable? Certainly not if only a priori justification is given. Other possibilities exist as performance variables, and to suppose that a distinction made on the basis of another metatheory will ipso facto be of use in cognitive psychology is to make a serious error. On the other hand, to view a distinction from a related field as a heuristic for guiding research is a valid pragmatic justification, but it must be remembered that heuristics are different from theoretical principles. We must clearly separate principles of discovery from principles of justification.

What do we mean when we say that a linguistic rule has "psychological reality"? Demonstrations that some observable, such as reaction time or memory errors, can be predicted in an orderly way on the basis of distinctions borrowed directly from linguistics constitute an exceedingly weak approach to the goal of explaining language performance. Perhaps this is where theoretical pressure from another sister field, computer science, may have a salutary effect. Programs for the understanding of natural language are necessarily performance models, designed to accomplish the pragmatic goal of actually working. Perhaps at the interface of these two fields, psychology and computer science, abstract and elegant theories of performance can emerge. To this extent, programs designed for language performance become a major methodological tool in psycholinguistics.

The tools for psychological research on language already exist, and most of them are very simple. Those methodological problems that remain have to do with the use of these tools in the construction of theories of psycholinguistic phenomena. From the trends evident in the short history of psycholinguistic research, these remaining problems will be difficult to crack.

Acknowledgments

Preparation of this chapter was supported in part by Public Health Service Research Grant MH-20021 from the National Institute of Mental Health to the second author. The authors thank Eve Clark for many helpful suggestions.

References

Abrams, K., & Bever, T. G. Syntactic structure modifies attention during speech perception and recognition. *Quarterly Journal of Experimental Psychology,* 1969, **21,** 280–290.

Anderson, J. R. Computer simulation of a language acquisition system: A first report. In R. L. Solso (Ed.), *Information processing and cognition: The Loyola Symposium.* Hillsdale, New Jersey: Lawrence Erlbaum Associates, 1975.

Anderson, J. R., & Bower, G. H. *Human associative memory.* Washington, D.C.: V. H. Winston, 1973.

Anglin, J. M. *The growth of word meaning.* Cambridge, Massachusetts: M.I.T. Press, 1970.

Anisfeld, M. False recognition of adjective-noun phrases. *Journal of Experimental Psychology,* 1970, **86,** 120–122.

Baird, R. On the role of chance in imitation-comprehension-production test results. *Journal of Verbal Learning and Verbal Behavior,* 1972, **11,** 474–477.

Bellugi, U. *How children say no.* Cambridge, Massachusetts: M.I.T. Press, in press.

Berko, J. The child's learning of English morphology. *Word,* 1958, **14,** 150–177.

Berko, J., & Brown, R. Psycholinguistic research methods. In P. H. Mussen (Ed.), *Handbook of research methods in child development.* New York: Wiley, 1960: Pp. 517–557.

Bertelson, P., & Tisseyre, F. Perceiving the sequence of speech and nonspeech stimuli. *Quarterly Journal of Experimental Psychology,* 1970, **22,** 653–662.

Bever, T. G. The cognitive basis for linguistic structures. In J. R. Hayes (Ed.), *Cognition and the development of language.* New York: Wiley, 1970. Pp. 279–362. (a)

Bever, T. G. The influence of speech performance on linguistic structure. In G. B. Flores d'Arcais & W. J. M. Levelt (Eds.), *Advances in psycholinguistics.* Amsterdam: North-Holland, 1970. Pp. 4–30. (b)

Bever, T. G. Serial position and response biases do not account for the effect of syntactic structure on the location of brief noises during sentences. *Journal of Psycholinguistic Research,* 1973, **2,** 287–288. (Abstract)

Bever, T. G., Lackner, J., & Kirk, R. The underlying structures of sentences are the primary units of immediate speech processing. *Perception and Psychophysics,* 1969, **5,** 225–234. (a)

Bever, T. G., Lackner, J., & Stolz, W. Transitional probability is not a general mechanism for the segmentation of speech. *Journal of Experimental Psychology,* 1969, **79,** 387–394. (b)

Bloom, L. *Language development: Form and function in emerging grammars.* Cambridge, Massachusetts: M.I.T. Press, 1970.

Bloom, L. Why not pivot grammar? *Journal of Speech and Hearing Disorders,* 1971, **36,** 40–50.

Bloom, L. *One word at a time.* The Hague: Mouton, 1973.

Blumenthal, A. L. Prompted recall of sentences. *Journal of Verbal Learning and Verbal Behavior,* 1967, **6,** 203–206.

Blumenthal, A. L. *Language and psychology: Historical aspects of psycholinguistics.* New York: Wiley, 1970.

Blumenthal, A. L., & Boakes, R. Prompted recall of sentences. *Journal of Verbal Learning and Verbal Behavior,* 1967, **6,** 674–676.

Bond, Z. S. Units in speech perception. Working Papers in Linguistics No. 9, Computer and Information Science Research Center, Ohio State Univ., July, 1971. Pp. viii–112.

Bowerman, M. F. *Early syntactic development: A cross-linguistic study with special reference to Finnish.* New York: Cambridge Univ. Press, 1973.

Braine, M. D. S. The ontogeny of English phrase structure: The first phase. *Language,* 1963, **39,** 1–13.

Braine, M. D. S. The acquisition of language in infant and child. In C. Reed (Ed.), *The learning of language.* New York: Appleton, 1971. Pp. 7–95.

Bransford, J. D., Barclay, J. R., & Franks, J. J. Sentence memory: A constructive versus interpretive approach. *Cognitive Psychology,* 1972, **3,** 193–209.

Bransford, J. D., & Franks, J. J. The abstraction of linguistic ideas. *Cognitive Psychology,* 1971, **2,** 331–350.

Bransford, J. D., & Johnson, M. K. Considerations of some problems of comprehension. In W. G. Chase (Ed.), *Visual information processing.* New York: Academic Press, 1973. Pp. 383–438.

Broadbent, D. E. *Decision and stress.* New York: Academic Press, 1971.

Brown, R. The development of Wh questions in child speech. *Journal of Verbal Learning and Verbal Behavior,* 1968, **7,** 279–290.

Brown, R. *A first language: The early stages.* Cambridge, Massachusetts: Harvard Univ. Press, 1973.

Brown, R., & Fraser, C. The acquisition of syntax. In C. N. Cofer & B. Musgrave (Eds.), *Verbal behavior and learning.* New York: McGraw-Hill, 1963, Pp. 158–197.

Brown, R., & Hanlon, C. Derivational complexity and order of acquisition in child speech. In J. R. Hayes (Ed.), *Cognition and the development of language.* New York: Wiley, 1970. Pp. 11–53.

Cairns, H. S., & Foss, D. J. Falsification of the hypothesis that word frequency is a unified variable in sentence processing. *Journal of Verbal Learning and Verbal Behavior,* 1971, **10,** 41–43.

Carroll, J. B., & Freedle, R. O. (Eds.) *Language comprehension and the acquisition of knowledge.* Washington, D.C.: V. H. Winston, 1972.

Cazden, C. B. The acquisition of noun and verb inflections. *Child Development,* 1968, **39,** 433–448.

Chapin, P. G., Smith, T. S., & Abrahamson, A. A. Two factors in perceptual segmentation of speech. *Journal of Verbal Learning and Verbal Behavior,* 1972, **11,** 164–173.

Chase, W. G., & Clark, H. H. Mental operations in the comparison of sentences and pictures. In L. Gregg (Ed.), *Cognition in learning and memory.* New York: Wiley, 1972.

Chomsky, C. *The acquisition of syntax in children from 5 to 10.* Cambridge, Massachusetts: M.I.T. Press, 1969.

Chomsky, N. *Syntactic structures.* The Hague: Mouton, 1957.

Chomsky, N. Formal properties of grammars. In R. D. Luce, R. R. Bush, & E. Galanter (Eds.), *Handbook of mathematical psychology.* Vol. 2. New York: Wiley, 1963. Pp. 323–418.

Chomsky, N. *Aspects of the theory of syntax.* Cambridge, Massachusetts: M.I.T. Press, 1965.

Chomsky, N. *Language and mind.* New York: Harcourt, 1968.

Chomsky, N. Deep structure, surface structure, and semantic interpretation. In D. D. Steinberg & L. A. Jakobovits (Eds.), *Semantics: An interdisciplinary reader in philosophy, linguistics and psychology.* New York: Cambridge Univ. Press, 1971, Pp. 183–216.

Chomsky, N., & Miller, G. A. Introduction to the formal analysis of natural languages. In R. D. Luce, R. R. Bush, & E. Galanter (Eds.), *Handbook of mathematical psychology.* Vol. 2. New York: Wiley, 1963. Pp. 269–321.

Clark, E. V. On the acquisition of the meaning of *before* and *after. Journal of Verbal Learning and Verbal Behavior,* 1971, **10,** 266–275.

Clark, E. V. Some perceptual factors in the acquisition of locative terms by young children. *Papers from the Eighth Regional Meetings of the Chicago Linguistic Society,* 1972, **8,** 431–439.

Clark, E. V. Non-linguistic strategies and the acquisition of word meanings. *Cognition,* 1973, **2,** 161–182. (a)

Clark, E. V. What's in a word? On the child's acquisition of semantics in his first language. In T. E. Moore (Ed.), *Cognitive development and the acquisition of language*. New York: Academic Press, 1973. Pp. 65–110. (b)

Clark, H. H. Some structural properties of simple active and passive sentences. *Journal of Verbal Learning and Verbal Behavior*, 1965, **4,** 365–370.

Clark, H. H. Linguistic processes in deductive reasoning. *Psychological Review,* 1969, **76,** 387–404.

Clark, H. H. How we understand negation. Paper presented at COBRE Workshop on Cognitive Organization and Psychological Processes. Huntington Beach, California. August, 1970.

Clark, H. H. The chronometric study of meaning components. Paper presented at the CRNS Colloque International sur les Problèmes Actuals de Psycholinguistique. Paris, December, 1971.

Clark, H. H. The language-as-fixed-effect fallacy: A critique of language statistics in psychological research. *Journal of Verbal Learning and Verbal Behavior,* 1973, **12,** 335–359.

Clark, H. H. Semantics and comprehension. In T. A. Sebeok (Ed.), *Current trends in linguistics.* Vol. 12. *Linguistics and adjacent arts and sciences.* The Hague: Mouton, 1975.

Clark, H. H., & Begun, J. S. The use of syntax in understanding sentences. *British Journal of Psychology,* 1968, **59,** 219–230.

Clark, H. H., & Begun, J. S. The semantics of sentence subjects. *Language and Speech,* 1971, **14,** 34–46.

Clark, H. H., & Chase, W. G. On the process of comparing sentences against pictures. *Cognitive Psychology,* 1972, **3,** 472–517.

Coleman, E. B. Generalizing to a language population. *Psychological Reports,* 1964, **14,** 219–226.

Collins, A. M., & Quillian, M. R. Retrieval time from semantic memory. *Journal of Verbal Learning and Verbal Behavior,* 1969, **8,** 240–247.

Collins, A. M., & Quillian, M. R. Experiments on semantic memory and language comprehension. In L. W. Gregg (Ed.), *Cognition in learning and memory.* New York: Wiley, 1972. (a)

Collins, A. M., & Quillian, M. R. How to make a language user. In E. Tulving & W. Donaldson (Eds.), *Organization of memory.* New York: Academic Press, 1972. Pp. 309–351. (b)

Conrad, C. Cognitive economy in semantic memory. *Journal of Experimental Psychology,* 1972, **92,** 149–154.

Cromer, R. F. 'Children are nice to understand': Surface structure clues for the recovery of a deep structure. *British Journal of Psychology,* 1970, **61,** 397–408.

Cromer, R. F. The learning of surface structure clues to deep structure by a puppet show technique. *Quarterly Journal of Experimental Psychology,* 1972, **24,** 66–76.

Danks, J. H. Grammaticalness and meaningfulness in the comprehension of sentences. *Journal of Verbal Learning and Verbal Behavior,* 1969, **8,** 687–696.

Danks, J. H., & Glucksberg, S. Psychological scaling of linguistic properties. *Language and Speech,* 1970, **13,** 118–140.

Davidson, R. E. Deep structure differences and transition error patterns. *Proceedings of the 76th Annual Convention of the American Psychological Association,* 1968, **3,** 11–12.

Davidson, R. E., & Dollinger, L. E. The effects of deep structure variations in sentences: Free recall and paired-associate learning. Technical Report No. 110,

Wisconsin Research and Development Center for Cognitive Learning, Univ. of Wisconsin, 1969.

Degerman, R., & Mather, R. S. Spatial representation of noun phrases. *Journal of Verbal Learning and Verbal Behavior,* 1972, **11,** 66–72.

de Villiers, P. A., & de Villiers, J. G. Early judgments of semantic and syntactic acceptability by children. *Journal of Psycholinguistic Research,* 1972, **1,** 299–310.

Donaldson, M. Developmental aspects of performance with negatives. In G. B. Flores d'Arcais & W. J. M. Levelt (Eds.), *Advances in psycholinguistics.* Amsterdam: North-Holland, 1970. Pp. 397–410.

Donaldson, M. Preconditions of inference. In J. K. Cole (Ed.), *Nebraska symposium on motivation,* 1971. Lincoln: Univ. of Nebraska Press, 1972. Pp. 81–106.

Donaldson, M., & Wales, R. On the acquisition of some relational terms. In J. R. Hayes (Ed.), *Cognition and the development of language.* New York: Wiley, 1970. Pp. 235–268.

Downey, R., & Hakes, D. Some psychological effects of violating linguistic rules. *Journal of Verbal Learning and Verbal Behavior,* 1968, **7,** 158–161.

Epstein, W. Recall of word lists following learning of sentences and of anomalous and random strings. *Journal of Verbal Learning and Verbal Behavior,* 1969, **8,** 20–25.

Ervin, S. M. Imitation and structural change in children's language. In E. H. Lenneberg (Ed.), *New directions in the study of language.* Cambridge, Massachusetts: M.I.T. Press, 1964. Pp. 163–189.

Ervin-Tripp, S. An overview of theories of grammatical development. In D. I. Slobin (Ed.), *The ontogenesis of grammar.* New York: Academic Press, 1971. Pp. 189–212.

Feldman, J. A., Gips, J., Horning, J. J., & Reder, S. Grammatical complexity and inference. Technical Report No. CS 125, Stanford Artificial Intelligence Project, Stanford Univ., June 1969.

Ferguson, C. A., & Slobin, D. I. *Studies of Child language development.* New York: Holt, 1973.

Fernald, C. D. Control of grammar in imitation, comprehension, and production: Problems of replication. *Journal of Verbal Learning and Verbal Behavior,* 1972, **11,** 606–613.

Fillenbaum, S. Memory for gist: Some relevant variables. *Language and Speech,* 1966, **9,** 217–227.

Fillenbaum, S. On the use of memorial techniques to assess syntactic structures. *Psychological Bulletin,* 1970, **73,** 231–237.

Fillenbaum, S. On coping with ordered and unordered conjunctive sentences. *Journal of Experimental Psychology,* 1971, **87,** 93–98. (a)

Fillenbaum, S. Psycholinguistics. *Annual Review of Psychology,* 1971, **22,** 251–308. (b)

Fillenbaum, S. *Syntactic factors in memory.* The Hague: Mouton, 1973.

Fillenbaum, S., & Rapoport, A. *Structures in the subjective lexicon.* New York: Academic Press, 1971.

Fillenbaum, S., & Rapoport, A. Verbs of judging, judged: A case study. *Journal of Verbal Learning and Verbal Behavior,* 1974, **13,** 54–62.

Foa, U. G., & Schlesinger, I. M. Syntactical errors in sentence recall: A reanalysis of Mehler's data. Unpublished paper, Israel Institute of Applied Social Research, 1965.

Fodor, J. A. The appeal to tacit knowledge in psychological explanation. *Journal of Philosophy,* 1968, **65,** 627–640.

Fodor, J. A., & Bever, T. G. The psychological reality of linguistic segments. *Journal of Verbal Learning and Verbal Behavior,* 1965, **4,** 414–420.

Fodor, J. A., Bever, T. G., & Garrett, M. F. *The psychology of language.* New York: McGraw-Hill, 1974.

Fodor, J. A., & Garrett, M. Some reflections on competence and performance. In J. Lyons & R. F. Wales (Eds.), *Psycholinguistic papers.* Edinburgh: Edinburgh Univ. Press, 1966. Pp. 133–154.

Forster, K. I. Visual perception of rapidly presented word sequences of varying complexity. *Perception and Psychophysics,* 1970, **8,** 215–221.

Forster, K. I., & Ryder, L. A. Perceiving the structure and meaning of sentences. *Journal of Verbal Learning and Verbal Behavior,* 1971, **10,** 285–296.

Foss, D. J. An analysis of learning in a miniature linguistic system. *Journal of Experimental Psychology,* 1968, **76,** 450–459.

Foss, D. J. Decision processes during sentence comprehension: Effects of lexical item difficulty and position upon decision times. *Journal of Verbal Learning and Verbal Behavior,* 1969, **8,** 457–462.

Foss, D. J. Some effects of ambiguity upon sentence comprehension. *Journal of Verbal Learning and Verbal Behavior,* 1970, **9,** 699–706.

Foss, D. J., & Cairns, H. S. Some effects of memory limitations upon sentence comprehension and recall. *Journal of Verbal Learning and Verbal Behavior,* 1970, **9,** 541–547.

Foss, D. J., & Lynch, R. H., Jr. Decision processes during sentence comprehension: Effects of surface structure on decision times. *Perception and Psychophysics,* 1969, **5,** 145–148.

Franks, J. J., & Bransford, J. D. The acquisition of abstract ideas. *Journal of Verbal Learning and Verbal Behavior,* 1972, **11,** 311–315.

Fraser, C., Bellugi, U., & Brown, R. Control of grammar in imitation, comprehension and production. *Journal of Verbal Learning and Verbal Behavior,* 1963, **2,** 121–135.

Frijda, N. H. Simulation of human long-term memory. *Psychological Bulletin,* 1972, **77,** 1–31.

Garner, W. R. *Uncertainty and structure as psychological concepts.* New York: Wiley, 1962.

Garrett, M., Bever, T., & Fodor, J. The active use of grammar in speech perception. *Perception and Psychophysics,* 1966, **1,** 30–32.

Gleitman, L. R., Gleitman, H., & Shipley, E. F. The emergence of the child as grammarian. *Cognition,* 1972, **1,** 137–164.

Glucksberg, S., & Danks, J. Grammatical structure and recall: A function of the space in memory or of recall delay? *Perception and Psychophysics,* 1969, **6,** 113–117.

Gold, M. Language identification in the limit. *Information and Control,* 1967, **10,** 447–474.

Greene, J. *Psycholinguistics: Chomsky and psychology.* Baltimore: Penguin, 1972.

Hakes, D. T., & Foss, D. J. Decision processes during sentence comprehension: Effects of surface structure reconsidered. *Perception and Psychophysics,* 1970, **8,** 413–416.

Herriot, P. *An introduction to the psychology of language.* London: Methuen, 1970.

Holmes, V. M., & Forster, K. I. Detection of extraneous signals during sentence recognition. *Perception and Psychophysics,* 1970, **7,** 297–301.

Holmes, V. M., & Forster, K. I. Click location and syntactic structure. *Perception and Psychophysics,* 1972, **12,** 9–15. (a)

Holmes, V. M., & Forster, K. I. Perceptual complexity and underlying sentence structure. *Journal of Verbal Learning and Verbal Behavior,* 1972, **11,** 148–156. (b)

Hörmann, H. *Psycholinguistics: An introduction to research and theory.* New York: Springer-Verlag, 1971.

Huxley, R., & Ingram, E. (Eds.) *Language acquisition: Models and methods.* New York: Academic Press, 1971.

Ingram, D. Transitivity in child language. *Language,* 1971, **47,** 888–910.

Johnson, S. C. Hierarchical clustering schemes. *Psychometrika,* 1967, **32,** 241–254.

Johnson-Laird, P. N. On understanding logically quantified sentences. *Quarterly Journal of Experimental Psychology,* 1969, **21,** 1–13.

Johnson-Laird, P. N. The interpretation of quantified sentences. In G. B. Flores d'Arcais & W. J. M. Levelt (Eds.), *Advances in psycholinguistics.* Amsterdam: North-Holland, 1970. Pp. 347–370. (a)

Johnson-Laird, P. N. The perception and memory of sentences. In J. Lyons (Ed.), *New horizons in linguistics.* Baltimore: Penguin, 1970. Pp. 261–270. (b)

Johnson-Laird, P. N., & Wason, P. C. A theoretical analysis of insight into a reasoning task. *Cognitive Psychology,* 1970, **1,** 134–148.

Just, M. A., & Clark, H. H. Drawing inferences from the presuppositions and implications of affirmative and negative sentences. *Journal of Verbal Learning and Verbal Behavior,* 1973, **12,** 21–31.

Kaplan, R. M. Augmented transition networks as psychological models of sentence comprehension. *Artificial Intelligence,* 1972, **3,** 77–100.

Karttunen, L. Implicative verbs. *Language,* 1971, **47,** 340–358.

Kerr, B. Processing demands during mental operations. *Memory and Cognition,* 1973, **1,** 401–412.

Kintsch, W. Notes on the structure of semantic memory. In E. Tulving & W. Donaldson (Eds.), *Organization of memory.* New York: Academic Press, 1972. Pp. 247–308.

Kintsch, W. *The representation of meaning in memory.* Hillsdale, New Jersey: Lawrence Erlbaum, 1974.

Klima, E. S., & Bellugi, U. Syntactic regularities in the speech of children. In J. Lyons & R. Wales (Eds.), *Psycholinguistic papers.* Edinburgh: Edinburgh Univ. Press, 1966. Pp. 183–207.

Kruskal, J. B. Multidimensional scaling by optimizing goodness of fit to a nonmetric hypothesis. *Psychometrika,* 1964, **29,** 1–27.

Labov, W. The logic of nonstandard English. In F. Williams (Ed.), *Language and poverty.* Chicago: Markham, 1970. Pp. 153–189.

Ladefoged, P. *Three areas of experimental phonetics.* New York: Oxford Univ. Press, 1967.

Ladefoged, P., & Broadbent, D. E. Perception of sequence in auditory events. *Quarterly Journal of Experimental Psychology,* 1960, **12,** 162–170.

Lehiste, I. The units of speech perception. Working Papers in Linguistics No. 12, Computer and Information Science Research Center, Ohio State Univ., June 1972. Pp. 1–32.

Levelt, W. J. M. A scaling approach to the study of syntactic relations. In G. B. Flores d'Arcais & W. J. M. Levelt (Eds.), *Advances in psycholinguistics.* Amsterdam: North-Holland, 1970. Pp. 109–121.

Lyons, J. *Noam Chomsky.* New York: Viking Press, 1970.

Macnamara, J. Cognitive basis of language learning in infants *Psychological Review,* 1972, **79,** 1–13.

Maratsos, M. P. How preschool children understand missing complement subjects. *Child Development,* 1974, **45**, 700–706.

Martin, E. Toward an analysis of subjective phrase structure. *Psychological Bulletin,* 1970, **74**, 153–166.

Matthews, N. A. Transformational complexity and short-term recall. *Language and Speech,* 1968, **11**, 120–128.

McNeill, D. *The acquisition of language.* New York: Harper, 1970.

Mehler, J. Some effects of grammatical transformations on the recall of English sentences. *Journal of Verbal Learning and Verbal Behavior,* 1963, **2**, 346–351.

Melton, A. W., & Martin, E. (Eds.) *Coding processes in human memory.* Washington, D.C.: V. H. Winston, 1972.

Menyuk, P. A preliminary evaluation of grammatical capacity in children. *Journal of Verbal Learning and Verbal Behavior,* 1963, **2**, 429–439.

Menyuk, P. *Sentences children use.* Cambridge, Massachusetts: M.I.T. Press, 1969.

Meyer, D. E. On the representation and retrieval of stored semantic information. *Cognitive Psychology,* 1970, **1**, 242–299.

Miller, G. A. *Language and communication.* New York: McGraw-Hill, 1951.

Miller, G. A. Some psychological studies of grammar. *American Psychologist,* 1962, **17**, 748–762.

Miller, G. A. Project grammarama. In *The psychology of communication: Seven essays.* Baltimore: Penguin, 1967. Pp. 125–187.

Miller, G. A. A psychological method to investigate verbal concepts. *Journal of Mathematical Psychology,* 1969, **6**, 169–191.

Miller, G. A. English verbs of motion: A case study in semantics and lexical memory. In A. W. Melton & E. Martin (Eds.), *Coding processes in human memory.* Washington, D. C.: V. H. Winston, 1972. Pp. 335–372.

Miller, G. A., & Chomsky, N. Finitary models of language users. In R. D. Luce, R. R. Bush, & E. Galanter (Eds.), *Handbook of mathematical psychology.* Vol. 2. New York: Wiley, 1963. Pp. 419–491.

Miller, G. A., & McNeill, D. Psycholinguistics. In G. Lindzey & E. Aaronson (Eds.), *Handbook of social psychology.* (2nd ed.), Vol. 3. Reading, Massachusetts: Addison-Wesley, 1969. Pp. 666–794.

Miller, G. A., & Selfridge, J. A. Verbal context and the recall of meaningful material. *American Journal of Psychology,* 1950, **63**, 176–185.

Miller, W., & Ervin, S. The development of grammar in child language. In U. Bellugi & R. Brown (Eds.), The acquisition of syntax. *Monographs of the Society for Research in Child Development,* 1964, **29**(Whole No. 92). Pp. 9–34.

Moore, T. E. (Ed.) *Cognitive development and the acquisition of language.* New York: Academic Press, 1973.

Moray, N. *Attention: Selective processes in vision and hearing.* New York: Academic Press, 1969.

Morganbesser, S. Fodor on Ryle and rules. *Journal of Philosophy,* 1969, **66**, 458–472.

Murchison, C., & Langer, S. K. Tiedemann's observations on the development of the mental faculties of children. *The Pedagogical Seminary and Journal of Genetic Psychology,* 1927, **34**, 205–230.

Murdock, B. B., Jr. *Human memory: Theory and data.* Hillsdale, New Jersey: Lawrence Erlbaum, 1974.

Nagel, T. The boundaries of innerspace. *Journal of Philosophy,* 1969, **66**, 452–458.

Norman, D. A. (Ed.) *Models of human memory.* New York: Academic Press, 1970.

Norman, D. A., & Rumelhart, D. E. *Explorations in cognition.* San Francisco: W. H. Freeman, 1975.

Olson, G. M. Memory for prenominal adjectives in ordinary English sentences. *Cognitive Psychology,* 1971, **2,** 300–312.

Olson, G. M., & Laxar, K. Asymmetries in processing the terms "right" and "left." *Journal of Experimental Psychology,* 1973, **100,** 284–290.

Olson, G. M., & Laxar, K. Processing the terms "right" and "left": A note on left-handers. *Journal of Experimental Psychology,* 1974, **102,** 1135–1137.

Palermo, D. S., & Eberhart, V. L. On the learning of morphological rules: An experimental analogy. *Journal of Verbal Learning and Verbal Behavior,* 1968, **7,** 337–344.

Palermo, D. S., & Howe, H. E. An experimental analogy to the learning of past tense inflection rules. *Journal of Verbal Learning and Verbal Behavior,* 1970, **9,** 410–416.

Palermo, D. S., & Parrish, M. Rule acquisition as a function of number and frequency of exemplar presentation. *Journal of Verbal Learning and Verbal Behavior,* 1971, **10,** 44–51.

Pfuderer, C. Some suggestions for the syntactic characterization of baby talk style. In Working Paper No. 14, The structure of linguistic input to children. Language-Behavior Research Laboratory, Univ. of California, Berkeley, 1969.

Pylyshyn, Z. Competence and psychological reality. *American Psychologist,* 1972, **27,** 546–552.

Quillian, M. R. Semantic memory. In M. L. Minsky (Ed.), *Semantic information processing.* Cambridge, Massachusetts: M.I.T. Press, 1968. Pp. 216–270.

Quillian, M. R. The teachable language comprehender: A simulation program and theory of language. *Communications of the ACM,* 1969, **12,** 459–476.

Reber, A. S. Implicit learning of artificial grammars. *Journal of Verbal Learning and Verbal Behavior,* 1967, **6,** 855–863.

Reber, A. S., & Anderson, J. R. The perception of clicks in linguistic and nonlinguistic messages. *Perception and Psychophysics,* 1970, **8,** 81–89.

Reed, C. E. (Ed.) *The learning of language.* New York: Appleton, 1971.

Reeker, L. H. A problem solving theory of syntax acquisition. *Journal of Structural Learning,* 1970, **2,** 1–10.

Rips, L. J., Shoben, E. J., & Smith, E. E. Semantic distance and the verification of semantic relations. *Journal of Verbal Learning and Verbal Behavior,* 1973, **12,** 1–20.

Rohrman, N. L. The role of syntactic structure in the recall of English nominalizations. *Journal of Verbal Learning and Verbal Behavior,* 1968, **7,** 904–912.

Rohrman, N. L. More on the recall of nominalization. *Journal of Verbal Learning and Verbal Behavior,* 1970, **9,** 534–536.

Rohrman, N. L., & Polzella, D. J. Recall of subject nominalizations. *Psychonomic Science,* 1968, **12,** 373–374.

Rubenstein, H., Garfield, L., & Millikan, J. A. Homographic entries in the internal lexicon. *Journal of Verbal Learning and Verbal Behavior,* 1970, **9,** 487–494.

Rubenstein, H., Lewis, S. S., & Rubenstein, M. A. Evidence for phonemic recoding in visual word recognition. *Journal of Verbal Learning and Verbal Behavior,* 1971, **10,** 645–657. (a)

Rubenstein, H., Lewis, S. S., & Rubenstein, M. A. Homographic entries in the internal lexicon: Effects of systematicity and relative frequency of meanings. *Journal of Verbal Learning and Verbal Behavior,* 1971, **10,** 57–62. (b)

Rumelhart, D. E., Lindsay, P. H., & Norman, D. A. A process model for long-term memory. In E. Tulving & W. Donaldson (Eds.), *Organization of memory.* New York: Academic Press, 1972. Pp. 197–246.

Sachs, J. Recognition memory for syntactic and semantic aspects of connected discourse. *Perception and Psychophysics*, 1967, **2**, 437–442.

Sachs, J. S. Memory in reading and listening to discourse. *Memory and Cognition*, 1974, **2**, 95–100.

Savin, H. B., & Perchonock, E. Grammatical structure and the immediate recall of English sentences. *Journal of Verbal Learning and Verbal Behavior*, 1965, **4**, 348–353.

Schank, R. C. Conceptual dependency: A theory of natural language understanding. *Cognitive Psychology*, 1972, **3**, 552–631.

Schank, R. C., & Colby, K. M. (Eds.) *Computer models of thought and language.* San Francisco: W. H. Freeman, 1973.

Scheffé, H. *The analysis of variance.* New York: Wiley, 1959.

Schwartz, D., Sparkman, J. P., & Deese, J. The process of understanding and judgments of comprehensibility. *Journal of Verbal Learning and Verbal Behavior*, 1970, **9**, 87–93.

Seitz, M. R., & Weber, B. A. Effects of response requirements on the location of clicks superimposed on sentences. *Memory and Cognition*, 1974, **2**, 43–46.

Shepard, R. N. The analysis if proximites: Multidimensional scaling with an unknown distance function. I. *Psychometrika*, 1962, **27**, 125–140. (a)

Shepard, R. N. The analysis of proximities: Multidimensional scaling with an unknown distance function. II. *Psychometrika*, 1962, **27**, 219–246. (b)

Shepard, R. N. A taxonomy of some principal types of data and of multidimensional methods for their analysis. In R. N. Shepard, A. K. Romney, & S. B. Nerlove (Eds.), *Multidimensional scaling: Theory and applications in the behavioral sciences.* Vol. 1. New York: Seminar Press, 1972. Pp. 21–47.

Shipley, E. F., Smith, C. S., & Gleitman, L. R. A study in the acquisition of language: Free responses to commands. *Language*, 1969, **45**, 322–342.

Siklóssy, L. A language-learning heuristic program. *Cognitive Psychology*, 1971, **2**, 479–495.

Siklóssy, L. Natural language learning by computer. In H. A. Simon & L. Siklóssy (Eds.), *Representation and meaning: Experiments with information processing systems.* Englewood Cliffs, New Jersey: Prentice-Hall, 1972. Pp. 288–328.

Siklóssy, L., & Simon, H. A. Some semantic methods for language processing. In H. A. Simon & L. Siklóssy (Eds.), *Representation and meaning: Experiments with information processing systems.* Englewood Cliffs, New Jersey: Prentice-Hall, 1972. Pp. 44–66.

Simmons, R. F. Answering English questions by computer: A survey. *Communications of the ACM*, 1965, **8**, 53–70.

Simmons, R. F. Natural language question-answering systems: 1969. *Communications of the ACM*, 1970, **13**, 15–30.

Simmons, R. F. Some semantic structures for representing English meanings. In J. B. Carroll & R. O. Freedle (Eds.), *Language comprehension and the acquisition of knowledge.* Washington, D.C.: V. H. Winston, 1972. Pp. 71–97.

Slobin, D. I. (Ed.) *A field manual for cross-cultural study of the acquisition of communicative competence (Second draft—July, 1967).* Berkeley: ASUC Store, Univ. of California, 1967.

Slobin, D. I. On the learning of morphological rules: A reply to Palermo and Eberhart. In D. I. Slobin (Ed.), *The ontogenesis of grammar.* New York: Academic Press, 1971. Pp. 215–223. (a)

Slobin, D. I. (Ed.) *The ontogenesis of grammar.* New York: Academic Press, 1971. (b)

Slobin, D. I. *Psycholinguistics.* Glenview, Illinois: Scott, Foresman, 1971. (c)

Slobin, D. I., & Welsh, C. A. Elicited imitations as a research tool in developmental psycholingunstics. In C. A. Ferguson & D. I. Slobin (Eds.), *Studies of child language development.* New York: Holt, 1973. Pp. 485–497.

Smith, K. H., & Braine, M. D. S. Miniature languages and the problem of language acquisition. In T. G. Bever & W. Weksel (Eds.), *The structure and psychology of language.* Vol. 2. New York: Holt, in press.

Smith, K. H., & Gough, P. B. Transformation rules in the learning of miniature linguistic systems. *Journal of Experimental Psychology,* 1969, **79,** 276–282.

Smith, P. T. Two experiments with artificial languages. *Quarterly Journal of Experimental Psychology,* 1970, **22,** 583–591.

Sternberg, S. The discovery of processing stages: Extensions of Donders' method. *Acta Psychologica,* 1969, **30,** 276–315.

Sternberg, S. Decomposing mental processes with reaction-time data. Invited address given at the Annual Meeting of the Midwestern Psychological Association, Detroit, May, 1971.

Suls, J. M., & Weisberg, R. W. Processing syntactically ambiguous sentences. *Journal of Experimental Psychology,* 1970, **86,** 112–114.

Taplin, J. E. Reasoning with conditional sentences. *Journal of Verbal Learning and Verbal Behavior,* 1971, **10,** 219–225.

Taylor, W. L. "Cloze procedure": A new tool for measuring readability. *Journalism Quarterly,* 1953, **30,** 415–433.

Trabasso, T., Rollins, H., & Shaughnessy, E. Storage and verification stages in processing concepts. *Cognitive Psychology,* 1971, **2,** 239–289.

Tulving, E., & Donaldson, W. (Eds.) *Organization of memory.* New York: Academic Press, 1972.

Wang, M. D. Influence of linguistic structure on comprehensibility and recognition. *Journal of Experimental Psychology,* 1970, **85,** 83–89. (a)

Wang, M. D. The role of syntactic complexity as a determiner of comprehensibility. *Journal of Verbal Learning and Verbal Behavior,* 1970, **9,** 398–404. (b)

Wanner, H. E. On remembering, forgetting, and understanding sentences: A study of the deep structure hypothesis. Unpublished doctoral dissertation, Harvard Univ., 1968.

Wason, P. C. Reasoning about a rule. *Quarterly Journal of Experimental Psychology,* 1968, **20,** 273–281.

Watt, W. C. On two hypotheses concerning psycholinguistics. In J. R. Hayes (Ed.), *Cognition and the development of language.* New York: Wiley, 1970. Pp. 137–220.

Watt, W. C. Competing economy criteria. Paper presented at the CRNS Colloque International sur les Problèmes Actuals de Psycholinguistique. Paris, December, 1971.

Wexler, K. N., & Hamburger, H. On the insufficiency of surface data for the learning of transformational languages. In J. Hintikka, J. M. E. Moravcsik, & P. Suppes (Eds.), *Approaches to natural languages: Proceedings of the 1970 Stanford workshop.* New York: Humanities Press, 1972.

Winer, B. J. *Statistical principles in experimental design.* (2nd ed.) New York: McGraw-Hill, 1971.

Winograd, T. Understanding natural language. *Cognitive Psychology,* 1972, **3,** 1–191.

Woods, W. A. Transition network grammars for natural language analysis. *Communications of the ACM,* 1970, **13,** 591–606.

Chapter 3

THE PRODUCTION OF SPEECH AND LANGUAGE

PETER MACNEILAGE AND PETER LADEFOGED

I. SPEECH AND LANGUAGE

Very little is known about the production of language; but we are beginning to understand a considerable amount about the production of speech;
and most of the physiological mechanisms involved in producing individual
speech sounds are now fairly well described. In order to make clear the
limits of our knowledge, we may consider a speech act to consist of four
stages. The first stage consists of the formation of an idea, the production
of a thought that has to be expressed. Second, this thought has to be ar-

ranged in terms of an appropriate phrase or sentence. This stage includes determining which lexical items should be used, and arranging these items within a suitable semantic and syntactic framework. The third stage involves devising a program of skilled motor movements so as to produce the speech sounds corresponding to this sentence. Finally, there is the execution of this program and the production of speech.

The first two stages constitute the production of language. They have to be achieved irrespective of whether the thought is finally expressed in terms of speech or writing. The sentence we have just written has, as far as we know, never been spoken by anybody. The third and fourth stages outlined above have never occurred. But there is no doubt that the words form a sentence in the English language. Thus we can distinguish between language and the medium of expression of that language. Speech is the medium of expression of spoken language (Abercrombie, 1967).

Even when we consider speech acts in which all four stages occur, there is evidence that the production of language is separate from the production of speech. The fact that an utterance may contain false starts, hesitations, and ill-formed sentences indicates that on these occasions the speaker had not entirely thought out what he intended to say before starting to talk. It is also a matter of common experience that it is possible to have an idea (whatever that may mean), to verbalize this idea and start saying something, and then to change one's mind (whatever that may mean), and say something different. However, although it is possible to make a clear distinction between the process of deciding what to say and the process of actually saying something, it is by no means certain that it is equally possible to separate the first two stages mentioned above, the process of determining the meaning to be conveyed, and that of deciding on the appropriate sentence or phrase. There are indications that these processes might be separable. Introspectively, it sometimes seems that one "knows" what one wants to say, but cannot "find" the right words. But it is possible that on these occasions the difficulty in finding the right words arises precisely because one does not really, in any sense, "know" what one wants to say. It may be the thought itself that is incomplete. In this sense it may truly be said that thinking consists of putting something into words.

In this chapter we will be concerned mainly with the production of speech—the mechanisms involved in producing an utterance after one has determined what one is going to say—rather than with the production of language, which may be inseparable from the process of thinking. Our understanding of the production of language is so small that there is nothing worthwhile that can be said here. It may be that in the future we can build on the work on word association (reviewed by Clark, 1970; see also Deese, 1966), on speech errors (reviewed by Fromkin, 1973), and on aphasia and other aspects of neurolinguistics (reviewed by Whitaker, 1971). It is also possible that descriptions of a speaker's linguistic competence on the lines proposed by Chomsky (1965, 1968) may one day be shown to be related to the processes that actually occur in the production of a sentence. But at the moment there is nothing like a comprehensive theory that will account for the production of language in the sense that we have been using this phrase.

The production of speech involves the concatenation of a number of skilled motor movements. Before we can consider the overall control of these movements, we must discuss the individual parts of the speech producing mechanisms. Using a traditional approach, speech may be considered to be the product of four separate processes: the airstream process, the phonation process, the oronasal process, and the articulatory process. As a first simplification we may associate these four processes with the actions of the lungs, the vocal folds, the velum, and the tongue and lips.

II. RESPIRATORY MECHANISMS

The source of power in nearly all speech sounds is the air that is pushed out of the lungs. The volume of air in the lungs is affected, first, by the action of the diaphragm, which is a large inspiratory muscle at the base of the rib cage; second, by the action of the external intercostal muscles, which are also inspiratory muscles in that they lift and enlarge the rib cage; and third, by all the muscles that can be used for expiration, the most important of which (from the point of view of speech production) are the internal intercostals, which pull the rib cage down and decrease its size. Ladefoged (1968) presents the following summary of the general course of respiratory events associated with an utterance:

> In general, we found that during the first part of an utterance beginning after a deep inspiration, the external intercostals remain in action, regulating the pressure of the air below the vocal cords by checking the descent of the rib cage, thus counteracting the relaxation pressure [the sum of the forces from the stretched lung tissues and other factors contributing to the elastic recoil of the lungs]. As the lung volume decreases, the action of the external intercostals diminishes and eventually ceases altogether when the lung volume is slightly less than the volume after a normal inspiration, at which moment the relaxation pressure is sufficient to provide the power required for a normal conversational utterance. From then on, expiratory activity is needed to maintain the pressure below the vocal cords, and accordingly the internal intercostals come into action with gradually increasing intensity. When the lung volume is a little below that at the end of a normal expiration, the action of the internal intercostals is supplemented by various other muscles, such as the external obliques, rectus abdominis, and latissimus dorsi [p. 141].

Ladefoged also noted that most speech is not preceded by deep inspiration or prolonged as long as in the example just cited. Under these conditions, no action of the external intercostals or of muscles other than the internal intercostals was usually observed.

The actions described here are necessary to preserve a relatively constant level of subglottal pressure during most of an utterance. However, typically superimposed on this average of subglottal pressure were found transient increases in pressure that were correlated with transient increases in activity of the internal intercostal muscles. The circumstances governing these occurrences are of particular interest. Perhaps the most well-known hypothesis related to this phenomenon is that of Stetson (1951) who believed that each syllable was accompanied by a "chest pulse," a belief that is still occasionally stated as fact in introductory textbooks (e.g., Gleason, 1967; Abercrombie, 1967). The work of Ladefoged and his associates (summarized in Ladefoged, 1967a) has shown quite conclusively that neither a burst of internal intercostal muscle action nor a transient increase in subglottal pressure is an invariant accompaniment of the syllable. Ladefoged et al. did find that a burst of intercostal muscle activity preceded each syllable during repetition of a single stressed syllable. However, during connected speech the bursts did not accompany every syllable, but occurred mainly preceding the principal stresses of the utterance, with some variation correlated with degrees of stress. Some other findings also deserve attention. Occasionally a single increase in muscle activity spanned a group of articulations including two vowels separated by a consonant closure (e.g., in *pity* or *around*). Sometimes two bursts of activity were observed in a single syllable, e.g., in *sport* and *stay* and other words beginning with a fricative–plosive sequence. Bursts of activity usually preceded [h] and long vowels. In other words, some aspects of intercostal activity appeared to be related to the pattern of individual articulatory segments as well as to stress. These latter findings contradict the usual conclusion that the subglottal mechanism is too sluggish to produce changes associated with individual segments.

A theory of stress that could account for this particular pattern of results is not known to us. In fact there is a good deal of difference of opinion about how to define stress, which is beyond the scope of this chapter but adversely affects any consideration of stress from the point of view of speech physiology. (Problems of stress are discussed from various points of view by Bolinger, 1958; Chomsky & Halle, 1968; Fry, 1970; Kent & Netsell, 1971; Ladefoged, 1971a; Lehiste, 1970; Lieberman, 1967, 1974; Ohala, 1970; Vanderslice, 1968; and Vanderslice & Ladefoged, 1972.) There is some agreement that in clear cases of stress four physical correlates are typically involved in English: fundamental frequency, intensity, segment duration, and vowel quality, with fundamental frequency being the most effective perceptual cue (Fry, 1970). What we require is a set of rules determining when stress is applied, how many different degrees of stress must be postulated, and the relative role of respiratory, laryngeal, and articulatory mechanisms in generating the above physical correlates. One of the main problems in the analysis of respiratory contributions to stress is that these contributions must be made in the context of entire utterances whose length and overall intonation contour also involve adjustments in the respiratory mechanism in order to maintain the required control of lung volume and subglottal pressure. We are at present a very long way from formulating these rules.

The role of physiological mechanisms in speech is to produce acoustic signals that have communicative significance. It is therefore of interest, in this context, to ask what are the acoustical effects of particular maneuvers of the respiratory system. It is well accepted that subglottal pressure (P_s), or, more accurately, amount of pressure drop across the glottis (transglottal pressure drop, P_T) is positively related to both intensity and fundamental frequency (F_0) of the speech signal. Hixon and his associates have recently done some elegant parametric work on the effect of changes in transglottal pressure drop (typically produced in natural speech by differences in subglottal pressure, at least during vocalic segments) on F_0 and intensity of the speech wave (Hixon, 1971; Hixon, Mead, & Klatt, 1970). By applying the output of a low-frequency loudspeaker either to the external entrance to the airway (the mouth) or to the body wall of the respiratory apparatus (enclosed in a body plethysmograph), they were able to effect sinusoidal variations in transglottal pressure drop in 10 subjects. Results of Hixon et al. concerning the relation between changes in transglottal pressure drop (P_T) and changes in F_0 $(\Delta F_0/\Delta P_T)$ add to a consensus arising from the work of several investigators (Fromkin & Ohala, 1968; Isshiki, 1959; Ladefoged, 1963; Ohala, 1970; Öhman & Lindqvist, 1966). They found that $(\Delta F_0/\Delta P_T)$ values exceeded 5 Hz/cm of H_2O in only one subject and in the speech range of F_0 they were typically 2–4 Hz/cm of H_2O. Their findings were similar whether the changes in P_T were induced via the body wall or the airway, and whether the subject was engaged in steady phonation or production of monosyllables. It is of special interest, in view of Lieberman's contention (1967, 1974) that effects of transglottal pressure drop quite often exceeded 5 Hz by considerable amounts, that Hixon et al. failed to replicate the range of 3–18 Hz/cm H_2O found by Lieberman, Knudson, and Mead (1969), even in the particular experimental subject used by Lieberman et al. Given a dynamic range of F_0 during speech of about one octave and a modal value of approximately 120 Hz in men, and given that the range of subglottal pressures observed during speech is approximately 8 cm of water, then a good deal of observed variance in F_0 cannot be accounted for in terms of respiratory influences on subglottal pressure. As we shall see in the next section, variations in laryngeal activity are responsible for most of the F_0 variations observed in speech.

III. LARYNGEAL MECHANISMS

In many sounds, the air from the lungs is turned into acoustic energy by the action of the vocal folds. The vocal folds are small, muscular folds in the larynx that can be set into vibration. In the formation of a voiced sound, the vocal folds are adjusted so that they are almost touching along their entire length. The result of air flowing through this constriction is that there is a suction effect (the Bernoulli effect), which draws the vocal folds together. But as soon as they are together there is no flow and consequently no action pulling them together; so they come apart and release the pressure that has been built up beneath them. But when they are apart they are again subject to the suction caused by the flow of air between them. So the cycle continues, producing the regular vibrations known as voice. We have already discussed the effect on the rate of vibration of the vocal folds of varying the subglottal pressure. We must now consider the actions of the larynx itself.

A. Variations in Fundamental Frequency

It is relatively well established that the main laryngeal maneuvers used to change the fundamental frequency of voiced sounds are changes in the length, thickness, and longitudinal tension of the vocal folds. Within the modal or chest register, which includes the range of fundamental frequencies observed in normal speech, it is generally agreed that most of the increase in vocal fold length is achieved by a maneuver known as "closing the cricothyroid visor."

The vocal folds run between the anterior part of the thyroid cartilage and the arytenoid cartilages, which are mounted on the posterior part of the cricoid cartilage. The cricoid cartilage can rotate about a horizontal transverse axis at the cricothyroid joint (Sonesson, 1970, Figs. 2, 3). This results in the anterior part of the cricoid being raised toward the anterior part of the thyroid cartilage (thus closing the visor). The posterior part of the cricoid is tilted backward. The result of this rotation will be lengthening of the vocal folds and an increase in their tension.

It appears that a further tension increase is produced by contraction of the muscles within the vocal folds themselves. In a particularly comprehensive recent study of steady phonation within the chest register conducted on 16 subjects, Shipp and McGlone (1971) have shown a positive relation between increase in fundamental frequency and increase in contraction of the cricothyroid and thyroarytenoid muscles, as judged from electromyograms. The cricothyroid muscle is likely to be the one most involved in the visor-closing action, and the thyroarytenoid muscle is situated within the vocal folds. As Sawashima (1974) points out, a number of earlier investigators have also come to similar conclusions.

The most far-reaching claims to be made recently about the relative role of the respiratory and laryngeal components in the control of prosodic aspects of speech are those of Lieberman (1967). He postulated the existence of an "archetypal unmarked breath group," which was supposedly an innate and universal maneuver of the respiratory apparatus and was reflected in the infant's cry. In adult speakers it was manifest in simple declarative sentences. *Joe ate his soup* was the main example used by Lieberman. It was Lieberman's contention that the characteristic changes in F_0 produced in sentences of this type were a result of subglottal pressure changes, with laryngeal maneuvers playing, by implication, a minor role. First of all, Lieberman pointed out that the subglottal pressure curve tends to match the F_0 curve in declarative sentences, remaining fairly constant through most of the sentence but falling considerably at the termination. Lieberman contended further that the phenomenon of prominence, or major sentence stress (which, for example, in *Joe ate his soup,* would be placed on *soup*), was also a result of changes in subglottal pressure. Finally, Lieberman postulated the "marked" breath group, which occurred in yes–no questions and took the form of a laryngeal maneuver to increase vocal cord tension and therefore F_0 in the terminal part of the sentence. His evidence for this contention was his observation that on these occasions, F_0 increased while P_s was decreasing, which, incidentally, provides further documentation of the possibility of the independence of laryngeal F_0 control from the respiratory component during speech.

One value of Lieberman's hypotheses is that at least some of them are sufficiently concrete to be specifically tested. Ohala (1970) has provided confirmatory evidence that F_0 increases in the terminal phases of yes–no question forms are produced by laryngeal maneuvers. Using electromyography, he found increases in activity in thyroarytenoid, cricothyroid, and lateral cricoarytenoid muscles paralleling F_0 increase and P_s decrease, which suggested that increases in vocal cord tension were occurring.

Other aspects of Lieberman's hypotheses have been called into question, particularly by Ohala (1970). From a reanalysis of the data Lieberman studied on infant cry, Ohala finds insufficient grounds for Lieberman's claim that these data provide evidence of an unmarked breath group. Ohala's dissatisfaction arose both from the small sample of data considered, and from the heterogeneity of those data with respect to the hypotheses. He also raised the question of whether infant *cry* was an appropriate homologue of adult speech.

In addition to confirming Lieberman's evidence that there are subglottal pressure increases accompanying major sentence stress or prominence as Ladefoged's work had shown earlier, Ohala and his associates (particularly Hirano) have found electromyographic evidence for concurrent F_0-raising laryngeal maneuvers. The electromyographic findings were analogous in pattern to those accompanying terminal F_0 raising, namely concurrent activity of the cricothyroid, vocalis, and lateral cricoarytenoid muscles. These findings, along with those of Hixon *et al.,* on the limitations of changes in P_T changing F_0, lead to the conclusion that there is a considerable amount of laryngeal contribution to the implementation of sentence prominence.

It does not provide a great advance in our knowledge to note that laryngeal maneuvers are more important in the pitch variations that occur in sentence prominence than Lieberman had supposed, for, as Ohala (1970) has pointed out, this view had a good deal of acceptance before Lieberman formulated his alternative view. What we require at this stage is research showing in more detail what the relative contribution of larynx and lungs to F_0 actually is under a variety of conditions. A step in this direction has recently been made by Lieberman, Sawashima, Harris, and Gay (1970). They were able to confirm the finding of laryngeal involvement in sentence prominence in simple declarative sentences by means of recording of cricothyroid muscle activity in one subject. But they did not observe cricothyroid activity accompanying sentence prominence in questions that involved terminal F_0 raising. An additional requirement at present is for studies of a number of subjects. The fact that it is possible to vary F_0 by more than one means tends to make suspect any generalizations about the relative role of lungs and larynx that are based on only one or a few subjects.

With respect to the terminal fall in F_0 in declarative sentences, Ohala has observed increases in activity of the sternohyoid muscle, suggesting again laryngeal involvement, this time of the extrinsic musculature, in F_0 control. But two recent reviewers (Harris, 1974 and Sawashima, 1974) have noted other studies that have not been successful in finding a relation between sternohyoid activity and F_0 lowering. Harris considers that the laryngeal contribution to F_0 lowering may be a passive one, consisting of cessation of activity in muscles mediating F_0 raising.

In summary, Lieberman appears to have been correct about the role of the larynx in terminal F_0 raising, wrong about the degree of laryngeal involvement in the pitch raising that accompanies sentence prominence, and, his hypothesis about terminal F_0 lowering is still being evaluated. In addition, no convincing evidence is available to support his notion of an innate universal archetypal breath group, partly because the notion is not formulated in a manner allowing its test (Ohala, 1970, p. 80).

B. Variations in Phonation Type

Laryngeal mechanisms are responsible for far more than fundamental frequency variations in speech. All known languages also use the difference between voiced sounds (such as the consonants in the words *buy, die, zoo*) and voiceless sounds (the consonants in *pie, tie, sue*). In voiced sounds the vocal folds are together (adducted), whereas in voiceless sounds they are so far apart (abducted) that they cannot be set into vibration by the flow of air between them.

We will now consider the operation of adduction and abduction of the vocal cords and more specifically the movements of the arytenoid cartilages that bring about these adjustments. It now seems clear from the morphology of the cricoarytenoid joint that the degree of posterior separation of the vocal cords is not controlled by the rotation of the arytenoid cartilages about a vertical axis as some earlier descriptions had suggested. As Sawashima (1974) puts it,

> The structure of the cricoarytenoid joint permits the arytenoid cartilages two principal types of motion. One of them, the main type, is a rotating motion around the longitudinal axis of the joint; the other is a longitudinal sliding motion parallel to the axis [p. 2312].

The cricoid facet of the cricoarytenoid joint is a convex surface the axis of which runs in a ventrolaterocaudal to dorsomediocranial direction. The arytenoid facet is a reciprocally concave surface. Sonesson (cited by Sawashima) considers the movements of the arytenoid cartilages to be controlled by the individual laryngeal muscles in the following manner:

> (1) the thyroarytenoid and the lateral cricoarytenoid muscles contribute to the adduction of the arytenoid cartilages and their linear sliding in the ventrolaterocaudal direction [for what he considers to be a maximum of 2 millimeters]; (2) the arytenoid muscle causes the adduction of the arytenoid cartilages and their linear sliding in the dorsomediocranial direction; (3) the posterior cricoarytenoid muscle contributes to the abduction of the arytenoid cartileges with little effect on their linear sliding motion [p. 2313].

Electromyographic (EMG) studies of segmental articulation have added to the broad outline of functions attributed by Sonesson to the intrinsic laryngeal muscles, although in this area there are still relatively few data available, where only *small* differences between muscles are reported, the findings should probably await replication. A study of two subjects by Hirose (1971) has shown quite clearly that the posterior cricoarytenoid muscle is active in the abduction of the vocal cords for voiceless stop consonants and fricatives in intervocalic position and for the voiceless stop [p] in final position. In addition, MacNeilage has found in an unpublished study of data from Shipp's laboratory that there was *always* posterior cricoarytenoid activity for intervocalic voiceless stops and fricatives in the records of a number of subjects producing disyllables in citation form. The abduction of the vocal cords for voiceless stop consonants and fricatives and their behavior for voiced obstruents has been observed in transillumination studies and direct photography, and the results of these studies have been summarized by Sawashima (1972).

Hirose (1971) has observed EMG activity of the vocalis, interarytenoid, and lateral cricoarytenoid muscles preceding the initiation of voicing in disyllables beginning with a vowel. These effects are visible in the results shown by Ohala (1970) in utterances beginning with [b], and have also been reported by Hiroto, Hirano, Toyozumi, and Shin (1967) and observed by MacNeilage (in the thyroarytenoid and interarytenoid) in Shipp's data. Hirose has also found that the interarytenoid appears to be more directly opposite in function to the posterior cricoarytenoid than the vocalis or the lateral cricoarytenoid. It shows much more reduction of activity preceding voiceless stops than preceding voiced stops, when the reduction is only slight. On the other hand, the vocalis and the lateral cricoarytenoid show only slight but equal reductions preceding both voiced and voiceless stop consonants. The interarytenoid also mirrors the posterior cricoarytenoid more than the other two muscles in showing more increase in activity (as posterior cricoarytenoid activity reduces) after voiceless stops than after voiced stops. These data, though requiring confirmation, suggest to Hirose that there may be a functional differentiation between these three muscles. Whereas the interarytenoid is more strictly an adductory muscle, the remaining two muscles may be concerned also with other adjustments. Elsewhere Hirose and his colleagues also have suggested that there may be a functional differentiation between the lateral cricoarytenoid and the vocalis (Hirose, Simada, & Fujimura, 1970). They found in one subject that "the vocalis is particularly active in voicing and has the characteristic of contracting and relaxing in a relatively fast manner, while the lateralis shows relatively continuous activity during the entire period of the utterance [p. 25]." It is of interest that the reduction in activity of all these muscles preceding voiced consonants is consistent with the hypothesis of Halle and Stevens (1967) that there may be a different mode of voicing during voiced stop consonants than during vowels. On the other hand the lack of difference in vocalis and lateral cricoarytenoid activity for voiced and voiceless stops (together with the fact that the cricothyroid muscle is minimally involved in segmental gestures [Hirose, 1971]) is contrary to the claim of Halle and Stevens (1971) that voiced and voiceless stops differ in vocal cord stiffness.

Numerous other states of the glottis remain to be investigated. In a review of the linguistic data, Ladefoged (1973) has shown that several languages use more than just the voiced and voiceless states of the glottis. In Hindi and many of the other languages of India some sounds are produced while the vocal folds are vibrating for part of their length, but the arytenoid cartilages are apart so that a considerable amount of air escapes between them. This kind of phonation is known as breathy voice, or murmur. Yet other languages have sounds in which the arytenoid cartilages are held tightly together so that only the anterior part of the vocal folds can vibrate. This kind of sound, which is usually very low pitched, is sometimes called creaky voice, or vocal fry. It is used to make contrasts between consonants in several American Indian languages. An additional glottal state that is widely used (e.g., in the Malayo–Polynesian languages of the Philippines) is a glottal stop, a tight closure of the two vocal cords. This articulation occurs also in many forms of English as the usual pronunciation of [t] in words such as *bitten* and *fatten*. If there is a glottal stop and the closed glottis is moved rapidly upward or downward, it can act like a piston pushing or pulling the air in the pharynx. When there is an upward movement of the closed glottis the resulting sound is called an ejective. Amharic, the national language of Ethiopia, uses this mechanism. A downward movement of the glottis is used in the production of implosive sounds, which occur in many American Indian, African, and other languages. The precise physiological mechanisms used in all these laryngeal gestures are not fully understood, but data on many of them are becoming available through the use of fiber optic techniques (Sawashima, 1974).

IV. ARTICULATORY MECHANISMS

The air passages above the vocal folds are known collectively as the vocal tract. They may be divided into the oral tract, within the mouth and the pharynx, and the nasal tract, within the nose. Many speech sounds are characterized by movements of the lower articulators, such as the tongue or the lower lip, toward the upper articulators within the oral tract.

The upper surface includes several important structures from the point of view of speech production. Fig. 1 illustrates most of the terms that are commonly used in describing the vocal organs. The *upper lip* and the upper *teeth* (notably the frontal incisors) are familiar structures and need no further comment. The *alveolar ridge* is a small protuberance that can easily be felt with the tongue just behind the upper front teeth. The major part of the roof of the mouth is formed by the *hard palate* in the front and the soft *palate* or *velum* at the back. The soft palate is a muscular flap that can be raised so as to shut off the nasal tract and prevent air from going out through the nose. When it is raised so that the soft palate is

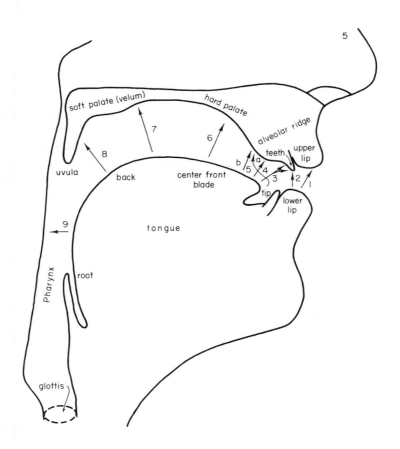

FIG. 1. Diagram showing the vocal organs and the possible places of articulation. (*1*) bilabial; (*2*) labiodental; (*3*) dental and interdental; (*4*) alveolar; (*5*) post-alveolar. (*a*) retroflex, (*b*) palato-alveolar; (*6*) palatal; (*7*) velar; (*8*) uvular; (*9*) pharyngeal.

pressed against the back wall of the *pharynx* there is said to be a velic closure. At the lower end of the soft palate there is a small appendage hanging down which is known as the *uvula*.

As may be seen from Fig. 1, there are also specific names for different parts of the *tongue*. The *tip* and *blade* are the most mobile parts. Behind the blade is what is technically called the *front* of the tongue; it is actually the forward part of the body of the tongue, and lies underneath the hard palate when the tongue is at rest. The remainder of the body of the tongue may be divided into the *center,* which is partly beneath the hard palate and partly beneath the soft palate, the *back,* which is beneath the soft palate, and the *root,* which is opposite the back wall of the pharynx.

A. Consonants

In the formation of consonants, the airstream through the vocal tract is obstructed in some way. Consonants can be classified according to the place and manner of this obstruction. Some of the possible places of articulation are indicated in Fig. 1 by the arrows going from one of the lower articulators to one of the upper articulators. The principal terms required in the description of English speech sounds are: *bilabial* (made with the two lips); *dental* (tongue tip or blade and the upper front teeth); *alveolar* (tongue tip or blade and the teeth ridge); *retroflex* (tongue tip and the back part of the teeth ridge); *palato-alveolar* (tongue blade and the back part of the teeth ridge); palatal (front of tongue and hard palate); and *velar* (back of tongue and soft palate). The additional places of articulation shown in Fig. 1 are required in the description of the sounds of other languages. Note that the terms for the various places of articulation denote both which part of the lower articulators (lower lip and tongue) and which part of the upper articulatory structure are involved. Thus *velar* denotes a sound in which specifically the back of the tongue and the soft palate are involved; and *retroflex* implies a sound involving the tip of the tongue and the back of the alveolar ridge. If it is necessary to distinguish between sounds made with the tip of the tongue, and those made with the blade, the terms *apical* (tip) and *laminal* (blade) may be used.

There are six basic manners of articulation that can be used at these places of articulation:

1. STOP

Closure of the articulators, so that the airstream cannot go out of the mouth results in a stop. This manner of articulation can be considered in terms of the two possibilities:

(a) NASAL STOP. If the soft palate is down so that air can still go out through the nose, there is said to be a nasal stop. Sounds of this kind occur at the beginning of the words *my, nigh.*

(b) ORAL STOP. If, in addition to the articulatory closure in the mouth, the soft palate is raised so that the nasal tract is blocked off, then the airstream will be completely obstructed, the pressure in the mouth will be built up, and an oral stop will be formed. When the articulators come apart the airstream will be released with a plosive quality. This kind of sound occurs in the consonants in the words *pie, tie, kye, buy, die, guy.*

Many authorities refer to these two possibilities simply as nasals (meaning nasal stops, the closure of the articulators in the oral tract being implied), and stops (meaning oral stops, the raising of the soft palate to form a velic closure being implied).

2. FRICATIVE

Close approximation of two articulators, partially obstructing the airstream and producing a turbulent airflow, results in a fricative. Examples of sounds of this kind are the consonants in the words *fie, thigh, sigh, shy.*

3. APPROXIMANTS

An approximant results when one articulator approaches another, but without the tract being narrowed to such an extent that a turbulent airstream is produced. The terms "frictionless continuant," "semivowel," and "glide" are sometimes used for some of the sounds made with this manner of articulation. The consonants in the words *we* and *you* are examples of approximants.

4. TRILL

A trill occurs when one articulator is loosely held fairly close to another articulator, so that it is set into vibration by the airstream. The tongue tip and blade, the uvula, and the lips are the only articulators that can be used in this way. Tongue tip trills occur in some forms of Scottish English in such words as *rye* and *ire.* Uvular trills are comparatively rare, but are used in some dialects of French (but not Parisian French). Trills of the lips are even rarer, but do occur in a few African languages.

5. TAP

One articulator is thrown against another, as when the loosely held tongue tip makes a single tap against the upper teeth or the alveolar ridge. The consonant in the middle of such words as *letter* or *Betty* is often made in this way in American English.

6. LATERAL

Obstruction of the airstream in the midline of the oral tract, but with incomplete closure between one or both sides of the tongue and the roof of the mouth results in a lateral. The sounds at the beginning and end of the word *lull* are pronounced in this way in most forms of American English.

B. Vowels

Vowels have traditionally been specified in terms of the position of the highest point of the tongue and the position of the lips. Figure 2 shows these positions for eight different vowels. The highest point of the tongue is in the front of the mouth for the vowels in *heed, hid, head* and *had*. Accordingly these vowels are classified as front vowels, whereas the vowels

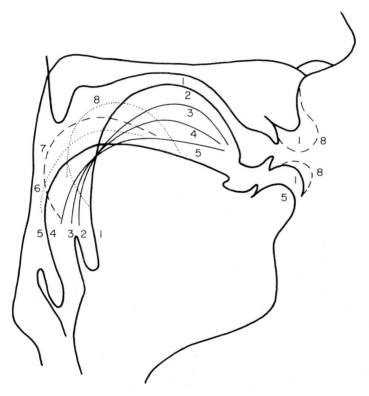

FIG. 2. Tongue positions for vowels in the words: (*1*) *heed*, (*2*) *hid*, (*3*) *head*, (*4*) *had*, (*5*) *hod*, (*6*) *hawed*, (*7*) *hood*, (*8*) *who'd*.

in *hod, hawed, hood* and *who'd* are classified as back vowels. The tongue is highest in the vowels in *heed* and *who'd* (which are therefore called high, or close, vowels), and lowest in the vowels in *had* and *hod* (which are called low, or open, vowels). The height of the tongue for the vowels in the other words is between these two extremes, and they are therefore called mid vowels. Lip positions may be described as being rounded (as in *who'd*), or unrounded and spread (as in *heed*).

The specification of vowels in terms of the position of the highest point of the tongue is not entirely satisfactory for a number of reasons. In the first place, it disregards the fact that the shape of the tongue as a whole is very different in front vowels and in back vowels. Second, although the height of the tongue in front vowels varies by approximately equal amounts for what are called equidistant steps in vowel quality, this is not true in descriptions of back vowels. Third, the width of the pharynx varies considerably, and to some extent independently of the height of the tongue, in different vowels.

V. ARTICULATORY DYNAMICS

During the past few years, there has been a rapid increase in the number of studies of articulatory dynamics (Laver, 1970) and the development of a number of new techniques for their measurement. Accompanying this work, there has been an increase in the realization, which began with the earlier acoustic phonetic studies, that there is enormous variability in articulatory gestures as a function of their phonetic and linguistic context. This has led in turn to an increasing realization of the inappropriateness of conceptualizing the dynamic processes of articulation itself in terms of discrete, static, context-free linguistic categories, such as "phoneme" and "distinctive feature." This development does not mean that these linguistic categories should be abandoned—as there is considerable evidence for their behavioral reality (Fromkin, 1971). Instead, it seems to require that they be recognized, even more than before, as too abstract to characterize the actual behavior of articulators themselves. They are, therefore, at present better confined to primarily characterizing earlier premotor stages of the production process, as revealed by speech errors, and to reflecting regularities at the message level (Fant, 1962) of the structure of language, such as those noted by phonologists. Parallel to this decrease in relevance of the linguistic theory to the dynamics of articulation, there has arisen a need for new concepts to characterize articulatory function, concepts more appropriate to the description of movement processes than of stationary states. It seems desirable that, in the future, these concepts be integrated with or made compatible with traditional linguistic unit concepts. But this should not be a one-way street. If a goal of linguistic theory is to characterize what speakers do, then the concepts of that theory must be compatible with the facts of speech production.

In the 1950s perhaps the major impetus to studies of articulatory dynamics came from the pioneering work of Haskins Laboratories researchers, in which they established the importance of formant transitions arising from articulatory dynamics and delicate timing cues arising from dynamic interaction of laryngeal and articulatory structures (Liberman, 1957) as cues to speech perception. These discoveries led to increasing interest in the articulatory processes underlying the cues. Concern with articulatory processes was given further impetus by the motor theory of speech perception (Liberman, Cooper, Harris, MacNeilage, & Studdert-Kennedy, 1967), which claimed that perception of some linguistic categories resulted from the listener making reference to a particular kind of motor information underlying his own articulation. In other words, the perceptual theory was accompanied by an assertion about the commands underlying speech production, which naturally invited tests. This in turn led to the initiation of electromyographic studies of articulation (Cooper, Liberman, Harris, & Grubb, 1958; Lysaught, Rosov, & Harris, 1961).

In the 1960s, perhaps the most important event was the publication of a monograph by a number of Russian authors (Chistovich, Kozhevnikov, Alyakrinskiy, Bondarko, Goluzina, Klass, Kuz'min, Lisenko, Lyublinskaya, Fedorova, Shuplyakov, and Shuplyakova) entitled: *Speech: Articulation and Perception* and translated by the U.S. Department of Commerce in 1965. This monograph came to grips, for the first time, with the *general* problem of articulatory dynamics, in the context of the production of entire utterances, and presented a number of very ingenious hypotheses and experimental approaches bearing on this problem. It demonstrated, perhaps for the first time, that conceptual tools appropriate to the study of articulatory dynamics could be formulated free from the inherent constraints imposed by static linguistic unit concepts that were themselves formulated primarily for reasons other than the explanation of articulatory processes.

These developments, along with a number of others, have given rise to the increasing interest in details of the articulatory process in the past few years. In the following paragraphs, we will attempt to summarize the present state of knowledge in this area and to evaluate the explanatory concepts that have arisen. Before beginning, we should emphasize that we are still primarily at a fact gathering stage in this area. Consequently, there are many facts available that appear to have no principled basis at present. Nevertheless, we will present many of these facts, rather than ignoring them, because we do not want to prejudge their ultimate significance.

A. The Soft Palate or Velum

In most languages the soft palate has only one linguistically distinctive function, namely to distinguish between nasal and nonasal segments. Thus, the only difference between the first consonant in *man* and that in *ban* is that, in the formation of [m], the soft palate is lowered so that the airstream can pass out through the nose. Because of its inaccessibility and its rather complex morphology and for clinical reasons, much effort has been expended in attempting simply to find out how the palate actually moves, and how this movement is controlled by contraction of the palatal musculature. There is a good deal of agreement that the radial movement of the velum in a posterior–superior direction, which results in a closure of the velopharyngeal port for nonasal segments, is achieved primarily by contraction of the levator palantini muscle. Combined cinefluorographic and electromyographic studies (Fritzell, 1969; Lubker, 1968) have shown correlation coefficients of approximately .8 between amount of velar elevation and amplitude of EMG activity in the levator palatini muscle. Velar elevation and levator palatini EMG amplitude have also been regularly shown to be directly proportional to vowel height, although not so regularly related to the front–back dimension of vowels (Berti, 1971). Lubker (1968) has suggested that the higher EMG levels for high vowels reflect a maneuver compensating for their greater susceptibility to nasalization. Palatal elevation and levator EMG activity have been found to be greater for obstruents than for vowels. But within the class of obstruents, no differences have been consistently observed. For example, Berti (1971) found higher EMG amplitudes for voiced stops than for voiceless stops in one of her two subjects, but no difference in the other. On the other hand, Lubker, Fritzell, and Lindqvist (1972) found higher EMG amplitudes during voiceless stops in the one subject they investigated intensively.

Both perseverative and anticipatory coarticulation effects have been observed in cinefluorographic studies of palatal movement and electromyographic studies of the levator palatini. Coarticulation effects stretching across more than one segment will be discussed later. The most systematic study of coarticulation effects of adjacent segments is a study of perseverative effects in EMG activity of their one subject by Lubker *et al.* (1971). It is extremely provocative that most of the numerical data they present on nonasal segments following other segments (see their Fig. IIA-4) is consistent with one generalization; the average amount of EMG activity for the second of two segments is proportional to the ratio between the average amount of peak activity observed during speech in general for segment two and segment one. For example, most activity is observed for voiceless stop consonants following nasals, as voiceless stops showed the most activity in general and nasals the least. Conversely, the nonnasal segments showing least activity in general were open vowels, and they showed their least activity when they followed voiceless stop consonants. These results, although based on only one subject, suggest two generalizations about perseverative coarticulation over adjacent segments in the levator palatini muscle that are probably applicable to other articulatory systems as well: (*1*) the production system is constrained to approximate a particular articulatory configuration for each member of a given class, whenever it occurs, at least in careful speech; (*2*) the amount of EMG activity associated with a segment on any given occasion is proportional to the mechanical work required to approximate the required articulatory configuration. This second generalization is perhaps stating the obvious. But what is of interest in this particular case is that the levator, unlike most other articulatory muscles, is only involved in one task during speech, so that its degree of contraction can be related in a straightforward manner to the accomplishment of that task.

When considering other muscles of the palatopharyngeal complex, we find that the present picture is not nearly as straightforward as it is with the levator palatini.

B. Labial and Mandibular Mechanics

Since the positions of the lips and the tongue depend to a great extent on the position of the jaw, we will consider the mechanics of jaw movements first. There is a considerable amount of data on the degree of jaw displacement in consonants. According to some investigators (Ohala, Hiki, Hubler, & Harshman, 1968; Kent & Moll, 1969; Perkell, 1969) the degree of opening in stop consonants is smallest for [t], next smallest for [p], and greatest for [k]. Other investigators (Abbs, Netsell, and Hixon, 1972) agree that [t] has the smallest opening, but found that for all three of their subjects [p] had a greater opening than [k]. Kent and Moll (1969) found the order of magnitude of jaw opening for some lingual consonants of different manners of articulation to be [g > j > d > z]. The amount of jaw opening decreases as the place of constriction moves forward in the oral cavity.

The relative jaw opening in vowels corresponded well to what has traditionally been called "vowel height," according to Ohala *et al.* (1968; one subject), Watkin and Abbs (1972; two subjects) and Lindblom and Sundberg (1971; one subject). Because the tongue shapes of the front vowels remained constant with respect to the mandible, Lindblom and Sundberg concluded that relative jaw opening was the primary factor for distinguishing height. However, this conclusion was found to be untenable when the behavior of additional subjects was considered. Four out of six subjects in the study by Ladefoged, DeClerk, Lindau, and Papçun (1972) did not use jaw opening as the primary mechanism for distinguishing vowel heights.

C. Tongue Positions

The tongue is the most complex of all the organs of speech. In a review of the anatomy and physiology of the tongue muscles, Ladefoged *et al.* (1972) have shown that there are numerous interacting forces. MacNeilage and DeClerk (1969), Smith (1971), and MacNeilage (1970) report considerable variation of EMG activity of muscles that are involved in different articulations; and it appears that even the shapes of the tongue in simple vowels are more varied than had been presumed by earlier investigators. According to Houde (1967; one subject), Perkell (1969; one subject), Lindblom and Sundberg (1971; one subject), and Kent (1972; two subjects), the tongue shapes of different vowels are very similar—at least for the body of the tongue. However, only two out of the six subjects studied by Ladefoged *et al.* (1972) accomplished tongue height differences by moving the jaw with a constant tongue shape, and even for these two subjects this was true for only a small subset of vowels. The six speakers employed different combinations of the mechanisms of jaw opening, advancing the tongue root, and lifting the tongue body within the mandible in order to achieve different tongue heights. Lindau, Jacobson, and Ladefoged (1972) also found all these three mechanisms to play a role in the control of tongue height in six different languages.

From an EMG study of action of the genioglossus, Raphael (1971) concluded that there was consistently greater genioglossus activity for the vowels [i], [e], and [u] than for their counterparts in the vowel triangle [ɪ], [ɛ], and [ɒ]: He remarks that this difference is, however, inseparable from differences in duration and quality. As the main result of genioglossus activity is to pull forward the root of the tongue, Raphael's data support a recent proposal credited to Halle and Stevens by Perkell (1971). According to this proposal the primary mechanism for tenseness in vowels is the advancing of the tongue root. Again, this proposal cannot be supported as a general mechanism for tenseness when more subjects are considered. Three of the six speakers used by Ladefoged *et al.* (1972) did separate tense and lax front vowels by advancing the tongue root and thus increasing the width of the pharynx. But the other subjects did not distinguish between these two groups of vowels in this way.

D. Segment Durations

Segment durations provide useful information about dynamics in that they provide clues as to the temporal organization of the serial ordering of speech production. Segments can be conceived of as possessing intrinsic durations that relate to the means of their own articulation (Lehiste, 1970, p. 18). Within the class of vowels, some of the variance in duration of different vowels in comparable contexts is accounted for by the amount of jaw opening, more open vowels having longer durations (House, 1961). The articulatory process thus *appears* to be subject to the mechanical constraints inherent in moving this large articulator increasing distances, as most consonants require relatively closed jaw positions. But it is of interest that partially successful efforts appear to be made to overcome this constraint. It has been shown that maximum velocity of jaw opening and closing movements is directly proportional to the amount of jaw opening required for the vowel in the set [i], [ɛ], [æ] (Sussman & Smith, 1971). Furthermore, Lindblom has shown compensatory vowel-shortening movements of the lower lip when open vowels are followed by bilabial stop consonants (Lindblom, 1968). It is as if the central mechanism strives for equality of segment duration, but with either an inability to achieve it or a lack of necessity for completely achieving it, which Lindblom has suggested may be based on perceptual tolerances (Lindblom, 1968).

When different phonetic contexts are considered, most of the variance in vowel duration is related to the identity of the following consonant, with voiced consonants preceded by longer vowels than voiceless, and fricatives by longer vowels than stop consonants. An important clue to the reason for these differences, at least in stop consonants, was provided by Chistovich *et al.* (1965). They found that average velocity of the lip closing movement was faster for voiceless bilabial stops than for voiced (140 versus 125 mm per second). On the basis of some measurements of this effect in English, Chen (1970) has concluded that the greater rate of lower lip movement in voiceless bilabial stops could make a difference of 27 msec in vowel duration. Chen found that this value was similar to the differences in vowel duration preceding voiced and voiceless stops in a number of languages. These differences in closure movements for bilabial stop consonants probably result from the fact that a more forceful articulator movement is required in the voiceless stop to counteract the greater aerodynamic forces about to be imposed on the upper articulators by air flow in the open glottal condition necessary for voicelessness.

However, rates of lip movement would not be expected to be relevant to differences in the voicing of alveolar and velar stops, as they do not actively involve the lips. In this connection, it must be borne in mind that rate of lower lip movement is a combined result of actual lower lip movement with respect to the lower jaw and lower jaw movement itself. Ohala *et al.* (1968) have concluded that rates of lower jaw closing movements are greater for voiceless stop consonants in general than for voiced, though they only presented a single illustration of each type of stop. Kim and MacNeilage (1972) gathered information on this question in three subjects, and found that although actual lower lip movement rates were not greater for bilabial voiceless stops, lower jaw movement rates for all three voiceless stops significantly exceeded those of their voiced counterparts when they followed the open vowel [a]. It appears then that velocity differences in jaw movement are related to the need to counteract aerodynamic forces. It therefore seems that mechanical constraints are responsible for differences in vowel duration due to following stop-consonantal context, just as they are responsible for durational effects of vowel openness. The interesting theoretical question thus becomes: Why does the means of coping with the aerodynamic contingencies result in a shortening of vowel segment duration in the voiceless case? It is not the only possible means.

An explanation in terms of mechanical constraints appears to cover the facts of the vowel duration effects of following stop consonants in many languages, but not all. It is well known that differences in vowel duration preceding voiced and voiceless stop consonants in English and French can considerably exceed 27 msec. House (1961), for example, finds a mean value of approximately 130 msec. It has been shown by Denes (1955) in an experiment using synthetic speech, that English-speaking listeners used the differences in vowel length as a major perceptual cue to the voicing of the following consonant. In fact in many pronunciations of the words *bat* and *bad* there is no difference whatsoever in the final segments, the entire distinction between the words being one of vowel length. Furthermore, it has been shown by Chen that in English utterances involving the sequence vowel-sonorant-stop as in *bant* and *band,* both the vowel and the sonorant are shorter in duration when they occur before a voiceless stop. This change in the vowel obviously cannot be due to any physiological effect of the terminal stop consonant.

Findings of this kind make it necessary to postulate that an inherent mechanical constraint on speech production has in some sense "triggered" larger differences in vowel duration in some languages so that these differences themselves come to have a distinctive function. This is a common phenomenon in linguistic change. There are many cases where the introduction of a small economy in articulation leads to a change in the phonemic system of a language. Thus the pronunciation of a forward articulation of [k] before a front vowel leads to the softening of the velar, so that we now have a difference in the first consonants in *child* and *cat*. A similar case of differences in F_0 associated with voiced voiceless stops "triggering" the development of differences in word tone, even though the earlier consonant distinction has disappeared, has been described by Mohr (1969).

So far, we have observed the effects of two different types of mechanical constraint on articulatory dynamics. In the case of intrinsic differences in vowel duration, there appears to be a simple constraint of articulatory mass, directly proportional to displacement and partially compensated for by velocity of movement. In the case of vowel duration differences conditioned by voicing of following stop consonants, we have observed an interaction between phonatory and articulatory mechanical contingencies. The greater vowel durations preceding fricatives than preceding stops appear to be associated with a third distinct type of mechanical effect—the effect of required precision of movement on rate of movement. Stevens and House (1963) have postulated, on the basis of spectrographic evidence, that articulator movements are slower during transitions from vowels into fricatives than in transitions from vowels into stops. They speculated that the slower movements for fricatives might result from the fact that a greater precision of articulator placement is required for fricatives—namely an optimally narrow constriction—than for stops where "overshoot" of an articulator following occlusion will have a negligible effect on the acoustic signal. Kim and MacNeilage (1972) have shown that, although the lower jaw does not appear to move more slowly for fricatives than for stops, the lower lip did move more slowly for labiodental fricatives than for bilabial stops in all three subjects. Thus, longer durations of vowels before fricatives might be at least partly due to longer durations of movements of the articulators directly involved in the fricative constriction, related to the precision required for fricative production. This would not be surprising in the light of Fitts's (1954) finding that in simple skilled movements there are tradeoff relations between the three variables: (1) speed of movement, (2) precision of the termination of the movement, and (3) amount of displacement required. It appears that, in this case, some speed may have been traded for precision.

Vowel durations are also affected by the place of articulation of the following consonant. Both Fischer-Jørgensen (1964) and Peterson and Lehiste (1960) have shown that vowels are shorter preceding bilabial stop consonants than before velar or alveolar stops. Peterson and Lehiste also found this effect of place of articulation for durations of both long and short vowels before fricatives, and for long vowels before nasals, i.e., the labiodental fricatives [f] and [v] and the bilabial nasal [m] were preceded by shorter vowels than other segments of comparable manner and voicing. There is also in this literature some tendency for vowels to be shorter before palatal and velar consonants than before alveolar consonants, though there are some exceptions to this trend.

These findings can be most profitably considered along with the durations of the consonants themselves, i.e., the time period of occlusion of the vocal tract for stops and nasals and the period of optimal vocal constriction for fricatives. There is a very good consensus that the period of occlusion is longer in all phonetic contexts for bilabial stops than for alveolar or velar stops (see summary in Lehiste, 1970, pp. 27–30). The fact that this effect is context-free suggests that it is an intrinsic property of bilabial stops. Still another mechanical contingency appears to be involved here. As the lips and jaw are to some extent mechanically independent of the tongue, which is the major articulator for vowels and most consonants, they are apparently under less time constraint than the tongue, which is often involved in several adjacent segments. The lips and jaw are therefore free to produce longer occlusions than the tongue. The fact that vowel duration is less before bilabials than before other stops, and the fact that vowels are shortened more by following stops than by preceding stops suggests that the mechanical freedom of the lip and jaw system is manifest more in anticipation of its target position for bilabial stops than in perseveration in that position. Of course, the fact that an articulator is free to produce a longer occlusion is not an explanation of the fact that it produces a longer occlusion.

Although the literature is less clear on this point than on the characteristics of bilabial stops, there is some consensus that vowels are short before velar stop consonants than before alveolars. And, as in the case of bilabials, there is some evidence that the consonants that shorten the vowel more—namely, velars—are themselves longer in duration than alveolars with comparable voicing. Lehiste (1970) has suggested a mechanical explanation for these findings, namely, that the tongue tip, being the more mobile articulator, can move faster, thus producing shorter closure durations. Whether this explanation is correct would seem to depend on the overall timing demands imposed on an utterance, which are not at present clear but will be discussed at greater length in later paragraphs. In the absence of that knowledge, one could equally well argue that, being a faster articulator, the tongue tip could carry out closing and opening gestures more quickly, thus leaving *more* time for occlusion than is available for velars.

E. Suprasegmental Influences on Segment Duration

So far, we have considered durational variations that are observable in monosyllabic words. But there remains an enormous class of durational effects associated with higher-order aspects of the production of utterances and indicating the existence of an elegant hierarchy of speech timing mechanisms. We will now outline some of these durational variations. They have recently been reviewed in more detail by Lehiste (1970). She also reviews contrastive uses of duration in languages other than English, but these will not be considered in detail here.

There is a tendency in many languages for the duration of syllabic nuclei to vary inversely with the number of syllables in a word. This tendency is quite marked, for example, in Hungarian (Tarnoczy, 1965, cited by Lehiste, 1970, p. 40) and also occurs in English (Lehiste, 1971b).

The lengthening of final syllables is another well-known suprasegmental effect, and has recently been systematically explored by Oller (1973). He has confirmed the popular impression that final syllable lengthening is greater when a word occurs in the final position of an utterance. He also finds a slight (20 msec) lengthening even when the word is produced in a nonfinal position in a phrase. In English, lengthening of the syllable appears to take place predominantly within the vowel. However, in a study of one dialect of Finnish, Oller found very little final vowel lengthening but relatively more final consonant lengthening. It appears then, that final syllable lengthening is not uniform in pattern in different languages, and this makes the phenomenon difficult to ascribe, in any straightforward way, to an inherent production constraint. It is also difficult to explain it as the provision of a perceptual cue (Oller, 1973).

In English, stress appears to be typically accompanied by lengthening of the syllable nucleus (Fry, 1955), and probably by systematic, though small, changes in surrounding consonants. In English, and some other languages, the longer duration of more heavily stressed syllables is accompanied by more movement of articulators toward target positions (Lindblom, 1963). Studies of articulatory dynamics have suggested that these articulator movements also tend to be of higher velocity for stressed syllables (MacNeilage, 1970; Kent & Netsell, 1971). Electromyographic studies have shown that stressed syllables are accompanied by higher levels of muscle activity in some articulators than are unstressed syllables (Harris, 1974; Harris, Gay, Sholes, & Liberman, 1968; Slis, 1971). Kent and Netsell's study suggests that these differences are not accompanied by differences in the amount of coarticulation of the affected gestures with adjacent gestures.

A final determinant of segment duration is speaking rate. Increases in speaking rate are accompanied by decreases in segment duration, with the decrease in the vowel being proportionately greater (Chistovich et al., 1965; MacNeilage & Declerk, 1969). These decreases are achieved not by an increase of rate of articulator movement—rates either remain constant (Lindblom, 1964; MacNeilage & DeClerk, 1969) or decrease (Chistovich et al., 1965)—but by a reduction in the amount of articulator displacement toward target. The consequences of speaking rate increase thus may be analogous to those of stress decrease.

It is of interest to note two variables that might have been imagined to have durational consequences but apparently do not. Lehiste (1971a) has concluded that morpheme boundaries and syntactic boundaries did not have any systematic effects on segment durations separable from effects that could be ascribed to the syllabic structure of the utterances.

F. The Chistovich *et al.* View of Articulatory Dynamics

We do not yet have available satisfactory theoretical formulations about any of the main individual aspects of articulatory timing that have been summarized here. In fact, general interest in articulatory timing within the field of speech physiology has developed only within the past few years, largely as a result of contributions by Lashley (1951), whose *general* view of the problem of output timing has, in our opinion, yet to be improved upon (MacNeilage & MacNeilage, 1973), and by Chistovich *et al.* (1965), Lenneberg (1967), Allen (1968), and Lehiste (1971b). Chistovich and her colleagues have made the most specific and influential attempts to develop a model of articulatory timing. A convenient and appropriate way to evaluate the present state of theorizing in this area is to summarize the views of the Russian group and then consider how subsequent studies, stimulated largely by the Russian work, bear on these views.

Chistovich *et al.* postulate that the largest unit of speech timing is the *syntagma*. It is not very easy to see precisely what they mean by this term: They define it as "a sentence or part of a sentence distinguished by meaning." It is produced as a single output bounded by pauses and has an average length in free speech of seven syllables.

Within the syntagma, Chistovich *et al.* postulate that the basic articulatory unit is the articulatory syllable, which differs considerably from traditional linguistic conceptions of the syllable. The articulatory syllable consists of a vowel and however many consecutive consonants precede it. This claim was based largely on the finding that the lip rounding gesture for the vowel /u/ began "simultaneously" with the first consonant when either one or two consonants preceded the vowel. This same result was still found, even when a conventional syllable or word boundary fell between the two consonants. The coincidence between lip rounding onset and the first consonant led Chistovich *et al.* to consider lip rounding onset as an objective sign of the beginning of the syllable. Further hypotheses govern the interrelations between gestures within the syllable. The most basic assumption is that all movements required for the syllable are "assigned" at the beginning of the syllable. Movements that are not antagonistic to other movements, such as lip rounding during consonants, are accomplished simultaneously (with a minor "triggering" rule to account for appropriate sequencing of consonant clusters). Where antagonism exists, movements required for the vowel are delayed.

A cineflourographic study by Daniloff and Moll (1968) confirmed the findings of Chistovich for one and two consonants preceding rounded vowels, and also found that the vowel rounding gesture extended back to the beginning of three and four consonant sequences as well (e.g., in the four-consonant sequence in *construe*).

More recently, Moll and Daniloff (1971) have discovered some rather damaging counterexamples to the Russian concept of the articulatory syllable, which show that English cannot be described in this way. They found that "in sequences in which a nasal consonant is preceded by one or two vowel sounds, the velar opening gesture for the nasal is initiated near the beginning of primary articulatory movement toward the first vowel in the sequence [p. 683]." In addition, Dixit and MacNeilage (1972) have found that, in Hindi, nasal vowels and nasal consonants exhibit similar anticipatory coarticulation effects that extend over at least three segments—consonants or vowels—as long as none of these preceding segments are obstruents.

It appears, therefore, that, although there is no reason to abandon the view of Chistovich *et al.* that the syllable is in some sense a basic articulatory unit, the position of the boundary before the syllable cannot be established by examination of anticipatory coarticulation effects alone. The question now arises as to what overall pattern the anticipatory effects exhibit. The principle suggested by Chistovich *et al.*, that movements not contradictory to other momements can be coarticulated with these movements, has some appeal from the intuitive point of view. For example, anticipatory nasality effects presumably do not extend into obstruents because the resultant nasal leak would prevent the formation of the aerodynamic prerequisites for some acoustic cues for obstruents, e.g., friction in fricatives, bursts in stops. But it is difficult to give a formal definition to the notion "contradictory."

Another question of considerable interest is: Why do anticipatory articulatory effects occur so long beforehand? It is obviously not due to mechanical demand in any simple sense of the term, because the "same" gestures that spread over four segments on some occasions are produced in little more than half a segment on others. Moll and Daniloff have suggested that anticipatory coarticulation may have perceptual benefits in that it may provide useful anticipatory cues to the identity of later segments. This possibility is consistent with the fact that perseverative effects appear to be typically a good deal more restricted in their temporal scope than anticipatory effects. There may be two perceptually based reasons for this finding. First, perseverative effects are restricted because there is little perceptual advantage in continuing to provide cues for segments whose main acoustic effects have already been transmitted. Second, the provision of such cues may, because of the potentially confusing effects of their cooccurrence with anticipatory cues for later segments, reduce the usefulness of the anticipatory cues.

This explanation should not be accepted uncritically. It has troubling teleological connotations. In addition, Dixit and MacNeilage (1972) have found that the perseverative effects of nasality in Hindi have a temporal scope at least equal to that of anticipatory effects, which is a counterexample to the general finding that anticipatory effects have greater temporal scope than perseverative effects. Nevertheless, it still appears that the overall pattern of both anticipatory and perseverative effects is better explained in terms of its perceptual consequences than in terms of any simple view of articulatory necessity. Furthermore, the apparent counterexample of Hindi may simply reflect the fact that the general principles governing the temporal scope of both types of coarticulation in a given language are a result of the total inventory of perceptual cues to segmental forms and their phonotactic distribution in that language. However, it should be noted that perceptually based solutions are not without theoretical inconvenience. The more comprehensive, and language specific, perceptually motivated articulatory events are, the more they are likely to mask inherent articulatory constraints on the production process. Furthermore, it should also be noted that this whole discussion of coarticulation effects has been based on the assumption that the central processes are organizing independent segments of the size of a consonant or a vowel. But we do not know if it is valid to characterize the production of speech in terms of units of this sort.

G. Correlation Studies

Chistovich et al. distinguished between two types of models or principles that could govern the temporal organization of speech output. In the first type of model, commands are issued from a central location at regular intervals. This has been called a *comb model*. In the second type, the timing of peripheral events subsequent to the first one is determined by some signal arising from the immediately preceding event (the so-called *chain model*). Note that there is an important difference in control principles between these two models. The first can be regarded as open loop, in that the commands and their timing are autonomously controlled from higher centers. On the other hand, the second is a closed-loop model in that the timing (although not the form) of output gestures is determined by feedback from previous events. Chistovich et al. attempted to make an empirical choice between these two models on the basis of the durations exhibited by speech segments in repeated productions of the same utterance. They reasoned that speech segment durations would be affected in two ways, depending on which type of model was controlling production. First, if the chain model was correct, there would be no reason to expect any correlation between the duration of a given segment and the duration of the immediately following one. On the other hand, the constant timing of higher-order outputs in the comb model was taken to mean that if the actual duration of a given peripheral gesture was shorter than its average, the manifestation of the next gesture would be correspondingly longer, as required for it to terminate as "planned" by a higher-order timing scheme. Second, the resultant negative correlation between adjacent durations in the comb case should result in the sum of the variances of individual segments in an utterance being larger than the variance of the total utterance. Both these predictions from the comb model were upheld in Chistovich's analysis. Sums of variance for syllables, and for individual segments, were greater than the variance of the entire utterance in the case of the phrase, *Tonya topila banyu* repeated 100 times by two subjects. Negative correlations were found between segments in the same syllable, for segments straddling the syllable boundary (V–C) that these investigators had postulated, and for adjacent syllables. The highest average negative correlation was between vowel and following consonant, and, although this was across the postulated syllable boundary, Chistovich *et al.,* made no comment on it. More recently, Lehiste (1971b) has also found generally higher and more consistent negative correlations between vowel and following consonant in English monosyllables (which, interestingly, decreased in magnitude if the "same" syllable was not the final syllable, e.g., *steady* instead of *stead*).

There are a number of reasons for interpreting the data with caution. First, there is reason to question whether there is a simple one-to-one relation between particular patterns of variance in unit durations and correlation between units, on the one hand, and either of the two models, on the other. Ohala (1970) has reviewed some of these questions. Second, Haggard (1971) has pointed out that the type of correlation to be expected depends partly on whether the two adjacent segments are homorganic, partly on whether the articulatory demands of the two gestures are compatible, and partly on whether the vocal tract is changing to a more open position between segments. For example, he argues quite convincingly that, in a sequence such as [pə], even if the events governing [p] closure, [p] closure termination, and [ə] termination in a series of repetitions are all random, there will still be a negative correlation between [p] and [e] durations, because the "earlier" the release of the [p] occurs, the longer the vowel will be, other things being equal. Haggard's attempt to predict the form of correlations from articulatory dynamics (and his claims to have confirmed some of these predictions) deserve study because they address themselves to a very important question in speech physiology, although one that has often been ignored because bothering with these extremely small variations in segment duration appears to some as mere bristle counting. The problem can be expressed in the following manner: The mechanism responsible for sequencing of speech sounds must program articulatory gestures that satisfactorily interface pairs of adjacent segments. Segment durations and details of articulatory dynamics give clues as to how this interfacing takes place. It seems quite clear at present that the means by which this interfacing is achieved is extremely complex and dependent on the type of segments being interfaced and their position in words. However, it also seems clear that simply attempting an either–or choice between comb and chain models of articulatory dynamics is far too superficial a way to approach the problem of speech organization. Furthermore, it is again worth recalling that all the models we have been considering presume that articulatory segments exist as independent entities. We may find that we cannot construct fully viable models without revising this assumption.

H. The Control of Gestures within a Syllable

A good deal of work has been done on the general question of the control principles underlying segmental articulatory gestures themselves. This work has been reviewed in detail elsewhere (MacNeilage, 1970; MacNeilage & MacNeilage, 1973) and merely will be summarized here.

In the early sixties a number of authors independently formulated models of speech production in which the phoneme (segment) was the basic unit. Segment production was conceived as either the issuing of a single invariant motor command (or one of a small subset of allophonic variants) per phoneme (Halle & Stevens, 1964; Liberman et al., 1967; Moll & Shriner, 1967; Öhman, 1966), or as the result of central specification of targets or vocal tract configurations (Ladefoged, 1967b; Lindblom, 1963; Stevens & House, 1963). These models were unanimous in attributing the well-known lack of phonemic invariance in the acoustic signal to mechanical and neuromuscular limitations of the production apparatus and temporal overlap in commands. In the few years since the formulation of these models it has become quite clear, largely from electromyographic studies of articulator movement (e.g., Fromkin, 1966; Öhman, 1967; MacNeilage & DeClerk, 1969), that the notion of invariant motor commands is untenable at the neuromuscular level and untestable (at present) at higher levels of the nervous system. The finding of a lack of invariance at the peripheral level is quite consistent with the review of data presented earlier on segmental influences on articulatory dynamics, which shows the interfacing of segments to be such a complex and context dependent process. In addition, this review suggests that, rather than being a passive victim of its neural and mechanical limitations, the articulatory mechanism has a host of elegant strategies that help it achieve its aim under different circumstances.

In 1969, Wicklegren put forward a different type of "motor command" hypothesis, namely that there are as many commands ("context sensitive allophones") as there are interfaces between segments. On a number of grounds, this hypothesis has drawn criticism like a magnet (Halwes & Jenkins, 1971; Lenneberg, 1971; MacKay, 1970; MacNeilage, 1970; MacNeilage & MacNeilage, 1973; Whitaker, 1970), mostly valid to varying degrees in our opinion. The most important of these criticisms are:

1. The hypothesis is little more than a restatement of the facts and is virtually untestable.

2. It contains no principle for distinguishing between different allophones and hence does not recognize important phonetic generalizations that emerge from the facts. To take a single example, the allophones of /p/, /t/, and /k/ following open vowels have in common a faster rate of jaw movement than their voiced cognates because they share aerodynamic contingencies related to voicelessness.

3. It disallows the potential for creativity in the production mechanism that allows it to reorganize its articulatory movements so as to remain intelligible in such situations as talking with the teeth clenched or with food in the mouth. Incidentally, this same criticism can also be leveled at the other "motor command" theories.

The alternative hypothesis, that there are targets governing segmental articulation, remains tenable in our opinion. There is a large body of evidence that we have "space coordinate systems" [Lashley's (1951) term] in the brain, which we use to conceptualize three-dimensional space and guide movements in three-dimensional space. One of the most important pieces of evidence for the existence of targets comes from our ability to speak with the teeth clenched, which can be done without changes of targets of moving articulators but requires on-the-spot generation of whole sets of new motor commands (MacNeilage, 1970). It was suggested (MacNeilage, 1970) that relatively invariant articulator positions might be achieved by operation of the so-called gamma loop (Matthews, 1964) which could allow a muscle to assume a single length for a given segment regardless of its segmental context. More recent work has suggested that the target mechanism must be a good deal more complex than had been proposed previously by MacNeilage (1970). Nooteboom (1970) and

Lindblom and Sundberg (1971) have pointed out that, in teeth-clenched speech, the fact that the jaw is fixed means that many muscles need to assume *different* lengths than usual in order to shape the vocal tract in a similar way for a given vowel. For example, muscles lowering the tongue for a low vowel (e.g., [a]), which involves considerable jaw opening, must shorten more when the jaw, to which the tongue is attached, does not lower. The gamma loop mechanism of equalizing muscle length is therefore inadequate to the task of obtaining an analogous vowel target position with the jaw fixed in position. Furthermore, Nooteboom has argued that we are able to produce quite different configurations of the resonant cavities of the vocal tract in order to produce a vowel with similar acoustic properties. This suggests to Nooteboom that there is an auditory perceptual component to the target assignment mechanism, because the match being produced under restriction is more an acoustic match than an articulatory match. This auditory–motor view of speech production has been elaborated by Ladefoged *et al.* (1972). They have also provided X-ray data showing the different articulatory gestures used by six speakers in the form of a subset of English vowels.

I. Closed-Loop Control of Articulation

The role of closed-loop, or feedback, control in articulation has been a recurrent theme in this chapter and in the area of speech physiology in general. It should be said at the outset that, despite a considerable amount of research and speculation on this subject, there is at present no simple yes-or-no answer to the question of whether closed-loop control operates during speech. If one considers the results of a large number of neurophysiological studies of sensorimotor function, the overwhelming impression is that closed-loop control is a universal property of behavior. But most neurophysiological studies are of limited direct relevance to speech in that they have been done on other species than man and under highly artificial conditions, typically including physical restraint. Furthermore, the activity being studied is initiated by the experimenter—often with electrical stimulation—rather than in a natural manner by the animal itself.

It seems unlikely that moment-to-moment *auditory* feedback plays an important role in the control of running speech, largely because speech movements for the most part precede their main acoustic effects in time, and the firing of the motoneurons controlling the muscles largely precedes the movement. Effects of delayed auditory feedback have been quite considerable, even to the point of reducing some subjects to complete incoherence. However in all these cases the intervention consists of *changing* the arrival time of most auditory input and not eliminating it, and the effects observed may be due to the nature of the changes, rather than to the fact that normal feedback is necessary. This interpretation is suggested by the fact that an optimal delay interval of a little less than 200 msec produces the maximum disturbance in delayed auditory feedback situations. Such a time-locked effect would not be predicted simply from the notion that normal feedback is essential to normal production. Thus it suggests that factors other than mere loss of sensory information are involved. In fact, the delay producing most disturbance does not even seem to be related to the structure of the speech material, as supposed by those who noted that 200 msec is similar to the duration of the syllable. Huggins (1968) has shown that the interval producing maximum disturbance does not change when the utterances spoken have particularly long or particularly short syllables.

With respect to *somatic sensory* control, it seems that closed-loop control is essential to the initiation of speech. The command necessary for an articulator to reach a fixed speech-initial position must be conditional upon the prespeech position of that articulator, which no doubt varies from occasion to occasion. It has been shown that this is true for the jaw in one subject (MacNeilage, Krones, & Hanson, 1969).

The sensory intervention studies have a number of methodological problems. Borden (1971) has provided evidence that the nerve block procedure used by Ringel and Steer (1963) and by Scott and Ringel (1971) to produce a characteristic spectrum of speech deficits short of unintelligibility may also paralyze certain muscles. However, it is at present difficult to reconcile the spectrum of deficits with the malfunction of the particular muscles that may be impaired. A selective block of gamma efferent fibers has been shown to affect the parameters of displacement, velocity, and acceleration of movements (Smith, 1969; Abbs, 1973), though apparently not affecting perceived fluency of speech (Abbs, 1973). There are two unanswered questions about these experiments. One is about the extent to which the changes in movement pattern are specific to the gamma block condition. The second is whether or not the pattern of effects could have been predicted from hypothesized operational characteristics of the gamma loop. With respect to the first question, Sussman has also found changes in velocity and displacement of jaw movements in subjects speaking under delayed feedback (Sussman & Smith, 1971) and following topical anesthesia of the *lips* (unpublished study), and some of these changes have been analogous to those found by Abbs and Netsell. Would white noise also produce such changes? In addition, it is necessary to ask whether Abbs and Netsell would have found similar changes in simple repetitive jaw movements (diadachokinesis) not involving speech control mechanisms.

Smith and Lee (1971) have produced evidence unfavorable to a gamma loop control hypothesis for speech. They showed that an artificially introduced increase in resistance to lip closure during the production of bilabial stop consonants is not followed in a few milliseconds by an increase in muscle contraction, as would be predicted from the load compensating property of the gamma loop. On the contrary, they observed EMG inhibition in many cases. These experiments may be contrasted with those of Sears and Davis (1968), who have shown that, 30 to 80 msec after introducing an unexpected resistance to air flow during forced respiration, there is an increase in muscle contraction in the internal intercostal muscles. This suggests to them that the gamma loop could operate in normal speech to compensate for changes in respiratory load resulting from changes in impedence at laryngeal and upper articulatory sites. However, similar changes have not yet been observed in speech (see for example McGlone & Shipp, 1972), and there is some question (Mårtensson, 1968) whether the latencies reported are short enough to be the result of gamma loop action.

VI. SPEECH PHYSIOLOGY AND CORTICAL FUNCTION

In considering the neurophysiology of speech in general, we again encounter the fact that, until very recently, most neurophysiological work on the motor system had limited relevance to normal voluntary behavior. Perhaps the most encouraging recent development in neurophysiology from the point of view of the speech physiologist has been the advent of studies involving simultaneous recording of single CNS neurons and electromyograms during the voluntary performance by animals of relatively skilled motor tasks, which can be considered similar to speech in some respects. The most well-known work of this kind has been done by Evarts and his colleagues (Evarts, 1967). They recorded from precentral motor cortex and points in cortico-cerebello-cortical pathways while monkeys made regular goal-directed flexion and extension movements of the wrist under various loads. The most typical motor cortex neuron from which they recorded exhibited firing patterns related to the force developed by the muscle, although a number of other less interpretable firing patterns were also observed. Another example of this approach is the work of Humphrey and his associates (Humphrey, Schmidt, & Thompson, 1970). They have succeeded in recording from up to five motor cortex neurons simultaneously and, using multiple regression procedures, have been able to predict the form of the corresponding peripheral movement from cortical neuronal firing patterns with a high degree of accuracy. Despite the recent tendency to deemphasize the relative importance of the precentral motor cortex in voluntary movement as opposed to the importance of other motor centers and pathways (Rosner, 1970), these results demonstrate again that the motor cortex plays an important role in normal voluntary movement. Furthermore, when it is considered that there are extensive monosynaptic links between the larger motor cortex neurons and motoneurons (Kuypers, 1964) and that there is a one-to-one relation between an action potential in a cranial motoneuron and the muscle action potential in the muscle fibers that it innervates, the possibility emerges that electromyographic studies of speech production may provide an important indirect index of cortical motor function—in fact, the least indirect neurophysiological link available in normal users of speech. This possibility may be explored by making electromyographic recordings of single motor units in the speech musculature. It is possible to "calibrate" single motor units in various muscles by observing their waveforms, and their firing rates under isometric (motor unit training as described by Basmajian, 1963) and isotonic (speech gesture) conditions, with special reference to the possibility of functional differentiation of motor units into tonic and phasic types (Granit, 1970). A central aim of this research is to determine the overall composition of a burst of firing accompanying a speech gesture and note the relative role of the two variables known to be involved—the time pattern of recruitment of motor units and their firing rates. The methodology and preliminary results of these studies have been described elsewhere (Hanson, 1971; MacNeilage, Sussman, & Hanson, 1972; MacNeilage & Szabo, 1972; MacNeilage, 1973; Sussman, Hanson, & MacNeilage, 1972). However, an example of one of the preliminary findings may be of some interest. In muscles running to the tongue and the hyoid bone from the anterior mandible, a rather wide range of firing rates (from 13 to 36 per second) has been observed for single motor units in motor unit training studies. However, some of these same units have been observed to fire at up to six times their modal isometric firing rates when involved in a speech movement, and there is scarcely any overlap between their isometric and isotonic firing rates. These latter firing rates, approaching 200 per second, are higher than any reported in the literature to our knowledge, with the exception of reports of firing frequencies of up to 350 per second from the extrinsic eye muscles (Marg, Tamler, & Jampolsky, 1962).

The division of firing into two frequency ranges is strongly reminiscent of the "primary" and "secondary" ranges of firing shown by Kernell (1965) with a more direct method of "calibration" of cat motoneurons, namely, by intracellular stimulation. This finding raises a number of interesting questions about possible differences in the means of motor control in the two cases. One possibility relevant to the issues already discussed in this chapter is that these two firing conditions make different use of closed-loop control from somatic sensory receptors. MacNeilage (1971) and Tokizane and Shimazu (1964) have suggested that slower, more regular rates of firing in a given muscle are relatively more under spinal (closed-loop) control, whereas faster firing rates are more under cortical (open-loop) control. They have partially documented their claim by showing that blockage of the gamma loop by procaine considerably impairs the regularity of motor units firing at low rates. An obvious implication of these findings and hypotheses for the question of closed-loop control of speech is that experiments should be done in which the effect of sensory block on single motor unit firing frequencies is observed in both isometric and isotonic conditions.

VII. SPEECH PHYSIOLOGY AND LINGUISTIC THEORY

A satisfactory theory of the physiology of speech production obviously must be compatible with the main phenomena of language function. One might imagine that the converse would also be self evident, namely that a satisfactory linguistic theory must be compatible with the main phenomena of speech physiology. However speech physiology, and for that matter phonetics in general, has occupied and still does occupy a rather marginal position within linguistic science. For example, from the standpoint of generative phonology, it has been made clear by Chomsky and Halle (1968) that many aspects of the speech signal are of little theoretical interest (coarticulation phenomena are specifically singled out for mention in this regard). They consider the linguistically significant aspects of speech to be embodied in a "phonetic transcription [p. 295]" according to the perception of the language user. Lisker (1974) has pointed out that this view involves an interest in speech that is confined to linguistically distinctive properties of parts of the speech signal, and that this in turn involves the characterization of the speech signal in terms of discrete static entities, a characterization that we hope this review has indicated to be unrealistic at the phonetic level in many ways. One consequence of the view, which was pointed out by Lisker (and also by Laver, 1970), is a lack of interest in the dynamics of speech production and of the important variable of timing in speech. As Lisker has put it in a discussion of the generative phonologists' "phonetic transcription":

> Underlying the linguist's graphical representation of a sentence is a model of the speech piece as a temporal sequence of articulatory states, their acoustic resultants or their neural-command antecedents, which are themselves largely "timeless" (Abercrombie, 1967, pp. 42, 80–81), in that a

particular segment is no more to be characterized by the time interval over which its defining physical properties are maintained than its graphical representative is by the space it may occupy on the line of print [Lisker, 1974, 2388–2388].

The generative phonologists' lack of concern with many aspects of the speech signal is one way in which they indicate their opinion that speech physiology has limited relevance to linguistic theory. The fact that aspects which are of interest are *perceptual* ones further reduces the relevance of speech physiology. This is especially so in the case of stress, in which it is implied that under certain conditions stress distinctions made on perceptual grounds might not have *any* basis in the speech signal:

A person will normally not be aware of many properties manifest in the signal, and, at the same time, his interpretation may involve elements which have no direct physical correlates [Chomsky & Halle, 1968, p. 294].

It would perhaps be possible to defend such an a priori restriction of the scope of linguistic theory if the resultant formulation did not seriously suffer from the restriction. A defense might be made on the tactical grounds that it is difficult at this early stage in the development of linguistic science to formulate a complete theory covering all linguistic phenomena. But in the present case the restriction of scope results in some serious limitations. As has been pointed out elsewhere (Ladefoged 1971b, 1972), one limitation is that a specification of the phonological component on perceptual grounds is not verifiable, in that it does not suggest means for objective test. Furthermore, Chomsky and Halle, in fact, attempt to specify the phonological component almost entirely in *articulatory* terms, not in perceptual terms, which reflects rather unfavorably on their arguments for the primacy of the perceptual approach to their theoretical framework. This inconsistency results from ignoring the needs expressed by a number of writers (e.g., Ladefoged, 1971a; Lieberman, 1970) explicitly to separate perceptual and articulatory explanations in phonological theory and to recognize that each has considerable explanatory power, but for different sets of linguistic data.

It is unfortunate that where Chomsky and Halle provide articulatory underpinnings to their phonological view the resultant formulations are in many cases not only uninformed with respect to current phonetic knowledge but lacking in obvious phonetic implications. For example, they state:

The feature "tenseness" specifies the manner in which the entire articulatory gesture of a given sound is executed by the supraglottal musculature. Tense sounds are produced with a deliberate, accurate, maximally distinct gesture that involves considerable muscular effort; nontense sounds are produced rapidly and somewhat indistinctly [p. 324].

Although the terms "deliberate," "accurate," "maximally distinct," "rapidly," and "somewhat indistinctly" have a number of vague mentalistic, physical and auditory-perceptual connotations, they are undefined in phonetics. In the case where an articulatory meaning most safely can be inferred, namely that tense sounds are produced with slower rates of articulator movement than lax sounds, the data that were available to Chomsky and Halle (Chistovich *et al.,* 1965) are contrary to the hypothesis (rates of movement are greater in closure for [p] than for [b]).

In addition, Lisker and Abramson (1971) have argued that the difficulty of including speech timing considerations in linguistic models has adversely affected Chomsky and Halle's attempt to specify the phonological component in phonetic terms. According to Lisker and Abramson, this is evidenced by Chomsky and Halle's use of combinations of four *simultaneous* articulatory features (often with questionable phonetic justification) to attempt to account for a number of aspects of stop consonant production that Lisker and Abramson account for quite well in terms of the *time relations* between release of occlusion and onset of voicing.

The work of Lisker and Abramson and a number of others (e.g., Lindblom, 1972; McAllister, 1972; Ohala, 1971; Öhman, 1967; Stevens, 1972) suggests that many aspects of the sound pattern of languages can be best understood in terms of facts of speech production dynamics. The fact that it has proven difficult to give a definition of phonological concepts like "least effort" and "naturalness" in terms of phonetic facts does not necessarily mean that phonetics is irrelevant to phonological concerns. It may just mean that these concepts have been formulated in a manner that does not allow phonetic evaluation, thus limiting their usefulness in phonology as well as in phonetics.

It seems likely that the integration of speech physiology with linguistic theory would be well served by following Ladefoged's (1972) suggestion that the proper goal of phonology is to attempt to describe the sound patterns that occur in a language. The adoption of this goal would place more value on verification of phonological hypotheses by reference to phonetic data. It would also deemphasize the distinction between competence and performance (Chomsky & Halle, 1968, p. 3), which too often in the past has been used as an excuse to ignore directly observable aspects of language function (as performance variables) that are inconvenient to a theoretical view. The value of acknowledging the importance of performance variables in the formulation of linguistic theory has been made especially evident by recent studies of speech errors (e.g., Boomer & Laver, 1968; Fromkin, 1971, 1973; MacKay, 1970). These studies provide important clues to the organizing principles that underlie the production of language and, by doing so, provide guidelines (well-stated in the above papers) for the construction of explanatory models in both speech physiology and linguistic theory, thus giving an important impetus toward a much needed unification of the two disciplines.

Acknowledgments

Preparation of this paper was supported in part by grants GU-1598 and GS-3218 from the National Science Foundation, and USPHS grant NS-09780. We would like to thank Prakash Dixit and Harvey Sussman, who read parts of the manuscript and made helpful comments; and Mona Lindau, who assisted in the preparation of the sections on the lips, jaw, and tongue. We would also like to thank Hajime Hirose for his comments on the sections on respiratory and laryngeal mechanisms.

References

Abbs, J. H. The influence of the gamma motor system on jaw movements during speech: A theoretical framework and some preliminary observations. *Journal of Speech and Hearing Research,* 1973, **16,** 175–200.

Abbs, J. H. Netsell, R., & Hixon, T. J. Variations in mandibular displacement, velocity, and acceleration as a function of phonetic context. *Journal of the Acoustical Society of America,* 1972, **51,** 89.

Abercrombie, D. *Elements of general phonetics.* Chicago: Aldine, 1967.

Allen, G. D. The place of rhythm in a theory of language. *UCLA Working Papers in Phonetics,* 1968, **10,** 60–84.

Basmajian, J. V. Control and training of individual motor units. *Science,* 1963, **141,** 440–441.

Berti, F. B. The velopharyngeal mechanism: An electromyographic study—a preliminary report. *Status Report on Speech Research* (Haskins Laboratories), SR-25/26, 1971, 117–129.

Bolinger, D .L. A theory of pitch accent in English. *Word,* 1958, **14,** 109–149.

Boomer, D. S., & Laver, J. D. M. Slips of the tongue. *British Journal of Disorders of Communication,* 1968, **3,** 1–12.

Borden, G. J. Some effects of oral anesthesia on speech: A perceptual and electromyographic analysis. Paper presented at the Annual Convention of the American Speech and Hearing Association, Chicago, 1971.

Chen, M. Vowel length variation as a function of the voicing of the consonant environment. *Phonetica,* 1970, **22,** 129–159.

Chistovich, L. A., Kozhevnikov, V. A., Alyakrinskiy, V. A., Bondarko, L. V., Goluzina, A. G., Klass, Yu. A., Kuz'min, Yu. I., Lisenko, D. M., Lyublinskaya, V. V., Fedorova, N. A., Shuplyakov, V. S., & Shuplyakova, R. M. *Rech': Artikulyatisiya i vospriyatiye,* ed. by Kozhevnikov, V. A. and Chistovich, L. A. Moscow and Leningrad: Nauka. [Trans. as *Speech: Articulation and perception.* Washington: Clearinghouse for Federal Scientific and Technical Information, 1965. JPRS. 30, 543.]

Chomsky, N. *Aspects of the theory of syntax.* Cambridge, Massachusetts: M.I.T. Press, 1965.

Chomsky, N. *Language and mind.* New York: Harcourt, 1968.

Chomsky, N., & Halle, M. *The sound pattern of English.* New York: Harper, 1968.

Clark, H. Word associations and linguistic theory. In J. Lyons (Ed.), *New horizons in linguistics*. London: Penguin, 1970. Pp. 271–286.

Cooper, F. S., Liberman, A. M., Harris, K. S., & Grubb, P. M. Some input-output relations observed in experiments on the perception of speech. *Proceedings of the Second International Congress of Cybernetics*, Namur, Belgium, 1958.

Daniloff, R., & Moll, K. Coarticulation of lip rounding. *Journal of Speech and Hearing Research*, 1968, **11**, 707–721.

Deese, J. *The structure of associations in language and thought*. Baltimore: Johns Hopkins Univ. Press, 1966.

Denes, P. Effect of duration on the perception of voicing. *Journal of the Acoustical Society of America*, 1955, **27**, 761–764.

Dixit, R. P., & MacNeilage, P. F. Coarticulation of nasality: Evidence from Hindi. Paper presented at the 83rd Meeting of the Acoustical Society of America, April, 1972.

Evarts, E. V. Representation of movements and muscles by pyramidal tract neurons of the precentral motor cortex. In Yahr & Purpura (Eds.), *Neurophysiological basis of normal and abnormal motor activities*. New York: Raven Press, 1967.

Fant, C. G. M. Descriptive analysis of the acoustic aspects of speech. *Logos*, 1962, **5**, 3–17.

Fischer-Jørgensen, E. Sound duration and place of articulation. *Zeitschrift für Sprachwissenschaft and Kommunikationsforschung*, 1964, **17**, 175–207.

Fitts, P. M. The information capacity of the human motor system in controlling the amplitude of movement. *Journal of Experimental Psychology*, 1954, **47**, 381–391.

Fritzell, B. The velopharyngeal muscles in speech: An electromyographic and cine-fluorographic study. *Acta Oto-laryngologica*, Supplement 250, 1969.

Fromkin, V. A. Neuromuscular specification of linguistic units. *Language and Speech*, 1966, **9**, 170–199.

Fromkin, V. A. The non-anomalous nature of anomalous utterances. *Language*, 1971, **47**, 27–52.

Fromkin, V. A. *Speech Errors as Linguistic Evidence*. The Hague: Mouton, 1973.

Fromkin, V. A., & Ohala, J. Laryngeal control and a model of speech production. *Reprints* of the Speech Symposium, Kyoto, 1968.

Fry, D. B. Duration and intensity as physical correlates of linguistic stress. *Journal of the Acoustical Society of America*, 1955, **27**, 765–768.

Fry, D. B. Prosodic phenomena. In B. Malmberg (Ed.), *Manual of phonetics*. Amsterdam: North-Holland Publ., 1970. Chapter 12.

Gleason, H. A. *An introduction to descriptive linguistics*. New York: Holt, 1967.

Granit, R. *The basis of motor control*. New York: Academic Press, 1970.

Haggard, M. P. Speech synthesis and perception. *Progress Report No. 5*, 1971, Psychological Laboratory, Cambridge, England.

Halle, M., & Stevens, K. N. Speech recognition: A model and a program for research. In J. A. Fodor & J. J. Katz (Eds.), *The structure of language*, Englewood Cliffs, New Jersey: Prentice-Hall, 1964.

Halle, M., & Stevens, K. N. On the mechanism of glottal vibration for vowels and consonants. *Quarterly Progress Report*, Laboratory of Electronics, M.I.T., 1967, **85**, 267–271.

Halle, M., & Stevens, K. N. A note on laryngeal features. *Quarterly Progress Report*, Research Laboratory of Electronics, M.I.T., 1971, **101**, 198–213.

Halwes, T., & Jenkins, J. J. Problem of serial order in behavior is not resolved by context-sensitive associative memory models. *Psychological Review,* 1971, **78,** 122–129.

Hanson, R. J. Computer aided analysis of single motor unit muscle action potentials. *Proceedings of the DECUS Fall Symposium,* San Francisco, November, 1971, 45–48.

Harris, K. S. Physiological aspects of articulatory behavior. In T. A. Sebeok (Ed.), *Current trends in linguistics* (Vol. 12, Part 10, Pp. 2281–2302. The Hague: Mouton, 1974.

Harris, K. S., Gay, T., Sholes, G. N., & Lieberman, P. Some stress effects on electromyographic measures of consonant articulation. In *Status Report on Speech Research* (Haskins Laboratories), SR 13/14, 137–152, 1968. (Also presented at the Kyoto Speech Symposium of the Sixth International Congress on Acoustics, August 29, 1968.)

Hirose, H. An electromyographic study of laryngeal adjustments during speech articulation: A preliminary report. In *Status Report on Speech Research* (Haskins Laboratories), SR-25/26, 1971.

Hirose, H., Simada, Z., & Fujimura, O. An electromyographic study of the activity of the laryngeal muscles during speech utterances. *Research Institute of Logopedics and Phoniatrics Annual Bulletin,* 1970, **4,** 9–26.

Hiroto, I., Hirano, M., Toyozumi, Y., & Shin, T. Electromyographic investigation of the intrinsic laryngeal muscles related to speech sounds. *Annals of Otology, Rhinology and Laryngology,* October, 1967, **76,** 861–872.

Hixon, T. J. Oral paper presented in the session on "Mechanical Aspects of Speech Production." Annual Convention of the American Speech and Hearing Association, Chicago, November, 1971.

Hixon, T. J. Respiratory function in speech. In F. Minifie, T. J. Hixon, & F. Williams (Eds.), *Normal speech, hearing, and language.* Englewood Cliffs, New Jersey: Prentice-Hall, 1972.

Hixon, T. J., Mead, J., & Klatt, D. H. Influence of forced transglottal pressure changes on vocal fundamental frequency. Paper presented at the 80th meeting of the Acoustical Society of America, Houston, November, 1970.

Houde, R. A. A study of tongue body motion during selected speech sounds. *Speech Communications Research Laboratory Mono. No. 2,* Santa Barbara, 1967.

House, A. S. On vowel duration in English. *Journal of the Acoustical Society of America,* 1961, **33,** 1174–1178.

Huggins, A. W. F. Delayed auditory feedback and the temporal properties of the speech material. *Zeitschrift für Phonetik,* Band 21, Heft 1/2, 1968.

Humphrey, D. R., Schmidt, E. M., & Thompson, W. D. Predicting measures of motor performance from multiple cortical spike trains. *Science,* 1970, **170,** 758–761.

Isshiki, N. Regulatory mechanism of the pitch and volume of voice. *Oto-Rhino-Laryngology Clinic* (Kyoto), 1959, **52,** 1065–1094.

Kent, R. D. Some consideration in the cinefluorographic analysis of tongue movements during speech. *Phonetica,* 1972, **26,** 16–32.

Kent, R. D., & Moll, K. L. Vocal-tract characteristics of the stop cognates. *Journal of the Acoustical Society of America,* 1969, **46,** 1549–55.

Kent, R. D., & Netsell, R. Effects of stress contrasts on certain articulatory parameters. *Phonetica,* 1971, **24,** 23–44.

Kernell, D. Synaptic influence on the repetitive activity elicited in cat lumbosacral motoneurons by long-lasting injected currents. *Acta Physiologica Scandinavica,* 1965, **63,** 409–410.

Kim, J., & MacNeilage, P. F. Unpublished observations, 1972.

Kuypers, H. G. J. M. The descending pathways to the spinal cord, their anatomy and function. In J. C. Eccles & J. P. Schade (Eds.), *Organization of the spinal cord.* Amsterdam: Elsevier, 1964, Pp. 178–202.

Ladefoged, P. Some physiological parameters in speech. *Language and Speech,* 1963, **6,** 109–119.

Ladefoged, P. *Three areas of experimental phonetics.* New York: Oxford Univ. Press, 1967. (a)

Ladefoged, P. Linguistic phonetics. In *UCLA Working Papers in Phonetics,* 1967, **6.** (b)

Ladefoged, P. Linguistic aspects of respiratory phenomena. In *Annals of the New York Academy of Sciences,* 1968, **155,** 141–151.

Ladefoged, P. *Preliminaries to linguistic phonetics.* Chicago: Univ. of Chicago Press, 1971. (a)

Ladefoged, P. The limits of phonology. In B. Spang-Thomson (Ed.), *Form and substance.* Copenhagen: Akademisk Forlag, 1971. (b)

Ladefoged, P. Phonological features and their phonetic correlates. *Journal of the International Phonetic Association,* 1972, **2,** 2–12.

Ladefoged, P. The features of the larynx. *Journal of Phonetics,* 1973, **1,** 73–83.

Ladefoged, P., DeClerk, J., Lindau, M., & Papçun, G. An auditory-motor theory of speech production. *UCLA Working Papers in Phonetics,* 1972, **22,** 48–75.

Ladefoged, P., Draper, M. H., & Whitteridge, D. Syllables and stress. *Miscellanea Phonetica,* 1958, **3,** 1–14.

Ladefoged, P., & McKinney, N. Loudness, sound pressure and subglottal pressure in speech. *Journal of the Acoustical Society of America,* 1963, **35,** 454–460.

Lashley, K. S. The problem of serial order in behavior. In L. A. Jeffress (Ed.), *Cerebral mechanisms in behavior* (the Hixon symposium). New York: Wiley, 1951.

Laver, J. The production of speech. In J. Lyons (Ed.), *New horizons in linguistics.* Baltimore: Penguin Books, 1970. Chapter 3.

Lehiste, I. *Suprasegmentals.* Cambridge, Massachusetts: M.I.T. Press, 1970.

Lehiste, I. The temporal realization of morphological and syntactic boundaries. Paper presented at the 81st Meeting of the Acoustical Society of America, Washington, D.C., April, 1971. (a)

Lehiste, I. Temporal organization of spoken language. In L. L. Hammerich, R. Jakobson, & E. Zwinnen (Eds.), *Form and Substance:* Phonetic and Linguistic Papers Presented to Eli Fischer-Jørgensen. Akademisk Forlag, Copenhagen, 1971. (b)

Lenneberg, E. H. *Biological foundations of language.* New York: Wiley, 1967.

Lenneberg, E. H. The importance of temporal factors in behavior. In Horton, D. L. & Jenkins, J. J. (Eds.), *The perception of language.* Columbus, Ohio: Charles E. Merrill, 1971. Pp. 174–184.

Liberman, A. M. Some results of research on speech perception. *Journal of the Acoustical Society of America,* 1957, **29,** 117–123.

Liberman, A. M., Cooper, F. S., Harris, K. S., MacNeilage, P. F., & Studdert-Kennedy, M. G. Some observations on a model for speech perception. In W. Wathen-Dunn (Ed.), *Models for the perception of speech and visual form.* Cambridge, Massachusetts: M.I.T. Press, 1967.

Lieberman, P. *Intonation, perception, and language.* Cambridge, Massachusetts: The M.I.T. Press, Research Monograph No. 38, 1967.

Lieberman, P. Towards a unified phonetic theory. *Linguistic Inquiry,* 1970, **1,** 307–322.

Lieberman, P. A study of prosodic features. In T. A. Sebeok (Ed.), *Current trends in linguistics,* Vol. 12, Part 10, Pp. 2419–2450, The Hague: Mouton, 1974.

Lieberman, P., Knudson, R., & Mead, J. Determination of the rate of change of fundamental frequency with respect to sub-glottal air pressure during sustained phonation. *Journal Acoustical Society America,* 1969, **45,** 1537–1543.

Lieberman, P., Sawashima, M., Harris, K. S., & Gay, T. The articulatory implementation of the breath-group and prominence: Crico-thyroid muscular activity in intonation. *Language,* 1970, **46,** 312–327.

Lindau, M., Jacobson, L., & Ladefoged, P. The feature advanced tongue root. *UCLA Working Papers in Phonetics,* 1972, **23,** 76–95.

Lindblom, B. E. F. Spectrographic study of vowel reduction. *Journal of the Acoustical Society of America,* 1963, **35,** 1773–1781.

Lindblom, B. E. F. *Articulatory activity in vowels.* STL-QPSR, 2/1964. Royal Institute of Technology, Stockholm, Sweden, 1–5.

Lindblom, B. E. F. *Vowel duration and a model of lip mandible coordination.* STL-QPSR, 4/1968. The Royal Institute of Technology, Stockholm, Sweden, 1–29.

Lindblom, B. E. F. Numerical models in the study of speech production and speech perception: some phonological implications. In A. Rigault & R. Charbonneau (Eds.), Proceedings of the Seventh International Congress of Phonetic Sciences, The Hague, Mouton, Pp. 63–93, 1972.

Lindblom, B. E. F., & Sundberg, J. Neurophysiological representation of speech sounds. Paper presented at the XVth World Congress of Logopedics and Phoniatrics, Buenos Aires, Argentina, August, 1971.

Lisker, L. On time and timing in speech. In T. A. Sebeok (Ed.), *Current trends in linguistics,* Vol 12, Part 10, Pp. 2387–2418, The Hague: Mouton, 1974.

Lisker, L., & Abramson, A. S. Distinctive features and laryngeal control. *Language,* 1971, **47,** 767–785.

Lubker, J. F. An electromyographic-cinefluorographic investigation of velar function during normal speech production. *The Cleft Palate Journal,* 1968, **5,** 1–18.

Lubker, J. F., Fritzell, B., & Lindqvist, J. Velopharyngeal function: An electromyographic study. In A. Rigault & R. Charbonneau (Eds.), Proceedings of the Seventh International Congress of Phonetic Sciences, The Hague, Mouton, Pp. 371–374, 1972.

Lysaught, G., Rosov, R. J., & Harris, K. S. Electromyography as a speech research technique with an application to labial stops. *Journal of the Acoustical Society of America,* 1961, **33,** 842 (Abstract).

MacKay, D. G. Spoonerisms: The structure of errors in the serial ordering of speech. *Neuropsychologia,* 1970, **8,** 323–350.

MacNeilage, P. F. Motor control of serial ordering of speech. *Psychological Review,* 1970, **77,** 182–196.

MacNeilage, P. F. Indirect inferences about somatic afferent control mechanisms from neuroanatomy and neurophysiology: The possibility of sensory influences on single motor unit firing patterns. Paper presented at the Annual Convention of the American Speech and Hearing Association, Chicago, November 1971.

MacNeilage, P. F. Preliminaries to the study of single motor units in speech in speech musculature. *Journal of Phonetics,* 1973, **1,** 55–71.

MacNeilage, P. F., & DeClerk, J. L. On the motor control of coarticulation in CVC monosyllables. *Journal of the Acoustical Society of America,* 1969, **45,** 1217–1233.

MacNeilage, P. F., Krones, R., & Hanson, R. Closed-loop control of the initiation of jaw movement for speech. Paper presented at the 78th meeting of the Acoustical Society of America, San Diego, November, 1969.

MacNeilage, P. F., & MacNeilage, L. A. Central processes controlling speech production during sleep and waking. In F. J. McGuigan and R. A. Schoonover (Eds.), *The Psychophysiology of Thinking.* New York: Academic Press, Pp. 417–448, 1973.

MacNeilage, P. F., Sussman, H. M., & Hanson, R. J. Parametric study of single motor unit waveforms in upper articulatory musculature. Paper presented at the 83rd meeting of the Acoustical Society of America, April, 1972.

MacNeilage, P. F., & Szabo, R. K. Frequency control of single motor units in upper articulatory musculature. Paper presented at the 83rd meeting of the Acoustical Society of America, April, 1972.

Marg, E., Tamler, E., & Jampolsky, A. Activity of a human oculorotary muscle unit. *Electroencephalography and Clinical Neurophysiology,* 1962, **14,** 754–757.

Mårtensson, A. In discussion of Sears, T. A. & Davis, J. N. *Annals of the New York Academy of Sciences,* 1968, **155,** 202.

Matthews, P. B. C. Muscle spindles and their motor control. *Physiology Review,* 1964, **44,** 219–288.

McAllister, R. The nuclear stress rule and the description of English stress. In A. Rigault & R. Charbonneau (Eds.), *Proceedings of the Seventh International Congress of Phonetic Sciences.* The Hague: Mouton, Pp. 966–973, 1972.

McGlone, R. E., & Shipp, T. Comparison of subglottal air pressures associated with /p/ and /b/. *Journal of the Acoustical Society of America,* 1972, **51,** 664–665.

Mohr, B. Intrinsic variations of acoustic parameters of speech sounds. *Project on Linguistic Analysis,* Univ. of California, Berkeley, 1969, 2.9, M 1–44.

Moll, K. L., & Daniloff, R. G. Investigation of the timing of velar movements during speech. *Journal of the Acoustical Society of America,* 1971, **50,** 678–684.

Moll, K. L., & Shriner, T. H. Preliminary investigation of a new concept of velar activity during speech. *The Cleft Palate Journal,* 1967, **4,** 58–69.

Nooteboom, S. G. The target theory of speech production. *IPO Annual Progress Report,* 1970, **5,** 51–55.

Ohala, J. J. Aspects of the control and production of speech. *UCLA Working Papers in Phonetics,* 1970, **15.**

Ohala, J. J. The role of physiological and acoustic models in explaining the direction of sound change. *Project on Linguistic Analysis,* Univ. of California, Bekeley, 1971, 2.15, 25–40.

Ohala, J. J., Hiki, S., Hubler, S., & Harshman, R. Transducing jaw and lip movements in speech. Paper presented at the 76th meeting of the Acoustical Society of America, Cleveland, Ohio, November, 1968.

Öhman, S. E. G. Coarticulation in VCV utterances: Spectrographic measurements. *Journal of the Acoustical Society of America,* 1966, **39,** 151–168.

Öhman, S. E. G. *Peripheral motor commands in labial articulation.* STL-QPSR 4/1967. Royal Institute of Technology, Stockholm, Sweden, 30–63.

Öhman, S. E. G., & Lindqvist, J. *Analysis-by-synthesis of prosodic pitch contours.* STL-QPSR 1/1966, Royal Institute of Technology, Stockholm, Sweden, 1–6.

Oller, D. K. The effect of position in utterance on speech segment duration in English. *Journal of the Acoustical Society of America,* 1973, **54,** 1235–1247.

Perkell, J. S. *Physiology of speech production: Results and implications of a quantitative cineradiographic study.* Cambridge, Massachusetts: M.I.T. Press, 1969.

Peterson, G. E., & Lehiste, I. Duration of syllable nuclei in English. *Journal of the Acoustical Society of America,* 1960, **32,** 693–703.

Raphael, L. J. An electromyographic investigation of the feature of tension in some American English vowels. *Status Report on Speech Research* (Haskins Laboratories), 1971, **28,** 179–191.

Ringel, R. L., & Steer, M. D. Some effects of tactile and auditory alterations of speech output. *Journal of Speech and Hearing Research,* 1963, **6,** 369–378.

Rosner, B. S. Brain functions. In P. H. Mussen & M. R. Rosensweig, *Annual Review of Psychology,* 1970, **21,** 555–594.

Sawashima, M. Laryngeal research in experimental phonetics. In T. A. Sebeok (Ed.), *Current trends in linguistics,* Vol. 12, Part 10, 2303–2348, The Hague: Mouton, 1974.

Scott, C. M., & Ringel, R. L. Articulation without oral sensory control. *Journal of Speech and Hearing Research,* 1971, **14,** 804–818.

Sears, T. A., & Davis, J. N. The control of respiratory muscles during voluntary breathing. *Annals of the New York Academy of Sciences,* 1968, **155,** 183–190.

Shipp, T., & McGlone, R. E. Laryngeal dynamics associated with vocal frequency change. Journal of Speech and Hearing Research, 1971, **14,** 761–768.

Slis, I. H. Articulatory effort and its durational and electromyographic correlates. *Phonetica,* 1971, **23,** 171–188.

Smith, J. L. Fusimotor neuron block and voluntary arm movement in man. Unpublished doctoral dissertation, Univ. of Wisconsin, 1969.

Smith, T. A phonetic study of the function of the extrinsic tongue muscles. *UCLA Working Papers in Phonetics,* 1971, No. **18.**

Smith, T. S., & Lee, C. Y. Peripheral feedback mechanisms in speech production models? Paper presented at the VIIth International Congress of Phonetic Sciences, Montreal, August, 1971.

Sonesson, B. The functional anatomy of the speech organs. In B. Malmberg (Ed.), *Manual of phonetics.* Amsterdam: North-Holland Publ., 1970. Pp. 45–75.

Stetson, R. H. *Motor phonetics.* Amsterdam: North Holland Publ., 1951.

Stevens, K. N. The quantal nature of speech: Evidence from articulatory-acoustic data. In E. E. David & P. B. Denes (Eds.), *Human communication: A unified view,* New York: McGraw Hill, 1972, Pp. 51–66.

Stevens, K. N., & House, A. S. Perturbation of vowel articulation by consonantal context: An acoustical study. *Journal of Speech and Hearing Research,* 1963, **6,** 111–128.

Sussman, H. M., Hanson, R. J., & MacNeilage, P. F. Studies of single motor units in the speech musculature: Methodology and preliminary findings. *Journal of the Acoustical Society of America,* 1972, **51,** 1372–1374.

Sussman, H. M., MacNeilage, P. F., & Hanson, R. J. Labial and mandibular dynamics during the production of bilabial stop consonants. Journal of Speech and Hearing Research, 1973, **16,** 397–420.

Sussman, H. M., & Smith, K. U. Jaw movements under delayed auditory feedback. *Journal of the Acoustical Society of America,* 1971, **50,** 685–691.

Tokizane, T., & Shimazu, H. *Functional differentiation of human skeletal muscle.* Springfield, Illinois: Charles C Thomas, 1964.

Vanderslice, R. The prosodic component: Lacuna in transformational theory. Paper presented at the RAND Corporation, Seminar in Computational Linguistics, sponsored by the National Science Foundation, June, 1968.

Vanderslice, R., & Ladefoged, P. Binary suprasegmental features and transformational word-accentuation rules. *Language,* 1972, **48,** 819–838.

Watkin, K. L., & Abbs, J. H. Dynamic behavior of the hyoid bone, mandible, tongue and thyroid cartilage during speech production. *Journal of the Acoustical Society of America,* 1972, **51,** 89.

Whitaker, H. A. Some constraints on speech production models. Paper presented at the First Essex Symposium on Models of Speech Production, September, 1970.

Whitaker, H. A. Neurolinguistics. In W. O. Dingwall (Ed.), *A survey of linguistic science,* College Park, Maryland: Univ. of Maryland Press, 1971. Pp. 136–251.

Wicklegren, W. A. Context-sensitive coding, associative memory, and serial order in (speech) behavior. *Psychological Review,* 1969, **76,** 1–15.

Chapter 4

NEUROBIOLOGY OF LANGUAGE

HARRY A. WHITAKER

I. INTRODUCTION

The topics that one might include under the heading neurobiology of language focus on communication in both animals and man, and range over neurolinguistics, neuropsychology, neuroanatomy, neurophysiology, and neurochemistry. The approaches are both species-specific and comparative. Since there are no traditional paradigms of inquiry with such a label, one typically finds a remarkable degree of eclecticism in the scholarly research in this area. A seminal work which is concerned primarily with human language and speech is Meader and Muyskens (1962). The majority of the recent research, particularly those studies which explore correlations between the communication systems of animals and man, is found in a scattering of articles in journals and anthologies. The theme of all of this research is the biological context of man's language capacity, and the particular interests include, but of course are not limited to, such topics as: the origins and evolution of language, aspects of language that are comparable to communication systems of other animals, the innate and the learned components of language, the relationships between the maturation of the nervous system and language development, and the specializations of the central and peripheral nervous systems that are correlated with language. A goal of studying the neurobiology of language is a biological theory of language—a model of the brain that literally bridges the gap between structure and function; as Marshall (1970) noted, however, no general theory has been proposed, despite a plethora of observations on man and other animals. While it may be plausibly argued that we are not on the brink of such a proposal, it is nevertheless clear that a good number of the component parts of a general theory are reasonably well established.

Certain concepts, distinctions, and assumptions which invariably appear in discussions of the neurobiology of language are sufficiently well established to be considered definitional preliminaries. Language, like all behaviors, has both an innate and a learned or acquired component [a discussion of the various meanings of these terms can be found in Lehrman (1970)]; therefore, the issue is not whether language is innate or learned but what contributions these two factors make to the adult's language capacity. Comparative biology focuses on both the disparities and the commonalities among species and, as clearly implied by the concepts of speciation and evolution, man is unique in his morphology (structure), behavior, and, perforce, his language (Sarles, 1972). The issue here is not to demonstrate that language is unique to *Homo sapiens* but to demonstrate which aspects of man's communicative behavior are homologous to the communicative behaviors of other species, which aspects are comparable but probably due to the effects of convergence, and which aspects have uniquely evolved in man. The criteria for establishing that a behavior is homologous are extremely complex but minimally involve a demonstration that a homologous structure underlies the behavior (Atz, 1970). This implies that to show homologies for language requires that one show homologies in certain parts of the central nervous system between, e.g., man and chimpanzee. "Convergence is the evolutionary development of similar characteristics by unrelated groups of animals in response to similar environmental needs [Atz, 1970, p. 54]." It obviously is much easier to make a case for the convergence of behaviors, at least among animals other than man. The concept of critical periods for language acquisition has been proposed (Lenneberg, 1967; Milner, 1967); these periods are determined by the successive stages of maturation of the central and peripheral nervous systems. Finally, the fact that certain structures in the nervous system characteristically are implicated in language and speech disorders (see Chapter 12 by Goodglass and Geschwind, and Chapter 13 by Whitaker, this volume) implies that they are the neural structures which underlie man's language capacity. Although one can easily point to gaps in knowledge as well as to areas of great understanding in all of these approaches to language, there is one gap which seems to be particularly germane to an understanding of the neurobiology of language: This is the relationship between electrical activity in the brain and concurrent linguistic behavior. The research on this problem is very recent but already promises to be a valuable supplement to aphasia research.

II. COMPARATIVE STUDIES

Students of animal communication, regardless of whether their operational paradigms are taken from the life sciences, the humanities, or the social sciences, must face the very important initial question of the validity of cross-species comparison of communicative systems. The appropriate answer to this question depends upon the level of analysis. Since language is a communicative system, general theories of communication will include it together with the communicative systems of other animals (Chomsky, 1968; Sebeok, 1968; Sarles, 1969). Such general theories are not necessarily devoid of interest to the student of human language. For example, the phenomenon of dialect variation is rather widespread in the animal world and could conceivably be related to commonalities in the effects of the environment on animals (convergence). Dialect variation may be thought of as the occurrence of systematic variants of some aspect of the communicative system of a species, such that a group within the species is socially isolated; presumably the isolated group eventually forms a subspecies and finally a new species. One of the more dramatic examples of this was presented by Marler (1970), who showed that in a region as small as the San Francisco bay area, the white-crowned sparrow developed three distinct regional variants of the mating song. Fledglings from one group who were allowed to mature in a second group's area developed the song of the second group, thus demonstrating an equipotentiality for any of the three dialects. The effect of the dialect is that males and females from different groups are unlikely to mate, since the song differences are quite significant to the birds. This leads naturally to a reproductive isolation and the formation of a stable gene pool, which seems to be important for maximal evolutionary adaptation. LeBoeuf and Peterson (1972) observed a comparable phenomenon in a population of elephant seals in the Pacific Ocean off the coast of California; in this case, threat vocalizations had regional dialect variants. Mating calls of widely different species such as frogs and fruit flies can be similarly viewed: changes in some aspect of the communication system such that individuals maintain reproductive isolation even though they can in fact interbreed and produce viable offspring. It remains to be seen whether such observations and the general models which incorporate them shed any light on the nature of dialect varation in human language, but the suggestions are tantalizing (Nottebohm, 1970; Whitaker, 1972). The question of the neurological substrates of these different communication systems, and thus by implication the question of homologies and convergence, can at least be raised, even though detailed answers are not yet available. Nottebohm (1970) has shown neural later-

alization of vocal control in passerine birds—the left branch of the hypoglossal nerve (cranial nerve XII in man; it controls the tongue musculature) innervates the syrinx, and severing the right branch will not affect
adult song patterns. Nottebohm also showed that lateralization develops,
it is not prewired: If the left branch is cut in the young fledgling then
the right branch will assume its function and the song patterns will mature
normally. The parallel between this type of neural lateralization (clearly
of central origin) and cerebral dominance for language in man is suggestive. Another series of experiments reported in Nottebohm (1970) is based
on the fact that normal adult song patterns evolve through a series of three
steps: subsong, plastic song, and the adult pattern. Deafening a bird at
one of these stages produces an effect on the final song patterns that reflects
the song stage the bird was in; Nottebohm suggests that the results are
analogous to the situation in human infants who are either born deaf or
become deaf by injury, and he implies a convergence model that is task
related, i.e., a model of vocal communicative behavior. A few studies have
extended the analysis to central nervous system structures. Delius (1971)
explored some of the central nervous system correlates of bird vocalizations
in a series of electrical stimulation studies on gulls and pigeons; vocalizations were elicited from the inferior colliculus, auditory thalamic nuclei,
and a medial nucleus of the hypothalamus. From these experiments and
a literature review, Delius concludes that the system of avian vocalization
seems to "correspond reasonably well with that mediating vocalization in
mammals [p. 78]," which suggests, of course, that the system has a long
evolutionary history. Interestingly, Delius did not find evidence for laterality in his study; in this context it should be noted that Nottebohm's research
was on a different species, the chaffinch. A study of macaque vocalizations
by Robinson (1967) also failed to find evidence for laterality in neural
control.

While the question of homologies remains moot with respect to species
widely removed from man on the evolutionary scale, the question is often
seriously raised with respect to the other primates. The research on monkeys and apes with respect to the neurobiology of language takes a number
of different approaches, including among others (1) attempting to show
or deny that the vocalizations of other primates bear any relationship to
the presumed evolutionary origins of human language, (2) comparing the
neuronal cytoarchitecture of the cortex of various primates, (3) analyzing
the anatomy of the vocal tract region of various primates in order to deduce
the possible range of vocalizations each tract might be capable of, and
(4) efforts to teach anthropoid apes some form of a human language.
While each of these approaches has its critics, it is quite clear that the
positive results have initiated a significant renewal of interest in, and, more
importantly, have necessitated drastic revisions of, previously held theories

of the neurobiology of language. Primate communication systems, both vocal and gestural, have been extensively analyzed and, in many papers, compared to various attributes of human communication (see, for example, Marler, 1965; Bastian, 1965; Marler, 1969; Lancaster, 1968; Peters, 1972). It is reasonable to view these and other studies in the light of general theories of zoosemiotics (Sebeok, 1968). Generally the success of arguing the point for or against human–nonhuman parallels in communication systems is a function of the sophistication of the general theory. From the standpoint of a neurobiology of language, however, there are some different lines of research that seem to be most promising. Analysis of the central nervous system substrates of social vocalizations of the squirrel monkey (Ploog, 1969), and in the macaque (Robinson, 1967) have shown that the essential structures are in the limbic system—thalamus, hypothalamus, midbrain, amygdala, and hippocampus regions. This system has been referred to by Magoun, Darling, and Prost (1960) as the "deep-lying mesencephalic system for emotional vocalization [p. 43]," a system that is undoubtedly present in man and may be partly implicated in the syndrome known as akinetic mutism. With due allowance for the fact that much more research remains to be done on other primates, it can be seriously proposed that

> No intimate relationship is known between this deep-lying mesencephalic mechanism, present widely through the animal kingdom, and the topographically distant cortical region for speech, which has only appeared with the relatively recent evolution of associational cortex in the human brain. In keeping with their phylogenetic differences, these two mechanisms display widely differing maturation times in the ontogeny of the human infant. The older, more stereotyped subcortical emotional mechanism is already functional at birth. By contrast, activity of the cortical mechanism in understandable speech only develops between one and two years after birth [H. W. Magoun. In C. H. Millikan & F. L. Darley (Eds.), *Brain mechanisms underlying speech and language,* New York: Grune and Stratton, 1967, p. 18].

A different line of research, which appears to provide the corollary to the above observations, has been undertaken by Lieberman and his colleagues (Lieberman, 1968; Lieberman & Crelin, 1971; Lieberman, Crelin, & Klatt, 1972; Lieberman, Harris, Wolff, & Russell, 1972; Lieberman, Klatt, & Wilson, 1964), who have studied the vocal tract shapes and the acoustic properties of vocalizations in several species of primate and in man. In addition, they have extrapolated this research to Neanderthal man and concluded that the most nearly humanlike vocal tracts, those of the Neanderthal man and the chimpanzee, are incapable of producing the range of phonetic contrasts made by normal adult humans. In fact, the phonetic abilities of chimpanzee and Neanderthal man seem to approximate those of the human neonate, who is also not capable of producing the full range of adult sounds. It ought to be noted here that the brain capacity of Neanderthal man is approximately the same as that of contemporary man; it is thus plausible that languagelike communication developed prior to so-called speech capacity. In view of the research on the mesencephalic vocalization system and the functional anatomy of the vocal tract, it is not surprising that efforts to teach human vocalizations qua language to a chimpanzee did not succeed. As is well known, however, efforts to teach visual and gestural representations of human language to a chimpanzee have been strikingly successful, on the one hand using colored plastic chips to represent morphemes (Premack, 1971) and on the other hand using the American Sign Language (Gardner & Gardner, 1969, 1971). The most thoughtful discussion of the cognitive and linguistic abilities of Premack's chimpanzee, Sarah, and the Gardners' chimpanzee, Washoe, can be found in the conference proceedings edited by Ploog and Melnechuk (1971); the objective observer, who is not committed to proving that Sarah and Washoe have failed to master a number of the essential properties of human language, will defer his judgment as to what is specifically human in human language until there has been further research on the chimpanzee. As Premack noted, "It is premature to assert what infrahuman and pathological human populations can and cannot learn [Ploog & Melnechuk, 1971, Appendix II, p. 692]."

Since it is probable that the chimpanzee is using cortical structures in the mastery of visual and gestural components of human language, it is relevant to note what is and is not known about the cerebral cortex of nonhuman primates in comparison with man. Lenneberg (1967) suggested that "language function is comparatively independent [in modern man] from both brain size and variations in cognitive capacities [p. 69]"; he presented some evidence that nanocephalic [bird-headed] dwarfs, with a brain size that approximates that of the chimpanzee, "acquire the rudiments of language including speaking and understanding and the majority master the verbal skills at least as well as a normal five-year-old child [p. 70]." But, in the light of the achievements of the chimpanzees Sarah and Washoe, one might reasonably ask if in fact there is a rather strong correspondence between brain size on the one hand and language and cognitive achievement on the other, making the assumption that these animals have in many respects reached a level of function comparable to a 5-year-old child. Support for the notion that overall brain size does reflect the volume of the cerebral cortex, the total number of neurons in the brain, and the degree of dendritic proliferation—in short, the information processing capacity of the brain—comes from the studies of Jerison (1969, 1970a, 1970b, 1971). In an extensive series of analyses, Jerison suggested that relative increases in brain size in various animals can be correlated with species diversification and the environmental–social demands on various information processing systems in the brain. The specific question of homologous structures in the cerebral cortices of man, macaques, and chimpanzee was addressed by Bonin and Bailey (1961). Interestingly enough, they found no evidence for histological uniqueness between man and chimpanzee in the parietal, occipital, or temporal lobes, but they did find an area in the frontal lobe which significantly differed in man's brain—Area 44, or Broca's area. Thus, with the exception of Broca's area, the main difference between man and chimpanzee cortex appears to be quantitative, and the principal quantitative differences are to be found in the temporal lobe, the inferior parietal lobe, and the frontal lobe anterior to Broca's area. The inferior parietal lobe and temporal lobe differences correspond to the regions which subserve the language function in man (Geschwind, 1965, 1968a, 1968b) and of course the unique Broca's area is also included in man's language system. Broca's area, however, is usually associated with speech production (see Goodglass & Geschwind, Chapter 12 this volume, and McAdam & Whitaker, 1971), and it has already been noted that this aspect of language is probably not comparable between man and the other primates. The picture that begins to emerge is one of a clearly distinct speech–vocalization system in man based on a species-specific neural structure (Broca's area) and anatomic structure (the vocal tract), coupled with a significant increase in the quantity of and the information processing capacity of the homologous cerebral cortex (inferior parietal and superior temporal lobes). Some further discussion of the role of Broca's area is taken up in the last section of this review.

III. DEVELOPMENTAL STUDIES

At birth the human brain weighs approximately 380 gm; the cerebral cortex for all intents and purposes is not functioning, even though it has its full complement of neurons. By puberty the brain will have grown to about 1400 gm, through the proliferation of the neuroglia that surround the cortical neurons and through the maturation of the neurons themselves. Neurons mature structurally in essentially two ways: the development of a myelin sheath around the transmitting axon and the multiplication of axo-dendritic synapses. There is also an internal, chemical maturation. Considering its final product, this physical maturity is paralleled by a development in information processing capacity that is presumed to be unmatched by any other animal, although it appears to begin with less than most other animals (at least, less than that of the other primates). Knowl-

edge of the maturation of the nervous system is an important adjunct to
the study of the neurobiology of language; such knowledge may suggest
constraints on the acquisition of language, insights into the various structures that underlie language ability, and clues as to which components of
language may be innate and which may be acquired. Although far from
complete, the knowledge that is currently available on development is sufficiently rich that a number of suggestive hypotheses have been framed. A
number of important studies that have contributed to this knowledge should
be mentioned. An early study correlating perceptual, motor, and language
development is Shirley (1933); several studies on the development of
myelin in the brain are Flechsig (1920), Yakovlev and Roch-Lecours
(1967), Savolainen, Palo, Riekkinen, Moronen, and Brody (1972); the
major study on neural maturation of the cortex is Conel (1939–1967);
a detailed and scholarly analysis of the available neural and behavioral
data with correlations between the two is Milner (1967); a short and lucid
résumé of brain maturation is Marshall (1968); two studies that correlate
stages of language acquisition with stages of neuronal maturation are Sloan
(1967) and Milner (1967); a brief overview of language acquisition and
the corresponding motor milestones can be found in Lenneberg (1967)—
he has a particularly interesting survey of some of the earlier literature
on acquired aphasia in children and some comments on the language development of both the profoundly deaf and children with Down's syndrome
[on this latter topic see also Berry (1972), Brown, Darley, and Gomez
(1967), Chappell (1970), Evans and Hampson (1968), Kastein and
Fowler (1960), Morley (1957), Shapiro, Fish, and Ginsberg (1972), and
Swisher and Pinsker (1971)]; some particularly detailed tables correlating
the development of nonverbal behavior and the comprehension of and use
of language in normal children up to 8 years of age are in Berry (1969)—
she concludes with five complete case histories of children with developmental disorders due to genetic deficit, general learning disability, central
nervous system lesion, cerebral palsy, and autism. These case histories of
Berry's are notable for their detail, including phonetic transcriptions of
actual utterances at different ages, scores on various tests of cognition and
perceptual ability, and observations on behavior.

A discussion of the sequences of normal language acquisition and the
details of acquired or developmental language impairment as represented
in the studies just cited is outside the scope of this review, although some
remarks will be offered on certain points. In children, damage to the central
nervous system structures associated with language is not directly comparable to similar lesions in adults, regardless of whether the injury is due
to traumatic insult, disease, or genetic errors. The typical result in children
is a delay in the various stages of acquisition, a much slower appearance

of stages, and, in cases of severe damage or severe genetic deficit, a final "plateau" of language capacity. It is frequently noted that the outright failure to develop rudimentary language ability is a consequence of only the most severe disruption in the central nervous system. The language-impaired child generally exhibits a reduction of output; it is rare but not unknown to find increases of output such as are found in certain cases of adult aphasia (Swisher & Pinsker, 1971), and it is also rare to find such impairments as phonemic or verbal paraphasias or other deficits associated with Wernicke's-type aphasia (Alajouanine & Lhermitte, 1965). While in the normal child there is a typical cooccurrence of motor and language milestones (Lenneberg, 1967; Milner, 1967) these two are not causally connected; disturbances can be found in either system that have little effect on the other, for reasons that will be made clear below. It has also been noted that receptive language capacity may develop in spite of a failure of expressive capacity (Lenneberg, 1962), suggesting that the primate or mesencephalic vocalization system may be selectively impaired in man without direct effects on the cortical elaboration of much of the language system proper. The fact that a fully normal receptive language capacity may not develop in such cases could be attributed to the lack of adequate sensory–motor feedback, as suggested by the animal studies of Held and Hein (1963). It is well known that adequate auditory input is required for a normal development of language, as evidenced by the impairment of the verbal language abilities of the profoundly deaf; if the loss of auditory inputs is due to bilateral lesions in the auditory pathways plus parts of the temporal lobe projection area (Landau, Goldstein, & Kleffner, 1960), language capacity may remain retarded even with extensive training. The loss of auditory inputs of course does not preclude the development of a rich and elaborate visual–gestural communication system, as is typical of the deaf; the difficulty that most deaf persons experience with written language, however, suggests that the effect of deprivation of auditory input is more general and not limited to verbal language capacity—a consequence not unlike that shown in the results of the animal studies of Hubel and Wiesel (1963, 1965). The successful behavioral maturation of the individual depends upon an intricate combination of genetic and experiential factors which may in gross respects be remarkably resistant to disruption but in finer details reflects rather directly any deficits.

The maturation of the nervous system constrains the acquisition of behavior, in that the structure subserving a particular function must be neurologically mature in order for the behavior to be manifested. The fact that normal maturation depends upon both innate and environmental factors led Jacobson (1969, 1970) to propose a theory of neuronal specificity in which three classes of neurons are distinguished. This theory assumes that genetic information specifies the developmental program, rather than the details of neuronal cytoarchitecture in the cortex, and it takes account of the fact that there is a progressive loss of modifiability as the organism matures. Class I neurons originate early in embryonic development and are generally macro-neurons: large neurons with long axons, that form the primary afferent and efferent systems in the brain, usually in a topographical arrangement. Class II neurons are interneurons, which originate later, are usually smaller, and continue to differentiate well into postnatal life. Class III neurons are specified slowly, postnatally, as the organism matures. Both Class II and Class III neurons depend upon specific sensory stimulation for their full and normal development and for the maintenance of their connections; hence the nature of their connectivity is quite variable compared to class I neurons. The critical periods (milestones) are periods of "functional validation" of the neurons of Classes II and III.

In terms of gross systems and levels within the central nervous system, neural maturation from birth onward proceeds in a cephalic direction, originating in the brainstem, which is reasonably mature and functioning at birth, and terminating in the cerebral cortex, which reaches full functional maturity no earlier than puberty and probably not until around 20 years of age. Bergstrom (1969) presented a model of this progression of levels, based upon an analysis of motor output. His model distinguishes "tonic" from "phasic" activity and assigns the former (graded) activity to lower, nonspecific systems, and the latter (punctate) activity to higher, specific systems. Bergstrom's model comprises a central reticular core surrounded by "shells" of neural structures: The first shell or circuit is situated nearest the core and is the pathway of the subthalamus–globus pallidus–red nucleus; the second shell is the pathway of the centromedian thalamic nucleus–corpus striatum–substantia nigra; the third shell is the pathway of the thalamus–cerebral cortex–pyramid tract. The nearer a circuit is to the periphery (third shell), the more "order" it has and the more it is involved in phasic activity, such as one might associate with language. The central circuits are more random and diffuse and involved in tonic activity, such as overall systemic control of the postural musculature.

Anokhin (1964) made an important observation supplementing the above models with respect to the completeness of maturity in various systems. He identified the principle of "systemogenesis" and illustrated the point with respect to the facial nerve. The sucking reflex is present at birth and of course depends upon adequate innervation of the lip musculature (orbicularis oris). Anokhin showed that the fibers of the facial nerve (cranial nerve VII) that innervate the orbicularis oris were myelinated at birth but the fibers of the facial nerve that innervate the other muscles of facial expression were not. He concluded that, "An organ does not mature simultaneously as a whole in all regions. Only those parts and structures of an organ which are necessary for performing the vital functions at the time of birth, mature selectively and with a higher speed [p. 65]."

These models provide a background against which the maturation of the cerebral cortex may be considered. The major work on the postnatal development of the cortex is Conel (1939–1967); the following sketch draws on his data, the correlation study of Milner (1967), and the resume of Marshall (1968). The schema of CNS maturation has two principal components: (1) the maturation of neurons within a particular cortical area and (2) the sequence of maturation of different cortical areas. The innermost neurons in the cortical mantle mature prior to the surface neurons (i.e., layer VI matures before layer I), with the result that major hemispheric connections are established first between the periphery and primary cortical zones (the sensory–motor, visual, and auditory cortices), later between primary and association zones [the pre-motor (Broca), anterior parietal sensory association, visual association, and auditory (Wernicke) association areas], and last between different association areas themselves (the long tracts, including the corpus callosum and Arcuate fasciculus). Inner cell layers of the cortex contain neurons whose axons form both the cortico–subcortical connections and the cortico–cortical connections. Since specific control areas (e.g., auditory or motor cortex) send information to and receive information from their respective peripheral structures earlier than they integrate information amongst themselves, the behavioral result is that auditory and visual inputs will be processed to some degree before they can become the appropriate stimuli for perceptions and hence motor response. The sequence of maturation in different cortical areas in the cerebral hemispheres begins in the primary projection zones and progresses to the secondary or association zones. The sensory–motor cortex (pre- and post-Rolandic fissure) is always the most mature area of the cerebral cortex up to 6 years after birth; there is a tendency for the motor portions to be more advanced than the sensory. Next in order of maturity is the primary visual cortex, and lagging furthest behind is the primary auditory cortex. Within the sensory–motor cortex, maturation proceeds from the region of the hand area, spreading upward toward the leg area and downward toward the head area. At the same time, maturation proceeds anteriorly through the frontal lobe, in the direction of Broca's area (which lies in front of the area for the lips, jaw, and tongue) and Exner's center (which lies in front of the area for the hand and fingers). There is a corresponding sequence proceeding posteriorly from the sensory cortex into the parietal lobe, proceeding anteriorly from the visual cortex toward both the parietal and temporal lobes, and finally, proceeding caudally (down) from the auditory cortex into the temporal lobe. The language regions, which are last to mature, include the supramarginal gyrus, angular gyrus, and Broca's area. This developmental sequence is summarized in Figs. 1 and 2; there are some simplifications in the diagram, and Conel (1939–1967), Flechsig (1920), Yakovlev and Roch-Lecours (1967), or Milner (1967) should be consulted for more specific information.

At birth the cortex of the human infant is not functional, and thus in effect he is a "midbrain" animal. The reflexes observed in neonates are essentially based upon circuits to and from the midbrain area, e.g., the counterrotation of the eyes when the head is moved to one side indicates that the vestibular nuclei have connections to the oculomotor and abducens nuclei. The responses to loud noises or to human voices presuppose that the cochlear nuclei are connected to motor nuclei in the brain stem and spinal cord. The gross indications of maturation from the midbrain to the cerebral cortex in the sequences described above, can be detected easily up to about 6 years of age. After 6 years of age there are changes, of course, but not as clearly of the landmark variety. There is a particularly critical stage somewhere between the ages of 6 and 15 months, usually around 1 year after birth, during which a number of parameters converge. This is the period referred to in Piagetian theories as the onset of inten-

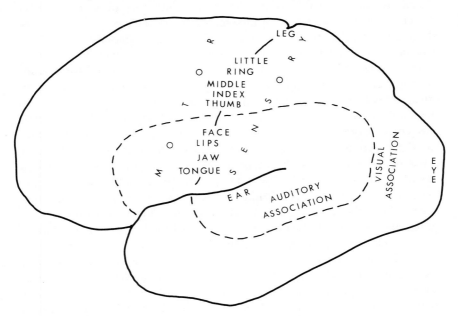

Fig. 1. Primary sensori-motor cortical zones (language area outlined with dotted line).

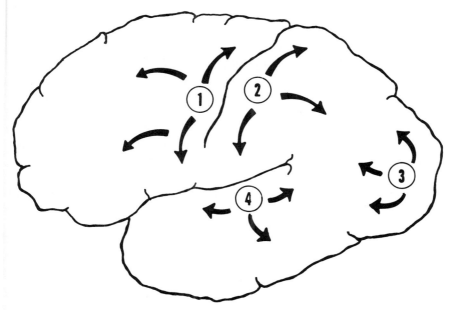

Fig. 2. Maturation sequence in cortex (compare to Figure 1).

tional behavior. It is the period during which babbling ceases and single words appear. It is the period during which the asynchrony of the electro-encephalographic activity (EEG) declines and the faster, lower-amplitude waves begin to gain in prominence. Some of the slowest maturing fibers in primary projection systems, the fibers running to the auditory cortex, complete their myelination at about this time. The microscopic appearance of various areas of the cortex, particularly layers IV and V, indicates that a significant increase has occurred in the number of axons both from other cortical areas and from subcortical structures. Meaningful sensorimotor coordination in the language system is developing, presumably because the fibers of the Arcuate fasciculus have matured sufficiently to transmit infor-mation from the recognition to the production language areas. In terms of the neuronal model of Jacobson, this would mark the conclusion of the development of genetically constrained neuronal connections and the onset of the establishment of those connections based upon functional vali-dation. This amounts to a hypothesis that the appearance of language from about 1 year up to 3 or 4 years of age is correlated with actual alterations in the connections between neurons in the CNS structures underlying lan-guage. This "environmentally determined" specificity is presumably the basis for native language habits, and the structural alterations would explain why these habits persist so well throughout life, even when the CNS is injured.

Speculations about the preword stages (before 12 months) in the CNS lead to even more interesting hypotheses. The amount of acoustic information that the auditory cortex and adjacent Wernicke's area can process prior to 12 months is severely limited, i.e., it is not likely that children during this time are learning words passively. A number of recent experiments have demonstrated that children as young as 4 weeks, however, can process/discriminate acoustic phonetic features such as voice onset time and second formant transitions, which are important in the perception of place and manner of articulation in speech (Eimas, Siqueland, Jusczyk, & Vigorito, 1971). It is also well established that young infants orient to intonation contours, the voice quality of the mother as opposed to strangers, loudness levels, changes in the filtering of frequencies, and even forward versus backward speech. The temptation to suggest that such discriminations are evidence for a genetically endowed acoustic speech processor (the innateness hypothesis) must be tempered by the following facts: The cerebral cortex is not functioning at this age, and there are strong reasons for doubting that subcortical parts of the auditory system do any linguistic processing (this evidence comes from the nonlinguistic nature of the auditory deficits produced by damage to subcortical structures subserving hearing). A crucial experiment would be to show that mammals have analogous acoustic discriminatory abilities. If, for example, one presented /pa/ to a cat until it had habituated to the signal and then switched to /ba/, it is likely that one would discover an orienting reflex in response to the acoustic changes. In fact, Walker and Halas (1972) performed a comparable experiment: Using chronically implanted electrodes in cats' dorsal cochlear and inferior colliculi nuclei, they recorded neuronal discharges when the auditory system was stimulated with human voices pronouncing words. The results were a unique pattern of neuron firing associated with a particular word, e.g., *five, seven,* etc.; this pattern was consistent for both male and female voices pronouncing the same word—demonstrating that the response is to the pattern and not to the specific frequencies—and was highly reliable across cats. Since no one would want to argue that a cat perceives the acoustic basis for discriminating English, the reasonable conclusion is that the mammalian ear/auditory system is capable of making an acoustic analysis which, in man, is the basis of speech perception. With some reservation, similar reasoning should apply to the other acoustic parameters that have been investigated in very young children.

During the period of 1 to 12 months, the assumption is that there are few functional connections between the auditory (Wernicke's) and vocal tract (Broca's) cortical centers. Therefore, it would be predicted that babbling, as well as any vocalizations occurring prior to babbling, is not in a direct sense the result of the infant practicing the sounds of his (future) native language, since the initiation of signals from motor or motor associa- tion cortex to the vocal tract musculature would not be guided nor influ- enced by any of the areas concerned with receptive language abilities. What then is babbling? A possible theory may be gleaned from the model pre- sented by Bergstrom (1969), from the maturational data of Conel (1939–1967) and Marshall (1968), and from an interesting theory of phonological acquisition proposed by Drachman (1970). Babbling could represent the increasing degree of phasic control over the vocal tract motor circuits by the cerebral cortex (the rooting and sucking reflexes seen at birth are prima facie evidence that some brain stem circuits are already functioning); this evolving control is clearly nonlinguistic, or better, non- phonological practice. As Broca's area matures sufficiently to begin to influ- ence the vocal tract and, at the same time, as the Arcuate fasciculus fibers from Wernicke's area begin to send coherent signals to Broca's area, there is a period of "readjustment." This apparently is often marked by a brief cessation of babbling and is comparable to the cessation of other reflex motor behaviors when the cortical control centers reach maturity. Once the genetically endowed or specified auditory–verbal connection is made [in Jacobson's sense (1969)], the stage is set for the functional validation of Class II and III neuronal connections. This could conceivably be achieved by a process analogous to the formation of the "auditory tem- plate" postulated by Marler (1970) to account for the acquisition of mat- ing songs by the white-crowned sparrow.

We may imagine that the peripheral circuit, genetically programmed to establish connections specific to the analyzed acoustic stimuli it receives, can and is actually preprocessing these stimuli along the most important parameters of speech perception. One of the more compelling aspects of Drachman's model is his postulation of the sequence of acquisition of phonological contrasts, once the child's language system is in its "linguistic mode"; this sequence matches the sequence of maturation in the sensory– motor cortex—vocalization, lips, jaw, tongue, pharyngeal region. However, until Broca's area is relatively mature, complex coordinations between mus- cle groups that are controlled in different regions of motor cortex is a diffi- cult accomplishment for the child. The histological evidence of cortical maturity suggests that these coordinations could be mastered by the ages of 4 and 6 years, and the behavioral evidence substantiates this. By age 4 to 6, the auditory habits of the child are fairly well rehearsed and under control, in fact, are approaching the automatic status of the adult's decod- ing system; it is surely not coincidental that this is the age at which later- alization can first be detected, as measured by dichotic listening experiments. A recent paper by Krashen and Harshman (1972) presents an array of evidence to support the notion that cerebral dominance (lateralization) is essentially complete by 5 years of age, although not necessarily fixed, since it is well established also that there is still a remarkable degree of plasticity in the location of cortical functions up to puberty. Molfese (1972) presented some additional data, based on a study of infants' auditory evoked responses (AER), that the AER to language compared to piano notes indicates that rudiments of lateralization may be detected in the first 12 months of life. The reasonable conclusion is that certain features of language acquisition may be considered rather directly dependent upon CNS maturation; although fairly speculative in nature, the sketch given here does have the virtue of being empirically testable along several parameters.

IV. NEUROLINGUISTIC MODELS

Of the variety of possible methods for investigating the language system in the brain, two have yielded the most relevant data: (*1*) the classical lesion approach, which includes analysis of the aphasias, electrical stimulation of the brain (ESB), and other neurosurgical procedures, and (2) EEG studies on normal subjects, including readiness and evoked potential recordings. Research based on animal studies has produced some interesting hypotheses but is only indirectly applicable to human language per se; in part this is attributable to the problem, noted above, of structural differences between the brain of man and that of the other primates, and in part this is attributable to the fact that no other primate has been shown to develop or be capable of learning a language system based upon the acoustic channel. The success in teaching chimpanzees a language system based on the visual channel, however, leads one to suppose that there will be fresh insights into animal–human comparative neurology in the near future. Of these two approaches to neurolinguistic models, the EEG studies are the most recent, even though the basis for such work can be traced back to the late nineteenth century, about the time when the aphasia studies were initiated. The relevance of EEG studies on normal subjects is obvious when contrasted with the aphasia studies. A lesion in some part of the brain may disrupt function either because that particular cortical area subserved the function or because of the lesion's disinhibitory–facilitative effect on some other part of the brain (diaschisis). This has led to certain problems in the interpretations of the aphasias, as well as neurosurgical procedures, frequently subsumed under the so-called "localizationist" controversy. On the other hand, demonstration of localized activity that is time locked to on-going language events may more plausibly be taken to indicate that the particular brain area being monitored is actually part of the language system.

The earliest observations on speech-correlated anticipatory EEG responses are reported in the work of Schafer (1967) and Ertl and Schafer (1967, 1969); there was no report in these studies of either lateralization or localization of activity. The first study to show that the EEG activity preceding verbalization was both lateralized to the left hemisphere and localized to the inferior frontal region (Broca's area) was McAdam and Whitaker (1971). Recent studies that essentially confirm the discovery of McAdam and Whitaker are Low, Wada, and Fox (in press) and Morrell and Huntington (1972). Of particular interest is the Low, Wada, and Fox study, which shows a correlation between the anticipatory slow negative potential over Broca's area and the carotid artery Amytal injection (the Amytal "test" indicates hemispheric dominance for language by temporarily blocking the expressive language function in one hemisphere for a period of approximately 10 minutes). In those subjects who were shown by the Amytal technique to have right hemisphere language dominance, the slow negative potential preceding speech was maximum over the right homologue to Broca's area. Morrell and Huntington's study is of interest in that it specifically controlled for artifacts due to movement-related electrical potentials (EMG). A number of studies have shown a lateralization, usually to the left hemisphere, of cortical electrical activity subsequent to the perception of linguistically meaningful stimuli; the EEG activity in this case is identified as an evoked response, and both visual and auditory evoked responses (VERs and AERs) have been analyzed. A study of the AER, which showed a hemispheric difference in response to identical stimuli depending on whether the stimuli were being processed linguistically or simply acoustically, is Wood, Goff, and Day (1971).

While the EEG research on language is still in its infancy and has not yet led to general models of the brain's language system, neurolinguistic analysis of the aphasias, together with neurosurgical evidence, has produced a rich body of data on the areas of the brain that subserve language and has further provided some evidence on the functional processing presumed to take place in these areas. These studies are considered in detail in Goodglass and Geschwind (this volume) and semiformalized in a flow-chart model in Whitaker (1971a,b). One aspect of the question of the brain's language system that is not analyzed in any detail in either of these references is the question of a cortical versus a cortical–subcortical model. This question can be pursued profitably regardless of whether the model being proposed emphasizes the connections between cortical language areas (see Geschwind, 1965) or the status of these areas as analyzers (see Luria,

1966), whether the model emphasizes a gestalt-function approach to the language system (cf. Goldstein, 1948) or a discrete linguistic-function approach (Goodglass & Geschwind, chap 12; Whitaker, 1971a,b), or whether the model emphasizes the plasticity of the cortex and the nondiscreteness of cortical language zones (Lenneberg, 1967) or the opposite (Whitaker, 1971a,b). In brief, the question of whether the language system in man's brain is essentially subserved by cortical structures alone or subserved by a combination of cortical and subcortical structures must be answered independently of the various issues of how the brain functions.

First, the distinction between language and speech-hearing must be made. Problems with making this distinction abound in the literature, in spite of the fact that it is a definitional matter more than an empirical one. The definition used in this review is as follows: Factors of speech-hearing are (a) those which can be assigned to the neural commands governing the vocal tract musculature subsequent to and dependent upon linguistic encoding and (b) those which can be assigned to the neural signals in the auditory pathways that reflect the acoustic analysis of the sound wave and are prior to linguistic decoding. Other aspects of man's communicative system are assigned to the language system, i.e., those factors which involve linguistic encoding and decoding. In terms of this distinction between language and speech-hearing, it is probably the case that the following structures of the central nervous system are *not* part of the language system: the ear, auditory pathways to Heschl's gyrus, lower motor neurons, cranial nerves and vocal tract musculature, the basal ganglia (excluding thalamic structures), the cerebellum, and the input and output pathways of the cerebellum. Clinically the sequelae of damage to these structures is typified as dysarthria or hearing losses (see Whitaker, this volume). The question of subcortical language structures thus becomes one of the role of the thalamus in linguistic encoding and decoding; the facts are by no means clear, but there is a reasonable body of literature containing very suggestive data. Penfield and Roberts (1966) argue that the more recently evolved cortex in man's brain is primarily connected with the phylogenetically older portions of the brain, particularly the thalamus, and thus permits an elaboration of the functions of the older brain. They write as follows (obviously using a definition of "speech" that in fact is analogous to the definition of "language" in this review):

> It is proposed, as a *speech hypothesis* [emphasis in original] that the functions of all three cortical speech areas in man are coordinated by projections of each to parts of the thalamus, and that by means of these circuits the elaboration of speech is somehow carried out . . . . Support for such a conception is given by the fact that removal of the gyri all about these two major cortical speech areas [sic] does not produce aphasia. Indeed, the map of the cortical speech areas shown in Figure X-10 was drawn from the negative evidence provided by successful excisions of gyri

close to the speech area, which resulted in no more than transient post-operative aphasia [pp. 207–209].*

As convincing as this sounds, the very next paragraph contains an admission that proof is still wanting:

> Such removals were carried to the bottom of each fissure but never deeper than the gray matter of the gyrus. The removals would not, therefore, interrupt the connections between other gyri and their own subcortical structures under any circumstances. They would also not ordinarily interrupt the more deeply placed transcortical connections in the white matter [pp. 209–210.]*

In short, pathways such as the Arcuate fasciculus, which play an important role in the model proposed by Geschwind (1965), Whitaker (1971a, 1971b) and Goodglass and Geschwind (Chapter 12), were not affected by these surgical procedures. Penfield and Robert's model depends upon two-way connections with the pulvinar, the large posterior nucleus in the thalamus; by their own admission, they assume that the pulvinar has the postulated connections with the posterior language areas in the cortex—the supramarginal gyrus, angular gyrus, and Wernicke's area. Geschwind (1965), on the other hand, argues that the unique fact about man's brain is the lack of such pathways; he claims that the inferior parietal and posterior temporal areas are connected to other association cortex but not significantly to the pulvinar. Indeed, most current neuroanatomical texts agree with this assumption: The pulvinar is usually represented as having connections with the superior parietal area only, an area not ordinarily implicated in the language system. The data that cast this into doubt and that support the model suggested by Penfield and Roberts (1966) come from neurosurgical lesions in the structures of the thalamus, introduced for the purpose of controlling certain aspects of involuntary movement disorders.

Ojemann and Ward (1971) produced anomia by stimulating the left lateral thalamus; the anomia took the form of an inability to name an object even though fluent verbal output was still evident, as well as a misnaming of objects, e.g., identifying a church as an "ace," an arm as a "balloon," and the like. In addition to demonstrating what was obviously a language disturbance, they also demonstrated lateralization to the left thalamus, which is consistent, of course, with the presumed left hemisphere dominance for language (their patients were right handed). A study that included surgery on basal ganglia structures as well as thalamic structures was reported in Riklan, Levita, Zimmerman, and Cooper (1969), using a definition of language versus speech-hearing that is comparable to the

---

* From *Speech and brain mechanisms* by Wilder Penfield and Lamar Roberts (Copyright © 1959 by Princeton University Press). Reprinted by permission of Princeton University Press.

one outlined above. They found that unilateral subcortical lesions were associated with *transient* language disturbances, primarily as sequelae to dominant hemisphere side operations; bilateral subcortical lesions were usually associated with speech disturbances of much longer duration and primarily related to articulations. These authors take the position that the role of the thalamus in the language system can be considered as facilitating a balance between nonspecific (reticular) and specific (cortical) physiological systems—a distinction which is reminiscent of Bergstrom's (1969) model. This implies that the participation of the thalamus in the language system of the brain is not one of mediating linguistic encoding and decoding. The data from Ojemann and Ward (1971) appear to be in direct conflict with this interpretation, which leaves the matter as yet unsettled. From the other data presented by Riklan *et al.* (1969) it can be concluded that other subcortical structures do not play a role in language per se, and thus the question of cortical versus subcortical linguistic processing appears to be principally a matter of the role of the lateral and posterior thalamic nuclei. The main issue seems to be the permanence of the language deficits associated with lesions in these parts of the thalamus; if it turns out that these deficits are transient, then it is clear that the role of the thalamus in the language system will be rather different from that of the classical cortical areas.

References

Alajouanine, T., & Lhermitte, F. Acquired aphasia in children. *Brain,* 1965, **88,** 653–662.

Anokhin, P. K. Systemogenesis as a general regulator of brain development. In W. A. Himwich & H. E. Himwich (Eds.), *The developing brain.* New York: Elsevier, 1964. Pp. 54–86.

Atz, J. W. The application of the idea of homology to behavior. in L. R. Aronson, E. Tobach, D. S. Lehrman, and J. S. Rosenblatt (Eds.), *Development and Evolution of Behavior.* San Francisco: Freeman, 1970, pp. 53–74.

Bastian, J. Primate signalling systems and human languages. In I. Devore (Ed.), *Primate behavior.* New York: Holt, 1965. Pp. 585–606.

Bergstrom, R. M. Electrical parameters of the brain during ontogeny. In R. J. Robinson (Ed.), *Brain and early behavior.* London: Academic Press, 1969. Pp. 15–41.

Berry, M. F. *Language disorders of children.* New York: Appleton, 1969.

Berry, P. B. Comprehension of possessive and present continuous sentences by nonretarded, mildly retarded and severely retarded children. *American Journal of Mental Deficiency,* 1972, **76,** 540–544.

Bonin, G. von and Bailey, P. Pattern of the cerebral isocortex. H. Hofer, A. H. Schultz and D. Starck (Eds.), *Primatologia.* Basel: Karger, 1961.

Brown, J. R., Darley, F. L., & Gomez, M. R. Disorders of communication. *Pediatric Clinics of North America,* 1967, **14,** 725–748.

Chappell, G. E. Developmental aphasia revisted. *Journal of Communication Disorders,* 1970, **3,** 746–755.

Chomsky, N. *Language and mind.* New York: Harcourt, 1968.

Conel, J. L. *The postnatal development of the human cerebral cortex.* Cambridge, Massachusetts. Harvard Univ. Press, 1939–1967.

Delius, J. D. Neural substrates of vocalizations in gulls and pigeons. *Experimental Brain Research,* 1971, **12,** 64–80.

Drachman, G. Physiology and the acquisition of phonology. Paper read to the Linguistic Society of America, summer meeting, 1970.

Eimas, P. D., Siqueland, E. R., Jusczyk, P., & Vigorito, J. Speech perception in infants. *Science,* 1971, **171,** 303–306.

Ertl, J., & Schafer, E. W. P. Cortical activity preceding speech. *Life Sciences,* 1967, **6,** 473–479.

Ertl, J., & Schafer, E. W. P. Erratum. *Life Sciences,* 1969, **8,** 559.

Evans, D., & Hampson, M. The language of Mongols. *British Journal of Disorders of Communication,* 1968, **3,** 171–181.

Flechsig, P. *Anatomie des menschlichen Gehirns und Ruckenmarks auf myelogenetischer Grundlage.* Leipzig: Thieme, 1920.

Gardner, R. A., & Gardner, B. T. Teaching sign language to a chimpanzee. *Science,* 1969, **165,** 664–672.

Gardner, B. T., & Gardner, R. A. Two-way communication with an infant chimpanzee. In A. Schrier & F. Stollnitz (Eds.), *Behavior of nonhuman primates,* Vol. 4. New York: Academic Press, 1971. Pp. 117–184.

Geschwind, N. Disconnexion syndromes in animals and man. *Brain,* 1965, **88,** 237–294, 585–644.

Geschwind, N. Neurological foundations of language. In H. Myklebust (Ed.), *Progress in learning disabilities,* Vol. 1. New York: Grune and Stratton, 1968. Pp. 182–198. (a)

Geschwind, N. The development of the brain and the evolution of language. In R. J. O'Brien (Ed.), *Selected papers on linguistics: 1961–1965.* Washington: Georgetown University Press, 1968. Pp. 133–147. (b)

Goldstein, K. Language and language disturbances. New York: Grune & Stratton, 1948.

Held, R., & Hein, A. Movement-produced stimulation in the development of visually guided behavior. *Journal of Comparative & Physiological Psychology,* 1963, **56,** 872–876.

Hubel, D. H., & Wiesel, T. N. Receptive fields of cells in striate cortex of very young, visually inexperienced kittens. *Journal of Neurophysiology,* 1963, **26,** 944–1002.

Hubel, D. H., & Wiesel, T. N. Receptive fields and functional architecture in two nonstriate visual areas (18 and 19) of the cat. *Journal of Neurophysiology,* 1965, **28,** 229–289.

Jacobson, M. Development of specific neuronal connections. *Science,* 1969, **163,** 543–547.

Jacobson, M. *Developmental neurobiology.* New York: Holt, 1970.

Jerison, H. J. Brain evolution and dinosaur brains. *American Naturalist,* 1969, **103,** 575–588.

Jerison, H. J. Brain evolution. New light on old principles. *Science,* 1970, **170,** 1224–1225. (a)

Jerison, H. J. Gross brain indices and the analysis of fossil endocasts. In C. R. Noback & W. Montagna (Eds.), *The primate brain: Advances in primatology,* Vol. 1. New York: Appleton, 1970. Pp. 225–244. (b)

Jerison, H. J. More on why birds and mammals have big brains. *American Naturalist,* 1971, **105**, 185–189.

Jerison, H. J. Evolution of the brain and intelligence. New York: Academic Press, 1973.

Kastein, S., & Fowler, E. P. Differential diagnosis of children with communicative disorders. *Folia Phoniatrica,* 1960, **12**, 298–312.

Krashen, S., & Harshman, R. Lateralization and the critical period. *UCLA Working Papers in Phonetics,* 22, Los Angeles: Univ. of California, 1972.

Lancaster, J. B. Primate communication systems and the emergence of human language. In P. C. Jay (Ed.), *Primates.* New York: Holt, 1968. Pp. 439–457.

Landau, W. M., Goldstein, R., & Kleffner, F. R. Congenital aphasia. *Neurology,* 1960, **10**, 915–921.

LeBoeuf, B. J., & Peterson, R. S. Dialects in elephant seals. *Science,* 1972, **166**, 1654–1656.

Lehrman, D. S. Semantic and conceptual issues in the nature-nurture problem. In L. R. Aronson, E. Tobach, D. S. Lehrman, and J. S. Rosenblatt (Eds.), *Development and evolution of behavior.* San Francisco: W. H. Freeman, 1970. Pp. 17–52.

Lenneberg, E. H. Understanding language without ability to speak. *Journal of Abnormal and Social Psychology,* 1962, **65**, 419–425.

Lenneberg, E. H. *Biological foundations of language.* New York: Wiley, 1967.

Lieberman, P. Primate vocalizations and human linguistic ability. *Journal of Acoustical Society of America,* 1968, **44**, 1574–1584.

Lieberman, P., & Crelin, E. S. On the speech of Neanderthal man. *Linguistic Inquiry,* 1971, **2**, 203–222.

Lieberman, P., Crelin, E. S., & Klatt, D. H. Phonetic ability and related anatomy of the newborn and adult human, Neanderthal man, and the chimpanzee. *American Anthropologist,* 1972, **74**, 287–307.

Lieberman, P., Harris, K. S., Wolff, P., & Russell, L. H. Newborn infant cry and nonhuman primate vocalizations. *Journal of Speech & Hearing Research,* 1972, **14**, 718–727.

Lieberman, P., Klatt, D. H., & Wilson, W. H. Vocal tract limitations on the vowel repertoires of rhesus monkey and other nonhuman primates. *Science,* 1969, **164**, 1185–1187.

Low, M. D., Wada, J. A., & Fox, M. Electroencephalographic localization of conative aspects of language production in the human brain. *Electroencephalography and Clinical Neurophysiology,* in press.

Luria, A. R. *Higher cortical functions in man.* New York: Basic Books, 1966.

Magoun, H. W. comments. In C. H. Millikan and F. L. Darley (Eds), *Brain mechanisms underlying speech and language.* New York: Grune & Stratton, 1967, p. 18.

Magoun, H. W., Darling, L., & Prost, J. The evolution of man's brain. In M. B. Brazier (Ed.), *The central nervous system and behavior.* New York: Josiah Macy, Jr. Foundation, 1960. Pp. 33–126.

Marler, P. Communication in monkeys and apes. In I. Devore (Ed.), *Primate behavior.* New York: Holt, 1965. Pp. 544–584.

Marler, P. Animals and man: Communication and its development. In J. D. Roslansky (Ed.), *Communication.* Amsterdam: North-Holland, 1969. Pp. 23–62.

Marler, P. A comparative approach to vocal learning: Song development in white-crowned sparrows. *Journal of Comparative & Physiological Psychology,* 1970, **71**, Number 2, Part 2.

Marshall, J. C. The biology of communication in man and animals. In J. Lyons (Ed.), *New horizons in linguistics.* Harmondsworth, Middlesex: Penguin Books, 1970. Pp. 229–241.

Marshall, W. A. *Development of the brain.* Edinburgh: Oliver and Boyd, 1968.

McAdam, D. W., & Whitaker, H. A. Language production: Electroencephalographic localization in the normal human brain. *Science,* 1971, **172,** 499–502.

Meader, C. L., & Muyskens, J. H. *Handbook of biolinguistics.* Toledo, Ohio: H. C. Weller, 1962.

Milner, E. *Human neural and behavioral development.* Springfield, Illinois: C. C Thomas, 1967.

Molfese, D. L. Cerebral asymmetry in infants, children and adults: Auditory evoked responses to speech and noise stimuli. Unpublished doctoral dissertation, Pennsylvania State Univ., 1972.

Morley, M. E. *The development and disorders of speech in childhood.* Edinburgh: Livingstone, 1957.

Morrell, L. K., & Huntington, D. A. Cortical potentials time-locked to speech production: Evidence for probable cerebral origin. *Life Sciences,* 1972, **11,** 921–929.

Nottebohm, F. Ontogeny of bird song. *Science,* 1970, **167,** 950–956.

Ojemann, G. A., & Ward, A. A. Speech representation in ventrolateral thalamus. *Brain,* 1971, **94,** 669–715.

Penfield, W. L., & Roberts, L. *Speech and brain mechanisms.* New York: Atheneum, 1966.

Peters, C. R. Evolution of the capacity for language: A new start on an old problem. *Man,* 1972, **7,** 33–49.

Ploog, D. Early communication processes in squirrel monkeys. In R. J. Robinson (Ed.), *Brain and early behavior.* London: Academic Press, 1969. Pp. 269–303.

Ploog, D., & Melnechuk, T. Are apes capable of language? *Neurosciences Research Progress Bulletin,* Volume **9,** Number 5. Brookline, Massachusetts: NRP, MIT, 1971.

Premack, D. Language in chimpanzee? *Science,* 1971, **172,** 808–822.

Riklan, M., Levita, E., Zimmerman, J., & Cooper, I. S. Thalamic correlates of language and speech. *Journal of Neurological Sciences,* 1969, **8,** 307–328.

Robinson, B. R. Vocalizations evoked from forebrain in maccaca mulatta. *Physiology and Behavior,* 1967, **2,** 345–354.

Sarles, H. B. The study of language and communication across species. *Current Anthropology,* 1969, **10,** 211–215.

Sarles, H. B. The search for comparative variables in human speech. Paper read to Animal Behavior Society, annual meeting, 1972.

Savolainen, H., Palo, J., Riekkinen, P., Moronen, P., & Brody, L. E. Maturation of Myelin proteins in human brain. *Brain Research,* 1972, **37,** 1972, 253–263.

Schafer, E. W. P. Cortical activity preceding speech. *Life Sciences,* 1967, **6,** 473–479.

Sebeok, T. A. (Ed.) *Animal communication.* Bloomington: Indiana Univ. Press, 1968.

Shapiro, T., Fish, B., & Ginsberg, G. L. The speech of a schizophrenic child from two to six. *American Journal of Psychiatry,* 1972, **128,** 1408–1414.

Shirley, M. M. *The first two years.* Minneapolis: Univ. of Minnesota Press, 1933.

Sloan, R. F. Neuronal histogenesis, maturation and organization related to speech development. *Journal of Communication Disorders,* 1967, **1,** 1–15.

Swisher, L. P., & Pinsker, E. J. The language characteristics of hyperverbal hydrocephalic children. *Developmental Medicine and Child Neurology,* 1971, **13,** 746–755.

Walker, J. L., & Halas, E. S. Neuronal coding at subcortical auditory nuclei. *Physiology and Behavior,* 1972, **8,** 1099–1106.

Whitaker, H. A. *On the representation of language in the human brain.* Edmonton, Canada: Linguistic Research, 1971. (a)

Whitaker, H. A. Neurolinguistics. In W. O. Dingwall (Ed.), *A survey of linguistic science.* College Park: Univ. of Maryland, 1971. Pp. 136–251. (b)

Whitaker, H. A. Comments on the innateness of language. In R. W. Shuy (Ed.), *The Georgetown linguistics forum.* Washington: Georgetown Univ, 1972. Pp. 95–120.

Wood, C. C., Goff, W. R., & Day, R. S. Auditory evoked potentials during speech perception. *Science,* 1971, **173,** 1248–1251.

Yakovlev, P. I., & Roch-Lecours, A. The myelogenetic cycles of regional maturation of the brain. In A. Minkowski (Ed.), *Regional development of the brain in early life.* Oxford, England: Blackwell Scientific Publications, 1967. Pp. 3–70.

Chapter 5

THE DEVELOPMENT OF SPEECH

JACQUELINE SACHS

I. INTRODUCTION

The development of the ability to speak and understand a language can be viewed as two interrelated processes: language learning and development. Though these processes are intertwined in the acquisition of language in children, they can be separated conceptually and considered as two factors that together determine the pattern of linguistic behavior at any point in a child's history. In "learning a language," the child must internalize a complex system for coding thoughts into sounds, and decoding sounds into thoughts. The system that the child will eventually control, a language, is infinitely productive. There is no upper limit to the number of ideas that can be communicated. Therefore, the language speaker cannot simply learn a large set of sound–meaning translations but must, instead, have a way of forming utterances to express ideas, and of discovering the meanings of utterances. Therefore, the child's speech and understanding at a particular time is determined partly by the level of his mastery of the linguistic system to which he has been exposed.

The other factor that limits the child's performance is his developmental stage. The characteristics of perception and of information processing, storage, and retrieval vary according to age (see, for example, Piaget, 1952; Bruner, Olver, & Greenfield, 1966; Conrad, 1972a,b). Compare the case of second language learning by an adult to first language learning by the young child. For the adult, there is also a linguistic system to acquire, but the adult's progress may be different from the child's. Knowing a language already, of course, the adult would benefit from the degree of overlap in linguistic rules between the two languages and suffer from interference when he had to master new rules. However, as well as these factors, the adult would have different cognitive abilities, which he would bring to bear on the task, and might have quite different language acquisition strategies from the child. Similarly, the learning of a first language by a 4-year-old might proceed differently from the learning of language by the infant, because the initial level of nervous system development, and therefore the level of cognitive processing, would be quite different. Unfortunately, the present state of knowledge does not generally permit the independent assessment of the contribution of these two factors, linguistic knowledge and developmental stage. For example, the "one-word stage" observed in normal language development may exist because of production constraints due to the developmental level, rather than because of a lack of linguistic knowledge.

In this chapter, we will explore some current approaches to the problems of how and why a child comes to be a speaker of a language.

II. LINGUISTIC ABILITIES IN INFANCY

A. Perception

Although the child does not begin to use words until around 12 months of age, it would be incorrect to refer to the period before that as a "prelinguistic" period, since many changes significant to language development occur during that time. The abilities of the child during this period have been reviewed recently by Kaplan and Kaplan (1971) and will be discussed only briefly here. From birth, the infant actively perceives and learns about the world about him, visually, tactually, and auditorily. Neonatally or shortly thereafter, the infant responds differently to the human voice from the way he responds to other sounds (Eisenberg, 1969; Molfese, 1972; Wolff, 1966).

Furthermore, some research suggests that certain of the sound categories used in languages are responded to in a special way. Eimas, Siqueland, Jusczyk, and Vigorito (1971) showed that 1- and 4-month-old infants perceived as different those sounds that adults perceived as different phonemes (/b/ and /p/). The infants could discriminate between synthetic speech sounds only 20 msec apart in voice onset time if the sounds fell into different phoneme categories, but did not show the discrimination between two sounds with the same physical difference if the sounds did not cross a phoneme boundary. These results have been supported by other discrimination studies by Moffit (1971) and Trehub and Rabinovitch (1972). Such findings suggest that certain aspects of the infant's perceptions may be specialized for language processing innately, rather than acquired through experience with language sounds. Such an inborn specialization is consistent with a growing body of research demonstrating a special "speech mode" of perception (Liberman, Cooper, Shankweiler, & Studdert-Kennedy, 1967).

B. Babbling

In the neonatal period, the sounds produced by the infant are very simple. For example, the cry is a result of changes in the larynx and in air pressure, but with no accompanying changes in the shape of the vocal tract (Lieberman, 1967; Lieberman, Harris, Wolff, & Russell, 1971). As the infant matures, both his anatomical structure and his central nervous system change, resulting in a gradual increase in the complexity of sounds he can produce.

Babbling with consonantal sounds typically begins by the sixth month, with production of single syllable utterances at first. Next the infant duplicates the syllable (e.g., *mama*), increases the number of sounds produced and the variety of sequencing, and eventually may produce quite complex strings of sounds with a variety of intonation patterns ("jargon" babbling). Babbling frequently overlaps the onset of speech, with children babbling and saying short utterances for a few months, but most children stop babbling by about 18 months.

It is not yet known whether babbling plays any functional role in the child's speech development. Mowrer (1952, 1960) and Staats and Staats (1963) argued that primary and secondary reinforcement during the babbling period "shapes" the child's sound productions to match the sound system of the language, and therefore is the first stage of language acquisition. This view is not supported by most recent psycholinguistic research, which suggests that there is some discontinuity between the babbling period and true speech, and that babbling is not necessary for later language development. If the babbling period represented the early stages of the child's learning of his language's sound system, we would expect the sounds used in babbling to come to match those in the model language. Weir (1966) reported studies in which listeners attempted to identify babies of different language backgrounds from tapes of their babbling. The judges could not discriminate among babies exposed to Arabic, Russian, and (American) English. Tapes of a 6-month-old baby of Chinese parents, however, sounded different from the others. It appeared that what the judges were responding to was the great differences in intonation patterns between English and Chinese, but they could discriminate no differences in segmental features on any of the tapes. The failure of naive judges to hear differences among the babies cannot be taken as evidence that no differences exist in the sounds babbled, of course, but the conclusions are supported by two studies using spectrographic analysis. Nakazima (1962) found little difference between the prelanguage sounds produced by American and Japanese babies. Differences in babbling began to emerge at about 1 year, when the babies started to use words, but again were differences in intonation rather than in segmental features. Preston, Yeni-Komshian, and Stark (1967) analyzed the production of stop consonants in 1-year-old babies exposed to Hungarian, Arabic, and English. The babies' productions did not differ according to the language they had heard, but all showed the same pattern of producing mostly stops with simultaneous voicing onset and consonant release.

Further evidence that the babbling period is not significantly involved in learning the sound system of the language comes from the observation that some babies babble sounds that they later have great difficulty in learning to control (Berry, 1969). Lenneberg (1967), too, argued that cooing and babbling are not necessary or useful as a practice period for the child. As evidence, he cited the case of a child who was tracheotomized for 6 months and therefore could make no sound. When the opening in the child's throat was closed at 14 months, he babbled appropriately for his age.

The evidence suggesting that babbling is not necessarily involved in learning the sound system of a particular language does not rule out the possibility that it is functional in other ways. Fry (1966) stated that babbling allows the child to discover the properties of his own articulatory system and to establish an "auditory feedback loop [p. 189]," that is, a connection between tactual–kinesthetic feelings and the auditory sensation of his sounds. This process seems, however, not to be a necessary one in Fry's view, because he also stated that a child could learn to speak without having babbled. If the child were exploring his own capabilities during the babbling period, then the sounds he made would not necessarily approach the model language, but his later phonological acquisition might be facilitated.

Babbling may also be functional in establishing interaction patterns and a rudimentary kind of communication system between the baby and his caretakers (Blount, 1969; Bullowa, 1970). This vocal type of interaction is not a necessary precursor to language development (as shown, for example, by the fact that hearing children of deaf parents learn language), but it might play some role in the normal developmental process. Toward the end of the babbling period, many children produce "jargon"—long strings of sounds that sound something like sentences without words. Though there has been little research on this phenomenon, many investigators believe it indicates that the child first believes language interaction to be the production of sounds with intonation patterns. Some children even use this type of babbbling in special situations in which they have heard adults producing monologues. My daughter used it when "reading" from a book or "talking" on the telephone.

C. Phonological Development

When the child begins to use and understand words, he does not simply imitate the pronunciation of adults (as would a parrot), but he must learn the sound system of his language. That is, he must discover what variations in speech sounds signal differences in meaning in his language. The most influential theory in research on phonological development has been the *distinctive feature* theory of Jakobson (1941). In this theory, the universal set of speech sounds is organized according to a set of binary features (characteristics specifying place or manner of articulation, such as dental–labial or voiced–voiceless). The features are ordered, so that some are more basic than others. This ordering implies that a language could never have contrasts that arise out of features at one point in the ordering without having contrasts that arise out of earlier features. For example, a language might have front consonants and no back consonants, but no language would have back consonants and no front consonants. The ordering of the features would also predict the frequency of phonemes across languages, because all languages would have the contrasts generated by the basic features, but few would have phonemes generated by contrasts at the end of the ordering.

Jakobson suggested this theory not only to explain the structure of the sound systems of the languages of the world, but also to explain the acquisition of these sound systems. According to the theory, the child does not learn individual sounds, but acquires features that allow him to generate contrasting sounds. For example, if a child already used the phonemes /b/ and /d/, when he acquired the feature voiced–voiceless he would be able to produce the contrast both between /p/ and /b/ and between /t/

and /d/. (Such a pattern of acquisition was, in fact, observed in a child studied by Velten, 1943.) The order of acquisition of the contrasts would presumably be predicted by the ordering of the features in the theory, would be the same across all children, and would reflect the frequency of use of the contrasts in the languages of the world rather than the frequency of use in the language the child hears. The first distinction the child would learn would be between vowels and consonants, and then he would further differentiate within these two categories. For example, within the consonants he would distinguish orals from nasals (/p/ from /m/), labials from dentals (/p/ from /t/), and so forth. The last contrasts to be mastered would be the ones that are also rare in the languages of the world.

Although the basic ideas of the distinctive feature theory are widely accepted, the theory as applied to language acquisition has not been substantiated in detail. The major source of information about phonological development is the detailed study of individual children. From these studies, there is evidence that children sometimes acquire contrasts that then apply to all cases for which that contrast is appropriate (Burling, 1959; Velten, 1943) but in some cases the contrast appears earlier for some sounds than for others (Moskowitz, 1970, 1973). Furthermore, the order of acquisition of features does not appear to be exactly the order suggested by Jakobson. Ervin-Tripp (1966) made the following tentative generalizations based on the evidence available from case studies:

(*a*) The vowel–consonant contrasts are probably the earliest.

(*b*) A stop–continuant (/p/ versus /m/ or /f/) contrast is quite early for all children, the continuant being a fricative or a nasal.

(*c*) Stops precede fricatives.

(*d*) If two consonants are alike in manner of articulation, one will be labial, the other dental or alveolar (e.g., /p/ versus /t/), resulting in the common lack of /k/.

(*e*) Contrasts in place of articulation usually precede voicing contrasts.

(*f*) Affricates (ch, j) and liquids (l, English r) usually appear later than stops and nasals.

(*g*) In Russian and French /l/ precedes a vibrant /r/.

(*h*) A contrast between low and high vowels (e.g., /a/ versus /i/ or /y/) precedes a front versus back contrast (e.g., /i/ versus /u/).

(*i*) Oral vowels precede nasal vowels, the contrast being acquired late.

(*j*) Consonant clusters or blends are usually late.

(*k*) Consonant contrasts usually appear earlier in initial position than in medial or final position [pp. 68–69].

Moskowitz (1970) analyzed the phonological structure in the speech of three English speaking children at 2 years of age. The data revealed some instances in which the child seemed to acquire a feature, as predicted by Jakobson's theory. However, the children were not always able to apply the feature to all of their sounds and had to learn to pronounce individual phonemes. Thus, Moskowitz argued that both the feature acquisition theory and the phoneme acquisition theory are oversimplifications, and a new theory is needed that specifies the order of acquisition in terms of an interaction between the phonological task and the phonetic task.

Data about children's perceptions of sounds would also be relevant for testing the distinctive feature theory, but unfortunately this problem has not been studied extensively as yet. Shvachkin (1948) investigated the discrimination of sound contrasts by 11- to 23-month-old Russian children. The method involved teaching the children to understand a set of words that had been specially constructed to differ by only one phoneme. The pattern of phonemic development was reported in terms of the acquisition of feature contrasts, and the sequence followed Jakobson's predictions very well. However, a study of American children at comparable ages, based on Shvachkin's methods (Garnica, 1973), did not replicate the earlier results. The study, in fact, revealed that the order of acquisition of discrimiation was different from the theoretical predictions and was also somewhat variable across children.

As well as learning the sound system of his language, the child also learns the rules governing combinations of sounds into words, or phonological rules. These include, for example, rules of permissible sequencing of sounds and sound changes as a function of stress changes (see Chomsky & Halle, 1968). Although the learning of these rules begins in early childhood (Braine, 1971; Morehead, 1971), this complex aspect of development continues well into the child's school years (Moskowitz, 1973). It has been suggested (Chomsky, 1970) that the knowledge of these phonological rules is important for the child who is learning to read and write. Some of the work relevant to this topic has been reviewed by Menyuk (1971, pp. 82–88) and by Braine (1970, Section 2.13 and 2.14).

III. THE TRANSITION TO LANGUAGE USE

A. Age of First Word

The first words are typically used around 12 months of age (Darley & Winitz, 1961; Lenneberg, 1967). Assuming that the child is exposed to a speaking community, the age at which speech begins is probably determined primarily by the level of central nervous system development, but no information is available yet concerning the specific determining factors. Lenneberg has noted the correlation between the onset of speech and walking in support of his maturational theory of language development.

Sometimes the first word is not an imitation but evolves out of a sound that is used in a semantically consistent way by the child. If the parent notices the child's usage, he may imitate the child and use this "word" even though there is no apparent relationship to the word used in the model language. For example, Leopold (1949) reported that his child said *dididi* to express disapproval. Even when the child imitates an adult's word, the first approximations are quite unlike the adult word in pronunciation. Lenneberg (1967) has remarked that the child's acquisition strategy does not have him wait for good articulatory control before he begins to speak. Rather he uses a variety of sounds equivalently, leading to an inconsistent and unclear pronunciation, a "crude replica of the adult word [p. 280]." This fact is evidence that the child does not learn the separate elements of language but learns general patterns. Often the idiosyncratic pronunciation of adult words makes it difficult to identify the exact time that the child says his first word. Bullowa, Jones, and Duckert (1964) reported that an analysis of sound films allowed them to trace back the rudimentary beginnings of a word (shoe pronounced as *tu*) earlier than it had been recognized as a word.

B. The Development of Meaning

The child's early utterances differ from the adult's words in meaning as well as in pronunciation. Although the child may learn a word by hearing it used with a particular referent, he does not consider the word to be the name of that one thing, but takes the word to refer to a category. Typically, the child's category does not match the adult's exactly, but includes things that the adult would refer to with other words. The child "overextends" the meaning of a word. Clark (1973) described a number of instances of overextension from the diary–study literature on child language and offered a theory of semantic development to account for this phenomenon. Clark suggested that the reason the child makes "errors" is that he does not have the same set of semantic features, or components of meaning, that an adult does for the word. For example, the child might use the word *doggie* at first to refer to any animal, and we might discover that the feature he identified with the word *doggie* was 'having four legs.' As the child learns more about the correspondence between words and their referents, he adds features, so that the meanings of his words become narrower and gradually approximate the adult meaning. The basic source of features for the young child seems to be perceptual characteristics. For the overextensions reported in the diary studies, the features involved were usually movement, shape, size, sound, taste, and texture. For example, in a series of overextensions that seemed to be related to texture, a child first learned the word *wau-wau* to refer to dogs, and then used it to refer to all animals, a toy dog, soft bedroom slippers, and a picture of a man dressed in furs (example cited in Clark; originally from Leopold, 1949). My daughter first used the word *hot* to refer to both hot and cold things, presumably having discovered that the word *hot* had to do with the feature "temperature different from room temperature," and only later acquired *cold* to refer to one end of the continuum. According to Clark, the difference in semantic features can account for children's misinterpretations of meanings at later stages, too, as shown in her discussion of the work of Donaldson and Balfour (1968), Donaldson and Wales (1970), Wales and Campbell (1970), Clark (1971), and others. (See also Clark, 1972, and Andersen, 1975, for further discussion of the role of semantic features in language acquisition.)

C. Reasons for the One-Word-at-a-Time Restriction

Most children continue to utter only one word at a time for several months. At this stage, even if the child is asked to imitate a longer utterance, he will repeat just one of the words. Length of the utterance seems not to be a critical factor, because the child will be able to say a two- or three-syllable word (*elephant*) but will be unable to say two one-syllable words together (*big dog*). Occasionally utterances that seem to be longer phrases may be found during the one-word stage, but these seem to be used as unanalyzed wholes, such as *I wan'it* or *what's dat?*.

There are at least two possible reasons for this limitation on utterance length. The first is that the child is functioning under an age-determined performance restriction that prevents him from sequencing the words he knows, even when he might have the linguistic knowledge that would generate two words at a time. The second possible reason is that the child's linguistic knowledge is limited and he does not know the rules for combining meanings.

The explanation based on a performance restriction has been supported by McNeill (1970), who claimed that the child's earliest utterances actually stand for complex ideas. The one-word stage had been described by many earlier researchers as the "holophrastic period"; that is, a word means a whole sentence. For example, the child who says *cookie* may mean that he wants a cookie, that the object he sees is a cookie, that the cookie fell down, or any number of other semantic intentions. In this framework, a child's one-word utterances cannot be viewed in isolation, but must be interpreted as a comment on some aspect of the current context. On the basis of data from de Laguna (1927), Greenfield, Smith, and Laufer (in press), and others, McNeill suggested that some of the child's earliest utterances are predicative, and that there is an orderly progression in the types of grammatical relations inherent in the one-word utterance. When two-word utterances appear, they are simply the outward expression of a grammar that already existed.

Such a view is quite susceptible to the criticism that the interpretation of the data may be guided by the theory. For example, in Greenfield's data reported in McNeill, it was claimed that the child said *ha* (for "hot") to an empty coffee cup and a turned-off stove. McNeill concluded from these data that the child is using *ha* to assert a property, rather than using it as a label. However, if Clark's (1973) semantic feature theory (see Section III,B) were applied to these data, they could easily be explained as cases of overextension of meaning. Using another of Greenfield's examples, it was claimed that the child knew the grammatical relation "object of preposition" at 15 months because she said *eye,* meaning 'water in my eye'. Such a paraphrase seems to be very weak evidence. The word *eye* could just as well mean 'my eye hurts' in this context.

The nature of the postulated "performance restriction" is not known, although many developmental psycholinguists have discussed the possibility of some kind of memory limitation. Another possibility is that the child might have problems in sequencing two units of behavior, and especially in inhibiting the expression of one thought until another has been expressed. Observations in my data support this hypothesis. The child went through a stage just as she started joining two words together in which she would begin to say the second word in the utterance, then stop herself and say the first, as in *ta—on table.* Such a sequencing problem might be analogous to a stage in the development of grasping skills, though of course at a much later point in development. Just after the baby is able to close his hand to grasp objects that are placed near him, he still has difficulty in obtaining things that he must reach out for. The problem is that he closes his hand first, then reaches with a closed fist and cannot pick up the object.

If the one-word stage is a result of a performance restriction, the child may continue to operate under similar kinds of restrictions at much later points in development when he is tired, frightened, overactive, and so on. The variability in the form of expression in young children is striking. The child who can already say complex sentences may be heard to use one-word utterances or even a regressive "baby talk" in some contexts. In my data, the mean length of utterance for a recording session seemed to be influenced by variables such as stress or activity. For example, the child's utterances tended to be longer if she was relatively still (as in a bathtub or car seat), as compared to times when she was moving around. The encoding of meaning into speech is a skill that is highly automatic in the adult, but perhaps during the acquisition period other cognitive or motor activities may interfere significantly with the ability to speak. The variability in children's speech forms has not been studied in detail but may offer some clues as to the reasons for length and complexity limitations (see Brown, 1973).

The explanation of the one-word-at-a-time restriction based on performance limitations has been challenged by Bloom (1973), who interpreted the one-word period as resulting from a lack of linguistic knowledge. She claimed that children use words to refer to various aspects of their experience that they conceptualize nonlinguistically. They must then learn the linguistic code (for example, word order or inflection) that represents these conceptualizations formally. Toward the end of the one-word period, the child studied by Bloom often used strings of single words, such as *Daddy. peach. cut.* Each word had a terminal falling pitch contour, and there were pauses between the words. These strings were not used in a consistent order. According to Bloom, these sequences of single words are evidence that the child is aware of relationships among different aspects of the situation, but that he is unable to express these relationships linguistically.

One potential source of evidence to help resolve the controversy concerning the child's linguistic knowledge at the one-word utterance stage would be studies of comprehension abilities during this period. If the reason for the restriction on utterance length is a performance limitation, we might find that the child would show evidence of his linguistic knowledge in a different task. Parents often feel that their children can understand much more than they can say, but they may overestimate the children's ability to understand language. For example, a baby might learn to respond correctly to a command such as "Touch your nose" or "Give me the ball" but not comprehend the sentence the way an adult would. His response might be determined by the parent's intonation pattern, by one word out of the sentence, or by a gesture that typically accompanied the command. Shipley, Smith, and Gleitman (1969) found that children in the one-word stage were most likely to respond to one-word utterances, rather than to sentences, suggesting that they attended best to their own level of language structure. Their experiment did not rule out the possibility, however, that the children could have demonstrated an understanding of longer utterances if the situation had called for it. Huttenlocher (1974) has reported that children in the one-word stage can follow commands involving more than one word. Also, Greenfield *et al.* (in press) and Parisi (1974) have used young children's responses to their mothers' speech to argue that the child "intends" more than one word before he can join words in sequence.

Analogous questions concerning length or complexity limitations could be raised at other stages in the development of speech: Does the child leave out certain items from his sentences because of a performance limitation (e.g., length or complexity) or because he does not know how to use the items? One can almost always paraphrase a child's sentence by a more complete adult sentence, but it is difficult to discover whether that paraphrase correctly reflects what the child "meant." The analyst of child speech must always find his way between two dangers, that of reading too much into the child's utterances on the basis of his knowledge as an adult, or on the other hand underestimating the child's knowledge by concluding that he knows no more than just what he says. In the extreme, the first view would lead to crediting the child who speaks in one-word utterances with the knowledge of the grammar of English. The second view might leave us with no more than a list of the utterances the child said.

IV. THE GRAMMATICAL STRUCTURE OF EARLY LANGUAGE

Around 18 months of age, the child begins to join two words together. The two-word utterances he says are neither simple imitations of adult utterances nor random combinations of the words he knows. Rather, they follow from the system that the child is using to express meanings at that time.

Most of our information about this stage of language development comes from detailed, longitudinal studies of children. Though many of the studies in recent years have used English-speaking children, there are data available for many other languages as well (see Slobin, 1972, for a comprehensive bibliography of studies of the acquisition of languages other than English). In many cases, the observer has attempted to write "grammars" for the children studied. In writing a grammar, one attempts to formulate a set of rules that will generate the utterances that the child could use at that stage of language development. The set of rules is a hypothesis about the nature of the child's linguistic knowledge. As linguistic theory has changed over the years, so has the form of child grammars.

Using distributional analysis, Braine (1963) and Ervin and Miller (1963) arrived at similar descriptions of the child's knowledge in the two-word stage. To use Braine's analysis, sentences consisted of words chosen from two grammatical classes, the "pivot class" and the "X class" (also called "open class"). The "pivot class" was a small set of words that could be combined with other words and always occurred in a fixed position in the utterance. Thus, the pivot class could be subdivided into pivot words that occurred in the first position (P_1 words), and pivot words that occurred in the second (P_2 words). The words that made up these classes might vary from child to child. For example, one child studied, Steven, had P_1 words such as *want, get,* and *it,* while his P_2 class included only *do.* For another child, Gregory, the word *it* was classified as a P_2 word. The other major class of words, the open class, consisted of a larger set of words that was rapidly growing in number. These words could appear in either position. Examples of open-class words used by Steven were *Mommy, car, doll,* and *doggie.* The grammatical rules proposed by Braine for this stage were very simple. Sentences consisted of P_1 + open-class word or open-class word + P_2. For the examples given for Steven, these rules would generate utterances like *want Mommy, get car,* and *doll do.* The formulation of a grammatical rule hypothesizes that any utterance generated by the rule would be an acceptable sentence to the child at that stage. As noted above, in Gregory's case, the word *it* was described as a P_2 word and therefore should combine with Gregory's open-class words to yield utterances like *Mommy it, egg it,* and *man it.* However, inspection of the data from which the word classes were derived might make one skeptical of the acceptability of these utterances to Gregory, for in fact the combinations in which *it* had occurred consisted of *do it, push it, close it, buzz it,* and *move it.* All of these utterances contain a word in the first position that would be classified as a verb in the adult grammar. To categorize both *Mommy* and *push* simply as open-class words would seem to underestimate the child's knowledge of English at this point.

The *pivot-grammar formulation* fails to describe the child's linguistic competence on other grounds as well. In collecting data on three young children, Bloom (1970) had recorded the context of the child's utterance and had obtained an interpretation of the meaning, as well as the utterance itself. From these data, Bloom argued that although some utterances used by the children seemed to be consistent with the pivot-grammar analysis, the use of that method would yield incorrect results in other cases. The children Bloom studied were clearly intending more complex meanings than merely looking at the distribution of the words would indicate. For example, on one occasion a child of 21 months said *Mommy sock.* The context of the utterance was that the child picked up her mother's sock and Bloom interpreted it as meaning 'Mommy's sock'. In the same language sample, the child again said *Mommy sock,* but in this instance the context was that the mother was putting the child's sock on the child. Bloom interpreted this utterance as a subject (Mommy) and object (sock), as in the phrase 'Mommy puts on sock'. To use the pivot-grammar analysis and call *Mommy* a pivot-word would neglect the fact that the word was probably being used by the child in quite different functions at different times. (Analyzing the utterances as consisting of two open-class words would yield no better insight into the differences between them.) Bloom suggested that one must attend not only to the form of the child's utterance, but to its function. In this case, *Mommy sock* in one instance could be analyzed as a genitive construction and in the other as subject–object.

The fact that different meanings can be expressed by the same form had been used in linguistic theory to argue for the distinction between "deep structure" and "surface structure" (Chomsky, 1965). Bloom argued that it is possible to make this distinction between meaning and form even at the two-word stage in language development. In the grammar Bloom formulated for her children's speech, the utterances they used (the surface structures) were generated from deep structures by rules, within the framework of generative transformational grammar. Bloom found that many types of functions were possible, even though only two words at a time were being used: for example, conjunction, genitive, subject–object, subject–verb, verb–object, attribution, location, and negation. No examples of the identity relation (*baby* [is a] *girl*), disjunction (an "either–or" relationship), or indirect object (*give* [to] *baby*) were found.

As the study of child language moved from such purely distributional descriptions as Braine's (1963) or Ervin and Miller's (1963) to the syntactic descriptions deriving from generative transformational grammar, interpretations of the child's meanings became more important. A number of investigators (e.g., Blount, 1969; Bowerman, 1973; Brown, 1973; Kernan, 1970; Schlesinger, 1971) have suggested that the description of this stage would be more accurate if semantics, rather than syntax, were considered as central to the acquisition process. Many of these researchers have been influenced by the movement within linguistics called *generative semantics,* in which it is claimed that rules can be formulated to show the coding of meaning directly into the surface structure of the sentence, without a syntactic deep structure level of representation. Fillmore's (1968) proposals for a *case grammar* have been by far the most influential to date.

Bowerman (1973) analyzed the language of three young children (two of whom were learning Finnish and the other English) using three different theoretical frameworks: the pivot grammar, generative transformational grammar, and case grammar (based on Fillmore, 1968). The pivot grammar was not adequate as a description of the data, and it did not reflect the knowledge that the child possessed about his language. The analysis following generative transformational grammar seemed to be a good theory of the child's knowledge in some respects. For example, the linguistic structures could be rich enough to capture the child's meaning. However, Bowerman found no evidence that the child had a knowledge of constituent structures of the sort that are assumed in generative grammar. Furthermore, notions such as "subject of sentence" seemed inappropriate for describing the child's knowledge at that stage. The analysis based on case grammar gave better results in general, but none of the analyses were entirely satisfactory. Bowerman suggested that in order to capture the nature of language acquisition a theory will have to allow for more flexibility in assigning linguistic structure than any currently do. For example, at one stage it might be appropriate to describe some aspect of the child's system in semantic concepts, but at some later point a syntactic description might be needed for the same data.

V. PROGRESS TOWARD THE ADULT LANGUAGE

As the child's utterances increase in length, his progress follows a pattern of development that has been described in detail in a number of sources (see especially Braine, 1970; Brown, 1973; Cazden, 1972). The child at first finds some way to communicate a meaning, even though it is probably not the "correct" way according to the adult model. Later, he attends to learning the correct form of expression. Some meanings can be found from the child's earliest utterances. For example, negation can be communicated with a one-word utterance. The semantic relationships of actor–action and action–object are found in the two-word stage. Other meanings do not appear until much later; for example, the subjunctive or the future perfect tense in English. Some forms are easy to learn (for example, regular plural endings) and some seem to be intrinsically more difficult (for example, the auxiliary verb system in English). The interplay between the discovery of meanings and the learning of linguistic forms to communicate those meanings determines the pattern of acquisition of a language, in terms both of the rate of acquisition and of the types of nonadult forms that are found.

Languages use a number of formal mechanisms for signaling meanings:

1. The most obvious is the use of words. Words have meanings even in isolation, although some words seem to derive their meanings from their use in sentences while others have more inherent meaning. It is easy to think about the meaning of words like *table, boy,* or *throw* (often called "content words"), whereas the meaning of words like *the, a, as,* or *any* are determined by their function within the sentence and are often therefore called "function words."

2. The meaning of a sentence also depends on the order of the words. *The bird chased the cat* has a different meaning from *The cat chased the bird.*

3. Inflections, or syntactic modifications of words, also affect meanings (*dog–dogs, man–men, walk–walked*).

4. Intonation changes alone can signal changes in meaning, as for example in questions like *He's really going?*

5. Stress and juncture may affect meaning, as in the contrast between *blackbird house* and *black birdhouse.*

In the two-word stage, several of these formal mechanisms are already used to signal differences in meanings. The child uses words in particular orders. He also uses intonational differences. For example, the earliest form of the question found is a sentence in standard order with a rising intonation contour, as in *Daddy home?* Stress is also used quite early, according to Miller and Ervin (1964), who found that some children used different structures: e.g., *báby chair* to mean 'baby's chair' or 'small chair' and *baby cháir* to mean that the baby is in the chair or does something to the chair.

During this period, the child has probably not correctly used any of the function words in English. Most children omit these words in their early speech. Even if such a word is used, there is no evidence that the child uses it to signal differences in meaning. For example, for a few weeks my daughter started each of her one-word utterances with *a*, producing *a-crayon, a-toy,* and *a-pin,* but there seemed to be no contrast in meaning intended by the *a*. The English-speaking child also does not use inflections to signal meanings at this stage, although some words might be learned in their inflected form (e.g., *running, fell, feet*).

As the child's utterances become longer, he initially continues to use the mechanisms already found at the two-word stage, with the use of words in particular orders being by far the most important means of signaling meanings. At first, the semantic relationships that were expressed in the two-word stage are combined to form longer utterances. The actor–action sentence combines with the action–object sentence to yield a basic sentence structure—actor–action–object, or, in syntactic terminology, subject–verb–object. This ordering in fact is derived from the sentences the child hears, because it is so frequent. For a time, this subject–verb–object rule directs both the child's sentence production and his comprehension (Bever, 1970; Fraser, Bellugi, & Brown, 1963; Slobin, 1971). An adult sentence that does not follow this order will be misinterpreted. For example, the young child may interpret *The man was chased by the dog* as "The man chased the dog."

Other semantic relationships found in the two-word stage can also be combined. For example, the actor–action sentence can be expanded to a three-word sentence by modifying the actor, yielding a sentence with an adjective, actor, and action. One interesting source of information about the internal structure of children's three-word and longer utterances is "replacement sequences" (Braine, 1970). A child's utterance may be followed by another utterance that is a paraphrase of the same content or that expands the original utterance. Some examples given by Braine are:

Car on machine . . . Big car on machine.
Build house . . . Cathy build house.
Stand up . . . Cat stand up . . . Cat stand up table.

Such examples have also been used by Bloom (1970) and Ervin-Tripp (1971) in analyzing the structure of early speech.

Inflections and function words ("grammatical morphemes") continue to be absent from the child's sentences for some time in English, giving the speech a "telegraphic" character (Brown & Bellugi, 1964; Brown & Fraser, 1963). The child's imitations, too, are typically reduced: *I am drawing a dog* would be imitated as *I draw dog.* Reasons for these omissions have been suggested by Brown (1973) in his detailed study of the acquisition of a number of grammatical morphemes. For example, one reason is that many of the meanings represented by inflections and function words in English are not among the first meanings discovered by children. If a language signals an important semantic distinction (like which noun refers to the actor) by an inflectional ending, that inflection will be learned early (Slobin, 1971). Also, inflectional endings are sometimes irregular in form, and this makes the learning harder. As noted for the learning of the order rules, the child is sensitive to the regularities in the language he hears. He attempts to discover a pattern or rule behind the examples, and then uses that rule in generating his own utterances. Since inflectional endings do follow rules to some degree, the child learns the rules. He then uses those rules to generate all endings, even though some will be incorrect. The child says *comed* instead of *came, mans* instead of *men,* because he knows the rule for forming past tenses and plurals. Ervin (1964) has shown that the child's preference for producing his linguistic behavior by rule is so strong that an incorrect form will displace a previously learned correct irregular form. That is, the child who already said *went* or *fell* at an earlier stage will abandon those forms and say *goed* and *falled* when he learns the rules for forming past tenses. What seems to be simply an error in the child's speech is actually evidence that the child is making progress in acquiring the language. The incorrect overregularizations are very resistant to change, and usually some persist until the elementary school age. The learning of isolated exceptions to general patterns is a very difficult part of language acquisition, even if those exceptions are very common words that are heard in their correct form every day.

As adult speakers, we know an elaborate code for incorporating many simple ideas or meanings into one sentence. Although the child learns much of the basic structure of his language in the preschool years, the acquisition of rules of embedding, complementation, pronominalization, and so on is not complete for some time.

The child may be able to comprehend certain syntactic structures before he is able to use them. Elicited imitations provide one kind of evidence of the child's comprehension (Slobin & Welsh, 1971). At one stage, my child used sentence-final relative clauses, such as *Here's the book I picked up,* but no embedded relatives. When she was given sentences with embedded clauses to imitate, she could not reproduce the structure, even though the sentence was no longer than sentences in her spontaneous speech. Her attempts at imitating revealed that she understood the meaning although she could not use the construction. For example, *The bathing suit grandma sent is pretty* was imitated as *The bathing suit is pretty that grandma gave—sent it. The bag your pretzels are in is green* was changed to *The bag it has pretzels in it is pretty.* Three months later, she started to use embedding in her own speech, and one of her first recorded attempts illustrates the problems a child may have with this complex structure: *That mommy is on the record is finished talked.*

The existence of exceptions to grammatical rules presents special problems for the child. In the case of irregular plural or past tense endings, the child's errors are obvious because these words are used frequently. In the case of certain syntactic irregularities, however, the child's lack of linguistic knowledge is not apparent, because he simply says what he wants to in the way he knows how, rather than using a structure incorrectly. C. S. Chomsky (1969) showed that comprehension tests can reveal that children between the ages of 5 and 10 have not mastered all the rules of English, no matter how correctly they speak. One of the constructions Chomsky tested is illustrated by the sentence *John promised Bill to leave.* In this sentence, John promises, and John would perform the act of leaving. Many other sentences that appear to be like this sentence in structure exist in English, but actually are quite different. For example, *John wanted Bill to leave* or *John asked Bill to leave.* In these sentences, John wants or asks, but Bill leaves. The sentence with the verb *promise* is an exception to a very general principle in English that holds for the other verbs such as *want, tell, expect, desire,* and so on. When children are tested for their understanding of a sentence like *John promised Bill to leave,* they often misunderstand the sentence and report that the second person named will do the activity, even though they understand the meaning of *promise.* They interpret the "promise" sentence according to the general principle that holds for most of the sentences they hear.

VI. FACTORS INFLUENCING THE RATE AND PATTERN OF DEVELOPMENT

A. Cognitive Development

In general, the pacesetter in language development is the child's cognitive development. As the child discovers new ideas, he seeks ways to express these ideas linguistically. In most cases, the source of the ideas seems to be the child's nonlinguistic experience. The child discovers that there are objects in the world and that these objects act and have effects on other objects. The child discovers that there may be more than one instance of an object or an action. He discovers that he can remember what has happened before and can predict certain events that will happen. These concepts arise independently of the child's linguistic experience. (See, for example, Sinclair-de-Zwart, 1969, 1971, for further comments on the child's conceptual development in relationship to language development.) Language may play a role in guiding the child's discovery of other meanings. For example, since English distinguishes between mass and count nouns, the child will discover what sorts of meanings fit into these two categories.

Whether a concept is discovered from experience or from contact with a language, the child cannot use a linguistic form appropriately until he has the concept behind it. The mere occasional use of a linguistic form is not an indication that the child knows the meaning. If a child used some words with plural endings but never used the same word in both singular and plural appropriately, or if he used both singular and plural randomly, we would not credit him with knowing the meaning of plurality. On the other hand, the use of an incorrect form can sometimes indicate that the child has a concept but lacks the appropriate linguistic form. For example, when my daughter first discovered the past tense, she signaled it with the word *yesterday,* so that *I go yesterday* meant 'I went.' When she discovered the past tense endings, the "yesterday" form disappeared.

Several recent studies have investigated the role of cognitive development in language acquisition. McNeill and McNeill (1968) and Bloom (1970) independently found similar patterns in the acquisition of types of negation in two languages, suggesting that the conceptual development, rather than the linguistic form, determined the order of learning. Cromer (1968) suggested that only an underlying change in children's cognition could account for the sudden emergence of certain linguistic forms expressing temporal relationships. Wells (1974) showed that the types of conceptual relations expressed by several children developed in a very similar pattern, and Edwards (1974) has tried to relate the content of children's early speech to a Piagetian framework.

B. The Mastering of Linguistic Forms

Although cognitive development is necessary for language development, it is by no means sufficient. However early a child expresses a meaning, he must eventually master certain formal rules. The acquisition of a few aspects of language have been studied longitudinally in detail. Bellugi's (1965, 1967) work gives a good idea of the complexity of formal rules necessary for the expression of two very basic concepts, interrogation and negation, in English. Her work also supplies more examples of the interaction of performance constraints and linguistic knowledge (Bellugi, 1971). In one stage in the acquisition of interrogative structures, a child could form interrogatives with modals correctly (*Why can the lady sing?*) and could form negations correctly (*The lady can't sing*), but, if the child was asked to form a negative question, his sentence form regressed to an earlier stage in which the auxiliary inversion was not performed (*Why the lady can't sing?*). Bellugi hypothesized that, although the child had the linguistic knowledge that should have enabled him to form the correct sentence, the complexity of the operations involved interfered with the ability. (But see R. Clark, 1974, for an interpretation based on an ability to modify only familiar routines.)

Some aspects of language seem to be intrinsically more difficult than others. The amount of time that intervenes between the first evidence of the child's intention to express a meaning and the point at which the child masters the correct form is one indication of the relative difficulty of different linguistic forms. Slobin (1971) cited the case of two children who were learning Hungarian and Serbo-Croatian simultaneously (originally reported by Mikeš, 1967, and Mikeš & Vlahović, 1966). The children started to use Hungarian case endings to express locative meanings long before they used the Serbo-Croatian prepositions that expressed the same ideas. If we assume that the child has a unitary cognitive development, rather than one developmental level in Hungarian and a different one in Serbo-Croatian, then the difference in time of mastering the form to express the idea must be a function of the formal complexity in each language. Slobin argued that we can use information about the relative difficulty of various linguistic forms to develop hypotheses about the reasons for the difficulty, and therefore about the process of acquisition. To this end, Slobin has surveyed patterns of acquisition across children and across different languages and suggested that certain *universals* can be found. To account for these universals, he proposed that the child must have certain processing strategies, which he calls *operating principles*. In the example cited above, the crucial difference between the two languages was believed to be that the semantic marking occurred after the content word in Hungarian but before it in Serbo-Croatian. Combining this observation with others yielded the universal that "for any given semantic notion, grammatical realizations in the form of suffixes or postpositions will be acquired earlier than realizations in the form of prefixes or prepositions [p. 336]." The operating principle, or processing strategy, involved is, "Pay attention to the ends of words [p. 335]."

The operating principles suggested by Slobin may in some instances be specific to language acquisition, although in other instances they are very likely the result of more general perceptual and information processing strategies of the child. For the example given here, the strategy of paying attention to the ends of words could be the result of the child's attentional mechanisms. Suppose that a child's interest was aroused to some level whenever speech was perceived, but that when a familiar, comprehensible word was heard, his attention increased markedly. If this were so, then whatever came directly after the more familiar content words would be within the span of the child's heightened attention and would more likely be noticed and stored. If something came before an interesting word, it would often go relatively unnoticed.

C. The Role of the Linguistic Environment

Until the last decade, the explanation for language learning typically given by American psychologists was that parents teach their children to speak by supplying examples to imitate and reinforcing the children's correct utterances. Much of the developmental psycholinguistic research of the 1960s consisted of demonstrations that this type of theoretical explanation was inadequate. One direction this work took was collecting the sort of data that have been reviewed in this chapter. These studies showed that children acquire a system for producing utterances, rather than acquiring a set of utterances. Children's sentences are not mere imitations of what they have heard. The role of reinforcement for the correctness of sentence structure in child language development was examined by Brown and his colleagues. Brown, Cazden, and Bellugi (1969) analyzed the interaction between children and their parents, to determine whether the parents offered positive and negative reinforcement contingent upon the grammaticality of the child's utterances. The results were dramatic. Parents almost universally paid no attention to the structure of the child's sentence but reinforced purely on the basis of the truth of the semantic content. Since it seemed possible that parents might negatively reinforce ungrammatical sentences by simply not responding to them (because they could not understand them), Brown and Hanlon (1970) analyzed mothers' reactions to well-formed and primitive utterances. They found that mothers understood their children's primitive utterances equally well and responded equally often to them. Children acquire the patterns of the language even though they are not required to do so in order to be understood.

To replace the concepts of imitation and reinforcement, developmental psycholinguists argued that the child was very active in the acquisition process and had special abilities designed just for this task. The strong environmentalist tradition had culminated in Skinner's book *Verbal Behavior* (1957) and the psycholinguistic reaction to this theoretical framework was begun by Chomsky's influential review of that book in 1959. Other theorists followed who argued for the complexity of the language, the abstractness of deep structures (Bever, Fodor, & Weksel, 1965), the necessity for postulating powerful acquisition devices and innate knowledge (McNeill, 1966), and the uniqueness of language among learned behaviors (Lenneberg, 1967). These writers and others were important and beneficial in furthering the concepts of a cognitively based psychology, but, because they emphasized the creative aspects of language acquisition, they tended to ignore or even reject the possible influence of the input.

The arguments that language is biologically based, that the child has special capacities for language acquisition, and that the child is active in the acquisition process are now widely accepted. However, the belief that the child is an organism that has evolved to be a language learner and language user does not logically preclude an interest in the language input, and recently investigators have challenged the view that the input is random and not modified to help children learn to speak. A fine review of this research can be found in Cazden (1972, Chapter 6) and it will be described only briefly here. Some researchers have analyzed naturalistic mother–child interaction data (Brown & Bellugi, 1964; Brown et al., 1969; Brown & Hanlon, 1970; Friedlander, Jacobs, Davis, & Wetstone, 1972). Others have examined various aspects of the language of adults in relation to children in more experimental situations (Phillips, 1973; Snow, 1972). The findings generally are that children do not receive a random sample of linguistic input but that the speech of an adult to a child is simpler and more redundant. For example, Snow found that both mothers and nonmothers, when talking to a 2-year-old child, as compared with an 8-year-old child, used shorter sentences, fewer complex sentences, fewer pronouns, and more repetition. Such input characteristics potentially are helpful to the child in his task of discovering the meanings of the language he hears and abstracting the structure of the language. However, we have at this point only a few studies which indicate that these input characteristics are necessary or even beneficial for language acquisition. Nelson (1973) and Newport (1974) found correlations between certain aspects of the adult's speech and the child's linguistic development. Sachs and Johnson (in press) reported a case of deviant language in a hearing child of deaf parents. The child had been exposed to speech on television, from playmates, and at nursery school, but very little speech had been addressed to him personally. The authors argued that the abnormal nature of the linguistic input could have contributed to the child's problem in language acquisition.

Slobin (1969) has suggested that the study of parent–child interactions in middle-class American homes may give a very biased idea of the role of the input in the acquisition process. Cross-cultural studies from widely separated areas indicate that most children may be exposed primarily to the speech of other children, rather than adults. This observation, however, does not necessarily contradict the idea that characteristics of the language input play a role in language development, for the speech of children to younger children shows many of the characteristics of the speech of adults to children (Shatz & Gelman, 1973).

Another aspect of parent–child interaction that has received renewed attention recently is imitation. Bloom, Hood, and Lightbrown (1974) found that some children imitated adults' utterances frequently, while others did not. There was no difference in rate of language acquisition for the two types of children. However, for those who imitated, the imitations were of words or structures that would soon appear in their speech. Thus, some children might use imitation of the adult's preceding utterance as one of their language acquisition strategies.

An interest in the language input does not indicate a return of psycholinguistics to the traditional environmentalists' view. Rather, it indicates that there is now an even deeper appreciation of the complexities of the acquisition process. We believe that humans have evolved a behavior uniquely suited for thought, communication, and socialization. Children undoubtedly are suited for acquiring linguistic systems, partly in terms of inborn characteristics (such as certain aspects of speech perception), partly in terms of their cognitive abilities, and partly in terms of the sorts of strategies they use to process the input they receive. It would not be surprising, in view of these specializations for language acquisition and use, if certain patterns of social interaction and forms of adult speech had developed to help the child in his task of learning how to talk.

References

Andersen, E. S. Cups and glasses: Learning that boundaries are vague. *Journal of Child Language,* 1975, **2,** 79–103.

Bellugi, U. The development of interrogative structures in children's speech. In K. Riegel (Ed.), *The development of language functions.* Report No. 8. Ann Arbor:

Univ. of Michigan Center for Human Growth and Development, 1965. Pp. 103–137.

Bellugi, U. The acquisition of negation. Unpublished doctoral dissertation, Harvard Univ., 1967.

Bellugi, U. Simplification in children's language. In R. Huxley & E. Ingram (Eds.), *Language acquisition: Models and methods.* New York: Academic Press, 1971. Pp. 95–119.

Berry, M. F. *Language disorders of children.* New York: Appleton, 1969.

Bever, T. G. The cognitive basis for linguistic structures. In J. R. Hayes (Ed.), *Cognition and the development of language.* New York: Wiley, 1970. Pp. 279–362.

Bever, T. G., Fodor, J. A., & Weksel, W. On the acquisition of syntax: A critique of "contextual generalization." *Psychological Review,* 1965, **72,** 467–482.

Bloom, L. M. *Language development: Form and function in emerging grammars.* Cambridge, Massachusetts: M.I.T. Press, 1970.

Bloom, L. M. *One word at a time: The use of single word utterances before syntax.* The Hague: Mouton, 1973.

Bloom, L., Hood, L., & Lightbrown, P. Imitation in language development: If, when and why. *Cognitive Psychology,* 1974, **6,** 380–420.

Blount, B. G. Acquisition of language by Luo children. Unpublished doctoral dissertation, Univ. of California, Berkeley, 1969.

Bowerman, M. F. *Early syntactic development: A cross-linguistic study of early syntactic development with special reference to Finnish.* New York: Cambridge Univ. Press, 1973.

Braine, M. D. S. The ontogeny of English phrase structure: The first phase. *Language,* 1963, **39,** 1–13.

Braine, M. D. S. The acquisition of language in infant and child. In C. Reed (Ed.), *The learning of language.* New York: Appleton, 1970. Pp. 7–95.

Braine, M. D. S. An inquiry into the nature of the morphophoneme in preliterate children. Paper presented at Conference on Developmental Psycholinguistics, Linguistics Institute, Buffalo, New York, 1971.

Brown, R. *A first language: The early stages.* Cambridge, Massachusetts: Harvard Univ. Press, 1973.

Brown, R., & Bellugi, U. Three processes in the child's acquisition of syntax. *Harvard Educational Review,* 1964, **34,** 133–151.

Brown, R., Cazden, C., & Bellugi, U. The child's grammar from I to III. In J. P. Hill (Ed.), *Minnesota symposium on child psychology.* Vol. 2. Minneapolis: Univ. of Minnesota Press, 1969. Pp. 28–73.

Brown, R., & Fraser, C. The acquisition of syntax. In C. N. Cofer & B. S. Musgrave (Eds.), *Verbal behavior and learning.* New York: McGraw-Hill, 1963. Pp. 158–197.

Brown, R., & Hanlon, C. Derivational complexity and order of acquisition in child speech. In J. R. Hayes (Ed.), *Cognition and the development of language.* New York: Wiley, 1970. Pp. 11–53.

Bruner, J. S., Olver, R., & Greenfield, P. M. *Studies in cognitive growth.* New York: Wiley, 1966.

Bullowa, M. The start of the language process. *Actes du Congres International des Linguistes, Bucharest, 28 aut-2 september 1967, III.* Bucharest: Editions de l'Academie de la Republique Socialiste de Roumanie, 1970. Pp. 191–200.

Bullowa, M., Jones, L. G., & Duckert, A. R. The acquisition of a word. *Language and Speech,* 1964, **7,** 107–111.

Burling, R. Language development of a Garo and English speaking child. *Word*, 1959, **15**, 45–68.

Cazden, C. *Child language and education*. New York: Holt, 1972.

Chomsky, C. S. *The acquisition of syntax in children from 5 to 10*. Cambridge, Massachusetts: M.I.T. Press, 1969.

Chomsky, C. S. Reading, writing, and phonology. *Harvard Educational Review*, 1970, **40**, 307–308.

Chomsky, N. A review of B. F. Skinner's *Verbal behavior*. *Language*, 1959, **35**, 26–58.

Chomsky, N. *Aspects of the theory of syntax*. Cambridge, Massachusetts: M.I.T. Press, 1965.

Chomsky, N., & Hale, M. *The sound pattern of English*. New York: Harper, 1968.

Clark, E. V. On the acquisition of the meaning of *before* and *after*. *Journal of Verbal Learning and Verbal Behavior*, 1971, **10**, 266–275.

Clark, E. V. On the child's acquisition of antonyms in two semantic fields. *Journal of Verbal Learning and Verbal Behavior*, 1972, **11**, 750–758.

Clark, E. V. What's in a word? On the child's acquisition of semantics in his first language. In T. E. Moore (Ed.), *Cognitive development and the acquisition of language*. New York: Academic Press, 1973.

Clark, R. Performing without competence. *Journal of Child Language*, 1974, **1**, 1–10.

Conrad, R. Speech and reading. In J. F. Kavanaugh & I. G. Mattingly (Eds.), *Language by ear and by eye*. Cambridge, Massachusetts: M.I.T. Press, 1972. Pp. 205–240. (a)

Conrad, R. The developmental role of vocalizing in short-term memory. *Journal of Verbal Learning and Verbal Behavior*, 1972, **11**, 521–533. (b)

Cromer, R. F. The development of temporal reference during the acquisition of language. Unpublished doctoral dissertation, Harvard Univ., 1968.

Darley, F. L., & Winitz, H. Age of first word: Review of research. *Journal of Speech and Hearing Disorders*, 1961, **26**, 272–290.

Donaldson, M., & Balfour, G. Less is more: A study of language comprehension in children. *British Journal of Psychology*, 1968, **59**, 461–472.

Donaldson, M., & Wales, R. J. On the acquisition of some relational terms. In J. R. Hayes (Ed.), *Cognition and the development of language*. New York: Wiley, 1970. Pp. 235–268.

Edwards, D. Sensory-motor intelligence and semantic relations in early child grammar. *Cognition*, 1974, **2**, 395–434.

Eimas, P., Siqueland, E. R., Jusczyk, P., & Vigorito, J. Speech perception in infants. *Science*, 1971, **171**, 303–306.

Eisenberg, R. Auditory behavior in the human neonate: Functional properties of sound and their ontogenetic implications. *International Audiology*, 1969, **8**, 34–45.

Ervin, S. Imitation and structural change in children's language. In E. H. Lenneberg (Ed.), *New directions in the study of language*. Cambridge, Massachusetts: M.I.T. Press, 1964, Pp. 163–189.

Ervin, S., & Miller, W. Language development. In H. W. Stevenson (Ed.), *Child psychology (62nd yearbook of the National Society for the Study of Education, Part I)*. Chicago: Univ. of Chicago Press, 1963. Pp. 108–143.

Ervin-Tripp, S. Language development. In M. Hoffman & L. Hoffman (Eds.), *Review of child development research*. Vol. 2. Ann Arbor: Univ. of Michigan Press, 1966. Pp. 55–105.

Ervin-Tripp, S. An overview of theories of grammatical development. In D. I. Slobin (Ed.), *The ontogenesis of grammar.* New York: Academic Press, 1971. Pp. 189–212.

Fillmore, C. J. The case for case. In E. Bach & R. T. Harms (Eds.), *Universals in linguistic theory.* New York: Holt, 1968. Pp. 1–90.

Fraser, C., Bellugi, U., & Brown, R. Control of grammar in imitation, comprehension and production. *Journal of Verbal Learning and Verbal Behavior,* 1963, **2,** 121–135.

Friedlander, B. A., Jacobs, C. J., Davis, B. B., & Wetstone, H. S. Time-sampling analysis of infants' natural language environments in the home. *Child Development,* 1972, **43,** 730–740.

Fry, D. B. The development of the phonological system in the normal and the deaf child. In F. Smith & G. A. Miller (Eds.), *The genesis of language.* Cambridge, Massachusetts: M.I.T. Press, 1966. Pp. 187–206.

Garnica, O. K. The development of phonemic speech perception. In T. E. Moore (Ed.), *Cognitive development and the acquisition of language.* New York: Academic Press, 1973.

Greenfield, P. M., Smith, J. H., & Laufer, B. *Communication and the beginnings of language.* New York: Academic Press, in press.

Huttenlocher, J. The origins of language comprehension. In R. L. Solso (Ed.), *Theories in cognitive development.* Potomac, Maryland: Lawrence Earlbaum Associates, 1974. Pp. 331–368.

Jakobson, R. *Kindersprache, Aphasie, und allgemeine Lautgesetze.* Uppsala: Almquist and Wiksell, 1941. (English trans. by A. Keiler. *Child language, aphasia and general sound laws.* The Hague: Mouton, 1968).

Kaplan, E., & Kaplan, G. The prelinguistic child. In J. Eliot (Ed.), *Human development and cognitive processes.* New York: Holt, 1971. Pp. 358–381.

Kernan, K. Semantic relationships and the child's acquisition of language. *Anthropological Linguistics,* 1970, **12,** 171–187.

de Laguna, G. *Speech: Its function and development.* New Haven, Connecticut: Yale Univ. Press, 1927.

Lenneberg, E. H. *Biological foundations of language.* New York: Wiley, 1967.

Leopold, W. F. *Speech development of a bilingual child.* 4 vols. Evanston, Illinois: Northwestern Univ. Press. 1939–1949.

Liberman, A. M., Cooper, F. S., Shankweiler, D. P., & Studdert-Kennedy, M. Perception of the speech code. *Psychological Review,* 1967, **74,** 431–461.

Lieberman, P. *Intonation, perception and language.* Cambridge, Massachusetts: M.I.T. Press, 1967.

Lieberman, P., Harris, K. S., Wolff, P., & Russell, L. Newborn infant cry and non-human primate vocalizations. *Journal of Speech and Hearing Research,* 1971, **14,** 718–727.

McNeill, D. Developmental psycholinguistics. In F. Smith & G. A. Miller (Eds.), *The genesis of language.* Cambridge, Massachusetts: M.I.T. Press, 1966. Pp. 15–84.

McNeill, D. *The acquisition of language.* New York: Harper, 1970.

McNeill, D., & McNeill, N. B. What does a child mean when he says "no"? In E. Zale (Ed.), *Proceedings of the Conference on Language and Language Behavior.* New York: Appleton, 1968. Pp. 51–62.

Menyuk, P. *The acquisition and development of language.* Englewood Cliffs, New Jersey: Prentice-Hall, 1971.

Mikeš, M. Acquisition des catégoires grammaticales dans le langage de l'enfant. *Enface*, 1967, **20**, 289–298.

Mikeš, M., & Vlahović, P. Razvoy gramatičkih kategorija u dečjim govoru. *Prilozi proučavanju jezika, II.* Novi Sad, Yugoslavia, 1966.

Miller, W. R., & Ervin, S. The development of grammar in child language. In U. Bellugi & R. Brown (Eds.), The acquisition of language. *Monographs of the Society for Research in Child Development*, 1964, **29**, 9–33.

Moffit, A. R. Consonant cue perception by twenty- to twenty-four-week old infants. *Child Development*, 1971, **42**, 717–731.

Molfese, D. L. Cerebral asymmetry in infants, children and adults: Auditory evoked responses to speech and noise stimuli. Unpublished doctoral dissertation, Pennsylvania State Univ., 1972.

Morehead, D. M. Processing of phonological sequences by young children and adults. *Child Development*, 1971, **42**, 279–289.

Moskowitz, A. I. The two-year-old stage in the acquisition of English phonology. *Language*, 1970, **46**, 426–441.

Moskowitz, A. I. On the status of vowel shift in English. In T. E. Moore (Ed.), *Cognitive development and the acquisition of language.* New York: Academic Press, 1973.

Mowrer, O. H. The autism theory of speech development and some clinical applications. *Journal of Speech and Hearing Disorders*, 1952, **17**, 263–268.

Mowrer, O. H. *Learning theory and the symbolic processes.* New York: Wiley, 1960.

Nakazima, S. S. A comparative study of the speech developments of Japanese and American English in childhood (1)—a comparison of the developments of voices at the pre-linguistic period. *Studia Phonologica*, 1962, **2**, 27–39.

Nelson, K. Structure and strategy in learning to talk. *Monographs of the Society for Research in Child Development*, 1973, **38**, (1–2, Serial No. 149).

Newport, E. L. Motherese: The speech of mothers to children and its relation to the child's acquisition of language. Unpublished doctoral dissertation, Univ. of Pennsylvania, 1974.

Parisi, D. What is behind child utterances. *Journal of Child Language*, 1974, **1**, 97–105.

Phillips, J. R. Syntax and vocabulary of mother's speech to young children: Age and sex comparisons. *Child Development*, 1973, **44**, 182–185.

Piaget, J. *The origins of intelligence in children.* New York: International Univ. Press, 1952.

Preston, M. S., Yeni-Komshian, G., & Stark, R. E. Voicing in initial stop consonants produced by children in the prelinguistic period from different language communities. *Annual report, Neurocommunication Laboratory.* The Johns Hopkins Univ. School of Medicine, 1967. Pp. 307–323.

Sachs, J., & Johnson, M. L. Language development in a hearing child of deaf parents. In W. von Raffler Engel (Ed.), *Proceedings of the International Symposium on First Language Acquisition.* Brussels: Univ. of Brussels Press, in press.

Schlesinger, I. M. Production of utterances and language acquisition. In D. I. Slobin (Ed.), *The ontogenesis of grammar: A theoretical symposium.* New York: Academic Press, 1971. Pp. 63–101.

Shatz, M., & Gelman, R. The development of communication skills: Modifications in the speech of young children as a function of listener. *Monographs of the Society for Research in Child Development* 1973, **38** (5, Serial No. 152).

Shipley, E. F., Smith, C. S., & Gleitman, L. R. A study in the acquisition of language: Free responses to commands. *Language*, 1969, **45**, 322–342.

Shvachkin, N. Kh. Development of phonemic speech perception in early childhood. *Izvestiya Akad. Pedag. Nauk. RSFSR,* 1948, Vyp. 13. [Abstracted by Slobin, D. I., in F. Smith & G. Miller, *The genesis of language,* Cambridge, Massachusetts: M.I.T. Press, 1966. Pp. 381–382.]

Sinclair-de-Zwart, H. Developmental psycholinguistics. In D. Elkind & J. H. Flavell (Eds.), *Studies in cognitive development: Essays in honor of Jean Piaget.* New York: Oxford Univ. Press, 1969. Pp. 315–336.

Sinclair-de-Zwart, H. Sensorimotor action patterns as a condition for the acquisition of syntax. In R. Huxley & E. Ingram (Eds.), *Language acquisition: Models and methods.* New York: Academic Press, 1971. Pp. 121–130.

Skinner, B. F. *Verbal behavior.* New York: Appleton, 1957.

Slobin, D. I. Questions of language development in cross-cultural perspective. In Working Paper No. 14, Language-Behavior Research Laboratory, University of California, Berkeley, 1969.

Slobin, D. I. Developmental psycholinguistics. In W. O. Dingwall (Ed.), *A survey of linguistic science.* College Park, Maryland: Linguistics Program, Univ. of Maryland, 1971. Pp. 298–400.

Slobin, D. I. *Leopold's bibliography on child language: Revised and updated.* Bloomington: Univ. of Indiana Press, 1972.

Slobin, D. I., & Welsh, C. Elicited imitation as a research tool in developmental psycholinguistics. In C. S. Lavatelli (Ed.), *Language training in early childhood education.* Urbana: Univ. of Illinois Press, 1971. Pp. 170–185.

Snow, C. Mothers' speech to children learning language. *Child Development,* 1972, **43,** 549–565.

Staats, A. W., & Staats, C. K. *Complex human behavior: A systematic extension of learning principles.* New York, Holt, 1963.

Trehub, S. E., & Rabinovitch, M. S. Audio-linguistic sensitivity in early infancy. *Developmental Psychology,* 1972, **6,** 74–77.

Velten, H. V. The growth of phoneme and lexical patterns in infant language. *Language,* 1943, **19,** 281–292.

Wales, R. J., & Campbell, R. On the development of comparison and the comparison of development. In G. B. Flores d'Arcais, & W. J. M. Levelt (Eds.), *Advances in psycholinguistics.* Amsterdam: North-Holland Publ., 1970. Pp. 373–396.

Weir, R. Some questions on the child's learning of phonology. In F. Smith & G. A. Miller (Eds.), *The genesis of language.* Cambridge, Massachusetts: M.I.T. Press, 1966. Pp. 153–172.

Wells, G. Learning to code experience through language. *Journal of Child Language,* 1974, **1,** 243–269.

Wolff, P. H. The natural history of crying and other vocalizations in early infancy. In B. M. Foss (Ed.), *Determinants of infant behavior.* Vol. IV. London: Methuen, 1966. Pp. 81–109.

Part II

Coding, Perception, and Hearing

Chapter 6

THE PERCEPTION OF SPEECH

C. J. DARWIN

I. INTRODUCTION

One of the most striking phenomena in the perception of speech is the degree to which our conscious experience follows the semantic intention of the speaker. Our conscious perceptual world is composed of greetings, warnings, questions, statements, while their vehicle, the segments of speech, goes largely unnoticed, and words are subordinated to the framework of the phrase or sentence. Nor is this "striving after meaning" a mere artifact, confined to situations in which we want to understand rather than to analyze, since our ability to analyze speech into its components is itself influenced by higher-level units. The basic physical dimensions of the stimulus and even, under normal listening conditions, the segments of speech are inaccessible to us directly. This is evident in experiments on the perception of prosody and in experiments in which subjects listen for a particular phonemic segment. The results of these experiments parallel in an interesting way the perception of three-dimensional objects in vision.

Lieberman (1965), for example, studied whether the intonation contours transcribed by linguists trained in a particular transcription system corresponded with the objective pitch present in the stimulus. He found that many of the pitch features described by his linguists were not in fact present but were introduced by the perceived syntactic structure of the sentence. The pitch the linguists heard was often that which their system told them should accompany a particular syntactic structure. Somewhat similar results have been reported by Hadding-Koch and Studdert-Kennedy (1964). They found that subjects' judgments about whether or not a short utterance has a rise in pitch at the end were influenced by the pitch contour in the earlier part of the utterance in a way that is thought to reflect aerodynamic constraints on spoken pitch (Lieberman, 1967). In a similar vein, Huggins (1972a) found that subjects had lower thresholds for detecting changes in the duration of segments of speech from "normal" when they based their judgments on the rhythm or stress of the utterance than if they tried to listen for duration itself. Even such familiar dimensions as pitch and duration seem to be relatively inaccessible to conscious experience. There is perhaps a parallel here with the problems that face a painter trying to represent a three-dimensional object in two dimension. Gombrich (1960) describes how different stylistic schools resort to a repertoire of visual tricks or schemata to achieve the two-dimensional representation of a scene, attaining, like Lieberman's linguists, a representation determined as much by their training as by the object portrayed. In both cases a more objective representation can be attained by resort to artificial aids, which distract attention from the meaning of the elements portrayed. Dürer illustrates one extreme way of doing this in his woodcut of a draughtsman drawing a reclining nude by viewing her from a fixed point in space through a transparent grid which corresponds to a similar grid on his canvas (Gombrich, 1960, p. 306). In the same way Daniel Jones transcribed intonation contous by lifting the needle from a phonograph record in midsentence and judging the last-heard pitch. In both these cases some external segmentation has been imposed on the perceptual whole to remove some of the changes caused by semantic interpretation. Without this aid the listener can only reconstruct properties of the stimulus from what he knows about higher level categories.

This reconstruction also appears to be operating in experiments where the subject is asked to listen for a particular speech segment. Following traditional phonetics we will use the term "phoneme" to refer to the smallest segment of speech that distinguishes two words of different meaning. The intuitive value of this concept outweighs, for the purposes of this chapter, the theoretical problem that it raises. The words *kine* and *Cain* thus share initial and final phonemes (/k/ and /n/, respectively) but differ in the medial diphthong. When subjects listening to a list of two-syllable words are asked to press a key whenever they hear a particular phoneme, they do this more slowly than when they are asked to detect a whole syllable; this in turn is slower than detecting a whole word (Foss & Swinney, 1973; Savin & Bever, 1970). Moreover, the time taken to detect a given phoneme at the beginning of a syllable is shorter if that syllable is a word than if it is not (Rubin, 1975). Here the subject's performance is influenced by larger units of analysis, despite the needs of the task. If these higher levels are removed so that phonemes are being targeted for in lists of phonemes, and syllables in lists of syllables, then the smaller units are in fact detected faster than the larger (McNeill & Lindig, 1973). Our conscious awareness, then, is driven to the highest level present in the stimulus, allowing lower levels to be accessible only as a subsequent operation on these higher units.

This somewhat paradoxical finding, that conscious decisions at a higher level can be made before decisions at a lower level, though striking in speech, is also encountered in written language. Letters embedded in words are identified more accurately than letters in nonword strings or in isolation (Reicher, 1969; Wheeler, 1970) provided, again paradoxically, that subjects do *not* know in which position in the word the letter that they have to report will occur (Johnston & McClelland, 1974). Although both the speech and the written language results demand an interpretation that stresses the importance of higher-order units in perception, there are interesting differences between the two modalities.

First, subjects are quicker at detecting an isolated phoneme than one embedded in a word (McNeill & Lindig, 1973); in vision, isolated letters are identified less accurately than those in words (Wheeler, 1970). Second, knowing where in a word a target will appear does not abolish the relative difficulty of detecting that phoneme, compared with detecting the whole word (Foss & Swinney, 1973; McNeill & Lindig, 1973); in vision, on the other hand, knowing where in a string the target letter will appear reverses the usual advantage of the string being a word (Johnson & McClelland, 1974). This latter discrepancy, may perhaps be taken as illustrating the relative ease with which spatially defined portions of a visual stimulus may be attended to compared with temporally defined portions of an auditory stimulus. A more attractive explanation is that these differences arise because of the basically different nature of spoken and written language.

Embedding a phoneme in a syllable, or a syllable in a word, is very different from embedding a letter or string of letters in a typewritten word. The whole physical representation of the phonemic element can be completely restructured in a way that prevents the subject from being able to attend to it or detect it without also taking account of the context in which it occurs.

To appreciate the implications of this restructuring for perception, let us follow the changes that take place in semantic elements as they are described linguistically at different levels. The choice of linguistic systems is to some extent arbitrary, and we will dip both into contemporary generative phonology and into acoustic and articulatory phonetics.

II. THE STRUCTURE OF SPEECH

There is growing psychological evidence that the morpheme is a significant unit in word recognition. It is more powerful than the word at explaining frequency effects in perception (Morton, 1968) and seems to be able to explain effects of word length on perception that have previously been attributed to number of syllables (Coltheart & Freeman, personal communication). This evidence is primarily from studies of the written word, but it is probable that similar effects could also be obtained for speech, particularly as in generative phonology the systematic phonemic level bears a striking similarity to the written word. The systematic phonemic level represents the linguistic message as an ordered sequence of elements that preserve morphemic invariance but can be mapped, using the particular rules of a language or dialect, into a phonetic representation; from such a representation, using for example a speech synthesis-by-rule program, an intelligible utterance could be derived. At the systematic phonemic level the words *courage* and *courageous* can be represented as /koræge/ and /koræge+as/, forms that bear an interesting resemblance to the spelled word (Chomsky, 1970; Chomsky & Halle, 1968; Gough, 1972). Quite specific to speech, though, is the restructuring that takes place between this systematic phonemic level and the phonetic level to give strings such as [kʌrəj] and [kərêyjəs] (Chomsky & Halle, 1968, p. 235), forms from which an articulatory specification and thence an acoustic signal could be derived. This variation between the systematic phonemic level and the phonetic is one that, though not generally accessible to the naive listener, is nonetheless readily distinguished by a phonetician. In the example cited above, the change in the second vowel is not difficult to apprehend, but more subtle changes are covered by the same level of rules (such as the change in aspiration of the /p/ in *pit* and *spit*), which are difficult to perceive as such except by the trained ear. This variation has been termed *extrinsic* allophonic variation (Ladefoged, 1966; Wang & Fillmore, 1961), as distinct from *intrinsic*, which is not accessible even to the trained ear of the phonetician. To appreciate the problems raised by intrinsic allophonic variation we need to consider in outline the mechanisms by which speech is produced.

In normal (rather than whispered) speech, the main source of sound is the vibration of the vocal cords. These are set into vibration by airflow from the lungs, the frequency of the vibration being determined jointly by the stiffness of the cords and the pressure drop across them (see Mac-Neilage & Ladefoged, this volume). The waveform of the sound at this stage is roughly an asymmetrical triangle whose spectrum, for a continuously held pitch, is a series of harmonics of the fundamental that decrease in amplitude with increasing frequency. The effect of the cavities of the mouth (and of those of the nose when they are coupled in, as during nasal consonants and nasalized vowels) is to change this spectrum, so that well-defined, broad peaks occur in it that correspond to the resonant frequencies of the system of cavities. These broad peaks are *formants,* and their frequencies and amplitudes vary in a well-understood way (Fant, 1960) with the changing shape of the vocal tract, as the various articulators move to give formant transitions. The value of the formants is independent of the pitch of the voice, although the accuracy with which a formant peak can be estimated from the harmonic structure depends on the particular pitch present. For unvoiced consonants, such as /p, f/, or in whispered speech, the vocal cords do not vibrate, instead, the sound source is noise from turbulent air either at the glottis (for /h/ aspiration and whisper) or at some other point of constriction. Peaks corresponding to the vocal tract resonant frequencies still exist, but the spectrum will be continuous, rather than composed of harmonic lines. The peaks found in the noise spectrum will reflect mainly the resonances of cavities in front of the point of constriction at which the noise is generated.

The acoustic speech signal reflects only indirectly the movements of the individual articulators of the vocal tract. These articulators can move with a large degree of independence: The lips move independently of the tongue, different parts of the tongue have some independence (Öhman, 1967), and whether the vocal cords vibrate or not depends but little on the movements of the supralaryngeal tract, provided the airflow is not blocked. This ability of independent movement of the articulators would present little problem if speech consisted of a sequence of rigidly defined vocal tract positions, with every distinctive linguistic unit having a concomitant vocal tract configuration. Unfortunately this is not the case. Only in the production of continuously held vowels does the vocal tract come close to this ideal, in that a change in the position of any articulator will modify the quality of the vowel. For consonants, though, the situation is much more complicated. They are produced by constricting the vocal tract at a particular place—the place of articulation—and in a particular manner. The constriction formed by different manners of articulation can be complete (as for the stops /b,d,g,p,t,k/), complete for the oral cavities but with the soft palate lowered to allow airflow through the nose (as for the nasals (/m,n,ŋ/), incomplete but sufficiently close to give turbulent noise (as in the fricatives /f,s,ʃ,v,z,ʒ/), with complete closure in the midline but with space for airflow at the sides (as with the lateral /l/), or so incomplete as to approximate extreme vowel positions (as in the semivowels (/w,j/). Definition of the place and manner of the articulation is sufficient together with voicing, to define the consonant; provided this articulation is accomplished, the articulatory mechanisms not involved with this gesture are free to get on with whatever the forthcoming phonemes require. It is this property of coarticulation that is one source of the intrinsic variation between the signal and the phoneme. A well-known extreme example is the syllable /stru/, in which the lips are free to round in anticipation of the vowel *three* phonemes later, irrespective of word boundaries (Daniloff & Moll, 1968). Similar and perceptually significant coarticulations occur with nasality (Moll & Daniloff, 1971; Ali, Gallagher, Goldstein, & Daniloff, 1971), which are also unconstrained by word boundaries (Dixit & Mac-Neilage, 1972).

A related source of variation is the fact that for most of the time the vocal tract is moving from one target position to another; thus, information about which targets are being approached or left is carried by transitional information, which, of its very nature, depends both on the immediately adjoining and on the more distant targets. For example, the formant transitions produced by the rapid movement away from a point of constriction into a subsequent vowel can be a sufficient cue to the location of that point of constriction (Cooper, Delattre, Liberman, Borst, & Gerstman, 1952).

A further complication comes from the articulation of vowels in normal fast speech being considerably less differentiated than in the citation of individual words (Shearme & Holmes, 1962). In addition, in rapid speech, the target articulation position for a vowel may not be reached before the tongue must move back toward the target position for the next phoneme. This articulatory undershoot necessarily implies a corresponding acoustic undershoot, so that instead of reaching and holding a target position the formants go through maxima and minima short of their target (Lindblom, 1963).

These examples illustrate some of the production mechanisms responsible for "intrinsic" allophonic variation. But they do not exhaust the sources of variation, for, as Studdert-Kennedy (1974) points out, between-speaker but within-dialect variation is not covered by either of the categories intrinsic or extrinsic. The problem here is that different speakers have different-sized heads, so that the formants produced when a child articulates a particular vowel are higher in frequency than those produced by an adult. Even within normal adults there is a variation of about 20% (Peterson & Barney, 1952). Moreover, this is not a simple scaling problem. The values of the individual formants for different vowels change by different proportions for male and female speakers in a way that suggests that men have proportionately larger pharynxes than women (Fant, 1966).

III. CUES TO PHONEMIC CATEGORIES

There is abundant evidence that articulatory mechanisms structure the acoustic signal in such a way that, in general, there is no simple relationship between a phonetic category and those sounds that are sufficient to cue it. Work on the perception of synthetic speech has made this point elegantly, enabling us to understand the relationship between phonetic categories and their cues sufficiently well to produce intelligible speech automatically from a phonetic symbol input (Holmes, Mattingly, & Shearme, 1964; Kuhn, 1973; Lieberman, Ingemann, Lisker, Delattre, & Cooper, 1959). What is perhaps less well understood is the degree to which the cues that have been shown to be important in synthetic speech are also important in natural speech. Subjects can be variable in the way that they react to synthetic speech, and yet natural speech retains its intelligibility under a wide range of distortions. It is possible that this discrepancy is due to the fact that natural speech contains a wider variety of cues than has been investigated systematically with synthetic speech and also to the fact that different listeners use the particular cues used in the synthesis to differing extents. But another factor is undoubtedly that we do not yet understand sufficiently the changes in the cues to segments that occur with context. While this has been emphasized for such effects as that of the neighboring vowels on a consonant (Delattre, Liberman, & Cooper, 1955; Öhman, 1966), other interactions, such as cues to consonants in clusters, changes that occur with word boundaries, and changes that occur with differing stress patterns and speaking rates have until quite recently received very little attention in perceptual experiments.

A. Vowels

Although vowels produced in isolated syllables can be adequately distinguished by the steady-state values of their first two or three formants,

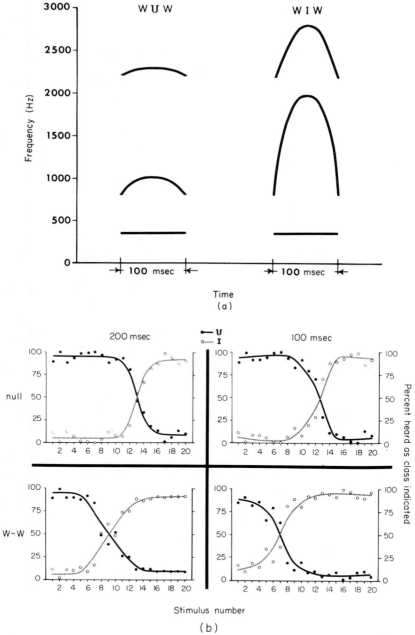

FIG. 1. Part (a) shows stylized spectrograms of synthetic syllables differing in the maximum values attained by the second and third formants. Part (b) shows how subjects heard vowels distributed along a continuum between these maxima. The

it is unlikely that vowel perception in running speech can be dealt with in such a simple way. Normal continuous speech introduces at least two complications, speaker change and rapid articulation. Using synthetic two-formant patterns, Ladefoged and Broadbent (1957) showed that varying the range of frequencies used in a precursor sentence influenced the vowel quality attributed to a fixed-formant pattern at the end of the sentence. Similar effects have been found for consonants (Fourcin, 1968). A particular formant pattern is thus perceived relative to some frame that is characteristic of the particular speaker. Information about this frame can be provided either by a precursor sentence or, it seems, by the syllable that contains the test vowel itself. Shankweiler, Strange, and Verbrugge (in press) have shown that a potpourri of vowels produced by many different speakers is more intelligible if the vowels are flanked by consonants than if they are spoken in isolation without the consonants. The dynamic information from the consonant transitions may more effectively limit the possible tract configurations that could have produced the syllable than could a steady state, or it may simply allow the formants to be detected more accurately.

Embedding a vowel between consonants can, at rapid rates of articulation, prevent the articulators—and hence the formant pattern—from reaching the target values (Lindblom, 1963). Nevertheless, the perceptual system appears able to compensate for this, so that a vowel is perceived whose steady-state formant values would have been more extreme than those actually reached in the syllable (Lindblom & Studdert-Kennedy, 1967). This is illustrated in Fig. 1.

B. Stops

Stop consonants in intervocalic position are characterized by an abrupt and complete closure (or stopping) of the vocal tract at some point of articulation, followed by an abrupt release of this closure. With voiceless stops, the vocal folds cease vibrating at closure and do not start again until some time after release. The period of closure is thus silent. For the voiced stops, though, the vocal chords continue to vibrate throughout the period of closure (provided it is not too long), producing a low-amplitude, low-

---

null condition vowels lack transitions: They have steady-state formants at the maximum values attained by the "w–w" patterns. As may be seen from the leftward shift of the /ʊ–I/ boundary in the "w–w" as opposed to the null condition, subjects display "perceptual overshoot": They identify patterns from the middle of the "w–w" series in the same way as steady-state patterns having formant values *beyond* their maxima. This "overshoot" is greater for fast (100 msec) than for slow (200 msec) patterns (Studdert-Kennedy & Cooper, 1966).

frequency sound. The abrupt changes in amplitude at closure and release are cues to the presence of a stop consonant; *slit* will change to *split* if a brief period of silence is introduced between the friction and the vowel (Bastian, Eimas, & Liberman, 1961). Other distinctive acoustic events that mark the presence of a stop consonant are the burst of energy at release and, for voiced stops, the rapid rise in the first formant after release.

When a stop is released, there is a sudden drop in pressure in the mouth cavity and a rapid flow of air through the widening constriction. The initial drop in pressure gives an impulsive excitation to the mouth cavities, which is followed by a brief period of frication from the turbulent airflow through the constriction. As the constriction widens, the airflow becomes smooth, and then the only source of excitation is that from the glottis. For voiced sounds this excitation will be air pulses; for voiceless sounds it will be noise produced by turbulent airflow at the glottis. The spectrum of the emergent sound is predominantly determined by the cavities in front of the source of energy. Formant structure similar to that for voiced sounds appears in the noise originating from the glottis (aspiration), but to a much lesser extent in the noise originating at a supraglottal place of articulation (burst and frication), which reflects predominantly the resonant frequency of the cavity in front of the place of articulation. The formant pattern changes as the articulators move away from the point of articulation into the position appropriate for the next segment.

A voiceless stop can be cued simply by putting a burst of noise at a suitable frequency a short time in front of a vowel. What place of articulation is heard depends on the frequency of the noise and on the vowel that follows. It is possible to make the same burst of noise sound like two different consonants by placing it before different vowels, e.g., /pi/, /ka/, /pu/ (Liberman, Delattre, & Cooper, 1952). Similarly, the significance in the change of the formant pattern depends crucially on what vowel the formants lead to (Delattre *et al.*, 1955). The reason for this dependency is partly that the formants have to lead into the vowel, but it is also because, during closure, the articulators are in a position that anticipates the forthcoming vowel. Because of this coarticulation, the formant pattern at release will vary with the vowel. Kuhn (1975) points out that the formant transition which appears to carry the burden of cueing the place of articulation of the stop is the one which is, for that particular stop-vowel combination, associated with the mouth cavity. The curiosity of the burst of noise at 1400 Hz that cues /pi/, /ka/, and /pu/ is described by Kuhn as follows:

> Before /i/ this burst appears to be interpreted as part of the rise in frequency of the front cavity resonance as it moves up to F_3. Before /a/, the

> burst appears to be interpreted as part of the fall in frequency of the front
> cavity as it moves to a slightly lower value in F_2. Before /u/ it appears to
> be interpreted as part of a flat, lip-release spectrum and was a somewhat
> weaker cue [p. 432].

For intervocalic stops with different vowels on either side (e.g., /idu/),
it has been shown by Öhman (1966) that the formant transitions both
into and out of the stop closure are jointly influenced by both vowels. However, the perceptual significance of this observation is not entirely clear.
Two independent experiments have failed to find any perceptual correlate
of this coarticulation effect. Fant, Liljencrants, Malac, and Borovickova
(1970), using both natural and synthetic speech, could find no general
effect of this coarticulation on intelligibility, while Lehiste and Shockey
(1972) found that listeners could not judge the missing vowel when played
the VC part of natural VCV utterances, even though these researchers
claim that coarticulation effects similar to those observed by Öhman could
be seen in spectrograms of their stimuli. These two experiments are particularly interesting, since they are a rare example of perception seemingly
not being sensitive to articulatory constraints.

1. INVARIANT CUES FOR STOPS?

The issue has been revived recently by Cole and Scott (1974a,b) as
to whether or not in natural speech there exist invariant cues or combinations of cues that uniquely specify particular consonants, independent of
the succeeding vowel. The claim made by Cole and Scott (1974b) is that
"place of articulation [for stops] is signaled by a set of cues which form
invariant patterns for /b/, /d/, /p/, /t/, /k/ in initial position before
a vowel in a stressed syllable . . . [p. 359]."

This claim is clearly at odds with the results from synthetic speech, which
show that neither the burst (Liberman *et al.,* 1952) nor the formant transitions (Delattre *et al.*, 1955) of adequate synthetic syllables are invariant
with vowel context. One resolution of this difference is to presume that
the synthetic speech studies have missed some important cue, or combination of cues, that is responsible for invariant perception in natural speech.
A closer inspection of the data on which Cole and Scott's conclusion is
based, however, suggests that there is no real discrepancy. Their conclusion
is made possible only by their being selective in the results they consider,
by a loose interpretation of "invariant," and an ambiguous use of the term
"burst."

Briefly, the evidence is this: If the *burst* (excluding the aspiration) from
a natural voiceless stop produced in syllable-initial position before one
vowel is spliced onto a different aspirated vowel—one that starts with a

brief period of aspiration without formant transitions (as formed in producing /h/)—then a stop is heard whose place of articulation will vary with the choice of vowels in a way that is consistent with the results from synthetic speech (Liberman *et al.,* 1952; Schatz, 1954). In particular, the same burst will be heard as /p/ before /i/ and /u/, but as /k/ before /a/. If, instead of just the burst, a longer portion of the sound from a voiceless consonant is removed and translated onto a different steady-state vowel, then again subjects' percepts do not change if the set of vowels interchanged is /i/ and /u/, but they are also relatively little affected if the vowel /a/ is included in the set (Cole & Scott, 1974a). The discrepancy here is readily explicable if we examine what information is being translated from one vowel context to another. In Cole and Scott's experiment, the duration of sounds translated were /b/, 20 msec; /d/, 30 msec; /g/, 40 msec; /p/, 50 msec; /t/, 80 msec; and /k/, 100 msec. With the possible exception of /b/ and /d/, these durations are sufficient to give considerable information about the following vowel by virtue of formant transitions within the aspiration. Indeed an experiment cited by Cole and Scott in support of their claim demonstrates this point. Winitz, Scheib, and Reeds (1972) removed all but the burst and aspiration from natural tokens of /p/, /t/, and /k/ spoken before the vowels /i/, /a/, and /u/, and played the resulting sounds to subjects for identification, either in isolation or followed by a 100-msec steady state of the *same* vowel before which they had been spoken. The mean durations of the translated segments were 70, 77, and 93 msec for /p/, /t/, and /k/, respectively. Subjects were asked to identify in both these types of sound either the consonant or the vowel. The results showed that for the sounds consisting only of the burst and aspiration the correct consonant was identified 65% of the time, and the correct *vowel* 64% of the time. Adding the steady-state vowel raised the scores to 71% and 86%, respectively. In these data, the consonant appears to be no more identifiable than the vowel. Cole and Scott's procedure is sufficiently close to that of Winitz and his colleagues to let us presume that similar results would have been obtained with Cole and Scott's sounds, had they asked their subjects to identify the vowel in the isolated sounds. Although Cole and Scott claim that only the burst was translated, the durations used in their sounds clearly allow for the acknowledged possibility that their sounds contained formant transitions. However, they claim (*pace* Winitz, Scheib, and Reeds) that these transitions should not have aided perception, citing the claim by Liberman, Cooper, Shankweiler, and Studdert-Kennedy (1967, p. 436) that formant transitions are not commutable between vowels. In fact, the claim made by Liberman is that in formant transition patterns there is no commutable *stop-consonant segment,* since a slice from the beginning of a formant pattern of a complete syllable will either be heard as a nonspeech sound or as a stop consonant *followed by some vowel*. This does not of course imply that following formant transitions by an inappropriate steady-state vowel prohibits the perceptual system from using the transition information to interpret the previous burst, just as it does when there is no additional vowel spliced on. Indeed, for some of the stimuli used by Cole and Scott (1974a), it is likely that listeners heard *two* vowels.

The apparent discrepancy between Cole and Scott's experiment on the one hand and those of Schatz and the Haskins group on the other is thus attributable to the longer stimuli, excised by Cole and Scott, carrying information about the following vowel. Since these stimuli probably contained sufficient information for the following vowel to be identified, Cole and Scott are no closer to demonstrating perceptual invariance of stop consonants with vowel context than if they had removed none of the vowel.

C. Fricatives, Nasals, and Liquids

The perception of fricatives and nasals is less controversial. In both fricatives and nasals, in syllable-initial position, there is a long period of steady state followed by transitions into the following vowel. The nature of the steady state provides the main cue to the manner of articulation of the consonant and also provides some information on the place of articulation. The nasal murmurs produced at different places of articulation are quite similar, since the oral cavity acts only as a side chamber to the nasal cavities from which the sound is radiated. The different nasals *can* be distinguished on the basis of their nasal murmurs alone, but the bulk of the place information is carried by the formant transitions (Liberman, Cooper, Delattre, & Gerstman, 1954; Malecot, 1956).

In contrast to nasals, fricative spectra (with the exception of /f/ and /θ/ and their voiced cognates /v/ and /ð/) are markedly dissimilar (Strevens, 1960) and carry the bulk of the perceptual load for place of articulation. Harris (1958) segmented naturally spoken fricative-vowel syllables into a fricative portion and a transition + vowel portion, which were then commuted. She found that, except for the /f–θ/ and /v–ð/ distinctions, the place of articulation was perceived according to the fricative spectrum, rather than according to the formant transitions.

Steady-state friction is the nearest that speech comes to a one-to-one mapping between sound and phonetic category. Yet even here there is variation with speaker and context, which, though not sufficient to cause confusion between the fricative categories, can serve to distinguish speaker sex (Schwartz, 1968) and, through weak formant transitions within the noise, to cue place of articulation of subsequent stops (Schwartz, 1967).

The liquids /r/ and /l/ are characterized by having a brief (or in some contexts nonexistent) steady state with a low first formant, followed by a rather slow transition into the following vowel. The speed of the transition, together with changes in the second and third formants, cues the presence of the liquid segment, but /r/ seems to be distinguished from /l/ primarily by changes in the third formant (Lisker, 1957b; O'Connor, Gerstman, Liberman, Delattre, & Cooper, 1957).

D. Voicing

The dimension of voicing has received intensive study recently, and it provides perhaps the best example of the intimate relationship between the articulatory–acoustic constraints that shape the stimulus and the mechanisms used to perceive the phonemic category. In final consonants, voicing can be cued by the duration of the preceding vowel (Denes, 1955; Raphael, 1972), and in poststressed intervocalic stops by the duration of the stop closure (Lisker, 1957a); however, the perception of stops in prestressed utterance-initial position has received the most attention.

Lisker and Abramson (1964) exploited the concept of voice onset time (VOT) to describe the differences in speech production between the various categories of voicing in stop consonants. This dimension classifies a particular stop utterance according to the time difference between the vocal chords starting to vibrate and the stop closure being released. For English voice stops [b,d,g] in utterance-initial position, this time is usually either around zero or positive (the vocal folds start to vibrate slightly before the stop is released), while for the English voiceless aspirated stops [p^h, t^h, k^h] (as in *pot, tot, cot*) there is a lag of between 20 and 100 msec from the release of the stop to the onset of voicing. The value of this dimension is twofold. First, it adequately describes the categorization of differently voiced stops from many languages. Different stops from similar contexts fall in well-separated clusters along the VOT continuum; these clusters are nonoverlapping for stops at the beginning of isolated words and show only slight overlap for words spoken in sentences (Lisker & Abramson, 1967b). Second, it explains the changes in the acoustic cues that accompany different stop-consonant voicings. A voiceless stop will normally have a more intense burst, a longer period of aspiration, and a weaker first formant during the aspiration than does the voiced homologue. All these changes can be adequately explained by the effect of changing the time for which the vocal folds are held apart, inhibiting voicing. Abduction of the vocal folds allows a greater pressure to build up within the oral cavity, leading to a stronger burst on release. In addition, it provides noise excitation which is weaker in low-frequency energy than is voicing, and it acoustically couples the trachea to the oral cavities; these last two factors are responsible for reducing the intensity of the first formant. Spectrograms of real speech illustrating three different values of VOT are shown in Fig. 2.

Perceptually, this complex of cues resulting from a single articulatory dimension raises the question of which cues are used and how they are combined. Lisker and Abramson (1967a) have shown that synthetic syllables that differ in some of the concomitant acoustic cues of voice onset time are perceived as differing in voicing. The syllables that they used varied both the time of onset of voiced excitation and the intensity of the first-formant transition. It can be shown that both these acoustic correlates of voice onset time are perceptually important. It was clear from the early synthetic studies of voicing that to produce a good token of /p, t, k/ there had to be present both aspiration during the initial period of formant transitions and a reduction (or cutback) in the amplitude of the first-formant transition (Liberman, Delattre, & Cooper, 1958). The importance of the first-formant transition has reappeared in recent work by Stevens and Klatt (1974) and by Summerfield and Haggard (1974). At a given VOT, perceived voicing can be influenced by a first-formant transition after the onset of voicing or by the amount of energy in the aspirated portion of the first formant. Interesting questions are raised by the known variation in VOT with such contextual factors as rate of articulation (Summerfield, 1974; Lisker & Abramson, 1967b) and the nature of the following segment (Lisker, 1961; Klatt, 1973). Although the use of the first-formant transition as a cue may allow the increase in VOT brought about by the presence of a lateral after the stop to be compensated for directly (Darwin & Brady, 1975), it is also likely that other context effects demand a change in the weightings attached to the various cues (Summerfield & Haggard, 1974).

E. Syllable Boundaries

A phonemic representation of speech needs to include some way of representing the perceptible difference between such phrases as *I scream* and *ice cream*. This is done in both traditional and generative phonology by introducing a juncture marker (#) (/aɪ#skrim/ versus /aɪs#krim/). The phonetic changes that accompany a change in juncture have been studied by Lehiste (1960) and by Gårding (1967), who show that some changes in juncture are perceptually easy to distinguish; but they do not show directly which cues are actually used. One of the most obvious allophonic changes that occur with a change in juncture is that of the aspiration of voiceless stop consonants. When Helen enters in Act IV, Scene 5, of *Troilus and Cressida,* she is greeted by a fanfare and the shout "The

Troyans' trumpet!" The aspiration of the word-initial /t/ and the voicing of the word-final /s/ are the phonetic cues that potentially protect her from insult. Using politically less sensitive material, Christie (1974) has shown that the aspiration of voiceless stops *is* used as a cue to juncture, since adding aspiration to a /t/ in the context /asta/ increases by about 30% listeners' judgments that the word boundary occurs after, rather than before, the /s/. Malmberg (1955) has also shown that the presence of formant transitions either before or after closure can influence whether

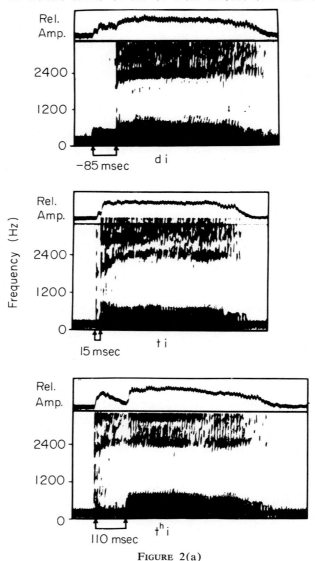

FIGURE 2(a)

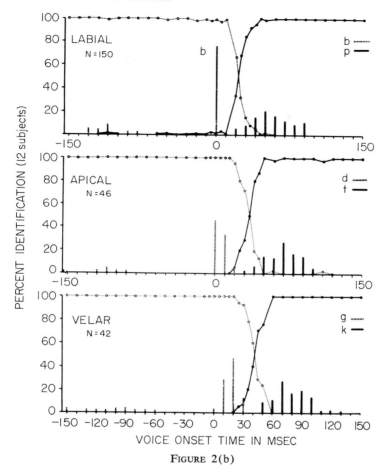

FIGURE 2(b)

FIG. 2. Part (a) illustrates three conditions of voice onset time found in Thai stops. The upper spectrogram is of a stop for which the vocal folds start to vibrate 85 msec before the stop is released. In the lower two spectrograms voicing starts 15 msec and 110 msec, respectively, after stop release. Part (b) shows a correspondence between production and perceptual data for English subjects. The bars show the distribution of voice onset times for the two categories of English stops in prestressed word-initial position for the three different places of articulation. There is very little overlap between voiced and voiceless stops for each place of articulation, although the boundary between the two categories changes with place. The superimposed identification functions are for a synthetic voice onset time continuum. The perceptual boundary corresponds well with the production boundary (Lisker & Abramson, 1964, 1967a).

a consonant is heard as coming after the first vowel or before the second vowel in a disyllable such as /ipi/. Malmberg's results have been amplified by Darwin and Brady (1975). They examined the cues underlying the distinction between *I made rye* and *I may dry,* and found that, provided the stop closure is quite short, appreciable formant transitions can occur after closure without shifting the juncture to before the /d/. The perceptual system here takes into account coarticulation effects across word boundaries that are also stop closures.

IV. AUDITORY GROUPING AND FEATURE EXTRACTION

How do we group together sounds which are to be analyzed as from a single source? The extensive literature on auditory selective attention has identified a number of variables that contribute to our remarkable ability to listen to one voice among many. The best known are pitch and location.

A. Pitch

Fletcher (1929, p. 196) was the first to show that the ears will fuse together sounds from different parts of the spectrum when they originate from a common source. Broadbent and Ladefoged (1957) amplified Fletcher's finding and showed that fusion will occur when the sounds at the two ears have the same pitch; if, on the other hand, the two ears receive signals that are amplitude modulated at different rates, then two sources will be heard, one at each ear (Broadbent & Ladefoged, 1957). The importance of this phenomenon in speech is clearly that this effect provides a mechanism whereby the different formants from a particular speaker can be grouped together as a separate perceptual channel from those belonging to other speakers, who will in general be speaking at a different pitch (Broadbent & Ladefoged, 1957). The breakdown of this mechanism can be noticed both in the concert hall, when two different instruments play at the same pitch and the resultant timbre sounds like neither (Broadbent & Ladefoged, 1957), and, more esoterically, when, in dichotic listening experiments, two different synthetic speech sounds with the same pitch are led one to each ear. Here the impression is of a single sound, but curiously subjects tend to report the sound at the right ear more accurately, indicating that the autonomy of the two sounds is to some extent preserved (Darwin, 1969; Shankweiler & Studdert-Kennedy, 1967). A demonstration of this autonomy-preserving fusion comes from Rand (1974) who played to one ear of his subjects a stop-vowel syllable from which the second-formant transition had been removed. This transition, which provided the only cue to place of articulation /b/, /d/ or /g/) was led to the opposite ear, but on the same pitch and in the correct temporal relation to the main stimulus. He found that subjects could distinguish the place of articulation of the consonant *and* hear an additional nonspeech noise in the ear receiving the transition.

Grouping by a common pitch may be a special case of a more general phenomenon of grouping together sounds by time of onset (with each laryngeal pulse marking a new event), since the normal fusion of two sounds with a common pitch can be overridden if the two components start at different times. For example, if we first listen to formant 1 of a vowel and then add formant 2, both formants can be heard in the resultant timbre. This is not true of the vowel that can be heard by starting both formants simultaneously (Liberman, personal communication). The concert hall again furnishes an illustration. Turning on a radio in the middle of a sustained orchestral chord yields a timbre that is not decomposable into its component parts but that separates out as soon as the instruments change notes.

Pitch plays a further role in auditory grouping at a more complex level. Bregman and Campbell (1971) have shown, although the principle was well known to baroque composers, that when a sequence of six notes of which three are high in pitch and three low is played rapidly, the impression is of two separate tunes, one high and one low. This impression only occurs for fast presentation rates (the crucial rate depends on the pitch intervals employed) and is objectively confirmed by subjects being unable to judge *between* tunes as to which note preceded which, although this ability is good *within* tunes for notes the same time apart. This effect might derive from a speech perception mechanism, enabling a listener to remain listening to a particular voice over periods of silence or pitchlessness in competition with other voices at different pitches. A recent unpublished experiment by myself and Davina Simmonds supports this idea. Simmonds asked her subjects to shadow a passage of prose presented to one ear with instructions to ignore what was presented to the other ear. Unknown to the subject at some time during the passage, the one they were supposed to be shadowing might change to the opposite ear giving a semantic discontinuity on the shadowed ear. Treisman (1960) had previously shown that in this situation subjects occasionally made errors in which they continued to shadow the same passage after it had switched to the "wrong" ear. Simmonds's contribution was to show that whether these errors occurred or not depended on whether the intonation pattern switched between the ears. If the passages were prepared by being read continuously so that intonation was continuous across the semantic break, few intrusion errors occurred from the opposite ear, although subjects tended to hesitate. The intrusions did occur, though, when the intonation switched ears. Moreover, intrusions still happened even when there was no semantic break. Continuity of intonation thus seems to be an important factor in determining which part of the auditory input is to be treated as belonging to the currently attended channel. It remains to be seen how much this is due to such short-term effects as those found by Bregman and Campbell and how much it is due to predictions of the expected prosodic pattern based on more complex aspects of the preceding input.

This extensive use of pitch in grouping auditory elements together suggests that it might be extracted by a different mechanism from that which is concerned with extracting information about the formant structure or timbre. This seems to be the case. Many speech signals have little or no energy at the fundamental (corresponding to the rate of vocal cord vibration), and yet the pitch is clearly heard. This problem, the missing fundamental, has indicated the need for a pitch mechanism other than the detection of place of excitation on the basilar membrane. Licklider (1951) first suggested autocorrelation as a possible mechanism for extracting this "periodicity pitch" and his idea has recently been revived by Wightman (1973), who claims that autocorrelation can handle a number of strange effects previously rather hard to explain (see Small, 1971). Autocorrelation involves quite simply a comparison (correlation) of the signal with copies of itself delayed by varying amounts. The correlation will be a maximum when one signal is delayed relative to the other by an amount equal to the periodicity of the waveform. Thinking of autocorrelation in this way leads to a realization of a possible mechanism in terms of a neural delay line (Licklider, 1951); but another mechanism, which is mathematically equivalent, is based on the observation that periodic signals have spectra with periodic peaks, the spacing between the peaks being related to the periodicity. Thus, a device for recognizing regular patterns of excitation along the basilar membrane, rather after the manner of spatial fourier analyzers in the visual system (Campbell & Robson, 1968), could also achieve autocorrelation. This latter type of mechanism is favored by Wilson (1973) and seems to have the advantage of achieving a first stage toward the required grouping of the individual components, prior to analysis of the formant structure. Autocorrelation has also been used as the basis for automatic pitch extraction devices that are less prone to errors (such as jumping up an octave) than traditional pitch meters, which operate on a principle closer to "place" theories (e.g., Lukatela, 1973).

B. Location

It has been known for some time that angular separation of auditory sources helps selective attention to one rather than the other (Broadbent, 1958), provided that other cues such as pitch do not override the usefulness of location. It appears also that localization is important in determining the effect that one sound can exert on another that precedes it. If a consonant–vowel syllable is played to one ear, followed (say 60 msec later) by another syllable, differing in the consonant, to the other ear, then the second consonant will be reported more accurately than the first (Studdert-Kennedy, Shankweiler, & Schulman, 1971). The question now arises, if one sound masks its predecessor, how do we ever perceive a continuous flow of speech? And, since the effect also occurs in nonspeech tasks (Darwin, 1971b), how do we perceive *any* rapidly changing sound? The answer perhaps lies in the observation that these masking effects are less easily obtained when the two sounds come from the *same* location (Porter, 1971); any masking that does occur then tends to be more symmetrical, with less predominance of backward over forward. Perhaps then, the auditory system is using location as a heuristic to decide whether two sounds are to be treated as part of the same gestalt or whether they should be distinguished and the processing of the first discarded in favor of the second.

So far there has been no indication that any of the mechanisms outlined exist exclusively for speech, even though one might argue that they have arisen because of the needs of speech perception. This is not altogether surprising, but this distinction becomes more important when considering subsequent stages of analysis.

C. Adaptation

The discovery of single cortical cells selectively sensitive to simple properties of a visual (Hubel & Wiesel, 1962) or an auditory (Evans & Whitfield, 1964) stimulus lent physiological credence to theories of pattern recognition which suggested that the organism first detects basic stimulus properties of a perceptual object and subsequently uses this information as a basis on which to construct a percept (Selfridge & Neisser, 1960). It also renewed interest in perceptual aftereffects, since some of these perceptual distortions could be neatly explained by appealing to the adaptation of detector units similar to those discovered electrophysiologically. The basic methodological axiom here is that repeated exposure to a particular stimulus weakens the subsequent response of detectors that have responded to that stimulus. This weakening then causes a distortion in the subsequent perception of any stimulus that would normally be capable of exciting those detectors. The degree to which the perception of different test stimuli is affected by previous exposure to some other stimulus thus gives an indication of what types of properties are being detected by the sensory system (e.g., Blakemore & Campbell, 1969).

This approach has been applied recently to auditory perception. Kay and Matthews (1972) have found, in adaptation experiments, evidence for detectors sensitive to a tone that is frequency modulated at a particular rate, thus providing one auditory analogue to the suggestion by Blakemore and Campbell (1969) that the visual system contains detectors sensitive to luminance that is amplitude modulated at particular spatial frequencies. Experiments on adaptation to speech sounds have multiplied rapidly since a seminal experiment by Eimas and Corbit (1973).

This study used stop consonants differing in voicing and with one of two different places of articulation. For each place of articulation they constructed a continuum of sounds varying in VOT. Their subjects first identified isolated sounds from these two continua, then they adapted to a token of /b/, /p/, /d/, or /t/ taken from the appropriate end of the VOT continuum by listening to it 150 times in 2 minutes. Their perception of the two VOT continua was then retested in a series of trials, each of which involved listening to a further 75 presentations of the adapting stimulus (in 1 minute) followed immediately by a test stimulus. The results showed that, irrespective of the place of articulation of the test and adapting stimuli, the voicing boundary moved toward the adapting stimulus, a slightly greater shift being found for voiceless than for voiced adapters. In a subsequent paper, Eimas, Cooper, and Corbit (1973) showed that this shift in the voicing boundary persists if the adapting and test stimuli are led to different ears. The effect, then, is central, rather than peripheral, but what type of detector is responsible? Is it a linguistic feature detector specific to speech, or is it an acoustic feature detector that can also subserve nonspeech distinctions? Eimas and his colleagues tackled this question by using as an adapting stimulus a voiced stop-vowel syllable with all but the initial 50 msec removed. This stimulus preserves the information that voicing starts at the beginning of the sound but does not sound like speech—"just a noise" in the words of the subjects. As predicted by the linguistic feature detector notion, adaptation to this sound gave no significant shift in the voicing boundary, even when the subjects were instructed to hear the sound as speech. However, Cooper (1975), in a review of the adaptation work, cites an unpublished study of Ades who does find some adaptation in this case.

The question of whether the adaptation effects obtained were due to the adaptation of a complete linguistic feature or to adaptation of the particular cues that can subserve it has been pursued by Bailey (1973). He used a linguistic dimension with well-understood multiple cues. Place of articulation for voiced stop-consonants can be cued by the second- and third-formant transitions. Bailey first showed that the adaptation effect could not be occurring at the level of a detector responding to place of articulation per se, since, when subjects adapted to the syllable /be/, they showed more shift along the /be/–/de/ continuum than along the /ba/–/da/ continuum. They did show some shift in the latter case, and Bailey's second experiment suggested why. Here, rather than changing the subsequent vowel, the particular formant transition used to cue the place distinction was changed. One set of stimuli used formants 1, 2, and 4 (F_4 had no transition), with the place distinction being cued only by changes in the second formant. The other set of stimuli used all four formants but with a neutral F_2 transition, so that the place distinction was being cued by changes in the third formant. Adaptation had a significant effect on the phoneme boundary when both adapter and test were from the same set. However, when they came from different sets there was only an effect when the adapting stimuli differed in a formant that was present in the test stimulus. When the adapting stimulus varied in F_3 but the test stimulus had no F_3, then no adaptation effect was observed. Here there could be no processing of F_3 transitions to reveal the underlying distortion of such processing by the adapting sequence. In a subsequent experiment Bailey showed that some effect of adaptation returned if the test stimulus was given a flat third formant.

These results give clear evidence that adaptation can occur at the level of detectors for specific acoustic features that precede the subsequent pooling of these features for a decision about the linguistic dimension. This conclusion has been confirmed by a number of recent studies. The boundary for place of articulation for stop consonants can be shifted by presentation of the isolated second- and third-formant transitions (Ades, 1973; Tartter, 1975) or by the second- and third-formant transitions accompanied by an inappropriate, nonspeech-like first-formant transition (Tartter, 1975). Provided, then, that the adapting stimulus contains cues that distinguish the items on the test continuum, the adapting stimuli themselves need not be heard as speech sounds.

Adaptation of specific acoustic cues can also explain why adaptation fails to generalize between initial and final consonants. Adapting to /bæ/ will shift the /bæ–dæ/ boundary but will have no effect on the /æb–æd/ boundary, and vice versa (Ades, 1974a). The reason for this is that, for the synthetic speech sounds used in this experiment, the formant transitions that cued the initial stop consonant were mirror images of those that cued the final stops, so presumably they were served by different auditory detectors. This explanation has been strengthened by an experiment by Tash (1974). Tash placed the formant transitions appropriate for initial stops at the end of a steady vowel-like sound whose formant values were the same as the *start* of the transitions. This gave nonspeech sounds with the transitions in final position. These sounds *were* effective at shifting the boundary for initial stops. Thus, provided the direction of the transitions is preserved, adaptation can occur between initial and final positions.

Adaptation at the auditory feature level, though undoubtedly present, is not the whole story. Stop consonants, differing only in place of articulation, can be synthesized to have identical first-formant transitions so that they are distinguished only by the second- and third-formant transitions. If adaptation were occurring only at the auditory feature level, we might expect that the presence of the (constant) first-formant transition would be irrelevant to the adaptation effect of place of articulation, since it does not carry any distinguishing information. However, it is clear that, although the isolated second and third formants do shift the place of the articulation boundary, this effect is much less than if the first formant is included (Ades, 1973; Tartter, 1975).

To explain this dependency we need to consider levels above the auditory feature. Let us assume that a number of auditory feature detectors map in a hierarchical way onto some higher-level unit. For example, three rising—formant detectors might map onto a detector for labial place of articulation or onto a particular syllable; at least one of these, the rising—formant detector, will presumably also map onto units at this higher level that have different places of articulation.

After adapting to a complete speech sound with all three formants present, all three of the auditory feature detectors will have been fatigued, but after adapting to the sound without the first formant, only the second and third formant detectors will have adapted. There are now two ways to explain the greater boundary shift with the complete stimulus. We can assume that through some nonlinearity in the system the adapted first formant leads to a greater reduction in the firing of the higher-level unit that is already receiving a reduced input from other (adapted) detectors than in the firing of a unit that receives unadapted input. Alternatively, we can assume, following Tartter (1975), that some adaptation is occurring in the higher-level unit itself. Although on the basis of the data presented so far the former hypothesis is perhaps more economical, additional adaptation at a higher level is made more likely by two types of study, split formants and cross modality. In the split-formants experiment, the first formant of a syllable is led to one ear while the other two are led to the opposite ear. If the two sounds are played simultaneously then the entire syllable is heard, but if they are played one after the other then two nonspeech sounds are heard. In an ingenious experiment, Ades (1974b) showed that there was greater adaptation when the sounds were presented simultaneously than when they were played at different times. Playing the components at different times should have no differential effect on the adaptation to the detectors of those components, but it would prevent adaptation to the higher-level category, since that is never heard. The greater adaptation for simultaneous presentation thus argues for adaptation also occurring at some level above the auditory feature level. The second type of evidence comes from cross-modal adaptation. Repeated *visual* presentation of a syllable that the subject reads *silently* gives a shift in the boundary for voicing (Cooper, 1975), which is specific to position within the syllable (Eimas, personal communication) so that a visually presented "bæ" will adapt the auditory [bæ–dæ] boundary but not the [æb–æd] boundary.

What then might be the level of this higher category? We can put forward three candidates, the feature, the phoneme, and the syllable. A number of authors have proposed that adaptation effects can occur at the phonetic feature level (Ades, 1974a; Cooper, 1974; Tartter, 1975), the argument being that there is some generalization for adaptation to place of articulation across vowels (Ades, 1974a; Cooper, 1974; Tartter, 1974) and across manner of articulation (Cooper & Blumstein, 1974). But these arguments are not strong, since this generalization can perhaps be handled by adaptation at the auditory level (see Cooper, 1975 for a discussion of this and related issues). Cooper and Blumstein find significant shifts in the [bæ–dæ] boundary after adaptation to [bæ, mæ, væ] (Fig. 3c) but very little after adaptation to [wæ] (Fig. 3k). Since all these sounds except [wæ] contain similar formant transitions, whereas [wæ] has slower transitions, the observed adaptation effects can be explained in terms of rate-specific formant-transition detectors. Rather more difficult to explain are the cross-vowel adaptation effects, but these can perhaps also be handled at the auditory level. Using synthetic speech adapters, Tartter (1975) has confirmed a finding by Cooper (1974) that adapting to a stop consonant in front of one vowel gives some shift in the boundary for place of articulation of a consonant in front of another vowel. Tartter used three-formant syllables with the third formant common to both vowels. Since third-formant transitions are cues to place of articulation it is not surprising that some cross-adaptation occurred.

Indeed, in Tartter's experiments it is possible to compare directly the extra adaptation effect attributable to the syllables sharing a common phoneme while controlling for common acoustic cues. Tartter finds that the third formant from a [bæ] produces a significant shift in the [bæ–dæ] and the [dæ–gæ] boundaries. This shift is in opposite directions for the two boundaries, since [bæ] and [gæ] both have rising third formants while [dæ] has a falling third formant. However, Tartter also examines the shift in these boundaries after adaptation to [bi] and [gi]. These stimuli are of interest since they both have the same third formant as [ba], but different first and second formants. On purely auditory grounds then we would expect [bi] to have the same effect on a [bæ–dæ] boundary as the [bæ] third

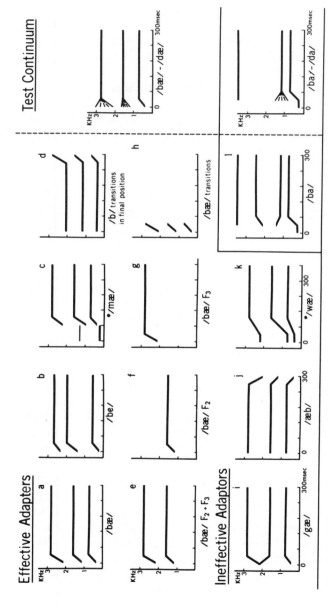

Fig. 3. Adapting with any of the "effective adapters" gives a significant shift in the boundary between /bæ/ and /dæ/ along the test continuum shown in the upper right, so that more sounds are heard as /dæ/ after adaptation than before. This shift is considerably greater for the original /bæ/ than for the others. Adapting with any of the first three "ineffective adapters" (i, j, k) gives no significant shift in the /bæ/–/dæ/ boundary along the same test continuum. In addition, adapting with the last of the "ineffective adapters" (which has an F_2 transition on the /b/–/d/ boundary) gives no shift in the lower test continuum (which has no F_3). The two spectrograms marked with an asterisk (c, k) illustrate experiments that used natural speech adapters. The other spectrograms are schematic illustrations of synthetic speech adapters. The experiments illustrated in this figure are all referred to in the text.

200

formant, while if some adaptation were occurring at the feature or phoneme level, [bi] should have a larger effect on the [bæ–dæ] boundary than the isolated third formant. A similar prediction can be made *mutatis mutandis* for [gi]. In fact, the average adaptation effect when the phoneme is shared is only 20% greater than when auditory factors alone are contributing to the adaptation.

If adaptation is occurring at some level beyond the auditory feature, then it would appear that the most appropriate level, at least for stops cued by formant transitions, is the *syllable*. This would explain why an entire speech sound is a more effective adapter than the acoustic discriminanda alone and also why *cross-modal* adaptation is specific to initial or final position. By assuming that some adaptation occurs at both an auditory and a higher level one is also able to explain why the [bæ–dæ] boundary does not shift after adaptation to [gæ] despite significant shifts being found after adaptation to the third formant, which [bæ] and [gæ] have in common (Cooper, 1974; Tartter, 1975).

There are a number of lines of evidence to suggest that auditory feature detectors are specific to a sound's spatial location. Ades (1974b) found that he could adapt the two ears simultaneously to different sounds using dichotic presentation. Thus, one ear received [bæ] at the same time as the other ear heard [dæ]. The direction of the shift in the [bæ–dæ] boundary was different for the two ears. Ades also showed that, after adapting to a sound presented to one ear alone, there was incomplete (55%) transfer to the opposite ear. Although Ades interpreted these results in terms of peripheral versus central adaptation, it would be equally valid to interpret them in terms of location-specific auditory detectors. Recent support for this notion comes from an experiment on the verbal transformation effect (Warren, 1968). Repeated listening to a word causes it to lose its meaning and change its sound so that it is perceptually transformed into another word. It seems likely that at least part of this effect is due to adaptation at the acoustic level (see Lackner & Goldstein, 1974). Warren and Ackroft (1974) have shown that if the same word is presented to the two ears but slightly offset in time so that two distinct utterances are heard, then different transformations can be heard in the two ears. This suggests again that there are different sets of detectors for different spatial locations.

Such wanton proliferation of auditory detectors might seem unwarranted and unnecessary, but without multiple detectors for identical sounds it is difficult to see how two separate streams of speech could be handled at the same time. That this does appear to be the case is shown by studies of selective attention. If a subject has to shadow a prose passage read to one ear while at the same time trying to make a manual response whenever a target word is played into either ear, he will fail to detect the vast majority of targets on the unattended ear, while successfully responding to those on the shadowed ear (Treisman & Riley, 1969). However, if the subject is conditioned before the experiment by being subjected to an electric shock each time he hears a word belonging to a particular semantic category and subsequently has to respond manually to words belong to that semantic category while shadowing, then, although virtually none of the words on the unattended ear produce a manual response, over a third give a galvanic skin response (Corteen & Wood, 1972). Thus, although the semantic properties of words on an unattended channel rarely reach consciousness, yet it can be shown that their semantic properties have been extracted. Some basic perceptual processing can occur for different speech streams at the same time.

In summary, then, the work on adaptation gives good evidence for detectors tuned to complex auditory patterns, such as particular formant transitions, which may exist in multiple sets, each set being maximally responsive to sounds from a particular location. The adaptation work gives evidence also for units at a more complex level than the auditory feature. While it is not yet clear what level these additional units are at, it is suggested that the available evidence is not incompatible with formant transition information being mapped directly onto a syllabic unit.

As a cautionary footnote to the work on adaptation, it is possible that some of the phoneme boundary shifts found in adaptation experiments might be due to factors other than the adaptation of various detectors. In particular, it is possible that some of the observed effects can better be looked on as criterion shifts brought about by a change in the *range* of stimuli recently presented to the subject. Brady and Darwin (personal communication) have found that, when subjects have to classify stop consonants presented in blocks of 16 trials during which all the stimuli come from a subrange of the voicing continuum, the phoneme boundary moves as a function of the location of the subrange used in that block (Fig. 4) and the subrange used in the preceding block. This is true whether the subjects have heard sounds from the entire range at the beginning of the experiment or not (although the effects are larger when they have not). The direction of the shift is such that sounds near the boundary are heard as being more voiceless when they occur in a range that extends towards the voiced end. It is unlikely that these range effects can themselves be explained by adaptation, since Sawusch, Pisoni, and Cutting (1974) have failed to find a similar shift in the voicing boundary when they varied the probability distribution of the stimuli presented, rather than their range. These authors used two different probability distributions, one in which the most voiced stimulus was four times as likely to occur as any of the other stimuli to be identified and another in which the most voiceless stimu-

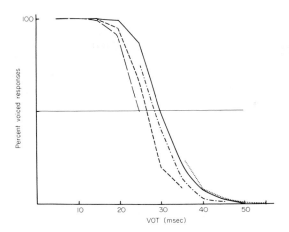

FIG. 4. Identification functions for stops differing in voice onset time, presented to subjects, in blocks of trials confined to a particular range of voice onset times. Each ogival segment extends over the range of sounds used in a particular block, and the solid line shows subjects' responses to stimuli in a block that covered the whole range. With changing range, there is a significant change in the voicing boundary.

lus was the more probable. Their experimental design differs from our range experiment in that it always includes some tokens from each end of the range. Since the number of these tokens is very small, it seems unlikely that they could be causing much of a change in the adaptation state of property detectors, rather we should perhaps conclude that they are sufficient to cause a shift in some criterion setting used to evaluate the phonetic significance of the output of the property detectors.

D. Dichotic Masking

Although less well developed than the work on adaptation, some experiments on dichotic masking are compatible with the idea that the extraction of acoustic features can be interrupted by the subsequent presentation of another sound that shares similar features.

The initial impetus to this work came from the previously mentioned experiment by Studdert-Kennedy et al. (1970), which showed that when two different stop-consonant–vowel syllables were presented one to each ear with a temporal offset between them, the second syllable tended to be reported more accurately than the first, over a range of offsets from 15 to 120 msec. Although initial interpretation of this effect was in terms of the interruption of some special speech processing device, on the grounds that vowel sounds were less prone to this masking (Porter, Shankweiler,

& Liberman, 1969), it now seems likely that the effect arises at the acoustic feature extraction stage after the initial grouping process. The reasons for this are first that the vowel–consonant dichotomy seems irrelevant, since Allen and Haggard (1974) have shown, confirming a prediction by Darwin and Baddeley (1974), that acoustically similar vowels suffer greater backward than forward masking, whereas acoustically different vowels do not. Second, greater backward than forward masking occurs for sounds distinguished by rapid transitions, irrespective of whether these transitions cue a linguistic distinction or not (Darwin, 1971b). Third, Porter and others (personal communication) have found that the stop consonant in a CV syllable can be masked by subsequent contralateral presentation of the syllable's second formant; again this shows greater backward than forward masking.

Reasons for supposing that these masking effects are due to the *interruption* of the extraction of some acoustic feature rest on analogies with visual masking. Here it is possible to distinguish between two types of masking, integration and interruption. Integration masking, which is at a prior stage to interruption masking, is more evident if target and mask are presented to the same eye, it then depends mainly on the relative energies of target and mask and to a much smaller extent on the contour relationship between the two. On the other hand, interruption masking occurs equally whether target and mask are presented to the same or to different eyes, and appears to be independent of the relative energies of the target and mask; but it does require that the two share similar contours (Turvey, 1973). Darwin (1971b) pursued the analogy between auditory and visual masking by distinguishing between the sets of sounds used for the target and the mask. Previous experiments had confounded the two by drawing both target and mask from the same set of sounds and then asking the subject to report either both sounds or the one on a particular ear (Kirstein, 1970). Darwin used the syllables /be, pe, de, te/ as a target set and one of four masks (/ge, e, ɔ/, and a nonspeech steady-state timbre) presented on the opposite ear either 60 msec in front of or 60 msec behind the target. He found that for place of articulation the amount of forward masking was the same for all the masks and rather small, on the other hand the amount of backward masking did depend on which mask was used, being very much greater for the /ge/ mask than for the others, which showed only minimally greater backward than forward masking. The perception of voicing showed only slightly greater backward than forward masking, and this was the same for all the masks used. As in vision, then, there is greater backward than forward masking only when the mask shares some features with the target.

The question of what type of features the target and mask must share has been taken up by Pisoni and McNabb (1974; Pisoni, 1975). Their experiment uses as a target set /ba, da, pa, ta/, and six different masks /ga, ka, gæ, ge, ke/. They, too, find that the amount of backward masking depends on the similarity between the target and the mask; backward masking is much greater when the mask has the same vowel as the targets.

This result is compatible with the idea that backward masking is sensitive to the particular auditory features present in the consonant, rather than to its phonetic features, since only the former vary when the vowel is changed. However, in a subsequent experiment they show that similar results also apply in *forward* masking, when the mask precedes the target. This result causes them to interpret both their experiments in terms of an integration hypothesis, since it is crucial for the interruption hypothesis that backward masking should be greater than forward masking but it is possible to accommodate the effect of target–mask similarity into an integration theory. This interpretation is appropriate for Pisoni and McNabb's results (although their data do show a slightly greater effect of backward masking), but it cannot be used, as Pisoni (1975) claims, as an interpretation of those results that have shown appreciably greater backward than forward masking. How can we reconcile these results? It is clear from the experiments which do show greater backward than forward masking that some forward masking is occurring (Studdert-Kennedy *et al.*, 1971) so it may not be inappropriate to suggest that some integration masking is present. Indeed this would not be entirely surprising, since the sounds used in all these experiments have a common pitch and so are likely to fuse together to some extent, depending on their onset asynchronies. The important question is, Why do some experiments show much more backward than forward masking (Darwin, 1971b; Kirstein, 1970; Porter, 1971; Studdert-Kennedy *et al.*, 1971), whereas others do not (Pisoni & McNabb, 1974)? The answer probably lies in the different tasks required of the subject. Pisoni and McNabb's experiment is unique in that the subject always knew into which ear the target would come and whether it would precede or follow the mask, whereas in all the experiments that have shown greater backward than forward masking the subject was in doubt either as to the ear on which the target sound would arrive or as to whether it would be the first or the second sound. The presence of both these physical cues may then allow the subject to stop the second sound from interrupting the processing of the first.

In summary, the data on dichotic masking of speech sounds suggest that both integration and interruption processes are occurring and that in both types the similarity of the target and the mask can affect the amount of masking obtained. However, in circumstances where interruption masking is clearly occurring (more backward masking than forward), the evidence suggests that it is occurring at the level of auditory features. Little more can be said at present from these experiments about the nature of these features, and it is unlikely that the masking experiments will provide as direct an access to them as adaptation experiments have, both because of the different types of masking that may occur and also because of the contribution that other factors, such as echoic memory, may play in performance on masking experiments (Allen & Haggard, 1974; Darwin & Baddeley, 1974). However, the comparative ease with which backward masking effects are shown for rapid acoustic transitions, compare with the unreliable and small effects for vowels and pure tones (Cudahy & Leshowitz, 1974; Massaro, 1970; Pisoni, 1972) suggests that the auditory features are likely to be complex or time-varying.

Objective methods then are beginning to provide a way of defining psychologically important auditory features. An interesting question is whether these will turn out to be the same as those that seem to be important for other reasons. Fant (1964) stresses the importance of looking in the speech signal for "auditory patterns" that might serve either as a direct indication of a segment's identity (as in /s/) or, more usually, that might provide the raw materials for the more complex processes required to interpret them in terms of linguistic categories.

V. MODELS OF SPEECH PERCEPTION

We are now in a position to see the magnitude of the problem that speech perception, even at the phonemic level, poses. Because of effects such as coarticulation, the speech signal resists any effort to segment it into acoustically defined portions that are influenced only by a particular phone, except in a very restricted set of cases. Some segmentation is possible according to purely acoustic criteria (Fant, 1967), and we have seen that there is growing evidence that auditory features are extracted as part of the perceptual process. But where do we go from here? What type of process mediates between the auditory feature and the phonetic category?

Formant transitions do not provide a simple invariant cue of the form: *a slightly rising transition lasting 40 msec* (Cooper et al., 1952), but can we say that they do not provide a set of invariant exclusive disjunctions of the form *a falling second formant lasting 40 msec ending around 800 Hz or a slightly rising second formant lasting 40 msec ending around 2700 Hz . . . etc.?* Rand (1971) has provided a simple demonstration that this type of invariance is not sufficient. He constructed two sets of synthetic syllables whose vowels had the same second formant but different first formants; in one case the vowel sounded like an /æ/ produced by a child, and in the other an /ɛ/ produced by an adult. Each of these vowels was preceded by formant transitions to give the three stops /b, d, g/. Rand found that the best transition for a /d/ response varied as a function of the apparent vocal tract size. The significance of a particular second-formant transition thus depends on the interpretation of the formant pattern as a whole, rather than on the value of the formant that it leads to.

The main dichotomy in models of speech perception has been between active (analysis by synthesis) and passive models. The distinction between these two types of model is that, while the passive model sees the primary categorization process as being due to some filter network whose decision criteria change relatively slowly with time (Morton & Broadbent, 1967), the active model sees it as being the result of matching the input signal to an internally generated representation that can change rapidly relative to that signal (Liberman, Cooper, Harris, & MacNeilage, 1962; Stevens & House, 1972).

A. Active Models

One of the motivations behind active models of speech perception (e.g., Liberman *et al.,* 1962; Stevens & House, 1972) is that of economy. Given that the processes of speech production and perception are both highly complex and formally similar, would it not be an economical solution to combine the two? Economy of description, though a fundamental criterion for the linguist, is not an infallible guide for the psychologist, and indeed there is no shortage of evidence for the independent operation of perceptual and production mechanisms. Listening to speech while speaking oneself is commonplace, but it is not readily explained away by active models. The more extreme example, of simultaneous translation from one language to another (Neisser, 1967, p. 217), illustrates this point well; here the very language of perception and that of production are different. Other examples of independence may be found in the clinic. Patients with the two hemispheres separated, by cutting the corpus callosum, can show by activities of the left hand that they comprehend instructions presented to the right hemisphere, but they cannot show this by speaking (Gazzaniga & Sperry, 1967). Congenitally anarthric individuals appear to have normal speech perceptual abilities (Lenneberg, 1962), and children who by virtue of an articulatory defect are unable to make a particular articulatory distinction show no corresponding perceptual impairment (Haggard, Corrigall, & Legg, 1971). Such experiments as these suggest that the ability to perceive speech comes through "the distinctiveness of the speech wave which we have acquired by being exposed to language in the first place and by reference to our own speech only in the second place [Fant, 1967, p. 113]."

Combining the mechanisms of production and perception also offers no way of accounting for variables that change between speakers. That inter-speaker variation is a significant perceptual problem is indicated both by experiments on speaker normalization (Ladefoged & Broadbent, 1957) and by the impaired performance of automatic speech recognition devices when tested on more than one speaker (see Hyde, 1972, for a review).

Although the problem of the lack of acoustic–phonetic invariance is cited as one reason why an active model is needed, it is not clear that it does in fact solve the problem. The trouble lies in deciding what is to be compared with what. The acoustic signal is presumably represented in terms of auditory parameters, while the internally generated articulatory representation is in terms of articulatory parameters. Before any direct comparison can be made there must be some translation between the two. To get around this problem, Stevens and House propose that a "catalog of relations between acoustic and articulatory instructions [of approximately syllable length] is built up in a child at an early age . . . . As the child produces new and different articulatory movements, new items are added to the catalog [1972, p. 53]." But if the mature speaker has this catalog, why bother with analysis by synthesis at all? Could you not simply look up the acoustic pattern in the catalog? Analysis by synthesis itself gets us no closer to solving the invariance problem.

Analysis by synthesis is also seen as a way of using the constraints of the language to aid perception. This is dealt with later, but, in anticipation, experimental evidence indicates that context is not used in the way suggested by active models, at least at the word level.

Both the Haskins model (Liberman *et al.,* 1967) and the Stevens and House model emphasize that different perceptual mechanisms are needed for phonemes that do or do not have invariant acoustic cues. Stevens and House perform a preliminary analysis on the signal in order to guide the subsequent synthesis, while the Haskins model allows only the more variable or "encoded" sounds to engage the speech processing mechanism. The perceptual significance of this dimension of "encodedness" has been claimed from a range of different experimental paradigms. These experiments have shown that stop consonants (the least invariant phonemes) produce different results from vowels (the most invariant phonemes), while other phonetic categories fall somewhere in between.

B. Perception of Different Phonetic Categories

The earliest demonstration of this difference between phonetic classes was a set of experiments comparing the categorization and discrimination of synthetic speech sounds. Since the second-formant transition can act as a sufficient cue for initial stop consonants, a continuum of sounds can be constructed varying in the extent and direction of this transition. Subjects will then label with some consistency sounds taken from this continuum as b, d, or g, depending on their position along it. If pairs of sounds adjacent on this continuum are then played to subjects, their ability to discriminate between the members of a pair will be rather poor, unless the pair happens to straddle the boundary between sounds labeled as different phonemes. For a continuum consisting of vowels, on the other hand, discrimination is good throughout the continuum (Fry, Abramson, Eimas, & Liberman, 1962; Liberman, Harris, Hoffman, & Griffith, 1957). Other paradigms that have shown differences between stops and vowels include laterality and dichotic masking experiments. After simultaneous dichotic presentation, stop consonants are recalled more accurately from the right than from the left ear, whereas vowels show the effect less reliably (Shankweiler & Studdert-Kennedy, 1967). Similarly, if two different sounds are led one to each ear but with a temporal offset of around 60 msec, the second sound is recalled more accurately than the first, for stops but not for vowels (Studdert-Kennedy *et al.*, 1970). Other classes of speech sounds have given results in the laterality paradigm intermediate between stops and vowels. For example, place of articulation for fricatives is cued mainly by the spectrum of the friction, but intelligibility is increased if appropriate formant transitions are added (Harris, 1958). The friction is a comparatively invariant cue to place of articulation, whereas formant transitions are more variable. In keeping with the predictions for active theories, Darwin (1971a) found that place of articulation for fricatives was only reported better from the right ear if formant transitions were present. Similarly, Cutting (1972) has shown that liquids (/r, l/), which can be regarded as having an intermediate amount of invariance, show an ear difference between that for stops and vowels.

That these experimental differences should be attributed to the relative amounts of invariance or encodedness of different phonetic classes has been questioned. Fujisaki and Kawashima (1968) offered an alternative explanation of the discrimination experiments. They observed that the discrimination of short-duration vowels showed clearer peaks at the phoneme boundary than did long-duration vowels. On the basis of this evidence, they proposed that performance in a discrimination task is determined both by the categorization process and by uncategorized information held in a buffer store. Pairs of sounds that differ in terms of the categorization process can be judged different on that basis, but if they are categorized as the same phoneme then comparison is made between their representations in the buffer store. Fujisaki and Kawashima showed that short vowels were perceived more categorically than long vowels. They suggested that a less accurate comparison could be made between the buffer store representations of stop consonants and brief vowels than between those of long vowels, on account of their duration. This result has since been confirmed by Pisoni (1971), who has also shown (Pisoni, 1973) that the accuracy of discrimination between pairs of long and short duration vowels decreased as the interstimulus interval increased, whereas the discrimination of pairs of stop consonants remained stable with time. There was a marked difference between the within-category discrimination scores for stop consonants and for vowels of the same duration. Clearly, cue duration of itself is not an adequate explanation of the discrepancy. One explanation of these effects (Liberman, Mattingly, & Turvey, 1972; Pisoni, 1973) is that a special mechanism responsible for the perception of stop consonants precludes the subsequent use of auditory information for nonphonetic judgments. If this explanation is valid, then Fujisaki and Kawashima's model needs to be altered to prevent auditory information being used after it has been categorized in a particular way. This explanation also renders the hypothesis of a special processing mechanism for stop consonants immune from attack along the lines proposed by Fujisaki and Kawashima.

This question of the relationship between the categorization process and the buffer memory trace from which it is derived has been examined in a different context by Darwin and Baddeley (1974). They proposed, as a result of experiments on acoustic memory based on recency effects in immediate recall of lists of items (Crowder, 1971; Crowder & Morton, 1969), that acoustic memory is not influenced by the categorization process but is simply an analogue representation of the acoustic stimulus, which becomes degraded with the passing of time (Darwin, Turvey, & Crowder, 1972). The result of this degradation is that acoustically fine distinctions are lost before acoustically coarser ones. They suggested that the various experiments that had purported to show differences in categorization mechanisms for different phonetic classes merely reflected differential contributions from acoustic memory because of the different acoustic confusability of items within different phonetic classes. Little useful acoustic information about place of articulation for a stop consonant can be obtained from acoustic memory a short time after its arrival, not because it has been categorized as a stop but because it is acoustically very similar to other stops with different places of articulation. However, this information will be less useful in distinguishing between different stop consonants than will similarly degraded information, which need only be put into categories that are acoustically coarser.

According to this account, the reason that some speech sounds show laterality effects where others do not is because the vocabulary of sounds used is sometimes sufficiently acoustically different for useful information to persist for some time in acoustic memory, thus giving the left hemisphere more time to categorize a left-ear signal, which, by virtue of poorer neural connections to that hemisphere, is degraded, compared with a right-ear signal (Darwin, 1973). Similarly, the reason that some sounds show more backward masking than others is because for acoustically distinct vocabularies the categorization mechanism can use the information in acoustic memory to take a second pass at a previously interrupted categorization. This hypothesis predicts that there should be a three-way correlation between laterality, dichotic masking, and acoustic memory experiments, so that the greatest evidence of acoustic memory (in, for example, recency experiments) is shown by vocabularies of sound that show the least laterality effects and the least dichotic backward masking effects. This correlation has been shown in a number of experiments.

Acoustically similar vowels (such as /ɪ, ɛ, æ/) show little evidence of useful acoustic memory in recency experiments (Darwin & Baddeley, 1974), in contrast to acoustically distinct vowels (such as /ɪ, æ, u/). Similarly, acoustically similar vowels show a significant right-ear advantage whilst acoustically distinct vowels do not (Godfrey, 1974), and acoustically similar vowels show more dichotic backward masking than do acoustically distinct ones (Allen & Haggard, 1974). Syllable-final consonants show more recency than syllable-initial consonants if they are acoustically distinct (/g, ʃ, m/; Darwin & Baddeley, 1974) but not if they are acoustically similar (/b, d, g/; Crowder, 1973), and, likewise, syllable-final consonants show more right-ear advantage than syllable-initial consonants if they are cued by slow transitions (/r, l/; Cutting, 1972) but not if they are cued by fast ones (/b, d, g/; Darwin, 1969). In stop consonants, voicing shows less backward masking than does place of articulation (Darwin, 1971b) but more recency (A. Thomasson, personal communication). Adding appropriate formant transitions to fricatives makes them show a right-ear advantage for place of articulation (Darwin, 1971a) but gives no increase in the size of their recency effect (Crowder, 1973).

The success of this hypothesis rests not only on showing that the utility of auditory information depends on the acoustic similarity of the items used rather than on their phonetic class but also on showing that under suitable circumstances auditory information *is* available from sounds belonging to acoustically similar categories, such as the stops. An experiment by Pisoni and Tash (1974) gives direct evidence that some auditory precategorical information is available from stop consonants. They used a same–different reaction time paradigm (Posner & Mitchell, 1967), measuring subjects' reaction times to pairs of sounds drawn from a continuum between /b/ and /p/. Subjects had to decide whether the two sounds were the same phoneme or not. Their reaction times showed that it took them longer to decide that the two sounds were the same phoneme when the sounds were physically slightly different (but still within the same phoneme category) than when they were identical. They also found that the time to decide that the two sounds were different was faster when the sounds differed by a larger distance on the continuum than when they differed by a smaller distance, even though the sounds always fell within different phoneme categories. Some precategorical information must have been available to the subjects over the half second or so that separated the onsets of the two sounds.

It would be premature then to claim that we have any psychological evidence for different phonetic classes of sound being perceived by different types of *categorizing* mechanisms. This does not mean of course that there are no differences, it merely shows that the paradigms used so far are not sensitive to what differences there may be. Deprived of this empirical support, active models become less plausible. But in rejecting the active model as a mechanism for categorization we must be careful not to reject it as a statement of the problem. The active model is correct in emphasizing that knowledge of the vocal tract must be used in order to categorize speech, but it appears to be incorrect in suggesting that the mechanism by which this is done is an active analysis by synthesis. Failure to use knowledge of the mechanisms and acoustics of the vocal tract is an important reason why contemporary attempts at machine recognition of speech have been unsuccessful (see Hyde, 1972, for review). The success of programs of analyzing visual scenes is related to the sophistication of the geometrical constraints that they have employed (Clowes, 1971; Guzman, 1969; Mackworth, 1973). Perhaps we can expect a similar improvement in speech recognition with the use of more sophisticated knowledge about the vocal tract. Although this knowledge exists in a variety of forms, including programs to synthesize speech by rule (Holmes *et al.,* 1964; Kuhn, 1973; Mattingly, 1968) it has not yet been applied systematically to perceptual problems.

Computational procedures exist that allow the cross-sectional area function of the vocal tract to be estimated directly (without recursive procedures) from the acoustic waveform (Atal, 1974). The advantages to the perceptual system of performing such a transformation are clear, in that many of the problems raised by coarticulation evaporate. But is it likely that this is a first stage in perception? For reasons outlined in Haggard (1971), such a process would be more likely to appear in the perception of vowels, where the spectrum is simpler, than for consonants, with their additional sources of acoustic energy. Haggard suggests that the acoustically complex consonants may be perceived by heuristics that map directly from acoustic features to phonetic categories (as we have seen suggested for voicing), while vowels may use a procedure that computes something like the vocal tract area function. Evidence from vowel perception, however, indicates that if the perceptual process passes through an articulatory representation of the vowel, this is perceived heuristically, or by "rules of thumb" that do not achieve a representation as detailed as a vocal tract area function.

Carlson, Granstrom, and Fant (1970) report the results of experiments in which subjects are asked to adjust the second formant of two-formant vowels to match vowels composed of four formants. The value of this F_2' lies between the values of the matched vowel's second and third formants (except for [i:] where it is above F_3), in a position that Carlson, Fant, and Granstrom (1973) show is predictable from the output of a model of the cochlea. The finite bandwidth of this model causes the peak of the second formant to be influenced by higher formants. A possible articulatory correlate of F_2', suggested by Kuhn (1975) is that it may indicate the length of the mouth cavity (the cavity anterior to the point of maximum tongue constriction), at least for the more constricted vowels. Kuhn also suggests that emphasis on the mouth cavity as a perceptual variable may help in speaker normalization, since Fant (1966) had deduced from acoustic data that the difference in shape (as opposed to size) between male and female vocal tracts lies more in the pharynx than in the mouth cavity, which is more linearly scaled between different sized vocal tracts. The implication of all this is that the perceptual system uses much cruder information than is needed to completely specify an area function, to perceive a vowel category.

There is another reason why a heuristic approach to vowel perception might be advantageous. Stevens has shown that places of articulation for consonants and vowels (Stevens, 1972) occur at points where a small perturbation in articulation gives a minimum of perturbation in the acoustic output. If the perceptual system were capable of deriving an exact area function from the acoustic data, then this choice could be a disadvantage. However, if perception operates heuristically, the advantages of a sloppy articulation producing a relatively stable acoustic output, which is then mapped onto some idealized articulation, becomes obvious. Studies of articulation under abnormal conditions, such as might occur with a pipe held between the teeth (Lindblom, 1972), indicate that the articulation is drastically changed in order to attain a more nearly constant acoustic result. In addition, X-ray studies of vowel articulation (Ladefoged, De-Clerk, Papçun, & Lindau, 1972) show that different speakers use very different tongue positions to produce the same phonetic vowel—again suggesting that some acoustic criterion must be satisfied. If, then, perception is mediated by articulatory variables, this articulation is unlikely to be equivalent to that of the speaker—as application of algorithms such as Atal's would lead to—or to that of the listener—as implied by motor theories—but rather, we must assume some more abstract form, which is neither subject to their limitations nor capable of their variations.

C. Context and Prosodic Variables

Although this chapter has concentrated on the problems of speech perception at the phonemic level, it would be misleading not to mention the further complications introduced by considering the perception of speech over segments longer than the isolated syllable or word.

Normal continuous speech varies from word to word in the precision with which it is articulated, and there appears to be an intimate relationship between the articulatory precision afforded a word and the ease with which that word could have been predicted by the listener. A word isolated from a predictable context is not as intelligible as the same word isolated from a less predictable context (Lieberman, 1963). The complement of this observation is that listeners can use context to make up for poor articulation (Lieberman, 1963; Rubenstein & Pollack, 1963).

The ability to use context as an aid to perception is one virtue of an analysis-by-synthesis model of perception, but an impressive quantitative account of the interaction between context and stimulus information has been given within a passive framework by Morton (1970). In this model (see Fig. 5), contextual constraints are seen as imposing a variable criterion on the decision mechanisms underlying word recognition, so that expected words are subject to a laxer criterion than are unexpected and so require less sensory information to produce a percept. Morton (see also Morton & Broadbent, 1967) contrasts this type of model with active models, which he maintains would predict a change in sensitivity, rather than a change in criterion setting. This is presumably because the more expected word would be put up as a candidate to the analysis-by-synthesis comparator earlier than the less expected word, and so would find the stimulus trace in a less decayed or overwritten form.

But there is more to the perception of connected speech than the use of the context which it supplies, for if words spoken in isolation are concatenated, the intelligibility of the resulting speech is very low (Stowe & Hampton, 1961). This is particularly striking, as Huggins (1972b) has observed, when one considers that the intelligibility of the individual words that constitute this speech is higher than that of the same words spoken fluently. Presumably, then, perception of connected speech does not proceed solely as a sequence of serial decisions of phonemic or word size helped by phonological, syntactic, and semantic constraints, rather, it is

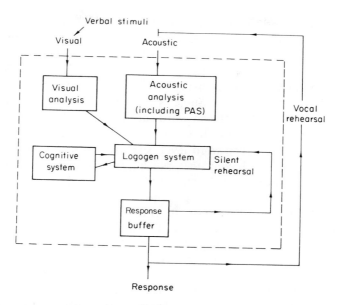

FIG. 5. Morton's "Logogen Model." While this model makes no attempt to describe the auditory-to-phonemic stage in speech perception it provides a useful summary of possible mechanisms before and after this stage. The persistence of a brief, over-writable, precategorical acoustical store (PAS) is used to explain modality-specific recency effects in short-term serial recall, and it is invoked in this chapter to explain perceptual differences between different phonetic classes of speech sound. The logogen system provides an interface between sensory information and knowledge of the language and the world. The system consists of morpheme-sized units that can be biased by the cognitive system on the basis of its expectancies. This aspect of the model handles, quantitatively, changes in the recognition accuracy of words with changing frequency, context and signal-to-noise levels. [From Morton (1970).]

augmented by suprasegmental factors, such as intonation and rhythm. Prosody obviously provides such information as where stress falls in a sentence, whether or not a question is being asked, what the mood of the speaker is and so on (see review by Fry, 1970), but it perhaps also plays a more dynamic role in perception. It may serve to direct the listener's attention toward potentially informative parts of the speech stream and to segment the stream up into chunks, which are then candidates for higher-level units of analysis.

Experimental evidence on the importance of prosodic variables in perception is scattered, but what is available suggests that they have been unjustly neglected. Martin (1972) has discussed the theoretical implications of rhythm in perception, and Huggins (1972b) has provided a brief but useful review of the perceptual significance of prosody in connected speech. One of the points to emerge from this review is that listeners can put more trust in prosodic information than they do in segmental, when the two are in conflict. Wingfield and Klein (1971) examined this question by playing to subjects sentences whose intonation indicated that a major syntactic boundary was occurring at a point that was incompatible with the words in the sentence. Subjects' transcriptions of these mismatched sentences occasionally included word substitutions, which changed the syntactic structure to be compatible with the intonation. Prosody seems also to be trusted more at the word level, since words read in a foreign accent tend to be heard as having the spoken, though incorrect stress pattern, even if this sacrifices useful segmental cues (Bansal, 1966; cited in Huggins, 1972b). This strategy is perhaps a wise one when we consider the relative resistance to distortion of prosodic and segmental information. Speech which is so severely band limited that the overall intelligibility is only 30% still carries enough prosodic information for the stress pattern of the words to be correctly perceived (Kozhevnikov & Chistovich, 1965). The same is true for hummed speech (Svennson, 1974), which carries no segmental information. Using spectrally rotated speech, which again gives no segmental information, Blesser (1969) has found that for some sentences the syntactic structure of the transcribed sentence corresponds closely with that of the original.

While these experiments indicate that prosody furnishes useful information about stress patterns, and perhaps about syntactic structure, in the absence of segmental information, there has been little attempt to model how the interaction between syntactic information obtained lexically and that obtained prosodically is achieved. However, there are two approaches to sentence perception that might provide a suitable framework for approaching this interaction.

Bever (1970) has described a heuristic approach to the perception of sentences in which words are grouped together according to strategies based mainly on the grammatical class of the words. These strategies suggest how the major constituents of a sentence could be extracted, and provide a possible theoretical link between syntactic processing mechanisms and the use of prosodic information. If indeed prosody can help to determine syntactically useful segments, then strategies using this information could readily be incorporated into the type of scheme that Bever suggests. Experiments by Scholes (1971a,b) provided a start on delimiting the usefulness of prosodic information for resolving syntactic ambiguity, and in a similar vein work on the use of prosodic information as an aid to automatic speech recognition by Lea (1973) shows that the ends of major syntactic constituents (except noun-phrase–verbal boundaries) can be detected quite reliably by looking for a drop in the pitch contour.

Perhaps the most explicit model for the perception of sentences is the computer program by Winograd (1972) that allows typed communication in English about a world of colored blocks. The program uses a grammar—based on Halliday's (1967a, 1970) systemic grammar—which permits a rich interaction between syntactic and semantic constraints during the process of understanding an input sentence. Its dynamic use of semantic information provides a valuable constraint on the possible syntactic parsings of a sentence, since semantically anomalous parsings can be rejected rapidly. For example, an attempt to parse *He gave the boy plants to water* as if it had the same structure as *He gave the house plants to charity* would be rejected when the semantic anomaly between *boy* and *plants* was detected. While such semantic constraints could also guide the perception of spoken language, there will be additional constraints imposed by the prosodic information in the spoken sentence. Halliday's own work (1967b) on the relation between grammar and intonation might serve as a starting point for this link, particularly as Smith and Goodenough (1971) have found Halliday's analysis useful in explaining the time it takes subjects to answer questions about statements spoken in a variety of intonations following different introductory sentences.

VI. CONCLUDING REMARKS

The experiments reviewed in the middle sections of this chapter have had some success at describing in information-processing terms possible mechanisms at early stages in the perception of brief, syllable-length segments of speech. Their success is to some extent a reflection of the success of information-processing ideas in vision (e.g., Turvey, 1973), since the paradigms or the methodology have often been taken directly from visual work (e.g, Darwin *et al.,* 1972; Pisoni & Tash, 1974). However, the success of information-processing approaches in vision has been largely confined to "perception at a glance," a term that equally describes the scope of the speech work. We should ask whether our present enthusiastic pursuits with information-processing techniques are more likely to secure a golden fleece or a red herring. Are the tools at our disposal likely to lead to any real understanding of the true complexity of speech perception? What little we know about the perception of extended utterances and what little we know about the way in which the cues to phonological categories change when they occur in fluent speech both give pause to any simple attempt to relate auditory "perception at a glance" to the perception of fluent speech. Here, as elsewhere, the techniques of the experimental psychologist fall short of the task that faces him. Too often do psychological techniques that promise to illumine basic perceptual processes end up, instead, raising problems confined to their own methodology, which shed comparatively little light on the original problem.

What is needed is a way of modeling the speech perceptual process that is at once sufficiently complex to allow the richness of the system to be adequately represented and yet sufficiently transparent to provide insight. Computer programs for the synthesis of speech by rule already provide such a modeling medium for the phonologist (Mattingly, 1971), but interaction between speech psychologists and those concerned with automatic recognition of speech has until recently been minimal (Hyde, 1972; Newell, 1971), partly because of the tremendous technological problems of dealing with auditory signals. However, as these problems are overcome, perhaps we could look forward to program-based models of the perceptual process being used to stimulate, and in turn be modified by, observations by psychologists on how the human brain perceives speech.

Acknowledgments

Part of this chapter was written while the author was on leave of absence at the University of Connecticut and Haskins Laboratories. He is indebted to Alvin Liberman, Gary Kuhn, Ignatius Mattingly, and Peter Eimas for discussion and comments, to Michael Studdert-Kennedy for putting him on the trail of the Troyan strumpet, and to his wife Kate for finding her for him.

References

Ades, A. E. Some effects of adaptation on speech perception. MIT, Research Laboratory of Electronics, *Quarterly Progress Report,* 1973, **111**, 121–129.

Ades, A. E. How phonetic is selective adaptation? Experiments on syllable position and vowel environment. *Perception and Psychophysics,* 1974, **16**, 61–66. (a)

Ades, A. E. Bilateral component in speech perception? *Journal of the Acoustical Society of America,* 1974, **56**, 610–616. (b)

Ali, L., Gallagher, T., Goldstein, J., & Daniloff, R. Perception of coarticulated nasality. *Journal of the Acoustical Society of America,* 1971, **49**, 538–540.

Allen, J., & Haggard, M. P. Dichotic backward masking of acoustically similar vowels. *Speech Perception,* 1974, Series **2**, No. 3, 35–39 (Queen's Univ., Belfast).

Atal, B. S. Towards determining articulatory parameters from the speech wave. Paper presented at International Congress of Acoustics, London, 1974.

Bailey, P. Perceptual adaptation for acoustical features in speech. *Speech Perception,* 1973, Series **2**, No. 2, 29–34 (Queen's Univ., Belfast).

Bansal, R. K. The intelligibility of Indian English. Unpublished doctoral thesis, London Univ., 1966.

Bastian, J., Eimas, P. D., & Liberman, A. M. Identification and discrimination of a phonemic contrast induced by a silent interval. *Journal of the Acoustical Society of America,* 1961, **33**, 842 (Abstract).

Bever, T. G. The cognitive basis for linguistic structures. In J. R. Hayes (Ed.), *Cognition and the development of language.* New York: Wiley, 1970.

Blakemore, C., & Campbell, F. W. On the existence of neurons in the human visual system selectively sensitive to the orientation and size of retinal images. *Journal of Physiology,* 1969, **203,** 237–260.

Blesser, B. Perception of spectrally rotated speech. Unpublished doctoral dissertation, MIT, Cambridge, Massachusetts, 1969.

Bregman, A. S., & Campbell, J. Primary auditory stream segregation and perception of order in rapid sequences of tones. *Journal of Experimental Psychology,* 1971, **89,** 244–249.

Broadbent, D. E. *Perception and communication.* Oxford: Pergamon, 1958.

Broadbent, D. E., & Ladefoged, P. On the fusion of sounds reaching different sense organs. *Journal of the Acoustical Society of America,* 1957, **29,** 708–710.

Campbell, F. W., & Robson, J. G. Application of Fourier analysis to the visibility of gratings. *Journal of Physiology,* 1968, **197,** 551–566.

Carlson, R., Fant, G., & Granstrom, B. Two-formant models, pitch and vowel perception. Symposium on Auditory Analysis and Perception of Speech, Leningrad, Aug. 21–24, 1973.

Carlson, R., Granstrom, B., & Fant, G. Some studies concerning perception of isolated vowels. STL-QPSR 1970/2–3, 19–35. Royal Institute of Technology, Stockholm.

Chomsky, N. Phonology and reading. In H. Levin & J. P. Williams (Eds.), *Basic studies on reading.* New York: Basic Books, 1970.

Chomsky, N., & Halle, M. *The sound pattern of English.* New York: Harper, 1968.

Christie, W. M., Jr. Some cues for syllable juncture perception in English. *Journal of the Acoustical Society of America,* 1974, **55,** 819–821.

Clowes, M. B. On seeing things. *Artificial Intelligence,* 1971, **2,** 79–116.

Cole, R. A., & Scott, B. The phantom in the phoneme: Invariant cues for stop consonants. *Perception and Psychophysics,* 1974, **15,** 101–107 (a)

Cole, R. A., & Scott, B. Toward a theory of speech perception. *Psychological Review,* 1974, **81,** 348–374. (b)

Cooper, F. S., Delattre, P. C., Liberman, A. M., Borst, J. M., & Gerstman, L. J. Some experiments on the perception of synthetic speech sounds. *Journal of the Acoustical Society of America,* 1952, **24,** 597–606.

Cooper, W. Adaptation of phonetic feature analyzers for place of articulation. *Journal of the Acoustical Society of America,* 1974, **56,** 617–627.

Cooper, W. Selective adaptation to speech. In F. Restle, R. M. Shiffrin, J. N. Castellan, H. Lindman, & D. B. Pisoni (Eds.), *Cognitive theory.* Potomac, Maryland: Erlbaum Press, 1975.

Cooper, W. E., & Blumstein, S. A "labial" feature analyzer in speech perception. *Perception and Psychophysics,* 1974, **15,** 591–600.

Corteen, R. S., & Wood, B. Autonomic responses to shock-associated words in an unattended channel. *Journal of Experimental Psychology,* 1972, **94,** 308–313.

Crowder, R. G. The sound of vowels and consonants in immediate memory. *Journal of Verbal Learning and Verbal Behavior,* 1971, **10,** 587–596.

Crowder, R. G. Representation of speech sounds in precategorical acoustic storage. *Journal of Experimental Psychology,* 1973, **98,** 14–24.

Crowder, R. G., & Morton, J. Precategorical acoustic storage (PAS). *Perception and Psychophysics,* 1969, **5,** 365–373.

Cudahy, E., & Leshowitz, B. Effects of a contralateral interference tone on auditory recognition. *Perception and Psychophysics,* 1974, **15,** 16–20.

Cutting, J. E. Ear advantage for stops and liquids in initial and final position. *Haskins Laboratories Status Report on Speech Research,* 1972, **SR-31/32,** 57–65.

Daniloff, R., & Moll, K. Coarticulation of lip-rounding. *Journal of Speech and Hearing Research,* 1968, **11,** 707–721.

Darwin, C. J. Auditory perception and cerebral dominance. Unpublished Ph.D. thesis, Univ. of Cambridge, 1969.

Darwin, C. J. Ear differences in the recall of fricatives and vowels. *Quarterly Journal of Experimental Psychology,* 1971, **23,** 46–62. (a)

Darwin, C. J. Dichotic backward masking of complex sounds. *Quarterly Journal of Experimental Psychology,* 1971, **23,** 386–392. (b)

Darwin, C. J. Ear differences and hemispheric specialization. In F. O. Schmitt & F. G. Worden (Eds.), *The neurosciences, third study program.* Cambridge, Massachusetts: MIT Press, 1973. Pp. 57–63.

Darwin, C. J., & Baddeley, A. D. Acoustic memory and the perception of speech. *Cognitive Psychology,* 1974, **6,** 41–60.

Darwin, C. J., & Brady, S. A. Voicing and juncture in stop-lateral clusters. Paper presented to Acoustical Society of America, Austin, Texas, April 1975.

Darwin, C. J., Turvey, M. T., & Crowder, R. G. An auditory analogue of the Sperling partial report procedure: Evidence for brief auditory storage. *Cognitive Psychology,* 1972, **3,** 255–267.

Delattre, P. C., Liberman, A. M., & Cooper, F. S. Acoustic loci and transitional cues for consonants. *Journal of the Acoustical Society of America,* 1955, **27,** 769–773.

Denes, P. Effect of duration on perception of voicing. *Journal of the Acoustical Society of America,* 1955, **27,** 761–764.

Dixit, R. P., & MacNeilage, P. F. Coarticulation of nasality: Evidence from Hindi. *Journal of the Acoustical Society of America,* 1972, **52,** 131 (Abstract).

Eimas, P. D., Cooper, W. E., & Corbit, J. D. Some properties of linguistic feature detectors. *Perception and Psychophysics,* 1973, **13,** 247–252.

Eimas, P. D., & Corbit, J. D. Selective adaptation of linguistic feature detectors. *Cognitive Psychology,* 1973, **4,** 99–109.

Evans, E. F., & Whitfield, I. C. Classification of unit responses in the auditory cortex of the unanesthetized and unrestrained cat. *Journal of Physiology,* 1964, **171,** 476–493.

Fant, C. G. M. *Acoustic theory of speech production.* The Hague: Mouton, 1960.

Fant, C. G. M. Auditory patterns of speech. STL-QPSR 1964/3, 16–20. Royal Institute of Technology, Stockholm.

Fant, G. A note on vocal tract size factors and nonuniform F-pattern scalings. STL-QPSR 1966/4, 22–30. Royal Institute of Technology, Stockholm.

Fant, G. Auditory patterns of speech. In W. Weiant-Dunn (Ed.), *Models for the perception of speech and visual form.* Cambridge, Masschusetts: MIT Press, 1967.

Fant, G., Liljencrants, J., Malac, V., & Borovickova, B. Perceptual evaluation of coarticulation effects. STL-QPSR 1970/1, 10–13. Royal Institute of Technology, Stockholm.

Fletcher, H. *Speech and hearing.* Princeton, New Jersey: Van Nostrand-Reinhold, 1929.

Foss, D. J., & Swinney, D. A. On the psychological reality of the phoneme: Perception, identification and consciousness. *Journal of Verbal Learning and Verbal Behavior,* 1973, **12,** 246–257.

Fourcin, A. J. Speech source inference. *IEEE Transactions on Audio- and Electroacoustics,* 1968, AU-16, 65–67.

Fry, D. B. Prosodic phenomena. In B. Malmberg (Ed.), *Manual of phonetics.* Amsterdam: North-Holland, 1970.

Fry, D. B., Abramson, A. S., Eimas, P. D., & Liberman, A. M. The identification and discrimination of synthetic vowels. *Language and Speech,* 1962, **5,** 171–189.

Fujisaki, H., & Kawashima, T. The influence of various factors on the identification and discrimination of synthetic speech sounds. Paper presented at 6th International Congress on Acoustics, Tokyo, Japan, August 1968.

Gårding, E. *Internal juncture in Swedish.* Travaux de L'Institut de Phonétique de Lund *VI.* Lund: Gleerup, 1967.

Gazzaniga, M. S., & Sperry, R. W. Language after section of the cerebral commissures. *Brain,* 1967, **90,** 131–148.

Godfrey, J. J. Perceptual difficulty and the right-ear advantage for vowels. *Brain and Language,* 1974, **1,** 323–336.

Gombrich, E. *Art and illusion.* Princeton, New Jersey: Princeton Univ. Press, 1960.

Gough, P. B. One second of reading. In J. F. Kavanagh & I. G. Mattingly (Eds.), *Language by ear and by eye.* Cambridge, Massachusetts: MIT Press, 1972.

Guzman, A. Computer recognition of three-dimensional objects in a visual scene. MAC Technical Report *59,* Project MAC, MIT: Cambridge, Massachusetts, 1968.

Hadding-Koch, K., & Studdert-Kennedy, M. An experimental study of some intonation contours. *Phonetica,* 1964, **11,** 175–185.

Haggard, M. P. Theoretical issues in speech perception. *Speech Synthesis and Perception,* 1971, **4,** 1–16. Psychological Laboratory, Cambridge.

Haggard, M. P., Corrigall, J. M., & Legg, A. E. Perceptual factors in articulatory defects. *Folia Phoniat,* 1971, **23,** 33–40.

Halliday, M. A. K. Notes on transitivity and theme in English. *Journal of Linguistics,* 1967, **3,** 37–81 and **4,** 179–215. (a)

Halliday, M. A. K. *Intonation and grammar in British English.* The Hague: Mouton, 1967. (b)

Halliday, M. A. K. Functional diversity in language as seen from a consideration of modality and mood in English. *Foundations of Language,* 1970, **6,** 3–2–361.

Harris, K. S. Cues for the discrimination of American English fricatives in spoken syllables. *Language and Speech,* 1958, **1,** 1–17.

Holmes, J. N., Mattingly, I. G., & Shearme, J. N. Speech synthesis by rule. *Language and speech,* 1964, **7,** 127–143.

Hubel, D. H., & Wiesel, T. N. Receptive fields, binocular interaction and functional architecture in the cat's visual cortex. *Journal of Physiology,* 1962, **160,** 106–154.

Huggins, A. W. F. Just noticeable differences for segment duration in natural speech. *Journal of the Acoustical Society of America,* 1972, **51,** 1270–1278. (a)

Huggins, A. W. F. On the perception of temporal phenomena in speech. *Journal of the Acoustical Society of America,* 1972, **51,** 1279–1290. (b)

Hyde, S. R. Automatic speech recognition: An initial survey of the literature. In E. E. David & P. B. Denes (Eds.), *Human communication: A unified view.* New York: McGraw-Hill, 1972.

Johnston, J. C., & McClelland, J. L. Perception of letters in words: Seek not and ye shall find. *Science,* 1974, **184,** 1192–1194.

Kay, R. H., & Matthews, D. R. On the existence in human auditory pathways of channels selectively tuned to the modulation present in frequency-modulated tones. *Journal of Physiology, London,* 1972, **225,** 657–677.

Kirstein, E. F. Selective listening for temporally staggered dichotic CV syllables. *Journal of the Acoustical Society of America,* 1970, **48,** 95 (Abstract).

Klatt, D. J. Voice-onset time, frication and aspiration in word-initial consonant clusters. *Quarterly Progress Report,* Research Laboratory of Electronics, M.I.T., 1973, **109,** 124–136.

Kozhevnikov, V. A., & Chistovich, L. A. *Speech: Articulation and perception.* Moscow-Leningrad. English translation J.P.R.S., Washington, D.C., 1965.

Kuhn, G. M. A two-pass procedure for synthesis-by-rule. *Journal of the Acoustical Society of America,* 1973, **54,** 339 (Abstract).

Kuhn, G. M. On the front cavity resonance and its possible role in speech perception. *Journal of the Acoustical Society of America,* 1975, 58, 428–433.

Lackner, J. R., & Goldstein, L. M. The psychological representation of speech sounds. *Cognition,* 1974, **2,** 279–298.

Ladefoged, P. The nature of general phonetic theories. *Languages and Linguistics,* 1966, Monograph No. **18,** 27–42 (Georgetown Univ.).

Ladefoged, P., & Broadbent, D. E. Information conveyed by vowels. *Journal of the Acoustical Society of America,* 1957, **29,** 98–104.

Ladefoged, P., DeClerk, J. L., Papcun, G., & Lindau, M. An auditory-motor theory of speech production. *Working Papers in Phonetics,* 1972, No. **22,** 48–75. Los Angeles: UCLA, Linguistics Department.

Lea, W. A. An approach to syntactic recognition without phonemics. *IEEE Trans. Audio and Electroacoustics,* 1973, **AU-21,** 249–258.

Lehiste, I. An acoustic-phonetic study of internal open juncture. *Phonetica,* 1960, **5,** Suppl.

Lehiste, I., & Shockey, L. On the perception of coarticulation effects in English VCV syllables. *Working Papers in Linguistics,* 1972, No. **12,** 78–86 (Ohio State Univ.).

Lenneberg, E. H. Understanding language without ability to speak: A case report. *Journal of Abnormal and Social Psychology,* 1962, **65,** 419–425.

Liberman, A. M., Cooper, F. S., Harris, K. S., & MacNeilage, P. F. A motor theory of speech perception. *Proceedings of the speech communication seminars,* Vol. 2. Stockholm: Royal Institute of Technology, 1962.

Liberman, A. M., Cooper, F. S., Shankweiler, D. P., & Studdert-Kennedy, M. Perception of the speech code. *Psychological Review,* 1967, **74,** 431–461.

Liberman, A. M., Cooper, F. S., Delattre, P. C., & Gerstman, L. J. The role of consonant-vowel transitions in the perception of the stop and nasal consonants. *Psychological Monographs,* 1954, **68** (8, Whole No. 379).

Liberman, A. M., Delattre, P. C., & Cooper, F. S. The role of selected stimulus variables in the perception of the unvoiced-stop consonants. *American Journal of Psychology,* 1952, **65,** 497–516.

Liberman, A. M., Delattre, P., & Cooper, F. S. Some cues for the distinction between voiced and voiceless stops in initial position. *Language and Speech,* 1958, **1,** 153–167.

Liberman, A. M., Harris, K. S., Hoffman, H. S., & Griffith, B. C. The discrimination of speech sounds within and across phoneme boundaries. *Journal of Experimental Psychology,* 1957, **54,** 358–368.

Liberman, A. M., Ingemann, F., Lisker, L., Delattre, P. C., & Cooper, F. S. Minimal rules for synthesizing speech. *Journal of the Acoustical Society of America,* 1959, 31, 1490–1499.

Liberman, A. M., Mattingly, I. G., & Turvey, M. T. Language codes and memory codes. In A. W. Melton & E. Martin (Eds.), *Coding processes in human memory.* New York: Wiley, 1972. Pp. 307–334.

Licklider, J. C. R. A duplex theory of pitch perception. *Experientia,* 1951, **7,** 128–134.

Lieberman, P. Some effects of semantic and grammatical context on the production and perception of speech. *Language and Speech,* 1963, **6,** 172–187.

Lieberman, P. On the acoustic basis of the perception of intonation by linguists. *Word,* 1965, **21,** 40–54.

Lieberman, P. Intonation, perception and language. *Research Monograph,* No. 38. Cambridge, Massachusetts: MIT Press, 1967.

Lindblom, B. E. F. Spectrographic study of vowel reduction. *Journal of the Acoustical Society of America,* 1963, **35,** 1773–1781.

Lindblom, B. Phonetics and the description of language. *Proceedings of the Seventh International Congress of Phonetic Sciences.* The Hague: Mouton, 1972. Pp. 63–93.

Lindblom, B. E. F., & Studdert-Kennedy, M. On the role of format transitions in vowel recognition. *Journal of the Acoustical Society of America,* 1967, **42,** 830–843.

Lisker, L. Closure duration and the intervocalic voiced-voiceless distinction in English. *Language,* 1957, **33,** 42–49. (a)

Lisker, L. Minimal cues for separating /w,r,l,y/ in intervocalic position. *Word,* 1957, **13,** 256–267. (b)

Lisker, L. Voicing lag in clusters of stop plus /r/. Appendix A-II, Speech Research and Instrumentation, Ninth Final Report, Haskins Laboratories, 1961.

Lisker, L., & Abramson, A. S. A cross-language study of voicing in initial stops: Acoustical measurements. *Word,* 1964, **20,** 384–422.

Lisker, L., & Abramson, A. S. The voicing dimension: Some experiments in comparative phonetics. *Proceedings of the Sixth International Congress of Phonetic Sciences.* Prague: Academia, 1967. Pp. 563–567. (a)

Lisker, L., & Abramson, A. S. Some effects of context on voice onset time in English stops. *Language and Speech,* 1967, **10,** 1–28. (b)

Lukatela, G. Pitch determination by adaptive autocorrelation method. *Haskins Laboratories Status Report on Speech Research,* 1973, **SR-33,** 185–193.

Mackworth, A. K. Interpreting pictures of polyhedral scenes. Third International Joint Conference on Artificial Intelligence, 1973.

Malecot, A. Acoustic cues for nasal consonants. *Language,* 1956, **32,** 274–284.

Malmberg, B. The phonetic basis for syllable division. *Studia Linguistica,* 1955, **9,** 80–87.

Martin, J. G. Rhythmic (hierarchical) versus serial structure in speech and other behavior. *Psychological Review,* 1972, **79,** 487–509.

Massaro, D. M. Preperceptual auditory images. *Journal of Experimental Psychology,* 1970, **85,** 411–417.

Mattingly, I. G. Synthesis by rule of General American English. Supplement to *Haskins Laboratories Status Report on Speech Research,* April 1968.

Mattingly, I. G. Synthesis by rule as a tool for phonological research. *Language and Speech,* 1971, **14,** 47–56.

McNeill, D., & Lindig, L. The perceptual reality of phonemes, syllables, words and sentences. *Journal of Verbal Learning and Verbal Behavior,* 1973, **12,** 417–430.

Moll, K. L., & Daniloff, R. G. An investigation of the timing of velar movements during speech. *Journal of the Acoustical Society of America,* 1971, **50,** 678–684.

Morton, J. Grammar and computation in language behavior. In J. C. Catford (Ed.), *Studies in language and language behavior.* Ann Arbor, Michigan: Univ. of Michigan, 1968.

Morton, J. A functional model for memory. In D. A. Norman. (Ed.), *Models of human memory.* New York: Academic, 1970.

Morton, J., & Broadbent, D. E. Passive versus active recognition models, or is your homunculus really necessary? In W. Wathen-Dunn (Ed.), *Models for the perception of speech and visual form.* Cambridge, Massachusetts: MIT Press, 1967.

Neisser, U. *Cognitive psychology.* New York: Appleton, 1967.

Newell, A. Speech-understanding systems: Final report of a study group. Computer Science Department, Carnegie-Mellon Univ., 1971.

O'Connor, J. D., Gerstman, L. H., Liberman, A. M., Delattre, P. C., & Cooper, F. S. Acoustic cues for the perception of initial /w,j,r,l/ in English. *Word,* 1957, **13,** 24–43.

Öhman, S. E. G. Coarticulation in VCV utterances. *Journal of the Acoustical Society of America,* 1966, **39,** 151–168.

Öhman, S. E. G. Numerical model of coarticulation. *Journal of the Acoustical Society of America,* 1967, **41,** 310–320.

Peterson, G. E., & Barney, H. L. Control methods used in a study of the identification of vowels. *Journal of the Acoustical Society of America,* 1952, **24,** 175–184.

Pisoni, D. B. On the nature of categorical perception of speech sounds. Supplement to *Haskins Laboratories Status Report on Speech Research,* 1971.

Pisoni, D. B. Perceptual processing time for consonants and vowels. *Haskins Laboratories Status Report on Speech Research,* 1972, **SR-31/32,** 83–92.

Pisoni, D. B. Auditory and phonetic memory codes in the discrimination of consonants and vowels. *Perception and Psychophysics,* 1973, **13,** 253–260.

Pisoni, D. B. Dichotic listening and processing phonetic features. In F. Restle, R. M. Shiffrin, N. J. Castellan, H. Lindman, & D. B. Pisoni (Eds.), *Cognitive theory,* Vol. 1. Potomac, Maryland: Erlbaum Associates, 1975.

Pisoni, D. B., & McNabb, S. D. Dichotic interactions and phonetic feature processing. *Brain and Language,* 1974, **1,** 351–362.

Pisoni, D. B., & Tash, J. Reaction times to comparisons within and across phonetic categories. *Perception and Psychophysics,* 1974, **15,** 285–290.

Porter, R. J. The effect of temporal overlap on the perception of dichotically and monotically presented CV syllables. *Journal of the Acoustical Society of America,* 1971, **50,** 129 (Abstract).

Porter, R. J., Shankweiler, D. P., & Liberman, A. M. Differential effects of binaural time differences on perception of stop consonants and vowels. Paper presented at 77th meeting of American Psychological Association, Washington, D.C., 1969.

Posner, M. I., & Mitchell, R. F. Chronometric analysis of classification. *Psychological Review,* 1967, **74,** 392–409.

Rand, T. C. Vocal tract size normalization in the perception of stop consonants. *Haskins Laboratories Status Report on Speech Research,* 1971, **SR-25/26,** 141–146.

Rand, T. C. Dichotic release from masking for speech. *Journal of the Acoustical Society of America,* 1974, **55,** 678–680.

Raphael, L. J. Preceding vowel duration as a cue to the perception of the voicing characteristic of word-final consonants in American English. *Journal of the Acoustical Society of America,* 1972, **51,** 1296–1303.

Reicher, G. M. Perceptual recognition as a function of meaningfulness of stimulus material. *Journal of Experimental Psychology,* 1969, **81,** 275–280.

Rubin, P. Semantic influences on phonetic identification and lexical decision. Ph.D. dissertation, University of Connecticut, 1975.

Rubinstein, H., & Pollack, I. Word predictability and intelligibility. *Journal of Verbal Learning and Verbal Behavior,* 1963, **2**, 147–158.

Savin, H., & Bever, T. G. The nonperceptual reality of the phoneme. *Journal of Verbal Learning and Verbal Behavior,* 1970, **3**, 295–302.

Sawusch, J. R., Pisoni, D. B., & Cutting, J. E. Category boundaries for linguistic and nonlinguistic dimensions of the same stimuli. Paper at 87th meeting of the Acoustical Society of America, New York, April 1974.

Schatz, C. The role of context in the perception of stops. *Language,* 1954, **30**, 47–56.

Scholes, R. J. *Acoustic cues for constituent structure.* The Hague: Mouton, 1971. (a)

Scholes, R. J. On the spoken disambiguation of superficially ambiguous sentences. *Language and Speech,* 1971, **14**, 1–11. (b).

Schwartz, M. F. Transitions in American English /s/ as cues to the identity of adjacent stop consonants. *Journal of the Acoustical Society of America,* 1967, **42**, 897–899.

Schwartz, M. F. Identification of speaker sex from isolated voiceless fricatives. *Journal of the Acoustical Society of America,* 1968, **43**, 1178–1179.

Selfridge, O. G., & Neisser, U. Pattern recognition by machine. *Scientific American,* 1960, **203** (Aug.) 60–68.

Shankweiler, D. P., Strange, W., & Verbrugge, R. Speech and the problem of perceptual constancy. In R. Shaw & J. Bransford (Eds.), *Perceiving, acting and comprehending: Toward an ecological psychology.* Potomac, Maryland: Erlbaum Associates, in press.

Shankweiler, D. P., & Studdert-Kennedy, M. Identification of consonants and vowels presented to left and right ears. *Quarterly Journal of Experimental Psychology,* 1967, **19**, 59–63.

Shearme, J. N., & Holmes, J. N. An experimental study of the classification of sounds in continuous speech according to their distribution in the F1-F2 plane. In *Proceedings of the 4th International Congress of Phonetic Science, Helsinki, 1961.* The Hague: Mouton, 1962.

Small, A. M. Periodicity pitch. In J. V. Tobias (Ed.), *Foundations of modern auditory theory,* Vol. II. New York: Academic Press, 1971.

Smith, F., & Goodenough, C. Effects of context, intonation and voice on the reaction time to sentences. *Language and Speech,* 1971, **14**, 241–250.

Stevens, K. N. The quantal nature of speech: Evidence from articulatory-acoustic data. In E. E. David & P. B. Denes (Eds.), *Human communication: A unified view.* New York: McGraw-Hill, 1972.

Stevens, K., & House, A. S. Speech perception. In J. V. Tobias (Ed.), *Foundations of modern auditory theory,* Vol. 2. New York: Academic Press, 1972.

Stevens, K. N., & Klatt, D. Role of formant transitions in the voiced-voiceless distinction for stops. *Journal of the Acoustical Society of America,* 1974, **55**, 653–659.

Stowe, A. N., & Hampton. D. B. Speech synthesis with pre-recorded syllables and words. *Journal of the Acoustical Society of America,* 1961, **33**, 810–811.

Strevens, P. Spectra of fricative noise. *Language and Speech,* 1960, **3**, 32–49.

Studdert-Kennedy, M. The perception of speech. In T. A. Sebeok (Ed.), *Current trends in linguistics,* Vol. XII: Phonetics. The Hague: Mouton, 1974.

Studdert-Kennedy, M. and Cooper, F. S. High performance reading machines for the blind. In *Proceedings of the International Conference on Sensory Devices for the Blind,* St. Dunstan's, June 1966.

Studdert-Kennedy, M., Shankweiler, D., &Schulman, S. Opposed effects of a delayed channel on perception of dichotically and monotically presented CV syllables. *Journal of the Acoustical Society of America,* 1970, **48,** 599–602.

Summerfield, A. Q. Toward a detailed model for the perception of voicing contrasts. *Speech Perception,* 1974, Series **2,** No. 3, 1–26 (Queen's Univ., Belfast).

Summerfield, A. Q., & Haggard, M. P. Perceptual processing of multiple cues and contexts: Effects of following vowel upon stop consonant voicing. *Journal of Phonetics,* 1974, **2,** 279–295.

Svennson, S-G., Prosody and grammar in speech perception. *MILUS,* 1974, No. **2.** Institute of Linguistics, University of Stockholm.

Tartter, V. C. Selective adaptation of acoustic and phonetic detectors. M.A. Thesis, Brown Univ., 1975.

Tash, J. Selective adaptation of auditory feature detectors in speech perception. M.A. dissertation, University of Indiana. In *Research on Speech Perception,* Progress Report No. 1. Bloomington: Indiana Univ., Department of Psychology, 1974.

Treisman, A. M. Contextual cues in selective listening. *Quarterly Journal of Experimental Psychology,* 1960, **12,** 242–248.

Treisman, A. M., & Riley, J. G. A. Is selective attention selective perception or selective response? A further test. *Journal of Experimental Psychology,* 1969, **79,** 27–34.

Turvey, M. T. On peripheral and central processes in vision. *Psychological Review,* 1973, **80,** 1–52.

Wang, W. S-Y., & Fillmore, C. Intrinsic cues and consonant perception. *Journal of Speech and Hearing Research,* 1961, **4,** 130–136.

Warren, R. M. Verbal transformation effect and auditory perceptual mechanisms. *Psychological Bulletin,* 1968, **70,** 261–270.

Warren, R. M., & Ackroft, J. M. Dichotic verbal transformation: Evidence of separate neural processes for identical stimuli. *Journal of the Acoustical Society of America,* 1974, Suppl. **56,** 554.

Wheeler, D. D. Processes in word recognition. *Cognitive Psychology,* 1970, **1,** 59–85.

Wightman, F. L. Pattern-transformation model of pitch. *Journal of the Acoustical Society of America,* 1973, **54,** 407–416.

Wilson, J. P. Psychoacoustical and neurophysiological aspects of auditory pattern recognition. In F. O. Schmitt & F. G. Worden (Eds.), *The neurosciences: Third study program.* Cambridge, Massachusetts: MIT Press, 1973.

Wingfield, A., & Klein, J. F. Syntactic structure and acoustic pattern in speech perception. *Perception and Psychophysics,* 1971, **9,** 23–25.

Winitz, H., Scheib, M. E., & Reeds, J. A. Identification of stops and vowels from the burst portion of /p,t,k/ isolated from conversational speech. *Journal of the Acoustical Society of America,* 1972, **51,** 1309.

Winograd, T. *Understanding natural language.* New York: Academic Press, 1972.

Chapter 7

PHONETIC CODING AND SERIAL ORDER[*]

WAYNE A. WICKELGREN

I. INTRODUCTION

This chapter will discuss the theoretical units of encoding that are useful in accounting for speech recognition and articulation phenomena. In doing this, it is necessary to give some attention to the processes (mechanisms) by which speech recognition and articulation are accomplished.

Although the ultimate goal of speech is to communicate meanings from one person to another, the primary concern of the present chapter is largely with the phonetic (structural) means by which this communication of ideas is accomplished. Thus, although there will be some discussion of the inter-

[*] The work presented in this chapter was supported by Grant MH17958 from The National Institute of Mental Health.

action of syntax and semantics with the phonetic aspects of speech communication, the emphasis will be on the nature of phonetic representation and its role in speech recognition and articulation.

The assumption that speech and language can be subdivided into phonetics and phonology, on the one hand, and syntax and semantics, on the other hand, is an assumption frequently made in linguistics and speech communication. This assumption has considerable empirical motivation, some of which will be made clear in the present chapter. What I call the phonetics of speech and language consists of that part of speech communication starting with a set of concept representatives (formatives, words) at some high level of the speaker's nervous system, the various stages of decoding of this set of concepts into a sequence of phonetic segments, and specification of the articulatory features of each segment, then continuing to an acoustic representation of the information, thereafter to an auditory representation in the nervous system of the hearer, and finally terminating in a set of concept representatives in the hearer.

I assume that, when a speaker plans an utterance, he selects concepts and organizes them into a syntactic structure in a manner that is part of the syntactic and semantic domain of speech and language. Similarly, when a hearer understands a spoken message, I assume that at the terminal stage he has a set of concepts organized into a syntactic and semantic structure, hopefully in a manner that in some way corresponds to what the speaker intended to communicate. This aspect of speech recognition is in the syntactic and semantic domain and outside the scope of the present chapter. The phonetic domain, which is the scope of the present chapter, includes everything in speech articulation and recognition between the syntactic–semantic domain of the speaker and that of the hearer. In particular, it will be assumed that a string of concept representatives is transformed into a string consisting of a much larger number of phonetic segments (phonemes, allophones, or syllables). These segments are, in turn, analyzable as a set of simultaneously present features. The decoding of concept representatives into segments and sets of features constitutes the necessary information for controlling the articulatory musculature to produce speech. Having produced speech, one has a physical acoustic representation of the message. This physical acoustic representation of the message is transformed into a set of simultaneously present auditory features in the hearer. These features change over time and can be organized at some stage in the speech recognition process into a set of segments in the auditory recognition process. If a sufficient number of auditory segments composing a word are recognized in an utterance, then the word will be recognized. In the present chapter I will not be concerned with anything beyond the recognition of individual words. Thus, in particular, I will not be concerned with how we recognize phrase structure at the most superficial syntactic level, to say nothing of how we recognize what Chomsky refers to as deep or underlying structure in an utterance.

The present chapter will attempt to account for the principal facts of speech recognition and articulation. No attempt will be made to account for phonological phenomena. Precise definition of phonology in linguistics varies from linguist to linguist. Chomsky and Halle's (1968) definition of phonology is in some ways similar to the definition of the phonetic domain of language just offered. However, the types of phenomena for which we are attempting to account are almost completely different. The following are examples of the types of regularity for which phonological theories attempt to account: (*a*) the accent patterns of different words, especially different words that are composed of some of the same basic concepts (stems, morphemes), such as *permit* and *permit, torment* and *torment;* (*b*) regularities in the combination of stems and affixes, such as in forming the plurals of nouns and the past tenses of verbs; (*c*) the phonetic relationships between various words that share a common stem (morpheme), such as *divine* and *divinity, communicate* and *communication;* and (*d*) stress patterns over phrases and sentences. Finally, Chomsky and Halle's (1968) phonology also attempts to characterize lexical elements by the minimum number of phonetic features, with the complete set of phonetic features necessary to specify the articulatory segments being supplied by the phonological rules. All of these matters are outside the scope of the present discussion.

II. LEVELS OF LINGUISTIC CODING

The primary units of linguistic coding of concern in this chapter are the concept level, the segment level, the articulatory feature level, and the auditory feature level. In addition, phrases, clauses, sentences, and the possibility of abstract feature representatives will be briefly discussed.

Concepts are units of meaning, and the concept is usually represented in language by a single word or very short phrase. Thus, *dog* is a concept, *little black dog* is a concept, *sit* is a concept, *slowly* is a concept, etc. Crudely speaking, the concept level is the word level, though many concepts can be referred to by more than one word or phrase and the same word often stands for a variety of different concepts (sometimes similar to one another, sometimes not). Consider the word *bank* meaning a financial institution or as in a river bank.

The spoken representative of a concept (word) is an ordered set of articulatory gestures that translate themselves into a temporally varying acoustic output. It is usually assumed that the articulatory and auditory representations of a word can be considered to be an ordered set of phones, allophones, phonemes, or syllables, though at peripheral articulatory and acoustic levels, it is often rather difficult to specify exactly where one segment ends and the next segment begins. However, it seems likely that, at some level of the nervous system, words are "spelled" in terms of smaller structural units in either ordered or unordered sets. These smaller structural units can be referred to in a very general way as *segments*.

An articulatory segment must produce a set of instructions to the articulatory musculature to assume a particular position appropriate, say, for production of the consonant phoneme /p/. Thus, a segment representative must activate a set of simultaneously present articulatory feature representatives. For example, the phoneme /p/ is unvoiced (vocal cords not vibrating), produced by closure of the lips (frontal place of articulation), not nasal (velum is closed so that little or no sound is transmitted through the nose), and the manner of articulation is that of the stop consonant (vocal tract completely closed at some point in the articulation). All of these articulatory features must be present for an individual to produce the segment that we identify as /p/. Of course, we cannot hear stop consonants such as /p/ in isolation, unaccompanied by a preceding or succeeding vowel, but that is largely irrelevant to the discussion of articulatory features.

However we analyze the temporally distributed acoustic information associated with a word, it is clear that we will have to analyze that information in terms of a number of auditory features characteristic of each segment of the word. Such features include the principal frequency components present at any point in time and the changes in these frequency components that occur over short periods of time. The detectors for these auditory features are considered to comprise the auditory feature level of the verbal modality.

III. CONCEPTS AND WORDS

A. Neural Representation of Attributes and Concepts

No one knows at the present time what the best definition of the term "concept" will turn out to be for analysis of the human mind. However, I will give what I consider to be the best definition available at present.

Work in sensory neurophysiology has made it quite clear that the nervous system encodes peripheral sensory input and motor output in terms of certain innate attributes. There are single neurons that respond vigorously when a stimulus with the appropriate properties (features, attributes) is presented. For example, there are known to be neurons in the auditory system that respond selectively to particular frequencies, neurons encoding frequency changes (e.g., Whitfield & Evans, 1965), and neurons that encode the direction of a sound source by responding to phase and intensity differences in the signals arriving at the left and right ears (e.g., Hall, 1965). On the motor side, a single motor neuron controls the activity of a single motor unit in a muscle. At higher levels of the motor system, there is evidence to indicate that certain more complex patterns of movement may be encoded in single neurons as well, though there will surely be redundant coding across many neurons, just as there is within the sensory nervous systems. Thus, it is reasonable to assume that on both the sensory and motor side there are feature representatives: units in the nervous system that represent particular features (attributes) of the sensory input and motor output. There is evidence that many of these attribute representatives are innately specified (e.g., Hubel & Wiesel, 1963).

Even if much of the peripheral representation of attributes is innate in human beings, it is clear that there cannot be representation of all human concepts by innately specified single neurons. The reason for this is that there are too many different types of concepts that human beings appear able to possess, perhaps an infinite number. Setting reasonable upper limits on the rate at which human beings might be expected to learn new concepts, say one new concept every second there are still more than enough neurons in the human brain (there are around 10^{10}) to have one neuron for every concept, provided that the specification of a neuron to stand for a concept is learned rather than innate. There is no experimental evidence to support the hypothesis that all concepts are represented by single neurons in the manner in which a single neuron can represent a straight line at a certain angle at a certain position in the visual field. However, this is a relatively clear, precise way to think of the representation of concepts in the nervous system, and I know of no other equivalently clear way to think of this representation. Thus, it seems reasonable to me to adopt this as a working hypothesis; but one should note that there is no direct experimental support for this hypothesis and many theorists consider the hypothesis outrageous.

B. Psychological Definition of Concepts

Irrespective of the neural representation of concepts, we still need to formulate some hypothesis concerning the logical relation between concepts and attributes. It will not do to say that concepts are simple conjunctions of attributes. It may be possible for a precise thinker to give some definition of a concept such as the concept of the species dog in terms of a conjunction of attributes possessed by all dogs. However, this is not the same as saying that whenever we perceive or think of the concept *dog,* it is because that conjunction of attribute representatives has been activated. Rather, we can think of the concept *dog* when we see a particular dog in a particular perspective with a conjunction of attributes that are quite different from those that would be present seeing the same dog from a different perspective, seeing a different dog, seeing a different species of dog, seeing the word *dog,* or hearing the word *dog.*

To explain how we are able to recognize examples of concepts, it is sufficient to consider that a concept is a disjunction of a large number of conjunctions of attributes. That is, there are large number of sets of attributes that are individually sufficient to activate the concept *dog* in our minds. It should be noted that defining a concept to be a disjunction of conjunctions of attributes is not necessarily the ideal way to define concepts. However, it appears to me at present to be a sufficient way of defining concepts, and I know of no other way that is sufficient to handle the problems of concept recognition. This description of concepts and the arguments for it are described in greater detail in Wickelgren (1969b).

It is worth pointing out that the representation of concepts proposed by Katz and Fodor (1963) is essentially a theory that characterizes a concept by a simple conjunction of attributes, which we have noted is not adequate to account for the perceptual recognition of concepts. What role if any such "dictionary" or "scientific" definitions of concepts may play in human thought or human perception and cognition is another question, but the dictionary definition is clearly not sufficient to define concepts as people actually use them.

Furthermore, Katz and Fodor (1963) postulate word representatives, which encode all the different possible meanings of a concept, rather than concept representatives, which encode only a single meaning.

Another important issue in discussing the representation of concepts concerns whether or not there is any unique representative for each concept separate from the set of representatives of any of its component attributes. As we have seen, no single conjunction of attributes is sufficient to define concepts as people use them, but perhaps a large number of sets of attributes would be sufficient to stand for the concept, without any need to specify a single unique representative for any of these sets of attributes. The issue can be stated in terms of whether there is a single neuron somewhere that stands for the one or more conjunctions of attributes that define the concept or whether the representation of the concept is simply by the set of representatives for each of its attributes. This problem is discussed at some length in Wickelgren (1969b), where it is concluded that there would be severe associative interference problems if the only representation of a concept was by a set of attribute representatives with a no single concept representative. Attribute representation of concepts simply creates too much confusion in an associative memory. Thus, it appears to be necessary to assume that individuals can "chunk," in the sense of Miller (1956), a set of attributes to form a new representative for each chunk. Then perhaps humans associate several different chunk representatives into a single concept representative to stand for the disjunction of these chunks. According to this theory, the process of concept learning results from two component processes: (a) chunking of the attributes within any given conjunction and (b) associating the different chunks together to form their disjunction, which is the concept.

C. Evidence for Concept Representatives

There is abundant evidence for the existence of concept representatives that stand for meanings in addition to representation of verbal concepts only by their segmental components (phonemes, allophones, syllables, etc.). In long-term recognition memory for single words, false-recognition errors are consistently higher for words that are either semantically or phonetically similar to previously presented words than they are for control (neutral) words (Ainsfeld & Knapp, 1968; Grossman & Eagle, 1970; Kimble, 1968; Klein, 1970; Underwood, 1965).

Although I know of no formal experimental evidence to support this, personal experience suggests that associations learned to a concept signaled by a particular set of cues will transfer to the same concept signaled by a different set of cues. Since the cues may have nothing in common from a perceptual or structural point of view this can only be mediated by some type of concept representative that uses semantic (meaningful) encoding.

Additional evidence for the existence of concept representatives comes from studies in conceptual recognition of words. Miller, Heise, and Lichten (1951), Rubenstein and Pollack (1963), and Stowe, Harris, and Hampton (1963) found that content words (nouns, verbs, adjectives, adverbs) are more easily recognized when presented in a grammatical sentence than when spoken in isolation. Although I cannot prove this definitely, it seems extremely unlikely that this effect could be mediated by the grammatical sentential context biasing a particular set of phonemes or syllables or other structural elements of the correct words. The number of possible words that could be presented in most sentential contexts is generally very large, and all structural elements (phonemes, syllables, etc.) must be represented many, many times in these different words. Rather it seems necessary to assume that the effect is mediated by a contextually induced bias (set) for concept or word representatives that can appear in the particular context of other words in some sentence. Miller and Isard (1963) obtained an intelligibility advantage for words spoken in either grammatical sentences or partially grammatical (anomalous) sentences versus words presented in ungrammatical strings. The number of possible alternatives for each position in the anomalous strings is even greater than in the perfectly grammatical strings, making it seem very improbable that the effect could be mediated by setting oneself for particular syllables, phonemes, features, etc. Similarly, Bruce (1955) and Rubenstein and Pollack (1963) found that the intelligibility of a word was enhanced when it was known to come from a particular conceptually defined set, such as the set of all foods, rather than being any possible word in the language. Again, since the reduction in the set of alternatives is based on semantic criteria, rather than on phonetic criteria, it seems very unlikely that the effect could be obtained unless there were concept representatives in some semantic system, in addition to phonetic representatives of the components of words.

Finally, the word frequency effect (e.g., Brown & Rubenstein, 1961; Howes, 1957; Pollack, Rubenstein, Decker, 1959; Rosenzweig & Postman, 1957), in which more frequently occurring words in a language are more easily recognized than less frequently occurring words, seems difficult to explain without assuming that there are concept or word representatives and that we are biased (set) to either perceive or emit more familiar words, as compared with less familiar words. It seems unlikely that very much of this effect could be attributed to systematic differences at the structural (phonetic) level between frequently occurring and infrequently occurring words. However, Fredericksen (1971) has presented some limited evidence that there may be some systematic phonetic differences between frequently and infrequently occurring words, so perhaps the issue cannot be considered closed. Nevertheless, there is an enormous amount of converging evidence for the reality of concept representatives, in addition to the possibility of segmental and feature representatives, at lower levels of the verbal modality.

D. Concept Representatives versus Word Representatives

Finally, there is evidence to indicate that these semantic units are concept representatives that encode one meaning of a word as postulated by Wickelgren (1969b), not word representatives that encode all the meanings of a word, as postulated by Katz and Fodor (1963).

When words to be learned were originally presented in a sentence context that biased a particular meaning, rather than other meanings, for each word, false recognition rates were elevated for words related to the correct meaning but not for words related to the other meanings of each presented word (Perfetti & Goodman, 1970). Light and Carter-Sobell (1970) and Tulving and Thomson (1971) have demonstrated that correct recognition memory for a word is decreased by changing from learning to testing the verbal context in which it is presented, in a manner that presumably changes in some cases the meaning the subjects attach to the word.

Also, MacKay (personal communication) found that associative responses to ambiguous words (words with multiple meanings, such as *sound*) took longer than responses to "unambiguous" words (words with one primary meaning or closely related meaning such as *clock*). MacKay controlled for length, frequency, emotional tone, and "other factors" that he thought might possibly confound the comparison. As MacKay concludes, this indicates that associations are not between word representatives but between concept representatives.

IV. PHRASES, CLAUSES, AND SENTENCES

Although I know of no relevant evidence, it is reasonable to conjecture that familiar (frequently occurring) phrases may be represented by single units at the concept level, just as words are. That is to say, the phrase *black bird* may be represented as a single concept, just as is the single word *blackbird*.

Since human beings are capable of consistently identifying the phrases, clauses, and sentences in a long utterance, there is reason to believe that these constitute "units" in *some* sense in the nervous system. However, I know of no evidence to indicate that each distinct phrase, clause, or sentence is represented by a single unit in the nervous system in the sense used for concept representatives. Considering that most of the phrases, clauses, and sentences that we speak are novel (never before uttered by the speaker), it seems extremely unlikely that there are single representatives for each distinct phrase, clause, or sentence that we can produce. Rather, what seems more likely is that we have representatives for a variety of types of phrases, clauses, sentences, etc. and also for the relationships that can obtain between phrases, clauses, sentences, etc. These more general concepts probably play an important role in our understanding and production of speech, but further discussion of these matters is beyond the scope of the present chapter.

V. FEATURES

A. Articulatory Features

The production of the sounds of speech depends upon the movement of air through the vocal tract in a manner analogous to the production of a musical sound by the passage of air through a complex pipe. The vocal tract has two channels (pipes) through which the air may pass, namely, the oral tract and the nasal tract. The vocal tract begins above the larynx (glottis, voice box) with a single cavity (pipe) known as the pharynx, which branches to form two cavities, the nasal cavity (through the nose) and the oral cavity (through the mouth).

1. CHEST

The production of the airstream essential for speech takes place primarily by operation of the chest muscles, which force air from the lungs, through the glottis, and then into the vocal tract. Alternate mechanisms for the production of an airstream are used in some languages.

Once an airstream has been produced, the acoustic characteristics of the sound one hears depend on the configuration of the vocal tract. In contrast to the usual pipe or system of pipes, however complex, the vocal tract is capable of a modification of its characteristics at a large number of places by means of muscular activity controlled by motor neurons.

2. LARYNX

In the larynx, the vocal cords may be in a variety of states. One state is that used in the production of voiced sounds, including all English vowels and the consonants /b/, /d/, /g/, /z/, /m/, /n/, etc. In the case of all voiced sounds, the vocal cords are in vibration, producing a characteristic pitch (fundamental frequency) that can be heard in association with these sounds. A second state of the larynx is that characteristic of voiceless aspirated sounds in English, such as the consonants /p/, /t/, and /k/, when these sounds occur in the initial or terminal position of syllables. A third state of the larynx is the voiceless unaspirated state. This state is used in producing such sounds as /p/, /t/, and /k/ in many interior positions of syllables, such as /p/ in the word *spot,* /t/ in the word *stove,* or /k/ in the word *ski.* It is quite easy to tell for yourself whether a sound such as /p/ is aspirated or unaspirated. Put your hand in front of your mouth during the pronunciation of a word that contains the sound /p/ and feel whether or not a puff of air hits the palm of your hand during the pronunciation of /p/. Aspirated /p/, as in *pit,* is accompanied by a puff of air;

unaspirated /p/, as in *spit,* is not. A fourth state of the larynx is that characteristic of whispered voice.

3. VELUM

Another modifiable aspect of the vocal tract is whether the soft palate (velum) is up or down. When the velum is up, the nasal cavity is shut off from the vocal tract and the airstream passes only through the oral cavity. In English, most sounds are strictly oral, including such consonants as /p/, /b/, /t/, /d/, /k/, /g/, /s/, /z/, /r/, /l/, /w/, etc. When the velum is down, the airstream passes through both the nose and the mouth. Such sounds are known as nasals and, in English, include only the phonemes /m/, /n/, /ŋ/, where /ŋ/ is the terminal phoneme in /ing,/ /ang/, /eng/, /ong/, etc.

4. JAW

Another modifiable aspect of the vocal tract is the jaw, which partly controls the degree of openness of the vocal tract (principally the volume of the oral cavity). Other factors, including principally lip and tongue position, also control the openness of the vocal tract, and it is not clear to what extent jaw position is modified to control openness.

5. LIPS

Lip position, including whether the lips are closed or opened and also whether the open position of the lips is spread or rounded, is another important characteristic of the vocal tract. For example, the consonant phonemes /p/, /b/, and /m/ are all produced by a complete closure of the lips. The consonant (semivowel) /w/, is characterized by a rounded, open lip position.

6. TONGUE

Finally, the most important modifiable aspect of the vocal tract is the position of the tongue. Muscles in the tongue exert considerable control in determining the openness of the vocal tract. In addition, the tongue can be elevated at many different places, markedly changing the relative configuration of the oral and pharyngeal cavities. The point at which the vocal tract is maximally constricted is known as the place of articulation. Place of articulation is an important feature dimension of both vowels and consonants, and the tongue is the principal articulator determining place.

Vowels and consonants differ in place of articulation, but whether the places of articulation for the vowels in any way correspond to the places of articulation for consonants is unknown. The question is difficult, since the degree of openness (largely determined by the degree of elevation of the tongue) for vowels is much greater than that for consonants. Similarly, semivowels, including the sounds /w/, /r/, /l/, /y/, and possibly /h/, are generally characterized by a degree of openness of the vocal tract intermediate between that for vowels and consonants. Once again, although it is possible to make some type of identification of the places of articulation of semivowels with corresponding places for consonants, this identification is extremely tentative, at present.

B. Auditory Features

1. NARROW-BAND FREQUENCY CUES

There is considerable neurophysiological evidence to support the existence of neurons at many levels of the nervous system that respond selectively to certain frequencies or frequency components of complex sounds. These neurons typically have a "tuning curve," responding maximally to a tone of a particular frequency and responding progressively less well to frequencies farther away from the "ideal" frequency for that neuron. Thus, there are frequency detectors to represent the fundamental frequency and also those relatively narrow-band resonances of the vocal tract known as formants, which are considered to be distinctive features for the perception of vowels (Delattre, Liberman, Cooper, & Gerstman, 1952; Peterson & Barney, 1952).

2. FREQUENCY TRANSITIONS

In addition, some neurons have been discovered at higher levels of the auditory nervous system that seem to respond to various frequency transitions (Suga, 1965, 1968; Whitfield & Evans, 1965), raising the possibility that there is unitary internal representation for each type of frequency transition. For example, there might be a set of neurons that respond selectively to a transition from 400 to 700 Hz, occurring over a 20–100 msec interval, a different set of neurons responding primarily to a transition from 400 to 900 Hz, still another group of analyzers responding selectively to transitions from 1400 to 1000 Hz, etc. Since changes in the formant frequencies (formant transitions) are known to be good cues for identifying consonants that precede or follow a vowel (see Liberman, Cooper, Shankweiler, & Studdert-Kennedy, 1967, for a review), single units representing these features would be very helpful. To my knowledge, there is no direct evidence that formant transitions have a unitary feature representation in the human nervous system. Virtually all of the work that has been done on the auditory nervous system has been done on animals other than man, for obvious reasons.

3. Broad-Band Formants

The formants and formant transitions that provide the important acoustic features for the perception of stop consonants, semivowels, and vowels are relatively narrow-band concentrations of energy around maxima at certain characteristic frequencies. By contrast, fricatives and affricates (f, v, θ, ð, s, z, š, ž, etc.) are characterized by extremely broad-band concentrations of energy in different frequency regions of the spectrum (Heinz & Stevens, 1961; Hughes & Halle, 1956; Jassem, 1965). The exact cues that distinguish fricatives and affricates are less well established than the cues for other English sounds. However, it does appear that concentrations of energy over frequency regions of many thousands of hertz are more characteristic cues for fricatives (especially s, z, š, and ž, see Harris, 1958) than local maxima (formants) with bands on the order of tens or hundreds of hertz. In part, this may be a consequence of the fact that most of the friction noise present in fricatives and affricates is at much higher frequencies than the fundamental frequency or the first-, second-, and third-formant frequencies characteristic of other speech sounds. The friction noise in fricatives and affricates is to a very large extent contained between 2000 and 12,000 Hz. It is well established that a given degree of discriminability of pure tones requires a progressively greater absolute (but not relative or percentage) separation in frequency as the frequency of the tones increases (e.g., Harris, 1952). Along this line, it is reasonable to suppose that frequency detecting units have broader bands at higher frequencies, measured in absolute frequency units (hertz).

While the friction noises characteristic of fricatives and affricates can be prolonged, there are other brief noise cues, called noise bursts, that provide useful cues in the recognition of stop consonants (Liberman *et al.*, 1967).

4. Silence

When a stop consonant, such as /p/ or /t/, is articulated, there is a short period of silence during which the vocal tract is completely closed and no sound can be heard. This period of silence is known to be an important cue for the perception of the stop consonants (Liberman *et al.*, 1967). Of course, the period of silence occurs at a different point in time than the formant transitions to or from the following or preceding vowel. Thus, in recognizing a phoneme we must assume that the features used in recognition do not all occur at exactly the same points in time but, instead, are spread over some small region in time on the order of 100 to 500 msec.

5. Duration

The duration of different periods of silence, noise bursts, broad-band formants, narrow-band formants, formant transitions, etc. may be cues of some importance in speech recognition at a given rate of speaking. Studies of the duration of different phonemes or other classes of speech segments invariably indicate systematic differences between different phonemes or other classes of speech sounds (e.g., Kozhevnikov & Chistovich, 1965; Lehiste, 1970b). However, it is often difficult or impossible to determine any particular point in time where one phoneme ends and the next phoneme begins. The cues for a given phoneme are intermixed in time to a large extent with the cues for adjacent phonemes. This being the case, it is not clear from peripheral articulatory or acoustic measurements what underlying psychological duration should be assigned to each segment (phoneme).

Although segmental duration may be a relatively meaningless concept in speech recognition, feature duration is known to be an important cue in discriminating between certain phonemes. Lisker (1957) has shown quite conclusively that the duration of stop consonant closure is a critically important cue for the distinction between voiced and unvoiced consonants /p/ versus /b/. The acoustic cue for the duration of stop-consonant closure is, of course, a period of relative silence, with voiceless consonants such as /p/ having closing durations in the Lisker study ranging from 90 to 140 msec (averaging 120 msec) and closure durations for the voiced consonant /b/ varying from 65 to 90 msec (averaging 75 msec).

Furthermore, Bolinger and Gerstman (1957) have shown that silence duration is an important cue for juncture (in this case, word segmentation) in distinguishing such phrases as *lighthouse keeper* and *light housekeeper.* The results are that the tendency to put *lighthouse* together is enhanced by having a short silent period between *light* and *house,* relative to the silent period between *house* and *keeper.* Conversely, the tendency to hear *housekeeper* as a single word is enhanced by making the silent period between *light* and *house* long, in relation to the silent period between *house* and *keeper.*

Given that rates of talking are variable, it is probably necessary for the listener to take speech rate into account in some way to make maximal use of duration cues. Relative durations of some kind are probably more critical than absolute durations.

6. INTENSITY

Integrating over all audible frequencies, phonemes differ systematically in their acoustic intensity (Lehiste, 1970b). Of course, we have already mentioned that an important cue for distinguishing different phonemes or allophones is the intensity in different (narrow or broad) regions of the frequency spectrum. Whether any type of integration over the entire audible frequency spectrum is an independently significant cue for speech recognition is not known. To establish this, we would need to know how intensity in different frequency regions is weighted by the "loudness" units in the nervous system assessing overall intensity. Furthermore, as with the duration cue, absolute intensities (air pressure levels) differ very considerably with different degrees of stress and different emotional states, even for the same speaker, to say nothing of differences across different speakers.

It was once thought that intensity was the primary cue for the suprasegmental stress feature, but the status of intensity as a cue to stress is now quite debatable (Bolinger, 1957–1958; Lehiste, 1970b; Lieberman, 1967; Morton & Jassem, 1965). It now seems generally agreed that fundamental frequency is the primary cue to stress (frequency changes of several types cueing stress; Bolinger, 1958), with duration being of some significance (greater duration indicates greater stress). Intensity, if it is a cue at all, is far less important than either fundamental frequency (intonation) or duration. It seems conceivable that the function of intensity variation in speech is largely a matter of achieving the appropriate signal-to-noise ratio for speech to be heard under different conditions of background noise. Overall intensity may be of no significance whatever, at either a segmental or suprasegmental level, as a cue to the meaning of the utterance.

C. Abstract Linguistic Features

Phonetics would be greatly simplified, if there were a simple relation between each articulatory feature and some auditory feature.

In some cases, there is a relatively simple relation. For example, the voicing state of the larynx is correlated with the presence of a fundamental frequency component in the acoustic signal. For steady-state vowels, there is a fairly simple relation between the openness and the frequency of the first formant and between place of articulation and the frequency of the second formant (e.g., Peterson & Barney, 1952). However, it should be noted that openness of the vocal tract and place of articulation are not simple articulatory feature dimensions to the same extent as is voicing.

At the other extreme, place of articulation for consonants is determined by a number of different muscles in both the tongue and the lips (and possibly the jaw), and the acoustic features of the "same" place differ for different phonemes and for the same phoneme in different phonemic environments. For example, the acoustic cues for the place of articulation of the /d/ phoneme differ greatly depending upon whether it is followed (or preceded) by the vowel /i/ or the vowel /ɑ/. (See Liberman *et al.,* 1967, for a more complete discussion of this issue.)

At present, there is no accepted theory of the articulatory and auditory features of speech sounds and the relation between them. Instead of having two feature analyses, one auditory and one articulatory, what we have are a variety of somewhat similar proposals for a single abstract (linguistic) feature analysis of those abstract classes of speech sounds known as phonemes (e.g., /p/, /z/, /o/, etc.).

Phonological arguments can be given for one distinctive feature system as opposed to another, but these are beyond the scope of the present chapter, and the psychological reality for articulation and recognition of much of phonology is in doubt (see Ladefoged, 1970).

One way to justify assuming an abstract feature level is if the sensory and motor aspects of speech unite at the feature level, as opposed to the segmental level or the concept level. According to such a theory, there should be a definable relation between articulatory and auditory features, so that the same feature representatives receive sensory input during perception, and control motor output during articulation. The last 20 years of research on speech perception and production make it seem very unlikely that such a relation can be defined (Liberman *et al.*, 1967). The theory defended in subsequent sections is that the sensory and motor aspects of speech unite at a segmental level, assuming that the segmental units are allophones (auditory and articulatory variants) of phonemes.

Conventional linguistic distinctive feature systems (excluding such purely phonological systems as that of Chomsky and Halle, 1968) may only be a convenient way of representing the average similarity of the phoneme classes of allophones at a segmental level. This average similarity might be jointly determined by both auditory and articulatory feature similarity in a manner too complex for present determination.

There is no doubt that some kinds of features have psychological reality, since articulatory and auditory features are needed for the speech production and perception processes, respectively. Furthermore, Hintzman (1967) and Wickelgren (1965, 1966) have demonstrated that errors in short-term memory for single phonemes are nonrandom in ways that can be described by distinctive feature systems, though these data do not permit a decision regarding the auditory, articulatory, or abstract nature of the features (Wickelgren, 1969d). However, there is no compelling evidence for the psychological reality of units representing abstract features, and existing feature systems include dimensions that may not represent either real articulatory or real auditory feature dimensions.

These latter dimensions are place and manner (openness) of articulation, which sound like articulatory dimensions (and may be at some central level), but which do not appear to be single dimensions at the peripheral motor neuron level.

Nevertheless, conventional linguistic feature systems serve the very useful function of representing, in at least an approximate way, the similarity of different phoneme classes of allophones. Furthermore, it is conceivable that such systems have articulatory or abstract linguistic reality (though it is very unlikely that they have auditory reality). For these reasons, a distinctive feature analysis of vowels is presented in Table 1 and a distinctive feature analysis of consonants is presented in Table 2. Arguments for something like this feature analysis can be found in Denes and Pinson (1963), Flanagan (1965), Gleason (1955), Ladefoged (1971), Pike (1947), Wickelgren (1965, 1966), and many other places.

Basically three or four feature dimensions are used to analyze the vowels. First, the major distinction is between simple vowels and complex vowels. Simple vowels refer in essence to a single configuration of the vocal tract, which is maintained in some sense throughout the vowel phoneme (though, of course, there are transitions from the preceding phoneme and transitions to the succeeding phoneme). In the case of complex vowels (complex syllable nuclei, diphthongs), the place of articulation or degree of openness or both change during the articulation of the vowel. In some cases, this change is extensive, as in the case of the complex vowel /ī/, where the initial portion of /ī/ is similar to the vowel /ɑ/, as in *hot,* but the terminal portion of /ī/ is similar to the semivowel /y/. In other instances, notably /ē/ or /ō͞o/, and possibly /ō/, the degree of alteration of the vocal tract configuration during the complex vowel is less dramatic,

TABLE I

DISTINCTIVE FEATURES OF ENGLISH VOWELS

Openness	Place		
	Front	Middle	Back
	Simple Vowels		
Narrow (High)	ı (h*i*t)	ɨ (b*ir*d)	ʊ (f*oo*t)
Medium (middle)	ɛ (s*e*t)	ʌ (h*u*t)	o ([a])
Wide (Low)	æ (h*a*t)	ɑ (h*o*t)	ɔ (*a*ll)
	Complex Vowels		
Narrow	ē or i or ıy (h*ea*t)	er or ɨr (b*ir*d)	ō͞o or u or Uw (b*oo*t)
Medium	ā or e or ɛy (h*a*te)		ō or ow (b*oa*t)
Wide		ī or ɑy (*i*ce)	oi or ɔy (*oi*l)
		and	
		ou or ɑw (c*ou*ch)	

[a] To my knowledge, short "o" does not appear in my English dialect, except as a part of the long vowel "ow."

TABLE II

DISTINCTIVE FEATURES OF ENGLISH CONSONANTS

Openness (Manner)	Place							
	0	1	2	3	4	5	6	7
Stops								
UV	p			t		k		
V	b			d		g		
N	m			n		ŋ		
Affricates								
UV		f	θ		č			
V		v	ð		j			
Fricatives								
V				s	š			
				z	ž			
Semivowels								
UV							h	
V	w			r	l	y		

NOTE: /θ/ = /th/ in "*th*ink", /ð/ = /th/ in "*th*e", /č/ = /ch/ in "*ch*eck" /š/ = /sh/ in "*sh*ook", /ž/ = /zh/ in "a*z*ure", /ŋ/ = /ng/ in "bri*ng*" UV = unvoiced, V = voiced, N = voiced nasal

to the point where some phoneticians have considered these vowels to have a single vocal tract configuration. (For a further discussion of this unresolved issue regarding which vowels are complex and the general relationship between various complex vowels and "corresponding" simple vowels and semivowels, see Lehiste, 1964, and Ladefoged, 1965.)

The other two distinctive feature dimensions for vowels, namely, the degree of openness and the place of articulation, are reasonably well established by comparison to the simple versus complex dimension. However, there are some disagreements regarding the classification of place and openness shown in Table 1. One question is whether /ɑ/, as in *hot,* should be classified as a middle-wide vowel (as in Table 1) or as a back vowel with a wider degree of openness than /ɔ/.

In general, for a given speaker there is no guarantee that the vowels found in the same row have the same degree of openness. Nor is there any guarantee that vowels found in the same column have the same place of articulation. The values of openness and place may be only relative to other entries within the same row or column, respectively. That is to say, within the front simple vowels, /ɪ/ is narrower than /ɛ/, which is narrower than /æ/, but /ɪ/ and /ʊ/ do not necessarily have the same degrees of openness of the vocal tract. It is not even clear from an articulatory standpoint, given the different shape of the tongue for front versus back vowels, what it means to have the same degree of "openness." Nevertheless, this type of relative classification with regard to the values of place and openness has proved to be of substantial value in understanding many of the differences between vowels.

Disregarding such features as aspiration, which are not critical in a logical sense for distinguishing any pair of words in English, English consonants can be analyzed in terms of four distinct feature dimensions: openness, place of articulation, voicing, and nasality.

The openness dimension in Table 2 refers to how much the vocal tract is constricted at the place of maximum constriction. This varies all the way from complete closure for stop consonants to a rather open vocal tract in the case of semivowels. Fricatives have a sufficiently narrowed vocal tract so that the air passes through a very narrow passage producing considerable friction noise. Affricates are somewhat intermediate between stops and fricatives, and their exact status in relation to stops and fricatives is not definitely decided.

Place of articulation varies in a more extreme manner for consonants than for vowels, namely, there are some consonants, such as /p/, /b/, /m/, and the semivowel /w/, that have their place of articulation at the lips. In the case of /p/, /b/, and /m/ this is by means of complete lip closure. Other consonants are produced by putting the lower lip against the upper teeth, as in the case of /f/ and /v/, or by placing the tip of the tongue against the upper teeth, as in /θ/ and /ð/, all the way back to /h/, which is made by pushing the root of the tongue against the back wall of the pharynx.

The number of different values of the place dimension could be reduced from the number used in Table 2 by collapsing place values 0 and 1, place values 2 and 3, and place values 6 and 7, since the more detailed analysis shown in Table 2 is not logically necessary for assigning a distinct set of feature values to each phoneme. However, since the places of articulation are reasonably different, a relatively arbitrary decision was made to adopt the more finely differentiated set of values on the place dimension. On the other hand, the feature analysis shown in Table 2 ignores many additional important characteristics of each consonant. For example, nothing in Table 2 indicates that /w/ has lip rounding, rather than the spread lip configuration. Nothing in Table 2 indicates some of the distinctive characteristics of the shape of the tongue for the phonemes /r/ and /l/. Aspiration is ignored, and so on.

Voicing and nasality have been represented in Table 2 as if they were a single dimension with three values. This reduction in the complexity of the table is possible for English, since all nasal consonants are voiced. However, logically speaking, voicing refers to a state of the vocal cords, while nasality refers to whether the velum is up or down.

VI. SEGMENTS

A. Phonemes

Although this analysis is currently being challenged within transformational generative phonology (e.g., Chomsky & Halle, 1968), linguists traditionally analyze a word or phrase that represents a concept into a sequence of structural units called phonemes. Thus, the English word *struck* would be analyzed to consist of the following ordered set of five phonemes /s/, /t/, /r/, /u/, /k/. The six letters used to spell the word *struck* in English orthography are often referred to as graphemes. The spelling of a word in written English is an ordered set of graphemes (letters). Although there is a rough correspondence in English between graphemes and phonemes, the relationship is very far from one-to-one.

Whereas words stand for concepts that have meaning, phonemes stand for structural components of words and have, in general, no meaning at all. This is a general characteristic of the segmental level of analysis, namely that the segments themselves are purely structural units with no meaning. Communication of concepts from one individual to another virtually requires representation of words by a succession of segments, since the number of unique, hearable, positions of the vocal tract is many orders of magnitude less than the number of different concepts that human beings possess. Since the human vocal system is essentially a one-sound-at-a-time system, it is necessary to construct sequences of sounds (vocal tract positions) in order to represent all of the concepts human beings possess.

There are usually considered to be approximately 40 consonant and vowel phonemes in the English language (for my listing of 41 consonant and vowel phonemes see Tables 1 and 2). Although there is some disagreement regarding the exact inventory of phonemes characteristic of English (particularly concerning whether complex vowels should be considered phonemes), there would be little disagreement concerning how any particular word ought to be spelled phonemically, within any given system of phonemes.

The primary theoretical justification for phonemes is that they constitute a theory of the segmental representation of words at some central level in the nervous system. Three properties of this representation bear explicit mention. First, the inventory of segments is relatively small in comparison to the number of words in English. Second, the segments are nonoverlapping. Knowledge that a word contains a given segment does not logically restrict what other segments might be used in the spelling of the word. [In regard to this second point it must be mentioned that, if we have statistical data on the spelling of words in the language, then we can make statements concerning conditional probabilities that certain phonemes will be found preceding or following or otherwise occurring in the same word with other phonemes. Furthermore, if we have some additional restrictions added to the phonemic theory regarding what phonemes are permitted to appear in association with what other phonemes in words (namely, a theory of phonology), then we also have a basis for making predictions. However, for the moment I am assuming that we lack both statistical and phonological information. My point is that spelling words in terms of ordered sets of phonemes does not logically require that there be nonrandom orderings of the segments across the dictionary of words in a language.] Third, the spelling of a word is by an *ordered set* of segments (phonemes) not by an *unordered set* or a two-dimensional tree structure, etc.

Note that, thus far, nothing has been said regarding the articulatory or acoustic representation of phonemes, though clearly the fundamental purpose of a segmental representation of words (concepts) is to permit communication by a sequential output device (the vocal tract) to a sequential input device (the ear).

The simplest relation between abstract phonemes and peripheral articulatory and acoustic events would be for a sequence of phonemes to translate into a discrete sequence of vocal tract configurations and, therefore, a discrete sequence of acoustic patterns characteristic of each phoneme. In this simple system, if there were 40 phonemes, there would be 40 vocal tract configurations (or 40 short sequences of vocal tract configurations) and 40 different acoustical events, one for each phoneme. Any given phoneme would have the same vocal tract configuration and the same acoustical properties independent of its context. That is to say, the articulatory and acoustic features of a phoneme would be independent of what other phonemes occurred next to it or in other positions in the same word. Furthermore, the vocal tract configurations and acoustic events characteristic of each phoneme would be nonoverlapping in time. That is, the articulatory and acoustic features of each phoneme would be presented during a period of time that in no way overlapped with the articulatory and acoustic features of any other phoneme. If speech segments had these two properties, we might say they were "context free" and temporally segmentable.

In actual fact, at an articulatory and acoustic level, speech does not consist of context-free segments, nor is it temporally segmentable. The vocal tract configuration and associated acoustic representation of a given phoneme vary considerably with the context, primarily the immediate left and right phonemic environment. That is to say, the phoneme /d/ will be very different in both articulatory and acoustic features depending on whether it is preceded or followed by the phoneme /ɛ/ or the phoneme

/ɑ/. Furthermore, there is not even a core of invariant acoustic features for each phoneme across all different contexts. (For a review of the extensive literature supporting these conclusions, see Liberman *et al.*, 1967; MacNeilage, 1970; Wickelgren, 1969a.)

There are two good reasons for this context-conditioned variation (coarticulation), which are inherent in the properties of the speech musculature: (*a*) inertia (the vocal tract cannot move instantly from one configuration to another) and (*b*) starting position (different muscular contractions are required to achieve the same terminal position of an articulator from different starting positions). Given these properties of the speech apparatus, one could only realize a sequence of invariant articulatory and acoustic segments by ignoring the transition regions between adjacent speech sounds and concentrating only on some invariant central period of time during which the vocal tract configuration and acoustic cues might be invariant for a given phoneme in all different contexts. This later, somewhat weaker type of context-free, temporally segmentable, phonemic coding does not obtain either. Given the neural and mechanical limitations of speech articulation, speech, if it were required to have these context-free, temporally segmentable properties, would be incapable of occurring at as rapid a rate as it occurs (Liberman *et al.*, 1967). Instead, the acoustic cues characteristic of the transitions between target positions for successive phonemes constitute extremely important cues for the recognition of both the prior and the subsequent phonemes (Liberman *et al.*, 1967). Under these circumstances, it is often rather arbitrary and absurd to try to decide some particular point in time at which one phoneme ends and the next phoneme begins.

It is possible to subdivide speech into a number of discrete segments, but these segments have no simple relationship to the phonemes. For example, a stop-consonant plus vowel utterance contains at least four different distinguishable segments: a silent period during the complete occlusion characteristic of the stop consonant, the fricative burst characteristic of the very short period of time following opening of the consonant (during which there is only a very narrow opening in the vocal tract), the "vowel-like" period of the transition to the target vowel position, and finally, if the speech rate is slow, the steady-state vowel period. The acoustical cues inherent in the transition to the vowel contain information regarding both the consonant and the vowel, so there is no particular point in time at which one could decide that the consonant portion has ended and the vowel portion has begun. Furthermore, in rapidly articulated speech, steady-state target positions for vowels may never be reached, which further complicates analysis.

What ability we do have to segment speech acoustically derives from the fact that certain underlying features of speech are relatively discrete, in the sense of having only two or a few states, with relatively rapid transitions from one state to the other. Examples of such discrete features include voicing (whether the vocal cords are vibrating or not), nasality (whether the nasal cavity is open to the passage of sound or not), whether the vocal tract is completely occluded or not, and, to a lesser extent, the presence versus absence of fricative noise. The very important features of tongue position and the degree of openness of the vocal tract, for any period other than the complete occlusion phase of stop consonants, are relatively continuous features with a large number of different states and relatively gradual transitions between the states. Since some of the continuous feature cues are among the most important for the identification of speech segments, the impossibility of segmenting the values on these feature dimensions effectively precludes the segmenting of speech into discrete phonemes. Even the discrete features are of no value in segmenting speech when adjacent phonemes have the same value on that discrete feature dimension, such as when adjacent phonemes are voiced. In such cases, the voicing is simply maintained continuously, without any break to indicate a separation between the two phonemes. Such discrete features as the voicelessness of the preceding consonant may extend well into the transition to a following vowel, and the anticipatory presence of features characteristic of subsequent phonemes is also observed. For example, sometimes a vowel adjacent to a nasal consonant will be itself nasalized throughout its entire duration. This is just one example of what is meant by saying that the features characteristic of phonemes at a peripheral articulatory and acoustic level are not independent of the nature of the adjacent phonemic context. Note that this also contributes to the impossibility of segmenting speech into nonoverlapping phonemes at a peripheral articulatory or acoustic level. (See Fant, 1962, for a further discussion of the segmentability of certain speech features and the lack of segmentability of other features and of phonemes.)

Consistent with the lack of segmentability and the context-conditioned variation in the acoustic cues for phonemes, it is known to be impossible to achieve highly intelligible speech by cutting "phoneme-size" segments from recording tape and splicing them together in new combinations to form new words. Such techniques have been tried several times and do not work (Harris, 1953). The smallest size units that can be cut and spliced from recorded utterances to produce intelligible speech are roughly a half syllable in length, and these half syllables must mesh properly in order to produce intelligible speech (Peterson, Wang, & Sivertsen, 1958). That is to say, an /ni/ half syllable must mesh with an /ic/ half syllable to produce natural and intelligible speech. Thus, speech at the vocal tract and acoustic cue level is not composed of successive, context-free segments. That is to say, speech at these levels is not phonemic.

Of course, this in no way implies that speech is not phonemic at some higher level of the nervous system. However, in subsequent sections, arguments will be presented to suggest that phonemic coding is not used at any level of the nervous system in normal adult speech recognition and articulation.

B. Context-Sensitive Allophones

A number of problems in speech recognition and articulation can be solved by making an assumption regarding the segmental encoding of words that is an alternative to the phonemic coding assumption (Wickelgren 1969a,c). Instead of assuming that a word such as *struck* is encoded as an ordered set of context-free phonemes /s/, /t/, /r/, /u/, /k/, one could assume that a word such as *struck* was encoded by an unordered set of context-sensitive allophones: $/_\#s_t/$, $/_st_r/$, $/_tr_u/$, $/_ru_k/$, $/_uk_\#/$. Each of the context-sensitive elements in this code essentially contains a little bit of local information concerning the ordering of this element in relation to other elements in the set.

If there were a unit in the nervous system for each such context-sensitive allophone, then the representation of the word could be by an unordered set of such units whenever this was convenient for speech recognition and articulation, since the information concerning the ordering of these elements can be derived from the unordered set in all cases for single English words. For example, one first looks for the only element that has $\#$ as its initial element, then this initial allophone provides the information that the next allophone is of the form $/_st_-/$, where "–" stands for an unknown phoneme, and so on until all the allophones in a word are correctly ordered. It is much like assembling a linear jigsaw puzzle. With phonemic coding, the same unordered set of phonemes can often be ordered to form two or more words. However, with context-sensitive allophonic coding it is a remarkable fact that there is, at most, one way of making an English word out of any unordered set of context-sensitive allophonic symbols.

Even if one were to take rather long phrases consisting of many words and scramble their context-sensitive allophonic segments, it will almost always be possible to reorder the symbols to form a unique reconstruction of the ordering of the allophones to form words in the phrase. This is especially true, if the terminal segment of the ith word is sensitive to the initial segment of the $(i + 1)$st word and the initial segment of the $(i + 1)$st word is context-sensitive to the terminal segment of the ith word. Such a context-sensitive coding would be said to "cross" word boundaries. For such an encoding of the phrase *Jim struck,* the terminal segment of *Jim* would be $/_im_s/$ and the initial segment of struck would be $/_ms_t/$.

Other mechanisms for achieving the correct ordering of words (sets of allophones) without context-sensitive coding crossing word boundaries are presented in Wickelgren (1969a) and in the section on suprasegmental components later in the present chapter.

Even for a completely artificial language with random selection of symbols for the spelling of "words" with ordered sets of symbols from a relatively small vocabulary of letters or phonemes (on the order of 20 or more), it is very improbable that the information concerning the ordering of these letters could not be recovered from the overlapping-triple type of context-sensitive coding proposed here. It came as a considerable surprise to me to realize how much of the information concerning the ordering of very, very long sets of elements can be communicated by this type of extremely local information concerning the relative order of adjacent elements. (For a further discussion of the mathematical properties of context-sensitive coding see Wickelgren, 1969a,c.)

The number of context-sensitive allophones (phoneme triples) that would be required for English can be determined by a count of the number of different phoneme triples that occur in the language. One such count is that of Hultzén, Allen, and Miron (1964) who found a total of 3,083 different phoneme triples in their sample of 20,032 consectuvie phonemes. This analysis considered accented and unaccented vowels to be different phonemes, and this two-level lexical accent system is probably completely adequate. Nevertheless, these figures probably underestimate by a factor of two or three (surely less than ten) the number of different triples occurring in English. This is because the sample size is too small. However, it seems likely from these data that there are no more than about 10 or 20 thousand phoneme triples in English. If syllable boundaries are marked in the manner suggested in the next section, then less than 5 or 10 thousand context-sensitive allophone representatives would probably be required. While such a number is large in comparison to 40–100 phonemes as the segmental units of the language, it is small in relation to the number of neurones in the nervous system (about 10^{10}), so that there is no need to be concerned about the number of segmental representatives that must be assumed by this theory.

The assumption that context-sensitive allophones are the primary internal representatives used at the segmental level in speech recognition and articulation solves the two previously discussed problems with the assumption of phonemic segmental coding. First, context-sensitive coding solves the problem of segmenting speech at a peripheral articulatory and acoustic level. Since the segments are now overlapping, rather than nonoverlapping, by definition, there is no need to segment speech into nonoverlapping portions of time. Second, there obviously can be context-conditioned variation in the articulatory and auditory features of the allophones within each phoneme class. No invariant core of articulatory or auditory features is required to define a phoneme, because the units are allophones of each phoneme, which may be different in these features for every different immediate left and right phonemic environment. There should be a core of articulatory and auditory features for each allophone that are invariant over variations in more remote phonemic context. This latter requirement has not been adequately tested. However, remote context-conditioned variation is known to be far smaller than immediate context-conditioned variation, so this prediction is probably valid.

In the control of speech articulation, there could be activation of a sequence of context-sensitive allophone representatives at some central level of the nervous system that would translate into a smoothly flowing sequence of articulatory movements at a peripheral level. Since each segmental control unit is sensitive to ("knows") the target position for the previous and the succeeding segments, the instructions to the articulatory muscles can take prior and subsequent target positions into account in trying to achieve approximately the same target position for the currently articulated allophone as for any other allophone within the same phoneme class. For example, the motor intructions (features) for the $/\upsilon d_{\varepsilon}/$ allophone can be different from the motor instructions for the $/_{\alpha}d_{I}/$ allophone in just the manner necessary to achieve approximately the same target position for both allophones of the /d/phoneme. According to the context-sensitive coding theory, the peripheral articulatory features of each phoneme class of allophones should exhibit context-conditioned variation. Also, it should be difficult or impossible to segment the stream of motor commands or vocal tract configurations, since the (allophonic) control elements are essentially overlapping phoneme-triples. Furthermore, the turning-off of one allophonic control unit and the turning-on of subsequent allophonic control units could be temporally overlapping to some extent. Thus, context-sensitive coding is consistent with these basic facts concerning speech articulation.

In speech recognition, all context-sensitive allophone representatives could be operating in parallel "looking" for the set of features needed to activate them with the requirement that features all be presented over some maximum unit in time. That maximum unit of time might well be variable for different perceived rates of talking. With such a parallel speech recognition scheme, there would be no need for prior segmentation of the speech stream. Also, with context-sensitive allophone detectors, the presence of context-condition variation in the acoustic cues for different "segments" would be an aid to speech recognition by increasing redundancy, rather than a hindrance to speech recognition.

It bears mentioning again that the results of Peterson *et al.* (1958), that the smallest segments that can be used for speech synthesis by the cutting and splicing technique are properly meshed half syllables, is precisely what one would expect on the view that the principal segmental representatives are context-sensitive allophones.

C. Syllables

The syllable has sometimes been proposed as an important unit in the segmental analysis of words. Thus, a word like *construct* is analyzable into two syllables: /con/, /strukt/. There are rather serious definitional problems in the case of segmental analysis of words into syllables, due to the fact that intuitions are far more variable regarding the syllabic analysis of words than the phonemic (and allophonic) analysis of words. A word such as *syllabic* might be subdivided into syllables by one person as /sil/, /lab/, /ik/; another might analyze it as /sil/, /ab/, /ik/; still another might analyze it as /sil/, /lab/, /ik/; another might analyze it as /si/, /lab/, /ik/; yet another might analyze it as /sil/, /ab/, /ik/; still another might analyze it as /sil/, /la/, /bik/, and so on. More sophisticated higher-level linguistic arguments can sometimes be given for a particular mode of syllabic analysis as opposed to another, but there is considerable disagreement at this level also regarding what, if any, syllabic analysis of words is useful. Personally, my intuition regarding *syllabic* is that there are no definite syllable boundaries in this word, though there clearly are three vowels and a definite accent pattern.

Context-sensitive allophonic coding is in a sense a type of overlapping syllabic coding, which would assert that there was a reality to all the different ways of analyzing a word such as *syllabic* into syllables. By contrast, syllabic coding requires analysis of a word into nonoverlapping segments. Syllabic coding provides no information regarding the ordering of syllables within a word. Furthermore, it is not at all clear how the assumption of syllabic coding could provide information regarding the ordering of the phonemic (allophonic) constituents of a syllable. So, although there are some superficial similarities between context-sensitive allophonic coding and syllabic coding, there are a greater number of differences.

Syllabic coding has sometimes been suggested as a way to provide invariant segmental units for auditory recognition, to get around the enormous effects of the immediate left and right phonemic context on the acoustic cues for the single phonemes. However, to the extent that initial and terminal phonemic (allophonic) segments of syllables are sensitive to terminal and initial phonemic segments of adjacent syllables, this solution is not satisfactory. Nevertheless syllabic coding would to some extent get around the problem of context-conditioned variation in the acoustic cues for each phoneme (Mattingly & Liberman, 1969). Segmentability problems would be reduced (but not eliminated), since there would be a need to segment only at syllable boundaries.

Often it has been suggested that the syllable is an important unit in the timing of speech. At one time it was thought that each syllable was the result of a separate chest pulse of air, but this is now known to be false (Ladefoged, 1971).

Recently, a rather complex statistical analysis of temporal compensation in the pronunciation of words and phrases has been used to argue for the reality of the syllables (and the higher word and phrase levels) as being important units in the timing of speech (Kozhevnikov & Chistovich, 1965; Lehiste, 1970a; Shockey, Gregorski, & Lehiste, 1971). The method for determining the existence of timing units in articulation consists of looking for negative correlation between the durations of different segments within a word or a phrase. The notion is that if a syllable is a timing unit in the nervous system, then a single syllable such as /kon/ should be pronounced in a certain amount of time, given a particular rate of talking. If, in repeated pronunciation of the syllable /kon/, the speaker prolongs the /k/ phoneme more at some times than at other times, and if the syllable is a unit of timing in speech articulation, then the longer /k/ phoneme should be compensated for by a shorter /o/ phoneme or a shorter /n/ phoneme within that particular utterance of the syllable. The previously mentioned studies have found many examples of this negative correlation or temporal compensation within syllables, words, and even phrases.

However, all of the previously mentioned studies, except Lehiste (1970a), used a completely inappropriate method of data analysis. They selected from all of the utterances those that maintained the closest approximation to some particular time for the entire utterance. This, for statistical reasons, guarantees negative correlation between segmental components of the entire utterance. Since this negative correlation is guaranteed by selecting utterances of approximately the same total length, the finding of negative correlation gives no evidence for the psychological reality of any unit.

When such statistical selection was not used, as in Lehiste (1970a), a greater mixture of positive and negative correlation was found, though there were some consistent negative correlations, such as between a vowel and a subsequent consonant. However, even such findings are questionable, since speakers were instructed to maintain a constant rate of talking. Whatever the causes of differences in rate of speaking in normal conversation, instructing a subject to maintain a constant rate of talking may induce artificial types of temporal compensation that ordinarily never take place. For example, in these experimental tasks, where the subject is to produce the same short utterance tens or hundreds of times at a constant rate of talking, it is possible for subjects to maintain a constant rate by controlling either rate of talking or the total duration of their utterances. Subjects may attempt to maintain a constant duration of talking in short utterances by *changing* their rate of talking at various points during the utterance. It may be quite erroneous to interpret constant durations of short utterances to indicate constant rates of talking. It is conceivable that constant rates of talking may be more achievable under natural conversational conditions with longer utterances. The foregoing studies may have guaranteed negative correlation simply by the instructions to the subject, with the results indicating nothing regarding the functioning units in ordinary speech production. I do not see how to solve this problem within the context of this type of study. Until it is satisfactorily resolved, it seems to me we can place no confidence in the results that have been obtained.

Allen (1972) presents similar criticisms of these studies and reports also that he and Ohala have failed to replicate many of the negative correlations. In addition, Allen (1972) and Kozhevnikov and Chistovich (1965) point out that any measurement error in locating segment boundaries will automatically produce negative correlation between adjacent segments. Given the difficulties of segmenting speech at an acoustic level, this is a serious problem.

Further reason for rejecting these findings as evidence for the psychological reality of syllables comes from studies by Huggins (1968a,b), who found no evidence for the perceptual reality of temporal compensation. Huggins found that, when an adjacent vowel was lengthened or shortened, there was no compensatory change in the subject's preferences for the duration of an accompanying consonant in the same syllable.

Savin and Bever (1970) and Warren (1971) found, surprisingly enough, that it took less time to identify either a monosyllabic word or a nonsense syllable target than it took to identify single phoneme targets. This provides further evidence of concept (word) representatives in the nervous system. The nonsense syllable versus phoneme comparison is also evidence of some units more extensive than a single phoneme being primary in the speech recognition process. However, these units could either be syllables or context-sensitive allophones (phoneme triples). In Warren's study, CV bigrams were recognized almost as quickly as entire nonsense syllables, suggesting that phoneme triples would be recognized just as quickly as entire syllables.

D. Syllable Juncture

The strongest evidence known to me for the psychological reality of the syllable comes from studies of errors in speech articulation. There has been repeated confirmation of the law stated by Boomer and Laver (1968), that "segmental slips obey a natural law with regard to syllable-place; that is, initial segments in the origin syllable replace initial segments in the target syllable, nuclear replace nuclear, and final replace final [p. 7]." Besides Boomer and Laver, this law has been supported by Fromkin (1968, 1970), MacKay (1970a,b), and Nooteboom (1967, 1968).

Another finding reported by MacKay (1970a,b) is that reversals (transpositions, spoonerisms) of phonemes more frequently involve the initial consonants of different syllables, whether the reversals are within a word or between words. This latter effect was extremely large, indicating that the transition from the terminal consonant of one syllable to the initial consonant of the following syllable is the weakest link in the ordering of phonemes in an utterance.

While the above findings regarding speech errors indicate that *syllable boundaries* must be taken into account in representing the phonetic encoding of words and phrases, these data do not show that the *syllable* as an ordered set of phonemes is a basic segmental unit in speech production. Occasionally one observes a transposition or substitution of an entire syllable, but "subsyllabic" (phonemes or clusters of phonemes) substitutions and transpositions account for almost all speech errors at a segmental level.

As an example of how one might mark syllable boundaries within the context-sensitive allophonic coding theory described earlier, consider the following analysis of the word *segment:* $/_\#s_e/$, $/_se_g/$, $/_eg_+/$, $/_+m_e/$, $/_me_n/$, $/_en_t/$, $/_nt_\#/$. This type of context-sensitive analysis marks the initial, medial, and terminal allophones in syllables in a manner that explicitly indicates similarity to other allophones that occupy initial, medial, or terminal syllable positions. Thus, errors should tend to preserve syllable position, as reported by the above investigators. In addition, it should be obvious that the encoding of order information is weakest across syllable boundaries, according to the above analysis. This is consistent with MacKay's finding that reversal errors frequently involve syllable-initial position. An additional assumption should probably be made that word juncture ($\#$) has high similarity to syllable juncture ($+$).

Marking syllable boundaries explains the previous speech error findings without requiring the syllable to be a segmental unit. However, the legimate question can be raised as to what purpose is served for the organism by the marking of syllable boundaries. It has just been observed that marking a syllable boundary reduces the integrity of the order information across that boundary, linking the last allophone of one syllable less uniquely to the initial allophone of the following syllable. This hardly seems like a desirable property for a speech production system. The only functional reason I can think of for marking syllable boundaries in this way is that it would substantially reduce the number of context-sensitive allophones required to be learned and represented in the system. There are few restrictions concerning what phonemes can follow what phonemes across syllable boundaries in English, but there are very substantial restrictions on the phoneme sequences within syllables.

Another way to look at somewhat the same point is to argue that phoneme sequences that cross syllable boundaries are not coarticulated to the same extent as phoneme sequences within syllables, and that this fact ought to be represented in the coding theory at a phonetic level. Along this line, one would argue that the /dwi/ phoneme triple in *sandwich* (assuming one does pronounce all of the phonemes indicated in the spelling of this word) and the /dwi/ sequence in *dwindle* are somewhat different in their allophonic coding. Namely, the /w/ allophone in *sandwich* is /$_+$w$_i$/ and the /w/ allophone in *dwindle* is /$_d$w$_i$/. According to this hypothesis, different acoustic cues would be associated with the two different /w/ allophones. The relatively small number of intrasyllable consonant clusters that we have in English are acquired developmentally later than the consonant vowel clusters. The pronunciation of consonant clusters may well be more difficult, due to mechanical properties of the vocal tract, and/or the perception of consonant clusters might be more difficult. This could mean that it is dysfunctional for a language to require coarticulated representations of all the possible consonant transitions. In any event, it seems in accord with both data and intuition to mark syllable boundaries in the manner indicated.

Furthermore, a slight modification of the above hypothesis would preserve considerably more of the order information across syllable boundaries in a manner that is still qualitatively consistent with the evidence for syllable boundaries derived from speech error data. The alternative hypothesis can most easily be explained by giving an alternative encoding of the word *segment:* /$_\#$s$_e$/, /$_s$e$_g$/, /$_e$g$_+$/, /$_g$+$_m$/, /$_+$m$_e$/, /$_m$e$_n$/, /$_e$n$_t$/, /$_n$t$_\#$/. By this analysis, syllable juncture is considered to be more than a conditioning factor on the syllable-terminal and syllable-initial allophones. Syllable juncture is also a context-sensitive allophonic segment in and of itself, conditioned by the terminal phoneme of the preceding syllable and the initial phoneme of the succeeding syllable. Such syllable-boundary segmental units would play an important role in preserving order information across syllable boundaries for speech articulation and recognition. In addition, if there are explicit cues for syllable boundaries, as there must be if the /w/ allophones in *sandwich* and *dwindle* are different, then there exist cues adequate for the acoustic definition of such syllable-juncture segments. In some words, with difficult transitions from the terminal phoneme of one syllable to the initial phoneme of the next syllable, the syllable juncture allophone might be associated with a short pause or transition region in speech. However, there is *no* need for the articulatory output of the syllable boundary segment to occupy any appreciable period of time. Within context-sensitive allophonic theory, it is simply not necessary to have each segment associated with some particular period of time that does not overlap with the period of time occupied by other segments.

Another point about the current theory of representing syllable juncture is that there is no need to assume that a word with n vowels has n syllables or $n - 1$ syllable junctures. Syllable juncture is not introduced to mark off nonoverlapping domains of different vowels, as necessary units of the speech production or recognition processes. Rather, syllable juncture is introduced to separate consonants that are not be coarticulated. In a word such as *syllabic,* there may be no syllable junctures at all in my dialect, though conceivably there might be one or more syllable junctures in someone else's dialect.

E. Suprasegmental Components

In addition to the traditional segmental components of speech, there is another class of articulatory features that are considered to be important phonetic components of speech. These factors are often grouped together and referred to as suprasegmental or prosodic features of speech. They include such linguistic notions as the intonation (pitch) contour of an utterance, stress, accent, rhythm, etc.

Intonation contours serve as important cues for the meaning of a message. For example, in English, a falling pitch contour at the end of an utterance is typical for statements, and a "not-falling" intonation contour is typical for questions. In addition, certain words in an utterance will be stressed more than other words. For example, articles, prepositions, and other grammatical "function" words are typically the most weakly stressed words in an utterance, and the other words in an utterance differ among themselves in judged degree of stress. In at least some utterances, linguistic intuition will be reasonably consistent in distinguishing three or four levels of what we shall here call "stress," which is the stress placed on one entire word, as opposed to another entire word, in the utterance.

Stress is thought to be primarily realized in conjunction with a particular syllable or vowel of the stressed word, the "accented" syllable, or the "accented" vowel. To reduce the possibility of confusion between word "stress" and segmental "accent," I have followed Bolinger (1958) in giving them different names. If the syllable has no reality, then "accent" should probably be assumed to be a distinctive feature of vowels. People make remarkably consistent judgments of vowel (syllable) accent, so there is little doubt concerning its psychological reality as a feature. For example, in the word "fundamental," the third vowel has the primary accent, while the first vowel has the secondary accent, and the second and fourth vowels are least accented. It is possible that there are only two distinctive levels of vowel accent, accented and unaccented.

Regarding the domain of the accent feature, it should be noted that considering accent to be a feature of vowels automatically conditions the (immediately) preceding and subsequent phonemes adjacent to the vowel. This could somewhat stretch out the articulatory and acoustic realization of the effects of different levels of accent. In addition, the anticipatory (priming) mechanism described earlier would further increase the articulatory and acoustic time domain of accent on an articulatory and acoustical feature level.

When a word is stressed, as for example when it is produced in isolation, there are measurable articulatory and acoustic features that differentiate different levels of vowel accent. However, when a word is relatively unstressed in continuous speech, there are frequently no observable acoustic differences between accented and unaccented vowels in such an unstressed word. Thus, the accent and stress systems are closely linked, with accent reflecting the different potential of the vowels in a word for exhibiting the effects of word stress.

Linguists, especially Chomsky and Halle (1968) have the intuition that every sentence has a normal word stress pattern. Accounting for this normal word stress pattern is part of the task of their theory of phonology. For example, in a sentence such as *Joe ran into a green door*, the word *door* would be judged by me to have primary stress, with *Joe, ran,* and *green* having secondary stress, and the function words *into* and *a* being unstressed. However, under appropriate circumstances, one could place primary stress on any word of the utterance, even the grammatical function words. Chomsky and Halle wish to account for "normal" stress patterns and leave these other stress patterns outside their theory, attributing them to different mechanisms. Beyond the linguistic intuition that there is one "most typical" stress pattern for virtually every sentence, I know of no other reasons to justify assuming different stress mechanisms in the two cases. The stress pattern judged "normal" for a sentence may simply be that which is appropriate for the most probable set of conditions for the utterance (intended meaning and assumed prior knowledge of the hearer). Thus, I do not find the evidence for assuming different mechanisms to be at all compelling. In any event, I am not concerned with accounting for any particular stress patterns for the words in an utterance. I shall take them to be given by the concept level as input for the phonetic level. My only concern is to ask how this word stress pattern is represented at the phonetic level and what its interaction is with the segmental aspects of speech.

We could characterize the stress pattern in an utterance as an ordered set of three or four stress levels. Thus, if 3 indicates the highest stress level, 2 the next highest, and 1 the lowest, we could characterize the stress sequence in *Joe ran to the green door* as (2,2,1,1,2,3). However, for reasons similar to the assumption of context-sensitive allophonic coding for segmental representatives, it seems preferable to assume that stress pattern is not represented at a phonetic level by an ordered set of context-free stress representatives but is, instead, represented by an unordered set of context-sensitive stress representatives. For example, in the above sentence, the context-sensitive stress coding would be $(_{\#}2_2)$, $(_22_1)$, $(_21_1)$, $(_11_2)$, $(_12_3)$, $(_23_{\#})$. Such a sequence of context-sensitive stress representatives could be input from the concept level to the phonetic level, either simultaneously or successively. In either case, the correct order of stress representatives would be activated by long-term associations between such context-sensitive stress representatives, even though the temporal ordering of stress representatives was not maintained at all times at the phonetic level. With only a small number of different stress representatives (probably only three or four), it is not clear whether such context-sensitive coding would always unambiguously encode the temporal ordering of stress levels (the intonation contour). However, input from the concept level to the phonetic level could be not simultaneous but successive, with each word and its associated stress level being output from the concept level to the phonetic level, in temporal order. In this case, the short-term associations among stress levels and between them and their associated words would help the stress representatives successfully traverse the ambiguous transitions. At present, the assumption that input to the phonetic level from the concept level is word-by-word successive seems slightly more reasonable than the assumption of parallel input. However, there is no real evidence on the point.

There is a reason for assuming that the ordering of stress representatives is at least partially (if not completely) independent of the ordering that might be induced by their associations with the successive words in an utterance. Evidence for this comes from Boomer and Laver (1968) and Fromkin (1970), who observed a number of speech errors in which subjects transposed words in an utterance but the stress patterns remained the same. That is to say, the sequence of stress representatives remained the same, though the words came out in the wrong order. This resulted in the "wrong" stress being assigned to words that appeared in the wrong positions in the utterance. If stresses do not have some representation of their ordering independent of their association with ordered word representatives, this should not happen. This constitutes some evidence for the validity of the context-sensitive associative-chain theory of serial ordering of stress representatives, as previously described, though of course other theories of the ordering of stress representatives could also account for this fact.

Although it seems desirable to assume that stress representatives have their own encoding of order to account for the above findings, it seems very desirable to assume that each stress representative has an association to its appropriate word (set of allophone representatives at the phonetic level). Although it is possible to assume that the representation of the order of words and the order of stress representatives are two separate systems that operate in parallel, this sort of system would probably lead to some coordination difficulties, unless there were interaction between the two sequences to keep them in proper phase. Assuming associations between stress representatives and sets of allophone representatives could probably be used to achieve this coordination. In addition, such a correlation would help to replicate the ordering of stress representatives and of the sets of allophone representatives for adjacent words, improving the accuracy of transitions from the terminal phoneme of a word to the initial phoneme of the following word.

References

Allen, G. D. Timing control in speech production: Some theoretical and methodological issues. Paper presented at Phonetics Symposium, Univ. of Essex Language Centre, January, 1972.

Anisfeld, M., & Knapp, M. Association, synonymity, and directionality in false recognition. *Journal of Experimental Psychology,* 1968, **77,** 171–179.

Bolinger, D. L. On intensity as a qualitative improvement of pitch accent. *Lingua,* 1957–58, **7,** 175–182.

Bolinger, D. W. A theory of pitch accent in English. *Word,* 1958, **14,** 111–149.

Bolinger, D. W., & Gerstman, L. J. Disjuncture as a cue to constructs. *Word,* 1957, **13,** 246–255.

Boomer, D. S., & Laver, J. D. M. Slips of the tongue. *British Journal of Disorders of Communication,* 1968, **3,** 2–12.

Brown, C., & Rubenstein, H. Test of response bias explanation of word-frequency effect. *Science,* 1961, **133,** 280–281.

Bruce, D. J. Effects of content upon intelligibility of heard speech. In C. Cherry (Ed.), *Information theory,* Third London Symposium: 1955. New York: Academic Press, 1956. Chapter 26, pp. 245–252.

Chomsky, N., & Halle, M. *The sound pattern of English.* New York: Harper, 1968.

Delattre, P., Liberman, A. M., Cooper, F. S., & Gerstman, L. J. An experimental study of the acoustic determinants of vowel color; observations on one- and two-formant vowels synthesized from spectrographic patterns. *Word,* 1952, **8,** 195–210.

Denes, P. B., & Pinson, E. N. *The speech chain.* Bell Telephone Laboratories: Waverly Press, 1963.

Fant, C. G. M. Descriptive analysis of the acoustic aspects of speech. *Logos,* 1962, **5,** 3–17.

Flanagan, J. L. *Speech analysis, synthesis, and perception.* New York: Springer-Verlag, 1965.

Frederiksen, J. R. Statistical decision model for auditory word recognition. *Psychological Review,* 1971, **78,** 409–419.

Fromkin, V. A. Speculations on performance models. *Journal of Linguistics,* 1968, **4,** 47–68.

Fromkin, V. A. Tips of the slung—or—to err is human. *UCLA Working Papers in Phonetics,* 1970, No. **14,** March, 40–79.

Gleason, H. A. *An introduction to descriptive linguistics.* New York: Holt, 1955.

Grossman, L., & Eagle, M. Synonymity, antonymity, and association in false recognition responses. *Journal of Experimental Psychology,* 1970, **83,** 244–248.

Hall, J. L. Binaural interaction in the accessory superior-olivary nucleus of the cat. *Journal of the Acoustical Society of America,* 1965, **37,** 814–823.

Harris, C. M. A study of the building blocks in speech. *Journal of the Acoustical Society of America,* 1953, **25,** 962–969.

Harris, K. S. Cues for the discrimination of American English fricatives in spoken syllables. *Language and Speech,* 1958, **1,** 1–7.

Harris, J. D. Pitch discrimination. *Journal of the Acoustical Society of America,* 1952, **24,** 750–755.

Heinz, J. M., & Stevens, K. N. On the properties of voiceless fricative consonants. *Journal of the Acoustical Society of America,* 1961, **33,** 589–596.

Hintzman, D. L. Articulatory coding in short-term memory. *Journal of Verbal Learning and Verbal Behavior,* 1967, **6,** 312–316.

Howes, D. On the relation between the intelligibility and frequency of occurrence of English words. *Journal of the Acoustical Society of America,* 1957, **29,** 296–305.

Hubel, D. H., & Wiesel, T. N. Receptive fields of cells in striate cortex of very young, visually inexperienced kittens. *Journal of Neurophysiology,* 1963, **26,** 994–1002.

Huggins, A. W. F. The perception of timing in natural speech I: Compensation within the syllable. *Language and Speech,* 1968, **11,** 1–11. (a)

Huggins, A. W. F. How accurately must a speaker time his articulations? *IEEE Transactions on Audio and Electroacoustics,* 1968, **AU-16,** 112–117. (b)

Hughes, G. W., & Halle, M. Spectral properties of fricative consonants. *Journal of the Acoustical Society of America,* 1956, **28,** 303–310.

Hultzén, L. S., Allen, J. H. D., & Miron, M. S. *Tables of transitional frequencies of English phonemes.* Urbana: Univ. of Illinois Press, 1964.

Jassem, W. The formants of fricative consonants. *Language and Speech,* 1965, **8,** 1–16.

Katz, J. J., & Fodor, J. A. The structure of semantic theory. *Language,* 1963, **39,** 170–210.

Kimble, G. A. Mediating associations. *Journal of Experimental Psychology,* 1968, **76,** 263–266.

Klein, G. A. Temporal changes in acoustic and semantic confusion effects. *Journal of Experimental Psychology,* 1970, **86,** 236–240.

Kozhevnikov, V. A., & Chistovich, L. A. *Speech: Articulation and perception.* Translated by J.P.R.S., Washington, D.C., No. JPRS 30, 543. Moscow-Leningrad, 1965.

Ladefoged, P. Acoustical characteristics of selected English consonants. *Language,* 1965, **41,** 332–338.

Ladefoged, P. The phonetic framework of generative phonology. *UCLA Working Papers in Phonetics,* 1970, No. **14,** March, 25–32.

Ladefoged, P. Phonetics. *UCLA Working Papers in Phonetics,* 1971, No. **20,** March, 1–28.

Lehiste, I. Acoustical characteristics of selected English consonants. *International Journal of American Linguistics,* 1964, **30:**3, Part 4, 34, pp. xi–197. Bloomington: Indiana University.

Lehiste, I. Temporal organization of spoken language. *Working Papers in Linguistics,* 1970, No. 4, Ohio State Univ., 95–114. (a)

Lehiste, I. *Suprasegmentals.* Cambridge, Massachusetts: M.I.T. Press, 1970. (b)

Liberman, A. M., Cooper, F. S., Shankweiler, D. P., & Studdert-Kennedy, M. Perception of the speech code. *Psychological Review,* 1967, **74,** 431–461.

Lieberman, P. *Intonation, perception, and language.* Cambridge, Massachusetts: M.I.T. Press, 1967.

Light, L. L., & Carter-Sobell, L. Effects of changed semantic context on recognition memory. *Journal of Verbal and Verbal Behavior,* 1970, **9,** 1–11.

Lisker, L. Closure duration and the intervocalic voiced-voiceless distinction in English. *Language,* 1957, **33,** 42–49.

MacKay, D. G. Spoonerisms: The structure of errors in the serial order of speech. *Neuropsychologia,* 1970, **8,** 323–350. (a)

MacKay, D. G. Spoonerisms of children. *Neuropsychologia,* 1970, **8,** 315–322. (b)

MacNeilage, P. F. Motor control of serial ordering of speech. *Psychological Review,* 1970, **77,** 182–196.

Mattingly, I. G., & Liberman, A. M. The speech code and the physiology of language. In K. N. Leibovic (Ed.), *Information processing in the nervous system.* Springer Verlag, 1969. Pp. 97–114.

Miller, G. A. The magical number seven, plus or minus two: Some limits on our capacity for processing information. *Psychological Review,* 1956, **63,** 81–97.

Miller, G. A., Heise, G. A., & Lichten, W. The intelligibility of speech as a function of the context of the test materials. *Journal of Experimental Psychology,* 1951, **41,** 329–335.

Miller, G. A., & Isard, S. Some perceptual consequences of linguistic rules. *Journal of Verbal Learning and Verbal Behavior,* 1963, **2,** 217–228.

Morton, J., & Jassem, W. Acoustic correlates of stress. *Language and Speech,* 1965, **8,** 148–158.

Nooteboom, S. G. Some regularities in phonemic speech errors. *IPO Annual Progress Report II* (Instituut Voor Perceptie Onderzoek), 1967.

Nooteboom, S. G. The tongue slips into patterns. *Nomen, linguistic and phonetic studies.* The Hague, Mouton, 1968.

Perfetti, C. A., & Goodman, D. Semantic constraint on the decoding of ambiguous words. *Journal of Experimental Psychology,* 1970, **86,** 420–427.

Peterson, G. E., & Barney, H. L. Control methods used in a study of the vowels. *Journal of the Acoustical Society of America,* 1952, **24,** 15–24.

Peterson, G. E., Wang, W. S.-Y., & Sivertsen, E. Segmentation techniques in speech synthesis. *Journal of the Acoustical Society of America,* 1958, **30,** 739–742.

Pike, K. L. *Phonemics: A technique for reducing languages to writing.* Ann Arbor: Univ. of Michigan Press, 1947.

Pollack, I., Rubenstein, H., & Decker, L. Intelligibility of known and unknown message sets. *Journal of the Acoustical Society of America,* 1959, **31,** 273–279.

Rosenzweig, M. R., & Postman, L. Intelligibility as a function of frequency of usage. *Journal of Experimental Psychology,* 1957, **54,** 412–422.

Rubenstein, H., & Pollack, I. Word predictability and intelligibility. *Journal of Verbal Learning and Verbal Behavior,* 1963, **2,** 147–158.

Savin, H. B., & Bever, T. G. The nonperceptual reality of the phoneme. *Journal of Verbal Learning and Verbal Behavior,* 1970, **9,** 295–302.

Shockey, L., Gregorski, R., & Lehiste, I. Word unit temporal compensation. *Working Papers in Linguistics,* 1971, No. **9,** Ohio State Univ. 145–165.

Stowe, A. N., Harris, W. P., & Hampton, D. B. Signal and context components of word-recognition behavior. *Journal of the Acoustical Society of America,* 1963, **35,** 639–644.

Suga, N. Functional properties of auditory neurones in the cortex of echo-locating bats. *Journal of Physiology,* 1965, **181,** 671–700.

Suga, N. Analysis of frequency-modulated and complex sounds by single auditory neurones of bats. *Journal of Physiology,* 1968, **198,** 51–80.

Tulving, E., & Thomson, D. M. Retrieval processes in recognition memory: Effects of associative context. *Journal of Experimental Psychology,* 1971, **87,** 116–124.

Underwood, B. J. False recognition produced by implicit verbal responses. *Journal of Experimental Psychology,* 1965, **70,** 122–129.

Warren, R. M. Identification times for phonemic components of graded complexity and for spelling of speech. *Perception and Psychophysics,* 1971, **9,** 345–349.

Whitfield, I. C., & Evans, E. F. Responses of auditory cortical neurons to stimuli of changing frequency. *Journal of Neurophysiology,* 1965, **28,** 655–672.

Wickelgren, W. A. Distinctive features and errors in short-term memory for English vowels. *Journal of the Acoustical Society of America,* 1965, **38,** 583–588.

Wickelgren, W. A. Distinctive features and errors in short-term memory for English consonants. *Journal of the Acoustical Society of America,* 1966, **39,** 388–398.

Wickelgren, W. A. Context-sensitive coding, associative memory, and serial order in (speech) behavior. *Psychological Review,* 1969, **76,** 1–15. (a)

Wickelgren, W. A. Learned specification of concept neurons. *Bulletin of Mathematical Biophysics,* 1969, **31,** 123–142. (b)

Wickelgren, W. A. Context-sensitive coding in speech recognition, articulation, and development. In K. N. Leivovic (Ed.), *Information processing in the nervous system.* New York: Springer-Verlag, 1969. Pp. 85–95. (c)

Wickelgren, W. A. Auditory or articulatory coding in verbal short-term memory. *Psychological Review,* 1969, **76,** 232–235. (d)

Chapter 8

SEMANTICS: CATEGORIZATION AND MEANING*

JAMES DEESE

I. INTRODUCTION

It is no longer unusual to hear it claimed that perception and cognition have an underlying structural identity. Arnheim (1972) so argues. Garner (1966) points out that to perceive is to know and that the conditions which determine perception also determine cognition. Deese (1969) argues that the cognitive categories underlying semantic relations are derived ultimately from modes of perceiving. Furthermore, there is widespread agreement with the notion that cognitive and perceptual categories are based upon universal and innate characteristics of the cognitive–perceptual system. Generally, the argument goes, some intellectual and perceptual modes are natural, easily demonstrated, and universal, other modes of perceptual and intellectual activity are difficult to acquire, demonstrate large individual differences, and are by no means culturally universal. The natural abilities appear to have well-defined developmental histories not to be confused with the changes that are associated with practice and other conditions of learning. Piaget and his followers have, by now, convinced nearly everyone that certain perceptual and intellectual abilities unfold themselves in an invariant and natural sequence. To attempt to teach a 3-year-old the

* This chapter was prepared with the partial support of funds from NIMH Grant No. 23957.

principle of conservation would appear to be the height of folly, for the interaction of experience and development would not yet have reached the point at which so young a child could understand the principle. A 3-year-old might be able to produce the "correct" responses in some particular conservation test, but it would be in much the same way that such a child could be taught to produce the logarithms of certain numbers.

Semantic relations are both cognitive and perceptual. There are abstract relations, for example, that define logical propositions paired with or perhaps underlying sentences and phrases. At the same time, it appears that perceptual modes also define certain kinds of semantic relations. The long history of the attempt to base the meaning of the words and phrases in ideas upon images testifies to the belief in the relation between perceptual modes and semantics. More recent is the point of view that images and sentences have a common origin in some more abstract structural relations. Many of the attempts to apply ideas derived from generative semantics to memory for and the process of understanding of sentences implicitly draw upon such a point of view.

This chapter is based upon the assumption that at least some of the categories of perception, particularly those relating to images, and of cognition, particularly those relevant to semantics, are basically the same. It takes the point of view that the problem in the analysis of the psychological character of semantics is not so much that of looking for differences between perception and thinking as it is to find those aspects of both perceptual and cognitive tasks that are determined by the same underlying structures. The problem is to separate those tasks that are universal and require little or no tuition from those tasks that are culture bound and require extensive tuition, usually of a formal variety. Semantic categories need not be characterized as perceptual or abstractly intellectual, but may be regarded as being determined by the same relations that also determine the character of human perception and thought.

The notion that we need not draw the traditional distinction between perception and cognition gives us a different point of departure for the study of semantics in a psychological context. It means we do not need to draw a hard line between the abstract and the concrete, the intellectual and the perceptual, the imageable and the unimageable. At the same time, it will be necessary to draw some new distinctions, distinctions that isolate the purely linguistic features of semantic relations from the cognitive and perceptual relations that determine their use.

Many linguists and a few psychologists have tried to apply some particular universal categorical structure to the description of semantic organization. Usually their efforts have been directed toward characterizing the

meaning of segments of language. Two linguistic segments have been selected for special attention: the word and the sentence. Modern linguistic
theory, of course, recognizes the morpheme. However, it is usually argued
that the user of English, or any other language for that matter, stores
words, rather than morphemes, though he knows and uses the rules for
forming words from morphemes (Halle, 1973). Despite the primacy of
the sentence, it is becoming increasingly apparent (see, for example, Bransford & Franks, 1972; Olson, 1970) that some transcendent level or levels
may be necessary before we can fully appreciate the precise sense of a word
or a sentence. Literary criticism has, of course, always recognized the importance of contextual analysis in determining the precise reading of some
term or phrase, and structural analysis is coming to recognize the same
need.

Meaning at the sentential level has received less attention from students
of language than meaning at the level of the word or morpheme. More
recently, meaning at the sentential or phrase level has been treated as a
problem to which various logical calculi should be applied (e.g., Lakoff,
1971; McCawley, 1971). It is sometimes, though not always, assumed that
a logical analysis of sentential meaning is also a psychological one. Both
Lakoff and McCawley say that the rules permitting efficient generalizations
about the semantic structure of sentences and its derivations are also rules
about how people understand, perform, believe, and generally operate
upon those sentences. To the extent that such a view is correct, these rules
are psychologically as well as linguistically and logically significant. It is,
however, not possible to demonstrate that the rules arising from the application of some logical calculus to the semantic structure of sentences are
identical to or even paired in a consistent way with the processes underlying
production and understanding. All that the facts of human communication
demand is that the processes underlying production and understanding lead
to outcomes correlated with those derived from the application of a well-
formed logical system. Lakoff and McCawley argue that the primary step
in a semantic analysis at the phrase level (the distinction between phrase
and sentence is necessary because surface sentences may interrelate independent propositions) is to determine the extent to which some semantic
representation is logically well formed. Alternatively, one might determine
the nature of a semantic representation by reference to some psychological
principle. For example, we might assume that all children of a certain age
naturally and inherently assign animistic character to the perception and
interpretation of motion. In the main, while there must be some correspondence between the logic used to determine the well formedness of a particular semantic representation and the psychological process of interpretation,

the correspondence need be only approximate. It must have some, but not necessarily complete, ecological validity.

II. THE STRUCTURE OF THE LEXICON

One of the consequences of the revolution created by generative theory was the shift from the word as the primary linguistic structure to the sentence. Sentences were no longer regarded as mere concatenations of words but as structures, more or less independently defined, into which words were placed by the application of various rules. The work of the past few years leads many of us to believe that, as a primary linguistic element, the sentence, or the underlying deep structure corresponding to particular simple sentences, has at least as many shortcomings as the word. Generative theory showed us that sentences are not agglutinations of words, and now it seems equally obvious that discourse is not an agglutination of sentences.

Nevertheless, words or morphemes and sentences or phrases do have an independent existence. We do have a lexicon that will serve indiscriminately in an indefinite number of sentential structures, and we do have sentential structures that will serve indiscriminately in any discourse. Corresponding to words and sentences, then, are semantic structures. Words have particular meanings, and sentence structures have grammatical functions that are, in the last analysis, intended to represent propositional meanings. Therefore, any account of the categories of meaning will deal at least with words and sentences, whatever else it may deal with. Because historical tradition reveals more concern with the semantics of words than with the semantics of sentences, it is the natural place to begin. Such a beginning has no theoretical implications. It is simply a matter of convenience.

The problem of the semantic structure of the lexicon received comparatively little attention from nineteenth-century philologists, despite their great interest in etymologies and comparative linguistics. Nineteenth century students of language were mainly concerned with words and their histories, and not with general principles by which the lexicon of a language becomes organized and is used. However, the nineteenth century did see a host of philosophers, amateurs, and plain eccentrics who were concerned with the problem of finding a universal classification of knowledge, and it is really these individuals who are the ancestors of contemporary linguistic theorists concerned with semantic structures. Also, as Aarsleff (1970) points out, Locke's analysis of simple and compound associations directly anticipates the contemporary concern with semantic features as the basic element in semantic structures.

A. Analytic Techniques

The problem of semantic structure of the lexicon is to describe its internal organization. The best-known and most influential scheme for giving an account of the internal semantic organization of English is that devised in the nineteenth century by the English physician Peter Mark Roget. The first edition of Roget's famous *Thesaurus of the English Language* was compiled over a period of more than half a century (Emblan, 1970), and subsequent editions have been in print ever since. Roget's *Thesaurus* is a classification system in which all concepts represented by words in the language are divided into six categories. These are (*1*) abstract relations, (*2*) space, (*3*) matter, (*4*) intellectual faculties, (*5*) voluntary powers, and (*6*) sentient and moral powers. Each of these is further categorized. Some of these classifications have three additional levels and some have more. All have large and varying numbers of branches at each level. The net result is that all words dominated by a particular pathway of nodes are grouped together. It is these that provide the entries to the *Thesaurus* proper.

A superficially different problem attacked in the nineteenth century was that a devising a scheme for the classification of books in libraries. It is superficially different from Roget's problem, in that the object of the classification is book titles instead of words. The general principles adopted by the various nineteenth-century classifiers, however, were essentially those of Roget. Knowledge was organized in the form of a (generally weak) hierarchical tree. Concepts functioned as semantic markers, and, just as in Roget's application words having similar meaning have similar or identical paths through the tree of markers, books on similar topics have similar or identical classification numbers. It is strange that it is only very recently that anyone has commented on the close resemblance between lexical storage and a library (see Norman, 1971, for an exposition of such a simile).

The description of semantic organization enters linguistic theory first as the result of developments in ethnolinguistics, and ethnolinguistics itself has developed a set of techniques and associated theory for the study of semantic structures, known as componential analysis. Independently, the emergence of generative theory in linguistics proper gave rise to the need to provide an explicit account of the semantic component of linguistic structures. While the concern of ethnolinguists is largely pragmatic and aimed towards the understanding of empirical anthropological data, the concern of generative theorists among the linguists is abstract and quite general. The structural linguists, who heavily influenced ethnolinguists, seldom addressed themselves to the problem of the internal organization of the lexicon. Bloomfield (1933), who was greatly concerned with the internal structure of grammar and phonology, dismissed the internal structure of semantics by saying: "In practice, we define the meaning of a linguistic form, wherever we can, in terms of some other science [Bloomfield, 1933, p. 140]." In short, Bloomfield argued, the structure of meaning is simply the structure of knowledge. There is nothing particular about the internal organization of the lexicon, and meaning really is only marginally a linguistic or a psychological problem. Bloomfield was a behaviorist and an associationist. He waited for learning theory to solve all the problems of how we acquire knowledge, and knowledge itself was simply determined by the organization of fields of investigation. However, generative theorists could accept no such point of view, and semantic theory became an essential component of linguistic theory. At the same time psychologists began to interest themselves in the structure of meaning, rather than the acquisition of meaning.

1. SEMANTIC FEATURE ANALYSIS

The best known of the early attempts to develop a theory of semantic structure within the framework of generative theory is that of Katz and Fodor (1963). The semantic component of generative theory, according to these authors, operates to provide a complete account of the interpretation of a sentence, an account that a syntactic analysis only begins. The semantic component provides, along with the grammar, possible readings of the sentence in question. The structure of the semantic component itself consists of two elements: semantic markers and semantic distinguishers. These are arranged in a weakly hierarchical tree, with the distinguishers always being the terminal branches. A weakly hierarchical tree is one in which some particular label or marker may appear at two or more nodes.

Each terminal branch of the tree gives a unique reading of some word having multiple meanings, so any particular tree is limited only to those markers applicable to a particular word. In this respect, the tree greatly differs from the general or universal classificatory tree proposed by Roget and the devisors of the various schemes for the universal categorization of knowledge. A complete account of the lexicon of some language by the conception established by Katz and Fodor would then be an ensemble or thicket of such trees. I do not mean to imply that Katz and Fodor do not suppose the lexicon to have any internal organization, indeed they say to the contrary. However, the semantic feature analysis they present is limited to the structure of individual members of the lexicon.

In each hierarchically arranged tree, more general markers, such as (+) concrete or (+) human, dominate less general markers, such as (+) young or (+) male. Semantic distinguishers are markers of less generality. In fact they apply only to a unique reading. They are not necessarily systematic for a language, but instead, specify something about the particular reading of the lexical entry they describe. Associated with the tree is a set of rules, the projection rules, that specify how to apply the particular markers, in order to arrive at an interpretation of sentences, by operating on the deep syntactic structure of the sentences.

The account given by Katz and Fodor has been criticized on a number of counts. Bollinger (1965) points out that the distinction between semantic markers and semantic distinguishers is spurious, and, what is worse, there is no principled way to provide a limit to the number of semantic markers that might be required to arrive at all the particular readings appropriate to a word in the context of any sentence in which it might occur. The number of markers required for any given entry will depend upon the particular context, but not in a way that can be specified in advance. In fact, any clever person can nearly always come up with additional readings, upon seeing those that someone else believes to exhaust the possibilities. It is this kind of problem that has induced more recent theorists to examine contexts beyond the limits of sentences, in an effort to provide more limits on possible readings and resulting lexical structures.

Related to the notion of the semantic marker as conceived by Katz and Fodor are a number of other formal and quasi-formal theories. Quillian (1968) has provided a model of semantic structure aimed at the particular problem of describing semantic storage in memory. In Quillian's scheme, markers or features are coded onto lexical entries in an unordered way. In this respect the theory differs from that of Katz and Fodor. It also contrasts with the notions of Katz and Fodor in that the lexical entries themselves are arranged in an orderly way. They are hierarchically arranged, as in Roget's *Thesaurus.* This kind of semantic structure, Quillian points out, enormously reduces the amount of information to be stored in memory, because it takes account of the existence of information to be stored in memory and because it takes account of the existence of hierarchical relations among words themselves. Thus, certain essential features associated with the word *typewriter* (capable of producing printed text, etc.) are stored with the entry in an unordered way, but the general features associated with the class to which the word belongs, namely *machine,* are stored with the word *machine* or some deep equivalent (to permit the semantic relations between such forms as *machine* and *mechanical*). Quillian points out that his model does not assume some predetermined hierarchy of classes (and in this respect it does differ from Roget's system) but that every word starts its own hierarchy when some search process requires it. Quillian explicitly says that such a system must be supplemented by some kind of nonsemantic storage—visual imagery, for example. Thus, he implies that knowledge is stored in two ways, linguistically and nonlinguistically. In this respect, Quillian seems to be in disagreement with the assumption stated at the outset of this chapter, namely that perceptual, linguistic, and cognitive structures are derived in part at least from the same source. However, the contrast is more superficial than real, for, in generating the meaning of words in particular contexts, there is certainly an important surface distinction between lexical storage as such and conceptual reconstruction. The same underlying categories may apply to both, however. Generic theories of the image might well be described by the same structure that Quillian uses to describe semantic storage. We shall return to some of the questions raised by Quillian in the section on categorical analysis.

Bierwisch (1971) has presented yet another version of a semantic marker or feature theory of the structure of the lexicon. Bierwisch points out that the uninterpreted, unordered grouping of semantic features proposed by Katz and Fodor will not do. Semantic features must be taken as predicates assigned to suitable arguments. Thus, he embeds the notion of features and feature analysis into a general and more logical scheme. Semantic representations require (1) a set of variables to which linguistic expressions refer and (2) semantic features classified into several subsets. One subset of semantic features are predicative. Predicative features represent the properties and relations ascribed to the variables of the object represented. They are further classified into places they may require in predication. Thus, the verb *buy* may require as many as four arguments, while *give* may require three, and *hit* only two (*Bill bought the book from Joe for three dollars; Bill gave Joe the book; Bill hit Joe*). Another subclassification of predicative features depends upon the type of arguments they take—true objects, facts, propositions, parasitic objects, etc.—in a manner resembling the characteristics of selectional features. Another classification characterizes the set of objects referred to by quantity and by the operations that constitute these sets. These are delimiting features, and they correspond to the operators of modern logic.

In substance, Bierwisch's proposal represents a formalization of the method employed by Katz and Fodor, and it enables him to deal with logical problems inherent in certain sentences. It is difficult to see, however, how it does not suffer from the fatal defects associated with the Katz and Fodor representation as a model for semantic storage in memory. It does not preclude the necessity for an indefinite number of features, and that must mean that, psychologically, semantic information cannot be stored in the form of features but must be stored in some representation (images, for example) from which features may be extracted. The problem is complicated by the fact that the contexts that demand the extension may not themselves necessarily be linguistic in nature. Completely nonlinguistic events surrounding a particular sentence often force interpretations upon that sentence which require some contrasts that can be recovered only by knowing the environmental circumstance.

Perhaps formal theories of the semantic component of language reach for too much. One can imagine a syntactic component of language having a completely self-contained existence, but any complete explication of a particular sentence may need to take into account the fact that the sentence was spoken under a particular set of circumstances. In short, the specification of the possible readings for all possible sentences may be an impossible task. How far, however, formal semantic theories are to be carried as purely linguistic enterprises has not been much at issue among linguistic theorists. The result is that the critic who sees psychological and epistemological problems in semantic analysis is likely to be frustrated by the very abstract and formal approach these theorists have taken. It is not the abstractness or the formal nature of the theories that is the problem, it is the fact that many semantic theorists among linguists have failed to tell us the domain to which their theories are to apply.

2. COMPONENTIAL ANALYSIS

Componential analyses are more or less empirical versions of the kinds of semantic feature notions we have discussed thus far. However, they arise in studies in empirical ethnography and thus are used for very different purposes. Various particular componential analyses (see Hammel, 1965) are related to formal semantic theories in a number of ways. However, that fact is less important than the fact that they are generally addressed to problems other than linguistic. The problems that give rise to componential analysis are very much more likely to be psychological in nature than are the problems that give rise to formal semantic analysis in linguistics. Componential analysis is, among other things, designed to give us an ethnography of the structure of human ideas.

Problems tackled by ethnographers are attempts to discover the features necessary to account for the distinctions made within some particular semantic field by the users of a particular language or dialect. Semantic fields are limited domains of experience that share referential properties and that may be unrelated to other domains of experience. An ideal semantic field is one that is completely self-contained and that requires no context for identification. It is no accident that the limited domain to which componential analysis has been most often applied is kinship. To a lesser extent, anthropologists have been interested in the semantic structure of the domain of color names and of such taxonomic categories as plants and animals. These limited interests avoid the problem that Bollinger (1965) pointed to in his criticism of semantic feature theory. There is no limit to the number of potentially contrastive features in all possible semantic domains. By limiting analysis to a self-contained semantic field, the number of features required is finite and specifiable.

The quasi-arbitrary nature of the delimitation of semantic fields is not always appreciated by ethnologists. Color, as a semantic field, has a quality of arbitrariness about it. The major contemporary ethnographic study of color, that by Berlin and Kay (1969), appears to ignore that fact, however. Color, in modern Western culture, is a semantic field defined by particular psychophysical operations and associated psychophysical theory. Color is described by three mathematical specifiable attributes, hue, saturation, and brightness. These can be rigorously defined in such a way as to specify color completely, but they do not completely specify all aspects of the visual appearance of surfaces. As David Katz pointed out long ago, microstructure, gloss, and other features of the appearance of surfaces enter into our perception of color as much as do the three psychophysically specified dimensions. Thus, the Western concept of color itself refers to an abstraction of the total visual impression. Color concepts of other cultures do not limit themselves to these three aspects, nor do the names assigned to colors permit an easy reduction to the characteristic scheme (the color solid) for representing color in the Western sense (see, for example, Conklin, 1955). In fact, one observer (Bornstein, 1973) has argued that certain cross-cultural differences in color are associated with physiological differences that would make the psychophysical dimensions of color not universally applicable.

It is a cultural universal that certain features of human relations, such as generation, consanguinity, sex, etc., are abstracted from the total set of potential relations to make abstract concepts of kinship. All languages code some of the possible kin relations on to simple or unmarked lexical elements. The particular set of relations so coded, however, will differ from language to language. Less used kin relations or ones of secondary importance in a given culture must be referred to or described by compounds, marked terms, or even whole phrases. The extent to which relations are coded into simple terms is regarded as being important to the understanding of the social structure of a given society. For example, though the significance is largely negative in character, it must be of some importance that the kinship system of Western societies in general do not differentiate between mother's brother and father's brother. The single term *uncle* suffices.

Plant and animal taxonomies are also studied by anthropologists. Animal taxonomies are of interest because of totem systems and the dependence of some primitive economies upon particular animals. Plant taxonomies are of economic and medical interest. It is worth mentioning plant and animal taxonomies because they illustrate an important point. The actual conceptions people have concerning the referents of the lexical elements in question may not be revealed in a particular componential analysis. The work of Henley (1969), using multidimensional scaling techniques, shows that American college students think of the similarities among animals in other than the commonly accepted taxonomic features. The two features that turn out to be important in describing her data are *size* and *wildness–tameness*.

While our kinship terms, except when used metaphorically, code a strictly limited set of features, animal names apparently do not. Thus, the application of a componential analysis to the domain of animal names, like the application to color, undoubtedly produces an incomplete description of the way in which people in a particular culture think about the concepts in question. In fact, it may be that kinship is the only semantic field for which it is possible to provide a complete description by the application of componential analysis. The number of primary terms in kinship structures is generally limited, and the features that specify those terms are likewise limited in number.

Componential analysis is closely related to the problem of forming taxonomies. The distinction between componential and taxonomic analysis, when it is observed, is a distinction between nested sets, or set membership based upon a hierarchy of features or markers and set membership determined by an unordered set of features or markers. In one case, certain features dominate or are more general than others, while in the other case there is no particular order among the features that specify the concepts or terms. There is reason to believe that biotaxonomies are universally hierarchical in nature (see Kay, 1971), though, interestingly enough, the most generic term in such taxonomies (the concept of *plant* or *animal* itself) is not always realized lexically. The biotaxonomies of Western biology are not prisoners of Darwinian biology or of Linneus's version of the Great Chain of Being, it would seem, but they are simply concordant with some natural human tendency to think of living things as being grouped into genera and families.

In general, then, componential analysis is to be distinguished from analysis deriving from semantic feature theory by the fact that it is not concerned with the problem of devising a universally adequate formal system for describing the semantically well formed structures of language in general. The universals sought in linguistics by the semantic theorists are universals of linguistic theory, while the universals sought by ethnolinguists are cross-cultural generalities about human experience. Anthropologists are less concerned than linguists about generalizations concerning language itself at some deep level. Ethnolinguists are not disturbed by the fact that linguistic theorists have not solved all the problems associated with feature-based semantic theories. They want to know only whether or not a particular technique works and whether or not it has psychological validity (Wallace, 1965). In this respect, the work of psychologists who study semantic fields and the work of anthropologists are more similar in aims and methods than are either of these to the work of theoretical linguists. Anthropologists have borrowed psychological techniques (e.g., Romney & D'Andrade, 1964), and the term "componential analysis" has been widely used by social psychologists as well as by psycholinguists. Because psychologists are more concerned with the nature of the cognitive processes behind the use of language than are anthropologists, they have investigated more thoroughly the nature of particular eliciting techniques than have anthroplogists.

3. Psychological Studies and the Subjective Lexicon

There is, then, a continuity between componential analysis and the various psychological studies of semantic fields. The term "subjective lexicon" was coined and popularized by G. A. Miller as the way to describe the outcome of psychological studies of semantic fields. There are, however, some important differences between the general notion of a subjective lexicon and the kind of conceptions that have resulted from the work of the ethnolinguists. The psychologists have been interested in doing a semantic feature analysis as such. As a result they have placed more emphasis upon highly controlled techniques for eliciting information from informants. Ethnolinguists have, by and large, adopted the basic principle behind semantic feature theory, namely, the notion of minimal contrast. Psychologists, however, have been concerned with the cognitive status of minimal contrast. Features are said to be distinctive when some element (a phoneme in phonological theory, a concept in semantic theory) can be contrasted with some other element by the presence or absence of a single feature. Distinctive features are those that make minimal contrasts between two elements. Nondistinctive features, while having the potential for so doing, do not.

Thus, implicit in a feature analysis is the principle of binary contrast. Psychologists have, from time to time, adopted the principle of binary contrast as being fundamental to semantics (and to associations; see Deese, 1965; McNeill, 1966), but more generally psychologists have allowed their views about the structure of the subjective lexicon to be more determined by available psychological techniques of investigation than by the relentless application of a single principle. In fact, it is the existence of a variety of techniques of measurement developed over the past century by psychologists, techniques such as factor analysis, paired comparisons, and multidimensional scaling, that has made possible the wealth of psychological material on the subjective lexicon. In a sense, it is the theory of psychological measurement that provides the theoretical underpinning of the subjective lexicon, not linguistic theory. With one conspicuous exception and a couple of less well known exceptions, these techniques of measurement have not been invented particularly and expressly for psycholinguistic investigations but rather have been adopted for such investigations.

The one well-known exception, of course, is the semantic differential, and that is but an adaptation and generalization of rating scale techniques. The semantic differential was specifically invented for psycholinguistic purposes, and its inventors (Osgood, Suci, & Tannenbaum, 1957) asserted that its development came squarely out of mediational learning theory. The derivation from mediation learning theory and its relation to that theory is less apparent than it once was, and, indeed, in recent years it would appear that the theory of the semantic differential might more reasonably be said to rest in semantic feature theory than in any particular psychological theory.

As is well known, the semantic differential consists of a more or less fixed set of scales having anchors defined by contrastive adjectives (*good–bad,* etc.). Subjects rate concepts on these scales, and the results are subjected to a factor analysis or some other linear analysis designed to reduce the dimensionality of the original set of scales. The particular fixed set of scales currently in widest use was the result of trying to find those adjectives in English that appeared to have the greatest generality in their application to lexical concepts at large. Given that attempt, it is not surprising that the adjectives mainly tap subjective or connotative reactions to lexical elements. Factor analyses of semantic differential scales usually result in three principal dimensions, generally labeled as evaluation, potency, and activity.

The technique of using a fixed set of scales to evaluate a set of concepts does not always lead to a solution revealing these three dimensions. The outcome will depend, of course, upon the adjectives that anchor the scales. And even when the adjectives are the ones used in the original form of the semantic differential, whether one finds the three well-known dimensions associated with the technique or not depends upon the sample of concepts being evaluated. There is no explicit theory behind the particular collection of adjectives that are commonly used, nor is there any principled way of telling us how to form appropriate contrastive sets of concepts to which to apply the scales. It just happens that emotional evaluations are the common denominator of interpretations of concepts. Over some large and random set of concepts, referential features either cancel one another out or do not apply to a wide enough range of concepts to allow them to emerge as primary factors in a factor analysis.

The semantic differential belongs to a large family of possible ways by which words as concepts can be characterized by descriptive adjectives. Adjective checklists of various sorts have been used. In adjective checklists, a set of concepts will be characterized by the frequency with which people check some descriptive adjective as appropriate to a particular concept. As with the semantic differential, most psychological applications of adjective checklists have attempted to reduce the complexity of the description achieved in the raw data by applying factor analysis and similar techniques. Adjective checklists do not have the limitation imposed in the semantic differential by using a fixed set of adjectives that are scalable and have well-defined opposites. Strangely, however, none of these techniques, the semantic differential included, have played a major role in determining the nature of structures in the subjective lexicon.

Fillenbaum and Rapoport (1971) have provided a comprehensive summary of almost all of the recent empirical work, including their own, aimed at discovering the structure of limited portions of the subjective lexicon by the application of a variety of psychological techniques. The applications have been to a number of semantic fields, from color names to the meaning of such grammatical classes as that of English prepositions. There are a large number of methods for exploring the subjective lexicon, and it would not serve a useful purpose to provide an inventory of them, particularly since it is now abundantly clear that the brute force application of such techniques cannot provide a general or comprehensive picture of the subjective lexicon as a whole. However, in order to characterize the nature of these techniques and their applications to semantic studies, we shall have to examine some of the better-known methods.

Multidimensional scaling has been more widely applied to semantic studies than to anything else. It has been used both by anthropologists (Romney & D'Andrade, 1964; Wallace & Atkins, 1960) and by psychologists (Clark, 1968; Henley, 1969; Richards, 1971). Typically, the Young–Torgerson (Young & Torgerson, 1967) program for the Shepard–Kruskal scaling analysis has been used, but others have been used as well. Generally, the use of multidimensional scaling has resulted in representations, in Euclidean space or generalized Minkowski space, of configurations among words. From the configurations it is usually possible to determine, with some degree of intuitive satisfaction, the principal dimensions used by people in judging the degree of similarity among words in some semantic field. For example, Henley's (1969) study of similarity judgments among animal names revealed two primary dimensions—anchored by the contrasts *tame–ferocious* and *large–small*. Henley's study is unusual, incidentally, in the use of associations and other techniques in order to establish a kind of convergent validity for the analysis achieved.

There are a number of serious problems with the application of scaling methods. One, of course, is the labor connected with the study of any sizable semantic field. Anything more than 50 terms is impossible to manage. More serious is a problem associated with any purely empirical semantic discovery technique. The introduction of new words into the set from which the configuration has been determined may change the configuration itself. There seems to be no way of knowing whether or not the addition of some new elements, requiring perhaps the addition of a new dimension, may alter the whole configuration. Sometimes it does happen and sometimes it does not (see Fillenbaum & Rapoport, 1971). This is a most serious problem if the spatial representations achieved are to be taken as models of the relations among words in the minds of the persons providing the judgments upon which the scaling is based. In general, the validity of the representation appears to depend upon three aspects of the scaling: (1) whether or not some statistical criterion of goodness of fit is met with some particular number of dimensions, (2) whether or not adding new elements (words) changes the configurations among the old ones, and (3) whether or not the results accord with intuition. The last point, of course, raises questions about the whole use of the application of sophisticated scaling techniques to the problem of studying the subjective lexicon in the absence of any theory. Richards's (1971) scaling of interpersonal verbs (*attack, please,* etc.) produced results that agree very closely with an a priori analysis of the feature structure of these verbs by Osgood (1970). Osgood's analysis is based upon himself as an informant, and though it did incorporate certain theoretical presuppositions, it appears as though the very strong agreement between Richards's scaling data and the feature analysis is one more example, perhaps the most carefully documented, of agreement between scaling and intuition. The outcome of scaling seems to be that carefully done intuitive descriptions of semantic relations are valid.

There are many ways of obtaining the judgments upon which multidimensional scaling is based. The precise nature of the judgments may influence the representation achieved. For example, in discussing some of the differences between their own work and that of Clark (1968), Fillenbaum and Rapoport (1971) point out that asking people to judge how similar pairs of opposites are will result in the pairs being separated in the resulting configurations, while asking whether or not the pairs are related in meaning will result in a configuration in which they are much closer. The trouble is, as Fillenbaum and Rappaport seem to be pointing out in their concluding discussion, there is no way of obtaining data that is, either from a psychological or a linguistic point of view, the correct one.

One word should be said about a methodological innovation introduced by Fillenbaum and Rappaport. Taking advantages of certain properties of networks in graph theory, they were able to arrive at multidimensional configurations of semantic fields by asking people to indicate the relations in meaning among words by drawing lines between pairs of words and then adding additional words and connecting lines until a structured network is produced. The networks themselves can be subjected to a nonmetric multidimensional scaling. The principal advantage of the technique is that it does not require an act of judgment that itself has a particular set of semantic characteristics associated with it, as do judgments of similarity, relatedness, etc.

Multidimensional scaling is not the only way of representing the relationships among concepts behind words. There are a variety of techniques that result in hierarchical patterns. The best known of these is that devised by Johnson (1967), and it has been revised, altered, and supplemented for use in a variety of situations (see Fillenbaum & Rapoport, 1971). Something like Johnson's program will take a set of measures of relatedness among words and impose upon them a hierarchy. That produces the basic problem. Such programs impose hierarchies no matter what. In general, this is the basic problem with the application of any automatic data analysis. Solutions of a sort will always occur, but the problem remains as to whether or not the solutions reflect an intrinsic organization determined by basic psychological principles or whether the solutions are arbitrary distortions introduced by the nature of the analysis itself. To date, two methods have been used to try to decide this question. One is purely intuitive: Do the solutions appear to be correct? This has the appearance of making the application of elaborate and time-consuming data analysis superfluous. The other is to make an attempt at concurrent validity or to use the data to "predict" such derived measures as rate of learning when the words in the semantic field are organized according to the structures discovered in the analysis, as opposed to rates when the words are organized counter to these structures (Deese, 1965). It is by no means clear whether or not these these efforts at concurrent validity represent but another bootstrap operation.

Nearly all techniques for discovering the configurational or hierarchical structure among some set of words require the combination of data from different individuals. Some of the more recent programs for multidimensional scaling do take into account individual differences by the application of a clustering analysis (see Carroll & Wish, 1974). Once again, however, these techniques are not based upon any understanding of the methods used by particular individuals in making judgments of similarity or relatedness but instead rely on correlations among the patterns of judgments made by individuals. Given this and other problems, it would seem to be the case that we have about reached the limits of application of techniques of psychological scaling to the discovery of the semantic structures of portions of the lexicons of various languages. Any large-scale or universal subjective lexicon obtained through multivariate and related analyses would appear to be a very improbable development.

One somewhat different technique deserves mention, however, if for other reason than it seems to have practical applications. At least it has been used to assess the acceptability of new brand names, among other things. It is a technique of sentential cooccurrence (Stefflre, Reich, & McClaran-Stefflre, 1971). A standard set of test frames is generated by any one of a variety of techniques. Words are then systematically substituted in these frames and tested for acceptability. A measure of the degree of similarity among the words is calculated from the agreements among frames in the words they accept. Finally, the word-by-frame matrix can be rearranged so as to group together those words that are closely related to one another. The result is a pictorial display of groups of words and contexts with similar distributional properties.

The technique is a purely empirical discovery procedure of the sort that linguistic theorists of the past 20 years have been telling us will not work for a general solution of the problem of semantic structure. That is true. But it is also true that the method produces intuitively satisfying groupings among words, and, while it is time consuming, it is not absolutely impossible for it to handle very large numbers of words, as is the case with multidimensional scaling and other techniques that depend upon linear analysis and iterative procedures. The groupings achieved by Stefflre's method appear to correspond, to the extent that the comparison is possible, to results achieved with the scaling procedures.

A final word about the psychological reality of the results achieved with all of these techniques. It is naive to suppose that they provide us with pictures of the way in which semantic information is stored in the head. They do provide us with pictures of the results of activation of that information. It is impossible at present to give any generally acceptable account of how semantic information is stored. However, we can give an account of the varieties of representations that are possible, given that information. Such an account is what is called here a categorical semantic analysis, and that is he subject of the next section.

4. CATEGORICAL ANALYSES

The methods we have discussed thus far can be labeled analytic because they are designed to provide an account of the structure of any given lexical element as well as the rules governing the relations among lexical elements. Those analytic techniques based in linguistic theory contain an implicit assumption to the effect that the particular technique in question has universal application and that, in theory at least, it would be possible to provide an account by application of that technique which would completely describe the regular or "competence" determined portion of ordinary usage. In short, it is the goal of at least some of those who have developed semantic theory to provide a description of just how semantic information is stored. However, the fact that psychologists and ethnolinguists make use of a variety of different methods in their attempts to describe in psychologically meaningful ways portions of the lexicons of various languages suggests an alternative, namely, that different kinds of relations may apply to the decomposition of particular lexical elements used in particular contexts. Instead of assuming that there is a concept paired with each lexical element, we may assume that comprehension of that element is generated by applying some one of a small set of operations to the content of experience. This begs the question as to how that content is stored in memory, but it allows for the fact that, in our conscious experience, individual concepts may seem to have a variety of types of relations to other concepts.

A large number of operations are possible, but, at the very least, they should include the kinds of operations that have been used to generate portions of the subjective lexicon. These include predication or feature specification, classification or hierarchical arrangement of features, and relations of similarity. For the latter we must assume that the basis of judgment is some unspecified number of features shared by two concepts. These operations will describe the nature of sentences which have at their base such propositions as *X is a* (   ), *X is* (   ), or *X is similar to* (   ). However, not all sentences can be so reduced. Furthermore, there are other possible intellectual operations, operations that do not so neatly correspond with possible base phrase markers or sentence types. Relations of magnitude and of order, as well as two- and three-dimensional spatial representations are possible in thought, and these may well be reflected in semantic relations.

Ordinary dictionary definitions reflect such an approach to the specification of semantic relations. The dictionary on my desk defines a *coloratura* (*soprano*) as "a high soprano voice of clearness and flexibility." The relations specified, in order, are those of magnitude or intensity (high is not properly an intensifier but it expresses a relative position in this case on a specific dimension—that of pitch), class relations (kind of voice) and feature specification ("clearness and flexibility"). Such definitions are characteristic of entries for nouns and verbs. Entries for adjectives characteristically give other adjectives similar in meaning or phrases meant to describe features. For example, the entry for *supporting* (*adj.*) is "that props up; confirms, etc." The trouble is that beyond the very general qualification imposed by grammatical class (a qualification by no means consistently or uniformly applied), there is no ready way to tell what particular kind of relations should enter the definition for any given word. Nor, except in the case of defining sentences of the sort mentioned above, is it at all certain what relations are implied by a particular use. That remains locked in the relation between what is in the speaker's head and the context, both linguistic and conceptual.

Dictionary entries are useful in a most general way, and their form reveals that generality. It is efficient, judging from the frequency of the examples, to define a concept by a class marker plus some features that identify it uniquely for many if not all circumstances. To this may be added some quantifier or dimensional descriptor ("high," "red," etc.). There is no way, so far as linguistic theory is concerned, of finding out what the most efficient class marker is for definitions in general. Shall we define *sycamore* as a tree or a plant? Intuition opts for *tree,* and indeed my desk dictionary so defines the word. This decision is clearly not out of some principled rule applied with regularity, for the same dictionary contains an entry for *aspen* that begins "any of several poplars . . . ." The users of English are apparently satisfied with all the markers dominated by the node *tree* in one instance and with the node *poplar* in another. The features following the class marker (or modifying it) serve to tell us which markers dominated by *tree* or *poplar* do not apply, though, once again, the information is only approximate.

Some of the information provided in such a definition must serve purely abstract purposes. Other information, however, serves the function of identifying stable characteristics that form the bases for generic images. Images themselves, however, are not generic. When I am asked to image some concept explicitly, the image always contains features not defining for the concept in question. This seems to be universally the case, and it is possible to establish feature norms for images. Thus one can ask a class of students to image a horse and then ask for the color of the horse. For American college students the horse will most often be brown, followed by white, black, piebald, etc. Not all images are in color of course (in fact a substantial minority of imagers refuse to assign a color to the image of *horse*), however, there will almost certainly be some irrelevant features in what has been described as the generic image. In the case of *tree,* the most commonly reported feature irrelevant to the generic concept is that of shape.

It seems highly unlikely that explicit images enter into very much of our production and comprehension of language. However, the fact that both explicit images and definitions, honed by the uses to which dictionaries are put, both contain features irrelevant to the concepts imaged or defined suggests that the understanding of those concepts and the production of images have a common origin. If that is the case, images may be defined by generic markers, but, to give these the concreteness that explicit imagery

demands, they are fleshed out with features only some of which are relevant
to the concept named. What is more, these images assume some point of
view. Thus, as I change my image from that of *sycamore* to that of *pine,*
not only do the shape and other characteristics of the image change but
the vantage point changes. My image of a *sycamore* is of an entire tree
at a distance, and my image of a *pine* is one of a close-up of a part of
a tree. To this I must add, of course, that the point of view of images
of generic concepts will surely change from instance to instance. But that
same point of view is embedded in the context of any lexical element whenever it occurs. The point of view, in fact, may concentrate on a limited
set of features, so that in the intellectual processes behind some particular
use, the class marker, almost always found in the dictionary definition,
may entirely disappear. Such is characteristically the case in similes and
metaphors. The meaning of the phrase *with coloraturalike agility* is entirely
independent of the fact that the term *coloratura* has a generic definition
of type of voice. Instead, the phrase captures the characteristics of flexibility, clearness, etc.

The makers of ordinary dictionaries operating largely out of intuition
have come closer to describing the subjective lexicon than have psychologists and anthropologists using their specialized techniques. Among formal
linguistic proposals for describing the structure of the lexicon, that of Quillian (1968) comes closer to the scheme apparent in ordinary dictionaries
than any other. In Quillian's scheme, concepts are specified by a class
marker. That class marker contains the necessary generic information, and,
as we have seen ordinary dictionaries do, it starts at any convenient point
in the general classificatory hierarchy. The concept is specified by the necessary identifying features. This scheme, which is meant to provide a formal
model for lexical storage in memory, works well for most concrete nouns
and perhaps some verbs, but it works less well for abstract nouns and adjectives. However, a more telling point is the fact that human intellectual
processes do not always proceed in the same way. Sometimes we may start
with the most generic information and sometimes we may arrive at that
generic information only as a kind of afterthought.

III. UNDERSTANDING LARGER LINGUISTIC SEGMENTS

The past decade has seen the development of several theories designed
to describe the understanding of larger segments of language, usually segments of the length of simple sentences, or of the propositions that are
thought to be at the base of simple surface sentences. Many of these theories
are not designed for psychological purposes. Some are concerned with

problems of machine language or man–machine interaction. Also, many of these theories, such as that devised by Weizenbaum (1966), seem not to be attempts to produce the structures that lie at the base of understanding, but rather, attempts to produce surface discourse that, in certain ways will appear to mimic genuine discourse. Other explicit programs have been more directly concerned with giving an account of the nature of understanding.

A. Theories of Understanding

One of the most thoroughly developed of the attempts to write a theory of understanding is that of Schank (1972a,b). Schank has devised what he calls a theory of conceptual dependency. In it a conceptualization consists of concepts and the formal relations among them. Underlying every sentence is at least one conceptualization, so that a conceptualization is close in practice to what used to be called a complete idea. Complex and compound sentences contain more than one conceptualization, and, since conceptualizations may exceed the boundaries of surface sentences, they may interrelate sentences. Schank's notion is thus only loosely tied to the linguistic definition of a sentence.

Concepts are either nominal or verbal or they function as modifiers of nominal or verbal concepts. These correspond only loosely to the surface linguistic notions of noun and verb or adjective and adverb, respectively. Schank's definitions of them are psychological. Thus, nominal concepts are picture producers (presumably by this Schank means potential image producers), modifiers are descriptors, either of actions or of picture producers, and actions are simply the names for actions and events. There are dependency relations among these in conceptualizations. A dependency relation exists when one concept cannot be understood without the presence of another. Nominal and action concepts are inherently governing concepts, though in a particular conceptualization even these become dependent upon other concepts in the conceptualization. Thus, in a sentence such as *John hit the ball,* the concrete subject and the verb are governing concepts, but the conceptualization itself produces a two-way relation between them. *Ball* is a governing concept, but in the sentence it is dependent upon the action *hit.* Modifiers always depend upon the concepts they modify, as do such relations as "possessed by" (e.g., *his*), adverbials of time, etc.

Conceptualizations, in order to be expressed in surface language, require syntactic processing. The main problem in syntactic processing is to find the main noun and main verb in a sentence and then to establish the syntactic dependencies between these and other parts of the sentence. A set of heuristics then proceeds to check these hypotheses. For example, when a decision is made as to the most likely main noun and verb, the correct verb sense is chosen by finding the most explicit semantic category of the nouns as subject and object that apply to the correct type of verb. This information is then transferred to a dictionary, which picks the appropriate action.

Conceptual rules provide a list of permissible conceptual dependencies. Six basic rules are given. One of these provides the concept of a subject of a sentence in action (*John is sleeping*), another provides for a predicate adjective construction (*John is tall*), a third provides for a predicate nominative (*John is a doctor*), a fourth embeds the predicate adjective relation in a concept that has already been predicated (The tall man), the fifth relates concepts that generally receive prepositional treatment in the surface grammar of English to governing concepts, while the sixth describes the objective dependency. Finally, there is a seventh rule that has the function of assigning case relations of the various nominal concepts to the verb. The cases that result are similar to those proposed by Fillmore (1968). However, case relations are modified to permit an entire conceptualization to be the instrument of a given action. Thus, *The boy hit the dog with the stick* would have a conceptualization *The boy hit the dog* and embedded in that a conceptualization *The boy do (something with) the stick (to the) dog*. Further analysis of the action with the stick is then required.

The heart of the conceptualization is the nature of the action categories. There are a number of action categories. These reflect semantic relations, such as whether or not the action is physical, emotional, communicative, etc., and essentially grammatical categories, such as whether or not the action is reflexive, intransitive, etc. Finally, there are a set of conceptual relations that dominate the relations among conceptualizations. The most important of these is causality (*John cried when (because) Mary left him*). The other conceptual relations are time and location.

This scheme is an attempt to produce, within the confines of a program defined in such a way as to interrelate traditional grammatical and semantic categories, a process that duplicates those in the understanding of natural language by human beings. Schank deals not only with such questions as those just described, but he is concerned with contextual features of the sort recently examined by linguists, which relate to such questions as focus and presuppositions, topic and comment, etc. It is too much to suppose, however, that application of a program derived from this account of language would produce sentences of the sort one would be likely to hear in ordinary discourse. The problems of assembling the information in a conceptual dictionary are simply too great at this stage, and the problem of providing an interface between the conceptual–linguistic representation and the real world are not really touched upon by Schank. As a model it is important because it represents a thorough mixture of grammatical and semantic analyses of language with conceptual treatment. The semantic dictionary appears to be of the eclectic or mixed variety described in the preceding section. The grammar is conceptual and is more closely related to generative semantic theory than to what Chomsky calls standard theory. In short, there is a distinct secondary and late role assigned to syntax.

It is possible, however, to propose a scheme that parallels Schank's in some respects but departs from a syntactic base. Deese (1974) has suggested such a possibility. It differs from earlier attempts to use syntactic theory as a basis for describing the process of understanding, in that it explicitly requires a one-to-one pairing of each base phrase marker with some particular semantic interpretation. Understanding, therefore, must occur at least at two levels, as one would expect from the primacy given the concepts of the word (or morpheme) and the sentence (or complete thought) in linguistic theory. One level of understanding is achieved by the pairing of a particular propositional form with some base phrase marker whose meaning it expresses. The other level is achieved by the insertion of particular lexical entries to correspond to the elements Schank calls concepts. The two processes go on independently, though the insertion of particular lexical elements may decide what particular transformations are to be performed upon the base to arrive at the surface. That is to say, not all decisions as to what base the surface form is to be related to are independent of the lexical entries. The context, the intent of the speaker, and the speaker's knowledge of the hearer will determine what transformations will relate base and surface. The hearer understands this. The marking of the base that is achieved by hearing one transformation as opposed to another supplies information for the hearer. Such information, however, has nothing to do with the speaker's referents. Instead, it tells the hearer what to pay attention to or what the speaker assumes to be common knowledge or perhaps it conveys some evaluative judgment the speaker wishes to place upon the proposition in question.

There are problems with starting with a completely syntactic base. As Schank points out, one runs into the quagmire created by verb pairs of the sort, *buy* and *sell*. The sentence, *John bought the rug from Harry* is a complete paraphrase, from a propositional point of view, of the sentence *Harry sold the rug to John*. The only difference is the point of view or the emphasis the speaker wishes to convey and the interpretation of that emphasis made by the hearer. Yet, in syntactic theory they are derived from different base phrase markers. The underlying propositional meaning, however, is devoid of any conceptual content. For both sentences it would simply assert that some concept X, performed some action W entailing concept Y, with respect to (directed to or from) Z.

If we admit selectional restrictions in the base as well as a variety of propositional types (directional, locative, etc.), then there would be somewhat greater specificity to the meaning of the syntactic structure underlying the sentence. For example, a particular propositional relation might be limited by the concept in the subject position being marked as *human*. Because the underlying propositional meaning is so abstract, it is easy to overlook it in the analysis of the relations between the linguistic segment and the event that it describes. The event or object to be described always comes in some particular propositional form, and that form is the result of an interaction among the operational characteristics of the human mind, the requirements of logical relations, and the universal characteristics of language. So far as language is concerned, propositional forms seem chiefly to differ in the nature of the verb. Thus, there are *is* sentences (*Harry is old*), *is a* sentences (*Harry is a thief*), and action recipient sentences specifying direction or location (*Harry threw the ball under the table*). There may well be a difference between state and action verbs as well, but it is also possible that state verbs are either properly reducible to *is* sentences (or the reverse) or that they are metaphorical extensions of action, at least as far as the process of understanding goes. However, the concrete content of sentences must then be entirely specified by concepts associated with the positions into which lexical elements are placed.

The choice of some particular base phrase marker is determined by the topic–comment relations intended or by the linguistic and/or nonlinguistic context of the sentence. It should be pointed out in this connection that a theory that pairs an underlying propositional meaning with a particular base phrase marker is no more deficient or complicated in this respect than the kind of theory put forward by Schank. Not only do we have problems in both accounts with the paraphrase relations between *Harry sold the rug to John* and *John bought the rug from Harry* but we have problems with the relations between such sentences as *Harry wrote the book* and *Harry was the author of the book*. The choice of some base form as well as of transformations that give rise to the surface are determined by extralinguistic considerations, and it does not seem to be particularly important whether certain of those extralinguistic considerations determine the selection of a base or merely serve to modify the course of derivation of the surface sentence from the base.

B. Models of Artificial Language

The application of computer technology to language went through a period of neglect after an early and enthusiastic start in the 1950s. The neglect was the result of an awareness of the magnitude of the problems associated with, say, mechanical translation. Recently, however, there have been signs of a revival, as noted by Hunt (1971). Schank's account of the process of understanding is closely tied to the notion of a device for processing the information in sentences. There now exist a great many programs explicitly designed to mimic human linguistic functions, although all of these in so many ways fall short of providing a simulation of natural language, that none of them may be said to be anywhere near its goal. Many fall short because they do not attempt to relate a universe of discourse and linguistic structures but simply imitate surface distinctions in some area of discourse. It is a commentary on human communication and psychotherapy that it is possible to mimic the transactions in psychotherapy to a fair degree simply by tagging likely replies to particular syntactic forms. The replies a machine may give to a human being in such a transaction are not the results of a meaningful decoding of the human being's remarks by the machine but simply the dredging up of a stock remark contingent upon the occurrence in the human speech of particular words, such as *mother*.

More important to the problem of the relation between perception and the structure of language are attempts to build grammatical and semantic analyzing programs for limited domains of sentence structures and limited referential universes. Here, there can be a genuine attack upon the problem of the relation between the perceived world and the understanding of language, without having to deal with the limitless problems inherent in natural languages. The best-known attempt is that of Winograd (1972).

Winograd (1972) constructed a program that allows a computer (robot) to interact, in ordinary English, with an interrogator about a display. The display consists of objects of various sizes, shapes, and colors. These can be moved about and arranged with respect to one another, and the robot can relate itself to the objects in the display in various ways (it can be said to "own" objects, for example). The interrogator can ask questions, such as *Which object is on top of the red square?* and expect to receive a sensible answer. The sensibleness of the answer depends upon both syntactic and semantic information in the query. Thus, the robot would respond to the question *Does the table own the pyramid?* as if it were nonsense because, in its world, tables cannot own things. The program also responds to instructions about rearranging objects. In order to realize such a system—a system that literally understands an indefinite number of statements about the objects in the limited universe—a linguistic parsing program, a semantic program, and a program of inference rules must be designed. The system must be able to respond to, reason about, and inquire about a universe, in much the same way a human being does.

The linguistic portion of the system devised by Winograd relies heavily upon a feature analysis. The grammatical portion of the program is designed after Halliday's (1967, 1970) systemic grammar. This kind of grammar has the effect of the analyzing sentences into groups of words each dominated by some feature. Higher level groups are clauses (complete clauses in the commonly understood sense), and the lower level groups include nominal groups, verbal groups, prepositional groups, etc. Each group contains positions for determiners, adjectives, etc., as well as for nouns. Groups can be nested within groups, and clauses within clauses. Associated with the clauses are such sentential features as declarative, imperative, query, passive. The meaning of each syntactic unit is inherent in the features associated with it. Actual surface sentences are related to the underlying features by a set of transformational or realization rules. In the actual program, the first task accomplished is the identification of features associated with the different parts of the sentences presented to the robot, so that it may be determined whether or not the input consists of an actual sentence. The program parses sentences and more or less simultaneously operates on the semantic structure and the inference rules necessary to an understanding of the sentence.

The semantic analysis is so intimately associated with the syntactic analysis that it is difficult to disentangle them. It is mainly a matter of what starts the analysis. The syntactic parser initiates the analysis. As soon as the syntactic system has identified a group, say a nominal group, a semantic analysis makes sure that the noun group in question makes sense. If it does not, the syntactic parser is asked to make another try. The semantic program has the full power of the deductive (inferential) system at its command in trying to find out whether some particular combination of words identified as a group by the syntactic parser makes sense or nonsense. Since each structure is analyzed as it is parsed, it appears to be an approach from the bottom up analysis. However, the semantic analysis can be delayed until some larger unit is analyzed, if no solution is found at a lower level. The solution then automatically becomes a from-the-top-down solution. At each level, the joining of groups and clauses must make sense if the procedure is from the bottom up.

The whole program operates by identification of features, some of which are semantic (in that they refer to objects and events in the universe of discourse) and some of which are syntactic (in that they refer to the structure of language). All features are tested by a deductive system that applies a logical analysis to knowledge of the structure of the world and the structure of language. In actual practice, then, the program thoroughly interrelates semantic, syntactic, and logical analyses as well as linguistic and perceptual (in the sense of the robot knowing about conditions in the display) features. The whole thing can be described as a program that identifies features and makes inferences about those features based upon knowledge that it has. To this is added a subsidiary program of a much lower order of complexity, which allows the robot to respond in a reduced version of ordinary English.

It is the remarkable conceptual simplicity of the program that makes it interesting. Essentially, it is the operation of deductive inference rules upon features. The limited domain of the universe of discourse and the associated simplicity of the linguistic analysis make it work. Presumably, the program would reject "deviant" sentences that ordinary people can interpret correctly (by analogy, if Chomsky is correct). It tells us, however, that, at least conceptually, an identification of invariant linguistic and perceptual features is all that is necessary to the operation of the process of understanding. Whether understanding in human beings is that simple is another matter. The whole question of perception as the detection of invariant features is at issue. Also, of course, the complexity of the linguistic structures built into the program is of a lower order than that which ordinary people seem to grasp. Furthermore, the program is not designed to provide an understanding of deviant sentences—an ability that human beings have to a remarkable and important extent. Perhaps even more important is the fact that the basic principles behind the program would work as well with any kind of linguistic system, whether that system had many of the surface characteristics of human language or not. The way in which deep structures are resolved into the communicative act provides what is humanly unique about human languages.

IV. MEANING AND PERCEPTION

We have now examined a wide range of theoretical and empirical attempts to describe the way in which meaning is encoded in language. The one common theme that has run through the various topics we have considered is that of the relation between perception and semantic structures. How can the one be converted into the other? In asking that question we come full circle to our original proposition, namely, that semantic and perceptual structures have a common basis. It only remains to explore the implications of a common basis for perception and semantics being found in the various topics we have discussed.

Let us start with Winograd's program for understanding. The apprehension of meaning in Winograd's analysis consists simply of the identification of features and the application to them of inference rules. Winograd does make a distinction between relational and descriptive features, but for both of them the essential characteristic of the feature is the presence of some property that remains invariant over all transformations. I do not wish here to engage the problem of the extent to which perception may be accounted for by the assumption that perceptual analysis consists of the detection of invariant features, but it is necessary to deal with the question as to whether or not invariant semantic features lie at the basis of understanding and the use of language.

First of all, there is the matter of the relation between inference rules and features. Inference rules are the result of the application of some logical calculus to knowledge of the world. We need to know something about tables before we can infer that tables cannot own things. Both our knowledge and our logical analysis may be faulty. Some people operate, at least some of the time, in such a way, for example, as to lead us to suppose that they confuse certain logical quantifiers. For some people at some times, *some* appears to equal *all* or *every*. Further, our inferences may be based upon faulty information. Someone may have told us that, in the eyes of the law, ownership attaches to inanimate objects. From a cognitive point of view, such faulty information is only of mild interest, unless it reveals a lingering animism. However, faulty inferences are interesting. Consider the experiments on perception which tell us that many people identify some property of motion with causation. Michotte (1946) has argued that inferences of causation are inherent in certain perceptual configurations. Put another way, given a certain concatenation of perceptual features, we naturally and innately infer the existence of causation. If Michotte and others who have made similar arguments about the perception of motion, space, etc. are correct, features are not entirely at the mercy of knowledge of the world, and simple inference rules must stem in part from what might be called genetic presuppositions.

The problem of errors of logic would appear to be largely a matter of faulty instruction. After all, confusion between the words *some* and *all* does not mean that people are inherently incapable of making the distinction. But it is clear that, even when instructed, people persist in drawing faulty inferences when the circumstances invite them. A vast literature, extending before and after the discovery of the atmosphere effect, shows that those circumstances include the surface characteristics of language. It should be remembered that the atmosphere effect applies to grammatical agreement as well as to the distribution of quantifiers between the premises of a syllogism. Furthermore, we often appear to adopt special rules for particular circumstances. If we do this habitually, we may be labeled schizophrenic. But it does not take a schizophrenic to infer that, because two things belong together, are associated together, or are similar in certain respects, they are identical with respect to other features. The homeopathic fallacy has not entirely disappeared from the world. The overinclusiveness of schizophrenic thought is only an exaggeration of normal human thinking.

If that is the case, certain kinds of meanings to which people put words are going to resist any fixed application of what is ordinarily conceived to be a logical calculus of features. In short, a program that duplicates human thinking (and its manifestation in human language) would have to have, in addition to a logical calculus, a psychological calculus, one that would enable us to understand what von Domarus's patient meant when he said *I am Switzerland*.

So, at the very least, if we say that perceptual and linguistic analysis consists of the application of inference rules, we shall have to supplement these with special rules that describe the regular and predictable ways in which people deviate from these rules. Moreover, there are problems associated with the features upon which such inference rules are supposed to act. In perception, the problem is that of extracting features from the various transformations of reality presented to the senses. The comparable problem in semantic analysis is that of describing how the information required to use and understand words sensibly is stored. However, there are reasons for supposing that such a statement of the problem is too simple. It implies that we store a fixed set of features and that these features are retrieved by some call number when the semantic demands of understanding require them. It neglects at least two possibilities. One is that features may be invented on the spot. From a psychological point of view, then, features would have only a kind of analytic existence. Another possibility is that features have a psychological reality about them but that not all features relevant to understanding some lexical element are stored with that element. Some contextual information in the discourse in question or in the environment may be sufficient to generate a feature not stored with the element. This is saying nothing more than that meaning may be guessed from context. The world and our perception of it are organized so that we do not have to retrieve from storage the conceptual markers for each lexical element and its associated concept, in order to understand a given proposition or conceptualization. We may make inferences from what we know about the world by drawing upon the redundancies in the perceived world. It is by no means impossible that the rules for drawing such inferences are as inherent in linguistic understanding as the Gestalt principles are in form perception. If that is the case, the problem is to find the rules that give rise to new configurations, and the conditions under which these rules are evoked. The second possibility is that the nature of feature retrieval may vary from occasion to occasion, again under the control of contextual information. One occasion may force us to retrieve some class marker. Another occasion may require us to retrieve some feature in minimal contrast, or perhaps a feature nondistinctive for the concept in question, or perhaps even some affective attitude toward the concept.

It is useful to distinguish between construction and organization. The distinction is necessary to an account of both semantic structure and perception. A structure may be said to be organized when there exists a set of rules for arranging elements of the structure into unique and interpretable configurations. The rules automatically apply, given the presence of certain features, and the organization itself may be said to be the result of the application of the rules to the features. This description applies to the theories of understanding developed by Schank and by Winograd. A sentence is more than a concatenation of words. A set of rules imposes a unique configuration upon the elements of the sentence, so that it has a particular and unique interpretation. Likewise, a set of principles will convert a sensory input into an organized, unique, and interpretable perception. Both processes reveal organization but not creation.

However, investigators into thinking and perception, such as Bartlett or J. J. Gibson, have from time to time suggested that human beings engage in creative processes in the attempt to perceive and understand. In Bartlett's phrase, there is an effort after meaning. This means that there are auxiliary rules for the construction of elements or features, where these do not exist in the information presented to the understanding. The sensory input in perception is often so degraded that the percept itself must consist of more than the information supplied by the application of principles inherent in the perceptual apparatus and the sensory input of the moment. The semantic interpretation of segments of language is also dependent upon the information in the language itself being supplemented by assumptions, inferences, and other kinds of information not describable by markers or by rules defining and combining the elements in the language. This supplemental information is complex and not easy to characterize. It is, however, based upon knowedge about the world, and it is reasonable to suppose that the knowledge that enables us to add information to the sensory input of the moment is the same as that which may be used to interpret language. The term "unconscious inference" is an old one, and it is as good as any to describe the process of constructing information not given in the sensory input or associated with the semantic markers known to be stored with the lexical elements of discourse. Until we know the principles by which such unconscious inference works, we shall have only partial success in describing perceptual devices capable of imitating human perceptual interpretation and linguistic devices capable of imitating understanding. Our success with feature detectors of various sorts should not lead us to suppose that we know all of the basic principles of understanding and that all that is necessary is to work out the details. The programs of Schank and Winograd have made beginnings in this direction. Winograd makes use of logical inference rules that lead to "correct" interpretations of the world, but there is no reason why his program could not be extended so that, say, motion always gives rise to the inference of animistic causation. His program would then have a less than adequate understanding of the rules of the natural world, but it might be more human. Schank shows that it is possible and indeed necessary to build beliefs into a system for understanding.

Failure in understanding, or failure in perception, results either because the information coming in fails to conform to the pattern necessary for our decoding devices to operate upon it or because we are unable to mobilize in a willful way whatever processes lead to acceptable interpretation. Thus, some creative effort in understanding may be self-controlled to a degree. When we do not understand or cannot perceive something, it is often the case that a willful attention, through processes we ourselves cannot accurately report upon, will bring us to understanding. These processes are, in the sense described above, constructive in nature. Such constructive processes may not occur where the perceptual task or the task of linguistic understanding is an easy one. When a sensory input is badly degraded or when a text is particularly difficult, we may have to search for meaning. We easily and naturally invoke the intellectual apparatus necessary for a search for meaning. The additional insight gained through such an effort after meaning tells us that the processes of organization and construction operate at different levels and that the latter is under the control of some self-initiating device. Neither a perceptual system nor a language-processing system need understand, in the constructive sense, unless it has been furnished with the motivation for deriving meanings when none appear to exist upon a routine processing of information. It is a well-known fact that it is difficult to construct random arrays that are perceived as purely random (unless the elements approach the resolving power of the sensory system) and that people will place interpretations upon random strings of words or even of speechlike sounds when pressed to do so or even when simply motivated to do so.

At this stage we can do little more than point to the fact that, in understanding, the meaning we arrive at is possibly the result of creative processes as much as organizational ones. The material in this chapter suggests that we are beginning to understand the nature of organizational systems in understanding and that at least some of the avenues of study available to us suggest ways of applying creative processes. Almost certainly, it means that we shall have to construct rule-determined systems that misinterpret as well as interpret (where interpretation means the application of logical inference to feature structures), and we shall have to imagine systems that can deal much more adequately with degraded and deviant information than can any systems we now know how to construct.

References

Aarsleff, H. The history of linguistics and Professor Chomsky. *Language,* 1970, **46,** 570–585.

Arnheim, R. *Visual thinking.* Berkeley: Univ. of California Press, 1969.

Berlin, B., & Kay, P. *Basic color terms: Their universality and evolution.* Berkeley: Univ. of California Press, 1969.

Bierwisch, M. On classifying semantic features. In D. D. Steinberg & L. A. Jakobovits (Eds.) *Semantics: An interdisciplinary reader in philosophy, linguistics, and psychology.* London: Cambridge Univ. Press, 1971.

Bloomfield, L. *Language.* New York: Holt, 1933.

Bollinger, D. The atomization of meaning. *Language,* 1965, **41,** 553–573.

Bornstein, M. H. Color vision and color naming: A psychophysiological hypothesis of cultural difference. *Psychological Bulletin,* 1973, **80,** 257–285.

Bransford, J. D., & Franks. J. J. The abstraction of linguistic ideas: A review. *Cognition,* 1972, **1,** 211–249.

Carroll, J. D., & Wish, M. Multi-dimensional scaling models for measurement of human perception. In E. C. Carterette & M. P. Friedman (Eds.), *Handbook of Perception.* New York: Academic Press, 1974.

Clark, H. H. On the use and meaning of prepositions. *Journal of Verbal Learning and Verbal Behavior,* 1968, **7,** 421–431.

Conklin, H. C. Hanunoo color categories. *Southwestern Journal of Anthropology,* 1955, **11,** 339–344.

Deese, J. *The structure of associations in language and thought.* Baltimore: Johns Hopkins Univ. Press, 1965.

Deese, J. Conceptual categories in the study of content. In G. Gerbner (Ed.), *Communication and content.* New York, Wiley, 1969.

Deese, J. Towards a psychological theory of the meaning of sentences. In A. Silverstein (Ed.) *Human communication: Theoretical explorations.* Holt, 1974.

Emblan, D. L. *Peter Mark Roget: The word and the man.* New York: Crowell, 1970.

Fillenbaum, S., & Rapoport, A. *Structures in the subjective lexicon.* New York: Academic Press, 1971.

Fillmore, C. J. The case for case. In E. Bach & R. Harms (Eds.), *Universals in linguistic theory.* New York: Holt, 1968.

Garner, W. R. To perceive is to know. *American Psychologist,* 1966, **21,** 11–19.

Halle, M. Prolegomena to a theory of word formation. *Linguistic Inquiry,* 1973, **4,** 3–16.

Halliday, M. A. K. Notes on transitivity and theme. *Journal of Linguistics,* 1967, **3,** 37–81, 199–244.

Halliday, M. A. K. Functional diversity in language as seen from a consideration of modality and mood in English. *Foundations of Language,* 1970, **6,** 322–361.

Hammel, E. A. Formal semantic analysis. *American Anthropologist,* 1965, **67,** no. 5 (separate issue).

Henley, N. A psychological study of the semantics of animal terms. *Journal of Verbal Learning and Verbal Behavior,* 1969, **8,** 176–184.

Hunt, E. What kind of a computer is man? *Cognitive Psychology,* 1971, **2,** 57–98.

Johnson, S. C. Hierarchical clustering schemes. *Psychometrika,* 1967, **32,** 241–254.

Katz, J. J., & Fodor, J. A. The structure of semantic theory. *Language,* 1963, **39,** 170–210.

Kay, P. Taxonomy and semantic contrast. *Language,* 1971, **47,** 866–887.

Lakoff, G. On generative semantics. In D. D. Steinberg & L. A. Jakobovits (Eds.), *Semantics.* Cambridge: Cambridge Univ. Press, 1971.

McCawley, J. D. Where do noun phrases come from? In D. D. Steinberg & L. A. Jakobovits (Eds.), *Semantics.* Cambridge: Cambridge Univ. Press, 1971.

McNeill, D. A study of word association. *Journal of Verbal Learning and Verbal Behavior,* 1966, **5,** 548–557.

Michotte, A. *La perception de la causalité.* Louvain: Institute Supérieur de Philosophie, 1946.

Norman, D. A. The library and human memory. Mimeo., La Jolla: Univ. of Calif. at San Diego, 1971.

Olson, D. R. Language and thought: Aspects of a cognitive theory of semantics. *Psychological Review,* 1970, **77,** 257–273.

Osgood, C. E. Speculation on the structure of interpersonal intentions. *Behavioral Science,* 1970, **15,** 237–255.

Osgood, C. E., Suci, G. J., & Tannenbaum, P. H. *The measurement of meaning.* Urbana: Univ. of Illinois Press, 1957.

Quillian, M. R. Semantic memory. In M. Minsky (Ed.), *Semantic information processing.* Cambridge, Massachusetts: M.I.T. Press, 1968.

Richards, M. M. A multidimensional scaling analysis of semantic space with real and simulated data. Unpublished M.A. Thesis, Univ. Illinois, 1971.

Romney, A. K., & D'Andrade, R. G. Cognitive aspects of English kin terms. *American Anthropologist,* 1964, **66,** 146–170.

Schank, A. C. 'Semantics' in conceptual analysis. *Lingua,* 1972, **30,** 101–140. (a)

Schank, R. C. Conceptual dependency: A theory of natural language understanding. *Cognitive Psychology,* 1972, **3,** 552–631. (b)

Stefflre, V., Reich, P., & McClaran-Stefflre, M. Some eliciting and componential procedures for descriptive semantics. In P. Kay (Ed.), *Explorations in mathematical anthropology.* Cambridge, Massachusetts: M.I.T. Press, 1971.

Wallace, A. F. C. The problem of the psychological validity of componential analysis. *American Anthropologist,* 1965, **67,** no. 5 (separate issue).

Wallace, A. F. C., & Atkins, J. The meaning of kinship terms. *American Anthropologist,* 1960, **62,** 58–79.

Weizenbaum, J. ELIZA—A computer program for the study of natural language communication between man and machine. *Communications of the ACM,* 1966, **9,** 36–45.

Winograd, T. Understanding natural language. *Cognitive Psychology,* 1972, **3,** 1–191.

Young, F. W., & Torgerson, W. S. TORSCA, a FORTRAN IV program for Shepard-Kruskal multidimensional scaling analysis. *Behavioral Science,* 1967, **12,** 498.

Chapter 9

SENTENCE COMPREHENSION: A CASE STUDY IN THE RELATION OF KNOWLEDGE AND PERCEPTION

J. M. CARROLL AND T. G. BEVER

> *The perceiver . . . responds to the stimuli according to some organization that he imposes upon them.*
>
> —G. A. MILLER, 1951, p. 79.

I. INTRODUCTION

For several decades psychologists have been investigating the problem of speech perception as defined by G. A. Miller in the early 1950s. Miller and his colleagues showed that listening to speech involves simultaneous reference to a number of linguistic "levels," including the levels of the "sentence" and "meaning." A sample demonstration of this is the fact that a sequence of random words is harder to hear than the same words ordered into a sentence (Miller, 1951). The most striking aspect of this phenomenon is the fact that the words themselves seem to be acoustically clearer as a function of their role in the sentence. This suggested that the sentential structure is providing information that can guide the acoustic analysis of the signal. The question was, *How does this kind of interaction in speech perception occur?*

That question is with us today, still unanswered. However, it has stimulated a considerable body of research, which has advanced our understanding of how to answer it. There are several principles that guide virtually every kind of research program on speech perception:

1. The amount of information that can be stored in memory in a single form is extremely limited.
2. The structure of language specifies a number of forms in which speech information can be simultaneously represented. These forms are structurally ordered in a hierarchy of "levels."
3. The way to study the perception of a representation at a particular linguistic level is to vary the stimulus at another level and observe the changes in reports about the representation.

The linguistic levels applicable to an utterance include (at least) the following (ordered roughly according to a traditional and intuitive notion of increasing "abstractness"):

Psycho-acoustics: A physiological specification of the speech waveform as transmitted by the ear.

Phones: A segmentation of the signal into discrete categories of speech sounds, using universal features

Phonemes: A segmentation in terms of the categories of sounds and features used in the particular language.

Syllables: A segmentation of the sequence in terms of canonical acoustic forms that could be uttered in isolation (e.g., CVC, CV, VC).

Morphemes: A segmentation in terms of the (memorized) meaning-bearing units of the language.

Words: The minimal meaning-bearing units that can be uttered in isolation in universal categories (e.g., noun, verb).

Phrases: Hierarchical groupings of adjacent words into universal categories (e.g., noun phrase, verb phrase).

Clauses: Groupings of adjacent phrases in terms of the canonical external relations they bear to each other (e.g., subject, verb, object).

Propositions: Groupings of the phrases (not necessarily adjacent) in terms of the canonical internal grammatical relations they bear to each other (e.g., agent, action, object, modifier).

Semantics: Interpretation (usually of a sentoid) in terms of relations to other utterances with which it is synonymous, contradictory, etc.

Speech acts: Analysis of the utterance in terms of the act it performs (e.g., promise, request, inform).

Intentions: An analysis of what the utterance indicates to be the speaker's state of mind (often in universal terms, e.g., supportive, critical, assertive, submissive).

This list is by no means complete, nor is it the case that every school of linguistics claims that all of these levels are properly included within the domain of a formal "grammar." The fact remains that we can analyze even the simplest utterance simultaneously in terms of a large number of different kinds of knowledge. For example,

(1) *Can you take out the garbage tonight dear?*

can be represented in ways varying from an acoustic specification to a (possible) description of an act by a speaker who intends to indicate that he/she feels unwell.

In a logical sense, it might appear that each level of representation *must* be present before the next more abstract level can be fully specified: for example, how can one isolate the phonetic segments without first having fully analyzed the acoustic structure?

The answer is that *some* acoustic analysis must be available, not necessarily a complete one, but one which renders those specific parameters that are critical for phonetic analysis. Furthermore, the number of choices at a "lower" level are often restricted by the representations at "higher" levels of analysis. For example, lexical and sentential information renders almost completely predictable the phonetic segment following the fragment in

(2) *Can you take out the garba--.*

Almost *any* acoustic parameter of /j/ will be sufficient for its perception at that point. Thus, it is probably the case that perception at each level can facilitate perception at the other levels. The availability of such a large number of interacting kinds of simultaneous representation may effectively circumvent the limitations on any single mode of storage. Speech perception is at least not magic. But how does it in fact occur?

The studies of this process characteristically manipulate the stimulus at one level and observe the changes in the reported percept at another level. Most intense effort has been devoted to the role of acoustic parameters in syllable perception; to the role of acoustic, phonetic, and syllabic parameters in word perception; and to the role of word and phrase representations in the perception of sentences. The reasons for these choices are not accidental or arbitrary. Each of these perceptual levels is a relatively natural one for listeners to discuss in a laboratory setting—the syllable is the minimal pronounceable unit of sound, the word is the minimal memorized unit of meaning, and the sentence is the minimal unit of word combinations that can ordinarily stand alone. Despite the natural reasons to study these levels, there is no doubt that our understanding of many of the unconscious acts of perception has been obscured by the primary focus on these relatively conscious units of language.

The perception of sentence construction, for example, is only part of what listeners do when they understand speech. However, a detailed understanding of this part of the comprehension process will aid our understanding of comprehension in general. Linguistic analysis aids this process by offering a structural analysis of the sentence. Studying sentence comprehension this way is like starting the study of visual object recognition by close examination of the processes used in mapping three-dimensional percepts onto simple two-dimensional line drawings. Although this is only a part of normal visual perception, it has played an important role in the development of visual theories.

II. GENERAL BACKGROUND

The claim that the role of linguistic structure in sentence perception is a viable research problem has been assailed from two general points of view about psychological theory. The first of these, represented by Skinner (1957), Mowrer (1960), and others, derives from the position that language is describable with the mechanisms of stimulus–response (S–R) psychology. The second view, which we return to in Section III, asserts that sentence perception is exhaustively modeled by the theoretical apparatus of formal linguistics.

Much of the psycholinguistic research of the early 1960s spoke to the first of these viewpoints. The overwhelming conclusion of this work was that the sentence is a complex and abstract psychological object. In particular, syntactic variables became recognized as relevant behavioral variables (see, Epstein, 1961; Glanzer, 1962; Mandler & Mandler, 1964; Miller, 1962; Miller & Isard, 1963). The effect of these empirical findings was enhanced by a growing theoretical dissatisfaction in psychology with the S–R model of human knowledge and a commensurate development of interest in formally richer "cognitive" models (e.g., Miller, Galanter, & Pribram, 1960).

The finding that linguistic knowledge cannot be subsumed under the behavioristic learning theory model had two important consequences for psycholinguistics. First, it opened wide the door for experimental investigation of the organization of language behavior. Free of the methodological strictures and theoretical impoverishment of the S–R paradigm, psychologists could at last begin to broach these issues. The second consequence of the debunking of the S–R approach to the psychology of language was to leave psycholinguistics without a theory. Just at that time, however, a particularly exciting theoretical revolution was taking place in linguistic science. Chomsky's (1957) theory of transformational generative grammar was displacing the taxonomic approach of American descriptivism.

Chomsky rejected the taxonomic linguists' method of constructing tiered hierarchies of descriptive levels and their operationalist goal of automatic "discovery procedures" (see, Fodor, Bever, & Garrett, 1974, Chapter 2). He argued that the goal of linguistic theory was the construction of a formal grammar that would "generate" all and only the sentences of the language.

Chomsky elaborated the "transformational" model of sentence structure initially developed by Harris (1965). In this model actual sentences are generated from a set of kernel sentence structures by means of a set of transformations as blocked out in

(3) $\boxed{\text{Kernel Component}} \rightarrow \boxed{\text{Kernel Sentence Structure}} \rightarrow \boxed{\text{Transformational Rules}} \rightarrow \boxed{\text{Sentences}}$

The kernel sentence structures are close to simple declarative sentences like

(4) John past warn the boy

These structures can be transformed into other structures by optional transformations like

(5) *Passive:* $NP_1 + \text{tense} + V + NP_2 \rightarrow NP_2 + \text{tense} + \text{be}$
$+ \text{past participle} + V + \text{by} + PN_1$

or

(6) *Negative:* $\ldots V \ldots \rightarrow \ldots \text{neg} + V \ldots$ *

A final set of obligatory transformations convert the abstract structures to morphologically correct sentences:

(7) *Do-support:* $\text{tense} + \text{neg} \rightarrow \text{tense} + \text{Do} + \text{neg}$

(8) *Affix movemment:* $\text{affix} \ldots V \rightarrow V + \text{affix}$

* NP = noun phrase; V = verb; neg = not.

Each sentence is assigned a "derivation," consisting of its kernel structure and the transformations that apply to yield its surface appearance. Sample derivations are given in*

(9) a. John past warn the boy
         John warn + past the boy   (affix movement)
         John warned the boy   (morphological replacement)
     b. John past warn the boy
         John past neg warn the boy   (negative)
         John past Do neg warn the boy   (Do-support)
         John Do + past neg warn the boy   (affix movement)
         John did not warn the boy   (morphological replacement)
     c. John past warn the boy
         The boy past be past participle warn by John   (passive)
         The boy be + past warn + past participle by John
                                                        (affix movement)
         The boy was warned by John   (morphological replacement)
     d. John past warn the boy
         The boy past be past participle warn by John   (passive)
         The boy past be neg past participle warn by John   (negative)
         The boy be + past neg warn + past particple by John
                                                        (affix movement)
         The boy was not warned by John   (morphological replacement)

This model of language is quite simple. Nevertheless, it captures a number of regularities about sentences. For example, it represents the fact that the sentences in

(10) a. *John warned the boy*   Active (K)
      b. *John didn't warn the boy*   Negative (N)
      c. *The boy was warned by John*   Passive (P)
      d. *The boy wasn't warned by John*   Negative Passive (PN)

are all related by assigning them the same basic kernel structure. The model also proposes that the formal *source* for every sentence is an *abstract* kernel structure **which is not itself an actual sentence.** This claim, that sentences have abstract structures underlying them, was the focus of much controversy in linguistics and psychology; it was difficult to see how children

---

* The linguistic rules and derivations we present in this paper are included for purely expositional purposes, although they are similar to those proposed by Chomsky. The same is true of the three diagrams and bracketings presented in what follows. For further discussions of transformational grammar, see Chomsky (1957, 1965) and many other sources.

could "learn" that such abstract structures exist. This led Chomsky and others to postulate that the knowledge of such structures must be innate, which is a fundamental claim about human knowledge. Of course this claim is of interest only if the grammar is in some sense psychologically "real."

Indeed, Miller, Galanter, and Pribram (1960) take as pretheoretical the position that a formal grammatical derivation is literally a part of the "plan" involved in speaking. This assumption became routine in the psycholinguistic research of the early 1960s—research that was designed to establish the "psychological reality" of transformational grammar. It identified the rules of linguistic grammar directly with psychological processes.

III. THE DERIVATIONAL THEORY OF COMPLEXITY— EXPLICIT TRANSFORMATIONS ARE REAL

Consider one such study, which is paradigmatic, by Miller and McKean (1964) (a modified replication of a study by Miller, McKean, and Slobin as reported in Miller, 1962). In this study, subjects were tachistoscopically presented with a sentence. The sentence represented one of the four transformational types exemplified in (10). The subjects' first task was to change his mental representation of the presented sentence into one of the other transformational types. When he had done so, he pressed a button which tachistoscopically displated a search list of new sentences all of that type. The subject then searched the list for the transformed version of the originally presented sentence and again pressed the button when he had found it. For example, if presented with (10b) and told to apply the passive, the subject would first change it to (10d) and then press the button in order to search for (10d) in the search list.

The response times for the first task (i.e., the transforming task) suggested that transformations create additive increments of complexity in sentences. Response times for sentences that require two transformations are longer than those for sentences that require only one transformation. Response times for transforming K sentences into PN sentences were approximately equal to the sum of the response times for transforming K sentences into P sentences and K sentences into N sentences. Moreover, response times do not appear to be sensitive to the direction of the transformation. Thus, transforming K sentences into P sentences takes approximately as long as transforming P sentences into K sentences.

The Miller and McKean results appeared to confirm the view that psycholinguistic processes correspond to grammatical operations. In Chomsky's (1957) transformational grammar the P and N versions of a sentence are obtained by the application of transformational rules to the kernel sentence structure underlying the K version. What Miller and McKean found suggests that the application of transformational rules is a psychological process that can be measured. Even the distinguished status reserved for the K sentences in Chomsky's theory seems to be borne out. Sentence pairs that included a K sentence yielded especially rapid response times.

The hypothesis that the psychological complexity of a sentence is related to the number of transformations in its derivation has been called the *derivational theory of complexity,* or DTC. In its strongest form this view would hold that the greater the number of rules in a derivation, the greater the complexity of the sentence corresponding to that derivation. A series of studies followed Miller and McKean (1964) and provided results that converged on the DTC.

For example, McMahon (1963) presented subjects with the same four sentence types used by Miller and McKean. He found that when the subject is asked to decide whether a given sentence is true or false, passives and negatives require a longer time than do active affirmatives (K sentences). McMahon (see also Gough, 1965) obtained similar results in a task that required the subject to decide whether a given picture made a sentence true or false. In both studies, the passive took longer to verify than the corresponding active and the negative took longer than the corresponding affirmative. (For other relevant results and discussion see Compton, 1967; Gough, 1966; Mehler, 1963; Mehler & Miller, 1964; Savin & Perchonock, 1965.) Thus, it appeared initially to be the case that a transformational grammar is literally a psychological model. This stimulated the hope that linguistic and psychological research could become directly linked, so that new linguistic hypotheses could be subjected to direct experimental verification.

However, several qualifications are required of the initial results supporting DTC. First, there are theoretical problems with the original model. Second, there are confounding variables built into most of the DTC studies that call into question their conclusions. Finally, there are a variety of intuitive and empirical facts that are in conflict with DTC. We discuss these in order.

Recall that for Miller and McKean the translation of N sentences into P sentences is more complex (yields longer response times) than the translation (mapping) of N sentences into NP sentences. On their view, this is because for the first pair, the negative transformation must be undone and then the passive transformation applied (two transformations), whereas for the second pair, only the passive need be applied in order to complete the mapping (one transformation). However, in the grammar the passive transformation is ordered before the negative transformation. In fact, if passive applies after negative, ungrammatical strings like

(11)   *The boy didn't be warned by John.

will be generated by the grammar. Coming back to our example, *three* transformations, and not one, will be necessary for the mapping of an N version into an PN version (i.e., first undo negative, then apply passive, then apply negative). This reverses the prediction for Miller and McKean's results on DTC and hence converts their support for DTC into evidence against. It is important to note that ordering of transformations is not unique to this particular case, but rather a typical and essential property of the transformational grammars that these workers were using.

Furthermore, the sentence types studied in the DTC experiments have properties that confound the syntactic variables at issue. For example, the common result that negative sentences are more complex than their corresponding affirmatives could reasonably be ascribed to the semantic complexity of negation, and not necessarily to the addition of a transformational rule in the sentence derivation (see Wason, 1961). Besides semantic confounding, the DTC experiments confounded sentence length with syntactic structure. The result that passive sentences are more complex than their corresponding actives could be due in part to the fact that passive sentences are two words longer than corresponding active sentences.

The initial experimental demonstrations of DTC rested on a small number of types of constructions. Intuitive consideration of other types of sentences suggests that DTC is not true in general. For example,

(12) a. *The nice red wooden box fell.*

is clearly more complex transformationally than

(12) b. *The box that was nice and that was red and that was wooden fell.*

from whose structure it is derived. Yet, it is clearly *not* more complex psychologically. There is a large number of such examples.

There are also several experimental disconfirmations of the DTC. For example, Bever and Mehler (1967) found that sentences like

(13)   a. *Slowly the strongman picked the girl up.*

are recalled better than sentences like

(13)   b. *The strongman slowly picked up the girl.*

in a short-term memory task, even though these derivations include two additional transformations that move out the particle and adverb, respectively. This result, with sentence length and meaning controlled, directly contradicts DTC. Bever, Fodor, Garrett, and Mehler (1966) studied a variety of cases in which increased derivational complexity did not involve increased sentence length. They asked subjects to decide which one of four tones hear before a sentence was repeated immediately after the sentence. In this task no performance differences reliably correlated with transformational complexity of the stimuli.

The support for DTC rests, as we have seen, on results based almost exclusively on the negative and the passive transformations. Furthermore, the analysis of the results for these two rules is liable to a number of problems. When other rules are investigated, as in the Bever and Mehler study of particle shift and adverb postposing, predicted effects are not obtained. Jenkins, Fodor, and Saporta (1965) also failed to find the predicted results for the rule of comparative deletion. They measured tachistoscopic threshold for sentences like

(14)   a. *Harry eats more than Alice eats.*
                b. *Harry eats more than Alice.*
                c. *Harry eats more than Alice does.*

but found that the threshold was highest for (14a), which is transformationally the least complex.

What we have seen is that an initial surprising convergence between linguistic and psycholinguistic theories proved to be specious. Nevertheless, many studies following that of Miller and McKean suggest that people *are* sensitive to transformational relations when they are explicitly marked. Experiments by Clifton, Kurcz, and Jenkins (1965), Clifton and Odom (1966), Koplin and Davis (1966), and Smith (1965) support the psychological validity of transformational "sentence families" like those in (10). In these experiments subjects characteristically rated different sentences in the same "family" as being more similar than paraphrastically related sentences not in the same transformational family.

One conclusion drawn from the psycholinguistic research on the psychological reality of grammar by 1965 was that shared underlying structures are perceived as the basis for sentence similarity. However, there was no consistent evidence that the linguistically defined transformations corresponded to psychological operations. This focused research onto the behavioral basis of the different linguistically defined structures in a derivation and away from the formal operations that manipulate these structures.

This represents an important turning point in psycholinguistic theory, although in a sense it was a reflection of a revision in linguistic theory. In the original model (see Chomsky, 1957) kernel sentences ("simple declaratives") are close to the apparent source of all sentence constructions;

they are deformed and combined by transformations. The revised linguistic model (Chomsky, 1965), the *standard theory,* emphasizes a special prominence for two levels of linguistic description: *deep structure* and *surface structure.* Deep structure represents the underlying logical form of all sentences, whereas surface structure is the constituent analysis of the sentences' manifest form. On this model, "transformational families" like (10) can be described in terms of the similarity or identity of their deep structures and need not make reference to specific transformations that have applied in their derivations.

This revision in transformational theory had special complications for the representation of complex sentences (sentences with more than one underlying proposition). In the earlier model such sentences were described as the transformational combination of separate kernel sentence structures. For example

(15)   a. *The ball dropped*
               b. *The ball is red*

would be generated as separate kernel structures and then combined into

               c. *The ball that is red dropped*

or

               d. *The red ball dropped*

by a special transformation. In the later model, a sentence like (15c) derives from a single deep structure like

(16)

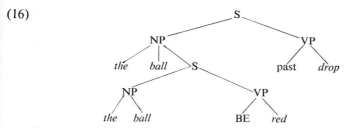

This form of analysis articulates two notions of "clause." At the deep-structure level, the clause structure represents the basic grammatical relations in each proposition (actor, action, object, modifier). That is, the actor of a predicate is the NP that is dominated by the S that dominates the VP that dominates the predicate (V); this complicated verbal description is simply represented by the following hierarchical tree:

At the surface level, the clause structure represents the hierarchical groupings of adjacent phrases, as shown in

(17)   a.

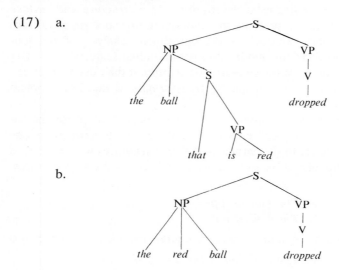

b.

Accordingly, the surface structure represents the hierarchical groupings of constituents that are created by the operation of the transformations on the deep-structure configurations.

The proposal that speaker–hearers are sensitive to both deep and surface structure but not necessarily to particular rules that relate these levels in formal linguistic theory is intuitively appealing. Deep structure in linguistic theory is the level at which all information relevant to semantic interpretation is represented (e.g., grammatical relations like "subject of," "predicate," and "object,"). If listeners are to understand sentences, it seems reasonable to assume that the computation of some such structure is involved. Indeed, at some level we understand a grammatical difference between sentences with superficially homonymous structures like

(18)   a. *John is eager to please.*
                   b. *John is easy to please.*

Only in (18a) is *John* the logical (i.e., deep) subject of the verb. Similarly, we understand that

(19)   *Murdering Cossacks can be horrifying*

expresses two different logical propositions even though this ambiguity cannot be represented in its surface structure.

IV. SURFACE AND DEEP STRUCTURES ARE PSYCHOLOGICAL OBJECTS

A. Surface Structures

A number of experiments have demonstrated the psychological perti-
nence of surface clause representations of sentences. Epstein (1961) found
that subjects could learn strings of grammatically inflected nonsense syllables more easily than they could learn strings of uninflected nonsense syllables—despite the greater length of the inflected strings. Glanzer (1962)
showed that mixed sequences of nonsense words and English words are
learned more efficaciously when they are interpretable as surface constituent frames. For example, (20a) and (20c) are more easily learned than
(20b) and (20d).

(20)
        a. YIG FOOD
        b. KEX AND
        c. WOJ AND KEX
        d. YIG FOOD SEB

Anglin and Miller (1968) found that printed prose passages are more
easily learned when the end of each line corresponds to a surface constituent boundary than when it does not. Suci (1967) and R. E. Johnson
(1970) report similar effects of facilitation of learning with surface constituent segmentation.

N. F. Johnson (1965) studied the patterns of errors made during the
learning of lists of sentences. He devised a measure called *transitional error
probability* (TEP). The value of TEP for a pair of words is the probability
that the second word is recalled incorrectly, given that the first word is
recalled correctly. Johnson found that the TEP for pairs of words adjacent
in surface structure increases sharply for the first word in a major constituent (e.g., noun phrase, verb phrase), and that a significant increase obtains
for the initial words of minor constituents as well. Johnson's central finding
is that surface clause structure can define the psychological units for learning sentences in lists.

A similar paradigm was used by Suci, Ammon, and Gamlin (1967).
In this study subjects were presented with a "probe" word immediately
following a sentence. The probe had occurred in the sentence, and the
subject's task was to supply the next word from his recollection of the sentence. Greatest response latencies were obtained for probe words that were
final words in a major constituent [e.g., "red" in (15c)]. Similar results
have been obtained by Kennedy and Wilkes (1968) and Ammon (1968).

Like Johnson's work, they suggest that the surface constituent is a psychologically real basis for organizing a sentence.

Mehler and Carey (1967) report surface structure effects with another paradigm. They presented subjects with sets of 11 sentences in noise. The first 10 sentences in the list had identical constituent structures, but in one condition, the last sentence had a different structure [contrast (21a) with (21b)].

(21)   a. *They are performing monkeys.*
                        b. *They are fixing benches.*

In this condition, subjects did not understand the final sentence in the list as well as in the condition in which it had a surface structure consonant with the preceding 10 sentences. Mehler and Carey attributed this result to a perceptual "set" for surface structure configuration induced by the first 10 sentences.

Fodor and Bever (1965) and Garrett (1965) studied surface structure effects using a paradigm derived from work by Ladefoged and Broadbent (1960). Ladefoged and Broadbent had noticed that subjects were less accurate in reporting the location of short bursts of noise (of about 30 msec) superimposed on recorded sentences than they were in reporting the location of these interruptions in recorded digit strings. They concluded that the perceptual units for digit strings were smaller than the units of perceptual analysis used for sentences. Fodor and Bever found that errors in click location were, in fact, sensitive to constituent structure. They found a greater location error for clicks not objectively located at constituent boundaries than for clicks objectively located in boundaries. Moreover, they found a reliable tendency for mislocated clicks to be placed in constituent boundaries.

Garrett, Bever, and Fodor (1966) controlled for acoustic artifact by constructing stimulus pair sentences like

(22)   a. *In her hope of marrying Anna is surely impractical.*
       b. *Your constant hope of marrying Anna is surely impractical.*

By cross-recording, the acoustic properties of the final six words are held constant while their syntactic configuration is manipulated. In (22a) the constituent structure break occurs between *marrying* and *Anna,* whereas in (22b) it occurs between *Anna* and *is.* Abrams and Bever (1969) constructed stimulus sentences by splicing together words that had been recorded in random word lists. These materials had no cues of stress, intonation, or pausing to reveal constituent structure. In both experiments the pattern of results from Fodor and Bever's study was replicated. (See also Berry, 1970; Holmes & Forster, 1970; Seitz, 1972; Scholes, 1969).

Stewart and Gough (1967) used a task in which a two-word probe was presented to the subject directly after a stimulus sentence. They measured the reaction time for a subject to decide whether or not the two-words had occurred in the sentence. Using materials like those used by Garrett *et al.*, they contrasted response latencies for cases in which the probe sequence "straddled" a constituent boundary with those cases for which it did not. For example, in (22b) *marrying Anna* does not straddle a boundary but in (22a) it does. Stewart and Gough found that reaction times for the straddling trials are greater than those for probes belonging to a single constituent. This again is consistent with the view that surface constituents (in this case, the surface clause) have a perceptual integrity.

As a final example of the reality of surface structure, consider a study by Levelt (1970). Levelt presented subjects with a sentence and then with a list of word pairs derived from the sentence. The subject rated the "relatedness" of each pair and the data were scaled by a "hierarchical clustering" analysis. Scaling structures obtained by using this procedure are highly similar to the surface analyses of the sentences further supporting the "reality" of surface structures.

B. Deep Structures

A number of studies also support the psychological pertinance of deep structure relations. For example, in some cases of Levelt's experiment, the scaling structures do not yield well-formed hierarchies. In these cases, Levelt found that subjects' judgments of relatedness were sensitive to deep grammatical relations. Thus, the chaotic scaling structure for

(23)   a. *Carla takes the book and goes to school.*

becomes very orderly when imposed on

(23)   b. *Carla takes the book and Carla goes to school.*

But, in fact, (23b) is similar to the deep structure organization of (23a) (i.e., before the linguistic rule of conjunction reduction that deletes the second *Carla*).

The same point holds for Stewart and Gough's results. Some of the reaction time asymmetries they found were not readily explainable in terms of surface constituent structure. In a subsequent study, Walker, Gough and Wall (1968) contrasted the effects of surface structure adjacency with those of deep structure relation. They used the two-word probe technique with sentences like

(24)   *The scouts the Indians saw killed a buffalo.*

Of the four probe types: *scouts saw, scouts killed, Indians saw,* and *Indians killed;* they found the fastest response latency for *scouts killed.* In general, probe words that are related in deep structure yielded faster response times than those which are not.

Davidson (1969) used the TEP measure to contrast full passives like

(25)   a. *Gloves were made by tailors.*

with truncated passives like

(25)   b. *Gloves were made by hand.*

He found no difference in TEP for words adjacent in surface structure (e.g., *made tailors* versus *made hands*). However, he found that the TEP for pairs related in deep structure like *tailors made* was lower than TEP scores for pairs not so related, like *hand made,* even though they had comparable surface structure positions. In sentences like (25a), the noun of the by-phrase is the deep structure subject of the verb; whereas in sentences like (25b), it is not.

A series of studies by Blumenthal, Boakes, and Wanner investigated the psychological reality of deep structure relations in prompted recall tasks. Blumenthal (1967) used sentences similar to those used by Davidson, finding that *tailors* was a significantly better prompt word than *hand.* This result, consistent with Davidson's, suggests the conclusion that deep subjects, like *tailors,* are more salient in the stored psychological representation of a sentence than are nouns in adverbial phrases, like *hand.* Blumenthal attributed this salience to the dominating position (or height) of subject nouns in linguistic deep structures.

To test the generality of the result, Blumenthal and Boakes (1967) tested other sentence structure types, like

(26)   a. *John is eager to please.*
                            b. *John is easy to please.*

in the same prompted recall paradigm. *John* was found to be a better prompt for sentences like (26a) than for sentences like (26b). This result is compatible with two interpretations, however. In (26a), *John* is the deep subject, whereas in (26b), it is not. Therefore, *John* is higher in the deep structure of (26a) than it is in the deep structure of (26b). But *John* also occurs twice in the deep structure of (26a) but only once in the deep structure of (26b). The two deep structures are glossed as

(27)   a. *John is eager for John to please someone.*

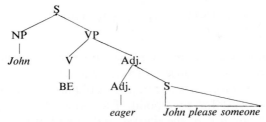

    b. *It is easy for John to please someone.*

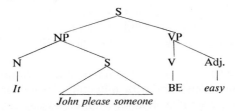

The Blumenthal and Boakes result cannot distinguish these two explanations of the differential prompt efficacy of *John*.

Wanner (1968) again using prompted recall sought to distinguish these two accounts. He used sentences like

(28)   a. *The governor asked the detective to prevent drinking.*
        b. *The governor asked the detective to cease drinking.*

and contrasted the prompt efficacy of *detective*. For both sentences, the noun has a position of equal height; however, in (28b) the noun occurs three times in the deep structure, while in (28a) it appears only twice. The two deep structures may be glossed as

(29)   a. [*The governor ask the detective* [*the detective prevent* [*someone drink*]$_s$]$_s$]$_s$
        b. [*The governor ask the detective* [*the detective cease* [*the detective drink*]$_s$]$_s$]$_s$

Wanner's results are persuasive support for the claim that the structures of the grammatical formalism are effective in the speaker–hearer's psychological representation of linguistic information. Wanner concluded that the number of deep structure propositions, or sentoids, that an item occurs in determines its value as a prompt for the matrix sentence. This, in turn, is consonant with the view that the psychological units recruited in a paradigm like the one used by Blumenthal, Boakes, and Wanner are deep structure sentoids. We will return to this position in the next section, when we discuss clausal analysis.

V. CLAUSAL ANALYSIS—THE SEARCH FOR SEMANTIC RELATIONS

Up to this point, we have reviewed evidence supporting the "psychological reality" of deep and surface structures but generally disconfirming the view that the explicit formal transformations of linguistic theory are psychologically real, at least for perception. The latter conclusion is somewhat equivocal, since any test of the derivational theory of complexity (DTC) must be intimately tied to some specific assumptions about grammar. In order to refute DTC decisively, one would need to demonstrate that no empirically adequate grammar could be formulated that would make correct predictions vis-à-vis the psychological reality of formal linguistic operations (see Watt, 1970).

We could attempt to recast the grammatical rules in order to accommodate them in a way consistent with differential behavioral complexity of sentences. However, even if such an attempt could succeed in specific cases, there is no known principled way to accommodate the full set of rules to the full set of complexity facts. The available evidence makes the prospects for such a grammar very dubious. Thus, each accommodation would be descriptive, but not explanatory.

In fact, there is reason to believe that no attempt to find such a principle could succeed. Transformations, in linguistic theory, operate on hierarchical phrase structures, not on strings of words or acoustic waveforms. The derivational theory of complexity must assume that the surface phrase marker of a sentence is specified in order for it to be detransformed into the corresponding deep structure. However the derivational theory of complexity gives no procedure for this. If such a procedure were part of the entire recognition process, it would presumably be a substantial contributor to complexity variation. Thus, DTC would be less subject to direct test: Even if the number of transformations *does* evoke a corresponding number of perceptual operations, their effect might be entirely masked by the perceptual processes involved in constructing a surface constituent structure.

Moreover, even given a surface phrase structure, how is the deep structure to be recovered? A random trial-and-error detransformation process is implausible: If it were true, it would also be inconsistent with a rigorous DTC. First, if the derivation of actual sentences involves a fraction of the number of transformations stated in the grammar (about 10^2), then a trial-and-error procedure would swamp the complexity difference between a sentence derivation with 10 transformations and one with 9. It cannot be replied that the transformations all apply virtually effortlessly and simultaneously, because then DTC itself could not make any empirical predictions.

The surface structure could be detransformed to the deep structure by way of an ordered set of inverse transformations. Indeed, one such computer model has been developed (see, Petrick, 1965). This model, however, is not directly consistent with DTC, because there is no particular number of inverse transformations corresponding to every linguistic transformation. Thus, the recognition of some sentences with 10 linguistic transformations could involve 10 inverse transformations, whereas the recognition of others could involve much more computation.

The considerations up to this point have established the following:

1. There is a variety of evidence for the psychological reality of linguistically defined surface and deep structure representations of sentences.
2. There is no consistent evidence for the perceptual reality of transformations as perceptual processes. Furthermore, there are formal arguments suggesting that no evidence could be found.

The question now is, given the "general reality" of surface and deep structures and the perceptual "unreality" of transformations, how do listeners in fact recover deep structures when they hear surface structures?

The simple diagram in (30) sketches the framework that has guided much research on this problem.

(30)
$$\left.\begin{array}{l}\text{Uttered}\\\text{Sequence}\end{array}\right\} \rightarrow \text{Store} \rightarrow \begin{array}{l}\text{Segmentation,}\\\text{Recoding,}\\\text{Labeling,}\end{array} \rightarrow \begin{array}{l}\text{Deep}\\\text{Structures}\end{array}$$

Basically, deep structures are constructed by active processes. Associated with the perceptual construction of each deep structure clause is a set of simultaneous behavioral phenomena; the perceptual segmentation of the corresponding surface sequence; the recoding of the sequence into a more abstract representation; and the labeling of the grammatical relations. These distinguishable behavioral phenomena should not be viewed as essentially independent from each other—rather, each reflects the active processes of constructing deep structures out of surface sequences. However, we shall discuss the behavioral phenomena separately for clarity of exposition.

A. Segmentation

One way to approach the problem of sentence perception is to ask: What is the primary unit of sentence perception? This question focuses on the clause as an obvious candidate—but the further question emerges immediately: Is it the clause at the surface or deep structure level that serves as a primary perceptual unit?

The deep structure clause, of course, is the more important of the two, in that it represents the information essential for the recovery of meaning (information about the relations between a sentence's logical propositions, grammatical relations, etc.). An interesting hypothesis, then, would be that deep structure propositions, or "sentoids," are the primary units of sentence perception. Such a view would predict that an early process in sentence perception includes grouping together surface structure items that belong to a common deep structure sentoid. It would predict perceptual effects of surface clause boundaries, since they always reflect deep structure clause boundaries [as in (15c)]. But it would also predict perceptual effects at positions in surface structure that, although they represent deep structure sentoid boundaries, are not marked by surface clause boundaries [as in (15d)]. We now review some studies that bear on this hypothesis.

Earlier, we discussed the click-location paradigm. Fodor and Bever (1965) had originally argued that all constituents in surface structure can function as perceptual units and can determine click mislocation. A reanalysis of their data (Fodor, Bever, & Garrett, 1974), however, shows that the experimental support for this claim comes from clicks placed at or near a major constituent (i.e., clause) boundary. In fact, Bever, Lackner, and Stolz (1969) and Bever, Lackner, and Kirk (1969) found no differential effects for minor constituent boundaries of various types. Moreover, the latter investigators found that much of the variance in the Fodor and Bever data is due to a tendency for clicks to be mislocated into surface positions corresponding to boundaries between deep sentoids.

These results are not consistent with the claim that it is the boundaries of surface structure clauses that are effective in perceptual segmentation. Note that although every surface structure clause boundary corresponds to a deep sentoid juncture, the converse is not always true. Bever, Lackner, and Kirk (1969) compared cases in which surface clause boundaries coincide with sentoid boundaries with those in which they do not. Compare

(31)   a. *John defied Bill to resign.*

and

(31)   b. *John desired Bill to resign.*

The two sentences have similar surface structures but different deep structures. In particular, the position between *desire* and *Bill* marks a sentoid boundary in (31b) whereas the corresponding position in (31a) does not mark any deep boundary. Bever *et al.* found the click effect to be reliably greater following the main verb in sentences like (31b) than in sentences like (31a). Of course, the interest of this particular result depends on the surface structure identity of sentences of the type of (31a) and (31b) but at present there are no conclusive linguistic arguments to the contrary. This result was replicated and extended by Fodor, Fodor, Garrett, and Lackner (1974).

The theoretical interest of the preceding findings rests on the methodological status of the click-location paradigm. Several investigators have suggested that the frequency of click location in the clause break is not a perceptual response to syntactic structure, but is actually due to a response bias. Reber and Anderson (1970) suggested that the mislocation patterns reflect a serial position bias for the middle of the sentence. Indeed, a serial position bias was reported in the original study by Ladefoged and Broadbent (1960). However, Bever, Lackner, and Kirk (1969) found no exaggeration of click mislocation into the major clause boundary when it coincided with the medial sentence position. Moreover, serial position has typically been controlled in the click location experiments we are reviewing.

A second possibility is that clause breaks are perceptually prepotent primarily because the redundancy of successive words increases (i.e., TEP decreases) in approaching a clause boundary but then decreases markedly in crossing the boundary. On this view, the clause acts as a perceptual unit because it is an island of relatively high transitional probability surrounded by boundaries of relatively low transitional probability. Bever, Lackner, and Stolz (1969) manipulated information redundancy, however, and showed that click mislocations do not occur into points of low transitional probability, when those positions do not coincide with a clause break.

A third possible alternative to the hypothesis that the click effect is truly perceptual response to syntactic structure is the claim that the location errors are due to a response bias in conjunction with recall error. Fodor and Bever (1965) had subjects recall stimulus sentences and then mark the perceived location of clicks. In fact, Ladefoged (1967) reported that when subjects are asked to guess the position of a subliminal (but in fact nonexistent) click, they manifest some predilection for locating it in a major constituent break. The issue, of course, is not whether the click location effect is a response bias for sentoidal boundaries, for this is just what all the results show. The question is whether it measures a truly perceptual effect.

A variety of data suggests that the effect cannot be attributed to recall error. First, when a recognition task is substituted for the recall task, there is no attenuation of the effect of the clause boundary on click location even though memory load is presumably decreased. Garrett (1965) and Holmes (1970) gave the subject a written script of the sentences after their auditory presentation and found the usual pattern of results. The conclusive study (to date) was carried out by Bever, Hurtig, and Handle (1976). They presented brief tones (rather than clicks) in a background of white noise during sentences. Subjects had to be prepared to write out the sentence, although on critical trials a script was given them after hearing the stimulus. On the preprepared script, the subject was given a response "window" four syllables wide, as shown in

(32)   a. *After the dry summer of /that year all crops/ were destroyed.*
        b. *After the dry summer /of that year all/ crops were destroyed.*
        c. *After the dry summer of that /year all crops were/ destroyed.*

The subject was told that the tone occurred somewhere in the window. The response window always straddled the location of the tone. [Hence, the three windows in (32) each correspond to a different tone location.] However, in certain cases *there was no tone present* (the purpose of embedding tones in noise was to make their apparent absence on certain trials less jarring to the subjects). Responses within the different response windows [as shown in (32a–c)] when tones were absent, gave a picture of the perception-free response bias subjects use. Bever *et al.* found that the response bias pattern does not account for the tendency to locate tones in the clause boundary. In brief, the click-location response patterns are shaped after listening and before responding a few seconds later (even when no writing is necessary).

Studies using other paradigms have also tended to converge on the conclusion that deep structure sentoids are perceptual units. For example, Forster (1970) and Forster and Ryder (1971) used the Rapid Serial Visual Presentation (RSVP) technique in which sentences are displaced word by word on successive frames of a film strip. In this technique, error rate can be manipulated by altering the rate of presentation. Forster finds that when length and semantic plausibility are controlled, sentences with only one deep sentoid obtain lower error rates than sentences having two sentoids in their deep structures. This follows from the view that sentences with more perceptual units ought to be more complicated than sentences with fewer of them.

B. Semantic Recoding

Although the studies we have just reviewed suggest that the clausal structure of sentences is effective in their perceptual segmentation, they do not address the behavioral role of clausal units during perception. A number of other studies shed some light on this question. Abrams and Bever (1969) found that reaction times to clicks located objectively at the ends of clauses are much slower than reaction times to clicks located immediately after a clause boundary. Bever (1968) varied click amplitude and found that, just before a break, detectability of clicks is lowest (replicated in Bever & Hurtig, 1975). These results support the conclusion that processing load in the perceptual system is high at the ends of clauses. Apparently, listeners are relatively preoccupied at the end of a clause. We have discussed the evidence that this preoccupation is reflected in perceptual segmentation. We turn now to evidence that at clause boundaries the acoustic information is recoded and integrated into more abstract levels of representation.

Jarvella (1971, 1973) had subjects listen to short stories that were interrupted without warning. The subject's task was to recall as much as he could of the story. Jarvella finds that rote recall is best for words in the clause immediately preceding the interruption, but that it falls off sharply for words in earlier clauses. There was no reliable serial position effect for words within clauses. However, when Jarvella tested for recall of meaning by questioning subjects on the content of the stories, he found virtually no difference as a function of clause position. These results, like those of Bever and of Abrams and Bever, are consonant with the view that sentences are perceptually integrated clause by clause. When a full clause has been parsed, it is recoded into some more abstract semantic store—its meaning is available but the exact form is not (see also Sachs, 1967).

A further result consistent with this analysis is reported by Caplan (1972). Caplan measured response time to decide whether a probe word presented after a stimulus sentence did or did not occur in that sentence. His sentences were constructed in the manner of Garrett *et al.* (1966) so that the clause in which the probe word occurred could be manipulated independently of intonational cues or distance from the end of the sentence. Response latencies for sentences with the probe word in the first clause were greater than those for sentences with the probe word in the second clause. This is the expected result on the view that as clauses are completed they are represented in a more abstract store. The same finding is reported by Shedletsky (1974), who systematically varied whether or not the first clause is a main clause or a subordinate clause.

With this viewpoint in mind, we now turn to a consideration of the case of ambiguous sentences. This topic has been of particular interest in psycholinguistics, since listeners must contend with many potentially ambiguous sentences every day. We will suggest that the clausal analysis view may be able to reconcile an apparent paradox in the literature about ambiguities. On the face of it, there seem to be two differentiable hypotheses about how ambiguous sentences are perceptually processed. First, one could hold that given a number of possible interpretations the perceptual system computes them all in parallel. On the other hand, it could be the case that only one interpretation is selected serially at a time for perceptual computation. For the case of unresolved ambiguities, the former model predicts that the perceptual complexity of a sentence ought to increase with the number of possible interpretations. In the latter model, the serial process model, ambiguity should only increase perceptual complexity when the interpretation selected first is incompatible with subsequent information. There are separate experiments supporting each of these models. We shall suggest that both models are correct, but at different times: During a clause listeners entertain a number of possible meanings in parallel; after the clause is completed only one meaning is recoded, and hence, only one meaning is retained.

Consider three studies that support the parallel model. MacKay (1966) presented subjects with sentence fragments and measured the time required to supply a completion. He found that ambiguous fragments took longer to complete than unambiguous fragments, even when the subject did not notice the ambiguity. This result supports the parallel view insofar as response time is assumed to be due to response interference.

Foss (1970) measured reaction times to prespecified phonemes in recorded sentence strings. He found slower reaction times following ambiguous material. Since "phoneme-monitor" times are taken as indications of computational load (see Foss, 1969; Hakes, 1971), this result is also amenable to the explanation that multiple readings are computed in parallel for ambiguous sequences.

Finally, Lackner and Garrett (1973) presented subjects simultaneously with an ambiguous sentence in one ear and disambiguating context in the other. Subjects were instructed to attend only to the ear to which the ambiguous material was presented. Following the stimulus presentation, subjects provided paraphrases of the attended material. Although both signals were easily understood in isolation, subjects were unable to report anything about the unattended (disambiguating) signal, except that it was speech. In particular, they did not notice the ambiguities of the attended signal. Nevertheless, Lackner and Garrett found a strong tendency for the paraphrase results to covary with the unattended biasing context material. The result seems to support the claim that both interpretations of an ambiguity are computed and available; otherwise, there would be no way that the biasing context could have an effect.

In contrast with the preceding findings, there are experiments that support the hypothesis that ambiguities are treated serially. Foss, Bever, and Silver (1968) presented subjects with sentences followed immediately by pictures. They measured the response time for the subject to decide whether the picture was true or false vis-à-vis the sentence. Foss *et al.* compared latencies for ambiguous and unambiguous sentences, finding that response time was greater for ambiguous sentences only if the picture favored the less frequent interpretation of the ambiguity. They concluded that subjects assign only one immediate interpretation to an ambiguous sentence (i.e., the more frequent). If that meaning is not appropriate to the situation then they may go back and reanalyze the sentence for another meaning. Supporting results have been reported by Cairns (1970).

Carey, Mehler, and Bever (1970) used the same paradigm as Foss *et al.* but pre-set subjects to expect a sentence with one of two phrase structures [see Mehler and Carey (1967), and sentences (21a) and (21b)]. Subjects then heard a sentence that was ambiguous between the two phrase structure interpretations. Subjects who later reported not having noticed the ambiguity and who heard the ambiguous sentence as having the phrase structure for which they had been "set" gave response times that were indistinguishable from those of subjects dealing with analogous but objectively unambiguous sentences. Subjects who noticed the ambiguity despite their "set" and heard the sentence as having the structure for which they had not been set, gave longer response times than subjects who heard the reading for which they had been set. Both of these results are incompatible with the parallel model. They suggest that the induced set can suppress the processing of one interpretation of an ambiguity.

There is a possibility that the conflicting results just reviewed can be reconciled by the clausal analysis view sketched earlier. On this view we might expect that many interpretations of an ambiguity are computed within a clause, but that when the clause is completed and recoded and dismissed from short-term storage, a decision is made as to the univocal semantic interpretation of the clause. This position has two sources of support.

First, it reconciles virtually all of the conflicts reviewed so far. A typical characteristic of the studies that support the parallel model is that they test for processing effects *within* a clause. On the other hand, the studies that tend to show support for the serial model typically measure an effect *after* the end of the sentence. In addition, Bever (1968) reanalyzed MacKay's data and showed that the effect of ambiguity reported by MacKay obtains only in sentence fragments that are incomplete clauses.

A second piece of evidence is a result by Bever, Garrett, and Hurtig (1973). Bever *et al.* used the sentence completion paradigm of MacKay but varied systematically the clausal properties of the fragments. One-third of their test fragments were incomplete clauses, one-third were clauses and one-third were completed clauses plus part of a following (unambiguous) clause. Only for the incomplete clause fragments were completion times reliably slower than for unambiguous control fragments. This result agrees with Bever's reanalysis of MacKay's data and supports the view that the computational complexity of ambiguous sentences may indeed be limited by clause boundaries. (See Foss & Jenkins, 1973, for further relevant results and discussion.)

C. Perceptual Strategies

We have reviewed some evidence that supports the claim that listeners are sensitive to both deep and surface linguistic structure. We have suggested that the deep sentoid, and therefore its surface realization, the clause, is the primary perceptual unit of sentence perception. We have explored the ways in which the clause may function as a perceptual unit and examined some of the literature on the particular issue of ambiguous sentences. We now turn to a consideration of the ways in which surface elements belonging to a common sentoid might become grouped together in perceptual analysis.

The canonical form of deep sentoids is subject noun followed by verb followed optionally by object noun. This is not to say that subject–verb–object (SVO) is universally preferred in all languages—the most frequent word orders are SVO and SOV. It is an interesting fact about English that very few surface sequences of the form noun–verb–(noun) do not represent the subject–verb–(object) of a common deep sentoid. It is reasonable to suppose that listeners might have internalized this fact and that they routinely employ what may be called the canonical-sentoid strategy, interpreting surface noun–verb–(noun) sequences as subject, verb and object of a common sentoid. The difficulty of sentences like

(33)   a. *The bomb rolled past the tent exploded.*
             b. *The pitcher tossed the ball tossed the ball.*

may be attributed to misapplication of the canonical-sentoid strategy. In these cases, the verb of a relative clause which has been reduced by the transformational rule of WHIZ Deletion is frequently misanalyzed as being the main verb.

This proposal also finds some empirical support. The first group of studies we will review deal with doubly self-embedded structures like

(34)   a. *The man the girl the boy liked hated laughed.*
       b. *The editor the authors the newspapers hired like laughed.*
       c. *The editor authors the newspapers hired liked laughed.*

    d. *The water the fish the man caught swam in was polluted.*
    e. *The reporter everyone I met trusts said Thieu will regain power someday.*

These constructions are rare in actual speech behavior. Like rare visually complex examples (e.g., the Kopferman cube, the "impossible pitchfork") they are important to consider because of what they reveal about the nature of speech perception and the relation between the grammar and behavior. It is an important achievement of a perceptual theory to explain such examples. Indeed, Miller and Chomsky (1963) recognized explicitly that center embedded constructions must be included in the set of grammatical sentences—there is no natural way of allowing single embeddings which are perfectly acceptable as in

(35)   a. *The girl the boy liked hated the man.*
          b. *The man the girl hated laughed.*

but blocking them from combining into unacceptable multiple embeddings. They suggested that such sequences tax short-term memory beyond its ability to store noun phrases at different phrase structure levels when the noun phrases are not yet organized in relation to verb phrases. Later research has been consistent with this general view. In particular, it has focused attention on listener's attempts to isolate appropriate sentoids with their grammatical relations.

    Blumenthal (1966) analyzed the errors of paraphrase responses to sentences like (34a) and found a strong tendency for subjects to treat them as noun–verb sequences in which both the noun and the verb were conjunctions (i.e., *The man, the girl and the boy liked, hated, and laughed.*). Bever (1968) reported a significant tendency for subjects to misanalyze sentences like (34c), assigning the deep relations subject–verb–object to the sequence *The editor authors the newspapers.* This tendency was resistant to learning effects. Finally, Schlesinger (1968) found that the difficulty of forms like (34a) is mitigated when predictable semantic relations obtain between corresponding nouns and verbs, as in (34d). Sentences like (34d) are sufficient to demonstrate that the center embedded construction is syntactically grammatical, independent of Miller and Chomsky's formal point that they cannot be formally differentiated from singly embedded sentences. This is further supported by the ease of comprehending such constructions when the three initial nounphrases are from different lexical classes, as in (34e). We return later to an explanation of *why* this is true. It is sufficient here to note that such cases indicate that we must accept center embedded sentences as grammatical, both for formal and empirical reasons. Why, then, are so many of them unacceptable?

If we adopt the clausal view of sentence processing, the inherent difficulty of self-embedded forms is explicable. On this view, listeners are searching for sentoids consisting of actor–action–object clusters. In the preceding sections, we discussed the phenomena of segmentation and abstract recoding associated with assigning a sentoid analysis. It is clear that there must also be a set of mapping operations that assigns the specific internal relations that obtain between lexical items and phrases. It is only as such relations are assigned that the sequences are recoded. To put it another way, surface items cannot be dismissed from short-term memory until they have been assigned to a deep structure sentoid. Self-embedded forms, then, place a special burden on short-term storage because they present the listener with three sentoids, in which only the most embedded has its members adjacent. Accordingly, it is true that the most embedded clause in these structures is typically the one most easily understood, since that is the only sentoid whose surface elements are juxtaposed. Blumenthal's and Bever's results show that with fewer cues or with misleading cues, listeners will attempt to impose a canonical order on the material, subject–verb–object. Thus, these considerations demonstrate that there are three factors in the assignment of sentoid grammatical relations—are the assigned phrases adjacent, are they semantically constrained to be related in only one way, and are they in a canonical SVO order?

The existence of such different factors is further supported by studies contrasting reversible (36a) and irreversible (36b) passives by Slobin (1966) and by Walker, Gough, and Wall (1968).

(36)   a. *The woman was chased by the dog.*
               b. *The car was repaired by the mechanic.*

These studies demonstrated the result that passives are more complex than their active counterparts. However, the result did not obtain when the passives were semantically irreversible. This outcome is consistent with the interpretation that passive versions are more difficult primarily because they deform the canonical order (i.e., reverse deep subject and object). When, as in the case of irreversible passives, the deep sentoid relations are univocally determined by semantic selection, the passive–active difference is not observed.

Experiments by Wanner and Maratsos (1971) and by Walker (1969) also marshall support for the canonical-sentoid strategy. Both of these studies found that sentences with subject relative clauses, like

(37)   a. *The man who hit John is a Rotarian.*

are easier than sentences with object relative clauses, like

(37)   b. *The man who John hit is a Rotarian.*

Only in the case of subject relatives can the canonical-sentoid strategy apply to the embedded clause (i.e., to the relative clause). Finally, recall that Bever and Mehler (1967) found a tendency for verb particles and adverbs to be displaced from their deep structure positions in an immediate recall task. This result is consonant with the view that preanalysis favors a sequencing of material to which the canonical SVO sentoid strategy can apply.*

As is clear from the results on semantically constrained self-embedded sentences and irreversible passives, the canonical-sentoid strategy cannot be the only heuristic device available to listeners for clausal analysis. We now review some of the ways listeners can use different kinds of lexical information in perceptually processing sentences. Our main point is that listeners are extremely sensitive to subtle differences in lexical surface form when those differences are important signals to sentoid relations.

Moore (1972) presented subjects with sentence frames from which one content word had been deleted. He then displayed a word to the subject and measured the time required to decide whether or not inserting the word in the blank made the sentence grammatical. The results showed that the decision times for verbs were greater than those for nouns. This is consistent with the claim that verbs play a greater role in determining the deep structure organization of a sentence than nouns do. This hypothesis is supported by Forster (1969) who found that subjects have greater difficulty in completing left-deleted fragments like

(38)   a. —————the man come running through the trees.

than they do with fragments like

(38)   b. —————saw the man come running through the trees.

In this case, the verb governs the neutralization of tense in the subordinate clause.

Fodor, Garrett, and Bever (1968) tested the hypothesis that the number of deep structure configurations with which a verb is potentially compatible is related to the difficulty in understanding sentences containing the verb.

---

* See also, Kaplan (1972) for an attempt to formalize the perceptual strategies in the style of a general purpose computer program originally developed by Bobrow and Fraser (1969) (an augmented transition network, ATN). Kaplan argues that modeling the strategies produces precise and testable claims about the comprehension process; indeed, Wanner and Maratsos (1975) have tested certain features of the particular ATN developed by Kaplan. The weakness of this approach is that the computer program can be arranged to simulate any conceivable result: Thus it cannot reveal or explain any internal properties of perception. It can only model them. Furthermore, all the empirical tests thus far are consistent with the canonical order hypothesis (e.g., Wanner and Maratsos, discussed above).

They contrasted verbs like *slap,* which can only occur with a direct object, with verbs like *like,* which occur with direct objects and a variety of complement types. They found that subjects were less accurate in supplying immediate paraphrases of self-embedded sentences with *like* type verbs than for those with *slap* type verbs. Similarly, subjects were less successful with *like* type verbs in a sentence anagram task (i.e., ordering a random array of words into a sentence).

Other investigators have also found much the same sort of results, although not all paradigms are sensitive to verb complexity. Hakes (1971) replicated Fodor, Garrett, and Bever's paraphrase result but failed to find an effect of verb complexity in the phoneme-monitor task (listening for the first instance of a particular sound). Holmes and Forster (1972) used the RSVP technique to show that one-clause sentences with complex verbs are more difficult than one-clause sentences with simple verbs. They also found some differences consistent with the other verb complexity results for several kinds of two clause sentences. Finally, the results of Bever, Lackner, and Kirk's (1969) click study can be shown to be almost entirely due to mislocations of clicks objectively in the verb. In the sentence types studied, the verb's properties are important cues to the probable location of sentoid boundaries in the surface sequence. It is possible to argue that since the main verbs of sentences like (31b) are more complex (i.e., compatible with more deep structure geometries) than the main verbs of sentences like (31a) subjects process the two verb types differently. The assumption that subjects use these cues will explain the Bever *et al.* data.

The canonical sentoid strategy and the use of lexical heuristics cannot even be the whole story. In those cases in which a surface item is amenable to more than one deep-structure analysis, the sentence surface structure must provide information to decide between alternatives. Knowing that sentences with *expect* type main verbs like (39) below are compatible with several different complement types will not in itself tell the listener which complement type has occurred in a given sentence. Clearly, it is to the listener's advantage to be sensitive to cues in the surface configuration which can narrow down the range of hypotheses about the deep structure of a sentence he is trying to understand.

Consider sentences like (39a–f).

(39)   a. *The woman expects that John will retreat.*
           b. *The woman expects John will retreat.*
           c. *The woman expects he will retreat.*
           d. *The woman expects him to retreat.*
           e. *The woman expects John to retreat.*
           f. *The woman expects John's retreating.*

These examples illustrate several surface structure cues which identify complement types. For example, in English, *that*-complements are the only complement types that both govern *tensed* subordinate clauses and permit free deletion of the complementizer *that*. Thus, the deletion of the complementizer and the tense marking in the subordinate clause uniquely identify the complement type in (39b). Furthermore, as in (39c), *that*-complements take subject pronouns in the subjective case. In contrast, notice that infinitival (*for–to*) complements take their subject pronouns in the objective case, as in (39d). In addition, these complements have the surface item *to*, which is a cue to their deep structure identity. Finally, note that *Poss–ing* complements may be recognized by the surface configuration *'s . . . ing*.

If such surface structure cues are effective in sentence perception, one would expect that the elimination or confusion of them would tend to increase perceptual complexity. Indeed, Fodor and Garrett (1967) found that when the relative pronouns of center-embedded sentences are deleted as in

(40) a. *The cow the horse the boy rode chased likes grass.*
      b. *The cow that the horse that the boy rode chased likes grass.*

subject's performance is impaired in a paraphrase task. This result has been replicated by Hakes and Cairns (1970). Hakes and Cairns and Hakes and Foss (1970) also found that phoneme-monitor times (the latency to identify a particular speech sound) are sensitive to this relative-pronoun deletion.

VI. CENTER EMBEDDED SENTENCES AGAIN

The preceding considerations suggest that listeners use perceptual strategies to map the grammatical relations among elements in surface sequences. We can schematize such strategies as shown in

(41) $. . . X P Y Q Z . . .$ ————$P(R_i)Q$.
        That is, "In a surface sequence in which P precedes Q, assign the grammatical relation R_i to $P \cdot \cdot \cdot Q$. (Note that X, Y, Z may be null, or may be specified, depending on the strategy.)

For example, the tendency to listen for the "canonical order" of grammatical relations can be formalized as in

(42)   NP V ———— NP (subject of) V.
                  V NP ———— V (object of) NP.

It is important at the present state of our understanding of these strategies not to take their formalization literally—it is not at all clear what the correct formalization is. Nevertheless, even an approximate formalization can express the fact that any NVN sequence (not already assigned other relations) is susceptible to being interpreted as SVO. This can lead to perceptual illusion in cases where the NVN in fact is not an SVO sequence. Consider

(43)   *The horse raced past the barn fell.

When presented with this sequence in isolation, most listeners reinterpret it either as a "sloppy speech" version of (44a), rarely (44b),

(44)   a. The horse raced past the barn and fell.
                  b. The horse raced past. The barn fell.

or as ungrammatical nonsense. If, however, (43) is preceded by either

(45)   a. The horse that was raced past the barn fell.

or

(45)   b. The horse ridden past the barn fell.

then it is immediately understood and accepted as grammatical. The difficulty of (43) is explained by the strategies in (42); since the past participle; raced, is homonomous with the simple past, listeners first treat the initial portion of the sequence as an SVO. it is striking that even when the word fell indicates that this analysis is incorrect, most listeners cannot break the SVO set and find the correct interpretation.

Now that the theory of speech perception has been somewhat more developed, we can examine its application to center-embedded sentences in detail. The action of another perceptual mapping rule does partially explain the initial complexity of double-embeddings. Consider the perceptual mapping rule that assigns the functions of underlying subject and object to noun phrases with relative clauses

(46)   In a surface sequence ". . . NP_1 NP_2 ($\neq$ who) (NP*) V
         ($\neq$ Be) . . ." NP_1 is the object of a sentoid of which NP_2
         is the subject.

This rule capitalizes on the fact that in clause initial (or postverbal) position two adjacent noun phrases followed by a verb other than BE (with other noun phrases optionally intervening) are uniquely related such that the first noun phrase is the object (direct or indirect) of an underlying clause of which the second noun phrase is the subject. For example, the initial sequence of noun phrases in (34a) would be assigned the appropriate relations by (46) as shown

(47)   *The girl   the boy   liked. . . .*
                Object$_i$ Subject$_i$

and

(48)   *The man   the girl   the boy   liked. . . .*
                Object$_i$ Subject$_i$
                            Object$_j$ Subject$_j$

Clearly (46) must apply twice to double-embeddings to mark the middle noun phrase as both a subject and an object. This double marking by the same perceptual rule lies at the heart of the difficulty of center-embedded sentences.

There is a logical restriction on the utilization of any conceptual dimension, given in the following principle:

(49)   A stimulus may not be perceived as simultaneously having
            two positions on the same classificatory relation.

This interacts with the double application of rules like (46) to double-embeddings. Principle (49) articulates the tautology that a stimulus cannot be perceived in two incompatible ways at the same time. For example, a noun phrase in the surface sequence cannot simultaneously be subject and object of the same nonreflexive verb. This principle, when applied according to the view of speech perception as a direct mapping of external sequences onto internal structures, will predict the difficulty of any sequence in which a phrase as a "double function" in such a mapping operation.

The general double-function hypothesis for speech perception following from (49) is this:

(50)   In a sequence of constituents x, y, z, if x has an internal
            asymmetric relation R_i to y and y has the same internal
            relation to z, and x, y, and z are superficially identical in
            construction type, then the stimulus is relatively complex.

This is due to y's double function in the perceptual mapping rule r_i in which y is both a p and a q. (Note that $R_i \neq$ conjunction)

$$(r_i) \quad pq \text{———} pR_iq$$

Thus, doubly embedded sentences are complex because they involve the second noun phrase in a double function with respect to the perceptual mapping rule (46).

It should be emphasized that the difficulty implied by (50) does not refer to all cases in which a single phrase has more than one role in the deep structure. For example, in

(51)   *The girl liked the sleeping boy Sam gave the sandwich to.*

the boy is simultaneously the underlying *subject* of *sleep,* the *object* of *like,* and the *indirect object* of *give.* Yet, the sentence is quite simple. Principle (50) applies only to those cases in which exactly the same perceptual mapping rule is used to assign different functions to the same phrase. That is, it is not the "double relation" of the middle noun phrase in the underlying structure which makes such sentences complex. It is, rather, the double application to it of the perceptual rule (46). In applying the rule the listener first categorizes the middle phrase as the right-hand member of a pair related by rule (46) and then must characterize it immediately as the left-hand member of the same kind of pair defined by the same rule. In the terms used in (50) the middle noun phrase of (34a) is simultaneously a p and q of the same mapping rule.

There are other examples of complex constructions explained by principle (50). Consider the relative complexity of sentences (52) and (53).

(52)   *?Maxine did not ask Harvey not to say he would not go.*

(53)   *Maxine did not ask Harvey to say he would not go.*

Sentence (52) is an example of triple negation, which has often been recognized as extremely complex, if acceptable at all. Like singly embedded sentences, sentences with only two negation markers are perfectly comprehensible and acceptable [as in (53)]. Principle (50) predicts the relative difficulty of sentences with three negations. The perceptual mapping operation corresponding to the negative marks the second *not* in (52) as *simultaneously* the scope of the first negation and the operator on the third negation. Following principle (50), any sequence containing such a double perceptual function is perceptually complex.

Principle (50) also explains some examples of perceptually complex constructions that are intuitively of the same sort as the preceding examples. Consider the sentences (54) and (55).

(54)   *?They were tired of discussing* **considering** *producing toys.*

(55)   *?They were tired of the discussion of* **the consideration** *of the production of toys.*

In each case, the sentences are extremely difficult to understand, if they are acceptable at all. As in double-embedding and triple-negation sentences, the complexity of these sentences is a function of the presence of three superficially identical phrases in which the second phrase is modified by the first phrase in the same way that the second phrase modifies the third phrase (in the underlying structure). Consider the relative perceptual ease of such constructions if only two phrases occur:

(56)   *They were tired of discussing producing toys.*

(57)   *They were tired of the discussion of the production of toys.*

Sentences like those in (54) and (55) are much easier to understand if the internal relations among the three critical phrases are varied as in

(58)   *They were tired of discussing ceiling producing toys.*

and

(59)   *They were tired of the discussion of the evolution of the pro-duction of toys.*

The explanation is that the middle phrase no longer has a double function, since *different* perceptual mapping rules relate the first two and second two verb phrases. [Note that in (58) the midddle phrase (*ceiling*) is the underlying structure object of the following phrase (*producing*), whereas the first (*discussing*) and second phrase are not directly related. In (59) the middle phrase (*evolution*) is the action carried out by the third phrase (*production*), but the object of the first phrase (*discussion*).]

Finally, (54) and (55) become perceptually simpler if the superficial form of the critical phrases is varied, even though the internal relations are held constant. The explanation for the relative ease of

(60)   *They were tired of discussing the consideration of producing toys.*

(61)   *They were tired of the discussion of considering the production of toys.*

is that the middle phrase does not have a double function with respect to the *same* exact perceptual mapping rule. The superficial difference in the middle phrase allows the listener to use a different mapping rule for relating the first two phrases than for relating the second two phrases.

It is striking that such a subtle difference in superficial form can have major effects on the perceivability of sentences, although it is just what the double function principle predicts. This raises the possibility that if we change the superficial form of the noun phrases in sentences like (34a) so that they differ from each other, then the sentences should become more comprehensible. Sentence (34e) is an example of this. We pointed out that most listeners find it immediately acceptable (although it is a center-embedded construction). Each of the initial noun phrases is of a different surface lexical type and thus differentiates the operation of strategy (46) into different rules. In fact, many listeners find

(62)   *The pictures a reporter everyone I met trusts took showed that arson caused the fire.*

to be acceptable though it is triply embedded;

(63)   *The banker your portrait an art dealer everyone I met trusts appraised belonged to knows nothing about art.*

a quadruply embedded sentence, may be acceptable because of the differences between the lexical form of the initial noun phrases.

The acceptability of (62) and (63) is not due to the fact that certain subject–object–verb relations are semantically facilitated (e.g., *reporter . . . take pictures; art dealer . . . "appraise . . . portrait"*). In the structurally parallel sentences

(64)   *The cricket the mouse the cat the dog barked at miawed at squeaked at chirped at midnight.*

(65)   *The hearth the cricket the mouse the cat the dog barked at miawed at squeaked at chirped at warmed the room.*

almost every subject–verb–object relation is semantically constrained but the sequences are not acceptable. This is due to the fact that the noun phrases are not superficially distinguished in the lexical class look-up phrase of perception and a number of them carry perceptual double functions.

This analysis modifies the Miller and Chomsky proposal that center-embedding is unacceptable due to the difficulty of extracting and holding two noun phrases in memory before they are attached to a verb in a sentoid. The present argument is that the memory difficulty is itself due to the fact that the middle noun phrase must be contradictorily coded by the perceptual mapping rules. This analysis, in turn, predicts new cases and even isolates critical examples of multiple embeddings that are comprehensible. Accordingly, the general model we have proposed for speech perception accounts for existing facts and predicts new facts as well. In this sense, our ability to deal with center-embedded sequences confirms the perceptual model.

VII. WHAT ARE THE PROCESSES THAT CREATE THE PERCEPTUAL ORGANIZATION?

It should be clear that most attention has been given to a *structural* definition of the sequences that are treated as points of perceptual segmentation, recoding, and functional labeling. The ultimate question for a psychological model concerns the processes that bring these organizational phenomena about. The view that we have outlined is roughly the following: During clauses, listeners use local lexical and semantic information to develop hypotheses about the possible sentoid mappings onto elementary grammatical relations. When a sufficiently clear mapping is possible, listeners recode the acoustic material into a more abstract form. This empties the immediate memory store for further speech material. In brief, listeners are continually playing "catch-up" with the speech stimulus—recoding the speech to a more abstract level whenever possible.

Several questions are suggested by this model. First, how will it treat degraded clauses (i.e., sequences whose surface realization does not explicitly include a full set of grammatical relations but whose underlying syntactic structure corresponds to a sentoid)? For example, the sentence

(66)   a. *After leaving, John regretted his harsh words.*

corresponds to the deep structure bracketing sketched in

(66)   b. [[*After John leave*]$_S$ *John regret John's harsh word*]$_S$
       c. *After John left, he regretted his harsh words*

After leaving does not explicitly mention the subject noun. The question is whether the initial sequence in (66a) will stimulate segmentation in the way that the clausal processing model predicts the initial sequence in (66c) will do so.

A second question concerns surface structure properties. We have reviewed evidence that surface structure cues can condition perceptual complexity (pages 328–329). Fodor, Fodor, Garrett, and Lackner (1974) tested pairs like

(67)   a. *This time of year anyone/who's rich enough takes a vacation.*
       b. *This time of year anyone/rich enough takes a vacation*

in a click location paradigm. They found that boundary effects (boundaries are indicated by a slash) were reliably stronger in the unreduced (67a) version. This result tends to complicate the sentence perception picture. It does not disconfirm the psychological reality of linguistic deep structure but it does eliminate the hypothesis that *only* deep structure variables are relevant in sentence perception. The linguistic difference between (67a) and (67b) is the reduction of a surface relative clause in (67a) to a postnominal modifier in (67b). Since (67a) and (67b) differ in surface structure but not in deep structure, the result suggests that although deep structure sentoid junctures determine potential points of perceptual segmentation, whether such a juncture is used as a perceptual unit boundary may depend on surface structure factors.

Another aspect of surface structure that may act as a segmentation variable is the clarity with which a clause is marked as an independent unit. Just as the grammatical relations within a clause must be integrated into a whole, so the various segmentation units must be integrated into a logical structure corresponding to the entire sentence. The listener's processing must be sensitive to the range of grammatical devices which mark subordination relations between clauses. Thus, in

(68)   a. **After Max ate steak,** *he became very tall.*
             b. **Max's eating steak** *made him very tall.*
             c. **Max eats more steak** *than he really ought to.*
             d. **Max eats a lot of steak** *and it made him beefy.*

surface markers signal the listener that the initial clause will have to be integrated with the following main clause: In (68a) the adverb *after,* in (68b) the sequence *'s . . . -ing* and in (68c) the comparative *more.* Subordinated clauses, like (68a), (68b), and (68c), cannot be as fully recoded as independent clauses, like (68d), because they must, at some subsequent point in processing, be integrated with their main clauses. The relative difficulty of the clause order subordinate–main versus the clause order main–subordinate seems to be consistent with these speculations (see Weksel and Bever, 1966; Clark & Clark, 1968; and Holmes, 1973). Moreover, noninitial markers [like those in (68b) and (68c)] might be less effective than initial markers [like that of (68a)] in cuing a suspended recoding strategy. Hence, the placement as well as the presence of surface structure marking may in part determine the likelihood that a given clausal sequence will stimulate segmentation.

The length (in words, syllables, phones, etc.) of clauses also seems to be a factor which could be expected to play a role in determining suitability as a segmentation unit. For example, a very short sentence-initial subordinate clause might just be parsed with its following main clause (i.e., it might not stimulate segmentation at all). Bever, Lackner, and Kirk (1969) suggest that even a proper noun (grammatically a single item) could serve as a segmentation unit if it were long enough. Sentences like

(69) a. *John told the man that the girl knew the answer.*
      b. *John told the obese and slovenly man the girl knew the answer.*

are ambiguous in that they may be interpreted as having a structure with a relative clause (i.e., *The man that the girl knew was told the answer by John.*) or with a complement clause (i.e., *That man was told by John that the girl knew the answer.*). Perhaps when short-term storage is over-taxed as in (69b) versus (69a), listeners will try to segment perceptually earlier. If this is true, then one might expect that sentences like (69b) will tend to be interpreted on the complement-clause reading more often than sentences like (69a). The relative-clause reading requires that *that the girl knew* be grouped into the initial clause as part of the indirect object of the main verb. Tanenhaus and Carroll (1975) have found that length does play a role in determining the usability of noun phrases as segmenta-tion units (longer noun phrases occasion stronger effects of closure).

Finally, semantic and lexical differences should be expected to play some role in determining how much linguistic material a listener will parse per segmentation unit. The grammatical difference between (70a) and (70b) is a trivial lexical alternation.

(70)   a. *Who who I know wants Sally to be at the party?*
         b. *Who that I know wants Sally to be at the party?*

However, (70b) seems much easier to understand (see, Bever, Carroll, & Hurtig, 1976). Similarly, recall the embedded sentences studied by Schlesinger (1968) [example (34d)]. In these sentences, difficulty seems to be related to the perspicuity of the pairings of nouns and verbs vis-à-vis semantic constraints. Finally, we have seen that the complexity and struc-tural characteristics of individual lexical items (specifically, verbs) can play an organizing role in sentence perception (pages 327–328). It is likely that more factors must be taken into account, to say nothing of the need for bet-ter specifying those factors that have been identified.

Tanenhaus and Carroll (1975) have attempted initially to integrate fac-tors like grammatical completeness, surface marking clause, length, and complexity in developing the notion of a *functional clause*. Using these factors, they have proposed a *hierarchy* of clause types, which scales the suitability of clausal structures as segmentation units. So, for example, they predict that main clauses are better functional clauses than are subordi-nates, which in turn are better than relative clauses, which are better than sentential subjects, which are better than nominalizations, etc.

Carroll and Tanenhaus (1975) argued that grammatical completeness (or in their term *functional completeness*) is the most important factor in defining the functional clause. They conducted two experiments using the "click location" technique. In their first experiment, they contrasted sentence-initial main clauses and subordinate clauses [(71a) and (71b), respectively] with headless nominalizations and noun phrases [(71c) and (71d), respectively].

(71)   a. *Harry insisted on his point / but nobody was swayed.*
       b. *Whenever I watch the news / I get depressed.*
       c. *Running down a city street / is a good way to get killed.*
       d. *The very old and worn shirt / was on sale.*

Main clauses and subordinate clauses are functionally complete in that they contain a complete and explicit set of grammatical relations. Headless nominalizations and noun phrases are functionally incomplete: Headless nominalizations lack an explicit subject noun and noun phrases lack an explicit verb.

Carroll and Tanenhaus found that brief tones superimposed on recorded sentences tend to be mislocated into or towards the clause-boundary [indicated in (71) by a slash] more often for functionally complete clauses [like (71a) and (71b)] than for functionally incomplete clauses [like (71c) and (71d)]. Following Fodor and Bever (1965) and Bever *et al.* (1969), they interpreted this as demonstrating that functionally complete clauses are better segmentation units than functionally incomplete clauses. The deep structure sentoid clausal processing model would not predict a difference between the clause types in (71) since *all* of them are derived from deep structure sentoids.

In their second experiment, Carroll and Tanenhaus contrasted relative clauses with noun phrases and headed nominalizations with headless nominalizations. Relative clauses contain a full set of grammatical relations [i.e., subject, copulative verb and predicate adjective, as in (72a)], but noun phrases with adjectives do not (72b).

(72)   a. *The man who is tall / played basketball.*
       b. *The tall man / played basketball.*
       c. *The army's destruction of the city / annoyed the senator.*
       d. *The destruction of the city / annoyed the senator.*

However, both are derived from the same deep structure configuration. Headed (72c) and headless (72d) nominalizations provide a critical test: at both surface and deep levels of syntactic description they have identical representations. They differ only in functional completeness.

Carroll and Tanenhaus found that relative clauses are better segmentation units than noun phrases with adjectives and that headed nominalizations are better than headless nominalizations. Their research with the click-location technique suggests that functional completeness and not deep and surface grammatical structure predicts the suitability of a linguistic sequence as a segmentation unit. And this, in turn, suggests that purely structural theories of segementation make the correct predictions only when they are in accord with functional theories.

VIII. CONCLUSION

The study of sentence perception can serve as a model for the study of the relationship between knowledge and behavior.

We mentioned in the introduction that treating the sentence as a perceptual object is like starting the study of three-dimensional visual perception with the perception of simple geometric forms. The same distinction arises between the formalization of the mapping between two dimensions and three and the actual visual processes that perceivers use to recognize three-dimensional objects. To take the grammatical rules as perceptual processes would be like taking the laws of perspective as direct models of psychological processes; to claim that the different levels of linguistic structure are perceived objects would be like claiming that a two-dimensional structure is analyzed independently of the three-dimensional object it represents. In both cases, the manifest stimulus is analyzed only insofar as the analysis supports a usable interpretation. Miller and his colleagues demonstrated that the sentence is a relevant unit in speech perception. Since there is an arbitrarily large number of sentences this required a theory that would describe the set of *possible* sentences: A generative linguistic grammar provided such a theory, and thereby became a hypothesis about the structure of linguistic knowledge. The grammar provides a structural description of each sentence, independent of perception. Such an independent description of what people *know* about a sentence sets the goal of what they must *discover* about a sentence when they comprehend it. This raised the question of how the grammar that describes linguistic knowledge is employed during sentence comprehension. The answer to this question offered by research has evolved in three phases. The first phase was to take the *grammatical transformations* literally as psychological processes. When this proposal broke down, the next phase was to argue that the linguistically defined *structures* are psychologically "real." Further research shows that structures are pertinent behaviorally only as a result of perceptual operations. Accordingly, our current focus must be on structures only insofar as they reveal properties of the psychological operations themselves.

References

Abrams, K., & Bever, T. G. Syntactic structure modifies attention during speech perception and recognition. *Quarterly Journal of Experimental Psychology,* 1969, **21,** 280–290.

Ammon, P. The perception of grammatical relations in sentences: A methodological exploration. *Journal of Verbal Learning and Verbal Behavior,* 1968, **7,** 869–875.

Anglin, J. M., & Miller, G. A. The role of phrase structure in the recall of meaningful verbal material. *Psychonomic Science,* 1968, **10,** 343–344.

Berry, R. A. A critical review of noise location during simultaneously presented sentences. Unpublished doctoral dissertation, University of Illinois, 1970.

Bever, T. G. A survey of some recent work in psycholinguistics. In W. J. Plath (Ed.), *Specification and utilization of a transformational grammar: Scientific report number three.* Yorktown Heights, New York: Thomas J. Watson Research Center, International Business Machines Corporation, 1968.

Bever, T. G., Carroll, J. M., & Hurtig, R. Analogy: or ungrammatical sequences that are utterable and comprehensible are the origins of new grammars in language acquisition and linguistic evolution. In T. Bever, J. Katz, & T. Langendoen (Eds.), *Integrated theories of linguistic ability.* New York: T. Y. Crowell Press, 1976.

Bever, T. G., Fodor, J. A., Garrett, M. F., & Mehler, J. Transformational operations and stimulus complexity. Unpublished, M.I.T., 1966.

Bever, T. G., Garrett, M. F., & Hurtig, R. Ambiguity increases complexity of perceptually incomplete clauses. *Memory and Cognition,* 1973, **1,** 279–286.

Bever, T. G., & Hurtig, R. Detection of a nonlinguistic stimulus is poorest at the end of a clause. *Journal of Psycholinguistic Research,* 1975 **4,** 1, 1–7.

Bever, T. G., Hurtig, R., & Handel, A. Response biases do not account for the effect of clause structure on the perception of nonlinguistic stimuli. In preparation, 1976.

Bever, T. G., Lackner, J. R., & Kirk, R. The underlying structures of sentences are the primary units of immediate speech processing. *Perception and Psychophysics,* 1969, **5,** 225–231.

Bever T. G., Lackner, J. R., & Stolz, W. Transitional probability is not a general mechanism for the segmentation of speech. *Journal of Experimental Psychology,* 1969, **79,** 387–394.

Bever, T. G., & Mehler, J. The coding hypothesis and short-term memory. *AF Technical Report,* Cambridge, Massachusetts: Harvard Center for Cognitive Studies, 1967.

Blumenthal, A. L. Observations with self-embedded sentences. *Psychonomic Science,* 1966, **6,** 453–454.

Blumenthal, A. L. Prompted recall of sentences. *Journal of Verbal Learning and Verbal Behavior,* 1967, **6,** 203–206.

Blumenthal, A. L., & Boakes, R. Prompted recall of sentences, a further study. *Journal of Verbal Learning and Verbal Behavior,* 1967, **6,** 674–676.

Bobrow, D., & Fraser, B. An augmented state transition network analysis procedure. In N. Walker & L. Norton (Eds.), *Proceedings of the International Joint Conference on Artificial Intelligence.* Washington, D.C., 1969. 557–568.

Cairns, H. S. Ambiguous sentence processing. Unpublished doctoral dissertation, The University of Texas at Austin, 1970.

Caplan, D. Clause boundaries and recognition latencies for words in sentences. *Perception and Psychophysics,* 1972, **12,** 73–76.

Carey, P. W., Mehler, J., & Bever, T. G. Judging the veracity of ambiguous sentences. *Journal of Verbal Learning and Verbal Behavior,* 1970, **9,** 243–254.

Carroll, J. M. & Tanenhaus, M. K. Functional clauses and sentence segmentation. Unpublished manuscript, 1975.

Chomsky, N. *Syntactic structures.* The Hague: Mouton, 1957.

Chomsky, N. Review of Skinner's *Verbal Behavior. Language,* 1959, **35,** 26–58.

Chomsky, N. *Aspects of the theory of syntax.* Cambridge, Massachusetts: M.I.T. Press, 1965.

Clark, H. H., & Clark, E. V. Semantic distinctions and memory for complex sentences. *Quarterly Journal of Experimental Psychology,* 1968, **20,** 129–138.

Clifton, C., Kurcz, I., & Jenkins, J. J. Grammatical relations as determinants of sentence similarity. *Journal of Verbal Learning and Verbal Behavior,* 1965, **4,** 112–117.

Clifton, C., & Odom, P. Similarity relations among certain English sentence constructions. *Psychological Monographs,* 1966, **80**(Whole No. 613).

Compton, A. C. Aural perception of different syntactic structures and lengths. *Language and Speech,* 1967, **10,** 81–87.

Davidson, R. E. Transitional errors and deep structure differences. *Psychonomic Science,* 1969, **14,** 293.

Epstein, W. The influence of syntactical structure on learning. *American Journal of Psychology,* 1961, **74,** 80–85.

Fodor, J. A., & Bever, T. G. The psychological reality of linguistic segments. *Journal of Verbal Learning and Verbal Behavior,* 1965, **4,** 414–420.

Fodor, J. A., Bever, T. G., & Garrett, M. F. *The psychology of language.* New York: McGraw-Hill, 1974.

Fodor, J. A., Fodor, J. D., Garrett, M. F., & Lackner, J. R. Effects of surface and underlying clausal structure on click location. *Quarterly Progress Report No. 113,* Research Laboratory of Electronics, M.I.T., 1974.

Fodor, J. A., & Garrett, M. F. Competence and Performance. In J. Lyons & R. Wales (Eds.), *Psycholinguistic papers.* Edinburgh: University of Edinburgh Press, 1966.

Fodor, J. A., & Garrett, M. F. Some syntactic determinants of sentential complexity. *Perception and Psychophysics,* 1967, **2,** 289–296.

Fodor, J. A., Garrett, M. F., & Bever, T. G. Some syntactic determinants of sentential complexity, II: Verb structure. *Perception and Psychophysics,* 1968, **3,** 453–461.

Forster, K. I. Visual perception of rapidly presented word sequences of varying complexity. *Perception and Psychophysics,* 1970, **8,** 215–221.

Forster, K. I. Linguistic structure and sentence production. Unpublished manuscript, 1969.

Forster, K. I., & Ryder, L. A. Perceiving the structure and meaning of sentences. *Journal of Verbal Learning and Verbal Behavior,* 1971, **10,** 285–296.

Foss, D. J. Decision processes during sentence comprehension: Effects of lexical item difficulty and position upon decision times. *Journal of Verbal Learning and Verbal Behavior,* 1969, **8,** 457–462.

Foss, D. J. Some effects of ambiguity upon sentence comprehension. *Journal of Verbal Learning and Verbal Behavior,* 1970, **9,** 699–706.

Foss, D. J., Bever, T. G., & Silver, M. The comprehension and verification of ambiguous sentences. *Perception and Psychophysics,* 1968, **4,** 304–306.

Foss, D. J., & Jenkins, C. M. Some effects of context on the comprehension of ambiguous sentences. *Journal of Verbal Learning and Verbal Behavior,* 1973, **12,** 577–589.

Garrett, M. F. Syntactic structures and judgments of auditory events. Unpublished doctoral dissertation, University of Illinois, 1965.

Garrett, M. F., Bever, T. G., & Fodor, J. A. The active use of grammar in speech perception. *Perception and Psychophysics,* 1966, **1,** 30–32.

Glanzer, M. Grammatical category: A rote learning and word association analysis. *Journal of Verbal Learning and Verbal Behavior,* 1962, **1,** 31–41.

Gough, P. B. Grammatical transformations and speed of understanding. *Journal of Verbal Learning and Verbal Behavior,* 1965, **4,** 104–111.

Gough, P. B. The verification of sentences. The effects of delay of evidence and sentence length. *Journal of Verbal Learning and Verbal Behavior,* 1966, **5,** 492–496.

Hakes, D. T. Does verb structure affect sentence comprehension? *Perception and Psychophysics,* 1971, **10,** 229–232.

Hakes, D. T., & Cairns, H. S. Sentence comprehension and relative pronouns. *Perception and Psychophysics,* 1970, **8,** 5–8.

Hakes, D. T., & Foss, D. J. Decision processes during sentence comprehension: Effects of surface structure reconsidered. *Perception and Psychophysics,* 1970, **8,** 413–416.

Harris, Z. Transformation theory. *Language,* 1965, **41,** 363–401.

Holmes, V. M. Some effects of syntactic structure on sentence recognition. Unpublished doctoral dissertation, University of Melbourne, 1970.

Holmes, V. M. Order of main and subordinate clauses in sentence perception. *Journal of Verbal Learning and Verbal Behavior,* 1973, **12,** 285–293.

Holmes, V. M., & Forster, K. I. Detection of extraneous signals during sentence recognition. *Perception and Psychophysics,* 1970, **7,** 297–301.

Holmes, V. M., & Forster, K. I. Perceptual complexity and underlying sentence structure. *Journal of Verbal Learning and Verbal Behavior,* 1972, **11,** 148–156.

Jarvella, R. Syntactic processing of connected speech. *Journal of Verbal Learning and Verbal Behavior,* 1971, **10,** 409–416.

Jarvella, R. Coreference and short-term memory for discourse. *Journal of Experimental Psychology,* 1973, **98,** 426–428.

Jenkins, J. J., Fodor, J. A., & Saporta, S. An introduction to psycholinguistic theory. Unpublished, 1965.

Johnson, N. F. The psychological reality of phrase structure rules. *Journal of Verbal Learning and Verbal Behavior,* 1965, **4,** 469–475.

Johnson, R. E. Recall of prose as a function of the structural importance of the linguistic units. *Journal of Verbal Learning and Verbal Behavior,* 1970, **9,** 12–20.

Kaplan, R. Augmented transition networks as psychological models of sentence comprehension. *Artificial Intelligence,* 1972, **3,** 77–100.

Kennedy, A., & Wilkes, A. Response times at different positions with a sentence. *Quarterly Journal of Experimental Psychology,* 1968, **20,** 390–394.

Koplin, J. H., & Davis, J. Grammatical transformations and recognition memory of sentences. *Psychonomic Science,* 1966, **6,** 257–258.

Lackner, J. R., & Garrett, M. F. Resolving ambiguity: Effects of biasing context in the unattended ear. *Cognition,* 1973, **1,** 359–372.

Ladefoged, P. *Three areas of experimental phonetics.* London: Oxford University Press, 1967.

Ladefoged, P., & Broadbent, D. E. Perception of sequence in auditory events. *Quarterly Journal of Experimental Psychology,* 1960, **13,** 162–170.

Levelt, W. J. M. A scaling approach to the study of syntactic relations. In G. B. Flores d'Arcais & W. J. M. Levelt (Eds.), *Advances in psycholinguistics.* New York: American Elsevier, 1970.

MacKay, D. G. To end ambiguous sentences. *Perception and Psychophysics,* 1966, **1,** 426–436.

Mandler, G., & Mandler, J. Serial position effects in sentences. *Journal of Verbal Learning and Verbal Behavior,* 1964, **3,** 195–202.

McMahon, L. Grammatical analysis as part of understanding a sentence. Unpublished doctoral dissertation, Harvard University, 1963.

Mehler, J. Some effects of grammatical transformations on the recall of English sentences. *Journal of Verbal Learning and Verbal Behavior,* 1963, **2,** 346–351.

Mehler, J., & Carey, P. Role of surface and base structure in the perception of sentences. *Journal of Verbal Learning and Verbal Behavior,* 1967, **6,** 335–338.

Mehler, J., & Miller, G. A. Retroactive interference in the recall of simple sentences. *British Journal of Psychology,* 1964, **55,** 3, 295–301.

Miller, G. A. *Language and communication.* New York: McGraw-Hill, 1951.

Miller, G. A. Some psychological studies of grammar. *American Psychologist,* 1962, **17,** 748–762.

Miller, G. A., & Chomsky, N. A. Finitary models of language users. In R. D. Luce, R. R. Bush, & E. Galanter (Eds.), *Handbook of mathematical psychology,* Vol. II. New York: Wiley, 1963.

Miller, G. A., Galanter, E., & Pribram, K. H. *Plans and the structure of behavior.* New York: Holt, 1960.

Miller, G. A., & Isard, S. Some perceptual consequences of linguistic rules. *Journal of Verbal Learning and Verbal Behavior,* 1963, **2,** 217–228.

Miller, G. A., & McKean, K. A chronometric study of some relations between sentences. *Quarterly Journal of Experimental Psychology,* 1964, **16,** 297–308.

Moore, T. M. Speeded recognition of ungrammaticality. *Journal of Verbal Learning and Verbal Behavior,* 1972, **11,** 550–560.

Mowrer, O. H. *Learning theory and the symbolic processes.* New York: Wiley, 1960.

Petrick, S. R. A recognition procedure for transformational grammars. Unpublished doctoral dissertation, M.I.T., 1965.

Reber, A. S., & Anderson, J. R. The perception of clicks in linguistic and nonlinguistic messages. *Perception and Psychophysics,* 1970, **8,** 81–89.

Savin, H., & Perchonock, E. Grammatical structure and the immediate recall of English sentences. *Journal of Verbal Learning and Verbal Behavior,* 1965, **4,** 348–353.

Sachs, J. Recognition memory for syntactic and semantic aspects of connected discourse. *Perception and Psychophysics,* 1967, **2,** 437–442.

Schlesinger, I. M. *Sentence structure and the reading process.* The Hague: Mouton, 1968.

Scholes, R. J. Click location judgments. *Quarterly Report, Department of Speech, University of Florida,* 1969, **7**(1), 33–38.

Shedletsky, L. Effects of some clause variables on memory scanning. Unpublished doctoral dissertation, University of Illinois, 1974.

Seitz, M. AER and the perception of speech. Unpublished doctoral dissertation, University of Washington, 1972.

Skinner, B. F. *Verbal behavior.* New York: Appleton, 1957.

Slobin, D. I. Grammatical transformations and sentence comprehension in childhood and adulthood. *Journal of Verbal Learing and Verbal Behavior,* 1966, **5,** 219–227.

Smith, F. Reversal of meaning as a variable in the transformation of grammatical sentences. *Journal of Verbal Learning and Verbal Behavior,* 1965, **4,** 39–43.

Stewart, C., & Gough, P. Constituent search in immediate memory for sentences. *Proceedings of the Midwestern Psychology Association,* 1967.

Suci, G. The validity of pause as an index of units in language. *Journal of Verbal Learning and Verbal Behavior,* 1967, **6,** 26–32.

Suci, G., Ammon, P., & Gamlin, P. The validity of the probe-latency technique for assessing structure in language. *Language and Speech,* 1967, **10,** 69–80.

Tanenhaus, M. K., & Carroll, J. M. The clausal processing hierarchy . . . and nouniness. In R. Grossman *et al.* (Eds.), *Papers from the parasession on functionalism.* Chicago: University of Chicago, 1975.

Walker, E. Grammatical relations in sentence memory. Unpublished doctoral dissertation, Indiana University, 1969.

Walker, E., Gough, P., & Wall, R. Grammatical relations and the search of sentences in immediate memory. *Proceedings of the Midwestern Psychological Association,* 1968.

Wanner, E. On remembering, forgetting, and understanding sentences: A study of the deep structure hypothesis. Unpublished doctoral dissertation, Harvard University, 1968. See also (same title) The Hague: Mouton, forthcoming.

Wanner, E., & Maratsos, M. An augmented transition network model of relative clause comprehension. Unpublished, 1975.

Wanner, E., & Maratsos, M. On understanding relative clauses. Unpublished paper, Harvard University, 1971.

Wason, P. C. Response to affirmative and negative binary statements. *British Journal of Psychology,* 1961, **52,** 133–142.

Watt, J. R. Two hypotheses concerning psycholinguistics. In J. R. Hayes (Ed.), *Cognition and development of language.* New York: Wiley, 1970.

Weksel, W., & Bever, T. G. Harvard Cognitive Studies Progress Report, 1966.

Woods, W. Transition network grammars for natural language analysis. *Communications of the A.C.M.,* 1970, **13,** 591–602.

Chapter 10

LANGUAGE AND NONVERBAL COMMUNICATION

JOHN LAVER

I. INTRODUCTION

It is a commonplace that the most frequent type of social interaction we experience is face to face communication in a conversational situation. "Conversation" is often loosely taken to mean the exchange of factual, propositional "semantic" information by verbal means, through the use of spoken language. In fact, conversation normally involves very much more than this. In addition to verbal communication of semantic information, many different types of information are conveyed by nonverbal means. For the purpose of this chapter, conversation will be interpreted as including both verbal and nonverbal communication.

The perceptual skills that allow us to participate successfully in face-to-face conversation are very complex. We are usually obliged to make a continuous stream of judgments, on the basis of the other participant's verbal and nonverbal behavior, about a wide spectrum of information. We not only have to decode what he is saying but also have to be able to draw conclusions about the speaker's personal characteristics, in terms of his physical, social, and psychological attributes and his momentary affective state, and shape our own behavior into an appropriate relationship with him. Also, since conversation requires an intricate temporal meshing together of the performances of the participants, we need to be able to judge when a speaker is coming to the end of his current contribution to the conversation and is expecting a reciprocal contribution from us as the listener.

It would seem reasonable to suppose that language and nonverbal communication should have a degree of mutual relevance and that one might therefore look to linguistics for a major point of entry into the study of nonverbal communication. Unfortunately, the implicit preeminence given to "language" over "nonverbal communication" in the title of this chapter is an accurate reflection of the view taken by most scholars working in linguistics of the relative importance (and hence the mutual isolation) of the study of these two areas. The last sentence in what is arguably the most influential book in linguistics, de Saussure's *Course in General Linguistics,* published in 1916, ends as follows: "The true and unique object of linguistics is language studied in and for itself [de Saussure, 1966, p. 232]." As Lyons (1970, p. 8) points out, this principle of autonomy has had the result of promoting the study of language as a formal system, to the great benefit of the subject; the sophistication of modern linguistic theories owes much to the concentrating effect of obedience to this dictum. An inevitable and regrettable consequence, however, has been that the nonverbal aspects of communicative behavior that accompany, support, and complement language have, until recently, received little attention from most linguists. Most of the major contributions to the study of nonverbal communication have come from psychology, psychiatry, anthropology, and sociology. Not surprisingly, research into conversational communication has not been the unified enterprise that it might have been in different historical circumstances; it has tended, rather, to be atomistic, with its focus normally on a single communicative channel.

Over the last decade or so, however, there seems to have been a swing toward a more broadly based attitude, promising a more productive union between linguistics and the other disciplines interested in social interaction (Argyle, 1969, 1973; Barnlund, 1968; Crystal, 1969; Duncan, 1969; Ekman & Friesen, 1969; Gumperz & Hymes, 1972; Hinde, 1972; Horton & Jenkins, 1971; Laver & Hutcheson, 1972; Moscovici, 1972; Sebeok, Hayes, & Bateson, 1964; Siegman & Pope, 1972; Smith, 1966; Sommer, 1967; Sudnow, 1972). It is becoming more accepted that behavior in face-to-face conversation can profitably be viewed as an interwoven complex of many different communicative strands and that these strands have an important degree of mutual relevance. Language is still seen as a principal strand, but nevertheless as only one among many strands contributing to the totality of the communication. The view is taken that the communicative function of language can be better understood in the context of the operation of the other strands than in isolation. All the means of communication capable of conventionally coded, short-term manipulation—language, tone of voice, gesture, posture, body-movements, spatial orientation, physical proximity, eye contact, and facial expression can be thought of as being woven together to form the fabric of a conversation, and we can understand the communicative texture of an interaction best by seeing the relationship of the different strands (Laver & Hutcheson, 1972, p. 11).

II. COMPONENTS OF NONVERBAL COMMUNICATION

The behavioral features that make up nonverbal communication have often been called *paralinguistic*. They are paralinguistic in the sense that they share some of the criterial characteristics of linguistic features (see Hockett, 1960; Crystal, 1969; Lyons, 1972), without sharing all of them—for example they share with language the characteristic of being arbitrary, convention-governed codes, but they lack the "duality of structure" intrinsic to language. They can be thought of as paralinguistic in another sense also, as being parasitic upon language, in the opinion at least of some writers, who see them as deriving relevance solely from their auxiliary relationship with linguistic communication.

There are almost as many interpretations of the term "paralinguistic" as there are writers on the subject (Crystal, 1971). Some writers, such as Crystal himself (1969), Crystal and Quirk (1964), and Trager (1958), restrict the term to the vocal features that accompany spoken language; others, such as Hill (1958) and Abercrombie (1968), apply it to both vocal and nonvocal features. In this chapter, we shall follow Abercrombie's usage and distinguish between the audible, vocal features of nonverbal communication and the visible, nonvocal features.

A. Audible paralinguistic features

Abercrombie divides paralinguistic features into those that can function quite independently of verbal behavior and those that have communicative function only when occurring simultaneously with verbal elements. He calls the former *independent* elements, and the latter *dependent* elements. Independent audible paralinguistic features include interjections, such as the click of impatience, that have to occur sequentially separate from the performance of verbal elements. Dependent audible paralinguistic features are much more varied and include everything normally referred to as comprising *tone of voice*. Tone of voice, one of the most powerful vehicles for the expression of emotion (Crystal, 1969; Davitz & Davitz, 1959; Dusenbury & Knower, 1939; Fairbanks & Pronovost, 1939; Kramer, 1963, 1964; Thompson & Bradway, 1950), constitutes to some extent a ground against which the figures of the verbal elements of language have to be perceived. This is because the vocal parameters upon whose use the perception of tone of voice depend are not substantially different in principle from those that serve the perception of verbal elements. The difference lies rather in the time scale involved. The vocal realizations of verbal elements are momentary, while those that act as evidence for tone of voice are rather longer-term. The phrase, "He spoke in an angry tone of voice," normally refers to a stretch of speech of at least one sentence and possibly many more. Because tone of voice relies on longer-term evidence than does verbal communication, one difference that does exist in the way that the vocal resources are exploited is that tone of voice is usually communicated by the perception of the range of a particular vocal parameter, while verbal identification is more a matter of the location of a speaker's momentary choice within that range. An example of this can be found in the control of loudness. In our culture, the attitude of anger is often paralinguistically communicated by boosting the overall range of loudness of speech production, compared with the lower range of loudness that characterizes emotionally neutral speech. In either case, of anger or of neutral emotion, the speaker manipulates loudness on a momentary basis within the relevant range when using contrastive stress to signal such verbal differences as the one between **im**port (noun) and im**port** (verb).

A paralinguistic feature similar to loudness range is pitch range. Others include the tempo and continuity of speech and the long-term control of the auditory quality of speech production. Within the control of quality in this sense there are two separable areas: first, auditory quality that derives from the shape of the vocal tract and, second, auditory quality that derives from the fine detail of the mode of vibration of the vocal cords. Vocal tract quality, when the effect persists over a number of verbal elements in an utterance, can be exemplified by the persistent nasality of "whining," the auditory coloring lent to a voice by the lips being held in a smiling position, or the tendency (mostly by female speakers) to keep the tongue raised toward the palate and the lips protruded and rounded when speaking to babies. Laryngeal quality, which derives from the mode of vibration of the vocal cords, when the effect persists over a number of verbal elements in the utterance (and where this is not a permanent characteristic of the speaker's voice production), can be exemplified by the so-called *breathy voice* in which confidential intimacies are often uttered or by the *harsh voice* associated with anger.

B. Visible Paralinguistic Features

1. PROXIMITY

Interpersonal distance is a paralinguistic feature that is surprisingly deli-cately controlled by participants in a conversation. Distances are chosen (sometimes to margins of accuracy of 2 in. or less in a standing face-to-face situation) that are appropriate not only to the status and intimacy relation-ship between the speakers but also to the particular phase (opening, me-dial, closing) of the interaction and to the physical and social locale in which the interaction takes place. The study of this feature has been given the name *proxemics* by Edward Hall, one of the major pioneers in its inves-tigation. More research has been carried out on proxemics (Hall, 1959, 1963, 1964, 1966; Little, 1965; Sommer, 1959, 1969; Watson & Graves, 1966) than on any other visible paralinguistic feature, with the exception perhaps of the group of features that are discussed below under the heading *kinesics*. Proximity is also very strongly a culturally-relative code. A "close" distance to an American is "distant" to an Arab (Hall, 1963), and in intercultural encounters of this sort a continual readjustment of proximity takes place, with each participant seeking to reestablish his cul-turally comfortable distance each time it is disturbed by the other partici-pant's movement.

2. SPATIAL ORIENTATION

It is obviously important for participants in face-to-face interaction to be able to see each other's faces, for facial expression and eye-contact pur-poses and, more generally, to be mutually available for visual inspection so that proximity, posture, body movements, and gestures can be registered and appropriately controlled. In most situations, participants have a certain degree of choice as to exactly how to arrange themselves spatially to achieve this. The choice they make is informative about their view of the nature of the interaction between them. Sommer (1965) has shown, for example, that people choose different seating arrangements depending on the type of task they are engaged in: At an oblong table, people tend to choose adjacent positions (either side by side or across a corner) if they are involved in a cooperative task but choose seats opposite to each other if they are in competition. (See also Argyle & Kendon, 1967; Mehrabian, 1967, 1969.)

3. KINESIC FEATURES

a. POSTURE. The choice of posture is as much a limited code of system-atic behavior as any other paralinguistic feature. Scheflen estimates that for Americans there are less than thirty "culturally standard postural configurations which are of shared communicative significance [1964, p. 316]."

There are nevertheless levels of choice within the posture parameter. If we consider an interview between a high-ranking officer and an enlisted soldier, the posture of each participant, though almost certainly different, will reflect a number of levels of systematic control. First, their posture will be appropriate to an interview situation. Second, it will signal their assessment of the degree of formality that obtains in that particular interview. Third, it will reflect their view of their status relationship.

The ability of posture to signal people's view of their relationship with each other (Mehrabian, 1968) is also visible in small group interactions, in mechanisms closely related to those of spatial orientation. Scheflen (1964) draws attention to the way that members of small groups tend to delimit the group and protect it from invasion by outsiders. Group members, when standing, tend to form a circle; when seated in a row, the members at each end tend to "turn inward and extend an arm or a leg across the open spaces as if to limit access in or out of the group [p. 326]." Scheflen calls this effect *bookending*. He also discusses how members of small groups covertly demonstrate sympathy with a particular fellow-member by choosing a similar, "congruent" posture, or antipathy by choosing a noncongruent posture.

Further possibilities of choice exist that have to do not with interpersonal relationships but with the temporal segmentation of the interaction. Scheflen points out that, where an interaction has a structured progression (as in a psychiatric interview), each major stage in the progression is associated with a different posture. A substantial change in posture is thus likely to be linked to a substantial thematic change in the linguistic structure of the interaction.

b. BODY MOVEMENTS AND GESTURES. Body movements and gestures are the moment-to-moment variations superimposed on an overall posture and can involve minor movements of the whole body or movements of only a part of the body, as in arm, hand, or head gestures. A major figure in the general study of bodily movement, to which he has given the widely accepted name *kinesics,* is the American anthropologist Ray Birdwhistell (1952, 1970).

In the terms introduced earlier, body movements and gestures as paralinguistic features have both independent and dependent aspects. Those conventional gestures that can stand for (or be replaced by) verbal elements (such as the head gestures of assent and dissent in our culture) are clearly independent. It is important to recognize, however, that there is no single independent gesture that has a meaning universally accepted by all cultures. Independent gestures are always part of a culturally relative arbitrary code (La Barre, 1947).

The dependent body movements and gestures, necessarily associated with speech, fall into two groups. The first group is used to regulate the exchange of speaker role, signaling either the incipient completion of a speech contribution or the incipient beginning of a contribution by the still silent listener. Kendon (1972) has called this a *regulative* function. Movements include the speaker raising his head to look directly at the listener, at the end of his contribution, and also turning his head to look away from the listener, either when beginning to speak or during points of silence where he wants to keep possession of the role of speaker (Kendon, 1967).

The second group of body movements and gestures is more closely connected to the speech material itself, in a variety of ways. First, they are said to be used in a function of linguistic support, in serving to identify the grammatical class of the verbal units involved. Birdwhistell (1970, pp. 121–126) has maintained that gestures that move away from the body (*distal* gestures), versus those that move toward the body (*proximal* gestures), are closely associated with verbal elements to do with distinctions of time and space and with various personal pronouns. Distal gestures accompany *he, she, it, those, they, that, then, there, any, some,* while proximal gestures accompany *I, me, us, we, this, here* and *now.* Past and future tenses are said to be linked to distal gestures, but with movement toward the rear and the front of the body, respectively. Birdwhistell goes on to suggest that characteristic gestures accompany plurality, such prepositions as *on, over, under, by, through, behind* and *in front of,* and such temporal adverbs as *slowly* and *swiftly.* He is supported in some of these findings by Kendon (1972).

Another function of body movements and gestures, noted by Birdwhistell, is to act as devices of emphasis, where the vocally most prominent verbal element in a stretch of speech tends to have a pattern of movement associated with it that stands in contrast to patterns of movement elsewhere. Body movements are also used to mark the semantic segmentation of a speaker's discourse, with each new development or new topic tending to be marked gesturally or with a slight body movement (Efron, 1942; Ekman & Friesen, 1969) or a small change in proximity (Erickson, 1975). This signaling of *thematic segmentation* is at a more delicate level than the grosser segmentation of topic signaled by large postural shifts mentioned earlier. Birdwhistell (1970) and Kendon (1972) would take this segmental signaling to an even more delicate level than thematic marking, however. They suggest that segmental units of speech, from groupings of phrases to individual phrases down even to the level of individual syllables, can be marked by distinct types of body movements and gestures. The marking by body movements of the rhythmic structure of speech at the level of the phrase is supported to some extent by Dittman and Llewellyn (1969) and by Dittman (1972).

If these findings about body movements and gestures being characteristically associated with both the grammatical identity and the syntactic structure of the speaker's linguistic performance are valid for the majority of speakers, then this provides the listener with a very important set of perceptual clues for decoding the verbal material of the conversation.

4. Gaze Direction and Eye Contact

Like proximity, with which it has an interactive relationship, gaze direction and eye contact is a paralinguistic parameter that participants in conversation control very delicately, and one to which they are very sensitive (Gibson & Pick, 1963; Kendon, 1967).

Eye contact seems to have three chief functions—monitoring the behavior of the other participant, regulating the progress of the interaction, and controlling the expression of mutual affiliation (Kendon, 1967; Argyle & Dean, 1965).

There are two regulative aspects. The first is captured in the everyday saying "to catch someone's eye." To establish mutual eye contact is normally a necessary prerequisite to interaction and has the effect of signaling acknowledgement that channels of communication are open. The second aspect, mentioned above in connection with head movements, is in regulating the time sharing of the interaction in negotiating moments of exchange of the speaker role. Eye contact on the part of the current speaker, when this is associated with appropriate intonation, body movement, and facial expression, offers the speaker role to the listener. A speaker's refusal to make eye contact signals resistance to giving up possession of the speaker role. Eye contact on the part of the listener, when an exchange of roles is offered by the current speaker, signals willingness to take over the speaker role, and a refusal to make eye contact declines the offered exchange. Characteristically, when a listener has accepted the offered speaker role by making eye contact, he then breaks eye contact as he begins to speak (Kendon, 1967).

During speech, the speaker looks intermittently at the listener, in order to monitor such details as whether or not the listener is attending to his messages and understanding them, whether or not the listener is making preliminary signals toward laying claim to the speaker role, and so forth. Correspondingly, the listener also makes intermittent eye contact, to offer appropriate signals of attention, comprehension, and agreement and, when relevant, to effect an exchange of speaker role. A participant becomes very uncomfortable when he can be seen by, but not himself see, the other participant (Argyle, Lalljee, & Cook, 1968).

The amount of mutual gaze between participants in a conversation is an index of the degree of their affiliation. The greater the affiliation, the greater the amount of eye contact, and vice versa (Argyle & Dean, 1965; Exline, 1963; Exline & Winters, 1965; Kendon, 1967).

The degree of affiliation between the participants, though a powerful factor, is not the only one that affects the amount of mutual eye contact. Within the generalization that eye contact lasts normally somewhere between 30% to 65% of the duration of the encounter, and that each glance lasts between 3 to 10 seconds (Argyle & Dean, 1965), such factors as the topic of conversation, the sex, and the proximity of the speakers have all been shown to influence the amount of mutual gaze. Exline, Gray, and Schuette (1965) have shown that eye contact is reduced when the topic becomes more personal. Women tend to engage in more eye contact than men, and same-sex pairs in more than opposite-sex pairs. When people are forced into greater proximity than is conventionally comfortable within the rules of the culture, the amount of eye contact decreases sharply to almost zero—as for example in a crowded elevator, where almost no eye contact is made during any conversation that might take place (Argyle & Dean, 1965).

5. FACIAL EXPRESSION

Together with tone of voice, facial expression must be one of the most powerful vehicles for the communication of emotion. Yet there is a surprising imbalance of research into facial expression as an independent paralinguistic parameter, compared with research into its use as a dependent parameter.

The major part of research has been directed toward facial expression as an independent parameter. The central controversy has been about whether communication of emotion by facial expression is universal or culturally relative. Birdwhistell (1970) is one worker who maintains that there is no single facial expression with a universally recognizable meaning, and that all facial expressions are culturally relative. His view is opposed by Tomkins (1962), Ekman and Friesen (1969), Ekman, Sorenson, and Friesen (1969), Eibl-Eibesfeldt (1970, 1972), and Ekman (1972). There is a good commentary on the "universalist" hypothesis in Dittmann (1972, pp. 58–62), and two recent books on the subject are Izard (1971) and Ekman, Friesen, and Ellsworth (1972).

There has been very much less research into facial expression as a dependent paralinguistic parameter. In this sense, facial expression can be considered dependent when used in support of verbal acts, such as interrogation, for example, with raised eyebrows. It would seem more profitable, however, to consider facial expression as being dependent not solely on verbal elements but, rather, on a combination of verbal elements and other nonnverbal parameters, such as posture, gesture, and eye control. This is to assert that, in its dependent aspect, facial expression is necessarily multi-valued and that a specific expression has communicative value only in conjunction with a constellation of particular values on both verbal and nonverbal parameters. This view can probably be extended to cover the dependent aspects of any nonverbal parameter, with dependency being to the total system of communication, rather than merely to the linguistic component of the total system.

III. INTERACTIONAL SYNCHRONY

We have seen above that, while language conveys primarily semantic information, nonverbal communication conveys a wide range of different sorts of information. Nonverbal elements do sometimes convey semantic information, as in the case of independent vocal interjections and independent gestures. But much of the information conveyed by nonverbal means has the function of assisting the process of linguistic communication, rather than substituting for it. The possibility of acts of linguistic communication taking place at all is facilitated by the regulative function of nonverbal behavior. We saw that this function served to open the channels of communication, as it were, and to manage the necessary meshing of performances in negotiating exchanges of the role of speaker; it also indicated the progressions within the interaction from one major stage to the next. It is at this point, where the structure of the interaction is paralleled by the thematic semantic structure of the linguistic interchange, that the regulative function of nonverbal communication begins to blend with what we might call its *demarcative* function. Nonverbal communication was seen to convey perceptual clues to the listener about the demarcation of linguistic boundaries at different levels—semantic, grammatical, and phonological.

In order for the regulative and the demarcative functions of nonverbal communication to succeed, various elements of nonverbal behavior have to be in synchrony with aspects of the speaker's linguistic behavior. This is particularly true of the visible paralinguistic features, all of which consist of very highly skilled muscular movements, as does speech itself. It is hardly surprising that there should be a high degree of temporal coordination of the different activities of vocal and nonvocal movement—to manage such an intricately skilled, multilevel performance on an asynchronous basis would be astonishing. So there is a synchronization in the majority of bodily movements of a speaker, such that, comparing speech and body movement, the "points of change in the flow of sound coincide with the points of change in body movement [Kendon, 1970, p. 103]."

What is perhaps more unexpected is that it has been found that self-synchrony of movements in the speaker is very often matched by an empathetic synchrony of movements by the listener, in what has been called *interactional synchrony*. The phenomenon was first described by Condon and Ogston (1966, 1967, 1971): It does not imply that the listener copies the movements of the speaker, merely that "the boundaries of the movement waves of the listener coincide with boundaries of the movement waves in the speaker [Kendon, 1970, p. 103]." The actual movements of the listener may be quite different from those of the speaker and are probably on a much smaller scale. One plausible and economical perceptual explanation offered for interactional synchrony by Kendon (1970, pp. 122–123) is that the linguistic output by the speaker is being decoded by the listener on an analysis-by-synthesis basis—that is, by intermittently sampling the speech output, setting up running hypotheses about future output, and checking from time to time for correct prediction (see Öhman, this volume; Neisser, 1967)—and that the resultant interactional synchrony is a reflection of the listener's empathetic processes toward this end.

Kendon also advances an interesting social explanation for the phenomenon, to do with mechanisms for signaling involvement in interaction, rather similar to the "bookending" phenomenon described by Scheflen (1964) and discussed earlier. Kendon (1970) writes:

> To *move* with another is to show that one is "with" him in one's attentions and expectancies. Coordination of movement in interaction may thus be of great importance since it provides one of the ways in which two people signal that they are "open" to one another, and not to others [p. 124].

IV. INTERACTIONAL EQUILIBRIUM

The discovery of interactional synchrony highlights the fact that conversation is an intricately controlled act of collaboration between speaker and listener. We might expect that such collaboration would have other interesting aspects, and one of these is the phenomenon of interactional equilibrium.

We saw earlier that participants in an interaction adjust their mutual proximity until they reach their culturally comfortable distance for the type of encounter in which they are engaged. There will be momentary oscillations around this distance, but an equilibrium is maintained, when the two participants come from the same cultural background. This is an example of collaboration in the maintenance of equilibrium on one interactional parameter. Argyle and Dean (1965) suggest that a more complex equilibrium process is managed, by participants manipulating the interplay of a number of conversational parameters. They write

> [A]n equilibrium develops for "intimacy," where this is a joint function of eye contact, physical proximity, intimacy of topic, smiling, etc. This equilibrium would be at a certain degree of intimacy for any pair of people. . . . [I]f one of the components of intimacy is changed, one or more of the others will shift in the reverse direction in order to maintain the equilibrium.

Some of the evidence for this was mentioned above, where increased intimacy of topic and increased proximity were both said to have the effect of decreasing the amount of eye contact. A similar compensation between parameters is where interactants standing uncomfortably close in a face-to-face position change their spatial orientation to face each other at right angles, or stand side-to-side (Argyle & Dean, 1965). Similarly, seated interactants, too far apart, lean forward in their chairs, in a compensatory change of posture.

V. INDEXICAL INFORMATION IN CONVERSATION

Explicit identification has been offered, so far in this chapter, of only three types of information communicated in conversation—semantic, demarcative, and regulative. But there is a fourth type of informational exchange, to which occasional allusion has been made, which is possibly the single most important aspect of conversation as a social act. This is the communication of information about aspects of the personal identity, attributes, and attitudes of the participants. A prime function of conversation is to enable the interactants to manage their psychosocial relationship, and this relationship is subject to continuous negotiation throughout each interaction (Cicourel, 1972); it is on the basis of the conclusions the interactants draw about each other's personal characteristics that such negotiation is conducted. Abercrombie (1967, p. 6), borrowing one meaning of the term from the nineteenth-century American pragmaticist philosopher C. S. Peirce, has called this sort of information *indexical,* and writes of different types of *index,* classified in terms of the particular characteristic indicated. He distinguishes between indices that signal group membership (such as a particular regional accent), indices that individuate a speaker within his group (such as an idiosyncratic aspect of pronunciation or a speech defect), and affective indices, that reveal changing states of the speaker's emotional condition (such as the loud, high-pitched, harsh voice of anger).

The examples of indices cited above all involve vocal evidence, but clearly indexical conclusions can also be drawn from nonvocal evidence. Gathering indexical information from a wide range of perceptual sources, we rapidly construct a profile of our fellow-participant in an interaction: first, about his physical characteristics of sex, age, size, physique, state of health, degree of fatigue, and so forth; second, about his social identity, in terms of regional origin, social status and associated social values, and possibly occupation; and third, about psychological details of his personality and momentary mood. We will also come to conclusions about his assessment of our own individual characteristics and of his attitude to the current encounter, and we shape our behavior accordingly, projecting the indexical persona (to the extent that it is within our control to do so) that we hope will achieve the effect we desire.

An account of indexical information in conversational interaction has to go beyond the verbal and nonverbal behavior considered so far. We make indexical judgments about a person from wider evidence than this—for example, from visible aspects, such as person's style of dress and his habitual gait, and from audible aspects, such as the characteristic individual quality of his voice. So, indexical information is to be found not only in linguistic and paralinguistic phenomena but in extralinguistic factors as well.

We all make indexical judgments about other people every day, and these judgments influence our social relationships very powerfully. We seldom question the validity of the judgments we make, yet there is considerable evidence that, in subjective judgments of this sort, particularly on the basis of such extralinguistic vocal information as the quality of a man's voice, we operate with stereotypes (Cantril & Allport, 1935; Eisenberg & Zalowitz, 1938; Fay & Middleton, 1939, 1940a,b; Kramer, 1963; Laver, 1968; Starkweather, 1964). We tend to "reach the same indexical conclusions from the same evidence, but the conclusions themselves may, on occasion, bear no reliable relation to the real characteristics of the speaker [Laver, 1968, p. 51]."

The stereotypic nature of indexical perception compounds the possibility of making wrong indexical judgments when dealing with vocal phenomena that are ambivalent between paralinguistic nonverbal communication and extralinguistic voice quality. Consider the case of a participant in a conversation speaking in a *whispery voice*. The listener has to decide whether the speaker is using whispery voice as a paralinguistic feature, signalling secretive confidentiality, or whether whispery voice is part of the speaker's voice quality (either habitually or because of temporary laryngitis). Listeners often draw the wrong conclusion, and sufferers from laryngitis have often had the experience of people whispering back to them, mistaking the physical, medical index of laryngitis for a psychological, attitudinal index of conspiracy.

VI. CONCLUSION

It has been argued in this chapter that language and nonverbal communication have an important degree of mutual relevance, if one views the communicative resources exploited in face-to-face interaction as a unified, total system, rather than in the more traditional atomistic way. The discovery of the phenomena of speaker synchrony, interactional synchrony, and interactional equilibrium lends support to this position. It was also said that nonverbal communication accompanies, supports, and complements language, and this was justified by appeal to the regulative and demarcative functions of nonverbal communication, in helping language to convey semantic information. The point was made, finally, that one of the most important functions of face-to-face interaction is to manage interpersonal relations, and that this is achieved largely by the communication of indexical information gathered from not only linguistic and paralinguistic but also extralinguistic aspects of behavior.

References

Abercrombie, D. *Elements of general phonetics.* Edinburgh: Edinburgh Univ. Press, 1967.

Abercrombie, D. Paralanguage. *British Journal of Disorders of Communication,* 1968, 3, 55–59.

Argyle, M. *Social interaction.* London: Methuen, 1969.

Argyle, M. *Social encounters.* Harmondsworth: Penguin, 1973.

Argyle, M., & Dean, J. Eye contact, distance and affiliation. *Sociometry,* 1965, **28,** 289–304.

Argyle, M., & Kendon, A. The experimental analysis of social performance. In L. Berkowitz (Ed.), *Advances in experimental social psychology.* New York: Academic Press, 1967. Pp. 55–98.

Argyle, M., Lalljee, M., & Cook, M. The effects of visibility on interaction in a dyad. *Human Relations,* 1968, **28,** 3–17.

Barnlund, D. C. (Ed.) *Interpersonal communication.* Boston: Houghton Mifflin, 1968.

Birdwhistell, R. L. *Introduction to kinesics.* Louisville, Kentucky: Univ. of Louisville Press, 1952.

Birdwhistell, R. L. *Kinesics and context.* Philadelphia: Univ. of Pennsylvania Press, 1970.

Cantril H., & Allport, G. W. *The psychology of radio.* New York: Harper, 1935.

Cicourel, A. V. Basic and normative rules in the negotiation of status and role.

In D. Sudnow (Ed.), *Studies in social interaction.* New York: Free Press, 1972. Pp. 229–258.

Condon, W. S., & Ogston, W. D. Sound film analysis of normal and pathological behavior patterns. *Journal of Nervous and Mental Disease,* 1966, **143,** 338–347.

Condon, W. S., & Ogston, W. D. A segmentation of behavior. *Journal of Psychiatric Research,* 1967, **5,** 221–235.

Condon, W. S., & Ogston, W. D. Speech and body motion synchrony of the speaker-hearer. In D. L. Horton & J. J. Jenkins (Ed.), *The perception of language,* Columbus, Ohio: Merrill, 1971. Pp. 150–173.

Crystal, D. *Prosodic systems and intonation in English.* New York: Cambridge Univ. Press, 1969.

Crystal, D. Paralinguistics. In T. A. Sebeok (Ed.), *Current trends in linguistics.* Vol. 12. The Hague: Mouton, 1971.

Crystal, D., & Quirk, R. *Systems of prosodic and paralinguistic features in English.* The Hague: Mouton, 1964.

Davitz, J. R., & Davitz, L. J. The communication of feelings by content-free speech. *Journal of Communication,* 1959, **9,** 6–13.

Dittman, A. T. *Interpersonal messages of emotion.* New York: Springer, 1972.

Dittman, A. T., & Llewellyn, L. G. Body movement and speech rhythm in social conversation. *Journal of Personality and Social Psychology,* 1969, **11,** 98–106.

Duncan, S., Jr. Nonverbal communication. *Psychological Bulletin,* 1969, **72,** 118–137.

Dusenbury, D., & Knower, F. H. Experimental studies of the symbolism of action and voice. *Quarterly Journal of Speech,* 1939, **25,** 65–75.

Efron, D. *Gesture and environment.* New York: Kings Crown Press, 1942.

Eibl-Eibesfeldt, I. *Ethology: The biology of behavior.* New York: Holt, 1970.

Eibl-Eibesfeldt, I. Similarities and differences between cultures in expressive movements. In R. A. Hinde (Ed.), *Non-verbal communication.* New York: Cambridge Univ. Press, 1972. Pp. 297–311.

Eisenberg, P., & Zalowitz, E. Judgements of dominance feelings from phonograph records of the voice. *Journal of Applied Psychology,* 1938, **22,** 620–631.

Ekman, P. Universals and cultural differences in facial expressions of emotions. In J. Cole (Ed.), *Nebraska Symposium on Motivation.* Lincoln: Univ. of Nebraska Press, 1972.

Ekman, P., & Friesen, W. V. The repertoire of nonverbal behavior: categories, origins, usage and coding. *Semiotica,* 1969, **1,** 49–98.

Ekman, P., Friesen, W. V., & Ellsworth, P. *Emotion in the human face.* New York: Pergamon, 1972.

Ekman, P., Sorenson, E. R., & Friesen, W. V. Pan-cultural elements in facial displays of emotion. *Science,* 1969, **164,** 86–88.

Erickson, F. An empirical investigation of one function of proxemic shifts in face to face interaction. *Proceedings of 9th International Congress of Anthropological and Ethnological Sciences, Conference on the Organization of Behavior in Face to Face Interaction, Chicago, 1973.* The Hague: Mouton, 1975.

Exline, R. V. Explorations in the process of person perception: Visual interaction in relation to competition, sex and the need for affiliation. *Journal of Personality,* 1963, **31,** 1–20.

Exline, R. V., Gray, D., & Schuette, D. Visual behavior in a dyad as affected by interview content and sex of respondent. *Journal of Personality and Social Psychology,* 1965, **1,** 201–209.

Exline, R. V., & Winters, L. C. Affective relations and mutual glances in dyads.

In S. S. Tomkins & C. E. Izard (Eds.), *Affect, cognition and personality*. New York: Springer, 1965. Pp. 319–350.

Fairbanks, G., & Pronovost, W. An experimental study of the pitch characteristics of the voice during the expression of emotion. *Search Monographs*, 1939, **6**, 87–104.

Fay, P. J., & Middleton, W. C. Judgment of Spranger personality types from the voice as transmitted over a public address system. *Character and Personality*, 1939, **8**, 144–155.

Fay, P. J., & Middleton, W. C. Judgment of Kretschmerian body types from the voice as transmitted over a public address system. *Journal of Social Psychology*, 1940, **12**, 151–162. (a)

Fay, P. J., & Middleton, W. C. Judgment of intelligence from the voice as transmitted over a public address system. *Sociometry*, 1940, **3**, 186–191. (b)

Gibson, J. J., & Pick, A. D. Perception of another person's looking behavior. *American Journal of Psychology*, 1963, **76**, 386–394.

Gumperz, J. J., & Hymes, D. (Eds.) *Directions in sociolinguistics: The ethnography of communication*. New York: Holt, 1972.

Hall, E. T. *The silent language*. New York: Doubleday, 1959.

Hall, E. T. A system for the notation of proxemic behavior. *American Anthropologist*, 1963, **65**, 1003–1026.

Hall, E. T. Silent assumptions in social communication. In D. McK. Rioch & E. A. Weinstein (Eds.), *Disorders of communication*. Baltimore: Association for Research in Nervous and Mental Diseases, 1964.

Hall, E. T. *The hidden dimension*. New York: Doubleday, 1966.

Hill, A. A. *Introduction to linguistic structures*. New York: Harcourt, 1958.

Hinde, R. A. (Ed.) *Non-verbal communication*. New York: Cambridge Univ. Press, 1972.

Hockett, C. F. The origin of speech. *Scientific American*, 1960, **203**, 89–96.

Horton, D. L., & Jenkins, J. J. (Eds.) *The perception of language*. Columbus, Ohio: Charles E. Merrill, 1971.

Izard, C. E. *The face of emotion*. New York: Appleton, 1971.

Kendon, A. Some functions of gaze-direction in social interaction. *Acta Psychologica*, 1967, **26**, 22–63.

Kendon, A. Movement coordination in social interaction: Some examples described. *Acta Psychologica*, 1970, **32**, 100–125.

Kendon, A. Some relationships between body motion and speech. In A. W. Siegman & B. Pope (Eds.), *Studies in dyadic communication*. New York: Pergamon, 1972.

Kramer, E. Judgment of personal characteristics and emotions from non-verbal properties of speech. *Psychological Bulletin*, 1963, **60**, 408–420.

Kramer, E. Elimination of verbal cues in judgment of emotion from voice. *Journal of Abnormal and Social Psychology*, 1964, **68**, 390–396.

La Barre, W. The cultural basis of emotions and gestures. *Journal of Personality*, 1947, **16**, 49–68.

Laver, J. Voice quality and indexical information. *British Journal of Disorders of Communication*, 1968, **3**, 43–54.

Laver, J., & Hutcheson, S. (Eds.) *Communication in face to face interaction*. Harmondsworth: Penguin, 1972.

Little, K. B. Personal space. *Journal of Experimental and Social Psychology*, 1965, **1**, 237–247.

Lyons, J. (Ed.) *New horizons in linguistics*. Harmondsworth: Penguin, 1970.

Lyons, J. Human language. In R. A. Hinde (Ed.), *Non-verbal communication*. New York: Cambridge Univ. Press, 1972. Pp. 49–85.

Mehrabian, A. Orientation behaviors and non-verbal attitude communication. *Journal of Communication*, 1967, **17**, 324–332.

Mehrabian, A. Inference of attitudes from the posture, orientation, and distance of a communicator. *Journal of Consulting and Clinical Psychology*, 1968, **32**, 296–308.

Mehrabian, A. Significance of posture and position in the communication of attitude and status relationships. *Psychological Bulletin*, 1969, **71**, 359–372.

Moscovici, S. (Ed.) *The psychosociology of language*. Chicago: Markham, 1972.

Neisser, U. *Cognitive psychology*. New York: Appleton, 1967.

de Saussure, F. *Course in general linguistics*. C. Bally, A. Sechehaye, & A. Riedlinger (Eds.), (trans. W. Baskin). New York: McGraw-Hill, 1966.

Scheflen, A. E. The significance of posture in communication systems. *Psychiatry*, 1964, **27**, 316–331.

Sebeok, T. A., Hayes, A. S., & Bateson, M. C. (Eds.) *Approaches to semiotics*. The Hague: Mouton, 1964.

Siegman, A. W., & Pope, B. (Eds.) *Studies in dyadic communication*. New York: Pergamon, 1972.

Smith, A. G. (Ed.) *Communication and culture*. New York: Holt, 1966.

Sommer, R. Studies in personal space. *Sociometry*, 1959, **22**, 247–260.

Sommer, R. Further studies of small group ecology. *Sociometry*, 1965, **28**, 337–348.

Sommer, R. Small group ecology. *Psychological Bulletin*, 1967, **67**, 145–152.

Sommer, R. *Personal space*. Englewood Cliffs, New Jersey: Prentice-Hall, 1969.

Starkweather, J. A. Variations in vocal behavior. In D. McK. Rioch & E. A. Weinstein (Eds.), *Disorders of communication*. Baltimore: Association for Research in Nervous and Mental Diseases, 1964.

Sudnow, D. (Ed.) *Studies in social interaction*. New York: Free Press, 1972.

Thompson, C. W., & Bradway, K. The teaching of psychotherapy through content-free interview. *Journal of Consulting Psychology*, 1950, **14**, 321–323.

Tomkins, S. S. *Affect, imagery, consciousness. Vol. 1. The positive affects*. New York: Springer, 1962.

Trager, G. L. Paralanguage: A first approximation. *Studies in Linguistics*, 1958, **13**, 1–12.

Watson, O. M., & Graves, T. D. Quantitative research in proxemic behavior. *American Anthropologist*, 1966, **68**, 971–985.

Chapter 11

LANGUAGE TEACHING AND LANGUAGE LEARNING

EVELYN HATCH

I. INTRODUCTION

The acquisition of language is, as Blumenthal (1970) notes, the most researched topic in psycholinguistics. It is to this literature and to the literature on the nature of language that language teachers have traditionally turned to find the most effective ways to teach languages. Our hope has been that, if we know what language is and know how it is possible for a person to acquire it (what language acquisition must consist of), then sensible language teaching techniques should not be all that difficult to discover.

Teaching techniques have reflected what linguists, psychologists, and philosophers have told us about language and language learning. Of course what we have been told has changed radically over time. Told that language equals words, we set children to copying vocabulary lists. Told that languages are learned via imitation and analogy, we had students "repeat-after-me" and waited—often in vain—for analogy to set in. Told that language learning is habit formation, we assigned students to trilling r's for 5 minutes, 3 times a day, 5 days a week, as if "piano practice" for tongue muscles were the answer. Told that languages, like plants, develop and flower, then decay and die, we fought language corruption and decay with rules, warning students to say *It is I* and that two negatives make an affirmative. There are few fields where changes in theory have had so immediate an effect in the classroom.

II. STRUCTURAL PERIOD

A. Theory

In the 1950s, after the success of the army language schools, teachers felt secure at last. Traditional and structural linguistics had given them teaching texts where language appeared carefully segmented and neatly classified. The sound system, the phonology of the language to be taught, was defined in detail. Illustrations were given to show how word forms change (morphological change) for such things as verb tense, adjective comparison, and possession and plurality, or how new word forms might be derived (magic, magical, magically, magician). And words were then combined into sentence patterns, the syntax of the language. The applied linguist also furnished the teacher with a comparison of the phonology, morphology, and syntax of the students' first language(s) and the target language to be taught. Depending on the thoroughness of the comparison, this contrastive analysis of the two languages isolated gross, and occasionally subtle, differences between the two languages. It was assumed that, at the points of difference, the first language would interfere with successful second language learning. The University of Chicago's contrastive structure series, particularly Stockwell, Bowen, and Martin's (1965) contrastive analysis of English and Spanish, is an example of contrastive analysis at its best. Most other works give a careful contrast of phonology and a few remarks on morphology, leaving syntax untouched.

Language-learning theory of the period was also straightforward. It was claimed that language learning was no different than any other learning skill: "We have no reason to assume . . . that verbal behavior differs in any fundamental respect from non-verbal behavior, or that any new principles must be invoked to account for it [Skinner, 1968, p. 10]." The student needed a model to imitate, he needed reinforcement of his correct repetitions or conditioning for closer and closer approximations to the model, and he needed "adequate" practice, to establish good language habits.

The tenets of language teaching for the period have been stated so frequently that it is difficult to attribute any of them to a particular source (see Brooks, 1960; Fries, 1945; Moulton, 1961); they were shared by scores of believers: (*1*) Language is habit. Language learning is habit formation. (2) Language is learned via imitation and analogy. (3) Habits are strengthened by reinforcement. (4) Oral language is primary; reading and writing are secondary skills. (5) Errors predicted by contrastive analysis allow the teacher to counteract negative transfer from the first language.

Linguists and psychologists seemed unanimous and confident in their answers. And, on these answers, teachers and textbook writers constructed elaborate pattern drills of all sorts—phonological, morphological, and syntactic. Language was frozen, snipped into instantaneous snapshots of sounds, words, and sentence patterns—a set of unreal pictures of language. Tapes sputtered and students around the world repeated their language lab lesson:

CUE:	*Lesson.*	STUDENT:	*The lesson is interesting.*
	Teacher.		*The teacher is interesting.*
	Book.		*The book is interesting.*
	Question.		*The question is interesting.*

as they mastered sentence patterns by habit formation.

The only room for real argument seemed to be over how to account for the failure of many students to learn. Students might be studying a language, but disappointingly few were learning it as well as had been predicted. The "special gift" myth, perpetuated by teachers as well as by students, was often invoked to explain success or failure. After agreeing that some students did not have the "special gift" and that others were not motivated or were intellectually fatigued (if not downright lazy), the teaching profession launched into a series of heated debates over the relative merits of various language teaching techniques.

B. Research

Research studies evaluating various methods—audio-lingual, cognitive code, traditional, direct—were reported in the journals. These large comparative studies suffered from all the usual problems of classroom research, but the most serious criticism was that methods were not accurately defined; nor was it possible to list the specific characteristics that separated one method from another in actual classroom practice. Even those studies that were carefully designed (Agard & Dunkel, 1948; Chastain, 1968; Scherer & Wertheimer, 1964; the Pennsylvania studies reported by Smith & Berger, 1968) do not compare mutually exclusive methods. For example, cognitive awareness of language does not necessarily conflict with the audio-lingual method, nor does language practice preclude use of cognitive code strategies in language learning. Lange, in his survey of this research

(1968), concluded, as had Carroll (1966) and Birkmaier and Lange (1966), that such evaluations, despite the tremendous amount of energy, time, money, and talent spent on them, offered little of significance to the language teacher.

Smaller studies promised more. Studies in verbal learning were much more carefully controlled. However, most of these were concerned with paired associate learning using English or nonsense words, rather than second-language data. Small studies that were concerned with language teaching found either nonreplicable differences or else nonsignificant differences between treatments. Nevertheless, teachers found the arguments about the relative merits of giving rules preceding, during, or after drills (Politzer, 1968), the value of language labs (Smith & Berger, 1968), the optimal number of vocabulary items per lesson (Crothers & Suppes, 1967), or when to introduce the printed word (Muller & Muller, 1968) worthy of attention. While these debates were and continue to be heated, they were minor compared to the shattering effect of the revolution in linguistics, the advent of transformational grammar, on language teaching and the direction of research.

III. TRANSFORMATIONAL PERIOD

A. Theory

In the early 1960s, theoreticians in both psychology and linguistics were simultaneously challenged on their claims about the nature of language and language learning. Not only were the inadequacies of traditional, structural, and taxonomic grammars shown but the general theories of language learning were declared inadequate as well. Chomsky and others assembled arguments to show that there are no principles of association, reinforcement, and generalization that can account for the learner's ability to "create language anew." (For a discussion of these issues, see Chomsky, 1967; McNeill, 1971; Palermo, 1971; Staats, 1971.)

Prior to transformational grammar, linguists had marveled at how languages differed in innumerable ways. Language teachers, using contrastive analysis to compare the language of their students with the language being taught, frequently felt the same way. With the revolution, linguists looked instead for similarities, the universals of language. According to transformational grammarians, these universals defined the constraints on the possible form of all languages. They were the wired-in, neurologically programmed part of language. This innate component would be set off by maturational factors as the child developed physically (Lenneberg, 1966).

The assumption that underlying principles of language are not learned

through training but are innate struck language teachers as extremely important to language teaching. Of course the notion of innateness was not
new. Blumenthal (1970) claims the notion of innateness can be traced
back all the way to Aristotle. And Stern and Stern discussed it in 1907.
Their final position was that imitation or innateness, taken alone, were
both too simplistic to account for language acquisition: "Both views are
capable of obscuring the real situation. . . . The real problem is not one
of imitation vs. spontaneity but rather concerns the extent that internal
tendencies and forces are working during assimilation, selection and internal processing of externally presented form [quoted in Blumenthal's translation, 1970, p. 86]."

Unfortunately, both for research workers in child language and for language teachers, the innateness argument polarized into an either–or position, with no compromise allowed. For some teachers, of course, these
were meaningless arguments compared to issues like contrastive analysis
and first-language interference Looking at the arguments and explanations
of transformational grammar, they saw it as just another way of segmenting
and classifying language—"It's what we've always taught." These teachers
went happily on their way claiming to use transformational grammar but
taking what Lakoff (1969) called "the hollow shell of formalism . . . re-
sorting to new forms of the same old mumbo jumbo [p. 129]."

Other teachers were not so fortunate. For them, the primary question
was: Does the second-language learner still have the built-in component
for language or does it atrophy somehow at puberty, as "optimal age" sup-
porters were claiming? If an innate component exists for the learner, what
strategies does he use to allow the innate abilities to interact with language
experience? Do these strategies coincide or conflict with teaching strategies? Most of all, teachers wanted to know whether or not it was true
that first languages are "acquired" but second languages must still be
"taught" in particular formalized ways.

1. REACTIONS TO APPLIED THEORY

Some answers seemed to be forthcoming. But the answers also split language teachers into quarreling camps. As linguists began working out what
the rules of a transformational grammar might look like for specific languages (for English, see Stockwell, Schachter, & Partee, 1968, many new
insights into the structures of languages were obtained. Some of these,
along with some ideas from Fillmore's case grammar, began to appear in
pedagogical articles and in textbooks (see Rutherford, 1968). Demonstrations of possible utilization of universal operations in teaching language
were given. See, for example, the discussion of relativization as a universal
process in languages by Schacter (1966) and the specific lessons on teach-

ing English relativization by McIntosh (1966). Some teachers were pleased to find descriptions of language that seemed to give genuine explanation of language facts rather than a catalogue of structures.

The earliest models of transformational grammar also suggested a sequence for teaching that seemed to make sense. Early psychological research on theory validation (Gough, 1965; Mehler, 1963; Miller & McKean, 1964) seemed to show that linguistic complexity (defined as number of transformations per sentence) also meant psychological difficulty for the learner. One could begin with the base sentences (sometimes called "kernel sentences" or "sentences of the propositional core"). Then the teacher could show how these sentences could be transformed into a variety of other sentences. Students would learn the operations involved in sentence negation, yes–no questions, why questions, tags, passives, imperatives, etc. Once the operations were familiar, they could be applied over and over again to a wide variety of sentence types. These sentences could then be expanded and put together in a variety of ways with other transformations, until the students acquired what Hunt (1970) has called syntactic maturity. Teachers found transformational drills easy to construct and easy to use in the classroom.

Unfortunately, later research failed to replicate some of the psycholinguistic literature on number of transforms as a reliable predictor of the psychological difficulty of sentences. Syntactic maturity in the sense of sentence variety as a global measure of language usage was also questioned (Moffett, 1968). And many authorities (Bolinger, 1972) questioned the wisdom of teaching transformations as mindless operations without reference to meaning change.

Nevertheless, teachers in this group felt that they now had a more creative set of materials. They could fit the exercises into their teaching frame of dialogues, questions, drills, and reading and writing practice. Many also appreciated the shift in attention from phonology to syntax.

A second group of teachers agreed with Chomsky's (1965) statement that, like everyone else, teachers are too willing to rely on experts, whether linguists or psychologists, for advice. For this group, language-learning theory, in both linguistics and psychology, was much too fragile to serve as the basis for language instruction. Most of them believed the arguments over innateness too vaguely stated ever to be empirically tested. Yet they believed, if not in innateness, then in the learner's natural capability to learn languages. For them, language teaching involved something other than learning a set of linguistic structures, whether the structures were specified by structural, transformational, case, or stratificational linguists. Many felt that language learners had been learning language in spite of, rather than because of, language teaching. They visualized language teaching as communication based, rather than centered on grammar structures. Some of them also proposed a move away from teacher-directed classrooms to student-centered learning.

To some extent, Newmark and Riebel became the leaders for this group of communication teachers. Others, particularly teachers of bilingual children, turned to the work of Moffett (1968) and of Postman and Weingartner (1969) and the literature of humanistic education.

Newmark and Riebel (1970) stated three basic assumptions for language learning: (1) exposing the learner to the systematically organized grammatical form of the language is neither necessary nor sufficient for his mastery of language; (2) presentation of particular instances of language in contexts that exemplify their meaning for use is both sufficient and necessary; and (3) systematic teaching of structure (as in structural drills) imposes formal rather than useful organization on language materials. What Newmark and others suggested was that we teach students how to use language by allowing them to observe and use language in context. The most efficient way to teach language, they argue, is not through structural grading of materials but by situational ordering. The teachers from student-centered classrooms agreed but insisted that the situation ordering had to be chosen by the learner, not the teacher.

Communication advocates argue that the learner should be exposed to the full range of grammatical structures from the start. Since the child acquiring a first language is able to abstract the general rules on exposure to language, the language learner with his natural learning abilities should be able to do the same thing. Just as the child acquires a first language by passing through a set of interim grammars, or stages of rule development, the student would also be allowed to form an interim grammar or several interim grammars as he developed hypotheses about the language. These would not be viewed as mistakes. The teacher would expand ("correct") the students' interim ("incorrect") utterances but not discourage them. This was based on the Cazden (1965) study on assisting the child's acquisition of his first language. Using this system, the teacher's role would be to accelerate the natural process of language learning and to help the learner use the language effectively, both for communication and for self-expression.

Needless to say, the communication model has come under strong attack, both from traditional structuralists and from teachers who wished to use transformational grammar as a base for new structure-centered lessons. Communication teachers were charged with irresponsibility for thinking their students could learn "by osmosis." The teacher has a responsibility to use the brief class time available in the most effective way; therefore, the critics charged, the structures of the language presented to the student must be carefully chosen and sequenced. As proof that learning by osmosis was impossible, they cited the numerous cases of children of bilingual parents who never learn the first language of their parents though they hear it frequently.

Such criticism overlooked the fact that the curriculum proposed by Newmark and Riebel is an active, not a passive one. They stated that the student must observe *and use* language in context; they did not advocate just listening. Students must practice using the language in the situations modeled for them. Class time is carefully scheduled; semantic content and contexts, but not the language structures, are carefully chosen and sequenced.

Proponents of structure practice, as they listened to teachers talk about communication classes, began to include more and more communication practice in their syllabus, moving from dialogues to role playing to context improvization. Teachers in the communication group began including a little pronunciation practice, more grammar explanation, and more formalized writing practice, as they saw it helped the learner. The two schools are slowly coming closer and closer together, as each tries to be more eclectic in approach. As they modify their programs, the approach to language teaching is less and less a dichotomy of either structure or communication practice, increasingly a combination of the two.

B. Research on Language Teaching

During this period, the focus of research, as might be expected, also changed. Comparative classroom research has not disappeared, but the interest has shifted away from what the teacher does to the learner himself. Observational studies of language learners have begun to appear. With the shift from language differences to language universals, tests on the validity of the contrastive analysis hypothesis were designed. Research in reading a second language gained a great deal of attention. (The reading research is too extensive to discuss here; for a review of the literature, see Hatch, 1974.) And finally, research on the relationship between motivation and second-language learning assumed a new importance. If second-language learning was not a "special gift" but something for which everyone has a natural ability, then motivation and attitudes might account for a large part of success or failure in learning.

1. ATTITUDE AND MOTIVATION

The motivation studies (a somewhat specialized meaning for "motivation") produced an interesting argument. By asking students why they wished to learn a new language, Gardner and Lambert (1959) had identified two major types of motivation. Motivation is said to be *integrative* when the learner wants to identify with the speakers of the language, to become a part of that culture group. *Instrumental* motivation includes learning a language as a skill for career purposes, for business, or in order to read literature in one's field. Integrative motivation was found to be significantly related to proficiency in learning the new language.

A second study, Anisfeld and Lambert (1961), produced contradicting results. Americans studying Hebrew in Israel were more proficient learners if they evidenced high instrumental motivation. However, the authors explained that since most of the students wished to become rabbis or Hebrew teachers, they really wished to be part of the Hebrew-speaking community. Lambert, Gardner, Barik, and Tunstall (1963) tested American students attending a 6-week French class. Their findings showed that the higher the scores on an acculturation measure, the higher their proficiency in French, again supporting the original findings.

Spolsky (1969) using an indirect measure of motivation, found that foreign students in this country who gave integrative responses performed better in English-language classes. Lukmani (1972), however, found that most students in her sample of Marathi-speaking students showed instrumental motivation for learning English and that the higher their instrumental scores, the higher their English proficiency scores. Her subjects held a high self-concept; language loyalty and culture loyalty were strong. Subjects wished to learn English as a means to a better standard of living, but they did not wish to adopt other aspects of Westernized culture. From the research, it is obvious that motivation, while related to language success, is much more complex than it seems on the surface.

Language-attitude studies attempt to identify students' attitudes towards speakers of the language they are studying. The assumption of teachers is that if students hold a positive attitude toward speakers of a language, it will be easier for them to learn that language. Bilingual speakers of native fluency in both languages are tape-recorded, reading a passage first in one language and then in the other (each language is called a "guise"; hence the term "matched-guise test"). With several bilingual speakers, the voices can be randomly ordered to allow the listener to believe he is listening to eight different voices, rather than four voices each speaking twice. The subjects listen to and rate the voices, using a rating sheet with pairs of adjectives in bipolar arrangement (semantic differential form):

kind——:——:——:——:——:——cruel

With this indirect measure, Lambert felt he had an instrument that could accurately measure the student's attitudes toward his own language and the language being learned.

The technique has been used with contrasting language groups, first with French and English (Lambert, Hodgson, Gardner, & Fillenbaum, 1960). Both English-speaking and French-speaking subjects rated English guises more favorably than French. The reactions of French Canadians to French and English voices were studied further by Anisfeld and Lambert (1961), with similar results, except that young children evidenced more language loyalty. Views of Jewish and Arabic high school students in Israel were studied in 1965 (Lambert *et al.*). In this case, Jews and Arabs were found to hold mutually negative views of each other's language. In addition, the Ashkenazic dialect of Hebrew was valued over the Yemenite dialect.

More recently, dialects of American English have been studied. Tucker and Lambert (1969) studied reactions to six American dialects (bidialectal speakers were not used in this study). Hensley (1972) reported on the reaction of high school Black students to Black speakers of standard English and Black English (bidialectal speakers). In the Hensley study, there is an indication that Black English was valued by women high school students, who felt that males who spoke Black English really "know what's happening"; otherwise, attitudes toward nonstandard dialects were uniformly negative.

What do these studies mean to the language teacher? Theoretically, if a student's attitude toward a language or a dialect is favorable, it should be easy for him to acquire that language or dialect. It has also been claimed that if you want to be like the speakers of a language, if you want to be part of that culture, then it will be simple to learn that language. But both claims are shaky. Controlling two dialects is not an easy accomplishment. Learning a new language may be easier if you want to be like the speakers of that language. Or it may be easier if you feel comfortable about being a member of your own group and want to use the new language simply to make your economic conditions better. The questions are interrelated, and the answers are not clear.

2. CONTRASTIVE ANALYSIS

The importance of contrastive analysis in explaining learning difficulties also came under attack in a number of research studies of this period. Banathy and Madarasz (1969) studied American subjects learning Hungarian. They performed a contrastive analysis and predicted difficulty for a variety of language structures. Results showed that language similarity could not be equated with ease of learning, nor differences with difficulties. Richards (1970) found that while contrastive analysis was important in some areas (particularly in pronunciation), errors made by a large variety of first-languages subjects learning English were strikingly similar. Working with error analysis, Richards claimed that interference between structures in English and the characteristics of language acquisition (overgeneralization, ignorance of rule restrictions, incomplete application of rules, and false concepts hypothesized) explained the errors much more efficiently than did contrastive analysis.

3. OBSERVATIONAL CASE STUDIES

Observational studies are beginning to give us a wealth of information on the characteristics of second-language acquisition. These preliminary studies are observations of children learning a second language without formalized language teaching. To many language teachers, the strategies used by these children are reminiscent of behavior they have observed in second-language learners regardless of age.

Huang (1971) studied the case of Paul, a 4-year-old Taiwanese child who arrived in this country with no knowledge of English. Paul was enrolled in a noninstructional playschool. Aside from this 12.5 hours a week for 4 months, his exposure to English was nil. The first 2 weeks, as can be seen in Table 1, were apparently unsettling because Paul said nothing while in school, though he responded to *hello* and *good morning*. He sang along during music, followed instructions by observing what the other children did, and made car noises in the playyard. His first English utterance, shown in Table 1, was a repetition: *Get out of here!* Two days later, when Mike tried to get a bike away from him, he remembered it: *Get out of here!* It worked. For the first month, it appeared that Paul was learning his second language by imitation. He might repeat the sentence immediately after it was said or he might remember and use it later in the appropriate situation.

Then during the second month, a second kind of utterance began to appear. Under the column labeled "rule formation," it may be seen that these utterances are exactly the same kind of data to be found in first-language acquisition. For example, when the two columns are scanned for negatives, it appears that those in the rule-formation column are the same as those reported for the first-language learner (Bellugi, 1964); they are quite different from the *Don't touch that* or *Don't touch* of the imitation column.

Clearly two separate and very distinct strategies were running along side by side, vindication for the Stern and Stern position that both imitation and rule formation are important strategies in language learning. After week 12, it became increasingly difficult to separate out imitation, since the rule stages moved so fast that Paul quickly caught up with the language spoken by the other children at the playschool.

Two other interesting processes used by Paul should not be overlooked. They are similar to techniques we use in language classrooms. When Paul

TABLE I

FOUR PROCESSES IN SECOND-LANGUAGE ACQUISITION: DATA ON A 4-YEAR-OLD
CHINESE CHILD ACQUIRING ENGLISH

Week	Imitation	Child language rule formation
2	Get out of here.*	
4	It's time to eat and drink.*	
	Let's go. Don't do that. Don't touch.	
6	Are your ready? See you tomorrow.	This+++kite.
	Excuse me. Hold my hand.*	Yeah, that+++bus.
	Kenny, sit down.	Ball+++no.
7	Are you going too?*	This+++money?
	It's time to go home.* Here we go.*	Paper+++this. Cow+++this.
	Scoot over.*	Mother+++no. Tree+++no.
		No+++ball.
		Wash hand? Two cat.
8	I'll see you. You shut up.	Kenny car.
	What do you like? Hi, how are you?*	This good. This ball?
	We are going home.	This+++boat. This+++paper.
		No ice cream. No candy.
9	How are you doing?*	No money. No turtle. No more truck.
	This is mine.	Paul+++baby. This+++freeway.
		This not box.
10	Get out of here. Scoot over.	
	All the birds up in the tree now	
	that spring is coming . . . (singing)	

Week	Sentence or Topic Expansion	Drill Practice Play
10	This ice cream. This is ice cream.	fish push baby Bobby Paul ball
	Bird. This is bird.	fish ship say see say see
	Wash hand. Wash your hand	Good boy doggy.
	Jim truck. Jim's truck.	Good boy sure.
		Good boy Brent.
11	Doggy jacket. Daddy's jacket.	bird happy birthday. Happy birthday to Jim.
	This mine. This is mine.	Happy birthday Paul Chen.
	Kenny. Kenny's	Baby pu-pu, Bobby pu-pu, don't pu-pu.
	This boat. This my boat.	Mommy money. This is + Noun practice.
12	I want this. I want this one.	Push it, push it, push it, pushing, push, pushing
14	Hand dirty. This hand is dirty.	This is telephone. Open the door.
	Let's go. Get out of here. Let's get out of here.	This is whistle. Open the window.
	Let's go. Let's go on the freeway.	Oh! Wonderful! I'm open the table.
		This is batman.
		Black hat. Yellow hat. Black cat.
		Dangerous. Freeway is dangerous.
		Car is dangerous.

SOURCE: Huang (1971).

* The utterance was repeated immediately after someone else had said it. All other imitations were delayed and used appropriately.

+++ indicates falling sentence intonation on each word.

was engaged in egocentric speech, he did something very close to simple substitution drills. He did a good deal of *This is (noun)* practice. One difference from language class drills is that few teachers ever put an *Oh! wonderful!* in the middle of a drill. The other practice is equivalent to our expansion drills. But here Paul does both the teacher *This ice cream* cue and the expansion, *This is ice cream.* Some of the data also consist of putting sentences tegether: *Let's go. Get out of here. Let's get out of here.* You almost expect transformational arrows to flash on. Weir (1962) noted this phenomenon in first-language acquisition as well. Substitution practice was common: *go for classes . . . go for them . . . go to the top . . . go throw . . . .*

McNeill (1970) in his discussion of this phenomenon in child language says it is doubtful that it has any effect on learning, since the child is playing with structures he has already acquired. If the forms are not adult forms, he does not correct himself. McNeill rules out this form of practice as language learning. Many of the practice data will, all the same, look very familiar to the teacher who uses backward build-up in language practice: *Block . . . Yellow block . . . Look at all the yellow block.*

The data collected by Huang show that at least two processes are at work in second-language acquisition. The person has a great capacity to create language. At the same time he is also capable of storing, repeating, and remembering large chunks of language via imitation. While he is still at the two-word stage in rule formation, he can recall and use longer imitated sentences. He also practices talking with techniques similar to those used in language classrooms.

Dato (1971) reported on the acquisition of Spanish as a second language by four American children living in Madrid. Using a transformational framework, he traced verb phrase development, particularly the order of acquisition of the aux system rule (AUX T (ha- + -do) (esta + -ndo) (haber)). He found that the children, aged 5:6 to 6:3, followed a similar order in acquiring person-number markers, tense, and other aux elements. More interesting, perhaps, is his observation that it is possible to relate the subject's utterances to intermediate structures generated in applying transformational rules. He claims that an utterance like **Yo quiere voy de mi clase* ('I want I go out of my class') could be considered a step from base to the surface structure *Yo quiero ir.* For language teachers, who hear such examples daily in the classroom, such errors have always been thought of as due to first-language interference, not as an interim-stage rule. It is an interesting area for further investigation.

These two studies looked at second-language acquisition in immersion, the first with 12.5 hours a week; the second with 35.5 hours a week. Most teaching programs offer much less exposure (5 to 10 hours). Limited class time has led teachers to question the relevance of such studies to language teaching.

Cathcart (1972) reported on a more typical situation, where children, in this case American children, began school in a second language. Their teacher taught them the regular kindergarten curriculum of colors, numbers, letters, and school rules in Spanish. The children were, of course, allowed to speak with each other in English; but the teacher spoke only Spanish. No formal language training was given to the children.

The children quickly learned to respond to commands with appropriate behavior (Table 2, Section A). They could easily rely on their intuition and the context to understand what was required. Later, their responses required comprehension of at least content words and interpretation of what was expected from the classroom situation.

At the same time, the children began to respond to their teacher's Spanish with English. Their responses (Section B) show they understood what was being said. In the third group of examples (Section C), the children responded in Spanish. Some responses reflected concepts taught in class (e.g., numbers and letter names). Others did not. Some were simple yes–no responses. Their Spanish utterances (Section D) were always directed to the teacher. Few examples, if any, were found of the children initiating Spanish conversation with peers. And, of course, there was no social reason for them to do so. The children tried to practice language courtesy. When speaking with their teacher, they would plug in Spanish content words as they acquired them. Usually Spanish word order was maintained, as in *I have a **bicicleta roja**.* They also tried to teach their teacher English: ***En ingles,*** *that's a dragon, Sra. W.* It is clear that these children mixed languages because they did not have the Spanish vocabulary they needed. In this case, mixing appears to be a language-learning strategy, a way of making communication possible. Others would call it language interference.

At first glance these data seem similar to the mixing data collected at a nearby kindergarten where Spanish-speaking children were attending a regular English kindergarten. Their responses (Section F), however, are not responses to the English-speaking teacher; they are peer conversations. The children are much more proficient in the two languages. They practice both switching and mixing, a very common phenomenon in their community. Lance (1969) has reported on switching and mixing in Spanish–English bilinguals in Texas; Uyekubo (1972) for Japanese–English bilinguals in Los Angeles. It is not an isolated phenomenon.

Why do bilingual children mix languages? One frequently hears teachers complain about children who "don't speak English and don't speak Spanish either," as though mixing languages showed that children were functionally incapable of using either language or of keeping them separated. Uyekubo

TABLE II

COMPREHENSION AND PRODUCTION OF SPANISH BY AMERICAN KINDERGARTEN CHILDREN

A. *Comprehension—behavioral response to teacher's Spanish*
Niñas, aquí. (Girls line up.) Niños, aquí. (Boys line up.)
Niños, a limpear la clase. (They begin to clean up.)
Pidele papel verde á la Sra. W. (Goes and asks in English).
Los más calladitos van primero en casa. (They all sit quietly.)

B. *Responses in English to teacher's Spanish*
No has terminado? *Not yet.*
Dónde está su yo-yo? *She don't have one.*
El jueves vamos a comér en la cafeteria. *Oh boy!*
Tienes calor? *No. I don't got my undershirt*

C. *Responses in Spanish.*
Cuantas flores estan aquí? *Cuatro*
Un Círculo mas chico. *No, mas grande!*
Para mamá y papá. *Y hermana?*
Ese es "b" grande. *Como "baño."*

D. *Self-initiated Spansih.*
Uno mas. Tengo uno mas.
Quieren otro lettras.
Yo es enferma. No es malo.
Es (e) es para la casa? (notes to parents)

E. *Mixing (a)*
Si, I think. I got a quarter for *leche.*
I'm gonna get a drink of *aqua.*
Tres more *dias* and we're going to the zoo.
I'm a *avion.* I have a *bicicleta roja.*
Es *his* casa.   En inglés that's a dragon.
Este es *you,* Sra. W.   Sra. W.
Es D. en mi casa with a t-shirt

F. *Mixing (b)*   Switching (b)
Yo tengo nueva *clay.*   Aquí, aquí, catch a car.
Pone *four.*   Cada uno? I'm gonna do two of 'em.
Va a ser una *butterfly.*   Hey, no. Es para la cocina. Get out! Shoo!
Esta *upside down.*

SOURCE: Cathcart (1972).

found her subjects switched languages according to the language of the interlocuter. When speaking with monolingual English speakers, they spoke English; when speaking with monolingual Japanese speakers, they used Japanese. Mixing was used only when speaking with other proficient bilinguals who also mixed languages. Teachers frequently feel that mixing occurs when the child has an impoverished vocabulary in the new language.

Certainly this was true with the Cathcart subjects, who were just acquiring Spanish. Lance and Uyekubo both have stunning examples of children switching back and forth between their two languages using the same vocabulary items in each language with ease. In the following example, Roy, a Spanish–English bilingual, uses *carreras* as well as *runs, batear* as well as *bat, ganaron* as well as *beat,* and numbers in both languages:

> C: *Cuentame del juego.* (Tell me about the game.)
> R: *Primero they were leading diez pa' nada. Then there was our team to bat and we made . . . 'cimos dos carreras. And then ellos fueron a batear. Hicieron una and then nosotros 'cimos cinco. And then they made dos and then it was our time to bat and we made . . . ah . . . five or six. And then they beat us by five runs* [Lance, 1969, p. 88]."

Vocabulary impoverishment cannot account for such mixing. When working with children who switch languages it is important to know that the child mixes languages in order to enhance his story-telling abilities and his sense of community membership with other proficient bilinguals who mix languages.

As teachers, we encourage students to learn how to switch from one language to another rapidly as social cues are given. Perhaps we also need to reexamine our feelings about language mixing by fluent bilinguals. It fulfills an important function and should not be confused with notions of language deficiency.

Data have also been collected on older subjects learning a second language without formal instruction. Butterworth (1972) observed a 13-year-old in his struggle, a very frustrating struggle, to learn English. The data showed that Ricardo went through many of the same phases as the child Paul in acquiring English. He tried juxtaposing content words in the usual two-word utterances of first-language acquisition: *Me good. He champion. This chair.* Few of the things he wished to say could be captured by this technique. Although little mixing occurred, he tried to use anything from Spanish that he could. Two which did not work very well were quickly replaced. *Possible + utterance,* which began as the Spanish *possible* and then changed to *possible* (*Possible is closed*), disappeared rapidly once *maybe* was learned. *Similar* (*Olympics similar ski* for 'Winter Olympics'; *He similar pull* for 'He fell down'; *He look TV similar newspaper* for 'he watches TV news') was quickly replaced by *for. For* proved to be very workable, the range of use (see Table 3) goes far beyond *por/para.* Some of the uses of *for* (e.g., as a conjunction) died out rather quickly; others were kept throughout the study.

There are many interesting facets to the data for Ricardo; the examples

TABLE III

AN ADOLESCENT'S ACQUISITION OF ENGLISH: EXAMPLES OF THE USE OF *for*

A. *Nominalizations*
  (1)* He for selling. (?) (he sells; he's a salesman)
  (3) In house one machine for hot. (a space heater)
  (3) One man is clean for clothes. (a laundryman)
  (3) He is for school. (a teacher)
  (4) This machine for envelopes for newspaper. (printing press)
  (4) These is shoes for water ice. (ice skates)
  (5) He champion in France for world. (World Champion)
  (5) This shoes for skiing. (ski boots)
  (6) . . . rooms for sleep. (bedrooms)
  (7) He's for English. (an English teacher)
  (9) One peoples cleans for floor, for carpet. (a janitor)

B. *For–to-ing nonagentive nominalizations*
  (1) For eat is good.
  (3) Finish for eat.

C. *In direct object position*
  (1) My father me go for lobster. (We fish lobsters.)
  (3) I do soap for clothes. (I wash clothes)
  (4) He looks the clocks for time, bang! (how he starts the race)
  (6) He for long hair ties it. (He ties back the long hair)
  (7) Maybe for Mr. Nixon pow! (Maybe someone will pow Mr. N.)
  (7) Maybe me for he one. (Maybe I'll hit him.)
  (9) He a match for one cigarette. (?he lit the cigarette; or *have* deletion)
  (10) He clean for teeth. (He brushes his teeth.)

D. *In indirect object position or benefactive*
  (6) Coffee for he. (They bring him coffee)
  (7) One hits him for he. (Someone hit him for him. Not reflexive)
  (9) Go for peoples for drink. (gets drinks for people)

E. *As preposition (to, into, near, down)*
  (2) In U.S. people go for San Silvestre. (to)
  (3) Is for South Laguna. (near)
  (3) Go for sands in car. (down the sand . . . a dune buggy)
  (5) Maybe go for Los Angeles. He go for Cali. (to)
  (7) You go for one girlfriend. (to)
  (9) One animal go for eye, for hair . . . . (animal = bug)
  (10) Me everydays go my dictionary for my house. (take it home)

F. *Duration*
  (3) Me working for 40 hours a week. (many examples)

G. *Conjunction*
  (3) You for me. (and)
  (4) You for me maybe? (We will play chess?)
  (6) Father for son. (and)

SOURCE: Butterworth (1972).
* Numbers in parenthesis refer to week of observation.

cited here illustrate only some of the differences that set it apart from the other studies.

4. UNIVERSALS OF LANGUAGE ACQUISITION

In the early 1970s, child language experts discussed a number of proposals on the universals of language acquisition. The most promising set for first-language acquisition is that proposed by Slobin (1971). Some of Slobin's principles are highly predictive of second-language acquisition as well. Others seem questionable in the second-language context.

Perhaps the most powerful operating principle that emerges from Slobin's list is that the word order of the input language will be followed by the language learner. Although this principle works for all the data on second-language acquisition, there are many exceptions. The most interesting variations were produced by Ricardo: *Two hours in car me. Maybe finish 11:30 Spanish. He in face one cloth.* (the TV wrestler was wearing a mask) *Me in play one hour possible. He for long hair ties it.* Despite his many examples of strange word order, frequently only the fact that word order was preserved made utterances understandable.

Ravem (1968) found that his subject followed the word order of the second language; that is, he did not try to impose Norwegian word order on English. Adams (1973), in her study of a group of Spanish speakers acquiring English, showed that word order was acquired even for some transformations before certain morphological endings were acquired. It seems quite likely, then, that second- as well as first-language learners attend to word order and that they acquire word order before learning morphological endings.

Slobin also proposed an order of acquisition for morphological endings with variant forms. First-language learners have been shown to begin with $\emptyset$ (zero) forms, move to appropriate marking in a few cases, then go to overgeneralization of forms, and finally sort the forms out as in adult language. For example, in acquiring the English plural morpheme, children frequently being with only number and no plural morpheme (*That two car*). Gradually they add plural endings in a few appropriate contexts. They may begin with the /s/ form (*That two cats* /kæts/), and a few /z/ forms (*That two dogs* /dɔgz/). When the more difficult /ɨz/ form is acquired, it tends to be generalized to other plurals (*two catses* /kætsiz/, *two dogses* /dɔgzɨz/, *two horses* /horsɨz/). After overgeneralization, the forms are sorted out again into the adult categories.

Paul moved rapidly through these stages. Regression to $\emptyset$ forms were, however, very common. Ricardo, on the other hand, simply did not mark semantic relationships by morphological endings. Instead, he juxtaposed words or used one of his *for* constructions. Verbs, for example, were not marked for tense. The semantic value of time was expressed with words like *now, today,* or *later* (*He play guitar now. Next year me come by high school. Yesterday me speak she over there.*) Possessives were also unmarked except by juxtaposition (*mother house, you girlfriend*). It could be said that his strategy worked so well that he just didn't bother with morphological endings. Or it may be that he had a very prolonged Ø stage.

A third principle proposed by Slobin and supported by our data was the avoidance of interruption and permutation of elements in an utterance. Just like first-language learners, Paul and Ricardo avoided permutation by forming questions as echo questions (Paul: *Wash hand?* Ricardo: *Me go? You tomorrow?*). But at the same time both subjects also had permuted forms for questions in utterances learned by imitation (Paul: *Are you ready? What are you doing,* Ricardo: *Where'd you go?*). And to avoid interruption, both subjects used external placement for negation (Paul: *No . . . ball.* Ricardo: *No sit down here*). At a later stage they began to move the negative into the sentence (Paul: *This not box.* Ricardo: *They no want bicycle*). Paul quickly acquired the *do*-support and neg attraction rules; Ricardo did not.

Many of the proposed universals of language acquisition do hold for second-language learning: word order, avoidance of permutation, learning of general class rules before subclass rules. However, many other strategies are used that are not included in such lists. The distinction between imitated and self-generated sentences in second-language acquisition seems quite clear. It is also clear that the second-language learner does not memorize these imitated sentences and then, by analogy, form like sentences. The fact that Ricardo had formula sentences with *do* in them did not mean that he could by analogy generate sentences with *do;* he could not. Neither could Paul, by analogy, form neg sentences like those he learned in imitation. The same is true for the American children, who could say in Spanish that it was time to go home but never tried to say it was time to do anything else. The subjects all arrived at new sentences of the same type only after going through a series of rule formation stages.

This research is, of course, extremely tentative, but it is important to language teachers. We expect students to learn language by imitation and analogy and we are often puzzled when analogy does not take place quickly. Little, if any, research has been conducted on the kinds of interim rules through which the learner works as he acquires the language.

5. LANGUAGE INPUT

There are many other areas to be investigated. One of these is the question of language input. Newmark and Riebel have assumed that if a child learning a first language can abstract the rules for the language from uncon-

trolled input, then there is no reason to limit the language input of a second-language learner. Yet, it is clear that parents speak differently to young
children acquiring language (Snow, 1972). Their language is more redundant, less complex, has fewer false starts and hesitations. Certainly foreign
students can force reduction of complex speech when they don't understand, as in this recorded example from my own teaching:

> TEACHER: *What I want you to do is to take the example, making it less,*
> *if you possibly can, like the model.*
> STUDENT: *Take . . . model?*
> TEACHER: *Take . . . the example.* (Points to page)
> STUDENT: *Yes.*
> TEACHER: *Yes, you see, and just make it a little less like the one here.*
> STUDENT: *Yes . . . ?*
> TEACHER: *Write . . . one . . . different.*
> STUDENT: *Write sentence different?*
> TEACHER: *Right.*

Controlled input studies are certainly easier in second-language learning
than in first; it should be possible to test the former area.

It should also be possible to test the effectiveness of correction giving.
Brown, Cazden, and Bellugi (1969) found that mothers correct the language of young children very rarely. Instead, they correct for content and
for truth value. In the audio-lingual method, teachers were warned against
allowing students to make errors in structure; they were not warned against
truth value errors (*The lesson is interesting,* when it is not).

We also need to know much more about how differences in the age
continuum change strategies in acquiring second languages. Ricardo may
be a unique case. Is his scheme for developing the noun phrase while ignoring the aux and verb system idiosyncratic? Itoh's (in progress) study of
a Japanese child learning English suggests that it is not. However, without
more data, there is no way to answer the many questions that this study
of an older learner has raised.

IV. CONCLUSION

We began this chapter by saying that teachers have looked with naive
hope to the fields of linguistics and psychology for answers to the problems
of language teaching. Certainly the hope is naive if we are looking for
final answers. And we are naive if we accept scientific breakthroughs—
whether disguised as language labs, watered-down transformational grammar, talking typewriters, or computer-assisted instruction—as wholesale
cures for the language-learning problems of our students. Yet teachers have

learned much of value from these two fields. While it is out of style at the moment to praise the work in contrastive analysis, we have gained an understanding of language interference problems from it. We also have learned much about the languages we teach from the papers written by transformational and case grammarians. Psychology literature, particularly that on language acquisition, is beginning to have an impact on our beliefs about the second-language learning process.

From these two fields we have also received sets of conflicting assumptions about the nature of language and language learning. With a commitment to research, many of these assumptions can be tested in a variety of interesting ways in the language classroom and language laboratory. It is time for the teaching profession to stop asking questions of others, to make a commitment to such research and begin looking for the answers ourselves.

References

Adams, M. Strategies used by elementary school children in the acquisition of English as a second language. Unpublished master's thesis, UCLA, 1973.

Agard, F., & Dunkel, H. *An investigation of second language teaching.* Boston: Ginn, 1948.

Anisfeld, M., & Lambert, W. E. Social and psychological variables in learning Hebrew. *Journal of Abnormal and Social Psychology,* 1961, **63,** 524–529.

Banathy, B., & Madarasz, P. H. Contrastive analysis and error analysis. *Journal of English,* 1969, **4,** 77–92.

Bellugi, U. The emergence of inflection and negation systems in the speech of two children. Paper presented at the New England Psychological Association, 1964.

Birkmaier, E., & Lange, D. L. Foreign language instruction. *Review of Educational Research,* 1966, **37,** 186–199.

Blumenthal, A. L. *Language and psychology, historical aspects of psycholinguistics.* New York: Wiley, 1970.

Bolinger, D. The influence of linguistics; plus or minus. *TESOL Quarterly,* 1972, **6,** 107–120.

Brooks, N. *Language and language learning.* New York: Harcourt, 1960.

Brown, R., Cazden, C., and Bellugi, U. The child's grammar from I to III. In P. Hill (Ed.), *Minnesota Symposium on Child Development,* 1969, **2,** 28–73.

Butterworth, G. A Spanish-speaking adolescent's acquisition of English syntax. Unpublished master's thesis, UCLA, 1972.

Carroll, J. B. Research in foreign language teaching: the last five years. In R. G. Mead (Ed.), *Reports of the working committees of the Northeast Conference.* New York: Modern Languages Association, 1966. Pp. 7–58.

Cathcart, R. Second language acquisition strategies of two groups of kindergarten children immersed in a second language. Unpublished master's thesis, UCLA, 1972.

Cazden, C. Environmental assistance to the child's acquisition of grammar. Unpublished doctoral dissertation, Harvard Univ., 1965.

Chastain, K. D. A comparison of the audio-lingual habit theory and the cognitive-code theory to the teaching of introductory college Spanish. Unpublished doctoral dissertation, Purdue Univ., 1968.

Chomsky, N. Linguistic theory. In R. G. Mead (Ed.), *Reports of the working committees of the Northeast conference.* New York: Modern Languages Association, 1965. Pp. 43–49.

Chomsky, N. Review of Skinner's verbal behavior. In L. A. Jakobovitz & M. S. Miron (Eds.), *Readings in psychology of language.* Englewood Cliffs, New Jersey: Prentice-Hall, 1967. Pp. 142–171.

Crothers, E., & Suppes, P. *Experiments in second language learning.* New York: Academic Press, 1967.

Dato, D. P. The development of the Spanish verb phrase in children's second language learning. In P. Pimsleur & T. Quinn (Eds.), *Psychology of second language learning.* New York: Cambridge Univ. Press, 1971. Pp. 19–33.

Fries, C. C. *Teaching and learning English as a second language.* Ann Arbor: Univ. of Michigan Press, 1945.

Gardner, R. C., & Lambert, W. E. Motivational variables in second language learning. *Canadian Journal of Psychology,* 1959, **13,** 226–273.

Gough, P. B. Grammatical transformations and speed of understanding. *Journal Verbal Learning and Verbal Behavior,* 1965, **4,** 107–111.

Gregoire, A. *L'apprentissage du language.* Paris: Droz, 1937.

Hatch, E. Studies in second language acquisition. Paper given at the Third International Congress of Applied Linguistics, Copenhagen, Denmark, 1972.

Hatch, E. Research on reading a second language. *Journal of Reading Behavior,* 1974, **6,** 53–61.

Hensley, A. Black high school students' evaluations of Black speakers. *Language Learning,* 1972, **22,** 2.

Huang, J. A Chinese child's acquisition of English syntax. Unpublished master's thesis, UCLA, 1971.

Hunt, K. W. *Syntactic maturity in schoolchildren and adults.* Chicago: Univ. of Chicago Press, 1970.

Itoh, H. A child's acquisition of two languages—Japanese and English. Unpublished master's thesis, UCLA, 1973.

Lakoff, R. Transformational grammar and language teaching. *Language Learning,* 1969, **19,** 117–140.

Lambert, W., Anisfeld, M., & Yeni-Komshian, G., Evaluational reactions of Jewish and Arab adolescents to dialect and language variations. *Journal on Personality and Social Psychology,* 1965, **2,** 84–90.

Lambert, W. E., Gardner, R. C., Barik, H. C., & Tunstall, K. Attitudinal and cognitive aspects of intensive study of a second language. *Journal of Abnormal & Social Psychology,* 1963, **47,** 114–121.

Lambert, W. E., Hodgson, R. C., Gardner, R. C., & Fillenbaum, S. Evaluational reactions to spoken languages. *Journal of Abnormal & Social Psychology,* 1960, **60,** 44–51.

Lance, D. M. A brief study of Spanish-English bilingualism. Research report, Texas A & M, Project #15504, 1969.

Lange, D. L. Methods. In Emma Birkmaier (Ed.), *The Britannica review of foreign language education.* Vol. 1. Chicago: Encyclopedia Britannica, 1968. Pp. 281–310.

Lenneberg, E. H. The natural history of language. In F. Smith & G. A. Miller (Eds.), *The genesis of language.* Cambridge, Massachusetts: MIT Press, 1966. Pp. 219–252.

Lukmani, Y. Student motivation for learning English in Marathi-medium schools. *Language Learning,* 1972, **22,** 261–273.

McIntosh, L. Language lessons based on transformational analysis. Paper given at the National Association of Foreign Student Affairs, Chicago, 1966.

McNeill, D. *The acquisition of language: The study of developmental psychology.* New York: Harper, 1970.

McNeill, D. The capacity for the ontogenesis of grammar. In D. I. Slobin (Ed.), *The ontogenesis of language.* New York: Academic Press, 1971.

Mehler, J. Some effects of grammatical transformations on the recall of English sentences. *Journal of Verbal Learning and Verbal Behavior,* 1963, **2,** 346–351.

Miller, G. A., & McKean, K. A chronometric study of some relations between sentences. *Quarterly Journal of Experimental Psychology,* 1964, **16,** 297–308.

Moffett, J. *Teaching the universe of discourse.* Boston: Houghton-Mifflin, 1968.

Moulton, W. Linguistics and language teaching in the United States, 1940–60. In C. Mohrmann, A. Sommerfelt, & J. Whatmough (Eds.), *Trends in European and American linguistics, 1930–60.* Utrecht: Spectrum Publishers, 1961. Pp. 86–89.

Muller, D. H., & Muller, T. The problem of interference in beginning Portuguese. *Language Journal,* 1968, **62,** 201–205.

Newmark, L., & Riebel, D. A. Necessity and sufficiency in language learning. In M. Lester (Ed.), *Readings in applied transformational grammar.* New York: Holt, 1970. Pp. 228–252.

Palermo, D. S. On learning to talk: Are principles derived from the language lab applicable. In D. I. Slobin (Ed.), *The ontogensis of grammar.* New York: Academic Press, 1971. Pp. 41–63.

Politzer, R. L. The role and place of explanations in the pattern drill. *International Review of Applied Linguistics and Language Teaching,* 1968, **6,** 315–331.

Postman, N., & Weingartner, C. *Teaching as a subversive activity.* New York: Delacorte Press, 1969.

Ravem, R. Language acquisition in a second language environment, *International Review of Applied Linguistics,* 1968, **6,** 175–185.

Richards, J. A noncontrastive approach to error analysis. Unpublished paper presented at the TESOL conference, San Francisco, 1970.

Rutherford, W. *Modern English: A textbook for foreign students.* New York: Harcourt, 1968.

Schachter, P. Transformational grammar and contrastive analysis. Paper given at National Association of Foreign Student Affairs, Chicago, 1966.

Scherer, G., & Wertheimer, M. *A psycholinguistic experiment in language learning.* New York: McGraw-Hill, 1964.

Skinner, B. F. *Verbal behavior.* Cambridge, Massachusetts: Harvard Univ. Press, 1968.

Slobin, D. I. Operating principles and universals in child language acquisition. Paper given at the Conference on Developmental Psycholinguistics, State Univ. of New York, Buffalo, August, 1971.

Smith, P. D., & Berger, E. An assessment of three language teaching strategies utilizing three language laboratory systems. Project 35-0683, U.S. Depart. of Health, Education & Welfare, Washington, D.C., 1968.

Snow, C. Mothers' speech to children learning language. *Child Development,* 1972, **43,** 549–566.

Spolsky, B. Attitudinal aspects of second language learning. *Language Learning,* 1969, **19,** 272–283.

Staats, A. W. Integrated-functional learning theory and language development. In
    D. I. Slobin (Ed.), *The ontogenesis of grammar.* New York: Academic Press,
    1971. Pp. 103–152.

Stern, C., & Stern, W. *Die Kindersprache.* Leipzig: Barth, 1907. Translated exerpts
    also appear in Blumental, A. L. *Language and psychology.* New York: Wiley,
    1970.

Stockwell, R. P., Bowen, J. D., & Martin, J. W. *The grammatical structure of English
    and Spanish.* Chicago: Univ. of Chicago Press, 1965.

Stockwell, R. P., Schachter, P., & Partee, B. Hall *Integration of transformational
    theories on English syntax.* Bedford, Massachusetts: U.S. Air Force, 1968.

Tucker, R. G., & Lambert, W. E. White and negro listeners reactions to various
    American-English dialects. *Social Forces,* 1969, **47,** 23–31.

Uyekubo, A. Language switching of Japanese-English bilinguals. Unpublished
    master's thesis, UCLA, 1972.

Weir, R. *Language in the crib.* The Hague: Mouton, 1962.

Part III

Disorders of Language and Speech

Chapter 12

LANGUAGE DISORDERS (APHASIA) *

H. GOODGLASS AND N. GESCHWIND

* The preparation of this chapter was supported in part by USPHS grants NS 06209 to Boston University and NS 07615 to Clark University.

I. DEFINITION

The ability to learn and use spoken and written language obviously depends on the integrity of auditory and visual perception and of the complex sensorimotor systems controlling the apparatus of articulation and writing. Other factors affecting the quality of speech are the motivation to communicate and the intellectual capacity to learn vocabulary and put the speaker's language skills to the most effective service of his intentions. The integrity of all these systems, however, is to no avail without the cerebral organization that acquires the symbol systems of language, mediating both their comprehension and their formulation into speech or writing. The term "language disorder" is applied here specifically to defects arising from lesions of these brain structures, defects that are subsumed under the term "aphasia." Aphasic disorders are those that are specific to the linguistic functions of the aforementioned sensory and motor systems. They are distinguished from disturbances due to muscular weakness or incoordination, to impaired hearing or vision, or to impaired intelligence, consciousness, or motivation.

Thus, the individual with an articulatory defect arising from impaired motor control mispronounces those sounds that depend on particular muscular movements—e.g., raising the soft palate to produce a stop consonant—but these errors are identical in all speech contexts, i.e., they are not contingent on the linguistic nature of the task. The aphasic, on the other hand may articulate a word perfectly as part of a memorized series (e.g., counting) but distort it beyond recognition in evoking it to answer a question. In the auditory sphere, analogously, reduced hearing expresses itself in failure to discriminate similar sounds, regardless of their linguistic context. When the sounds of a word are correctly perceived, comprehension is normal. In contrast, the aphasic with an auditory receptive defect may repeat a word out of context perfectly, but uncomprehendingly, yet respond to it appropriately as part of a familiar phrase.

The schizophrenic patient may withdraw from communication, either by withholding speech entirely (muteness) or by engaging in verbal play (schizophrenic jargon) that may have private symbolic value, while serving as a shield against contact with others. Both of these symptoms superficially mimic the outward effect of aphasia of different types, but without disorder of the language mechanism itself. The subjective feeling that the patient is withdrawing from interpersonal contact and the bizarreness of his behavior may be the only immediately obvious clue to distinguish him from an aphasic. The reversibility of the symptoms with spontaneous or drug-induced changes in emotional status are another indication that the language mechanism is intact. Maher (1972) provides a fuller discussion of schizophrenic speech.

Whether an aphasic patient is nearly mute or produces fluent jargon, one usually experiences a degree of emotional rapport with him that would be rare with a schizophrenic whose communication was so severely disordered. Even more compelling, however, is the very frequent (although not invariable) presence in aphasics of physical findings that confirm injury to the regions of the brain contiguous to the speech areas and the presence of associated nonlinguistic performance deficits produced by injury in the same regions that injure the language system.

II. THE ANATOMICAL BASIS OF LANGUAGE

Each case of aphasia represents an experiment of nature, revealing the way injury to a given region of the brain impairs or dissociates the components that function harmoniously and indistinguishably in the normal speaker. The vital importance of aphasic phenomena, however, lies in the fact that the natural lines of cleavage along which these components break down sometimes have no counterpart in normal experience and cannot be inferred from other avenues of inquiry, e.g., child language development or psycholinguistic studies of normal speakers. Thus, it is only from aphasia that we learn that fluent grammatical speech may be preserved when the ability to name common objects is lost; that grammatical capacity may break down independently of vocabulary; that writing may be preserved when reading is lost. These and many other paradoxical phenomena offer challenges for explanation at both the psychological and the physiological levels.

What lends these observations additional value is that they can often be correlated systematically with particular lesions. When such a correlation is established for a particular symptom, one can at least conclude that there is some uniformity across people in the structure–function relationships for the language system and that we have identified one of the aspects of language that is selectively vulnerable. The exact nature of the relationship between structural damage and resulting deficit, however, cannot be immediately inferred. Hughlings Jackson (1882) warned against the simplistic assumption that the missing function resided in the injured area. He pointed out that positive symptoms are the result of the activity of the remaining uninjured tissue.

There are various ways in which injury to a particular structure may produce a given outcome. In order to consider these alternatives some background on the functional anatomy of the cerebral hemispheres is necessary, and for this the reader is referred to Fig. 1.

The areas in Fig. 1 labeled M, A, S, and V represent zones with relatively fixed functions, prewired by major neural pathways, and having a one-to-one relationship with motor control (M), audition (A), somatosensory functions (S), and vision (V). These are the areas that control the peripheral modalities necessary for speech, reading, and writing—areas whose injury may produce sensory or motor deficits interfering with the mechanics of input or output, but not with language.

The one-to-one arrangement in these primary sensory and motor zones is so thoroughgoing that parts of the body can actually be mapped out on the primary motor and sensory zones, and segments of the visual field mapped onto the primary visual area. Significantly, the body is oriented head down on this cortical map, so that the mouth, tongue, and fingers are represented at the lower end of both the motor and sensory areas. Adjacent to the primary motor and sensory zones, and concentric to the auditory and visual areas, are their corresponding association areas. Here, among other functions, the experience of the primary zones is apparently codified and stored. Thus, the three sensory association areas are important

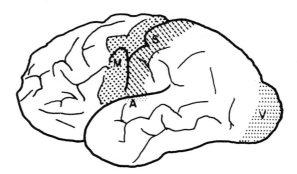

Fig. 1. Location of the primary motor and sensory regions on the cortex. M = motor; S = somatosensory; V = visual; A = auditory.

in the recognition of familiar configurations experienced through their respective modalities; the motor association areas are important in the organization of purposeful movements. We do not know what the nature of the code is, but it appears to be such that an entire association zone participates in each process, much as every part of a holographic plate contains information for the reconstruction of an entire picture.

Referring to Fig. 2, we can see that the anterior language zone (*Broca's area*) occupies the lower end of the motor association area, adjacent to the primary zone for the mouth and hand. Logically enough, injuries in this area appear to implicate most directly (but not exclusively) the phonological and graphic aspects of language. The posterior language zone (*Wernicke's area*), adjacent to the primary auditory center, appears to be critical for the comprehension of language, even though hearing as such is not interfered with by lesions in this area. As we shall see, such lesions rarely disturb comprehension alone but also change the character of speech production and the capacity for reading and writing.

The association area concentric to the primary visual zones plays an important part in the processing of all types of meaningful visual input. However, lesions of this region *alone* do not selectively impair the *linguistic* aspect of written language, although the recognition of letters, as well as that of other familiar forms, may be impaired (visual agnosia). It is the region of the *angular gyrus* of the left hemisphere that appears to be most critical for the linguistic elaboration of written symbols. Since visual language is normally based on the prior establishment of the spoken language code, the angular gyrus has most appropriately evolved between the auditory and visual association areas and appears to function as a second-order association area. This is the only region in which a lesion may destroy both reading and writing without significantly affecting either speech or

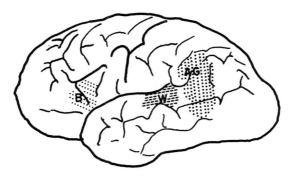

Fig. 2. Location of the principal language zones on the cortex. B = Broca's area, W = Wernickes area, AG = Angular gyrus.

comprehension. This region is critical for other functions in addition to written language.

While the phenomenon of cerebral lateralization of language will be treated at some length later in this chapter, it is important to review it briefly in the context of the localization of language. Briefly, it is observed that as language develops in the average individual, its functions are pre-empted by the language zones of the dominant left hemisphere, so that aphasia appears but rarely in conjunction with right-hemisphere injury. Most instances of aphasia caused by right-hemisphere injuries occur in left-handers. These facts have important implications when we consider that stimulus input may be directed to either cerebral hemisphere but can be processed linguistically only in the left hemisphere. Similarly, language-related output (e.g., left-handed writing, left-handed response to a written or verbal stimulus) may be executed under the *motor* control of the right hemisphere, but only with direction from the language zones of the left hemisphere. The major connecting link that carries this information be-tween the two cerebral hemispheres is a massive collection of fibers called the *corpus callosum*. The fibers that link homologous functional regions of the two hemispheres are localized within the corpus callosum, so that for example, the connection between the two visual association areas oc-cupies its posterior end, the *splenium*. The defects arising from injuries to these interhemispheric pathways are of great theoretical importance and will be described in a later section.

Since language apparently does not exist to any significant extent in the natural state in any subhuman species, although some capacity for the learning of language exists in chimpanzees (Gardner & Gardner, 1969; Premack, 1971) and since it is not possible to perform experimental brain ablations in humans, nearly all of our knowledge of the neurophysiology of language has been accumulated painfully in the last century on the basis of those occasional instances in which postmortem examinations revealed clearly-defined lesions in the brains of individuals who had demonstrated well-documented aphasic syndromes before death.

The best type of pathological material (Geschwind, 1970) comes from vascular lesions that have destroyed circumscribed areas. While vascular lesions are common, well-studied cases of isolated lesions that have under-gone careful postmortem study are not common.

III. BRAIN LATERALITY

As we have noted, the left hemisphere alone is responsible for language in the overwhelming majority of right-handed adults. Current estimates are that no more than 2% of aphasias in right-handers are due to unilateral right-cerebral lesions. Observations of children and of left-handers, however, make the problem appear complex indeed. The simplistic "classical theory of cerebral dominance," dating to the work of Broca (1865), held that language dominance lay in the hemisphere opposite the preferred hand. However, the study of series of cases of left-handed aphasics (Goodglass & Quadfasel, 1954; Penfield & Roberts, 1959) made it evident that aphasia in left-handers occurred at least as often with left- as with right-cerebral lesions. However, the paucity of negative cases (i.e., left-handers with cerebral lesions without aphasia) in these series made it impossible to decide between two alternatives: (1) that left-handers had unilateral dominance that might be on one side or the other or (2) that left-handers were vulnerable to aphasia from lesions of either hemisphere, i.e., that they had bilateral speech representation in the brain. The repeated reports (Goodglass and Quadfasel) of milder and more transient aphasias in left-handers lent some credence to the point of view that their speech is not so strongly lateralized as that of right-handers. Direct support for this position was finally provided by Gloning, Gloning, Haub, and Quatember (1969) in a series of 57 left-handed and 57 right-handed patients, matched as to site of lesion, and including both positive and negative cases. These data showed that for left-handers a lesion in *either* hemisphere was as likely to produce aphasia as a left-sided lesion in a right-handed patient. The data of both Gloning *et al.* (1969) and Luria (1970) also support the notion that left-handers, on the average, recover better from aphasias produced by right- than left-hemisphere lesions.

The role of the family handedness background was first pointed out by Foster Kennedy (1916), who noted that right-handers who developed an aphasia after a right-cerebral lesion were likely to be members of a left-handed family. Luria (1970) reports that aphasias in right-handers with a left-handed family background were milder than aphasias in right-handers without such family histories.

While the predisposition for language to lateralize toward the left hemisphere is believed to be genetically determined, the actual course of development can be reversed with early acquired injury to the left brain. Thus, children who have an infantile right hemiplegia, with an atrophic left hemisphere, develop normal language in the right hemisphere. Shifts in brain laterality are possible with lesions acquired after language has developed. Lenneberg (1967) documents the decreasing capacity to recover from aphasia with increasing age.

Until recently, the only sure index of language laterality was the occurrence of aphasia after a unilateral lesion. In 1960, Wada and Rasmussen described the results of a procedure, introduced by Wada, in which a transient aphasia could be produced experimentally by an injection of a barbiturate into the circulation of one cerebral hemisphere at a time. The most extensive series of Wada tests reported (Milner, Branch, & Rasmussen, 1966) produced a distribution rather similar to that of natural lesions, but sufficiently different to leave some unanswered questions. Thus, only 90% of right-handers showed left-hemisphere dominance, and 70% of left-handers had unilateral left-hemisphere dominance.

An anatomical basis for language laterality was demonstrated by Geschwind and Levitsky (1968) when they found that in 65% of adult brains Wernicke's area was larger on the left than on the right, while the corresponding region was larger on the right side in only 11% of adult brains. Here again, the difference in percentage from the evidence of aphasia-producing lesions has to be explained. Correlation with handedness is as yet unknown.

The most successful psychological laboratory technique for investigating lateralization of cortical functions is the method of dichotic listening, introduced by Kimura (1961). Simultaneous presentation of competing verbal information (digits) to the two ears results in superior report of right ear information. Kimura (1964) later showed that competing musical segments were better retained from the left ear. Studdert-Kennedy and Shankweiler (1970) compared competing vowels and competing consonants, finding that the lateralization of consonants was much more marked than that of vowels. Thus, it appears that the phonological components of speech may be differentially processed in the two hemispheres.

IV. THEORIES OF LANGUAGE REPRESENTATION

The literature on theories of aphasia includes a number of writers who dispute the multifactorial aspect of aphasia and, with it, the possibility of relating selective symptoms to site of lesion. Even more vehemently, they deny the further possibility of constructing a model of specialized centers and connecting pathways that would account for and predict the possible combinations of symptoms. The most important figures on the side of the holists are Jackson (1882), Marie (1926), and Head (1926). In the holistic tradition, Schuell and Jenkins (1959) reported that a factor analysis of aphasia test scores yielded a single overwhelming general language factor.

There are many elements in the test situation that tend to obscure the evidence for independently vulnerable components in aphasia. These obscuring factors are maximized when unselected, successive aphasic subjects are pooled in the sample, as in the study of Schuell and Jenkins. The bulk of the clinical material in such quantitative studies comes from vascular cases with large lesions, which implicate functionally diverse regions. Furthermore, the great majority of these cases have disease within the distribution of the middle cerebral artery. Even if it is true that the neural subsystems of language are selectively vulnerable at certain anatomical points, they are almost certainly intermingled in other areas of the cortex. Hence, the larger the lesion, the greater the number of functions affected. Furthermore, with respect to the collection of performance data, it is difficult to devise a single task that can be passed or failed through only one process. When, as in the study of Schuell and Jenkins, the test battery is weighted with a large number of complex speech production tasks, the contribution of a few "pure" tasks is lost in the variance that depends on scores derived from multiply determined tasks. As Luria (1970) points out, the emphasis on the treatment of language as a global psychological function forecloses the investigation of the brain mechanisms underlying normal and disturbed speech.

While it is uncommon to find aphasias that are extremely selective to one input or output modality (i.e., "pure"), the fact that well-described cases of pure phasia have repeatedly been reported has served as an impetus to the formulation of anatomic schemata of the cerebral language system. Such schemata were put forth by Charcot (1887) and by Bastian (1898), but the most influential has been that of Wernicke (1874). Wernicke's scheme depends on the primacy of an auditory language comprehension center (Wernicke's area), which functions both in the decoding of spoken messages and in the evocation of the acoustic model that guides the spoken output. This center is connected by a transcortical pathway to the anterior speech center (Broca's area), which controls the organs of speech. In Wernicke's theory, information from written symbols is transferred to Wernicke's area, where it is decoded into auditory form. Conversely, writing originates in acoustic form in Wernicke's area, and is then transmitted to the anterior speech center. This theory is consistent with the massive evidence that written language is encoded in acoustic form, as well as with the clinical observations that both reading and writing are damaged by lesions of Wernicke's area.

Rigorous support of Wernicke's theory requires, on the one hand, the identification of the anatomic pathways postulated and, on the other, the demonstration that lesions of the pathways between cortical centers produce distinctly different symptom pictures from those due to lesions of the centers alone.

The most dramatic support for Wernicke's theory comes from cases of injury to the interhemispheric connections, i.e., the corpus callosum or pathways to or from it. In these instances, a patient may be able to see the stimulus with his right hemisphere in the left visual field but not to read or name it (Gazzaniga & Sperry, 1967; Trescher & Ford, 1937). He may be able to recognize an object by touch, in his left hand, but unable to say what it is (Geschwind & Kaplan, 1962). He may be able to write with his right hand but produce gibberish with his left (Geschwind & Kaplan, 1962; Liepmann & Maas, 1907). These cases, in which the anatomical evidence has been well documented, make it clear that language depends on the transmission of information between the primary association areas and the language zones of the left hemisphere; further, that this information is conveyed over discrete neural pathways, whose injury produces a dissociation between the perceptual process and its linguistic elaboration.

The evidence for explaining syndromes through *intrahemispheric* disconnections between the language zones is less well established. One syndrome that seems to fit this requirement is called *"conduction aphasia,"* (see Section IV,D for details), attributed to the injury of the long fibre bundle (the arcuate fasciculus) connecting Broca's and Wernicke's areas. In theory, such a lesion should leave intact the fluency of articulation and auditory comprehension, while damaging selectively the ability to repeat auditorily presented stimuli. A syndrome displaying these features is recognized by many investigators, although the anatomical and behavioral interpretation of this disorder are still controversial at the present time.

Given the current obstacles to accepting a thoroughgoing anatomic–associationistic model of language, many writers consider it sufficient to correlate symptoms with language zones. Thus, Luria's (1970) fivefold system of aphasias is based on the concept of such cortical zones. Each of these zones is critical for one basic aspect of language, and injury within its boundaries results in a particular configuration of speech symptoms characteristic for that zone. The temporal or acoustic zone is virtually identical with the classical Wernicke's area, and the zone for "efferent motor aphasia" matches the classical Broca's area. Luria reports consistent evidence for a second, "afferent," form of motor aphasia, due to lesions at the foot of the primary somatosensory area. These correspond in lesion location, although there are some discrepancies in symptomatology, to the findings reported in conduction aphasia. The fourth zone is in the region anterior to Broca's area and its injury appears to affect the ability to initiate and shift ideas; thus, its manifestation in speech is in the form of an absence of spontaneous speech but retained ability to give short responses to specific stimuli. The fifth zone coincides approximately with the angular gyrus, and Luria acknowledges the aforementioned relation of reading and writing to lesions of this zone. However, for him, the basic process in this area is the perception of relationships—in the visual spatial, quantitative, logical, and grammatical spheres.

V. THE COMPONENTS OF APHASIA: CLINICAL, LINGUISTIC, AND EXPERIMENTAL APPROACHES

Clinically, the speech behavior of aphasic patients often follows one of several commonly observed forms, based on the particular cluster of deficits associated with a lesion site and on the characteristic adaptation of the individual to this configuration of defects. Nevertheless, the component deficits vary independently to such an extent that it is useful to regard them as potentially autonomous. In fact, they must be approached in this way when we go about examining the patient systematically. In this section, we step away from the patient as a whole performing organism, to look at his possible deficits one by one.

A. Articulation

Under the heading of articulation, we consider disturbances in the production of the codified gestures that constitute the standard phonemes of the speaker's language, with their normal allophonic variants, determined by the phonetic context. Articulatory disturbances, at their most severe, appear as a total inability to initiate or imitate the articulatory movements, even when shown how. When, as often is the case, the patient can count aloud or swear, we have dramatic evidence that this severe defect is not due to simple paralysis or ataxia of the speech organs but is a function of the linguistic context. However, even such automatic utterances as counting or swearing may be absent at the beginning.

As the patient begins to recover, various subtypes of articulatory difficulty become manifest. He may show groping oral movements, as he attempts to zero in on each sound and in this way express himself laboriously and haltingly. This type of patient benefits little from the opportunity to repeat after the examiner. His prosody is reduced to word by word recitation. More typically, patients recover facile articulation for an increasing repertory of common words and stereotyped phrases, while continuing to articulate awkwardly, with distortions and substitutions of phonemes in other, less common words. This type of patient is greatly aided by the opportunity for repetition. Both types of patients may eventually recover to the point where most of their speech is easily produced, with only occasional articulatory slips.

In both of these varieties of aphasia, the breakdown, from the linguistic point of view, is at the phonetic level. They contrast with a higher level of phonological disorder, in which the elementary phonemes and phonemic sequences up to the syllabic level are easily produced. In this latter defect, the selection and ordering of phonemes is disturbed but the elementary articulatory components are intact. The first two disorders have been termed *phonetic disintegration* by Alajouanine (1956), and the latter, *phonemic disintegration*. The disorder of phonemic sequencing is referred to by the French writers as *"aphasie de la première articulation,"* as opposed to phonetic disintegration, which is *"aphasie de la seconde articulation."* This refers to the fact that the phonetic level is the final stage of organization before motor execution.

Even though the patient with phonetic or phonemic disintegration may produce automatized or exclamatory utterances normally, it is easy to be misled into attributing his disorder to the impaired control of oral movements that can often be demonstrated for nonverbal acts. Thus, the aphasic may be unable to blow, sip, cough, or lick his lips to command, demonstrating a facial *apraxia* (loss of purposeful movements without elementary motor disturbance). In fact, facial apraxia is most often seen in these patients. However, facial apraxia may exist with normal articulation and praxis may be normal with impaired articulation. Thus, it seems unreasonable to assign a causal relation to the nonverbal praxic disorder. Rather, the verbal and nonverbal defects are probably related through the contiguity of the brain structures subserving them.

Articulatory disorders of the phonetic type are associated primarily with injury at or near Broca's area and represent an almost invariable feature of the syndrome of Broca's aphasia. In fact, Luria (1970) emphasizes that the lesion of Broca's area is specifically associated with the second of the two forms described above, i.e., the variety in which the patient recovers the articulation of familiar words and phrases, but remains deficient in both articulation and grammar when longer sequential speech acts are required. He sees this problem as the verbal manifestation of a general characteristic of injuries to the premotor zone. These lesions, in his view, primarily affect the execution of organized sequential movements, not of elementary acts of positioning. A phoneme embedded in a word is part of a complex articulatory sequence, but this complexity increases enormously with the length of the sequence. Like all disorders of higher cortical processes, the articulatory aspect of aphasia is dependent on the overlearned or automatized nature of the act.

Of the leading aphasiologists, Luria is the only one to ascribe a post-Rolandic lesions locus to a form of a motor aphasia with primarily articulatory features. We are now referring to the patient who indulges in oral groping behavior and must be painfully retaught to articulate, sound by sound. These patients make many errors due to improper differentiation of the place of articulation. Luria believes that the sensory structures that are injured are particulatly important for the spatial organization of motor movements and that, even though post-Rolandic, they form an essential part of the motor speech apparatus.

Because of the motoric nature of this disorder and its close analogy, in the sphere of language performance, to the apraxia of oral movements, a number of writers have chosen to refer to it as "apractic aphasia." The term "apraxia of speech" is now widely used among American speech pathologists. The present authors prefer to restrict the term "apraxia" to disorders of purposeful movements of a nonlinguistic nature and to assign the term "aphasia" to behavioral defects that vary as a function of their linguistic nature. By the latter criterion, "apractic aphasia" becomes an internally contradictory term.

B. Linguistic Studies

Systematic studies of articulatory errors by motor aphasics date back to Boumann and Grünbaum's (1925) and Ombredane's (1927) studies of single patients. In 1939, Alajouanine, Ombredane, and Durand carried out a similar but more extensive study of four patients with the syndrome of phonetic disintegration. These writers emphasized that there were systematic tendencies in the sound confusions of these patients, but that these could not be given the status of unvarying rules. Among these tendencies are the shift in consonants from voiced to voiceless, from nasal to oral, and from spirant to stop. The influence of the phonetic environment is noted, in the form of anticipations of later consonants and assimilation to earlier consonants, /komãse/ → /komãke/.

One of the first theoretical linguists to write in this area was Roman Jakobson (1941), who emphasized the parallels between the order of dissolution of phonemic distinctions in aphasia, their order of appearance in child language, and their universality in languages of the world. Jakobson postulated an order of acquisition of consonants in which each successive stage presupposed the mastery of the preceding one. In essence this sequence is:

1. labial–dental stops
2. front–back stops
3. fricatives
4. affricates
5. laterals and resonants.

Shankweiler and Harris (1966), however, found little parallel between the sounds most difficult for aphasics and those failed by children. In this, they supported earlier observations by D. B. Fry (1959).

Blumstein (1973), working in the framework of Jakobson's concepts of *distinctive features* and of *markedness* found that both of these theoretical constructs had predictive value in determining the direction of articulatory errors in aphasia. Aphasics make many more substitutions of consonants that vary by a single distinctive feature from their target than they do of consonants that differ by two or more distinctive features. Thus, the substitution of /t/ for /d/ (differing in voicing only) is much more likely than the substitution of /t/ for /b/ (differing in both voicing and place of articulation). Furthermore, the *unmarked* or more basic member of a contrasting consonant pair is more stable than the marked form. Thus, voicing and nasality as consonant marking features are more often lost than gained. A particularly interesting feature of Blumstein's results is that the *direction* of errors is equally consistent in Broca's aphasics (phonetic disintegration) conduction aphasics (phonemic disintegration), and Wernicke aphasics, who exhibit very few articulatory errors but, rather, chiefly manifest phonemic substitutions.

C. Word Finding

Virtually all aphasics have some reduction in the repertory of words available for speech and require more time than normal to produce words in response to pictures or questions. Usually, the frequent words of the language are the first to recover, and have the shortest response latency. When, as in the severe Broca's aphasic, extreme poverty of vocabulary is seen in a context of laborious articulation and absent syntax, word-finding difficulty may appear to be merely one aspect of a general restriction of language. However, the autonomy of disorders of word finding emerges dramatically in a group of patients with lesions in the Wernicke and angular gyrus regions, who show a surprising absence of substantive words, while their fluency in articulation and grammar is virtually unimpaired. This selective loss of lexical words—primarily nouns, but verbs, adjectives, and adverbs as well—is called *anomia*. The form of aphasia in which it is the predominant symptom is *anomic* or *amnesic* aphasia. As seen in anomic aphasia, the symptom takes the form of fluent, but rambling and uninformative, speech sometimes called "empty speech." There are many indefinites, such as "thing" in place of nouns, or "do" in place of specific verbs. The ability to name objects or pictures is correspondingly poor, as the patient makes such comments as "I know what it is, I use it to do my . . . I have one right here. . . ." While most anomic patients quickly recognize the target word when it is offered, some fail to do so, as though they have a two-way dissociation between the concept and its acoustic representation.

Clinical impression suggests that word-finding difficulty is an inclusive term for several qualitatively different defects that are not distinguished by ordinary naming tests. Thus, the patient who appears to have dissociated the sound from the concept gives a very different impression from the patient who is slow but sure or the patient who acts convincingly as though he has recovered the inner sound of the word but has trouble in recovering the articulatory movements for it.

Goldstein (1948) describes a particular type of word-finding difficulty that he terms "amnesic aphasia" and which he attributes to an underlying defect in the "abstract attitude." He interprets the patient's behavior as a basic loss of the orientation to words as symbols that stand for concepts. While these cases present clinically the typical pattern of "empty," circumlocutory speech, they show in addition a striking inability to grasp the idea of searching for a particular word, but react to the word-finding task by commenting on the object with whatever associations come to mind. These patients are particularly poor in understanding abstract concepts and fail conspicuously in sorting objects or colors by category. There is some question as to whether Goldstein's "amnesic aphasia" is not a simple anomic aphasia combined with an intellectual deficit of a type often seen in brain-injured patients and well described by Goldstein and Scheerer (1941) as loss of the "abstract attitude." Certainly, this intellectual deficit is often seen without any associated word-finding difficulty, but it may well modify the patient's adaptation to a coexisting aphasic deficit.

Word-finding difficulty as a manifestation of disconnection of the sensory input to the language areas may appear as a sense modality-specific disorder. Freund (1889) described a case of "optic aphasia," in which objects recognized visually could nevertheless not be named until they were picked up and handled. A similar phenomenon has been demonstrated by Gazzaniga and Spe y (1967) after transection of the corpus callosum, including the splenium. Under these conditions, objects experienced in the left visual field and transmitted to the right hemisphere are isolated from the language area and cannot be named, although they can be selected by touch with the left hand. Modality-specific tactile aphasic limited to the left hand has also been demonstrated by Geschwind and Kaplan (1962) in a patient with callosal disconnection, a finding duplicated in the callosally transected patients of Sperry and his co-workers.

D. Anatomical Features

To the extent that there is uncertainty concerning the number of mechanisms for word-finding difficulty, there is corresponding doubt as to specific localizations (except in the case of the modality-specific disconnection aphasias described above). Typical anomic aphasias have been reported with brain tumors remote from the language areas, suggesting that word-finding is sensitive to raised intracranial pressure, without the necessity of a discrete structural lesion. As we have observed, word-finding difficulty compounded with articulatory problems is produced by lesions of the anterior speech area. When *isolated* word finding difficulty is associated with a discrete lesion, this lesion is almost always in the temporal or temporo-parietal area. Luria (1970) reports that the form of anomia that involves a two-way dissociation of sound from meaning is a feature of lesions in the inferior temporal lobe, involving the posterior portions of the first and second temporal convolutions.

E. Psycholinguistic Research

The vocabulary of the Broca's aphasic, even though reduced by his word-finding difficulty appears to be relatively well supplied with concrete or picturable nouns and verbs. These are sparser in the output of the anomic speech of the amnesic or Wernicke aphasia. Wepman, Bock, Jones, and Van Pelt (1956), after examining the word frequency distribution of anomic patients, felt that this disorder was not related to part of speech at all. Rather, they found an overuse of high-frequency words of all form classes in the speech of these patients. However, close examination of their data indicates that the effect of this word frequency shift is much greater for nouns than other words. Goodglass, Hyde, and Blumstein (1969) found that Broca's and fluent (Wernicke and anomic) aphasics did indeed differ in the proportion of picturable to nonpicturable nouns used but only in the highest-frequency range. Fluent aphasics use many more nonpicturable words that occur idiomatically, but without much informational value, in their free-flowing speech. Broca's aphasics have an equal overuse of frequent nouns, but these include more words of specific concrete reference.

There is even stronger evidence that word-finding is a function of the semantic category of the words involved. Goldstein (1948) had noted that numbers were sometimes exempted from the difficulty experienced in naming nouns. Goodglass, Klein, Carey, and Jones (1966) examined the order of difficulty of object names, body parts, actions, colors, numbers, and letters, in a test in which the patient was asked either to name a visual stimulus or to choose the correct visual stimulus in response to the spoken name. Objects were most often the hardest category, and letters most often the easiest category, to name. In auditory comprehension this relationship was however, reversed, eliminating the possibility of a simple explanation in terms of word frequency. The greatest discrepancies among semantic categories were observed in anomic patients, who had much less difficulty naming numbers and letters than they did naming objects or body parts. Patients with the Broca's speech pattern had little variability in naming. The authors conjectured that the disparity in phonological information between letters and numbers places a greater information encoding load on the speaker for numbers, but a greater load for decoding on the listener for letters.

Selective naming disturbance for colors has been reported repeatedly (e.g., Geschwind & Fusillo, 1966) in patients with the disconnection syndrome of "pure" word blindness. In this disorder, the left hemisphere visual area is disabled, while at the same time the callosal connection with right-hemisphere vision is interrupted. Colors, like written language, appear to be particularly vulnerable because their linguistic representation is associated exclusively with visual experience. In this respect they differ from objects, since the latter arouse associations in nonvisual modalities. Hence, visual object aphasia (Freund, 1889) is very rare.

The occurrence of occasional cases of sense modality-specific naming disorders led Spreen, Benton, and Van Allen (1966) to compare tactile and visual naming in a series of 21 patients. Three of these had significantly more errors in naming by touch than by vision, but for the overwhelming majority, difficulty was equivalent in both modalities. No significant differences in patients' ability to name in response to visual, auditory, tactile, and olfactory stimulation were found by Goodglass, Barton, and Kaplan (1968).

Another factor in the naming process is amount of information in the sensory input. Bisiach (1966) reported that obscuring the drawing of an object with extraneous lines reduced the ability of aphasics to name, even though recognition by multiple choice selection was intact. North (1971) similarly found that minimally blurred pictures, or objects presented tactually, wrapped in thin foam rubber, could not be named as well as could unblurred stimuli, even though all could be recognized by multiple choice. Blurred information presented simultaneously to both modalities was more effective than one blurred modality. These data suggest that multimodal concepts in the dominant hemisphere can be activated by any sensory modality. A greater level of concept activation is required for naming than for object recognition.

F. Auditory Comprehension

Auditory comprehension must be examined in terms of the level of linguistic organization at which failure occurs. Thus, the levels of phoneme discrimination, recognition of the whole word as a familiar linguistic element and semantic association to the word, are most consistently related to temporal lobe lesions. Other relevant dimensions of auditory comprehension are the appreciation of logico-syntactic relationships, which is more vulnerable to parietal lobe lesions, and the restriction of span and complexity.

There is a small group of patients who behave as though they do not recognize the ensemble of sounds that compose a word spoken to them, although their hearing and ability to identify various environmental noises is intact. These are the *pure word deaf*. Like the hard-of-hearing, they may ask for many repetitions, or misinterpret a word on the basis of a well-perceived fragment. The distinctive feature in this disorder is that when repeated presentation finally permits them to grasp and repeat the sounds of the word as a whole, comprehension is instantaneous. Pure word deafness thus involves no disturbance at the semantic level, and it is doubtful that it can be explained at the level of discrimination of individual phonemes. These patients may have virtually normal speech and written language. The anatomical basis for this disorder is believed to be disconnection of the outputs of both primary auditory centers from an intact Wernicke's area.

The most common form of comprehension disorder is that which follows injury to the temporal speech zones—Wernicke's area. Here, the inability to make a semantic association to the perceived sounds is the primary problem. The patient may repeat a test word without comprehending it any better than before. Moreover, it can easily be shown that the breakdown of comprehension is primarily along semantic lines, since patients usually grasp the class to which the target word belongs, without being able to specify the item. Thus, given the opportunity to respond to the word "green" by selecting from an array of objects, colors, and numbers, the patient usually chooses a color, but the wrong color. In response to "ear," he will point to some part of his face; in response to "ankle," he will reach toward his leg, but not exactly to his ankle.

The clinical speech behavior of these patients includes certain features that are probably secondary to their loss of comprehension. While their speech output may be fluent, it includes many wrong words, which the patients do not detect (paraphasic speech). They often seem unable to bring their sentences to an end and continue talking as though lacking the sense of closure from a completed thought.

The response of these patients to length and complexity is sometimes paradoxical, since a single word out of context may be more difficult to understand than a sentence. However, on closer analysis the critical feature appears to be the ratio of information given to information to be extracted. Thus, a descriptive sentence focusing on a single term may be superior to the word alone, because it supplies a number of connotative clues (e.g., "Show me the prickly cactus that grows in the desert." versus "Show me 'cactus' "). A sentence of similar length requiring discrimination and comprehension of relationships between several concepts is much more difficult.

While we have emphasized the semantic level of comprehension loss, phonemic discrimination is also more impaired in these patients than in other types of aphasia and word deafness, i.e., total nonrecognition of the word–sound sequence is part of the picture in severely impaired patients with Wernicke's aphasia.

G. Psycholinguistic Research

The role of impaired phoneme discrimination has been given primary importance in temporal lobe aphasia by Luria. We believe this is present, but not severe enough to contribute significantly to the clinical disorder. Nevertheless experimental data cited by Luria show convincingly that patients with temporal lesions fail to form conditioned responses based on discrimination between phonemes that differ in only one feature (e.g., /p/ versus /b/).

A recent study by Harris (1970) compared several groups of aphasics in their phonemic discrimination errors. Those who had been classified clinically as having "intermittent auditory imperception" made almost twice as many phonemic discrimination errors as the rest of the aphasic population (7% versus 4%). The disparity in the performance of this subgroup was contributed to disproportionately by stimuli presented monaurally to the right ear, and much of this difference is due to a tendency to choose an acoustically unrelated foil, i.e., it is due to an increase in essentially random choices to the right ear stimuli. It must be pointed out, however, that the total percentage of errors in the most impaired aphasic group was not overwhelming, considering that the stimuli were consonant–vowel–consonant (CVC) words chosen so as to maximize the likelihood of a phonemic misperception. The opportunity for such confusion occurs rarely in ordinary speech, again suggesting that phonemic confusion plays but a small role in the comprehension disorder of temporal lobe aphasia.

H. Disturbances of Syntax

Disturbances in grammar and syntax fall into two clinically distinctive categories. One involves the loss of relational and inflectional terms and the fragmentation of grammatical structure. The other involves confusions of inflectional and other small grammatical terms and the "spoiling" of grammar by the juxtaposition of semantically incongruous sentence components. The first, in which there is impoverishment and simplification of grammatical forms, is called *agrammatism* and is a by-product of lesions of the anterior speech area. The second form, called *paragrammatism* is one of the features of Wernicke's aphasia and related to temporal lobe lesions.

In this section we are concerned with agrammatism, in which there appears to be a loss of the ability to express grammatical relationships, in spite of the relative availability of a vocabulary of lexical words that can be used singly or juxtaposed with a minimum of structure. At the most severe levels of agrammatism, speech is limited to one-word sentences composed chiefly of nouns. The following extract of agrammatic speech represents the patient's effort to explain that he came into the hospital for dental surgery:

> Yes . . . ah . . . Monday . . er . . . Dad and Peter H . . . . (his own name), and Dad . . . er . . . hospital . . . and ah . . . Wednesday . . . . Wednesday, nine o'clock . . . and oh . . . Thursday . . . ten o'clock, ah doctors . . . two . . . an' doctors . . . . and er . . . teeth . . . yah.

Contrast this disconnected chain of substantive ideas with the paragrammatical, fluent, but empty speech of an anomic aphasic, who says: "The things I want to say . . . ah . . . the way I say things, but I understand mostly things, most of them and what the things are."

As the agrammatic patient improves, we first hear verb–object combinations, adverbial expressions of time ("one year ago") and eventually complete simple declarative sentences. Subordinating conjunctions are rare, and the relationship between clauses is expressed by simple juxtaposition, sometimes with the conjunction "and." For example, a patient expressing the idea that his mother died six months after his fifteenth birthday said, "My mother died . . . uh . . . me . . . uh, fifteen uh . . . oh, I guess, six month . . . . my mother pass away."

It has been argued by some that agrammatism is an artifact, resulting from the motor aphasic's voluntary economy of effort. Because it is so difficult for him to emit speech, the argument goes, he reduces his utterance to the essential words. It is true that, for some patients, partial improvement is possible when they are urged to make a complete sentence and when their omissions are pointed out. However, such improvement rarely extends beyond supplying an omitted copula or article. Careful clinical observation shows that the theory of economy of effort is untenable. The patients often struggle with repeated self-corrections, in order to make their output approximate standard English, without succeeding. Obviously their recognition of what sounds correct considerably exceeds their productive ability.

Agrammatism is a more conspicuous phenomenon in a highly inflected language, such as German, than it is in English, and cross-language comparisons are instructive. For example, English-speaking agrammatics typically use the unmarked verb, or the present participle in place of the verb marked for person and tense (e.g., "Tomorrow, go home" or "Tomorrow goin' home" for "I will go home tomorrow"). This raises the question as to whether the patient has merely omitted an auxiliary or has nominalized the verb, by using the infinitive or the gerund. The German-speaking agrammatic, however, in these circumstances often uses the infinitive (e.g., *"gehen"*) in place of the properly inflected form. Since the German infinitive, unlike the English, has an inflectional ending, this evidence supports the view that the agrammatic indeed is not merely dropping the person and tense markers in English, but rather shifting to a nominalized use of the verb. Indeed one of the features of the early stages of recovery from agrammatism is the paucity of verbs, especially the copula. Thus we hear "Wife and me . . . coffee," where the concept of drinking is included in the noun object.

Jakobson (1956) was the first of the linguists to attempt a theoretical interpretation of agrammatism, to which he assigned the label *contiguity disorder*. This is an inclusive concept by which he refers not only to the sequential juxtaposition of words in syntax but to the motoric sequencing of phonemes within a word. Jakobson's formulation of the deficits of contiguity disorder are very much in accord with our above observations: They include:

1. Reduction in the variety of sentences;
2. Loss of ties of grammatical coordination and subordination;
3. Loss of inflectional endings and of words endowed with purely grammatical functions, such as conjunctions, prepositions, pronouns, and articles.

I. Psycholinguistic Research on Agrammatism

Studies by Goodglass and collaborators (Goodglass, 1968; Goodglass, Berko, Bernholtz, & Hyde, 1972; Goodglass, Fodor, & Schulhoff, 1967; Goodglass & Hunt, 1958; Goodglass & Mayer, 1958) have attempted to define the operations that distinguish between the fluent paragrammatic speech pattern and the true agrammatism associated with anterior lesions. The most suggestive finding is that the agrammatic patient depends on a stressed or phonologically salient word in order to initiate an utterance. Thus the negative interrogative auxiliary in "Don't birds fly?" which is stressed, is better preserved than the unstressed simple interrogative auxiliary "do." Similarly, the stressed "Wh-" interrogative adverbs represent one of the best-recovered syntactic elements. Unstressed grammatical words are dropped in initial position but almost never omitted when they fall between two stressed words, e.g., "The open door" versus "Open the door" (Goodglass *et al.,* 1967).

Indeed we observe that agrammatics frequently adopt compensatory devices to overcome their difficulty in constructions that normally open with an unstressed word, e.g., the subject pronoun. One such patient, unable to begin a sentence with "he," repeated the target sentence "He works here" as "This guy works here."

Studies of English inflectional morphology show that all aphasics find the plural morpheme "s" much easier to produce than the morphologically identical possessive "s" or the "s" of the verbal third person singular. This corresponds to the sequence of children's acquisition of these forms. However, some characteristics of agrammatic speech reverse the order of difficulty observed in children. For example, the syllabic variants of the final "s" and final "d" (as in "hors*es*," "nurs*e's*," "watch*es*," and "wait*ed*") are more often retained than the nonsyllabic variants ("book*s*," "boy'*s*," "play*s*," and "play*ed*"). Here too, it is conjectured, the salience of the extra syllable makes it more available to the agrammatic patient.

J. Paraphasia

Paraphasia refers to the production of unintended phonemes, words, or word sequences during the effort to speak. It may predominate on the phonological level, in the form of sound transpositions, substitutions, or intrusions (*phonemic* or *literal paraphasia*). At the lexical level it refers to the substitution of wrong words—usually nouns or verbs. In running discourse, paraphasia may take the form of semantic nonsequiturs, in which grammatically organized sequences are juxtaposed without completing a sensible thought. Completely neologistic words may appear either as one-word responses or in the course of running speech. While all varieties of aphasics produce some forms of paraphasia, Wernicke's aphasics often produce all of them, and resulting output is called "paraphasic jargon" or "jargonaphasia."

This example of paraphasic jargon is from a patient's description of a scene in which two children are stealing cookies while the mother's back is turned:

> Well this is . . . mother is away here working her work out o'here to get her better, but when she's looking, the two boys looking in the other part. One their small tile into her time here. She's working another time because she's getting, too . . . .

Because of its multiple forms and levels of linguistic organization, it is difficult to conceive that paraphasia represents the failure of a single mechanism. It would appear that one mechanism, damaged in temporal lobe disease, involves selection and inhibition of associations which, if unchecked, allow the speech output system to run on unrestricted, producing nonsense. The impaired comprehension of the temporal lobe patient seems to be responsible for his often uncritical acceptance of paraphasic speech. However, this relationship is not absolute; there are patients who are paraphasic in spite of good comprehension and vice versa.

K. Determinants of Paraphasic Utterances

Verbal paraphasias, although most common in Wernicke's aphasia, occur in aphasics of all types. They usually involve the misnaming of objects with a word related in sphere. Thus "my wife" may become "my mother," "tomorrow" may become "yesterday," "a wallet" may become "a purse." Some patients have a recurring word that takes the position of the noun in all their sentences. Thus, one patient's empty paraphasic speech went: "Well I had that in one department, then they took me to another department . . . and they did that department . . . etc." Another patient used the word "automobile" in much the same way.

The relation between the paraphasic output and the target may be totally capricious and confabulatory, e.g., "Brazilian clothes-bag" for a cross and "beer can thing" for a metal ashtray. While such arbitrary paraphasias may occur with Wernicke's aphasia, they are uncommon.

Literal, or phonemic paraphasias are similar to the spoonerisms of everyday speech, although they involve more than the transposition of initial sounds. While they occur frequently in Wernicke's aphasia, their occurrence does not appear to be related to impaired comprehension. Literal paraphasias are common in Broca's aphasia and may be the unique expressive disturbance in conduction aphasia.

In the following examples from the speech of a conduction aphasic, the typical self-corrective efforts to cope with his frequent literal paraphasias are conspicuous:

> (What is your address?) Seventy Humfoldt Way, Ray . . . (for 'Humboldt Way') Marmel . . . Marble . . . hay . . . hay (for 'Marblehead') Massachusetts."
>
> (How did you get into the hospital?) Well my doctor called them up and I had to have sexes . . . that's sess and I had plenty of them. (Plenty of what?) Sex. That's sesx. Y-E-S-T-S. -sesx. Plenty of sest . . . tex (Tests?) Tests, that's right.
>
> (Were you sick, or what?) Well the first time I know, I had a piece of pa . . . paker like that and I rock . . . I locked the paper on the floor.

(You're retired?) But I do a fishing lies . . . ries . . . (for "I tie flies')
and also make rods (Flies?) No . . . that's right. Rie . . . rils . . . flials.
E-L-Y-S. (Flies?) Flies, that's right.

The important feature to be noted in these literal paraphasic errors is
that the elementary phoneme sequences are well-produced English syllables—but with an incorrect choice and sequence of phonemes. In this, they
differ from the distorted, awkward phonemes of articulatory impairment.

As reported earlier, Blumstein (1973) found that the direction of consonant substitutions in literal paraphasia could be explained in terms of preference for shifting by no more than one distinctive feature and for going
from the marked to the unmarked member of a distinctive feature pair.
In this respect, literal paraphasic errors follow the same rules as substitutions caused by impaired articulation.

L. Reading

Disturbances in reading, of some degree, are found in the overwhelming
majority of aphasic patients. The diverse nature and severity of these disorders has yielded some knowledge of the organization of the brain for
this complex process and, coincidentally, some awareness of the psychological operations that enter into it and that may be selectively impaired.
Yet this understanding is still relatively superficial.

Rather than attack the poorly understood process of how reading ability
develops in the child, we will analyze the stages of reading as they appear
to be operating in the individual who has already mastered this skill and
who may suffer brain injury.

The reading process obviously starts with the perception and discrimination of the elements of the written code and the recognition that they belong
to the class of letters, words, numerals, or other categories of symbols.
This is a prelinguistic level of reading, and disturbances here are found only
in the relatively rare instances of visual agnosia—caused by injury, usually
bilaterally, of the visual association areas, with impaired recognition of
visual configurations of all types, including objects and faces.

Beyond this level, a number of elementary processes appear to be operating concurrently. These are: (1) the appreciation of the separate identi-
ties of the letters, their equivalence across various styles of print and script,
and the association of the verbal labels to the letters; (2) the arousal of
direct conceptual associations to whole words as ideographs; (3) the
arousal of auditory associations to words, on the basis of phonetic decoding
of the letter values or of the phonetic translation of familiar syllables. In
the case of common words, the auditory association may be aroused directly

by the configuration of the whole word and, in turn, arouse the corresponding concept.

The evidence, both from aphasia and from studies of normal reading, suggests that the phonetic or auditory decoding process is dominant in readers of alphabetic languages, such as English, in which the written language maps the phonemic structure of speech. The direct ideographic arousal of concepts, without phonetic intermediation, is probably at a primitive level in the average reader. However, the ideographic level of word recognition is sometimes preserved in aphasia when the phonetic level is totally lost.

All of these elementary associations to the written code appear to depend, first of all, on the integrity of the angular gyrus region of the left hemisphere and its input from the visual association areas. Damage to this system also prevents the patient from understanding words spelled orally to him and from understanding, through the tactile sense, letters drawn on his palm.

However, reading rarely escapes intact from a lesion in any part of the language area. Slowness in recognizing words or in grasping the meaning of complex passages, failure to understand grammatical terms, and misperceptions of words may be seen, even in Broca's aphasia, where the lesion is remote from the angular gyrus. It has been suggested that the reader who premorbidly depended on subvocal reading is the most vulnerable to reading impairment secondary to a lesion of the anterior speech area. By the same token, highly literate individuals are often thought to be unlikely to suffer severe reading disturbance with anterior lesions.

M. Clinical Manifestations of Alexia

In its most severe form, alexia prevents even the recognition of letters by name or the ability to match across styles of script and print. Except for the comparatively rare cases of "pure alexia" it is invariably accompanied by a writing disturbance of comparable severity. Even the most severely impaired patients, however, can usually copy slavishly in the same style (block printing or longhand) as the model presented and, at milder levels, transcribe from printing to longhand. In most cases, the ability to recognize and name letters recovers before the ability to recognize words: yet, paradoxically, there are cases (literal alexia) in which oral word-reading and even some comprehension of connected text is possible without the ability to name letters aloud.

It can also be shown that many patients who cannot select a written word on either oral or pictorial presentation can pick out a word that is foreign to a list of related words (e.g., a fruit from a list of animals).

Similarly, patients may misname a written word with another from the same class (e.g., "blue" for "green"), where there is no structural similarity between stimulus and response. Both of these phenomena illustrate the direct arousal of semantic associations, without the intermediary of phonetic decoding.

However, most reading errors are based on partial recognition and confusion of words or letters of similar structure. This is demonstrated when patients are required either to read words aloud or to select them from similar-looking alternatives. Even when individual nouns, verbs, and adjectives are well understood, patients frequently exhibit confusion between the various common prepositions and personal pronouns. Confusion between "for" "by" and "to," for example, makes it difficult for the patient to grasp the grammatical sense of a written message even when the lexical words are recognized.

The comprehension of connected text, then, may be impeded by problems at many levels, not the least being slowness to grasp semantic relationships between parts of a sentence, even when all the elements can be recognized.

Oral reading must be clearly distinguished from reading comprehension, since whatever problems encumber the patient's speech may be reflected in his oral reading, without a corresponding effect on comprehension. Thus the patient with agrammatism omits the grammatical particles; the anomic may unexpectedly fail, in the midst of fluent reading, to recall the sound of a word that he can paraphrase.

N. Pure Word Blindness

Pure word blindness takes the form of a severe inability to interpret letter sequences visually. Orally spelled words are perfectly understood. Often, the recognition of individual letters is spared and, in these cases, 'reading' is possible by painstaking silent spelling, one letter at a time. Similarly, the reading of words drawn on the palm of the hand is usually intact. Number recognition is usually spared completely or relatively and, paradoxically, the very letters that cannot be grasped as parts of words are sometimes promptly understood in the form of roman numerals. The underlying lesion for this disorder was first demonstrated by Déjerine (1892) to involve destruction of the visual cortex of the left hemisphere, while, at the same time, the fibers carrying visual information across from the right hemisphere are damaged in the splenium of the corpus callosum.

By similar logic, one can predict that interruption of fibers in the splenium alone will produce alexia in the left visual field, since there is no way in which this right-hemisphere visual information can be decoded linguistically. Indeed, the syndrome of "hemialexia" has been reported repeatedly (Gazzaniga & Sperry, 1967; Maspes, 1948; Trescher & Ford, 1937).

O. Writing Disorders

Virtually all aphasics (except for the rare cases of pure word deafness and pure word blindness) have a writing disturbance, that is generally more severe than their speech defect. Analogously to speech, writing may be disturbed: (1) at the level of its mechanics—impaired recall of the movements required for forming letters, even in direct copying; (2) at the level of symbol recall—inability to recall how to write individual letters or how to spell familiar words on dictation; or (3) at the level of language formulation, i.e., word finding and sentence organization.

The fact that writing suffers with every variety of aphasia is perhaps evidence that all of the components of the language system participate in its mediation. Writing (except in the congenitally deaf) is oral language recoded into a visually learned, graphic system. Thus, agraphia of the most severe degree—impairing the recall of letter formation—may be seen with aphasias arising from Broca's area, from Wernicke's area, and together with alexia, from angular gyrus lesions. There is some dispute as to whether pure agraphia, as an isolated variety of aphasia, exists. The German neurologist, Exner, believed that it could be produced by a lesion of the motor association area adjacent to the representation of the hand in the motor cortex. This has not been confirmed by subsequent reports. Writing has been observed to be the first language function to be lost in organic confusional states, when it can deteriorate even to illegible scrawls, while spoken language remains intact.

The naive observer and sometimes the patient himself mistakenly attribute the loss of writing to paralysis of the former writing hand, which often accompanies aphasia. However, the incapacity of the left hand for writing is far beyond what can be explained by awkwardness. In fact, total agraphia may be present with a Wernicke's area or angular gyrus lesion, neither of which produces a corresponding weakness of the right hand.

Total agraphia, however, is not the rule with aphasia. It is in the incomplete forms of the disorder that we find interesting parallels with the character of the patient's oral language. As in the case of speech, the easiest and first recovered levels of performance are direct copying and the writing of memorized sequences, such as one's name and address. These are the prepropositional levels of writing.

Patients with agraphia produced by parietal lobe lesions may show a persistent inability even to copy letters slavishly, in conjunction with a generalized inability to reproduce any sort of geometric configuration. In other cases, a profound agraphia at the level of symbol formation is dissociated from any disturbance in copying forms. Thus, a patient of Nielsen's (1946) could not copy any figure that he perceived as falling into the class of numbers, although he could perfectly well reproduce geometric forms closely similar in shape. Typically, in the recovery of spelling, patients correctly reproduce the first letter of a target word but omit or confuse the order of subsequent letters. At this stage, one sometimes discovers that a patient can spell orally quite well but cannot guide his written production by his oral knowledge.

At milder levels of aphasia, some capacity for the writing of connected discourse may be present, and here we see considerable resemblance to the pattern of the patient's speech. The agrammatic patient typically omits grammatical particles and inflections, both on dictation and in free composition. The fluent paraphasic patient may produce a rambling, repetitious output, with neologistic words and meaningless juxtapositions of phrases, i.e., written paraphasic jargon. An illustration of such writing by a Wernicke aphasic appears in Fig. 3.

Goodglass and Hunter (1970) suggested that differences between the spoken and written output of the same patient could be explained by the relative slowness of the writing process, its consequent greater demand on memory for what has gone before, and the absence of the prosodic structure, which, in speech, continuously provides cues for the positioning of the small grammatical words.

P. Propositionality

Hughlings Jackson, noting that aphasics could often swear fluently or recite memorized sequences, observed that they had not lost their memory for words but, rather, the ability to use them to convey information, or "propositionize." Propositional and nonpropositional speech were two poles of a continuum, the former on a higher psychological level. The persistence of interjectional or automatized utterances in patients with severe left-hemisphere damage led Jackson to postulate that these primitive forms of language can be subserved by the right hemisphere, which is not, however, capable of propositional speech.

The observed general order of difficulty of tasks within a particular modality, e.g. speech, suggests that this order can be partially explained in terms of the degree of overdetermination of the behavior by the cues in the situation. Overdetermination may be a function of repeated practice of an exclusive stimulus–response sequence (naming of letters, reciting memorized sequences). It may be due to the provision of a model for im-

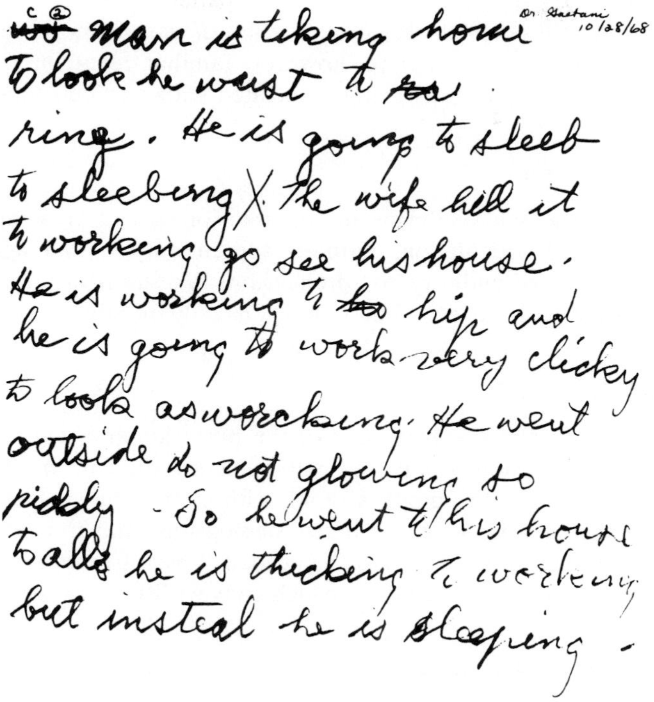

FIG. 3. Sample of writing by a patient with Wernicke's aphasia.

mediate reproduction (as in repetition). It may be in the form of an incomplete overlearned sequence ("Roses are red, violets are . . . ."). Self-initiation of language falls at the high-difficulty end of this hierarchy, while reactive speech, i.e., answering in response to a specific stimulus falls in between.

Goldstein's concept of abstract behavior, as applied to aphasia is virtually identical to propositionality. However, Goldstein holds that the act of naming an object makes a particular demand on abstract behavior, thus giving rise to his concept of "amnesic aphasia" as a manifestation of concrete behavior in language.

VI. SYNDROMES OF APHASIA

Many patients with aphasia have suffered extensive lesions involving both the anterior and posterior speech zones. If our acquaintance with the problem were limited to such cases, we would infer that language is an indivisible function of the brain, since these patients suffer severe impairment in all modalities. With the accumulation of data from more selective lesions within the left hemisphere, however, familiar recurring clusters of symptoms were recognized as being associated with particular lesion sites.

A. Broca's Aphasia

Broca's aphasia is a syndrome of the anterior speech area, marked by effortful, distorted articulation, reduced speech output, and agrammatic syntax but sparing of auditory comprehension. Writing is usually impaired commensurately with speech, but reading is only mildly disturbed.

B. Wernicke's Aphasia

Wernicke's aphasia is a syndrome of the posterior first temporal gyrus. Auditory comprehension is impaired, while fluency and ease of articulation are spared. While speech output is rapid, with many long syntactic strings, it is replete with errors of word choice, neologisms, and transpositions of sounds. The patient, unable to find the needed substantive words, produces a repetitious, often stereotyped flow, which conveys little information.

C. Anomic (Amnesic) Aphasia

Anomic aphasia is a syndrome of severe word-finding difficulty, in a setting of facile articulation and normal syntax. Auditory comprehension is not impaired. Inability to produce intended words usually results in circumlocution, rather than in paraphasic errors, the latter being more typical of Wernicke's aphasia. Reading and writing are unpredictable in this disorder, which is also least predictable as to lesion site.

D. Conduction Aphasia

Conduction aphasia is a syndrome that usually results from lesions of the parietal operculum, manifested by impairment of repetition disproportionate to the fluency of spontaneous speech, and in a setting of near normal auditory comprehension. Speech is marked by a predominance of literal paraphasia (phonemic substitutions and transpositions), especially during efforts to repeat. Word-finding difficulty and severely impaired writing are usually present. This syndrome is attributed to the anatomical dissociation of Wernicke's auditory speech area from Broca's area, thus disabling the guidance of speech output by auditory input. This effect is thought to be produced by an interruption of the arcuate fasciculus—the bundle of nerve fibers that has been identified as connecting the Wernicke and Broca zones.

E. Transcortical Sensory Aphasia

Transcortical sensory aphasia is the syndrome of preserved repetition in the absence of comprehension or meaningful expression. Efforts to elicit responsive conversations produce paraphasic jargon, well articulated, but largely irrelevant. Reading and writing are impossible. The preservation of repetition is dramatic and may be accompanied by the ability to recite the words to songs or other memorized material. The syndrome is thought to be due to an extensive lesion sparing Wernicke's and Broca's areas but isolating them, as a unit, from the surrounding cortex.

F. Transcortical Motor Aphasia

Transcortical motor aphasia is the syndrome of dramatically preserved repetition in a setting where spontaneous speech is absent and only brief responses can be elicited to specific stimuli, such as objects to be named. Auditory comprehension is intact, but writing shows the same impoverishment as speech. The lesion responsible for this disorder is generally in a portion of frontal lobe, just anterior to Broca's area. The syndrome is regarded as a manifestation, in speech, of the loss of initiative and general stasis of mental activity associated with more anterior frontal cortical damage.

G. Alexia with Agraphia

Alexia with agraphia is a syndrome produced by a lesion of the angular gyrus, which may be confined to the loss of reading and writing. In severe forms the loss is so severe as to prevent the recognition or the production of individual letters and numbers, although numbers are sometimes spared. The patient cannot grasp words spelled orally, nor recognize letters traced on his hand. He is likewise unable to spell aloud. Since this lesion is on the fringe of the speech area, it is often accompanied by some anomic difficulty, but without disturbance of auditory comprehension or of the phonologic or syntactic aspects of speech production.

H. Alexia without Agraphia

Alexia without agraphia is the least rare of the "pure" aphasias. In this syndrome only one linguistic modality is disturbed. The patient can no longer recognize configurations of letters presented visually but can spell aloud, understands orally spelled words and sentences, and recognizes cut-out letters by touch, as well as letters traced on his hand. Visual recognition of individual letters is often spared, and such patients may "read" by painstakingly spelling to themselves. Numbers are usually exempt from this disorder, with the paradox that roman numbers can sometimes be read while words composed of the same letters are failed.

Writing is either perfectly intact or relatively mildly disturbed, the patient being unable to read back what he has written.

As with all of the "pure" aphasias, we are dealing here with a disconnection syndrome—one that does not impinge on a language association area, but that involves the fibers bringing sensory input to the language zone. In this case, the usual lesion is one that damages the primary visual area on the left, while also producing an injury in the splenium of the corpus callosum that effectively isolates the right-hemisphere visual system from the language area.

I. Pure Word Deafness

Often referred to as "subcortical sensory aphasia," pure word deafness is a syndrome of isolated loss of auditory comprehension in a setting of normal speech output and normal reading and writing. It is believed to be due to disconnection, subcortically, of the fibers bringing acoustic information of Wernicke's area in the dominant hemisphere. Both Wernicke's area itself and at least one of the two primary auditory centers (Heschl's gyri) remain intact, since hearing is only slightly reduced. This is the rarest of the "pure" aphasias, probably because it is difficult for a lesion to be so placed that it injures only the subcortical tracts without impinging on the association area. Thus, word deafness associated with some of the features of Wernicke's aphasia—especially paraphasia—is less uncommon. In these cases reading and writing may still be well preserved.

J. Syndrome of the Corpus Callosum

Lesions in the corpus callosum have been reported as natural occurrences (Geschwind & Kaplan, 1962; Liepmann & Maas, 1907; Maas, 1907) and have also been produced in recent years by surgical section of the callosum for the treatment of epilepsy (Bogen & Vogel, 1962). The symptoms are entirely predicable by a model that assumes that linguistic operations are carried on predominantly in the left hemisphere and that input and output via the left side of the body is entirely or partially dissociated from language. Thus, the patient is unable to write meaningfully with his left hand, cannot name what he feels in his left hand, and, as a rule, cannot carry out verbal commands with that hand. Neither can he select named objects by touch with the left hand. When, as in the surgically sectioned patients, the splenium is cut, isolating the visual half fields from each other, it can be shown (Gazzaniga & Sperry, 1967) that objects and words flashed to the left visual field cannot be named, although they can be selected tactually with the left hand. Insofar as the right side of the body is concerned, the patient is totally normal, and without special test procedures one would not be aware of any aphasia-like defect.

VII. APHASIA IN CHILDHOOD

A. Acquired Aphasia

There are both parallels and differences between the pattern of aphasia in adults and its form in children who have suffered a brain lesion after having acquired normal speech. While it is claimed (Basser, 1962) that young children may lose their speech after either right or left hemisphere injury, this contention is not borne out either in Guttmann's series (1942) or in a series of 32 children between the ages of 6 and 15, reported by Alajouanine and Lhermitte (1965), in whom only left cerebral lesions were seen as a cause of aphasia. Thus, the likelihood is that by age 6, if not earlier, the adult pattern of dominance has been established.

There is, however, evidence that the organization of linguistic capacities within the speech zones is not quite the same in children as in adults. All writers agree that impoverishment of speech output is universal, and that markedly fluent, paraphasic speech is never encountered before age 10. There is a marked reduction in initiative and, at least initially, speech must be coaxed forth. As language begins to recover, it is in one-word or extremely simple sentences, resembling the agrammatic pattern of Broca's aphasia. Articulatory impairment, exclusively of the phonetic type is frequent in anterior lesions, but paraphasia of any type is rare. Vocabulary is restricted. Auditory comprehension may be disturbed, but less frequently than in adults. Reading and writing are universally severely damaged in the early stages of the illness.

In general, acquired childhood aphasias are distinguished by the absence of those features that represent the development of autonomous subsystems for the components of spoken language; consequently, the diverse syndromes of adult aphasia do not appear. Notably absent are the types of aphasia with fluent, grammatically complete but paraphasic speech. That is, Wernicke's aphasia is unknown in children. Thus it appears that the cerebral organization of language is less differentiated and less automatized in children than in adults. Finally, as noted earlier, rapid and complete recovery is far more common in children than in adults, although not universal. In many instances, after recovery, there is a detectable long-term deficit in written language skills, although normal schooling can generally be resumed.

B. Developmental Aphasia

Even in the absence of a detectable lesion, about 6% of children fail to develop normal speech at the expected time, i.e., single words by 12 months, simple sequences by 2 years and complete sentences by 4 years (Morley, 1965). Delayed development, culminating in normal speech by 6 or 7 years, is not uncommon and may be hereditary. However, of those who fail to show the normal language acquisition pattern, a small percentage have sufficiently severe and persistent disorders to be considered developmental aphasics. Knowing, as we do, that even massive congenital injury to one hemisphere does not prevent speech from developing, one must assume that these congenitally aphasic children have bilateral abnormalities in the development of their cortical speech areas.

The patterns of language deficit as they appear in developmental aphasia are usually even less differentiated than they are in acquired childhood aphasia, although more selective disorders occasionally occur. The child shows little or no babbling during infancy and does not progress from single words to word combinations until he is 4 years or older. While not grossly impaired in comprehension, he can easily be shown to have a reduced recognition vocabulary, a lack of understanding of prepositions, and a reduced auditory span, especially for retention of sequences. Even when sentences begin to appear, they have the agrammatic quality noted in acquired aphasia, with the omission of articles, auxiliaries, and inflections. A large proportion of these children are unable to learn written language, although there are a few who can read and spell at grade level.

The selective forms of developmental aphasia involve auditory imperception on the one hand and articulatory difficulty on the other. The child with auditory imperception initially often appears unaware of environmental sounds, except sporadically. Even the technique of conditioned galvanic response audiometry fails to confirm normal hearing. As he grows older, e.g., by age 5, his ability to listen matures, and speech begins to appear, although word-finding difficulties and agrammatism persist. Morley (1965) reports that reading ability may be well ahead of auditory comprehension in such cases. At the opposite pole are those children whose auditory comprehension is normal, yet who cannot master the articulation of sounds.

VIII. SPECIAL PROBLEMS IN APHASIA

Among the more challenging problems presented by aphasia are the occasional dissociations between symbol systems that, at least outwardly, make use of the same sensory and motor channels. These may be encountered in patients with special skills, such as polyglots, musicians, and users of language systems that have both ideographic and phonetic characters, such as do Japanese and the manual language of deaf-mutes.

A. Aphasia in Polyglots

In most cases, the effect of aphasia on all of a multilingual patient's languages is parallel in form and severity. However, the literature is rich in reports of selective recovery in one language. In some cases it is the mother tongue that remains, while the adopted language is lost; in other cases it is the reverse. In some instances patients have found themselves able to use only a language that they knew academically, that had never been a regular means of communication.

Minkowski (1963) cites a patient of Halpern's who was a native speaker of English and had emigrated to Palestine at age 20, having learned liturgical Hebrew as a child. He had become completely competent in Hebrew during his 22 years of residence in Israel, up to the time of his being rendered aphasic by a mine fragment in the left parieto-temporal area. For the first 2 months, in spite of a totally Hebrew-speaking milieu, he spoke and understood only English. More typical is a case, described in a personal communication by Quadfasel, of a French woman who had lived in New York for many years but made a great effort to maintain her contact with French culture through a circle of friends who spoke only French to each other. On becoming aphasic, her initial recovery was, to her chagrin, only in English, and she was unable to communicate at all in French.

Parallel recovery, even without practice, is illustrated in a case of Van Thal's (1960). The patient was a 68-year-old Dutchman who had lived in England for 50 years, making little use of the Dutch language. On becoming aphasic, he was treated only in English and made a moderate recovery. On the occasion of a planned visit to Holland, an assessment of his Dutch revealed that its recovery had kept pace with English.

Lambert and Fillenbaum (1959), who studied a large number of polyglot aphasics in Montreal, proposed that the degree of dissociation between their languages was a function of the similarity of the context in which they had been learned. Languages acquired in a common environment and interchangeably usable in that environment were "compound" and unlikely to be dissociated. Languages acquired and used in situations having different emotional significance to the patient were "coordinate" and more vulnerable to dissociation.

B. Aphasia in Musicians

The usual effect of aphasia on the capacity of a trained musician is illustrated by Alajouanine's report on the composer Ravel (1948). Fully able to recognize and appreciate music, including every detail of his own compositions, he was no longer able to read music or compose. It is a commonplace observation that aphasia usually leaves intact the patient's ability to sing a melody, even though the words are lost. In our personal experience with a number of trained musicians there has not been one who retained his ability to read music correctly after becoming aphasic. However, Luria (Luria, Tsvetkova, & Futer, 1965) has described the case of the Soviet composer Shebalin, who, although impaired in the auditory comprehension and formulation of language, continued to compose orchestral music of high merit. The fact that this patient retained his reading ability and a certain level of writing ability suggests that his lesion was relatively circumscribed.

C. Aphasia in Japanese

The Japanese language has developed two modes of writing, which have been observed to suffer different degrees of impairment in aphasic patients. Kanji characters are ideograms adopted from Chinese, and each character stands for a concept in its entirety. Kana characters, on the other hand, represent sounds (consonant–vowel syllables), and they may be used in combination to build up any word in the language, much as Western writing builds up words phonically by combining individual vowels and consonants. Imura (1943) and a number of other Japanese writers have reported the preservation of the ideographic Kanji characters in patients who could no longer use the Kana or phonetic transcription. Imura, Kido, Matsuyama, and Abe (1962) also report the reverse situation, which is less common. Sasanuma and Fujimura (1970) compared the production and recognition of the two forms of writing in a series of 20 aphasics. The syllabic characters were more difficult, both expressively and receptively, than the ideographic, and this disparity was most marked in the most severely speech handicapped.

D. Aphasia in Deaf-Mutes

The manual language of deaf-mutes bears a certain analogy to Japanese writing and manifests a corresponding similarity in the effects of aphasia.

Two forms of manual language exist in parallel—finger-spelling, which is a phonetic transcription of English spelling, and "signing" which consists of conventionalized ideographic gestures, each representing an integral concept. While there are only a few well-examined cases of aphasia in deaf-mutes in the literature, the cases of Critchley (1938) and of Tureen, Smolik, and Tritt (1951) illustrate the relative preservation of signs with respect to impaired finger spelling. On the other hand, Douglass and Richardson's case (1959) showed less recovery in universal sign language than in finger spelling.

IX. THE FUTURE OF RESEARCH IN APHASIA

Twenty-five years ago it was still fashionable in psychological circles to argue that the abnormal could not be understood until the normal had been fully clarified. Today, in a more tolerant atmosphere, it has become clearer that research on the normal and research on the abnormal can have a powerful mutually stimulating interest. One can consider one simple example. Broadbent introduced his technique of dichotic listening as part of a program of research on the capacity of individuals to shift attention from one channel to another. He deduced from his findings remarkable capacities of the nervous system that neither the neurophysiologist nor the student of the brain-lesioned had guessed at. This research was a triumph of classical "normal" psychological research. Kimura's modification of this technique to the study of patients undergoing cortical ablations for epilepsy illustrated in turn the power of study of the abnormal to illuminate the normal. The differential handling of music and words by separate hemispheres of the brain is one example of an unexpected and important finding.

The study of aphasia provides an opportunity for this type of interaction that is probably limitless in its scope. Particularly in the psychology of language, the continued interaction between studies of normal and of aphasic language may well provide an unexcelled opportunity for new insights into the nature of this curiously, although perhaps not exclusively, human capacity.

References

Alajouanine, T. Aphasia and artistic realization. *Brain*, 1948, **71**, 229–241.
Alajouanine, T. Verbal realization in aphasia. *Brain,* 1956, **77**, 1–28.
Alajouanine, T., & Lhermitte, F. Acquired aphasia in children. *Brain,* 1965, **88**, 653–662.

Alajouanine, Th., Ombredane, A., & Durand, M. *Le syndrome de la désintégration phonétique dans l'aphasie.* Paris: Masson, 1939.

Basser, L. S. Hemiplegia of early onset and the faculty of speech, with special reference to the effects of hemispherectomy. *Brain,* 1962, **85,** 427–460.

Bastian, H. C. *A treatise on aphasia and other speech defects.* London: H. K. Lewis, 1898.

Bisiach, E. Perceptual factors in the pathogenesis of anomia. *Cortex,* 1966, **2,** 90–95.

Blumstein, S. E. *A phonological investigation of aphasic speech.* The Hague: Mouton, 1973.

Bogen, J. E., & Vogel, P. J. Cerebral commisurotomy: A case report. *Bulletin of the Los Angeles Neurological Society,* 1962, **27,** 169–172.

Boumann, L., & Grünbaum, A. Experimentell-psychologische Untersuchungen zur Aphasie und Paraphasie. *Zeitschrift für des gesamte Neurologie und Psychiatrie,* 1925, **96,** 481–538.

Broca, P. Sur le siège de la faculté du langage articulé. *Bulletin de la Société d'Anthropologie,* 1865, **6,** 377.

Charcot, J. M. *Oeuvres complètes de Charcot.* Paris: Delahaye-Lecrosnier, 1887.

Critchley, M. Aphasia in a partial deaf mute. *Brain,* 1938, **61,** 163–169.

Déjerine, J. Des différentes variétés de cécité verbale. *Mémoires de la Société de Biologie,* 1892, Feb. 27, 1–30.

Douglass, E., & Richardson, J. C. Aphasia in a congenital deaf mute. *Brain,* 1959, **82,** 68–80.

Freund, C. S. Über optische Aphasie und Seelenblindheit. *Archiv. für Psychiatrie und Nervenkrankheit.,* 1889, **20,** 276–297, 371–416.

Fry, D. B. Phonemic substitutions in an aphasic patient. *Language and Speech,* 1959, **2,** 52–61.

Gardner, R. A., & Gardner, B. T. Teaching sign language to a chimpanzee. *Science,* 1969, **165,** 664–672.

Gazzaniga, M. S., & Sperry, R. W. Language after section of the cerebral commissures. *Brain,* 1967, **90,** 131–148.

Geschwind, N. The organization of language and the brain. *Science,* 1970, **170,** 940–944.

Geschwind, N., & Fusillo, M. Color naming defects in association with alexia. *Archives of Neurology,* 1966, **15,** 137–146.

Geschwind, N., & Kaplan, E. A human cerebral disconnection syndrome. *Neurology,* 1962, **12,** 675–685.

Geschwind, N., & Levitsky, W. Human brain: Left-right asymmetries in temporal speech region. *Science,* 1968, **161,** 186–188.

Gloning, I., Gloning, K., Haub, G., & Quatember, R. Comparison of verbal behavior in right-handed and non-right handed patients with anatomically verified lesions of one hemisphere. *Cortex,* 1969, 43–52.

Goldstein, K. *Language and language disturbances.* New York: Grune and Stratton, 1948.

Goldstein, K., & Scheerer, M. Abstract and concrete behavior. *Psychological Monographs,* 1941, **53,** No. 2.

Goodglass, H. Studies on the grammar of aphasics. In S. Rosenberg & J. Koplin (Eds.), *Developments in applied psycholinguistics research.* New York: Macmillan, 1968.

Goodglass, H., Barton, M. I., & Kaplan, E. Sensory modality and object naming in aphasia. *Journal of Speech and Hearing Research,* 1968, **11,** 488–496.

Goodglass, H., Berko, J. B., Bernholtz, N. A., & Hyde, M. R. Some linguistic structures in the speech of a Broca's aphasic. *Cortex,* 1972, **8,** 191–212.

Goodglass, H., Fodor, I. G., & Schulhoff, C. Prosodic factors in grammar-evidence from aphasia. *Journal of Speech and Hearing Research,* 1967, **10,** 5–20.

Goodglass, H., & Hunt, J. Grammatical complexity and aphasic speech. *Word,* 1958, **14,** 197–207.

Goodglass, H., and Hunter, M. Linguistic comparison of speech and writing in two types of aphasia. *Journal of Communication Disorders,* 1970, 3, 28–35.

Goodglass, H., Hyde, M. R., & Blumstein, S. Frequency, picturability, and the availability of nouns in aphasia. *Cortex,* 1969, **5,** 104–119.

Goodglass, H., Klein, B., Carey, P., & Jones, K. J. Specific semantic word categories in aphasia. *Cortex,* 1966, **2,** 74–89.

Goodglass, H., & Mayer, J. Agrammatism in aphasia. *Journal of Speech and Hearing Disorders,* 1958, **23,** 99–111.

Goodglass, H., & Quadfasel, F. A. Language laterality in left handed aphasics. *Brain,* 1954, **77,** 521–548.

Guttmann, E. Aphasia in children. *Brain,* 1942, **65,** 205–219.

Harris, C. M. Phonemic errors made by aphasic patients in the identification of monosyllabic words. Unpublished doctoral dissertation, Univ. of Minnesota, 1970.

Head, H. *Aphasia and kindred disorders of speech.* Longon: Cambridge Univ. Press, 1926.

Imura, T. Aphasia: Its characteristic features in the Japanese language (In Japanese). *Psychiatria et Neurologia Japonica.* 1943, **47,** 196–218.

Imura, T., Kido, K., Matsuyama, L. & Abe, Y. Impairment in reading sentences. *Journal of Psychiatry,* 1962, **3,** 759–765.

Jackson, J. H. On some implications of dissolution of the nervous system. *Medical Press and Circular,* 1882, **7,** 411. [Reprinted in J. Taylor (Ed.), *Selected writings of John Hughlings Jackson.* London: Hodder and Stoughton, 1932.]

Jakobson, R. *Kindersprache, Aphasie und allgemeine Lautgesetze.* Uppsala: Almqvist u. Wilsells, 1941.

Jakobson, R. Two aspects of language and two types of aphasic disturbance. In R. Jakobson & M. Halle, *Fundamentals of language.* The Hague: Mouton, 1956.

Kennedy, F. Stockbrainedness, the causative factor in the so-called 'crossed aphasias'. *American Journal of the Medical Sciences,* 1916, **152,** 849–859.

Kimura, D. Cerebral dominance and the perception of verbal stimuli. *Canadian Journal of Psychology,* 1961, **15,** 166–171.

Kimura, D. Left-right differences in the perception of melodies. *Quarterly Journal of Experimental Psychology,* 1964, **16,** 355–358.

Lambert, W. E., & Fillenbaum, S. A pilot study of aphasia among bilinguals. *Canadian Journal of Psychology,* 1959, **13,** 28–34.

Lenneberg, E. *Biological foundations of language.* New York: Wiley, 1967.

Liepmann, H., & Maas, O. Fall von linksseitiger Agraphie und Apraxie bei rechtsseitiger Lähmung. *Journal für Psychologie und Neurologie,* 1907, **10,** 214.

Luria, A. R. *Traumatic aphasia: Its syndromes, psychology and treatment.* The Hague: Mouton, 1970.

Luria, A. R., Tsvetkova, L. S., & Futer, D. S. Aphasia in a composer. *Journal of Neurological Sciences,* 1965, **2,** 288–292.

Maas, O. Ein Fall von linksseitiger Apraxie und Agraphie. *Neurologisches Centralblatt,* 1907, **26,** 789.

Maher, B. The language of schizophrenia: A review and interpretation. *British Journal of Psychology,* 1972, **120,** 3–17.

Marie, P. *Travaux et mémoires.* Vol. 1, L'aphasie. Paris: Masson, 1926.

Maspes, P. E. Le syndrome expérimental chez l'homme de la section du splénium du corps calleux. *Revue Neurologique* 1948, **2,** 101–113.

Milner, B., Branch, C., & Rasmussen, T. Evidence for bilateral speech representation in some right handers. *Transactions of the American Neurological Association,* 1966, 306–308.

Minkowski, M. On aphasia in polygots. In L. Halpern (Ed.), *Problems of dynamic neurology.* Jerusalem: Hebrew Univ., 1963.

Morley, M. E. *The development and disorders of speech in childhood.* Baltimore: Williams and Wilkins, 1965.

Nielsen, J. M. *Agnosia, apraxia, and aphasia.* New York, Hoeber, 1946.

North, B. Effects of stimulus redundancy on naming disorders in aphasia. Unpublished doctoral dissertation, Boston Univ. 1971.

Ombredane, A. Sur le mécanisme de l'anarthrie. *Journal de Psychologie Normale et Pathologique,* 1927, **61,** 940–955.

Penfield, W., & Roberts, L. *Speech and brain mechanisms.* Princeton, New Jersey: Princeton Univ. Press, 1959.

Premack, D. Language in chimpanzee? *Science,* 1971, **172,** 808–822.

Sasanuma, S., & Fujimura, O. Selective impairment of phonetic and nonphonetic transcription of words in Japanese aphasic patients: Kana vs. Kanji in visual recognition and writing. *Cortex,* 1970, **6,** 1–18.

Schuell, H., & Jenkins, J. J. The nature of language deficit in aphasia. *Psychological Review,* 1959, **66,** 45–67.

Shankweiler, D. F., & Harris, K. S. An experimental approach to the problem of articulation in aphasia. *Cortex,* 1966, **2,** 277–292.

Spreen, O., Benton, A. L., & Van Allen, M. Dissociation of visual and tactile naming in amnesic aphasia. *Neurology,* 1966, **16,** 807–814.

Studdert-Kennedy, M., & Shankweiler, D. Hemispheric specialization for speech perception. *Journal of the Acoustical Society of America,* 1970, **48,** 579–594.

Trescher, J. H., & Ford, F. R. Colloid cyst of the third ventricle. *Archives of Neurology and Psychiatry,* 1937, **37,** 959.

Tureen, L. L., Smolik, E. A., & Tritt, J. H. Aphasia in a deaf mute. *Neurology,* 1951, **1,** 237–244.

Van Thal, J. Polyglot aphasics. *Folia Phoniatrica,* 1960, **12,**& 123–128.

Wada, J., & Rasmussen, T. Intracarotid injection of sodium amytal for the lateralization of cerebral speech dominance. *Journal of Neurosurgery,* 1960, **17,** 266–282.

Wernicke, C. *Der aphasische Symptomencomplex.* Breslau: Franck u. Weigert, 1874.

Wepman, J. M., Bock, R. D., Jones, L. V., & Van Pelt, D. Psycholinguistic study of aphasia: revision of the question of anomia. *Journal of Speech and Hearing Disorders,* 1956, **21,** 468–477.

Chapter 13

DISORDERS OF SPEECH PRODUCTION MECHANISMS

HARRY A. WHITAKER

I. INTRODUCTION

Critchley (1970) has written an essay on the nomenclature of speech pathology that includes a semihistorical account of the definitions of *language* and *speech*. His recommendation for distinguishing these terms is based upon the notion of externalizing language in verbal-articulatory units, i.e., use of the auditory communication channel. It is generally agreed that useful definitions of *speech* emphasize its nonlinguistic character, which is to say that there should be a distinction between that aspects of human communication which is attributable to rule-governed encoding of (abstract) units and that aspect which is a realization or an externalization of the encoding. An operational definition of *speech* may be the most useful of all, particularly in the context of a discussion of speech disorders: Speech refers to structures and processes that are related to direct control of the vocal tract musculature. According to this definition, speech factors would have a direct relationship to the articulatory shapes that the vocal tract assumes over time, which in turn are directly mappable into acoustic waveforms. Nothing has been stated concerning meaningfulness, since this is not a speech factor. Therefore, the problem of the brain-damaged patient who says, in an articulatory clear and precise fashion, the following:

We used to nish; I used to nish, I used to fip in a fed batter on flesh island;
I always feshist in broad England [Buckingham & Kertesz 1974, p. 53].

is not a speech deficit but a language impairment; this patient has an
aphasia. The patient with a speech disorder is said to have *dysarthria.*
Luchsinger and Arnold (1965) provide the following definition:

> Dysarthrias are disorders of oral speech resulting from lesions within the
> cerebral centers, pathways and nuclei of the nerves that are involved in the
> speech event. From this definition results a fundamental difference between
> the dysarthrias, which represent disorders of the external speaking act, and
> the dysphasias, which indicate the loss of word and sentence formulation
> as well as word and sentence comprehension and thus interfere with the
> highest order of language function [p. 715].*

It should be noted that Luchsinger and Arnold also distinguish the *dys-
glossias,* which result from lesions to specific nerves or muscles and thus
alter pronunciation with respect to specific articulatory zones. In this review, these disorders are subsumed under the general heading of the dysarthrias, following usual clinical practice in the United States. Lesions that
produce dysarthria affect the control of the vocal tract muscles for all gestures, voluntary or otherwise; these effects are generally uniform (with certain exceptions to be noted below) and do not vary according to the complexity or difficulty of the gesture. This is the basis for the important
distinction between dysarthria on the one hand and an expressive motor
aphasia on the other (see Goodglass & Geschwind, Chapter 12). The expressive motor aphasia syndromes have been variously identified by different
researchers, e.g., Broca's aphasia, apraxia of speech, conduction aphasia,
phonetic disintegration, phonemic disintegration, etc. Because comprehension is typically fairly well preserved in patient's with such disorders, there
has been a notable tendency not to identify these as aphasia per se but
as some variety of speech disorder, although still distinct from dysarthria.
From a linguistic perspective, however, these disorders fall naturally into
the category of problems associated with the phonological component and,
consistent with the definitions of speech noted above, can be theoretically
distinguished from the dysarthrias which have to do with the actualization
or realization of the phonological component (see Whitaker, 1971). Phonological disorders may involve particular features of an articulatory gesture, such that in effect an incorrect phoneme is produced, e.g.,

> "tornado" pronounced a "dornado"
> "pineapple" pronounced as "poneapple"

* From *Voice–Speech–Language, Clinical Communicology: Its Physiology and
Pathology,* by Richard Luchsinger and Godfrey E. Arnold. © 1965 by Wadsworth
Publishing Company, Inc., Belmont, California 94002. Reprinted by permission of
the publisher.

or the error may be compounded by apparent substitutions, additions, or omissions of phonemes, such that the utterance is significantly distorted, e.g.,

> "hamburger" pronounced as "burpuggy"
> "Studebaker" pronounced as "stickermaker"
> "wheels" pronounced as "ways"
> "Episcopal" pronounced as "pickle"

With rare exceptions, the utterances of aphasic patients with phonological component disruptions obey the usual constraints of the sound system of these native language, i.e., these patients do not produce inadmissible consonant clusters and nonoccurring vowels or vocalic nuclei. Their speech is halting and effortful on occasion, the longer and more complex words are typically more distorted, they may or may not be able to repeat correctly, and they may or may not have a corresponding *oral apraxia* (which is the apparent loss of the knowledge of how to shape the facial muscles into such gestures as imitating sucking from a straw, blowing air, or kissing someone). The dysarthric patient, on the other hand, does produce consonants and vowels that do not appear in the phonetic repertoire of his native language, but it is clear that he does so because he cannot properly move the vocal tract muscles. In fact, the dysarthric patient will often produce speech that is atypical of any language, let alone his native one. Another way of illustrating the difference between a pure dysarthria and a pure phonological disorder is to consider how phonemes contrast in English to signal differences in meaning. The words "met," "bet," and "pet" differ basically in their initial phonemes, /m/, /b/, and /p/, and we can characterize the distinctions as one of [nasality] between /m/ and the others, and [voicing] between /p/ and the others. Therefore, the /m/ is marked as [nasal, voiced], the /b/ is marked as [nonnasal, voiced], and the /p/ is marked as [nonnasal, nonvoiced]. Typically the dysarthric patient, as well as the patient with phonological component disorders, can perceive the distinctions between all three words. The patient with phonological disorders will, on occasion, be unable to produce the various distinctions, however, and may instead of /m/ produce one of the other two initial consonants, or an even more unrelated segment such as an /l/ or an /f/. The dysarthric patient, on the other hand, may be unable to articulate any of the sounds accurately, but he will be able to produce some kind of audible distinction between the segments. Thus, if his velum is partially paralyzed, he obviously cannot produce the distinction between [nasal] and [nonnasal] consonants; but he will usually be able to alter the articulation of these segments in such a way as to signal a difference, for example, by making the targeted /m/ more breathy than the /b/, or perhaps by creating extra air turbulence. In sum, the lack of auditory intelligibility of the dysarthric is due to distortions in the usual features of contrast in his native language and can be deciphered by a listener, once the nature of the muscular deficits are identified; the patient with disorders of phonology is unintelligible for linguistic reasons—he misuses or misapplies the features of contrast.

II. THE DYSARTHRIAS

Classification of the dysarthrias may be approached in several ways. Emphasis can be placed on the distortions of the vocal tract and the resulting variation in acoustic waveform. The best example of this approach is Lehiste (1965), a very detailed study of the acoustic phonetic characteristics of speech disorders. One should be cautioned, however, that not all of Lehiste's subjects were dysarthric; it is apparent from both the clinical report and the phonetic analysis that some of the patients also suffered disordered phonological components. Definitive studies of the neurogenic or organic dysarthrias were done by the Mayo Clinic research team of Darley, Aronson, and Brown (Aronson, Brown, Litkin, & Pearson, 1968; Brown, Darley, & Aronson, 1968, 1970; Darley, Aronson, & Brown, 1968, 1969a,b), who studied 212 patients, each unequivocally diagnosed as exhibiting one of seven neurologic syndromes: bulbar palsy, pseudobulbar palsy, amyotrophic lateral sclerosis, dystonia, cerebellar disease, Parkinsonism, and choreoathetosis. Each patient was rated according to 38 different aspects of speech impairment, using a severity scale of 1 through 7. The speech dimensions were grouped into aspects of pitch control, loudness control, vocal quality (including breathiness, nasality, etc.), control of respiration, prosody (rate of speech, stress, duration of speech or pauses), and articulation (including the precision of consonant gestures, durations of the articulatory gesture, repetition of segments, fluency of gestures and distortion of vowels). Their clinical approach to the dysarthrias emphasizes the constellation of impairments associated with identifiable disease entities and of course is directly concerned with localizing the disease process to particular structures of the central and peripheral nervous system. From the standpoint of the contribution to speech production made by the different structures of the CNS and the PNS, a useful classification of the dysarthrias can be made on the basis of these structures themselves and the speech sequelae when they are diseased. Briefly, this system of classification will distinguish the speech impairments caused by lesions in three principal motor systems: the pyramid tract, the basal ganglia, and the cerebellum. The exclusion of the thalamus, and its inclusion in the brain structures for language proper, is discussed in Whitaker (Chapter 4 of this volume). The description of the dysarthrias is followed by comments on the neuroanatomic pathways of these structures and a neurolinguistic model of speech production that can be inferred from a consideration of the neuroanatomy and the speech pathology.

A. Pyramidal Tract: Lower Motor Neuron Lesions

The speech disorders resulting from lesions to the nuclei of the cranial nerves innervating the vocal tract musculature, the axons of these nerves, or the neuromuscular junction are generally identified as *flaccid dysarthria*. There is a pronounced reduction of the force of muscle contraction, sometimes to the degree of complete paralysis. The muscles are hypotonic (reduced tonus) or weak, and there is generally partial to complete atrophy of the affected muscle. It is characteristic of lower motor neuron lesions that only specific muscles are affected, depending of course upon which cranial nerves are affected by the lesion. This leads to three subclassifications, defined by the area of the vocal tract that is most affected: the laryngeal area, the velopharyngeal area, and the oral area. Involvement of cranial nerves IX and X, for example, can alter normal voice quality into a breathiness with audible inspiration, due to a weakness of the laryngeal muscles, or, a hypernasality with nasal emission due to weakness of the velopharyngeal muscles. Involvement of cranial nerves V, VII, and XII can result in an impreciseness of consonant articulation due to weakness of either the tongue or the lip–facial muscles.

B. Pyramidal Tract: Upper Motor Neuron Lesions

The speech disorders resulting from lesions to the neurons or their pathways that innervate the lower motor neurons (cranial nerves and spinal cord nerves) are generally identified as *spastic dysarthria*. Lesions may involve pathways to and from the basal ganglia, where they course with fibers of the pyramidal tract, but, by definition, do not include the basal ganglia themselves. The major characteristics of such lesions are muscle spasticity and hypertonicity (including hyperreflexia) and there is no muscle atrophy. This results in a pronounced slowing of movement and some reduction in the force and range of movement, but generally no disorders of rhythm or direction of movement. The effects are on movement patterns, rather than on specific muscles and muscle groups. Frequently noted is an insufficiency of pitch and loudness variation, a hypernasality associated with a spastic velum (or a hyponasality on the same basis), and a voice quality described as "strain-strangle harshness." Apparently due to the increased effort required to articulate, there is often a reduction in the length of the utterance as well. Another term for designating the dysarthria caused by upper motor neuron lesions is *pseudobulbar palsy,* contrasting with the term for the dysarthria from lower motor neuron lesions, *bulbar palsy.*

C. Basal Ganglia Lesions

Whereas the pyramidal tract clearly is the principal efferent pathway for skilled motor movements mediated by both the cranial nerve nuclei and the spinal motor neurons, the role of the basal ganglia in motor control is not as clear-cut. This system is frequently identified as the extrapyramidal system; it is phylogenetically older than the pyramidal system and appears to be mainly involved in postural synergies. A sophisticated introduction to the role of the basal ganglia in the control of movement can be found in Denny-Brown (1962), and a detailed study of movement disorders and the amelioration of them using neurosurgical techniques can be found in Cooper (1969). The basal ganglia may be considered from the standpoint of the long-term evolution of involuntary movement disorders associated with lesions in its principal structures: caudate, putamen, globus pallidus, and substantia nigra. The effects of lesions in these structures has been summarized by Denny-Brown (1962)*:

> We would focus attention upon the posture of general flexion accompanied by parkinsonian tremor, most characteristically seen in idiopathic paralysis agitans, associated with lesions of the globus pallidus. Lesions of the putamen, on the other hand, result in athetosis or asymmetrical dystonia leading to a more intensely rigid 'hemiplegic' posture of flexion of the upper limbs and extension of the lower limbs. Between these two extremes which we would designate as "pallidal" and "striatal" syndromes, there occur a variety of transitional states [p. 52].

Current research implicates the substantia nigra as the primary or essential locus of lesions that produce the parkinsonian symptomatology; clinically there is often an accompanying lesion in the globus pallidus, as Denny-Brown notes. There is a tendency for chorea-like symptoms to involve the caudate nucleus more than the putamen, a tendency for athetosis-like symptoms to involve the putamen more, and a tendency for parkinsonian-like symptoms to involve the substantia nigra more, particularly its efferent pathways. These symptoms may be outlined as follows:

Choreiform movements are extremely variable, purposeless, coarse,

* From D. Denny-Brown *The Basal Ganglia,* © Oxford University Press, 1962, by permission of the Oxford University Press, Oxford.

quick and jerky; they begin suddenly and show no rhythmiticity; when the movement is over the muscle group affected remains at rest and is relatively atonic until the next movement begins.

Athetoid movements are continuous, arrhythmic, slow, and "wormlike"; they are always the same in the same patient; the muscles are hypertonic and may show transient stages of spasm.

Dystonic movements are bizzare and twisting; some muscles are hypertonic, and there may be mobile spasms of axial and proximal muscles or a twisting-turning motion or a torsion spasm; these movements tend to involve larger portions of the body than choreiform or athetoid movements.

Parkinsonian tremor is a coarse, 3-to-6-per-second tremor of muscles when at rest; the tremor ceases when voluntary movement is initiated. It can be distinguished from cerebellar or *intention tremor,* which occurs during movement and is intensified at the termination of a gesture.

The speech disorders associated with basal ganglia lesions can be separated into two groups, using Denny-Brown's clinical descriptions and more recent neuroanatomical knowledge. (*a*) an *anterio-dorsal* group comprising lesions to the caudate and putamen (Denny-Brown's "striatal") and (*b*) a *posterio-ventral* group comprising lesions to the globus pallidus and substantia nigra (Denny-Brown's "pallidal"). *Anterio-dorsal* disorders are characterized by involuntary, distorted postural movements superimposed on articulation; they can be slowly evolving as in dystonia, rapidly evolving as in chorea, or continuously evolving as in athetosis. A choreiform disorder frequently results in long and inappropriate silences in speaking, as though all movement had ceased. The postural disorder which directly affects speaking may be a sudden sideways jerk of the head, a protrusion of the tongue, stenosis of the larynx, or a facial grimace. *Posterio-ventral* disorders are characterized by resting tremor, difficulty in initiating all movements, rigidity of musculature, and marked reduction in the range of possible movements. These apply to all muscles, including those of the vocal tract. Some cases give an impression of speeded-up speech rate; repetitive movements tend to be rather fast and tremulous, accompanied by the reduced excursion already noted.

D. Cerebellar Lesions

The salient characteristics of speech disorders resulting from cerebellar lesions are inaccuracy and randomness. The inaccuracy is marked by errors in timing of movements, errors in the range or distance of movements, and errors in the direction of movements. These errors appear at irregular intervals, that is, they are apparently quite random. The articulatory and prosodic aspects of speech are most noticeably affected; a frequently noted pattern is called "scanning speech" and can be described as a loss of major sentence and word stress, accompanied by an equalization of syllable durations. Thus, a syllable that should receive weak stress and be shortened, e.g., the middle and final syllables in the English word "character," might receive the same stress as the first syllable and be lengthened as well; the final production might be represented as CHAR –ACT –ER. This type of speech disorder is called *ataxic dysarthria*.

III. SPEECH PRODUCTION

The clinical interest in the dysarthrias, because of the significant localizing value of each cluster of speech disorders, has somewhat obscured the relevance of the neuroanatomy and speech pathology of the dysarthrias in the formulation of a model of speech production. The following sketch of such a model must be considered somewhat speculative due to the lack of detailed neuroanatomical data on human central nervous system pathways; however, it is reasonably consistent with the clinical evidence to date. We may first establish the a priori conditions that must be fulfilled in order that some part of the central nervous system, let it be called structure X, be considered a component in the speech production system.

1. A lesion in X causes a disruption of speech per se.
2. A lesion in X causes a disruption of speech independently of disorders in other motor systems.
3. There is anatomical–physiological evidence for either a localization of speech or a specialization for speech in structure X.
4. There are plausible anatomical pathways and inferred physiological mechanisms such that X could be a part of the speech production system.

On the basis of these criteria, it is clear that the pyramidal tract is the primary motor speech path in the brain. It partly originates in the large pyramidal neurons in cortical layers III and V, both in Broca's area, and in the head area of the Rolandic motor cortex. The fibers course into the midbrain, pons, and medulla, bilaterally innervating the cranial nerve nuclei, with the exception of the nuclei controlling the lower facial muscles, which are basically contralaterally innervated. Therefore, except for certain muscles of facial expression, each hemisphere's motor (Rolandic) and premotor (Broca) cortex is capable of controlling both sides of the vocal tract musculature, although it is traditionally argued that the dominant hemisphere (usually the left) in fact is responsible for speaking. At least two aspects of the pyramidal system are not well established: (*1*) the relationship between pre-motor and motor cortices as control centers and (2) the degree of plasticity of the nondominant homologous areas in the adult. On this latter point some interesting data is presented by Mohr (in press), documenting several cases of recovery from motor aphasia with demonstrable lesions (autopsied) of Broca's area.

A matter of current concern and study is the mechanism for feedback control of length and velocity parameters of the vocal tract muscles. The system of gamma efferents and muscle spindle afferents, from which the CNS may infer (subconsciously) the shape of the vocal tract, is generally assumed to mediate feedback of length and velocity sense in other (e.g., postural) muscles that have to act under varying load conditions in a semiautomatic manner (Curtis, Jacobson, & Marcus, 1972). It is debatable to what extent the gamma-loop system would be used in patterns of movement which require constant attention (volition) under no-load conditions, as is the case of some of the vocal tract muscles (e.g., the tongue). In any event the question has been raised frequently in discussions of models of speech production (see Bowman, 1971; MacNeilage, 1970; Sussman, 1972; Tatham, 1969). If we assume, as these authors do, that a gamma-loop system is in fact a control system for the vocal tract, there is a further question of determining the corresponding neuroanatomic pathways for feedback control. The classic muscle spindle afferents project to the cerebellum, which is presumed to be the center that utilizes information from the spindles to modify cortical output in the pyramidal system. Working independently of each other, Sussman (1972) and Bowman (1971) both came to the conclusion, however, that the muscle spindle system in the vocal tract musculature projects directly to the cortex, rather than to the cerebellum. This theory is schematically outlined in Fig. 1; the two authors should be consulted directly for the very ingenious details of reasoning and experimentation that led them to this conclusion. In addition to muscle spindle afferents, feedback control for speaking could be via tactile or proprioceptive afferents, or both, e.g., through the lingual nerve, which is a branch of the trigeminal (cranial nerve V), or, in the case of proprioception, from the facial (cranial nerve VII) through the mesencephalic root of the trigeminal. Ringel (1970) reviewed feedback mechanisms for speech, giving particular attention to the role of proprioceptive feedback; of special interest in his discussion of models of speech production that postulate two kinds of feedback—muscle spindle receptors, which are perhaps most important in vowel production, and cutaneous receptors, which are perhaps most important for consonant production. Cutaneous-tactile information clearly projects to the sensory–motor (rolandic) cortex through thalamic relays, and it also clearly projects to the cerebellum. This latter point is emphasized by Bowman (1971), who argues that the role of the

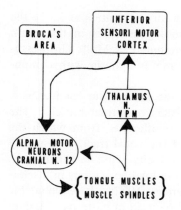

FIG. 1. Feedback circuit for motor speech (theoretical).

cerebellum in speech production may be more related to tactile feedback than to position and length–velocity sense feedback. His argument is based on a theory of the nature of the speech disorder from cerebellar lesions (ataxic dysarthria) in which he suggests that the primary disturbance is manifested *after* tactile contact of the articulators and that this disruption is the basis for the observed timing and sequencing errors.

Even from the preceding sketchy review, it is clear that the issue of the role of the cerebellum in speech production is closely bound up with the question of feedback control over the pyramidal tract. It does not seem possible at this stage of our understanding to propose any firm conclusions: the conservative position would be to assume that proprioceptive, cutaneous and muscle spindle receptors play some role in feedback control and that the circuits involved include both the cerebellum and a direct pathway to the sensory–motor cortex, via the thalamus. There are some other data to be considered with respect to the cerebellum, however, which clearly implicate it in speech production, regardless of its role in feedback. Brown *et al.* (1968, 1970) noted that lesions in the cerebellum may cause a speech disorder without necessarily any disorders in other motor systems. Usually cerebellar lesions cause clearly recognizable impairments of gait and skilled limb movements, in addition to the speech deficits. One of the criteria mentioned above (number 3) on the basis of which a structure could be assigned to the speech production system, was evidence for ana-tomical localization or specialization. Physiological specialization in the cerebellum for speech is evident from the isolated dysarthria that may fol-low circumscribed lesions; the anatomical evidence cited by Brown *et al.* (1970) implicates the midportion of the vermis (declive and culmen) and part of the paramedian lobule, as the regions of the cerebellum subserving speech. In this regard it should be noted that the cerebellum is somatotopi-cally organized (the homunculus) in these areas, and that there is a point-to-point projection from these areas to the ventrolateral nucleus of the thalamus, which is also somatotopically organized, all analogous to the somatotopic organization of the sensory–motor cortex surrounding the Fissure of Rolando. The nature of the afferent and efferent pathways of the cerebellum do not shed much more light on its role in speech production; most authors believe that the cerebellum exerts its influence on voluntary motor activity via the cerebello-cortical loop, which is schematically represented in Fig. 2. From the deep nuclei of the cerebellum, fibers project to the red nucleus and thalamus (ventrolateral nucleus) and thence to the sensory–motor cortex. Projections from the cortex first go to pontine nuclei and thence back into the cerebellum. The cerebellum also receives input from auditory and visual systems, both from the periphery as well as from the primary cortical projection areas. The other major input of interest in this context is the previously discussed spindle-afferent system. Konigsmark (1970), in contradistinction to Bowman (1971), suggests that there may be connections via the hypoglossal nerve to the hypoglossal nucleus (cranial nerve XII) and from there to the peri-hypoglossal nucleus and thence to the cerebellum. This system would be analogous to the more familiar routes of the spindle afferents. As has been noted, there are conflicting views on this, and the definitive research has yet to be done.

Fig. 2 also indicates the general schematics of the basal ganglia circuitry; these are elaborated somewhat in Fig. 3, in which the descending basal ganglia motor pathways (the extrapyramidal system) are differentiated from the basal ganglia-cortex loop pathways. It is not clearly established whether the effects of basal ganglia lesions on speech are due to disruptions in the cortical loop or in the descending pathways, or both. However, this question is not too important with respect to the speech production system, since the basal ganglia are not a major part of that system, according to the a priori criteria previously proposed. In the first place, there is very

FIG. 2. Anatomical pathways of the motor system (primary speech production system in heavy black).

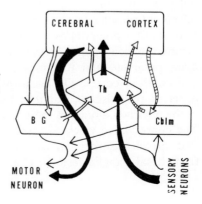

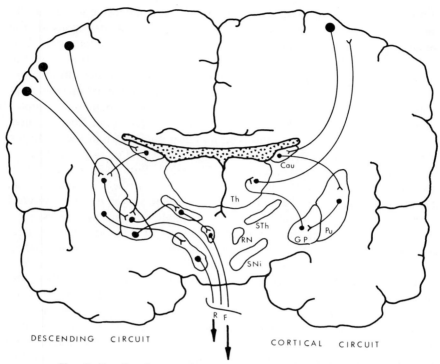

Fɪɢ. 3. Details of anatomical pathways of basal ganglia circuits.

little evidence that basal ganglia lesions can affect speech to the exclusion of other motor systems; rather, it usually is the case that the speech disorder is quite comparable to the involuntary movement disorder. In some cases, chorea in particular, the involuntary movement disorder is simply superimposed on all articulatory gestures—the gestures themselves are not impaired. In other cases, parkinsonian tremor for example, the disorder affects all muscles in the same manner, although not always in equal proportion. One potential exception is the case of Wilson's disease, a metabolic disorder which results in the deposition of protein-bound copper in the liver, putamen, and thalamus and, to a lesser extent, in the cerebellum and cerebral cortex. On occasion, dysarthria may be the first sign of the onset of this disease, but it is by no means clear that the abnormalities in the putamen alone are the lesions responsible for the early speech deficit. The conservative viewpoint would be that there is as yet no clear evidence that speech disorders in isolation from other motor disorders can result from basal ganglia lesions. Consistent with this is the fact that there is no clearly established somatotopic organization in any of the principal basal ganglia structures: caudate, putamen, globus pallidus, and substantia nigra. There is such organization in some nuclei of the thalamus, however, and for this and other reasons (see Whitaker, this volume) the thalamus is included in the central language system. The picture is somewhat clouded by the fact that some of the thalamic nuclei in which somatotopic organization has been demonstrated are ventroposteromedial (VPM) and ventroposterolateral (VPL)—relay nuclei for both cerebellar and basal ganglia pathways to the cortex. As Bowman (1971) noted, the issue then is whether (*1*) the activity of the thalamic nuclei in question is a summation of the various afferent inputs from spinothalamic and lemniscal tracts (tactile and spindle), basal ganglia, cerebellum, and internal thalamic pathways, as from pulvinar or whether (*2*) there are separate motor circuits and hence differentiable motor patterns in these thalamic nuclei. A great deal more information needs to be obtained before there can be clear answers to these questions.

References

Aronson, A. E., Brown, J. R., Litkin, E. M., & Pearson, J. S. Spastic dysphonia. II *Journal of Speech & Hearing Disorders,* 1968, **33,,** 219–231.

Bowman, J. P. *The muscle spindle and neural control of the tongue.* Springfield: C. C Tomas, 1971.

Brown, J. R., Darley, F. L., & Aronson, A. E. Deviant dimensions of motor speech in cerebellar ataxia. *Transactions of the American Neurological Association,* 1968, **93,** 193–196.

Brown, J. R., Darley, F. L., & Aronson, A. E. Ataxic dysarthria. *International Journal of Neurology,* 1970, **7,** 302–318.

Buckingham, H. W., & Kertesz, A. A linguistic analysis of fluent aphasia. *Brain and Language,* 1974, **1,** 43–62.

Cooper, 1. S. *Involuntary movement disorders.* New York: Hoeber, 1969.

Critchley, M. *Aphasiology.* London: E. Arnold, 1970.

Curtis, B. A., Jacobson, S., & Marcus, E. M. *An introduction to the neurosciences.* Philadelphia: W. B. Saunders, 1972.

Darley, F. L., Aronson, A. E., & Brown, J. R. Motor speech signs in neurologic disease. *Medical Clinics of North America,* 1968, **52,** 835–844.

Darley, F. L., Aronson, A. E., & Brown, J. R. Differential diagnostic patterns of dysarthria. *Journal of Speech & Hearing Research,* 1969, **12,** 246–269. (a)

Darley, F. L., Aronson, A. E., & Brown, J. R. Clusters of deviant speech dimensions in the dysarthrias. *Journal of Speech & Hearing Research,* 1969, **12,** 462–496. (b)

Denny-Brown, D. *The basal ganglia.* London: Oxford Univ. Pres, 1962.

Konigsmark, B. W. Neuroanatomy of speech. In *Speech and the dentofacial complex: The state of the art.* ASHA Reports 5. Washington: American Speech and Hearing Association, 1970. Pp. 3–19.

Lehiste, I. *Some acoustic characteristics of dysarthric speech*. Basel: S. Karger (Bibliotheca Phonetica, Fasc. 2), 1965.

Luchsinger, R., & Arnold, G. E. *Voice—speech—language*. Belmont, California: Wadsworth 1965.

MacNeilage, P. F. Motor control of serial ordering of speech. *Psychological Review,* 1970, **77,** 182–196.

Mohr, J. P. Rapid amelioration of motor aphasia. *Archives of Neurology,* in press.

Ringel, R. L. Oral sensation and perception. In *Speech and the dentofacial complex: The state of the art*. ASHA Reports 5. Washington: American Speech and Hearing Association, 1970. Pp. 188–206.

Sussman, H. M. What the tongue tells the brain. *Psychological Bulletin,* 1972, **77,** 262–272.

Tatham, M. A. A. The control of muscles in speech. *Occasional Papers #3*. Colchester: University of Essex, 1969.

Whitaker, H. A. *On the representation of language in the human brain*. Edmonton, Canada: Linguistic Research, 1971.

Part IV

Trends in Psychological Tests of Linguistic Theory

Chapter 14

DISINTEGRATING THEORETICIAL DISTINCTIONS AND SOME FUTURE DIRECTIONS IN PSYCHOLINGUISTICS

P. L. FRENCH

I. INTRODUCTION

The paradigmatic shift in theoretical approach to the study of human language from behaviorist to Chomsky's transformational grammar has been frequently said to be a scientific revolution, as described by Kuhn (1970) (e.g., Maclay, 1971; Searle, 1972). According to Kuhn, a paradigm provides essentially a world-view for the scientist in that it dictates the phenomena to be considered, and the methods of research into them. However, in providing the relevant empirical domain, methodology, etc., the paradigm not only provides a structure for research, but also determines to a great extent the nature of its "discoveries." A phenomenon lying outside the relevant empirical domain, or only discoverable with another methodology will not be uncovered. Moreover, findings within this domain and methodology will generally be interpreted in terms of the paradigm, whatever their nature. [See Crombie (1963, Part Four) for a more recent version by Kuhn and related commentary and criticism of his theory.] From this point of view, a scientific revolution such as Chomsky's entails a shift in the empirical domain, methodology, and ultimately, the world view of the scientist of language. Whereas formerly language was considered as a stimulus or response to be studied empirically (behaviorism), or a code to be broken down into its atomic elements and classified (structuralism), after Chomsky the topic was a nonempirical, formal competence. This abstract knowledge of the syntax of language was unobservable, and therefore required deductive, transformational methods.

An on-going view of psycholinguistics accords Chomsky an important position not only for his revolution in itself, but also for the (unintentional) initiation of an inexorable process in the evolution of psycholinguistic theory toward the inclusion of meaning. While structuralism studied the structure of the language code and behaviorism studied overt verbal behavior, meaning was not considered by either to be adequately characterizable for normal science research. Similarly Chomsky specifically excluded meaning also, characterizing "intuition about linguistic form" and "intuition about meaning" as "two terms that have in common only their vagueness and their undesirability in linguistic theory [Chomsky, 1957, p. 94]."

However, his successful shift of the domain of psycholinguistics from observable performance (speech behavior) to a nonobservable mental entity—competence (knowledge about the syntactic rules of the language) constituted an effective preliminary to the inclusion of meaning, another unobservable mental entity. Once such abstract knowledge was considered a proper subject for study, the only barrier to the study of other types of knowledge as well (i.e., meaning) was theoretical in the form of the competence–performance distinction. This distinction entailed two other more basic ones. The first is that syntax is autonomous from semantics (ensuring the formal, nonempirical, nature of the grammar) and the second even more basic one is that knowledge about language is separate from knowledge about the world (separating the domain of linguistics from that of cognitive psychology). The topic of this chapter is the erosion of these theoretical distinctions resulting in the present approach to the study of human language.

More recent formal argument in linguistics presents evidence not of the autonomy of syntax but of its inextricability from semantics for the generative semanticists, and the inseparability of knowledge about language and knowledge about the world for more radical linguists. The failure to find any direct reflection of syntactic competence in studies of performance has eroded support for the competence–performance distinction in experimental psycholinguistics. Increasingly, research demonstrates not the psychological reality of syntactic rules, or even of semantic rules, but rather the meaning of the utterance in context to the subject. This chapter, then, details the developments in linguistics and psycholinguistics after Chomsky's revolution, leading to what is perhaps an even more radical shift: the inclusion of meaning and its relation to nonlinguistic cognition in the study of human language.

II. COMPETENCE AND PERFORMANCE

A. Experimental Psycholinguistics

Miller's 1962 Presidential address to the Eastern Psychological Association presented essentially argument and evidence that the linguistic structure proposed by Chomsky was psychologically real. The comprehension of a sentence was described as the recovery of its underlying deep structure from its surface structure. Similarly, memory of a sentence was conceived of not as a configuration of words as did the behaviorists, but as an abstract representation of its syntactic base structure (i.e., its "kernel") plus tags indexing the proper transformations. In the 1960s, psycholinguists assumed that "actual speech behavior is some regular function of the abstract linguistic structure originally isolated in linguistic investigations [Bever, 1970, p. 270]," and studies of adult performance appeared to demonstrate such a direct relationship between competence and performance. Evidence was presented for the psychological reality of all three levels of Chomsky's model: surface structure, transformations, and deep structure.

1. SURFACE STRUCTURE

That constituents were psychologically perceived as more related than nonconstituents was demonstrated even before the Chomskyian paradigm began to direct psycholinguistic research. Maclay and Osgood (1959) found that hesitations in speech occur most frequently at constituent boundaries as do errors in recall (Johnson, 1968). A series of "click" studies demonstrated that such effects were also observed for perception. Clicks actually heard within constituent boundaries were perceived between them, indicating that constituents are psychological units that resist interruption (Garrett, Bever, & Fodor, 1966). However, these positive results for the psychological reality of surface structure are not necessarily evidence for Chomsky's transformational grammar, since surface structure and constituent structure were considered to have psychological reality by both structuralists and behaviorists.

2. TRANSFORMATIONS

Mehler (1963) was among the first to test these predictions. He did so by using a rote-memory task. Subjects learned eight sentences: A simple, active, affirmative, declarative ("kernel sentence"), a passive, a negative, and a question construction, and all combinations. It was assumed that the "kernel sentence" was understood and stored without transformation, and that therefore, the addition of passive, negative, or question transformations would increase memory load. It was predicted that this increase would be evidenced by simplification in memory toward the untransformed kernel sentence. So, these kernel sentences should be remembered most accurately, and errors in memory should increase in direct proportion to the number of transformations required. His results generally supported these assumptions and were considered to indicate a direct relationship between Chomsky's formal theory of syntax and memory for sentences. However, this evidence does not force such a conclusion. Since simple, active, affirmative, declarative sentences are overwhelmingly the most frequent (Goldman-Eisler & Cohen, 1970) a tendency to recall transformed sentences in terms of their kernels could also be explained by a response bias in favor of simple, active, affirmative, declarative sentences in general.

In the attempt to find evidence for transformations, it seemed that demonstrating a greater processing load for passive constructions than their corresponding active forms would be most readily accomplished, as studies such as Wright (1968) appeared to confirm. Since passive constructions require more words than their actives, this would be predicted by any performance theory (see Fig. 1). However, several studies found no such evidence. For example, Wright (1969) found that although active questions were more difficult to answer about passive sentences and vice versa, passive questions about passive statements were no more difficult to answer than active questions about active statements. Similarly, Slobin (1966) demonstrated that passives were no more difficult to understand than their corresponding actives if their semantic relations were unique.

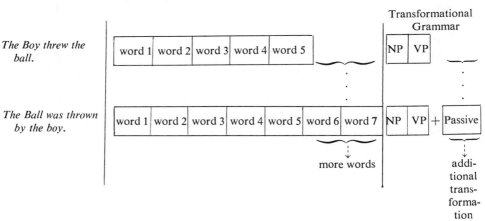

FIG. 1. Two alternative explanations for a greater processing time required by the passive form than by the active form of the same sentence.

While *The boy was kissed by the girl* was more difficult than *The girl kissed the boy, The leaves were raked by the boy* was no more difficult than *The boy raked the leaves.* This indicated to Slobin that ". . . part of the difficulty of understanding sentences is based on semantics [1971, p. 36]" again presenting evidence that a formal syntactic competence could not be directly related to performance.

A second type of experiment that supported Chomsky's theory as a model of performance was executed by Savin and Perchonock (1965). This experiment attempted to exploit the finite capacity of immediate memory to demonstrate that memory load is proportional to the number of transformations that must be stored. Recall of each sentence followed 5 sec after presentation of the sentence plus eight unrelated words. Results showed that the more transformations required by the sentence, the fewer unrelated words that could be recalled. The relative number of words that could be recalled after each transformational type allowed the authors also to infer the memory load imposed by different transformations. However, the immediate attempt to apply this technique to demonstrating the psychological reality of other transformations was unsuccessful (Bever, Fodor, Garrett, & Mehler, reported in Fodor & Garrett, 1966). Other researchers replicating Savin and Perchonock using the same transformations (e.g., Glucksberg & Danks, 1969; Matthews, 1968) found this result attributable to differences in time between presentation and recall, rather than any syntactic factor. Thus, strong evidence for the psychological reality of transformations remains to be presented. Other research (e.g., Fodor & Garrett, 1967) produced results which were frankly negative. Six additional transformations failed to produce a decrement in performance.

3. DEEP STRUCTURE

Attempts to provide evidence for a syntactic deep structure have been uniformly negative. If understanding a sentence is the recovery of its deep structure and remembering it is in terms of this structure also, then recall should be in terms of this structure. In recall of sentences, however memory for the *syntactic structure* (assumed to be the basis of memory) is poor, while memory for the *meaning* of the sentence is quite good (e.g., Fillenbaum, 1966, 1968). Fillenbaum (1968) demonstrated that errors in memory preserve meaning, while syntactic structure is not retained. In a survey of this literature, Fillenbaum (1973) concludes: "Sentences which are equivalent in meaning, although they differ in the basic grammatical relations in which their constituents enter and in their deep structure prepositions, are the ones most likely to be mutually confused [p. 56]." Furthermore, a series of studies demonstrate even less correspondence between deep structure and sentence memory. Bransford and Franks

(1971), Franks and Bransford (1972), and Bransford, Barclay, and Franks (1972) have shown that when subjects are presented with a number of meaningfully related sentences, they remember not the discrete sentences presented, but spontaneously integrate them into a "linguistic idea" and this is what is recalled. Thus, this series of experiments shows that memory is not only not for syntactic deep structure, and not necessarily even for sentences, but the meaning they convey.

4. SUMMARY

In the early 1960s, psycholinguists were confident that "actual speech behavior is some function of the abstract linguistic structure originally isolated in linguistic investigations [Bever, 1970, p. 270]." And, consistent with Kuhn's (1970) views on paradigms and normal science research, evidence was interpreted as confirmatory. While practically all confirmatory evidence advanced for the direct reflection of competence in adult performance could have been accounted for in terms of other (more obvious) factors such as a difference in memory load for more versus fewer words or for common versus less common sentence types, such alternative interpretations had extremely low visibility until the late 1960s (see Bever, 1970; Fodor & Garrett, 1966, 1967; Fodor, Garrett, & Bever, 1968). Since then, psycholinguists have increasingly rejected the notion that performance is in any way directly related to competence.

B. Developmental Psycholinguistics

At its inception, developmental psycholinguistics (McNeill, 1966) proceeded according to an essentially nativist theory. Following linguistics, an explanation of language ability was primarily an explanation for syntax. Since it was assumed that the child learns to produce all possible sentences in his language rather than only those he hears, and since the syntax, which relates meaningful elements, is not directly observable, it was concluded that this formal syntactic structure could not be learned, and therefore must be innate.

> It seems plain that language acquisition is based on the child's discovery of what from a formal point of view is a deep and abstract theory—a generative grammar of his language—many of the concepts and principles of which are only remotely related to experience by long and intricate chains of unconscious quasi-inferential steps. A consideration of the character of the grammar that is acquired, the degenerate quality and narrowly limited extent of the available data, the striking uniformity of the resulting grammars, and their independence of intelligence, motivation, and emotional state, over wide ranges of variation, leave little hope that much of the structure of the language can be learned by an organism initially uninformed as to its general character [Chomsky, 1965, p. 58].

Developmental psycholinguists in the 1960s essentially followed this position:

> " . . . It is now proposed that, first, children are born with a biologically based, innate capacity for language acquisition; secondly, the best guess as to the nature of the innate capacity is that it takes the form of linguistic universals; thirdly, the best guess as to the nature of linguistic universals is that they consist of what are currently the basic notions in a Chomskian transformational grammar. Metaphorically speaking, a child is now born with a copy of *Aspects of the Theory of Syntax* tucked away somewhere inside. Given the present state of knowledge regarding innate capacity and language universals, the above seem defensible guesses [Fraser, 1966, p. 116 (paraphrase of McNeill, 1966)]."

It was assumed that this innate structure was responsible for the ability to learn language and create and understand sentences. Developmental psycholinguistic research at this period consisted essentially of discovering evidence for the innate structure. Considering the effects of paradigms upon research (Kuhn, 1970), it is not surprising that such evidence was almost invariably found.

1. HOLOPHRASES

The interpretation of the child's first one-word utterances is a particularly good example of the effect of paradigms. Transformationalists (e.g., Lenneberg, 1967, p. 283; McNeill, 1966, p. 63; Menyuk, 1969, pp. 25–29) considered these utterances to be "holophrases"—one-word sentences— each of which could represent in surface structure a number of deep structures, depending upon intonation. Here, the child is credited with the innate knowledge of syntax independently of evidence in performance. Because such "evidence" derives from the paradigm's effects upon perception rather than data, no disproof or negative evidence could be forthcoming. However, other researchers (e.g., Bloom, 1973; Peng, 1975; von Raffler-Engel, 1970) who have rejected the transformational paradigm also reject this interpretation, considering these utterances to represent not an underlying syntactic competence, but the lack of it.

2. PRIMITIVE GRAMMARS

Evidence for a "primitive grammar" was discovered independently by Braine (1963), Brown and Fraser (1963), and Miller and Ervin (1964). These researchers examined the distributional structure of children's two-word utterances and found that privilege of occurrence divided the child's lexicon into essentially two classes which McNeill (1966) described as "pivot" and "open." Because these word classes do not correspond to those of the adult, but are rather constructed by the child, they are considered by McNeill (1966) to be evidence for the workings of an innate LAD (Language Acquisition Device). The child is perceived to create a primitive functor class from his competence rather than by learning the adult grammar, separating his vocabulary into two parts of speech.

> "Early speech of children . . . reflects a severely limited grammatical competence. However . . . these aspects of children's competence . . . are all properties of the base structure of sentences . . . children's earliest speech does not reflect the operation of transformational rules . . . Therefore, it is not too unreasonable to think of children "talking" base strings directly. We can conceive of their phonological rules as interpreting base structures rather than surface structure in the generation of sentences [McNeill, 1966, p. 51]. If the earliest syntactic competence comprises the base structure of sentences, then obviously the major portion of syntactic acquisition after this point will be taken up with the growth of transformations [McNeill, 1966, p. 53]."

Thus, after the primitive grammatical categories, "pivot" and "open" differentiate by successive approximations into the adult classes, the child is seen as developing transformations, which transform the base structures that he was "talking directly" into strings more nearly approximating adult surface structure. Here, the interpretation of children's language learning is already given by the paradigm. Children's increasingly well-formed sentences will be evidence for the development of transformations.

For researchers who accepted the transformational model, the above results were convincing evidence. However, such evidence for the existence of transformations requires the postulation of such structures, accepting which, almost any increase in well-formedness except rote learning can be interpreted as confirmatory. Assuming the existence of transformations to account for the gradual conformity of children's utterances to an adult model is an assumption, not an explanation. And such an assumption cannot be evidence for itself. This is the viewpoint of researchers who did not completely accept the Chomskian paradigm (and the entailed assumptions) and therefore did not "see" the confirmatory evidence (see von Raffler-Engel, 1970; Bloom, 1973; Peng, 1975).

Discussion of the holophrase or development of transformations was primarily theoretical, since their existence as evidence required the prior assumption of a transformational interpretation. But the pivot/open grammar appeared to present an emerging structure of the child's own creation, and as such, it provoked a substantive (rather than theoretical) debate. Although the theoretical interpretation of the pivot/open distinction (i.e., that pivot and open categories are the manifestation of an innate, universal hierarchy of word classes) can be neither proved nor disproved, objections were soon raised against the data themselves. The sum of the arguments raised by Bloom (1971), Brown (1973), and Bowerman (1973) amount to an indictment of the pivot/open distinction, and therefore any theoretical implications that could be drawn from it. First, they find that the generalization of privilege of occurrence which distinguishes the pivot-from the open-class word is faulty. From reexamination of this evidence, it was found that in no child's grammar, thus far, is the position of the pivot absolutely fixed. Pivots occur not only with open-class words, but also alone and in constructions with other pivots. Brown (1973) notes that this is a fatal flaw because

> . . . the pivot grammar depends absolutely on the nonoccurrence of P and P + P and on the restriction of certain pivots to initial position (P_1) and others to final position (P_z). If these restrictions were all removed, we should have as possible combinations: P, O, P + O, O + P, P + P, O + O. What this reduces to is the following:
>
> Sentence . . . . . (W) + W
>
> where W is any word. Which is no grammar at all. In short, the pivot structure does not exist unless the nonoccurrences implied by the rules are borne out by the facts [p. 97].

Finally, even the superficial distributional analysis allowing all of the above exceptions (pivots occurring alone and with other pivots) will not find a pivot/open distinction in all children (Bloom, 1970; Bowerman, 1973) (see Table I).

Furthermore, Bloom (1971), Brown (1973), Bowerman (1973), and Schlesinger (1971) all note that the analysis of the lexicon into two categories is superficial and descriptive—not functional or cognitive. The notion of the pivot- and the open-class word is a purely surface structure description, That is, it includes no notion of the meaning of utterances so constructed, or the relation between utterances with the same structure. Thus, although transformationally motivated, to the pivot grammar fall all of the shortcomings of the phrase structure grammar. Thus it is concluded by later researchers that not only did the pivot/open distinction not produce evidence for a direct relationship of Chomsky's model of competence to actual performance, but that its heuristic value is nil.

3. SUMMARY

In developmental psycholinguistics also, the mechanisms of the influence of paradigms upon research described by Kuhn (1970) is seen. Research was not simply a search for data on the mechanisms of language development, but rather a search for evidence supporting Chomsky's transformational account of the process. Given the prior acceptance of the paradigm's assumptions, the interpretation of data is already given. The child's earliest

TABLE I

AN EXAMPLE OF PIVOT/OPEN ANALYSIS OF PRIMITIVE GRAMMAR

Pivot class	Open class
see	*sleep*
more	*baby*
bye-bye	*cookie*
all gone	*Mama*
	truck
	horsie
RULES[a]	GRAMMATICAL SENTENCES
S → P + O	*see truck*
	all gone horsie
	more cookie
	bye-bye horsie
S → O + O	*Mama cookie*
	horsie sleep
	baby shoes
	horsie truck
S → P + P	UNGRAMMATICAL SENTENCES
	*all gone bye-bye
	*bye-bye see

[a] S = Sentence, P = Pivot-Class word, O = Open-Class word.

utterances—single words—will be interpreted as the surface structure manifestations of underlying base strings. Distributional accounts of two-word utterances will be described in terms of a pivot/open grammar: The surface manifestations of primitive transformations [e.g. $(S \rightarrow P + O)$]. Increasing grammaticality of utterances as the child becomes older will be described in terms of the development of transformations. Ultimately, the child's utterances will be identical with those of the adult, at which time he will have acquired all of the transformations of the language. As in experimental psycholinguistics, for those who accept the paradigm, the data were easily interpreted as confirmatory evidence. But for those who did not accept the assumptions of the paradigm, this evidence ranged from unconvincing to invisible.

Approximately 10 years of research in experimental psycholinguistics failed to find convincing evidence for the psychological reality of Chomsky's formal theory of syntactic competence that was independent of its assumptions. However, empirical evidence is essentially irrelevant to a formal theory. Chomsky himself made it clear that no relationship was to be expected between competence (postulated syntactic structure) and actual performance (production or comprehension of sentences) manifesting that structure.

> . . . [A] generative grammar attempts to specify what the speaker actually knows, not what he may report of his knowledge [Chomsky, 1965, p. 8].
> . . . [A] generative grammar is not a model for the speaker or the hearer.
> . . . When we say that a sentence has a certain derivation . . . we say nothing about how the speaker or hearer might proceed . . . [T]his generative grammar does not . . . prescribe the character or functioning of a perceptual model or a model of speech production [Chomsky, 1965, p. 9].

Thus, if no direct relationship is implied between competence and its empirical manifestation, performance, then empirical studies can generate an infinite amount of negative evidence for such a model without injuring its tenability.

However, while a formal theory is not vulnerable to empirical results, it is vulnerable to formal argument. A new faction of linguistic theorists—the generative semanticists—have presented arguments that a formal distinction between syntax and semantics cannot be maintained. The following section will attempt to summarize their arguments, showing also how collapse of a semantics–syntax distinction suggests also the inseparability of language and general cognitive abilities, which is the theoretical basis for more recent psycholinguistic research.

III. SYNTAX AND SEMANTICS

One of the most basic assumptions of formal systems (which include mathematics and logic as well as generative grammar) is that formal operations such as transformation and derivation do not change the meaning (or truth value) of the string upon which they are applied. For example $x(y - z)$ may be rewritten $xy - xz$ in algebra and in the predicate calculus, $\phi_1 \leftrightarrow \phi_2$ may be rewritten $(\phi_1 \wedge \phi_2) \vee (\sim\phi_1 \wedge \sim\phi_2)^*$, without affecting either the semantic interpretation or truth value assigned to the original string. If these operations did affect semantic interpretation or truth value of the strings to which they are applied, then their use would not be permissible in a formal system.

Thus, a formal theory of grammar must assert that transformations do not change the meaning of the strings to which they are applied. And, the passive is surely a transformation. In view of these two elementary as-

---

* The symbols "$\leftrightarrow$", "$\wedge$", "$\vee$", and "$\sim$" mean "if and only if," "and," "or," and "not," respectively.

pects of standard theory, Lakoff (1971a, p. 238) presents the following sentences:

(1)   *Many men read few books.*

(2)   *Few books are read by many men.*

While a theory of a purely syntactic deep structure must generate both (1) and (2) from the same base strings, the meanings of these two sentences are not the same. Generative semanticists respond to such examples by proposing not that transformations do not preserve meaning, but rather that such sentences are derived from different underlying structures. However, this would require that such structures cannot be purely syntactic, since the same deep structure would allow derivation of both (1) and (2).

The stage at which lexical insertion occurs is intimately related to this problem, also threatening the notion of a purely syntactic deep structure. Because lexical entries contain the features determining which transformations apply to strings containing them, lexical insertion cannot occur after transformation is complete. And, because "transformations cannot introduce meaning-bearing elements [Chomsky, 1965, p. 132]" if they are to be meaning-preserving, lexical insertion cannot occur during transformation. Since lexical insertion cannot occur either during or after transformation, in Chomsky's Standard Theory (and the 1971 revision), it must occur before the application of any transformations. Any other ordering of lexical insertion and transformation would violate the formal nature of the system. However, some generative semanticists have given examples of sentences that require alternative ordering of transformation and lexical insertion, given a purely syntactic deep structure. Lakoff and Ross (1967) and Lakoff (1971a) have demonstrated cases in which lexical insertion must occur after certain transformations have been applied, and Gruber (1965) has argued that some transformations occur before lexical insertion.

The accumulation of arguments such as these has pointed to the abandonment of deep structure. If accepted, the preceding arguments for variation in the order of lexical insertion and transformations destroy the formal nature of present linguistic theory unless the notion of a purely syntactic deep structure is dismissed. If deep structure is purely syntactic, then transformation must change meaning, a deadly and therefore unacceptable assumption for any formal theory. Furthermore, if lexical insertion and transformation stages cannot be separated, then the deep structure level, which supposedly segregates lexical insertion from transformation, is superfluous. Chomsky (1971) has considered these arguments and admitted their implications for deep structure. However, his term for describing the would-be status of deep structure is "not defined" rather than "superfluous" (Chomsky, 1971, p. 187). In general, his rebuttal of the generative semantics arguments has consisted of defining out of existence the problem their evidence poses:

> . . . suppose that one were to counterpose to the syntactically based standard theory a "semantically based" theory of the following sort. Whereas the standard theory proposes that a syntactic structure Σ is mapped onto the pair (P, S) (P a phonetic and S a semantic representation), the new theory supposes that S is mapped onto Σ, which is then mapped onto P as in the standard theory. Clearly, when the matter is formulated in this way, there is no empirical difference between the "syntactically based" standard theory and the "semantically based" alternative [Chomsky, 1971, p. 187].

However, this is not the way the generative semanticists such as Fillmore, Lakoff, McCawley, Postal, and Ross formulate the matter. If there is no level at which lexical insertion is complete without the operation of transformations, then there is no purely syntactic structure that can be considered as the sentence's antecedent (deep) structure. And, if such a deep structure level does not exist, then the generative semantic solution is to reject it rather than simply to call it "not defined." Far from accepting Chomsky's claim that there "is no empirical difference between the 'syntactically based' standard theory and the 'semantically based' alternative [Chomsky, 1971, p. 187]," the rejection of deep structure, which the semantically based theory requires, has serious consequences. If there is no level at which only syntactic considerations operate in the absence of semantic considerations, then Chomsky's basic assumption that "grammar is autonomous and independent of meaning [Chomsky, 1957, p. 17]" is in error. If deep structure is rejected for these reasons, it must be accepted that syntax and semantics are not independent. This is exactly what the generative semanticists have done. If deep structure does not exist, then a generative theory must still generate sentences from something. If this something is not a purely syntactic representation, then it must be a semantic representation also. This basic assumption spells the fundamental difference between standard theory and generative semantics.

In 1957, Chomsky remarked that "intuition about linguistic form [and] intuition about meaning" "have in common only their vagueness and their undesirability in linguistic theory [p. 94]." The notion that semantics may be relevant to grammatical description is passed off with ". . . the burden of proof . . . rests completely on the linguist who claims to have been able to develop some grammatical notion in semantic terms [p. 94]." Since then, linguists have taken their burden of proof and discharged it with enough success that several have suggested that sentences are generated from semantic representations and that a purely syntactic level of deep structure is superfluous (e.g., Fillmore, 1968, Lakoff 1971a, McCawley, 1968). Now the burden of proof has shifted and "rests with those who posit the existence of the extra level [McCawley, 1968, p. 165]." Generative semanticists would not accept that such proof has been offered thus far (Lakoff, 1971a, p. 283). Increasingly, linguistics are embracing the generative semantics position, which is "that syntax and semantics cannot be separated and that the role of transformations, and of derivational constraints in general, is to relate semantic representations and surface structures [Lakoff, 1971a, p. 232].

IV. KNOWLEDGE ABOUT LANGUAGE AND KNOWLEDGE ABOUT THE WORLD

But what is a "semantic representation"? Can such structures be defined in linguistic terms that distinguish them from other cognitive structures? They must, if the competence–performance distinction is to be preserved. However, that knowledge about language can be separated from knowledge about the world is a theoretical postulation based on the posited impossibility of handling the latter systematically rather than on any empirical evidence. Katz and Fodor (1963) make such an argument in "The Structure of a Semantic Theory":

> . . . since there is no serious possibility of systematizing all the knowledge of the world that speakers share, and since a theory of the kind we have been discussing requires such a systematization, it is ipso facto not a serious model for semantics [p. 179].

It is clear that "the semantic representations" of the generative semanticists must be richer structures than those of standard theory. For example, McCawley (1971) asserts that semantic representations must "separate a clause into a 'proposition' and a set of noun phrases which provide the material used in identifying the indices of the 'proposition' . . . [p. 224]." Lakoff (1971b) asserts the dependence of judgments of well-formedness upon presuppositions about the nature of the world. But he specifically rejects that this could be "considered as blurring the distinction between competence and performance. . . . Such a claim does not constitute the position that linguistic knowledge cannot be separated from knowledge about the world [p. 329]."

However, there are no discovery procedures for deciding what sort of knowledge is (linguistic) and therefore relevant to semantic representation and what is not. It is clear from the literature that whatever knowledge is found necessary for well-formedness will be considered linguistic with no other justification. And from present indications, the amount and complexity of this information will be staggering. Propositions and presuppositions about the nature of the world are a far cry from the semantic features that were so amenable to formal coding (Katz and Fodor, 1963). And when the notation of transformational grammar and the predicate calculus both are found inadequate to capture types of knowledge deemed necessary for semantic representations, the conclusion is drawn not that such knowledge resists inclusion into a formal theory because it is empirical, but that the notation is inadequate (McCawley, 1971, p. 222).

If whatever information is necessary will be assumed as part of semantic representation, then the distinction between linguistic knowledge and knowledge about the world is a theoretical assumption and, as such, will never be tested by linguists. It is already apparent that they are willing to accept as linguistic a great quantity of considerations that were formerly dismissed as "cognitive" or "performance variables" (see e.g., Lakoff, 1971b; McCawley, 1968).

If there is a type of semantic knowledge that is part of and specific to linguistic competence, then that type of knowledge should be assessed more easily than factual knowledge which lies outside of that system. It should be faster to verify that *A canary is a bird* than *A canary has wings,* since theoretically, the verification of the first sentence requires semantic information, whereas the second requires factive. This is the result of an experiment by Collins and Quillian (1969), which has been interpreted as upholding the semantic–factive distinction that Katz (1972) deems imperative to a linguistic theory. However, Conrad (1972) demonstrated that these results could easily be explained by the frequency with which one term is elicited by the other as an associate. Furthermore, these results could be viewed in terms of the relative latency of categorization (semantic) statements versus descriptive (factive) statements, to name one alternative explanation. Since, in the absence of some generally accepted definition, the results of such an experiment depend upon the experimenter's decision as to which types of information in the sentences are factive or semantic, it is unlikely that satisfactory evidence for the distinction will be provided in this manner.

V. FUTURE DIRECTIONS

Meanings, scientifically construed . . . were properly speaking the subject matter of psychologists. Alternatively they might be some mysterious mental entities altogether outside the scope of a sober science or, worse yet, they might involve the speaker's whole knowledge of the world around him and thus fall beyond the scope of a study restricted only to linguistic facts [Searle, 1972, p. 16].

Although the preceding excerpt is from a description of structuralism, it is equally relevant to the transformational approach. In fact, structuralism, transformationalism, and behaviorism all have in common the exclusion of meaning from their relevant empirical domains. So long as the domain is limited to the taxonomy of language elements, to overt behavior, or to syntax, the problems for normal science research entailed by meaning need not be handled. It is outside the empirical domain. The generative semanticists who argued successfully for the inclusion of semantics into transformational accounts of language are now faced with the difficulty, perhaps impossibility, of the formal characterization of the necessary semantic considerations for which they argued.

In the early 1960s, transformational grammar had provided a paradigm for both linguistic research and psycholinguistic research—formal deductive methods for linguistics and comparisons of the theoretical predictions with empirical results for psycholinguistics. The loss of this paradigm has put both linguistics and psycholinguists in a challenging position, with enormous freedom but no clear guide. Generative semanticists continue to labor at characterizing semantic aspects for inclusion into a formal theory, although the predicate calculus already appears to be inadequate for this purpose (McCawley, 1971, p. 222), and these semantic considerations appear to be indistinguishable from general cognitive knowledge about the world (Maclay, 1971, p. 180). More radical linguists (e.g., Chafe, 1973, R. Lakoff, 1972; Searle, 1972) appear to have abandoned the separation of knowledge about language and of the world entirely. These linguists write not of a formal characterization of language within a transformational framework as do the generative semanticists, but of language meaning.

Psycholinguists, in the absence of unified leadership from linguistics, have begun to use their own theorizing-equipment. Having lived through eras of both behaviorism and transformationalism, the shortcomings of each approach are still fresh in memory. Strict limitations to observable behavior cannot take account of cognitive processes, which are not observable. A purely formal account of competence is not and does not lead to an empirical account of performance. Furthermore, any model that excludes meaning cannot capture the basic character of human use of language.

The earliest departures from the transformational grammar paradigm in psycholinguistics was in terms of cognitive strategies. Slobin's (1971b) survey of cross-cultural language development suggested as candidates for innate specification strategies for acquiring grammatical structure rather than grammatical structure itself. Bever (1970) not only proposed such strategies rather than innate structures for language acquisition, but was among those who proposed the same interpretation for speech comprehension and production in adults somewhat earlier (Fodor, Garrett, & Bever, 1968). He specifically rejected the notion that language ability was either innate or autonomous from cognition. Similarly, Greenfield and Westerman (1974) find a correspondence between grammatical complexity and actual physical actions suggesting "cognitive capacities common to both language and action [p. 24]."

Although explanations were in terms of cognitive abilities rather than an autonomous syntactic structure, early studies of cognitive strategies still had the explanation for grammar as the primary goal. More recently, explaining grammar has become eclipsed by the study of meaning, as research moves increasingly farther from the generative model. Clark (1973) and Bowerman (1975) describe development of the meaning of words, while Nelson (1973), Greenfield and Smith (1976) and French (in press) describe what very young children select to talk about and what they ignore in terms of a cognitive semantic salience. Attention has become focused on the (syntactically uninteresting) one-word stage (Bloom, 1973; Greenfield & Smith, 1976) yielding cognitive explanations (via content) of a frankly incredible semantic competence at this stage such as the use of all of the adult's semantic relations as described by Fillmore (1968) [Greenfield (reported in Brown, 1973), Ingram (1971), and Bloom (1973)]. Rather than an uncharacterizable, irrelevant entity, meaning is now perceived to be the basis of language learning.

> "Infants learn their language by first determining, independent of language, the meaning which a speaker intends to convey to them, and by then working out the relationship between the meaning and the language. To put it another way, the infant uses meaning as a clue to language, rather than language as a clue to meaning [Macnamara, 1972, p. 1]."

A similar trend is observed in experimental psycholinguistics. Recent research increasingly presupposes the necessity of meaning in a description of the comprehension and production process and that this entails the inclusion of knowledge about the world. For example, Bransford and McCarrell (1974) in "A Sketch of a Cognitive Approach to Comprehension" write: "Comprehension results only when the comprehender has sufficient linguistic information to use the cues specified in linguistic input to create some semantic content that allows him to understand [p. 204]." They discuss real-world constraints of the structure of objects upon meaningfulness of utterances in which they are mentioned, and describe sentences as "instructions to create meanings [p. 201]." Olson (1970) in

"Aspects of a Cognitive Theory of Semantics" suggests that ". . . the choice of a word, is made so as to differentiate an intended referent from some perceived or inferred set of alternatives [p. 257]." Osgood (1971, p. 523) assumes that perceptual and linguistic signs share the same system and he provides evidence for a naturalness in the ordering of sentence elements in terms of the relative semantic salience of units (Osgood, 1971; Osgood and Bock, 1975; Osgood and Richards, 1973).

As the scope of psycholinguistics has expanded in depth to include knowledge about the world, it has also expanded in breadth to embrace all communicative behaviors including kinesics and paralanguage (see, e.g., von Raffler-Engel, 1964, 1975; Greenfield and Smith, 1976). Thus, this enlarged empirical domain now includes not only surface structure and syntax, but also semantics, pragmatics, accompanying nonverbal behavior, and nonlinguistic meaning. A new paradigm for this extended (empirical and nonempirical) domain must either define as irrelevant some of the above aspects or be much broader than either of the preceeding ones. In the latter case, nothing less than a thoroughgoing cognitive theory of human communication will suffice.

References

Bever, T. G. The cognitive basis for linguistic structures. In J. R. Hayes (Ed.), *Cognition and the development of language.* New York: Wiley, 1970.

Bloom, L. Why no pivot grammar? *Journal of Speech and Hearing Disorders,* 1971, **36,** 40–50.

Bloom, L. *One word at a time.* The Hague: Mouton, 1973.

Bowerman, M. *Early syntactic development.* Cambridge: Cambridge Univ. Press, 1973.

Bowerman, M. The acquisition of word meaning: An investigation of some current conflicts. Paper delivered at the Third International Child Language Symposium, London, 1975.

Braine, M. D. S. The ontogeny of English phrase structure: The first phase. *Language,* 1963, **39,** 1–14.

Bransford, J. D., Barclay, J. R., & Franks, J. J. Sentence memory: A constructive versus interpretative approach. *Cognitive Psychology,* 1972, **3,** 193–209.

Bransford, J. D., & Franks, J. J. The abstraction of linguistic ideas. *Cognitive Psychology,* 1971, **2,** 331–350.

Bransford, J. D., & McCarrell, N. S. A sketch of a cognitive approach to comprehension: Some thoughts about what it means to comprehend. In W. B. Weimer & D. S. Palermo (Eds.), *Cognition and the symbolic processes.* Hillsdale, New Jersey: Lawrence Erlbaum, 1974.

Brown, R. *A first language.* Cambridge, Massachusetts: Harvard Univ. Press, 1973.

Brown, R., & Fraser, C. The acquisition of syntax. In C. H. Cofer & B. Musgrave (Eds.), *Verbal behavior and learning: Problems and processes.* New York: McGraw-Hill, 1963, Pp. 158–201.

Chafe, W. L. Language and memory. *Language,* 1973, **49**, 261–281.

Chomsky, N. Three models for the description of language, *I. R. E. Transactions on Information Theory,* 1956, **II-2**, 113–124. (Reprinted in Smith, A. G. *Communication and culture.* New York: Holt, 1966.)

Chomsky, N. *Syntactic structures.* The Hague: Mouton, 1957.

Chomsky, N. *Aspects of the theory of syntax.* Cambridge, Massachusetts: MIT Press, 1965.

Chomsky, N. Deep structure, surface structure, and semantic interpretation. In D. D. Steinberg & L. A. Jakobovits (Eds.), *Semantics: An interdisciplinary reader in philosophy, linguistics, and psychology.* London: Cambridge Univ. Press, 1971.

Clark, E. V. What's in a word? On the child's acquisition of semantics in his first language. In T. E. Moore (Ed.), *Cognitive development and the acquisition of language.* New York: Academic Press, 1973.

Collins, A., & Quillian, M. Retrieval time from semantic memory. *Journal of Verbal Learning and Verbal Behavior,* 1969, **8**, 240–247.

Conrad, C. Cognitive economy in semantic memory. *Journal of Experimental Psychology,* 1972, **92**, 149–154.

Crombie, A. C. (Ed.), *Scientific change.* London: Heinemann, 1963.

Fillenbaum, S. Memory for gist: Some relevant variables. *Language and Speech,* 1966, **9**, 217–227.

Fillenbaum, S. Sentence similarity determined by a semantic relation: The learning of converses. *Proceedings of the 76th annual convention of the American Psychological Association,* 1968, **3**, 9–10.

Fillenbaum, S. *Syntactic factors in memory.* The Hague: Mouton, 1973.

Fillmore, C. J. The case for case. In E. Bach & R. T. Harms (Eds.), *Universals in linguistic theory.* New York: Holt, 1968.

Fodor, J., & Garrett, M. Some reflections on competence and performance. In J. Lyons & A. Wales, (Eds.), *Psycholinguistics papers,* Edinburgh: Edinburgh Univ. Press, 1966.

Fodor, J., & Garrett, M. Some syntactic determinants of sentential complexity. *Perception and Psychophysics,* 1967, **2**, 289–296.

Fodor, J., Garrett, M., & Bever, T. Some syntactic determinants of sentential complexity. II: Verb structure. *Perception and Psychophysics,* 1968, **3**, 453–461.

Franks, J. J., & Bransford, J. D. The acquisition of abstract ideas. *Journal of Verbal Learning and Verbal Behavior,* 1972, **11**, 311–315.

Fraser, C. Discussion of D. McNeill's "The creation of language by children." In J. Lyons & R. J. Wales (Eds.), *Psycholinguistics papers.* Edinburgh: Edinburgh University Press, 1966.

French, P. L. Perception and early semantic learning. In W. von Raffler-Engel (Ed.), *Child language today* (special edition of *Word*), in press.

Garrett, M., Bever, T. G., & Fodor, J. A. The active use of grammar in speech perception. *Perception and Psychophysics,* 1966, **1**, 30–32.

Glucksberg, S. and Danks, J. H. Grammatical structure and recall: A function of the space in immediate memory or of recall delay? *Perception & Psychophysics,* 1969, **6**, 113–117.

Gödel, K. Über formal unentscheidbare Sätze der Principia Mathematica und verwandter Systeme I. *Monatshefte für Mathematik und Physik,* 1931, **38**, 173–198.

Goldman-Eisler, F., & Cohen, M. Is N, P, and PN difficulty a valid criterion of transformational operations? *Journal of Verbal Learning and Verbal Behavior,* 1970, **9**, 161–166.

Greenfield, P. M., & Smith, J. H. *Communication and the beginnings of language: The development of semantic structure in one-word speech.* New York: Academic Press, 1976.

Greenfield, P. M., & Westerman, M. Some psychological relations between action and language structure. Unpublished manuscript, Dept. of Psychology, University of California, Los Angeles, 1974.

Gruber, J. Studies in lexical relations. Unpublished doctoral dissertation, Massachusetts Institute of Technology, 1965.

Ingram, D. Transitivity in child language. *Language,* 1971, **47,** 888–921.

Johnson, N. Sequential verbal behavior. In T. Dixon & D. Hoton (Eds.), *Verbal behavior and general behavior theory.* Englewood Cliffs, New Jersey: Prentice-Hall, 1968.

Katz, J. *Semantic theory.* New York: Harper and Row, 1972.

Katz, J., & Fodor, J. A. The structure of a semantic theory. *Language,* 1963, **39,** 170–210.

Kuhn, T. *The structure of scientific revolutions.* (2nd ed.) Chicago: Univ. of Chicago Press, 1970.

Lakoff, G. On generative semantics. In D. D. Steinberg & L. A. Jakovits (Eds.), *Semantics: An interdisciplinary reader in philosophy, linguistics, and psychology.* London: Cambridge Univ. Press, 1971. (a)

Lakoff, G. Presupposition and relative well-formedness. In D. D. Steinberg & L. A. Jakobovits (Eds.), *Semantics: An interdisciplinary reader in philosophy, linguistics, and psychology.* London: Cambridge Univ. Press, 1971. (b)

Lakoff, G., & Ross, J. R. Is deep structure necessary? Mimeograph, 1967. Cited in J. D. McCawley. The role of semantics in a grammar. In E. Bach & R. T. Harms (Eds.), *Universals in linguistic theory.* New York: Holt, 1968.

Lakoff, R. Language in context. *Language,* 1972, **48,** 907–927.

Lenneberg, E. H. *The biological foundations of language.* New York: Wiley, 1967.

Maclay, H. Linguistics: Overview. In D. D. Steinberg & L. A. Jakobovits (Eds.), *Semantics: An interdisciplinary reader in philosophy, linguistics, and psychology.* London: Cambridge Univ. Press, 1971.

Maclay, H., & Osgood, C. Hesitation phenomena in spontaneous English speech. *Word,* 1959, **15,** 19–42.

Macnamara, J. Cognitive basis of language learning in infants. *Psychological Review,* 1972, **79,** 1–14.

Matthews, N. A. Transformational complexity and short-term recall. *Language and Speech,* 1968, **11,** 120–128.

McCawley, J. D. The role of semantics in a grammar. In E. Bach & R. T. Harms (Eds.), *Universals in linguistic theory.* New York: Holt, 1968.

McCawley, J. D. Where do noun phrases come from? In D. D. Steinberg & L. A. Jakobovits (Eds.), *Semantics: An interdisciplinary reader in philosophy, linguistics, and psychology.* London: Cambridge Univ. Press, 1971.

McNeill, D. Developmental psycholinguistics. In F. Smith & G. A. Miller (Eds.), *The genesis of language: A psycholinguistic approach.* Cambridge, Massachusetts: MIT Press, 1966.

Mehler, J. Some effects of grammatical transformations on recall of English sentences, *Journal of Verbal Learning and Verbal Behavior,* 1963, **2,** 346–351.

Menyuk, P. *Sentences children use.* Cambridge, Massachusetts: The MIT Press, 1969.

Miller, G. A. Some psychological studies of grammar. *American Psychologist,* 1962, **17,** 748–762.

Miller, W. & Ervin, S. The development of grammar in child language. In U. Bellugi & R. Brown (Eds.), *The acquisition of language.* Monographs of the Society for Research in Child Development, 1964, **29**, 92:9–34.

Nagel, E., & Newman, J. R. *Gödel's proof.* New York: New York Univ. Press, 1958.

Nelson, K. Structure and strategy in learning to talk. *Monographs of the Society for Research in Child Development,* 1973, **38**, (1-2, No. 149).

Olson, D. R. Language and thought: Aspects of a cognitive theory of semantics. *Psychological Review,* 1970, **77**, 257–273.

Osgood, C. E. Where do sentences come from? In D. D. Steinberg & L. A. Jakobovits (Eds.), *Semantics: An interdisciplinary reader in philosophy, linguistics, and psychology.* London: Cambridge Univ. Press, 1971.

Osgood, C. E., & Richards, M. M. From yang and yin to *and* or *but. Language,* 1973, **49**, 380–412.

Osgood, C. E., & Bock, J. K. Salience and sentencing: Some production principles. In S. Rosenberg (Ed.) *Sentence production: Development in research and theory.* Hillsdale, New Jersey: Lawrence Earlbaum, 1975.

Peng, F. C. C. On the fallacy of language innatism. *The Language Sciences,* 1975, **37**, 13–16.

Savin, H. B., & Perchonock, E. Grammatical structure and the immediate recall of English sentences. *Journal of Verbal Learning and Verbal Behavior,* 1965, **4**, 348–353.

Schlesinger, I. M. Production of utterances and language acquisition. In D. I. Slobin (Ed.), *The Ontogenesis of grammar.* New York: Academic Press, 1971.

Searle, J. Chomsky's revolution in linguistics. *New York Review of Books,* 1972 (June 29), **18**(12), 16–24.

Slobin, D. I. Grammatical transformation and sentence comprehension in childhood and adulthood. *Journal of Verbal Learning and Verbal Behavior,* 1966, **5**, 219–227.

Slobin, D. I. *Psycholinguistics.* Glenview, Illinois: Scott, Foresman and Co., 1971. (a)

Slobin, D. I. Developmental psycholinguistics. In W. O. Dingwall (Ed.), *A survey of linguistic science,* College Park, Maryland: Univ. of Maryland Linguistics Dept., 1971. (b)

von Raffler-Engel, W. *Il prelinguaggio infantile.* Bresica, Italy: Paideia, 1964.

von Raffler-Engel, W. The inadequacy of the transformational approach to child language. *Word,* 1970, **26**, 396–401.

von Raffler-Engel, W. The relationship of kinesics and verbal factors in first language acquisition. In A. Kendon (Ed.), *The organization of behavior is social interaction.* The Hague: Mouton, 1975.

Wright, P. Sentence retention and transformation theory. *Quarterly Journal of Experimental Psychology.* 1968, **20**, 265–272.

Wright, P. Transformations and the understanding of sentences. *Language and speech,* 1969, **12**, 156–166.

AUTHOR INDEX

Numbers in italics refer to the pages on which the complete references are listed.

467

H

SUBJECT INDEX

A

Abstract attitude, 403
Abstract features, 242–245
Abstract lexical representation, related to phonetic representation, 7
Accent, 258–259
  patterns of, 229
Acoustic features of phonemes, 247–250
Acoustic memory, 210–211
Acoustic zone, 398
Action-object, in two-word stage, 159
Active constructions, processing load for, 448–449
Actor-action, in two-word stage, 159
Adaptation to speech sounds, 195–203
Adjective(s), contrastive, 277
Adjective checklists, 278
Adults
  grammars for children's speech and, 32
  laboratory analogies with, 37
  second language learning by, 146
  speech to children, 166–167
Affective indices, 356
Afferent motor aphasia, 398
Affiliation, eye contact and, 352–353
Affricates acquisition of, 150
  frequency cues for, 239
  openness of, 245
Age
  of first word, 151
  language learning and, 146
Agnosia, visual, 393
Agrammatism, 408–409, 414, 422
  psycholinguistic research on, 409–410
Agraphia, 415–416, 419
Airstream process, 77
Alexia, 412–414, 419–420
Allophones, context-sensitive, 105, 250–253
  syllable boundaries and, 256–258

Allophonic variation
  extrinsic, 179
  intrinsic, 179–181
Alveolar ridge, 86
  in tap, 88
Alveolar stops, 87
  duration of, 98
  vowel duration preceding, 97, 98
Ambiguity, 4
  concept representatives and, 235
  syntactic rules and, 9
  transformational rules and, 19–20
American Sign Language, chimpanzees and, 126
Amnesic aphasia, *see* Anomic aphasia
Amytal, hemispheric dominance and, 137
Analogy in language acquisition, 381
Analysis-by-synthesis, 207–208
  interactional synchrony and, 355
Analysis of variance, language in, 62
Angular gyrus, 132, 139, 398
  agraphia and, 415
  function of, 393–394
  lesions of, 419
  reading and, 413
  word finding and, 402
Animal taxonomies, componental analysis and, 274–275
Anomic aphasias, 402–403, 408, 414, 417, 418
  anatomical features of, 404
  thalamus and, 139
Anterio-dorsal speech disorders, 435
Anterior language zones, *see* Broca's area
Anticipatory effects, in speech timing, 101–102
Aphasia, 76, 390
  acquired, 128
  adult, 129
  agrammatism in, 408–410

481

relationship to articulatory features, 241–242

Auditory feature detectors, adaptation and, 198–202

Auditory feedback
babbling and, 148
role in control of articulation, 106–107

Auditory grouping, pitch and, 192–194

Auditory imperception, 422

Auditory quality, 348

Auditory receptive defect, 390

Auditory span, in aphasia, 422

Auditory stream segregation, 193

Auditory subcortex, 134

Auditory template, 135

Autocorrelation, auditory grouping and, 194

Automatized utterances, 416

B

Babbling, 147–149, 422
cessation of, 133, 135
function of, 135

Back vowels, 90

Backward masking, 204, 205–206

Basal ganglia lesions, 433, 434–435

Basal ganglia pathways, 439, 441

Base phrase markers, understanding and, 287–288

Basilar membrane, auditory grouping and 194

Bernoulli effect, vocal folds and, 80

Bilabial stops, 87
duration of, 98
gamma loop control and, 108
following open vowels, 95
vowel duration preceding, 97, 98

Bilinguals
communication-based teaching and, 369, 370
mixing and switching in, 376–378

Binary features, of speech sounds, 149–151, 276

Biotaxonomies, componental analysis and, 275

Birds
dialect variations in, 123
vocal control in, 123–124

Black(s), experimental situation and, 36

Black English, attitudes toward, 372

Blade of tongue, 87

Body movements in conversation, 350–352

Bookending, 350

Brace notation, for collapsing conventions, 10

Brain, see also specific brain structures
laterality in, 394–396
lesions of, 390–394
maturation of, 128
size of, language acquisition and, 126–127

Breath group
archetypal unmarked, 81
marked, 81

Breathy voice, 85, 348

Broad-band formants, 239

Broca's aphasia, 400, 404, 411, 418
articulatory errors in, 402

Broca's area, 127, 393, 397, 437
electroencephalographic studies of, 137
maturation of, 131, 132, 135

Bulbar palsy, 434

Burst, 184
stop perception and, 185–187

C

Case grammar, 158, 159, 367

Cat, acoustic discrimination in, 134

Categorical analysis, 281–284

Categorical perception, 208–214

Caudate lesions, 434

Causality
as conceptual relation, 286
inference of, 292

Cerebellum
lesions of, 433, 435–436, 438
tactile feedback and, 437–438

Cerebral cortex
anatomy of, 392–394
maturation of, 131–132, 134–136
primate comparisons of, 126–127

Chain model, 102–104

Chest, in speech production, 236

Chest pulse, 78

Childhood aphasia
acquired, 421–422
developmental, 422

I

HANDBOOK OF PERCEPTION

EDITORS: *Edward C. Carterette and Morton P. Friedman*

Department of Psychology
University of California, Los Angeles
Los Angeles, California

Volume I: Historical and Philosophical Roots of Perception. 1974

Volume II: Psychophysical Judgment and Measurement. 1974

Volume III: Biology of Perceptual Systems. 1973

Volume V: Seeing. 1975

Volume VII: Language and Speech. 1976

IN PREPARATION

Volume IV: Hearing

CONTENTS OF OTHER VOLUMES

Volume II: Psychophysical Judgment and Measurement